Volume TWO
since 1860

RANDOM
HOUSE

An American History: Freedom and Crisis

Volume TWO
since 1860

ALLEN WEINSTEIN, Smith College

R. JACKSON WILSON, Smith College

First Edition
98765432

Published in the United States by Random House, Inc., and simultaneously in Canada by Random House of Canada Limited, Toronto.

Library of Congress Cataloging in Publication Data
Weinstein, Allen.
Freedom and crisis.
CONTENTS: v. 1. To 1877.—v. 2. Since 1860.
1. United States—History. I. Wilson, Raymond Jackson, joint author. II. Title.
E178.W43 1974 973 73-18073
ISBN 0-394-31824-2

Manufactured in the United States of America

Grateful acknowledgment is extended to the following for permission to reprint previously published material:

Joan Daves:—From "I Have a Dream" by Martin Luther King, Jr. Copyright © 1963 by Martin Luther King, Jr.

Doubleday & Co., Inc.:—From *Six Crises* by Richard Nixon. Copyright © 1962 by Richard M. Nixon.

Alfred A. Knopf, Inc.:—From *In the Court of Public Opinion* by Alger Hiss. Copyright © 1957 by Alger Hiss.

Random House, Inc.:—From *Witness* by Whittaker Chambers. Copyright 1952 by Whittaker Chambers.

Charles Scribner's Sons:—From *The Spirit of St. Louis* by Charles A. Lindbergh. Copyright 1953 by Charles Scribner's Sons.

CONTENTS

SPECIAL FEATURES

MAPS AND CHARTS

NOTES ON SOURCES

Quotations by these foreign observers appear in the four Pictorial Essays. Minor adaptations have been made in some quoted material, chiefly to simplify selections. In the essays, the writer's name is followed by a date or dates. These represent the years in which the observations were made, if known. If the exact period is not known, the date represents the year in which the account was published.

Beauvoir, Simone de *(Essays 8, 9)* The noted French writer and philosopher made a nationwide tour of the United States between January and May 1947. *America Day by Day* (1953), based on her travels, shows her as an intelligent and sensitive reporter of the American scene.

Bremer, Fredrika *(Essay 6)* A Swedish novelist well known in her day, who traveled in America from 1849 to 1851. Her impressions, in the form of letters to her sister, appeared in *Homes of the New World* (1853).

Broughton, Morris *(Essay 9)* A South African journalist and editor of *The Cape Argus,* he came to the United States in 1956 as a guest of the State Department. By his estimation, he traveled over 10,000 miles and visited over thirty states during his three-month stay here.

Carpenter, Harry *(Essay 8)* An English sports expert, Carpenter was boxing and general sports columnist for *The London Daily Mail* from 1954 to 1962, as well as a full-time correspondent for the BBC. In his *Masters of Boxing* (1964) he spoke of Joe Louis as the "headmaster" of boxing.

Chesterton, G. K. *(Essay 6)* The English poet and novelist visited the United States on a lecture tour in 1921. His book, *What I Saw in America,* was published in London in 1922.

Colum, Padraic *(Essay 7)* This Irish man of letters made his home in the United States after 1914. He was a friend of many writers, including Robert Frost.

Cooke, Alistair *(Essay 9)* Of Anglo-Irish birth, this popular journalist and broadcaster has lived primarily in the United States since the 1930s, and became an American citizen in 1941. He is the author of many books on American culture. This selection comes from *Talk About America* (1968).

Corresca, Rocco *(Essay 6)* An Italian immigrant, he typified the penniless hopefuls who flocked to America to make their fortune. His "Biography of a Bootblack" appeared in a magazine, *The Independent,* in December 1902.

Dubos, René—See Ward, Barbara

Erkelenz, Anton *(Essay 7)* A member of the German parliament, he wrote a book called *America Today* (1927), in which he expressed an optimistic belief that the United States would some day create a culture uniquely its own.

Freymond, Jacques *(Essay 8)* On his first trip to the United States (1949-1950), Freymond, a Swiss historian, studied at Yale University and made an extended auto tour of the country. He returned for a two-month trip in 1955.

Galsworthy, John *(Essay 7)* The noted English writer gave a series of speeches in the United States that were published in a volume called *Addresses in America* (1919).

Graham, Stephen *(Essay 6)* A British traveler and journalist who visited the United States in 1913. These quotations are from his work *With Poor Immigrants to America* (1914).

Griesinger, Karl Theodor *(Essay 6)* This German historian spent five years in the United States, although he did not find the American form of democracy to his liking. His *Living Pictures from America,* published in 1858, is characterized by a cutting and ironical humor.

Hartog, Jan de *(Essay 9)* A Dutch author and playwright who made a leisurely voyage in 1958–61 from Houston to Nantucket, largely by inland waterways. He gives a charming account of his adventures in *Waters of the Western World,* published in 1961.

Hauptmann, Gerhart *(Essay 7)* In 1932 this German playwright, a Nobel prize winner, visited the United States. He remarked on leaving that the high points of his trip had been meeting O'Neill and attending *Mourning Becomes Electra.* The critique quoted here is from an interview the same year with an American correspondent.

Hawkes, Jacquetta—See Priestley, J. B.

Hilbersheimer, Ludwig and Udo Rukser *(Essay 7)* These German architects praised the innovations of American architecture and especially the work of Frank Lloyd Wright. Their article appeared in a 1920 issue of the German journal, *Art and Artist.*

Jarlson, Axel *(Essay 6)* The story of this Swedish farmer's immigration to America illustrates how the members of a single family helped each other to settle in the United States. Jarlson's narrative was published in the January 8, 1903, issue of *The Independent.*

Kipling, Rudyard *(Essay 7)* Between March and September 1889, the famous English writer (then only twenty-four) sent thirty-seven letters back to an Indian newspaper, as he traveled from India to England via the Far East and the United States. The last of his letters is titled "An Interview with Mark Twain." All this correspondence was published in *From Sea to Sea* (1890).

Kossenko, Zinaida—See Mikhailov, Nikolai

Labarca H., Amanda *(Essay 9)* A distinguished Chilean educator, feminist, and public servant, she visited the United States ten times between 1911 and 1952. She represented Chile in the first General Assembly of the United Nations in 1946.

Laski, Harold *(Essay 7)* A noted British socialist, he taught history at Harvard University from 1916 to 1920. After returning to England, he devoted himself to teaching, writing, and journalism. His *American Democracy* was published in 1948.

Leacock, Stephen *(Essay 8)* The Canadian humorist and man of letters was also a distinguished political scientist and professor at McGill University. This quotation is from *Stephen Leacock's Laugh Parade,* published in 1940.

Le Corbusier (Charles Edouard Jeanneret) *(Essays 8, 9)* This Swiss-born French architect has been called "the voice and conscience of modern architecture." He visited the United States several times during his lifetime. His book *When the Cathedrals Were White* (1947) was devoted mostly to his impressions of America.

Marias, Julian *(Essays 8, 9)* A Spanish philosopher, he helped found Madrid's Institute of Humanities. In 1951–52 Marias was a visiting professor at Wellesley College.

Maurois, André *(Essay 8)* The noted French critic and novelist was a frequent visitor to the United States, where he was a popular lecturer. In 1939 he published *Thirty-Nine States, Journal of a Voyage to America,* from which this quote is taken.

Mehdevi, Mohamed *(Essay 9)* An Iranian journalist and diplomat, he first became acquainted with the United States as a foreign student in Florida. *Something Human* (1962) was the result of his adventures hitchhiking from Florida to the West Coast.

Mikhailov, Nikolai and Zinaida Kossenko *(Essay 9)* This Russian geographer and his wife, a psychiatrist, made a tour of America in 1960. Their account first appeared in a Moscow publication the same year and was later published in the United States as *Those Americans, a Travelogue* (1962).

Münsterberg, Hugo *(Essay 7)* This German philosopher and professor at Harvard University wrote *The Americans* (1904) in order to dispel German prejudice against Americans.

Myers, Robert *(Essay 6)* A Jewish immigrant from Rumania, Myers came to the United States in 1913 and later became active in the labor movement. His recollections, *Stimmer* ["stutterer"]: *The Boy Who Couldn't Talk,* were published in 1959.

Newman, Ernest *(Essay 7)* From 1910 to 1940 he was the major British music critic. His review of Isadora Duncan quoted here was written in April 1921. Several years later, he moved to New York City, where he wrote music reviews for the *New*

York Evening Post. The November 17, 1924, edition carried his appreciation of Gershwin's *Rhapsody in Blue.*

Priestley, J. B. *(Essays 8, 9)* The English novelist and critic lived in the United States in 1935–36; *Midnight on the Desert* (1937) grew out of this experience. In 1954 he and his wife Jacquetta Hawkes (an author and anthropologist) traveled in the American Southwest. Their wry and amusing collaboration, *Journey Down a Rainbow,* for which each wrote alternating chapters, was published in 1955.

Pupin, Michael Idvorsky *(Essay 6)* Born in Yugoslavia, the brilliant physicist sold all his belongings in order to come to America. In 1924 he won a Pulitzer Prize for *From Immigrant to Inventor* (1923), the story of his life.

Rivera, Diego *(Essay 7)* In 1942 the celebrated Mexican artist spoke of his contemporary, John Sloan, to American art critic Walter Pach. Rivera himself had visited the United States in the 1930s, where he painted frescoes in Detroit, San Francisco, and New York. He was much impressed with American technology.

Rukser, Udo—See Hilbersheimer, Ludwig

Russell of Killowen, Lord *(Essay 6)* Born in Ireland, this lawyer first visited America in 1883 and wrote a *Diary of a Visit to the United States of America* (published in 1910). He served as lord chief justice of England from 1894 until his death in 1900.

Sarc, Omer Celâl *(Essay 8)* This Turkish economist has spent much time in the United States. In 1950 he visited universities across the country as a guest of the State Department. He also taught at Columbia University and worked for the United Nations.

Sheridan, Claire *(Essay 7)* A celebrated British sculptress, known for her busts of Lenin, Trotsky, and Gandhi. She met Sinclair Lewis in Washington, D.C., in April 1921. A vivid account of their meeting appeared in her book *My American Diary,* published the following year.

Stevenson, Robert Louis *(Essay 6)* The Scottish writer crossed the United States in 1879 to visit an American woman he had met in Europe (and whom he eventually married). *Across the Plains* was published in 1892.

Tyrmand, Leopold *(Essay 9)* A journalist born in Warsaw, Poland, he moved to the United States in the 1960s. Portions of his writings, dealing with his experiences as a European in America, appeared in *The New Yorker.* They were collected in *Notebooks of a Dilettante* (1967).

Vay de Vaya und Luskod, Count *(Essays 6, 7)* A Hungarian nobleman, he traveled widely as a diplomat for the Roman Catholic Church. Visiting the United States several times between 1903 and 1906, he described his travels in *The Inner Life of the United States* (1908).

Von Borch, Herbert *(Essays 8, 9)* This German writer's book *The Unfinished Society* (1960) was based on notes he made while working in the United States as a newspaper correspondent.

Ward, Barbara and René Dubos *(Essay 9)* Barbara Ward, an English social scientist, lectured frequently in the United States in the period after World War II. *Only One Earth* (1972) was written with the Pulitzer-prize winning microbiologist, René Dubos, who was born in France but moved to the United States in 1924.

Wells, H. G. *(Essay 6)* The famous English novelist visited Ellis Island during his first trip to the United States in 1905. He wrote of his impressions in *The Future of America* (1906).

West, Rebecca *(Essay 7)* Born in Ireland, she became known for her writings on history and politics. Her essay on Willa Cather was originally published by the *New York Herald Tribune* in September 1927, and was reprinted in *The Strange Necessity* (1928).

White, T. H. *(Essay 9)* Best known for his books on King Arthur, this English author kept a journal while on a lecture tour in the United States. It was later published as *America at Last, the American Journal of T. H. White* (1965).

Wolff, Albert *(Essay 7)* A French art critic, he wrote for the noted French newspaper, *Le Figaro.* This selection is quoted from his 1881 review of the Impressionists' sixth group exhibition.

AUTHORS' INTRODUCTION

Freedom and Crisis is a book of discovery about the American past. The reader will quickly recognize, by glancing at the table of contents or by flipping through the pages, that this book is different from the ordinary "text." The difference is embodied in the way that *Freedom and Crisis* organizes the American experience.

Units are arranged in pairs of chapters. Every pair opens with a dramatic narrative of a significant episode in the American past. Each episode was chosen not only because it conveys an exciting story but also because it introduces many aspects of American life during the period under investigation. The chapter that follows then locates the episode within its appropriate historical context, interpreting the major forces that shaped the actions described in the episode.

This remains the book's basic format: a narrative chapter on a single episode, based on fresh documentary research, followed by an explanatory chapter linking historical fact and interpretation to the episode itself. The account of Bacon's Rebellion in Chapter 1, for example, is followed by a chapter on seventeenth-century plantation colonies. Similarly, Charles Lindbergh's exciting trans-Atlantic flight serves as the basis for a chapter on technological changes in twentieth-century America.

The only exceptions to this pattern are the book's first and last chapters. The Prologue on the period of discovery and exploration and the Epilogue on the United States since 1960 cover a variety of themes. Such variety could best be presented, we felt, by means of a series of smaller dramas. Each of these "mini-episodes" then leads to a discussion of the historical setting of the event portrayed.

We have employed this novel approach to an introductory book on American history for one very good reason. Our primary concern from the start has been to write a book that would hold the interest of today's students, perhaps the most inquisitive but skeptical generation of students ever. To do this, we felt that a book had to be readable and realistic. *Freedom and Crisis* is both. The book dramatizes critical moments in the

 American democratic experience and deals candidly with both the extension and the denial of liberty at those times.

Freedom and Crisis is not a traditional book on United States history, then. Often such traditional books are written in the belief that there exists a certain body of data (election results, dates and outcomes of wars, treaties, major laws, and so forth) that comprises American history. We accept this idea only to the extent that most of the data of conventional texts can be found somewhere in this book. Sometimes, however, the information is located in maps, charts, and special features rather than in the text itself.

Frequently overlooked by students (and even by some teachers) is the point that this central body of data, the "facts," emerges only after a certain selection on the part of historians. There exists, after all, an almost infinite number of facts that could be chosen to represent the history of the human experience. In writing this book, we simply carried the usual selection process a step farther. Half the book is devoted to selected dramatic episodes. When linked to the accompanying chapters, the episodes form our bedrock of factual material. Using this foundation, students can then inquire into the fundamental questions of American history.

Most episodes can be read simply as absorbing stories. Thus readers will discover much about the country's past merely by studying such vivid incidents as the Boston Massacre, the Aaron Burr conspiracy, the New Orleans race riot, the Wounded Knee massacre, the Triangle fire, the Philippines revolt, the Bonus March, and the attack on Pearl Harbor. But by using the interpretative chapter accompanying each episode, students will develop the ability to extract greater meaning from the facts in these dramas and, at the same time, acquire an understanding of related historical events.

Freedom and Crisis moves chronologically through the American experience, but certain themes recur and receive particular attention. The book devotes several episodes, for example, to patterns of race and ethnic relations, especially the treatment of blacks, Indians, immigrants, and other oppressed minorities. The struggle for political liberties and economic betterment, class conflicts, territorial expansion, technological change, and basic ideological and cultural disputes are also treated.

The constant interplay of factual drama and careful interpretation is the book's distinctive feature. Facts and concepts cross paths on each page, thereby avoiding the usual unhappy classroom extremes of concentrating either on what happened or on why it happened. *Freedom and Crisis* has no room for empty historical abstractions that leave students without a factual anchor. Nor does an uncontrolled flood of rampaging facts lacking solid conceptual boundaries spill endlessly off the printed pages. The paired chapter format, we believe, avoids both these extremes.

The episodic-explanatory chapter pairs present a concise but comprehensive introduction to the history of the United States. Yet although the book covers the American experience, we wrote with less direct concern for coverage than for concreteness, drama, and interpretive depth. Almost every detail included in the narrative episodes has a larger meaning, so that students and instructors must work outward in this text from concrete detail to generalized understanding.

We make no apologies for this approach to studying and learning history, since professional historians use it daily. History as an act of inquiry involves putting great questions to small data, discovering general significance in particular events. *Freedom and Crisis* evolved from our belief that students are both willing and able to engage in the same process of inquiry as professional historians. In this manner each incident in the American odyssey, from the earliest European discoveries to our generation's exploration of the moon, can become a personal act of discovery for the reader, risky but rewarding.

The chapters that follow chart our personal roadmap through the American experience. The book will achieve its purpose only if it stirs the reader into beginning his or her own private journey through the past.

CIVIL WAR AMERICA

The formative period of modern America, from 1860 to 1900, began in civil war and ended in imperial conquest. The long, grueling war for national unity fought during this period freed the South's slaves only to abandon them, once freedmen, to still another form of bondage. At the same time, the country constructed the urban industrial society that forms the context of modern America's achievements and crises.

The terrible conflict that ushered in the era changed the character of both Southern and Northern life, as Chapter 20 makes clear. The problem of reconstructing the Union once the fabric of national politics had been torn apart emerged during the war itself and continued to disturb the nation for over a decade. What place should the freed Negro have in the American scene? What price should the South be expected to pay for losing its bid for independence? What new responsibilities did military victory impose upon the North? These basic issues and others emerge dramatically both in Chapter 19, the story of General Sherman's famous march and its aftermath, and in Chapter 20, which deals with the impact of Civil War and Reconstruction upon a transformed country.

CHAPTER

19

Sherman's March to the Sea

EARLY ON THE morning of November 16, 1864, the Union columns headed out of Atlanta, Georgia, bound southeast for the coastal city of Savannah. Northern troops, over 60,000 strong, with their horses, mules, and wagons, clogged the road. When they reached a hill outside Atlanta, it was natural for the soldiers to look back toward the town. Their commander, General William Tecumseh Sherman, recalled:

> Behind us lay Atlanta, smoldering and in ruins, the black smoke rising high in the air and hanging like a pall over the ruined city. Away off in the distance, on the McDonough road, was the rear of Howard's column, the gun-barrels glistening in the sun, the white-topped wagons stretching away to the south; and right before us the Fourteenth Corps, marching steadily and rapidly, with a cheery look and a swinging pace, that made light of the thousand miles that lay between us and Richmond. Some band, by accident, struck up the anthem of "John Brown's Body." The men caught up the strain, and never before have I heard the chorus of "Glory, glory, hallelujah!" done with more spirit, or in better harmony of time and place.

On that beautiful day of brilliant sunshine and clean, crisp air, the Civil War, already three-and-a-half years old, seemed exhilarating, if not remote. Sherman later recalled experiencing a "feeling of something to come, vague and undefined, still full of venture and intense interest. Even the common soldiers caught the inspiration, and many a group called out to me—Uncle Billy, I guess Grant is waiting for us at Richmond!"

Sherman's troops devastated much of central Georgia. Worse than the physical damage was the effect on Southern morale: With a Union army moving freely through their territory, few Southerners could still believe that the Confederacy might win the Civil War.

Tall, sharp-eyed, and red-haired, Sherman gained a reputation as a ruthless commander because of his march through the Confederacy. Actually, because he loved the South, he wanted to end the war quickly, and he opposed harsh reconstruction policies in the postwar era.

Although Richmond and victory for the Union were still five months away, Sherman had already made his mark in Georgia. The pall of smoke he and his troops saw above Atlanta came from the fires they had set in the town's railroad depot and machine shops. Flames soon swept into residential areas, destroying hundreds of dwellings. The general's reputation for toughness—"brutality" in the minds of most Southerners—took shape at Atlanta and on the subsequent campaign, his famous march to the sea. "We are not only fighting hostile armies," Sherman believed, "but a hostile people. We must make old and young, rich and poor, feel the hand of war."

Sherman, the tough-talking soldier, knew the South well. Born in Ohio in 1820, he attended West Point and, after graduation, spent most of his time on duty in military posts in the South. He resigned from the army in 1853. After working unsuccessfully as a bank manager in California and as a lawyer in Kansas, he tried to get back into the army. Rejected, he had to settle for the job of superintendent of a military academy in Louisiana. The school opened in 1859.

As the sectional crisis deepened, Sherman made it clear that, if Louisiana should secede from the Union, he would resign his post and do all he could to aid the national government. He kept his word when he heard of the Southern attack on Fort Sumter in April 1861. Secession, he thought, was "folly, madness, a crime against civilization." He immediately sought, and gained, reinstatement in the army. It was now more receptive to such applications, since so many regular officers had joined the Confederacy.

Sherman started as a colonel and rose rapidly in the Union high command. He served in the west as one of Grant's most trusted officers. By mid-1864, as a brigadier general, he was assigned the mission of striking from Tennessee into Georgia and seizing Atlanta. The town, though relatively small, was an important railroad center. Confederate troops under General Joseph E. Johnston and, later, General John B. Hood fought hard to hold Sherman back. They were defeated in July at two crucial battles, those of Peachtree Creek and Atlanta. After a siege of several weeks, Atlanta fell.

Sherman's troops entered the city on September 2. Although Hood at first moved south toward safety, he later wheeled northwest toward Tennessee, hoping to harass Sherman's communications so badly that his forces would have to retreat. Inadvertently, Hood's actions may have influenced Sherman in his later decision to move to the sea without regard for communications or established supply lines.

For the time being, however, Sherman wanted to rest his troops and observe Hood's movements. He decided that Hood could be kept at bay by some detachments of his own army, plus Union troops in Tennessee.

Sherman meanwhile undertook some indirect negotiations with the governor of Georgia, Joseph E. Brown. His aim was to separate the state from the Confederacy. There was reason to hope that Georgia might pull out of the war. Brown had already withdrawn his state's militia from the rebel army. And, like most Southern politicians, he detested Jefferson Davis, president of the Confederacy. Nothing came of the negotiations, though they may have impressed Sherman with the need for bringing the hardships of war home to the Southern civilian population.

When the war started, Atlanta—not then the state capital—had only 12,000 inhabitants. Many of them had fled as the Union troops approached. Others followed when Hood abandoned the town. When Sherman entered, he ordered the rest of the civilians to leave, since he did not want them clogging the town and interfering with his lines of communication. He and Hood agreed to a ten-day truce so that these civilians could move out.

By late October, Sherman had decided to march to the sea. On November 2 Grant wired: "I do not really see that you can withdraw from where you are to follow Hood without giving up all we have gained in territory. I say, then, go as you propose."

Sherman's bold plan called for his army of 62,000 men (5,000 of them cavalry) to move the 300 miles to Savannah without supply lines and without communications until they reached the Atlantic coast. There the Union navy could provide cover and supplies. Sherman's troops carried enough provisions for twenty or thirty days, but those were considered emergency rations. Food on the march would be "provided" by the local farms and plantations along the way—*not,* of course, on a voluntary basis. As a result, Georgia would be made to "howl."

Sherman's Special Field Order #120 detailed the procedure he hoped to establish. Brigade commanders were responsible for organizing foraging parties. Every morning they would move out from the four main columns under the direction of one or two "discreet officers." Foragers—or "bummers," as they soon came to be called (even by the Yankees themselves)—could seize available livestock and food supplies. They were not supposed to enter houses. Only corps commanders had the authority to order destruction of buildings, and then only in areas of resistance. Foragers for artillery units could take all the animals and wagons they needed.

If possible, foragers were to seize provisions from the rich planters rather than poor farmers. The wealthy were presumed to be more in favor of the rebellion than their humbler fellow Southerners. (This assumption fitted Northern views of secession as a conspiracy of the elite. It did not square with the facts of Southern political life.)

Sherman's field order directed his men to "forage liberally." They obeyed with a will. Men would go out in the morning on foot, seize a wagon, and then load it with everything valuable and movable they could find. One of Sherman's aides, Major Henry Hitchcock, described a foraging expedition in his diary:

> Plenty of forage along road: corn, fodder, finest sweet potatoes, pigs, chickens, etc. Passed troops all day, some on march, some destroying railroad thoroughly. Two cotton gins on roadside burned, and pile of cotton with one, also burned. Houses in Conyers look comfortable for Georgia village, and sundry good ones along road. Soldiers foraging all along, but only for *forage*—no violence so far as I saw or heard. Laughable to see pigs in feed troughs behind wagons, chickens swinging in knapsacks. Saw some few men—Whites look sullen—darkies pleased.

Stories of Union brutality, supposedly encouraged by Sherman himself, began to circulate. (They continued to circulate for generations.) But his march to the sea, devastating as it was, did not degenerate into an orgy of murder, rape, and arson. Sherman later acknowledged "acts of pillage, robbery, and violence" undoubtedly committed by some of his men. But, he argued, "these acts were exceptional and

A "bummer" goes his way, so loaded with booty that he cannot even hold the reins in his hands. For many of Sherman's men, the march through Georgia was a kind of holiday after months or years of difficult military life.

incidental. I have never heard of any cases of murder or rape; and no army could have carried along sufficient food and forage for a march of three hundred miles; so that foraging in some shape was necessary."

To Sherman, the march became just what he had ordered—harsh but, in the main, well-disciplined. The destruction of his "scorched-earth" policy centered on three main targets: railroads, the few factories on the route, and public buildings that could serve as temporary headquarters for military units.

Sherman marveled at the skill of his men in carrying out his order to "forage liberally." One fact among many proves how proficient they were: Sherman's army started the march driving 5,000 head of cattle; they ended it with over 10,000.

Where were the Confederate forces during these agonizing weeks? Some small cavalry units of the Confederate army did appear from time to time to raid foraging parties. But they had little overall effect. Hood's army had marched northwest to Tennessee and defeat. Since most Georgians of fighting age were serving with the Southern forces, the state militia had been reduced to several thousand old men and young boys. They tried to make a stand at the state capital, Milledgeville, but the Union forces swept them aside. After viewing the casualties, a northern officer wrote: "I was never so affected at the sight of dead and wounded before. I hope we will never have to shoot at such men again. They know nothing at all about fighting and I think their officers know as little."

Milledgeville fell on November 23. Georgia state officials had fled a short time before. The invading Yankee officers decided to mock the "sovereign state of Georgia." They pretended to hold a session of the state legislature, complete with resolutions and fire-eating oratory. Then they decided to repeal the ordinance of secession. When Sherman heard about these antics, he laughed. Meanwhile, his Milledgeville "legislators" ordered the burning of public buildings in the town.

Sherman's soldiers sliced a path forty to sixty miles wide through central Georgia. Every white family along the way underwent its own particular ordeal and emerged with its own sorrowful story. Tales of the devastation became commonplace: houses broken into and sacked, food and valuables hidden only to be found by the recurrent searches of intruding "bummers," treasured family possessions tossed into the flames, cotton gins and public buildings put to the torch. "Everything had been swept as with a storm of fire," wrote one Macon newspaper. "The whole country around is one wide waste of destruction."

Contrary to Sherman's conception of his foraging troops as skilled,

Mary Jones was one of the Southerners who felt the brunt of Sherman's attack. She wrote: "The foundations of society are broken up; what hereafter is to be our social and civil status we cannot see."

most Southerners in their path regarded them as greedy marauders. The experiences of two Georgia women, a mother and daughter, typified the ordeal. Mary Jones, the widow of a Presbyterian minister, owned three plantations in Liberty County, not far from Savannah. At the time of Sherman's march she and her daughter, Mary Jones Mallard, were living at the plantation known as Montevideo. Their letters and journals vividly portray the impact of war.

Mary Mallard's husband was captured on December 13 by Union cavalry near Montevideo. (Mrs. Mallard was then pregnant and expecting to give birth within days.) The first groups of "bummers" reached the Jones-Mallard household on December 15. They searched the house and made off with a number of family keepsakes. During the next two weeks, Union raiding parties—sometimes large detachments, sometimes only a few stragglers—arrived almost daily at the home. Each group searched the premises, insulted the two women, and took what food, supplies, or family items remained to be carted away.

Mary Mallard confided unhappily to her journal on December 17:

> The Yankees made the Negroes bring up the oxen and carts, and took off all the chickens and turkeys they could find. They carried off all the syrup from the smokehouse. We had one small pig, which was all the meat we had left; they took the whole of it. Mother saw everything like food stripped from her premises, without the power of uttering one word. Finally they rolled out the carriage and took that to carry off a load of chickens. They took everything they possibly could.

"Everything" included seven of the Jones family's slaves, who—like hundreds of blacks elsewhere along the army's line of march—were pressed into service as porters, laborers, or mule drivers. "So they were all carried off," Mary Mallard grieved, "carriages, wagons, carts, horses and mules and servants, with food and provisions of every kind—and, so far as they were concerned, leaving us to starvation."

Occasionally an officer would apologize for the behavior of his men. One friendly Union soldier, a Missourian, offered to show Mrs. Jones where to hide her things. Mary Mallard noted: "He said he had enlisted to fight for the *Constitution;* but since then the war had been turned into another thing, and he did not approve this abolitionism, for his wife's people all owned slaves." A few days later, a Virginian told Mrs. Jones that "there was great dissatisfaction in the army on account of the present object of the war, which now was to free the Negroes."

More often than not, however, the raiders stalked through the house indifferent to its inhabitants. Never knowing whether soldiers coming to the door would behave politely or insolently, the two women lived in constant fear. Several times, "bummers" threatened to return and burn down their house. Yet on other occasions, Union commanders offered them protection and safe-conduct passes to Savannah, which was still in Confederate hands. The women declined to leave, partly because of Mary Mallard's pregnancy. On January 4, 1865, she gave birth to a daughter. Her mother noted in her journal:

> During these hours of agony the yard was filled with Yankees. They were all around the house; my poor child, calm and collected amid her agony of body, could hear their conversation and wild halloos and cursing beneath her windows. After a while they left, screaming and yelling in a most fiendish way as they rode from the house.

Mary Jones' journal makes it clear that Sherman had achieved his major purpose in marching through Georgia—to demoralize beyond repair what remained of the Deep South's fighting spirit. She wrote in January 1865:

> As I stand and look at the desolating changes wrought by the hand of an inhuman foe in a few days, I can enter into the feelings of Job. All our pleasant things are laid low. We are prisoners in our own home. To obtain a mouthful of food we have been obliged to cook in what was formerly our drawing room; and I have to rise every morning by candlelight, before the dawn of day, that we may have it before the enemy arrives to take it from us. . . For one month our homes and all we possess have been given up to lawless pillage. Officers and men have alike engaged in this work of degradation. I scarcely know how we have stood up under it. God alone has enabled us to "speak with the enemy in the gates," and

A Confederate soldier returns to find his home a shambles in the midst of a devastated land. The artist who drew this scene was A. J. Volck, a German-born dentist who lived in Baltimore. He was the best-known satirist to interpret the Civil War from the Southern point of view.

> calmly, without a tear, to see my house broken open, entered with false keys, threatened to be burned to ashes, refused food and ordered to be starved to death, told that I had no right even to wood or water, that I should be "humbled in the very dust I walked upon," a pistol and carbine presented to my breast, cursed and reviled as a rebel, a hypocrite, a devil.

Troubling Mrs. Jones almost as much as the behavior of Sherman's soldiers was the reaction of her slaves. During the first days of Union occupation, most of them stayed on the plantation, perhaps out of fear, perhaps out of loyalty. But when it became clear that the Northern army firmly controlled the area, a number of slaves left to join the Union columns marching on Savannah. "Many servants have proven faithful," Mrs. Jones wrote in January 1865, "others false and rebellious against all authority or restraint."

Sherman himself pursued an ambiguous policy toward the ex-slaves, who were known as "contraband." He did not want them as soldiers, despite the good record of black regiments in battle when they were allowed to fight. He rejected the suggestion of General Ulysses S. Grant (by now in charge of all Union forces) that blacks be armed. He felt that his troops would object. And he had another reason. "My aim then," he later wrote, "was to whip the rebels, to humble their pride and make them fear and dread us. I did not want them to cast in our teeth that we had to call on *their* slaves to help us to subdue them."

Nevertheless, Sherman did order the formation of black "pioneer battalions"—construction units—for each army corps. "Negroes who are able-bodied and can be of service to the several columns may be taken along," Sherman instructed, "but each army commander will bear in mind that the question of supplies is a very important one, and that his first duty is to see to those who bear arms." In other words, the army was to keep blacks at a distance, using labor as needed but refraining from becoming a relief organization for ex-slaves who had left their plantations.

Sherman's prejudice against blacks was a crucial factor in his military policy. His brother John was an important antislavery Republican politician from Ohio, but William did not share his views. When still in Louisiana, he had assured Southerners that slavery was best for blacks. "All the congresses on earth," he said, "can't make the Negro anything else than what he is"—namely a slave, or a second-class noncitizen. In a letter he stated:

> I would not if I could abolish or modify slavery. I don't know that I would materially change the actual political relation of master and slave. Negroes in the great numbers that exist here must of necessity be slaves. Theoretical notions of

"Negroes leaving the plough" is the title given this drawing by Northern artist Alfred R. Waud, who reported the war for an illustrated journal. At the beginning of the war, Union policy toward fugitive blacks was so uncertain that many runaways were returned to their former masters.

humanity and religion cannot shake the commercial fact that their labor is of great value and cannot be dispensed with.

Whatever Sherman's own attitudes, it was clear that, from the moment his troops left Atlanta, they sparked the imagination of Georgia's slaves. As Sherman rode through the town of Covington, a day's march from Atlanta, he found that "the Negroes were simply frantic with joy." He later recalled that "Whenever they heard my name, they clustered about my horse, shouted and prayed in their peculiar style, which had a natural eloquence that would have moved a stone."

During the following weeks, as Northern troops foraged their way across Georgia, Sherman witnessed "hundreds, if not thousands, of such scenes." He wrote later that he could still see "a poor girl, in the very ecstasy of the Methodist 'shout,' hugging the banner of one of the regiments."

Thousands of slaves did more than simply greet the liberating Northern army. They joined it, striding alongside or in back of the troop columns. Wrote Mary Jones: "Negroes in large numbers are flocking to them. Nearly all the house servants have left their homes; and from most of the plantations they have gone in a body." The ranks of contraband included strong young men and women in the prime of life, mothers carrying children, and the white-haired elderly.

More than 30,000 blacks joined Sherman's army at one time or another during its four-week march. Yet only 10,000 remained with its ranks as it entered Savannah. Many were actively discouraged from remaining with the soldiers. Neither Sherman nor most of his officers and men wished to add the task of foraging to feed a huge contraband population from the food collected each day.

Sherman later remembered personally telling an old black man at one plantation that

> we wanted the slaves to remain where they were, and not to load us down with useless mouths. We could receive a few of their young, hearty men as pioneers. But if they followed us in swarms of old and young, feeble and helpless, it would simply load us down and cripple us in our great task. I believe that old man spread this message to the slaves, which was carried from mouth to mouth, to the

Black people followed Sherman's army on foot, on horseback, and in any kind of wheeled conveyance that could be found. No one in authority was well prepared to deal with the contraband situation, and many former slaves lacked adequate shelter, food, and clothing.

> very end of our journey, and that it in part saved us from the great danger we incurred of swelling our numbers so that famine would have attended our progress.

In any case, the thousands of slaves who remained with Sherman's forces did not all passively trudge along waiting to be fed and taken care of. Many played active roles. They carried supplies as porters and mule drivers. Some searched out food, animals, and equipment hidden by Confederates along the way. Others built roads or repaired bridges so that Sherman's men, equipment, and supply wagons could keep to their ten-mile-a-day pace across the swampy waterways of central Georgia. Still others helped the soldiers to destroy railroads and other strategic targets. (A favorite trick was to heat the heavy iron rails and twist them into "Sherman's neckties.")

Local blacks also served as reliable guides behind Confederate lines. One of Sherman's officers, General Oliver O. Howard, ordered one of his men to reach the Union fleet anchored off Savannah. After safely rowing a canoe past enemy posts along the Ogeechee River, the officer and his patrol

> found some Negroes, who befriended him and his men and kept pretty well under cover until evening. Then they went ashore to get a Negro guide and some provisions [after which they passed through Confederate lines]. Soon after this they came to quite a sizable Negro house, went in, and were well treated and refreshed with provisions. When they were eating they were startled by hearing a party of Confederate cavalry riding toward the house. Of course they expected to be instantly captured, but the Negroes, coming quickly to their rescue, concealed them under the floor. The coolness and smartness of the Negroes surprised even Captain Duncan, though he had believed and trusted them. The cavalry stopped but remained only a short time, and the Negroes guided our men back to their boats.

Although few blacks served the Union side so daringly during Sherman's march, the general himself acknowledged that the "large number employed as servants, teamsters and pioneers rendered admirable service."

Sherman's army marched into Savannah on December 21, along with the 10,000 black contraband. The general sent a playful telegram to "His Excellency," President Lincoln: "I beg to present you as a Christmas gift the city of Savannah, with one hundred and fifty heavy guns and plenty of ammunition, also about twenty-five thousand bales of cotton."

The message was quickly published throughout the North. Northerners had considered Sherman's army "lost" when the general had broken communication after leaving Atlanta. Sherman and his men instantly became popular heroes. "Our joy was irrepressible," said one high Washington official, "not only because of their safety, but because it was an assurance that the days of the Confederacy were numbered." Even to many Southerners, Savannah's capture seemed to foreshadow final defeat. Given the suffering Confederate soldiers and civilians had undergone by then, the prospect seemed almost welcome.

Sherman did not order the city's residents to leave, as he had done at Atlanta. With Union ships in the harbor and his troops in control of the surrounding countryside, he felt no useful military purpose would be served by evacuating or burning the city. In fact, Sherman decided to govern Savannah's 20,000 inhabitants mildly—much to their amazement and that of other Georgians. He gave people the choice of remaining or leaving for other cities still under Confederate control.

Sherman placed one of his generals in overall command of Savannah, but the Confederate mayor and city council handled most day-to-day matters. Relations between Northerners and Southerners were polite, almost cordial. Only a few hundred citizens left the city. Most people calmly went about their business. Relief ships organized by private citizens in the North arrived regularly in January 1865, bringing much-needed food and clothing. Supplies were distributed to freed blacks and needy whites. Local markets selling meat, wood, and other necessities reopened under military supervision.

"No city was ever occupied with less disorder or more system than Savannah," Sherman wrote on December 31. "Though an army of 60,000 men lay camped around it, women and children of an hostile people walk its streets with as much security as they do in Philadelphia." Confederate newspapers raged about the alleged "barbarities" of Sherman's forces on their march from Atlanta, exaggerating the amount of property burned, and the numbers murdered or raped. Meantime the "barbarians" occupied Savannah with little friction.

In Savannah, as on the march from Atlanta, Sherman became a hero to the liberated blacks. He wrote to his wife on Christmas Day: "They flock to me, young and old. They pray and shout and mix up my name with that of Moses and Simon and other scriptural ones as well as 'Abram Linkom.'" Hundreds of blacks hurried to see the general, wrote an aide. "There was a constant stream of them, old and young, men, women and children, black, yellow, and cream-colored, uncouth and well-bred, bashful and talkative—but always respectful and behaved—all day long."

It would have come as a great shock to the blacks of Savannah to learn that their hero was at that very moment being attacked in the North for his policy toward ex-slaves. Late in December General Henry W. Halleck wrote Sherman to congratulate him on the march through Georgia and his capture of Savannah. He also warned him that powerful individuals close to the President spoke critically of him, alleging that he "manifested an almost *criminal* dislike to the Negro." "They say," added Halleck,

> that you are not willing to carry out the wishes of the government in regard to him, but repulse him with contempt! They say you might have brought with you to Savannah more than fifty thousand, thus stripping Georgia of that number of laborers, and opening a road by which as many more could have escaped from their masters; but that, instead of this, you drove them from your ranks, prevented their following you by cutting the bridges in your rear, and thus caused the massacre of large numbers by Wheeler's cavalry.

Sherman defended his decision to discourage slave runaways from joining the march on the grounds that their presence would have overburdened his army and hindered its military success. In responding to Halleck, however, he acknowledged that his sympathy for freed blacks was limited:

> Thank God I am not running for an office and am not concerned because the rising generation will believe that I burned 500 niggers[1] at one pop in Atlanta, or any such nonsense. The South deserves all she has got for her injustice to the Negro, but that is no reason why we should go to the other extreme.

It was no surprise to Sherman when Secretary of War Edwin M. Stanton arrived in Savannah on January 9, aboard the Union ship *Nevada*. Stanton was supposedly traveling on a vacation cruise and to supervise the disposition of captured Confederate cotton supplies. Actually he came to check on Sherman's handling of matters involving blacks. Stanton strongly supported Sherman's military strategy in Georgia. But he disapproved of the general's rumored hostility toward the ex-slave population, and of his refusal to use blacks as soldiers.

Sherman denied that any of his officers or troops had been hostile to slaves on their march from Atlanta. But Stanton wanted to hear about Sherman's behavior from the blacks themselves. At his request, therefore, Sherman invited "the most intelligent of the Negroes" in Savannah to come to his rooms to meet the Secretary of War. Twenty black men attended the meeting with Sherman and Stanton on January 12, 1865.

[1] This term was considered only mildly discourteous in the 1860s. It was commonly used, even by antislavery Northerners.

Never before had any major American government official met with black leaders to ask what *they* wished for their people. Each man present began by introducing himself with a brief account of his life. The average age was fifty. Fifteen of the men were ministers—mainly Baptist and Methodist—and the other five were church officials of one kind or another. Five of the leaders had been born free. Of the others, three had bought their freedom; most of the rest had been liberated by Sherman's army.

Secretary of War Stanton sat at a table facing the black visitors, making extensive notes on their remarks. Sherman, restless and uneasy over the interview, stood with two of his aides apart from the seated group. He watched the proceedings warily, pacing across the room from time to time during the exchange. The blacks had selected as their spokesman sixty-seven-year-old Garrison Frazier, a Baptist minister. He responded firmly to each of Stanton's questions.

Stanton asked first whether the men were aware of Lincoln's Emancipation Proclamation. Frazier replied that they were.

> STANTON: State what you understand by slavery, and the freedom that was to be given by the President's Proclamation.
>
> FRAZIER: Slavery is receiving by irresistible power the work of another man, and not by his consent. The freedom, as I understand it, promised by the Proclamation, is taking us from under the yoke of bondage, and placing us where we could reap the fruit of our own labor, and take care of ourselves, and assist the Government in maintaining our freedom.

Stanton then asked how black people could best maintain their new freedom. Frazier suggested that young men should be able to enlist in the army, and that other blacks ought to receive land to farm: "We want to be placed on land until we are able to buy it, and make it our own."

The Secretary of War then asked whether the men believed that freed blacks "would rather live scattered among the whites, or in colonies by yourselves?" Frazier answered: "I would prefer to live by ourselves, for there is a prejudice against us in the South that will take years to get over; but I do not know that I can answer for my brethren."

Frazier and his black associates may have considered Stanton's next question offensive. The Secretary asked whether the ex-slaves of the South were intelligent enough to sustain their freedom while maintaining good relations with Southern whites. "I think there is sufficient intelligence among us to do so," Frazier replied simply.

The black minister was then asked what he believed were the causes and object of the Civil War, and whether blacks generally supported either side. He responded shrewdly and at length. Frazier told Stanton that blacks wished only to help the Union subdue the rebellious Confederacy. He acknowledged that the North's first war aim involved bringing the South back into the Union, that Lincoln had issued the Emancipation Proclamation mainly as a means toward achieving this end. Only the South's not freeing the slaves "has now made the freedom of the slaves a part of the war." Frazier noted that the thousands of runaways who followed the Union armies, "leaving their homes and undergoing suffering," spoke clearly for the pro-Union sentiments of blacks.

Stanton then indicated that he wanted to ask a question about Sherman. The general—silently furious—left the room. In Sherman's absence, Stanton inquired about "the feeling of the colored people in regard to General Sherman" and whether Negroes regarded "his sentiments and actions as friendly to their rights and interests." Frazier's answer probably surprised Stanton, considering the rumors current in Washington:

> We looked upon General Sherman, prior to his arrival, as a man in the providence of God, specially set apart to accomplish this work, and we unanimously felt inexpressible gratitude to him. Some of us called upon him immediately upon his arrival [in Savannah], and it is probable he did not meet the Secretary with more courtesy than he met us. His conduct and deportment toward us characterized him as a friend and a gentleman. We have confidence in General Sherman, and think that what concerns us could not be under better hands.

The meeting soon ended, after Stanton thanked his black visitors for their advice.

Stanton and Sherman spent the next three days discussing the problems of policy toward the freedmen. They agreed that Sherman would issue a field order on January 16, the day after Stanton's departure from Savannah.

Special Field Order #15 set aside confiscated or abandoned land along rivers emptying into the Atlantic and on the Sea Islands—nearby islands that lay along the coast from Charleston, South Carolina, to Jacksonville, Florida. These lands were to be used exclusively for settlement by freed blacks. A freedman and his family taking up such land were to be given a "possessory title" to "not more than forty acres of tillable land" until Congress should regulate the title.

Sherman clearly viewed this scheme as a temporary one in order to provide for freedmen and their families in the area during the rest of the war, or until Congress acted. "Mr. Stanton has been here," he confidently wrote his wife on the day of Stanton's departure, "and is cured of that Negro nonsense." By now Sherman was impatient to begin his march northward. He appointed General Rufus Saxton as Inspector of Settlements and Plantations for the entire area covered by his field order. On January 21 Sherman's army left Savannah, marching into South Carolina, the symbol of Confederate resistance.

Saxton energetically arranged to transport homeless blacks in Savannah to coastal farms. He wrote urgent letters to Northern sympathizers asking for food and supplies to help sustain the new agricultural settlements. By midsummer of 1865—with the war now over—Saxton and his aides had managed to settle more than 40,000 black people on lands covered in Sherman's order.

The people faced numerous hardships—neglected soil, old equipment (and little of it), poor seed, and shortages of supplies. But the hard-working freedmen, especially those on the Sea Islands of Georgia and South Carolina, successfully grew crops of cotton and various foodstuffs. They received support not only from Saxton and the military but also from Northern white teachers and missionaries, a number of whom traveled into the area to found schools.

Most of the planning and hard work, however, came from the freedmen themselves. Many started out with little more than the clothes on their backs. One party was led by Ulysses Houston, a minister who had been present at the interview with Stanton. Before leaving for Skidaway Island, he wrote a Northern reporter: "We shall build our cabins, and organize our town government for the maintenance of order and the settlement of all difficulties." The reporter later gave this account:

> He and his fellow-colonists selected their lots, laid out a village, numbered their lots, put the numbers in a hat, and drew them out. It was Plymouth colony repeating itself. They agreed if any others came to join them, they should have equal privileges. So blooms the Mayflower on the South Atlantic coast.

The impressive success of this resettlement led many Northerners to urge that Congress enact a general land distribution policy to help all freedmen. Landless ex-slaves also came to expect that, since 40,000 Deep South blacks had quickly and effectively settled new lands, others too would receive their forty acres in the near future. Such hopes were soon dashed.

Andrew Johnson became President after Lincoln was assassinated in April 1865. Many had believed that Johnson would be sympathetic to a generous land distribution policy once in the White House, since he had been sympathetic to black rights earlier as governor of Tennessee. But a proclamation of his in May 1865 completely shattered this belief. Johnson pardoned all former Confederates except for those whose taxable property exceeded $20,000 and those who had held high military or civil positions. (Even these groups could apply for special presidential pardon.)

For the great majority of white Southerners, Johnson's proclamation not only restored civil and political rights. It also restored their property—except for slaves—even if previously confiscated as a result of

A Northern teacher reads to two of her pupils at a school on St. Helena, one of the Sea Islands off the coast of South Carolina. These former slaves were among those resettled by Sherman's Order #15.

temporary wartime orders such as Sherman's. Not only did the new President say nothing about the freedmen in his proclamation. He clearly intended them to resume their second-class economic status in the South, although no longer as slaves. Johnson made it plain that he intended landowning blacks such as those under Saxton's jurisdiction to surrender their newly acquired lands and return them to their previous owners.

Saxton now administered the freedmen's new settlements in Georgia, South Carolina, and Florida as assistant director of the Freedmen's Bureau. This agency had been recently established by Congress to coordinate federal relief assistance to ex-slaves. Heading the bureau was Sherman's former subordinate, General Oliver O. Howard. He shared President Johnson's wish to conciliate the South. Unlike the President, though, he did not want to do so at the expense of the freedmen.

Both Saxton and Howard tried to resist and delay the restoration of black-occupied lands to their former white owners. They were supported by Stanton, who attempted various maneuvers to stave off the move. But Johnson was determined. Sherman's field order was revoked in June 1865. Saxton even traveled to Washington, but without success.

In September the former landholders of Edisto Island, then under Freedmen's Bureau control, petitioned Johnson for the return of their lands. The President directed Howard to visit the island and convince the freedmen to arrange a "mutually satisfactory solution." The President left little doubt that he wanted the blacks to pack up and leave.

Howard unhappily went to Edisto in late October. Trapped between his duty and his sympathies, he met with freed blacks in a local church. They crowded in, furious at the course of events. They refused to quiet down until a woman began singing the spiritual "Nobody Knows the Trouble I Seen."

The blacks then listened to Howard as he urged them to surrender their farms and return to work for the island's former white landholders. Angry shouts of "no, no" punctuated Howard's talk. One man in the gallery cried out: "Why, General Howard, why do you take away our lands? You take them from us who have always been true, always true to the government! You give them to our all-time enemies! That is not right!"

Howard patiently explained to his audience that their "possessory titles" to the land were not "absolute" or "legal." At his insistence, a committee was formed consisting of three freedmen, three white planters, and three Freedmen's Bureau representatives. It had authority to decide on the island's land ownership. (This practice was also adopted elsewhere on the Sea Islands.)

Howard still hoped to delay restoration of the property until Congress convened late in 1865. But the process of removing blacks from their assigned lands gathered momentum after he left the area to return north.

Saxton was still refusing to dispossess black landholders from the territories under his supervision, so Johnson removed him in January 1866. He was replaced by Davis Tillson, a Freedmen's Bureau official more sympathetic to presidential policy. Tillson issued an order allowing white owners to return to their former Sea Island farms and plantations. Tillson went so far as to charter a boat and accompany the first group, explaining personally to the blacks in residence that they would have to surrender their lands.

Blacks who were willing to sign contracts to work for white owners were allowed to remain. Others were driven from the islands either by Union troops or by white vigilante groups that began to terrorize black landholders throughout the Deep South during this period. One sympathetic New England schoolteacher later wrote of seeing all the freedmen on one Sea Island plantation leaving their newly acquired land with their hoes over their shoulders. "They told us that the guard had ordered them to leave the plantation if they would not work for the owners. We could only tell them to obey orders. After this many of the Sherman Negroes left the island."

For the moment, Howard's policy of delaying restoration had clearly failed. Yet shortly after Congress met in December 1865, the legislators debated the provisions of a new, postwar Freedman's Bureau Bill designed to protect the rights of ex-slaves in peacetime. The final version of that bill was enacted by Congress over the President's veto in July 1866. It allowed freedmen deprived of their land by Johnson's restoration policy to lease twenty acres of government-owned land on the Sea Islands with an option to buy cheaply within six years. By then, however, almost all of the "Sherman Negroes" had lost their lands.

By this time, too, Congress and Johnson were struggling bitterly over control of postwar policy toward the South. The outcome of that struggle would determine the nation's response to its millions of newly liberated blacks. Many of them probably shared the anguish of one Sea Island freedman who grieved shortly after his eviction: "They will make freedom a curse to us, for we have no home, no land, no oath, no vote, and consequently no country."

CHAPTER

20

Civil War and Reconstruction

On February 23, 1861 (at a time when Sherman had just left his post at the Louisiana military academy), Abraham Lincoln slipped secretly into Washington after an all-night train ride. His aides planned the night trip, fearing an assassination attempt at a previously scheduled stop in pro-Confederate Baltimore. On his special train the President-elect tried to sleep. But a drunken passenger kept singing the bouncy Southern melody "Dixie" over and over. Lincoln finally muttered to a companion, "No doubt there will be a great time in Dixie by and by." His concern over the impending showdown with the secessionist South was shared by most Northerners.

A thousand miles to the south the Confederacy's president-elect took a different type of journey to his own inaugural. Lincoln arrived in the nation's capital, according to one diplomat, "like a thief in the night." Jefferson Davis traveled from his Mississippi plantation to Montgomery, Alabama—first capital of the rebellious states—like a conquering hero.

Davis was a moderate Southerner. Like

Courtesy Chicago Historical Society

Abraham Lincoln, wrote George Templeton Strong, was "a most sensible, straightforward, honest old codger; the best President we have had since Jackson's time."

Jefferson Davis suffered from poor health throughout the war. Though he was strong-willed and irritable, his devotion to the South was unquestioned.

others, he had opposed secession until after Lincoln's election. Now this group had taken charge of the South's new national government, replacing many of the zealous fire-eaters who had spread the gospel of disunion during the 1850s. Southern moderates had selected Davis as their president largely because he wanted a peaceful settlement with the North. A West Point graduate, Davis had fought ably in the Mexican War, represented Mississippi in both the House and Senate, and served as President Pierce's Secretary of War.

FIRST STEPS

While Davis pondered his cabinet, the Montgomery convention that had chosen him for president wrote a Confederate constitution. For the most part the document copied provisions of the federal Constitution. It included a bill of rights, and it even prohibited the slave trade. Slavery was pronounced legal throughout the Confederacy, of course. In a significant speech at Savannah, the vice president-elect, Alexander Stephens of Georgia, spoke candidly of the new government: "Its foundations are laid, its cornerstone rests, upon the great truth that the Negro is not equal to the white man; that slavery, subordination to the superior race, is his natural and normal condition."

The new Confederate congress began its work by legalizing for the South all Union laws that did not conflict with its new constitution. For two months after Davis' selection as president, the Confederate government waited for some sign of how Lincoln intended to deal with the secession crisis. Then came Sumter—and war.

A "Brothers' War" When the Civil War began on April 12, 1861, Americans gave it various names. For secessionists it was a "War for Southern Independence" or "the War Between the States." Northerners, on the other hand, considered it "the War of the Rebellion" or simply "the War for the Union." Both sides agreed that, whatever else, it was a "brothers' war," severing links among families, personal friends, and public figures according to their sectional loyalties.

This deeply painful division reached even into Abraham Lincoln's family. A Kentucky officer named Ben Hardin Helm was the husband of Mary Todd Lincoln's sister. He spent several days at the White House talking to old West Point friends. Some of them were already preparing to head south and join the Confederate army. As Helm—still uncertain—concluded his visit, Lincoln gave him an envelope containing a major's commission in the Union army. The two men grasped hands warmly and exchanged good-byes. A few days later came the news that Helm had chosen the Confederacy.

But another Kentuckian, Fort Sumter's Robert Anderson, accepted Lincoln's promotion to brigadier general that same month. He then left for the Middle West to help keep his native state in the Union.

A third officer, a fervent Unionist, turned down Lincoln's offer to be commander of all Northern troops. Instead, he accepted command of the Confederacy's eastern force, the Army of Northern Virginia. "If Virginia stands by the old Union, so will I," Robert E. Lee remarked. "But if she secedes (though I do not believe in secession as a constitutional right, nor that there is sufficient cause for revolution) then I will follow my native state with my sword and, if need be, with my life." When Virginia finally broke with the Union, Lee followed.

In many ways the Confederate struggle for independence resembled the American revolt against British rule two generations earlier. Some revolutionists strive for colonial independence from a ruling country. This occurred in North America in the 1770s. Other revolutions result when one section of a country tries to break away from the whole nation, leading to an internal war between the nation and the section. Such separatist revolts often occur when the people of a particular region feel that their interests and values are directly threatened by those who control the national government. This was the case in the South after Lincoln's election.[1]

Both national uprisings, such as the American Revolution, and separatist revolts, such as the Civil War, usually take place only after great soul-searching among those rebelling. The American people do not shift their loyalties easily. Washington, Franklin, and other Revolutionary leaders had served the British Empire faithfully for decades in war and peace. Lee, Davis, and other key Confederate officials had served the national government before the South seceded. They finally revolted because they believed the Southern way of life—a culture based upon slavery—was directly threatened by Republican control of the central government.

Mobilization In the early months of the Civil War most Americans seemed to expect the conflict to be bloody but brief. Few realized what lay ahead. "No casualties yet, no real mourning, nobody hurt," wrote Mary Boykin Chesnut, the wife of a high Confederate officer, in June 1861. "It is all parade, fuss, and fine feathers."

A few leaders believed the situation was more serious. Among them were Lincoln and his generals and their counterparts behind the Southern lines. Jefferson Davis, wrote Mrs. Chesnut, informed her one evening that "either way, he thinks it will be a long war, that before the end came we would have many a bitter experience. He said only fools doubted the courage of the Yankees, or their willingness to fight when they saw fit."

Nor did most Southerners underestimate the extent of Northern resources. In almost every respect—population, capital, and raw materials—the Union had the advantage over the Confederacy. Most important, the North could produce endless supplies of guns, ammunition, ships, and other war equipment. The South, on the other hand, had increasing difficulty in keeping its soldiers supplied.

[1] More recently, separatist revolts took place in Nigeria (where the Ibo province of Biafra revolted unsuccessfully) and in Pakistan (where the Eastern Bengali area, now known as Bangladesh, won its independence).

Neither side began with much of an army, There were only 18,000 men in the regular army in 1860, with about 1,100 officers. Only a small number of these had significant combat experience, and most of them resigned to join the Confederate Army. These officers and their Northern counterparts prepared to fight a conflict far different, in strategy and tactics, from those for which they had been trained.

Both North and South started the war using a system of volunteer enlistments. At first they recruited men for a few months, since both sides believed that the war would be short.

As the fighting dragged on, it became apparent to both sides that volunteers would not provide enough manpower. Even the cash bounties offered to those who enlisted would not bring enough volunteers. Casualties mounted in 1862. First the undermanned Confederacy and then the Union turned to drafting soldiers by lottery. Wealthy or influential young men, North and South, could, and often did, avoid going to war. They could provide a paid substitute, who might cost as much as $600. Or they could claim exemption on grounds that their civilian work was essential. (Slaveholders who grew cotton, for example, could avoid service this way.) By the end of the war the South's troop shortage had become extreme. The Confederacy then began drafting and training thousands of slaves.

FIGHTING THE CIVIL WAR

Late in May 1861 the Confederate government moved its capital to Richmond. This was done partly because the large Virginia city could accommodate the growing Confederate bureaucracy more easily than Montgomery could. The move also dramatized the Confederacy's promise to defend the Upper South. Besides, Richmond was an important rail and road center. With Northern and Southern capitals and armies now only a hundred miles apart, the area of Virginia and Maryland became, for obvious reasons, the war's pivotal theater of operations.

A thick layer of gloom spread over Washington as Lincoln and his generals prepared for a Southern attack. There was talk that, for the second time in half a century, an American President might be forced to flee the White House, pursued by an invading army.

Southern Strategy Although a number of important battles were fought during the war, the Confederates generally used an overall guerrilla strategy that resembled Washington's in the American Revolution. A friend wrote Jefferson Davis complaining of the Confederacy's "purely defensive" strategy and of its reluctance to launch a full-scale attack on the North. Davis replied: "Without military stores, without the

RESOURCES OF THE UNION AND THE CONFEDERACY, 1861

	UNION	CONFEDERACY
Population	23,000,000	8,700,000*
Real and personal property	$11,000,000,000	$5,370,000,000
Banking capital	$330,000,000	$27,000,000
Capital investment	$850,000,000	$95,000,000
Manufacturing establishments	110,000	18,000
Value of production (annual)	$1,500,000,000	$155,000,000
Industrial workers	1,300,000	110,000
Locomotives	451,000	19,000
Railroad mileage	22,000	9,000

*Including 3,500,000 slaves

Lee was a vigorous fifty-five when the Civil War began. Like Washington, he fought against difficult odds and was much admired by his troops.

workshops to create them, without the power to import them, necessity, not choice, has compelled us to occupy strong positions and everywhere—selecting the time and place of attack—to confront the enemy without reserves." In other words, the South chose to conduct an "offensive defense." It tried to select the time and place for major battles carefully. At other times Southerners harassed Northern armies with cavalry raids led by such intrepid commanders as "Stonewall" Jackson, J. E. B. Stuart, Nathan B. Forrest, and John S. Mosby.

Confederate army commanders realized that it was impossible to prevent Union invasions of the South. They knew too that they had neither the manpower nor the resources to mount a full-scale invasion of the North. So the Confederates worked instead to maintain their armies in the field while fighting back the Union troops thrown against them. They hoped that a war-weary Northern public would finally force Lincoln's government to negotiate a peaceful settlement. Lee and Davis recognized, as Washington did during the 1770s, that a revolutionary army wins by not losing—that is, by displaying the capacity to endure.

Northern Strategy Recognizing the Southern strategy, Lincoln and his generals committed Northern armies from the beginning to a policy of total war against the South. They were dedicated to the complete destruction of Confederate military power and civil authority by every necessary means. George Templeton Strong wrote in his diary in November 1861:

> Were I dictator at this time, my military policy would be: (1) to defend and hold Washington, Western Virginia, Kentucky, Missouri; (2) to support Unionists in North Carolina and in eastern Tennessee; (3) to recover and hold (or destroy with sunken ships) every port and inlet from Hatteras to Galveston.

Strong's proposals resembled the North's actual strategy during the war, which was threefold: (1) to encircle the South in an ever-tightening military net by blockading its ports; (2) to divide the Confederacy in half by seizing control of the Mississippi and Tennessee rivers; (3) to capture Richmond and destroy the main Confederate armies in Virginia, where most Southern troops were concentrated. Strong believed, as did Lincoln and his officers, that if "the rebels of the South can be locked up and left to suffer and starve," victory would follow.

Superior to the South in its navy, the North was able to impose a blockade of Southern harbors. The Confederates counteracted with fast blockade-runners, joined by a number of private merchantmen. In the early years of the war they managed to slip past Union vessels in five out of every six attempts. But the Union blockade became increasingly effective. By 1865 it had choked off Southern cotton exports to Europe as well as imports of arms and supplies.

War in the East The outcome of the Civil War was decided not by naval encounters but by land battles. Northern armies began poorly but improved their performance every year. Confederate forces scored impressive victories at the first and second battles of Bull Run in July 1861 and August 1862. At Fredericksburg, Maryland, in December 1862, the North suffered a crushing defeat, with over 12,000 casualties.

In May 1863, at Chancellorsville, Maryland, outnumbered Southerners won another victory, though it cost them one of their best generals, "Stonewall" Jackson. They imposed a stalemate on the Virginia front and, several times, threatened to capture Washington itself.

Lincoln searched desperately for Union commanders capable of breaking the stalemate and executing major offensive operations. In the process he appointed a succession of commanding generals—George McClellan, John Pope, McClellan again, Ambrose Burnside, Joseph Hooker, and George Meade. One time, after McClellan had failed to pursue a retreating Confederate force, he received this letter: "My dear McClellan: If you don't want to use the Army of the Potomac, I should like to borrow it for a while. Yours respectfully, A. Lincoln."

The turning point of the Civil War in the east came in July 1863. Confederate troops under Lee marched into southern Pennsylvania, where they encountered a Union force near Gettysburg. After three days of costly fighting, Lee's invasion was repulsed decisively on July 3.

Each side had over 75,000 troops involved, and the South suffered almost 25,000 casualties. "The results of this victory are priceless," rejoiced the normally pessimistic Strong. "Philadelphia, Baltimore, and Washington are safe. The rebels are hunted out of the North, their best army is routed, and the charm of Robert Lee's invincibility broken."

Grubby-looking but brilliant, Grant was modest and reticent about his feelings. Of him Lincoln said: "I can't spare this man—he fights."

War in the West The South's strategy of tying down and wearing out Union forces worked reasonably well in the east. Elsewhere, however, better-equipped and better-led Union troops won a series of important victories.

In February 1862 federal troops and a

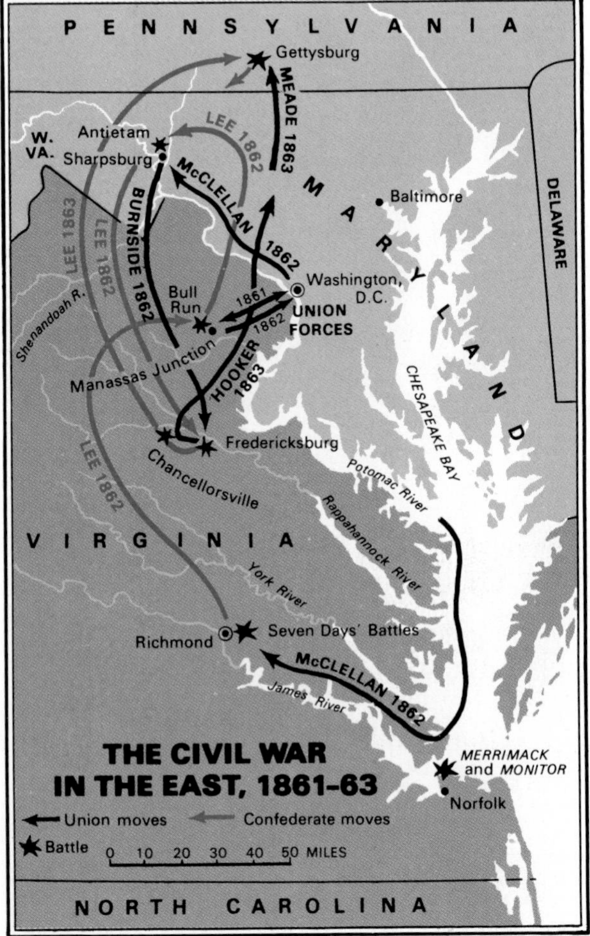

Fighting broke out on April 12, **1861**, when Confederate batteries opened fire on Fort Sumter in Charleston harbor. The Union quickly began a naval blockade of Confederate shipping. The first major engagement occurred on July 21, at Manassas Junction, Virginia. There an advancing Union army under Irvin McDowell was defeated in the first Battle of Bull Run and driven back to Washington, D.C.

The year **1862** witnessed the first naval battle between ironclads—the Union ship *Monitor* and the Confederate ship *Virginia* (formerly the *Merrimack*)—on March 9 near Norfolk, Virginia. The Union offensives of that year began in March with McClellan's Peninsula Campaign, an attempt to take Richmond from the southeast. He advanced slowly to within a few miles of the city. Confederate forces inflicted heavy casualties on his troops at the end of May. During the subsequent Seven Days' Battle (June 26-July 2) Lee and Jackson forced McClellan to retreat and abandon the campaign. The Confederate army moved northward to win the second Battle of Bull Run (August 29-30). From there Lee and Jackson advanced into Maryland. Near Sharpsburg, McClellan engaged the Confederates in the Battle of Antietam (September 17). Although militarily the battle was a draw, Lee withdrew to Virginia. McClellan was replaced as Union commander by Burnside, whose overwhelming force was shattered at Fredericksburg (December 13).

In **1863** Hooker took command of the Union army, only to be defeated at Chancellorsville (May 2-4). However, Confederate losses there included "Stonewall" Jackson. Lee marched into Pennsylvania and was defeated at Gettysburg by a Union army under Meade (July 1-3). Lee retreated to Virginia, his second offensive into Union territory a failure.

gunboat flotilla led by Ulysses S. Grant captured Fort Henry, on the Tennessee River, and Fort Donelson, on the Cumberland River. These moves forced Southern General Albert S. Johnston to abandon Kentucky and parts of Tennessee to the Union.

Admiral Farragut's capture of New Orleans in April 1862 and a series of Northern victories farther up the Mississippi—capped by defeat of the Confederate fleet at Memphis in June—brought most of the river under Union control. Arkansas, Louisiana, and Texas were thus isolated from the rest of the Confederacy.

In the west the decisive point was reached the day after Lee's defeat at Gettysburg. On July 4, 1863, Vicksburg fell. This key Confederate port surrendered after a six-week siege by Union troops. A final Confederate stronghold on the Mississippi—Port Hudson, Louisiana—fell later that same month.

Grant's remarkable success in this western campaign led to his appointment as Lincoln's seventh and last commanding general. Grant appealed to Lincoln for many of the same reasons he did to most Northerners. Wrote one admirer of Grant: "He talks like an earnest businessman, prompt, clearheaded, and decisive, and utters no bosh."

Final Campaigns Grant took command of the Union forces in the spring of 1864. In May he and Meade led a Northern force of 100,000 men against Lee's army, which had regrouped in Virginia after its Gettysburg defeat the previous year. It was in the same month that Union troops led by Sherman began their push to Atlanta.

For the remainder of the war Grant and

Meanwhile, in the west, the Union won a series of important victories in **1862**. In February Grant captured Fort Henry on the Tennessee River and Fort Donelson on the Cumberland. Moving southward in Tennessee, he was attacked at Shiloh (April 6-7), but Union reinforcements forced the Confederates to withdraw into Mississippi. Union forces also made progress in their drive to gain control of the Mississippi River. Farragut bombarded and captured New Orleans in late April and proceeded up the river to Baton Rouge. To the north, a combined naval and land expedition defeated the Confederate fleet at Memphis on June 6 and captured the city.

In **1863** the Union continued its campaign to secure mastery of the Mississippi. Grant began attacking the Confederate stronghold of Vicksburg in May, and the city surrendered on July 4. With the fall of Port Hudson on July 9, the entire Mississippi was in Union hands and the Confederacy split in two.

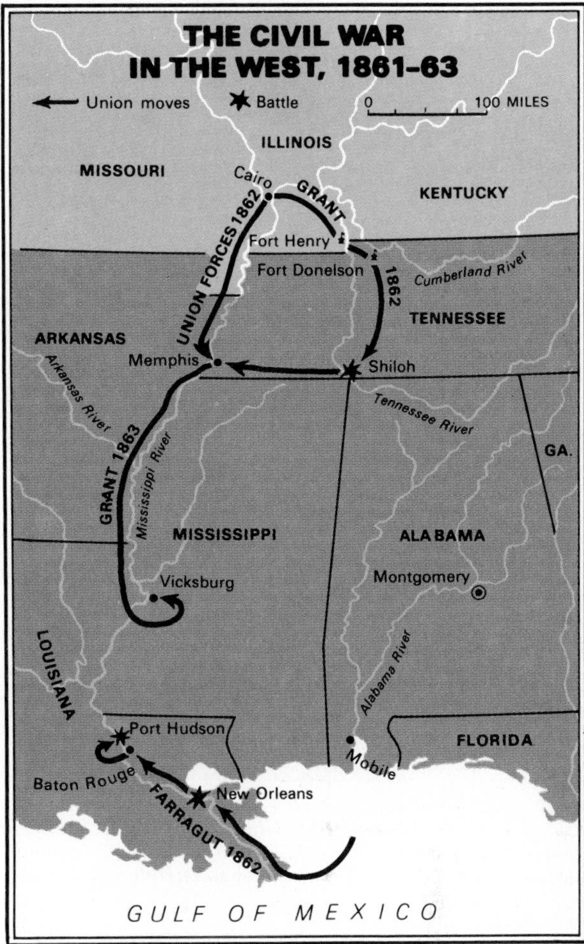

Sherman pursued the same strategy of wearing down the enemy that Davis and Lee had hoped earlier would win for the Confederacy. No longer did Union forces concentrate on capturing Richmond or other Southern territory for its own sake. Instead, Union forces struck directly at the remaining Confederate armies and resources, as Sherman did in Georgia. They aimed to inflict so heavy a price in casualties and physical devastation that a war-weary South would be forced to surrender.

Beginning in June 1864, Grant's army tied down most of Lee's forces near Petersburg, Virginia. That fall Sherman led his famous march to the sea from Atlanta to Savannah. From Savannah, Sherman's forces turned north and extended their scorched-earch tactics into South Carolina and North Carolina.

Grant's troops, meanwhile, left their Petersburg trenches for frequent assaults on Lee's thinly manned lines. By early April 1865 Grant had blocked Lee's effort to retreat southward. Lee's army had then been reduced by death and desertions from 54,000 to 30,000 men. Lee believed that further fighting was useless and that Confederate defeat was inevitable. He surrendered to Grant at Appomattox, Virginia, on April 9, 1865.

Despite pleas from Jefferson Davis for continued resistance, even if only by guerrilla bands in the Southern hills and forests, the rest of the Confederate armies still in the field surrendered by the end of May. Union troops finally occupied Richmond after Davis and other Confederate officials had fled. For all practical purposes Southern resistance had ended by the time Jefferson Davis was captured on May 10.

LIFE ON THE HOME FRONTS

In the long run it would have been far cheaper to have purchased the abolition of slavery, although such a course was unthinkable to both sides in 1861. Estimates of the war's total cost ran as high as $3 billion for the South and $5 billion for the North. This was three to four times the total estimated value of every slave in the Con-

(continued on page 415)

Many a Civil War battle exacted enormous tolls in men. Above, Confederate dead lie in a shallow trench at Chancellorsville. Union forces, below, attack on the third day of the combat at Gettysburg. Watching a similarly dramatic panorama earlier in the war, Lee had remarked: "It is well that war is so terrible—we would grow too fond of it."

The major military actions of the fall of **1863** occurred in the west. On September 9 Union forces maneuvered the Confederates out of Chattanooga, Tennessee, without a battle. Moving south into Georgia, the Union army was stopped at Chickamauga (September 19-20) and driven back into Chattanooga. In October Grant was given command of all the Union's western armies. At the Battle of Chattanooga (November 23-25) he defeated the Confederates in engagements on Lookout Mountain and Missionary Ridge.

In **1864** Grant, now in supreme command of the Union armies, took charge of the Virginia front. He began a campaign to destroy Lee's army and take Richmond. Grant struck again and again: at the Battle of the Wilderness (May 5-6), at Spotsylvania (May 8-12), and at Cold Harbor (June 1-3). Lee parried Grant's blows, inflicting heavy casualties on his opponent. In this one-month period the Union army lost approximately 60,000 men, a number equal to Lee's total strength at the beginning of the campaign. But the North could provide reinforcements of men and supplies; the South lacked reserves of both. Grant pressed on, moving south to Petersburg. He failed to capture it in a bloody four-day battle (June 15-18). However, his subsequent nine-month seige of the town cut Richmond off from the Deep South.

In the west, Union forces under Sherman moved out of Chattanooga in May 1864 to begin their invasion of Georgia. The opposing Confederate general, Joseph E. Johnston, fought a series of defensive actions but continued falling back toward Atlanta. John B. Hood, who replaced Johnston in July, suffered heavy losses in two pitched battles near Atlanta. It was occupied by Union forces on September 2. After the fall of Atlanta, Hood moved northwest to threaten Tennessee and the Union army's long lines of communication. Sherman sent part of his army to counter Hood's forces. He led the rest of his troops in a virtually unopposed march to the sea from Atlanta to Savannah, which fell on December 22. Meanwhile, Union forces shattered Hood's army at Nashville, Tennessee (December 15–16).

In **1865** Sherman continued his scorched-earth policy as he moved north from Savannah into North Carolina, where Johnston, restored to command, slowed his advance somewhat. In Virginia the Confederates, outnumbered more than two to one by Grant's reinforced army, were unable to lift the siege of Petersburg. On April 1, Lee's last attack (at Five Forks) was repulsed, and on April 2 he evacuated Petersburg and Richmond, moving westward. A Union army under Philip H. Sheridan, which had marched south through the Shenandoah Valley, blocked his path. Virtually surrounded by an overwhelming force, Lee surrendered to Grant at Appomattox on April 9. On April 18, Johnston surrendered to Sherman at Durham Station, North Carolina. Final Confederate capitulations occurred in Alabama (May 4) and Louisiana (May 26).

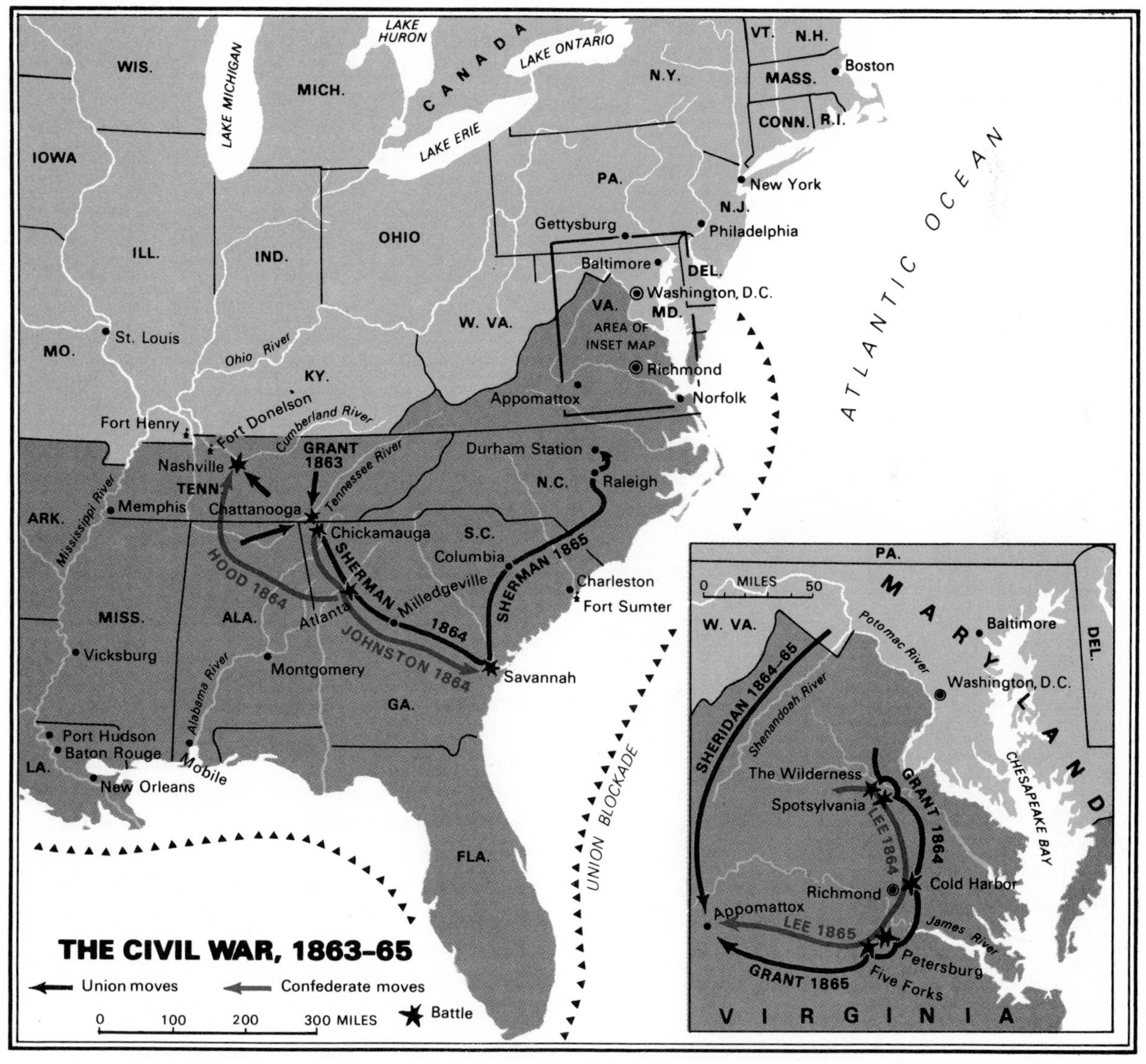

The First Modern War

"The Civil War was the first of the world's really modern wars," wrote the historian Bruce Catton. The weapons of this conflict were forerunners of today's standard military equipment. And the ways in which they were used foreshadowed modern techniques of warfare.

The basic weapon for the infantry, both Union and Confederate, was the single-shot, rifled musket. Because of its rifled (grooved) barrel, it had a range and accuracy two to three times greater than earlier, smoothbore guns. Troops could now engage in deadly fire from distances of a quarter to a half mile. Trench warfare came into being as close-range or hand-to-hand combat was no longer inevitable.

What did this mean for military tactics? The old-time massive assaults, with soldiers elbow to elbow rushing forward toward the enemy, became an invitation to slaughter. (Yet generals on both sides continued to demand this classic maneuver in spite of heavy human losses.) The increased firepower of the infantry threatened both artillery and cavalry. A bank of cannon could no longer offer a solid defense when outranged by enemy riflemen. And the dash of a cavalry charge became mere vainglory when riders could easily be picked off, one by one, from afar.

Civil War mortar

Breechloading rifles, improvements on the cumbersome muzzle-loaders, and repeating rifles were introduced during the war. Other innovations included rifled cannon and a form of machine gun. The Civil War marked the beginning of a new era in naval warfare, symbolized by the first battle between ironclad ships, the *Monitor* and the *Merrimack*. Other experiments in naval warfare included submarines—most were failures—and electrically controlled mines.

Transportation was modernized, with railroads used widely to move troops and supplies. The telegraph changed wartime communications. Union armies sent an estimated 6 million telegrams over 15,000 miles of wire set up by the Signal Corps. The most spectacular railroad supply system was that maintained for Sherman during his siege of Atlanta: 1,600 tons of supplies arrived daily in 16 trains from Union depots northwest of the city.

The Civil War was a modern war in the important sense that it required a break with traditional military thinking in order to achieve victory. Most Civil War generals on both sides regarded cities and territories—not enemy armies—as their objectives. They hoped to win by maneuvering rather than by fighting. By contrast, Lincoln's overall strategy was to move on all fronts simultaneously in order to crush the enemy's forces and gain control of his resources. This warfare of annihilation was a plan that tradition-bound generals scorned. Only in Grant and Sherman did Lincoln find generals who would employ his strategy successfully. They were willing to break the rules to play, and win, a new and deadly game.

federacy. Both the Union and the Confederacy had great difficulty in paying their enormous bills for war equipment, soldiers' salaries, and operating expenses. Both sides resorted to many similar financial measures: raising taxes, issuing various types of bonds, and printing vast quantities of paper money unsupported by gold or silver reserves.

Crisis in the South The overriding desire for victory led to sweeping measures in the South. Some affected the master-slave relationship. Southern slaveholders had defended their right to absolute control over their bondsmen in antebellum days. When war came, they watched helplessly as the Confederate government and Southern state governments transferred hundreds of thousands of slaves from private plantations to more urgent labor in the war effort. Slaves even became Confederate soldiers shortly before Appomattox. And throughout the war Southerners relaxed their close supervision of slave movements and activities.

Normal political life also came to a halt in the South during the war. There was no two-party system (as in the North). There was only one all-inclusive ruling, but unruly, "government party." Within the Confederacy there were people who opposed Davis' conduct of the war. They spoke their minds freely. Yet the demands of fighting a separatist revolt prevented any change in government.

The war not only changed master-slave relations and Southern politics. It also altered the Southern economy. The cherished doctrine of states' rights received rough treatment at the hands of Confederate leaders. These men were determined to assume every power they needed to wage war. Davis centralized and nationalized the economy to a remarkable degree. If occasion demanded, he interfered freely with the rights of capitalists. The Confederacy did more than seize slaves for war work. It closely regulated foreign commerce. It confiscated food and equipment from private farms for the army. It created government-run industries to produce military

CIVIL WAR MANPOWER

	UNION	CONFEDERACY
Total serving in armed forces	1,556,678	1,082,119
Killed in battle or died from wounds	110,070	94,000
Died from illness	249,458	164,000
Wounded	275,175	100,000

equipment. And it tightly controlled what was left of private enterprise.

The Confederacy even created a Cotton Bureau, which took over planters' cotton supplies. The Cotton Bureau paid a set price for the entire crop. By running the Northern blockade, the government acted as the sole Southern salesman in Europe. Government supplies of cotton were used as security for the Confederacy's foreign loans.

In spite of truly heroic effort and sacrifice the South was destitute by the end of the war. "We have no money, even for taxes, or for their confiscation," wrote Mary Chesnut in April 1865. "Our poverty is made a matter of laughing." Millions came close to starving. Confederate officials recommended the nutritional values of such fare as squirrels and rats to make up for the dire shortage of food. At the time of its surrender Lee's army had enough ammunition to provide each man seventy-five rounds—but no food.

Southern economic devastation by 1865 could be measured in many ways. Compared to 1860, there were 32 percent fewer horses, 30 percent fewer mules, 35 percent fewer cattle, and 42 percent fewer pigs. Cotton crops were destroyed or rotted unpicked in the fields. Few factories remained in operation. There was almost no trade. Only a handful of banks were left, and they were nearly empty.

Prosperity in the North "We hear they have all grown rich," Mrs. Chesnut complained about Northerners in 1865. "Genuine Yankees can

Richmond in April 1865. Only the shells of burned buildings surround the canal basin. Lee prepared to abandon the city on April 2, and mobs of its inhabitants set fire to the town on the eve of his evacuation.

make a fortune trading jackknives!" Industrial growth in the North began before the Civil War, of course. But it was vastly accelerated by wartime demands to equip and supply the army. The number of Northern factories increased from fewer than 140,000 in 1860 to over 250,000 by 1870. Railroad mileage doubled during this decade. The growth was aided not only by government contracts for arms and military supplies. It was helped also by wartime currency inflation, huge federal subsidies to railroads, and protective tariffs for industry.

The result was enormous inflation–high prices but also tremendous profits. There was rapid expansion in industries ranging from wool production to mining, from petroleum to iron manufacturing. Farmers prospered, too, because of the increased demand for every staple crop. Most merchants and shippers shared in the boom. Banking facilities were enlarged greatly after Congress passed several new banking acts. Senator John Sherman wrote his brother General William Sherman about the impact of the war on Northern capitalists: "They talk as confidently of millions as they formerly did of thousands." Aristocratic George Templeton Strong complained wistfully that the more sedate prewar culture of New York City was being "diluted and swamped by a great flood-tide of material wealth."

A shortage of manpower on Northern farms and in factories stimulated immigration from Europe. In 1865 alone, 180,000 new immigrants arrived on Union soil. In 1866 and 1867 the number spurted to 300,000 yearly.

Perhaps most important in the North, as in the Confederacy, was the role played by the government in stimulating economic growth. Southern Democrats had dominated Congress and the executive branch until the 1850s. They blocked measures such as the protective tariff, a national banking system, and railroad subsidies. Now the Republicans were in control. They favored industrialization and economic growth. To further their aims, they adopted the Morrill Tariff of 1861, which raised duties. They passed the National Banking Acts of 1863 and 1864; these aided national banks at the expense of state banks. In addition, Congress awarded land-grant subsidies to transcontinental railroads and stimulated western settlement with the 1862 Homestead Act, which offered land to settlers at nominal sums.

The Republicans changed not only the economic habits of the North but its political life as well. Lincoln found it no easier than Davis did to

Walt Whitman

At the outbreak of the Civil War Walt Whitman was forty-two years old. Bearded and graying, he worked off and on as a journalist in Brooklyn. Although his book of poems *Leaves of Grass* brought him little prestige and no income, he continued to revise it, writing poems whenever he could. In December 1862 he visited his wounded brother, a Union soldier in Virginia. He realized that he had to become part of the war effort. With a part-time government job in Washington, D.C., for support, he spent nearly all of the next three years serving the wounded in hospitals around the city and sometimes on the battlefields.

He described his role thus: "I have learnt a good deal of hospital wisdom. I adapt myself to each emergency, however trivial, however solemn—not only visits and cheering talk and little gifts—not only washing and dressing wounds but prayer at the bedside, etc." He entertained the veterans, both Union and Confederate, with recitations of poetry. He also led groups in "an amusing game called twenty questions."

For Whitman the essence of the war could be felt only "in the midst of its saddest results." His compassion for its victims was heightened by his own inner struggles. His optimistic views about mankind and democracy conflicted with the horror he felt toward the organized "butchery" of warfare. Not until the war ended did he resolve his own conflict. He accepted both war and peace, both evil and good, as parts of a divine plan.

In 1865 Whitman published *Drum Taps,* the poems he had written during the war. Some poems are martial outbursts—"Prelude," which describes the mobilization of the army in Manhattan, or "Beat! Beat! Drums! Blow! Bugles! Blow!" which lives up to its title. Others are quieter. They describe the cavalry crossing a ford, a bivouac, a field hospital, his own lonely vigils with the dying and the dead. In "A Sight in Camp in the Day-

break Grey and Dim," the poet lifts the shrouds of an old man, a youth, and a third figure. The last has a face "calm, as of beautiful yellow-white ivory":

Young man, I think I know you—
 I think this face of yours is the
 face of Christ himself;
Dead and divine, and brother of all,
 and here again he lies.

Drum Taps was being printed when the news of Lincoln's assassination reached Whitman. He was inspired to write the dirge that many critics consider his masterpiece. The poem stresses that peace and beauty triumph in death, for death brings a joining of man and nature. It begins:

When lilacs last in the door-yard bloom'd,
And the great star early droop'd
 in the western sky in the night,
I mourn'd—and yet shall mourn
 with ever-returning spring.
O ever-returning spring!
 trinity sure to me you bring;
Lilac blooming perennial,
 and drooping star in the west,
And thought of him I love.

 govern a country at war. Throughout the conflict the President was attacked from all sides of his wartime government coalition, which was known as the Union party. Abolitionist Republicans (known as Radical Republicans) denounced him for moving slowly on the question of emancipation, while War Democrats denounced him for moving at all on the problem. Moderate Republicans criticized the slow military progress of Northern armies.

Compared to the Confederacy, the North had a poor wartime record in the field of civil rights. In spite of Union victories, many Northerners opposed the war. Lincoln authorized a number of arbitrary military arrests of such civilians, especially Peace Democrats—called "Copperheads" by their enemies. He suspended the privilege of habeas corpus[2] to keep pro-Confederate Northerners in jail once arrested.

In both sections, North and South, the war interfered with civil liberties, but in different ways. Northerners were more likely to be thrown in jail for opposing the war. Southerners were more likely to be punished for resisting government confiscation of their property. These interferences involved of course the civil rights of *white* people. Neither government troubled itself much about the rights of blacks, free or slave.

FREEDOM FOR BLACK PEOPLE

As soon as the war broke out, Northern black men tried to enlist in the Union army. They were not allowed to do so, however, until the fall of 1862. Eventually, over 186,000 blacks served as Union soldiers—almost 15 percent of all Northern troops. They were usually led by white officers, and they were paid less than white troops. Union commanders were divided in their attitudes toward using black soldiers. Some welcomed them. Others, like Sherman, did not.

[2] This privilege, guaranteed by the Constitution, provides that an arrested person can demand that legal authorities show why he or she has been imprisoned. A writ of habeas corpus (Latin words meaning "you have the body") thus protects a person against being held in jail without cause.

The Emancipation Proclamation Northern policy toward slavery changed during the war. Many Republicans in the government believed sincerely in emancipation. Lincoln, though, had always regarded it as secondary compared to the overriding importance of winning the war and reuniting the nation.

Like most Americans at the time, Lincoln believed that blacks were inferior. He never felt certain that 4 million ex-slaves could reach full equality with whites in the United States. Throughout the Civil War he tried unsuccessfully to link his moves toward emancipation with efforts to colonize freed blacks. None of these efforts worked out.

Lincoln had been elected on a platform that pledged to restrict slavery but not abolish it. He moved cautiously toward emancipation mainly because of his military and political problems in conducting the war. Radical Republicans in Congress kept pressuring him for swift abolition. Even many moderate Northerners became fervent converts to emancipation as war casualties mounted, if only to punish the Confederacy. Such Unionists did not change their attitudes toward *black people* (and their supposed inferiority). They only changed their minds about *slavery*.

The situation was complicated by the fact that thousands of runaway slaves took refuge with the Union army. There they were often treated—as with Sherman's army—as both a help and a hindrance. Thousands of blacks, however, did join Union army ranks. Lincoln, along with most Northerners, grew more sympathetic to emancipation.

Congress took the first step by abolishing slavery in the federal territories in June 1862. Then, in September 1862, Lincoln issued a preliminary proclamation. In it he stated that he would issue a final document on January 1, 1863, freeing the slaves in all states then in rebellion. This final document was the Emancipation Proclamation.

The Emancipation Proclamation actually freed very few people when it was issued. It did not apply to slaves in border states fighting on the Union side. Nor did it affect slaves in Southern areas already under Union control. Naturally, the states in rebellion did not act on Lincoln's order. But the proclamation did show Americans, and the rest of the world, that the Civil War was now being fought to end slavery.

For all practical purposes the 3 1/2 million black slaves in the South found themselves free within days after Lee's surrender. It was only with final ratification of the Thirteenth Amendment, however, in December 1865, that slavery was ended completely throughout the United States.

Treatment in the North Though the Union—eventually, at least—fought to free black people, those who lived in the North faced many difficulties. In 1860 free Northern blacks numbered 225,000. Most of them were restricted to menial jobs. A rigid pattern of segregation in schools, hospitals, transportation, and other public facilities kept blacks and whites separated. Roughly 93 percent of Northern black people lived in states where they could not vote. (Only five New England states allowed blacks to cast ballots in 1865.)

Blacks were the victims of race riots throughout the North during the war. The most destructive took place in New York City in the summer of 1863. There, anger among the city's Irish working class at a new federal draft law exploded into violence during four days and nights of rioting. The new law allowed wealthy citizens to avoid the draft by buying the services of substitute soldiers—something poor laborers clearly could not afford.

Mobs of Irish workers rampaged over Manhattan Island from July 13 to July 16. They burned, looted, and killed. The rioters' main targets were free blacks and, to a lesser extent, white abolitionists and wealthy citizens. The city's outnumbered police force, also composed largely of Irishmen, fought the rioters with great bravery and discipline, finally putting down the rioting with the help of federal troops. By that time, some 1,200 persons, mostly black, had been killed. Many thousands were injured. Property worth millions was damaged or destroyed. Other Northern cities, especially in the Middle West, experienced similar draft riots.

After the War The Thirteenth Amendment did not settle the basic questions about the future status of black Americans, especially in the postwar South. Former slaves were now free. But free to *do* what? Free to *be* what? What did freedom mean to someone raised in slavery?

Many ex-slaves simply stayed on their plantations, working for the same masters. Their old habits altered little at first, although now the whites were often as poor as their former bondsmen. "The Negroes seem unchanged," Mrs. Chesnut wrote, referring to her one-time slaves. Other former slaves left their old homes, usually for an uncertain future.

Whatever the fate of individual freed slaves, one characteristic of Southern emancipation was its peaceful nature. Despite the fears of antebellum white Southerners, there were no blood

When the war ended, some Union commanders required surrendering forces to take an oath supporting the Constitution. These "Rebs" were sketched at Richmond.

baths, no vengeful attacks by ex-slaves on their former masters. Black people responded to their new freedom with dignity and grace.

Early in the twentieth century Benjamin Botkin and other folklorists traveled through the United States, recording the recollections of aged ex-slaves. One elderly man recalled:

> The end of the war, it come just like that—like you snap your fingers. Soldiers, all of a sudden, was everywhere—coming in bunches. Everyone was a-singing. We was all walking on golden clouds. Hallelujah! Everybody went wild! we was free. Just like that, we was free. It didn't seem to make the whites mad, either. They went right on giving us food just the same. Nobody took our homes away, but right off colored folks started on the move. They seemed to want to get closer to freedom, so they'd know what it was—like it was a place or a city.

The experience was exciting yet frightening for blacks, people like those who had joined Sherman's army on its march to Savannah. Many of them had never gone beyond the borders of their own farms. One ex-slave commented to Botkin:

> We knowed freedom was on us, but we didn't know what was to come with it. We thought we was going to be richer than the white folks, 'cause we was stronger and knowed how to work, and the whites didn't, and they didn't have us to work for them any more. But it didn't turn out that way. We soon found out that freedom could make folks proud, but it didn't make 'em rich.

As soon as the war was over, blacks began to organize and work for their own advancement. Historians sometimes overlook the fact that, even in 1860, there were 261,000 free blacks in the South. Tens of thousands of them were literate. These men and women—like the leaders who met with Stanton and Sherman—formed an important black leadership base at the end of the war. Many took part in black conventions held in a number of Southern cities in 1865 and 1866. They petitioned the federal government to assist freedmen by granting them the franchise, protecting their civil rights, and providing land and other economic help.

THE FIRST YEAR OF RECONSTRUCTION

The basic dilemma of Reconstruction for all those who lived through it, black and white, Southerner and Northerner alike, was its revolutionary nature. Like the Civil War itself, the postwar period had no examples on which to model itself, no constitutional provisions by which policy makers might be guided.

Compared with reconstruction periods that have followed more recent civil wars in Russia, Spain, and China, the American experience is notably mild. Confederate leaders were neither shot nor driven into exile. Indeed, many resumed their careers in American politics. Only a few, such as Jefferson Davis, were imprisoned, and these only for a brief period. No Confederate property was confiscated. Nor was there any forced redistribution of wealth imposed on the defeated South by the victorious North.

Lincoln's Approach In Lincoln's Second Inaugural Address, delivered a month before his death, he called for a generous settlement with the defeated South: "With malice toward none; with charity for all . . . let us strive on to finish the work we are in, to bind up the nation's wounds."

As early as 1862 Lincoln had indicated his desire to restore a defeated Confederacy quickly and without revenge against either its leaders or people. Lincoln suggested a basis for Reconstruction in December 1863. He called for amnesty[3] (except in the case of key leaders) for Southerners who pledged loyalty to the Union. Southern states in which 10 percent of the 1860 electorate took such a loyalty oath and accepted emancipation would be restored immediately to the Union.

Governments in Arkansas, Louisiana, and

[3] Amnesty is a form of pardon for offenses against the government—especially to a group of persons.

Tennessee met Lincoln's provisions in 1864. But Congress refused to seat their representatives. The problem was complicated by the fact that Lincoln believed that the executive branch should control Reconstruction, whereas Congress wanted this power for itself. Congressional attitudes were partly a reaction to the vast expansion of presidential authority under Lincoln during the Civil War.

Republicans in Congress were led by Radicals Thaddeus Stevens of Pennsylvania in the House and Charles Sumner of Massachusetts in the Senate. They were afraid that the Democratic party, led by Southern ex-Confederates, would quickly return to national power. So they offered a much tougher Reconstruction plan in a measure known as the Wade-Davis Bill. It provided that a majority of voters in each Southern state take an "ironclad oath" swearing to their *past* as well as to their *future* loyalty. Obviously, if the electorate were composed only of whites, no ex-Confederate state could honestly meet this provision. The bill also required that the Southern states abolish slavery in their constitutions, repudiate the Confederate war debt, and disfranchise Confederate leaders. Congress passed the Wade-Davis Bill on July 4, 1864. Lincoln killed the measure with a pocket veto. Then Congress passed the nonbinding Wade-Davis Manifesto, reasserting the provisions of the earlier bill.

Therefore, by mid-1864, the stage was set for a postwar confrontation between the President and Congress on Reconstruction policy. Was the South to be restored quickly, its new state governments falling into the hands of ex-Confederate whites with a minimum of federal interference? (This is what Lincoln wanted, though he did urge Southern whites to allow at least educated blacks to vote.) Or should the Southern states undergo fundamental political changes before they could rejoin the Union? Should they, for instance, allow blacks to vote and hold office, while disbarring ex-Confederate leaders and perhaps confiscating their land?

Assassination With the war almost over, Lincoln's thoughts had turned increasingly to the problem of reconstructing the South. After a trip to Richmond early in April 1865, he spent several days working out various programs.

On the night of April 14, Good Friday evening, President and Mrs. Lincoln went to Ford's Theater in Washington to see a popular play, *Our American Cousin.* Shortly after 10 P.M. a half-crazed Southern sympathizer named John Wilkes Booth shot Lincoln as he watched the play. Booth then stabbed another member of the President's party, leaped onto the stage, rushed from the theater, and rode away. (He was shot down on April 26 by Union troops that had pursued him into Virginia.)

The wounded Lincoln was taken from Ford's Theater to a nearby house. There family, friends, and government officials kept an all-night vigil. The President remained unconscious until his death at 7:22 the following morning. "Now he belongs to the ages," said Secretary of War Stanton, one of those at his bedside.

Word of Lincoln's assassination spread quickly via the telegraph. The first reaction to the event, shared by most Northerners and even many Southerners, was one of profound shock: "I am stunned," wrote George Templeton Strong, "as by a fearful personal calamity."

For Lincoln was highly popular in the North at the time of his death, a result of Union military victories beginning in 1863 and culminating in Lee's surrender. During the war itself, Southerners—as one might expect—had little affection for "Uncle Abraham." Many Northerners felt the same way, especially in the early years. One such person was Strong, an aristocrat and avowed snob. He never liked Lincoln's lack of polish and fondness for telling jokes. Yet these very qualities endeared the President to most other Americans. And even Strong, like other Unionists, responded to Lincoln's firm leadership and genuine anguish at the war's increasing toll in human suffering: "It must be referred to the Attorney General," Lincoln once told Strong about a request to pardon a criminal. "But I guess it will be all right, for me and the Attorney General's very chicken-hearted."

By the war's end, most Northerners prob-

Johnson was an honest but tactless man forced to cope with uniquely difficult circumstances. Born poor, he was a self-made man and touchy about it. Jefferson Davis said he had "the pride of having no pride."

ably agreed with Strong's high estimate of Lincoln's wartime achievement. The President's "weaknesses are on the surface," Strong wrote on April 11, 1865. "His name will be of high account fifty years hence, and for many generations thereafter."

Johnson's Plan Lincoln's death placed the burden of reconstructing the South on the shoulders of his former Vice President, Andrew Johnson. Johnson was a War Democrat from Tennessee and a one-time Radical on the Reconstruction issue. Once in the White House, however, he soon adopted Lincoln's basic proposals. Unfortunately, Johnson completely lacked Lincoln's basic sympathy for the problems of freed blacks. Also, he was a dogmatic man. He showed almost none of Lincoln's tact in dealing with political opponents.

Johnson, like Lincoln, believed that Reconstruction was a matter to be handled by the President. His position was strengthened by the fact that Congress was not in session for several months after he took office. Johnson readmitted the states of Arkansas, Louisiana, and Tennessee. In May 1865 he issued his own Reconstruction plan. It provided that whites in each Southern state who pledged their future loyalty to the Union could elect delegates to a state convention. This convention had to revoke the ordinance of secession, abolish slavery, and repudiate the Confederate war debt. Then the state would be restored to the Union. Johnson granted amnesty to almost all Confederates who took the oath of allegiance. The exceptions were wealthy people and high officials. Even they could apply for a presidential pardon. By late 1865 all the Southern states except Texas had complied with these provisions. (Texas did so early in 1866.)

Southern Regulation of Blacks Congress believed that the government had a duty to assist freedmen after the war. So in March 1865 it created the Freedmen's Bureau, a temporary federal assistance agency headed by Oliver O. Howard. The bureau distributed food and medicine to poor blacks (and whites), opened schools, supervised land distribution to freedmen, and tried to defend the civil rights of Southern blacks. (It exercised these functions in helping "Sherman's Negroes" in the resettlement program.)

The Freedmen's Bureau, however, could not protect the physical security of black Southerners without the help of Union troops. This problem was clearly a most urgent one. Brutal riots against blacks occurred in Memphis and New Orleans in 1866.

After Appomattox Union troops were mustered out of the army at a rapid rate. By the end of 1865 only 150,000 soldiers remained of the million serving six months earlier. Many of these were stationed on isolated western posts fighting Indians.

Under these conditions it was impossible for Union troops to offer the 4 million Southern blacks, most of them recently freed, any real protection. Most white Southerners had been raised to believe that blacks had no civil rights that whites were bound to respect. Killings, beatings, burnings, and other forms of physical terror directed against blacks—mostly to keep them out of politics—began soon after the war's end. Violence against blacks was often carried out by white secret societies. Several were formed after the war, primarily to keep blacks from voting. The most famous, the Ku Klux Klan, was founded in 1866. The turmoil increased during the 1870s.

Many whites in the South adopted other means to reduce black people to a state of virtual enslavement. In every Southern state new governments were elected by white voters according to the provisions of Johnson's Reconstruction plan. The Johnson state governments, as they were called, allowed no blacks to vote. They adopted so-called Black Codes to regulate the actions and bahavior of freedmen. Southern whites claimed that such codes were necessary because of the threat of social disorder as a result of emancipation. There had been no major instance, however, of blacks rioting against whites anywhere in the region.

The Black Codes had some provisions to protect blacks. They legalized marriages between blacks, for instance. They also gave blacks the

Stern, intense, and vindictive, Thaddeus Stevens attacked Lincoln throughout the war for not punishing the South harshly enough.

Charles Sumner, once admonished during an argument, "But you forget the other side," thundered in reply: "There is no other side!"

 right to sue and testify in court. But the codes consisted mainly of restrictions. They supervised the movements of blacks, prevented them from carrying weapons, and forbade intermarriage between blacks and whites. Contracts, sometimes for life, forced black people to remain at their jobs. In some states blacks could not own land or work at any job other than farming without a special license. Black children were forced into certain job apprenticeships.

Reaction in the North Northern Republicans, both Radicals and moderates, attacked the Johnson state governments. They denounced the Black Codes and called for their immediate repeal. Most Radicals believed that the defeated Southern states should be treated, in Thaddeus Stevens' phrase, like "conquered provinces," until more repentant leaders emerged.

When Congress reconvened in December 1865, representatives and senators elected under the Johnson state governments applied for admission. Republicans in Congress refused to admit them. These Southerners who now claimed loyalty to the Union included fifty-eight former Confederate congressmen, six of Jefferson Davis' cabinet members, and four Southern generals. Most amazing of all was the presence of Alexander Stephens of Georgia, who eight months earlier had been vice president of the Confederacy!

The 1866 riots in Memphis and New Orleans gave Northerners additional evidence that the white South remained unrepentant. Thus it seemed inevitable that there would be a power struggle between Johnson and congressional Republicans over who would control the Reconstruction process. Who was sovereign in the federal government, the President or Congress? Who could decide?

RADICAL RECONSTRUCTION

Congress answered these questions to its own satisfaction by taking the initiative completely out of Johnson's hands. By 1867 the legislature had won control. It dominated the government for the next ten years.

The Republicans who controlled Congress developed their strategy mainly through the Joint Committee on Reconstruction, which was dominated by the Radicals. This group asserted that Southern states could be readmitted only after meeting congressional requirements. The Joint Committee moved a series of measures through Congress between 1865 and 1867. Most of the bills were vetoed by the hapless Johnson, then repassed by a two-thirds majority.

First, in February 1866, came the new Freedmen's Bureau bill. It expanded the bureau's authority to protect Southern blacks, giving it the right to try in military courts persons accused of violating the civil rights of freedmen.

A Civil Rights Act of April 1866 granted the same civil rights to blacks as those enjoyed by whites. The measure also asserted the right of the federal government to interfere in state affairs to protect a citizen's civil rights.

In order to fortify their position, congressional Republicans in June 1866 adopted and sent to the states the Fourteenth Amendment. In effect, it gave blacks full citizenship. If a state denied the vote to blacks, its representation in the House would be reduced. The amendment also forbade ex-Confederate officials from holding federal or state office again without receiving congressional pardon. The Joint Committee declared that any Southern state wishing readmission would have to ratify the Fourteenth Amendment. The Johnson state governments in the South voted against ratification. (The amendment was eventually ratified in 1868.)

President Johnson hoped his Republican opponents would be defeated in the 1866 congressional election, and he campaigned personally against them. After a wild and bitterly fought campaign, however, anti-Johnson Republicans swept the election. They carried every Union state but three.

A Harsh Program When Congress met after the election, Republicans enacted their program into law. They began with the First Reconstruc-

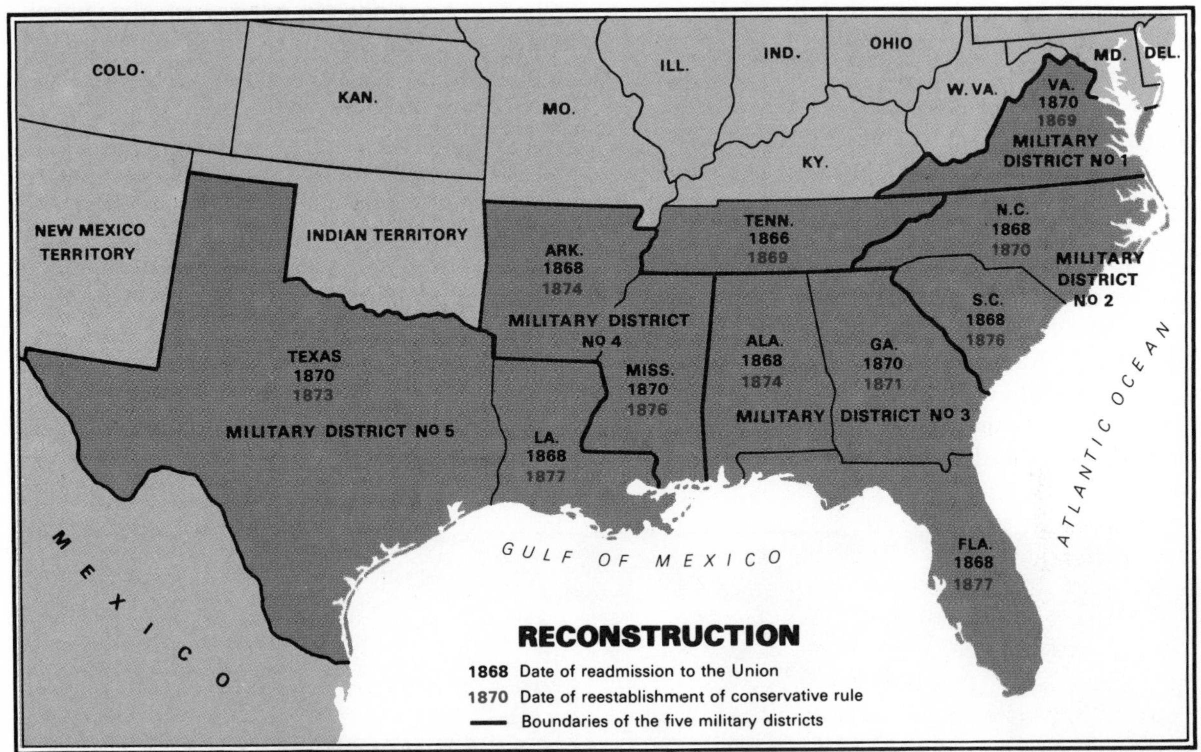

tion Act of March 1867. Significantly, the bill's final form came from a moderate, Republican John Sherman. By this time the moderates agreed with Radicals on most key issues of Reconstruction. This law abolished the existing Johnson state governments. It provided for universal manhood suffrage—that is, for black as well as white voting.

The First Reconstruction Act also authorized temporary military rule of the South. Ten former Confederate states were still outside the Union. (Tennessee had ratified the Fourteenth Amendment and had been readmitted.) These states were divided into five military districts. To rejoin the Union, a state had to call a constitutional convention elected by universal manhood suffrage. This body, in turn, had to create a new state government that would ratify the Fourteenth Amendment and guarantee black suffrage. Three subsequent congressional acts strengthened the powers of federal army commanders in the South.

The final aspect of the Radicals' Reconstruction program involved their attempt in 1867 to remove the President through impeachment. Congress was convinced that Johnson would sabotage its Reconstruction acts, so it called itself into special session, an unprecedented step. It passed two measures on March 2, 1867. One virtually deprived Johnson of command of the American army by requiring him to issue all military orders through the General of the Army, Ulysses S. Grant. The second bill was the Tenure of Office Act. It prohibited the President from removing officials whose appointments had been made with Senate consent without again securing Senate approval. This law meant that Johnson could not fire Secretary of War Stanton. This leading Radical was the man who—along with Saxton and Howard—had tried to block presidential interference with Sherman's land distribution policy. Johnson disregarded the measure and dismissed Stanton. Then the House passed a resolution impeaching

Johnson on eleven charges, including alleged violations of the two March 2 bills.

After a Senate trial the President was acquitted of the very flimsy charges. A two-thirds majority is needed to convict the President on an impeachment charge. Thirty-five senators voted for his conviction, while nineteen (including seven Republicans) voted for acquittal. Thus Johnson was saved by a one-vote margin.

The effort to unseat Johnson was the most daring episode in the Radicals' Reconstruction plans. A few Radicals such as Stevens tried to push through bills confiscating 394 million acres of land owned by the 70,000 chief leaders of the Confederacy. (Charles Sumner called the antebellum plantations "nurseries of the Rebellion.") But such measures found little support among the party's moderate majority, and therefore they did not pass.

Most aims of the Radicals were fairly limited. They worked chiefly for Republican political control of the national government. They also hoped that coalitions of black voters and friendly whites would dominate Southern politics, thereby preventing national revival of the Democratic party.

But Republicans did not have any direct social or economic goals. Only a small number of Radicals were committed to complete equality for black Americans. There was no large-scale

Southern blacks voted for the first time during Radical Reconstruction. Note, at right, a voter being paid off—a practice by no means limited to blacks or to Southern elections.

program to provide landless freedmen with an economic base. Many blacks had been promised "forty acres and a mule." But the thousands resettled on abandoned lands—such as "Sherman's Negroes" of the Deep South—were soon dispossessed.

After the attempt to impeach Johnson, Radicals left the problems of Reconstruction in the hands of federal commanders and new state governments in the South. The quarrel between legislative and executive branches over Southern policy ended in 1868, when Republican Ulysses S. Grant was elected President. By then the central drama of Reconstruction had shifted from Washington to the South itself.

The New Radical Governments Beginning in 1867, so-called Radical state governments were set up according to congressional regulations. New black voters made up a majority of the Radical electorate in five states—Alabama, Florida, Louisiana, Mississippi, and South Carolina. Elsewhere in the South, white Radical majorities were supported by black voters. By 1870 more than 700,000 blacks and 627,000 whites were registered as voters under the Radical state constitutions.[4]

Congress readmitted Louisiana and six other states to the Union under Radical rule in June 1868. By the end of 1870 all ten ex-Confederate states had been readmitted to the Union.

Throughout the South blacks filled public offices for the first time. These were not usually the highest offices, however. Nor did blacks hold office in proportion to their percentage of voters. Only one state legislature, that of South Carolina, ever had a black majority. No black ever became a Reconstruction Southern governor. (Some states, though, had black lieutenant governors.) There were two black United States senators and fifteen congressmen during the entire period of Radical rule.

[4] The Fifteenth Amendment, adopted in 1870, forbade any state from preventing citizens from voting because of race, color, or "previous condition of servitude." This was a clear effort to eliminate the hypocrisy of some Northern states that demanded suffrage for blacks in the South while continuing to deny it at home.

Many black political leaders were educated men. Some were among the most distinguished figures in the entire South. Francis L. Cardozo, for example, South Carolina's state treasurer, held degrees from the Universities of London and Glasgow, making him perhaps the best-educated politician in the South of either race.

Who were the Radicals in the South? They included many different groups. Some were Southerners, most of whom had been prewar Whigs or secret Union sympathizers during the war. Many Southern businessmen and even a few planters joined the Radicals. They hoped that the new governments would have enough help from Northern capitalists and Republican politicians to rebuild the South's shattered economy. Radicals also included nonslaveholding farmers, who, while they disliked blacks, hated ex-Confederates even more for having led them into what they considered "a rich man's war and a poor man's fight." These Southern-born Radicals were called scalawags (an often undeserved term) by former Confederates.

Other Radicals were Northerners. Tens of thousands of them went south after the war for a variety of reasons. Hostile whites referred to them bitterly as carpetbaggers, whose only aim was to fill their luggage with ill-gotten Southern wealth. Yet many were teachers—their carpetbags stuffed only with McGuffey's Readers. Like the people who went to the Sea Islands, their aim was to set up schools for the freedmen. Northern soldiers returned to the South seeking good land; 5,000 went to Louisiana alone. Businessmen sought opportunities to invest capital and to profit from the region's economic reconstruction. A number of politically ambitious people did arrive to take part in the Radical governments. But they were by no means all opportunists.

Charges of Corruption It has often been said that Radical state governments were corrupt. There is some truth to this charge. Legislators in South Carolina, for example, paid $200,000 for $18,000 worth of furniture for the state capitol. Louisiana's Radical governor H. C. Warmouth left the state with a personal fortune of half a million dollars, most of it acquired illegally. Similar fortunes were made throughout the South.

Several points should be noted in favor of the Radical governments, however. At this time scandals tainted the Grant administration and many Northern state and local governments. The historian John Hope Franklin has termed public dishonesty after the Civil War "bisectional, bipartisan, and biracial." (Actually, the blacks in Congress were not implicated in the Grant scandals, although many of their white colleagues were.) State governments everywhere ran up enormous debts. Postwar fortunes in the South were made by Radicals and ex-Confederates, Republicans and Democrats alike. Given the level of immorality in American politics, North and South, during Reconstruction, it seems fair to say that the Radicals were no more corrupt than other politicians at the time.

In fact, most Radical state funds were spent rebuilding a ruined economy. Somehow, the Radicals managed to begin reconstructing Southern highways, railroads, hospitals, and orphanages. They also began building schools; many Southern states had had no public-school system before the war. The rebuilding had to be done for an additional 3 1/2 million people. These were the ex-slaves, who were now citizens and entitled to the use of public facilities.

An Evaluation Historians have long debated whether Radical state governments in the South ruled poorly or well. Opinions on this question depend in part on attitudes about whether (or when) blacks should have been allowed the franchise and a role in governing. We tend to forget how short a time Radical governments actually ruled. Tennessee never underwent this type of control. Virginia, North Carolina, and Georgia returned to conservative hands by 1871. Arkansas, Alabama, and Texas did so by 1874. And it was all over by 1877.

Some provisions of the Radical state constitutions found approval even among ex-Confederates. The documents ended imprisonment for debt, for example, and did away with property qualifications for voting. Basically, ex-Confederate whites objected less to the corruption of Radical state governments than to their very existence—especially to the presence of blacks on the political slate. Radical rule did not end because of its failure to meet the economic and social problems of the South. Radicals were driven from power because of their insistence on meeting these problems through biracial political cooperation.

THE END OF RADICAL RULE

Two trends put an end to Radical Reconstruction. One was the increasing hostility of white Southerners. The other was the growing indifference of its Northern Republican sponsors.

Southern hostility not only increased, but it grew more violent. Thousands of blacks and white Radicals lost their lives to armed bands of whites such as the Ku Klux Klan and local "rifle clubs" that roamed the South during the 1870s. Federal troops and black state militia could suppress only a small number of these groups. Congress passed several Force Bills, making it a national offense to interfere with any citizen's civil rights (including his right to vote). But they had little effect, since only a few thousand federal troops remained in the South to enforce the laws against guerrilla groups like the Klan. To compound the Radicals' problem, Congress repealed its ironclad oath in 1871. No longer did Southerners have to swear that they had always been loyal to the Union. In 1872 a general amnesty restored civil rights (including the right to hold office) to all but about 600 high Confederate officials.

As white terrorists harassed the remaining Radical state governments, Northerners became indifferent. Republicans in Washington grew increasingly weary of the struggle to protect black civil rights. "The whole public," complained President Grant, "is tired of these outbreaks in the South."

The death or retirement of Radical leaders

Louisiana was one of five Southern states to have a majority of black voters. Between 1868 and 1896 the state had 133 black legislators—38 senators and 95 representatives. They were never numerous or strong enough to control political life in Louisiana, though Oscar Dunn (center) did lead a struggle against corruption and extravagance.

such as Stevens and Sumner helped restore control of Congress to more conservative, business-minded Republicans. A combination of Democrats and reform-minded "Liberal Republicans" nearly won the presidency in 1872 on a platform pledging an end to federal support for Radical regimes in the South. In 1874 the Democrats regained control of the House for the first time since before the war.

Public attention strayed even further away from the South after 1873, when a major depression swept the country. The business slump threw hundreds of thousands out of work and shifted political attention from postwar Reconstruction to the problem of economic recovery.

The Compromise of 1877 In 1876 both presidential candidates, Republican Rutherford B. Hayes and Democrat Samuel B. Tilden, promised even before the election to restore "home rule" to the South. Both pledged to remove federal support for the three remaining Radical state governments—those of Louisiana, South Carolina, and Florida. They implied that Southern whites could now handle all problems connected with blacks, including political rights.

The election ended in a unique stalemate. Two sets of returns arrived from the three states yet in Radical hands. The Radicals claimed that Hayes had won, while Democrats insisted on a Tilden majority. The nineteen doubtful electoral votes (including one disputed Oregon elector) meant the difference between a one-vote Hayes margin and a clear Tilden sweep. Congress finally accepted the recommendation of a specially appointed commission to award all the disputed votes to Hayes, thereby making him President. The South, in turn, received a pledge from Hayes that all remaining federal troops would be removed from the three Radical states, that federal subsidies would be provided for a Southern transcontinental railroad then under construction, and that a Southerner would be appointed to the Cabinet.

All these promises were met, and Radical rule promptly collapsed in the three remaining states. This so-called Compromise of 1877 marked the final surrender of the North's promise to defend black political and civil rights against the former white Confederates.

During the decades that followed, conservative governments defeated black efforts to participate in Southern politics. In every subsequent election fewer blacks voted.

Violence toward black people increased for the rest of the century. The great majority of Southern blacks farmed other people's lands as tenants or sharecroppers. They were forced into a subordinate place in Southern life, being neither slaves nor completely freedmen.

1. How did the Union and the Confederacy recruit soldiers at the beginning of the war? What changes took place in recruitment as time went on?
2. How did the basic military strategy of the Confederacy differ from that of the Union?
3. In what ways did the South change during the Civil War? Why did the absence of Southern representatives in Congress contribute to the industrial growth of the North?
4. Why was Lincoln's conduct of the war opposed by the Radical Republicans? By the War Democrats? How were people's civil rights affected in the North? In the South?
5. What were Lincoln's motives in issuing the Emancipation Proclamation? Why did it free few slaves? When did all the slaves gain their freedom?
6. Lincoln's Second Inaugural Address called for a generous settlement with the South. Did his Reconstruction plan bear this out? Why did Congress refuse to accept his program?
7. In what ways did Johnson's Reconstruction plan differ from Lincoln's?
8. What were the Black Codes and what was their purpose?
9. Why did Congress take over Reconstruction? What were the Radicals' most important moves?
10. Were the Radical Republicans truly radical in a political, economic, or social sense? Explain your answer.

Beyond the Text

1. Despite overwhelming odds, the Confederacy was able to carry on a war for four long years. Investigate the reasons for (a) its endurance, or (b) the eventual Northern victory. David Donald's collection of short essays in *Why the North Won the Civil War* can serve as a point of departure.
2. Lincoln had trouble finding good military leaders. Why was this so? Research and report to the class.
3. Blacks participated, both as voters and as legislators, in Southern politics for the first time during Reconstruction. How well did they perform?

Bibliography

Nonfiction

Catton, Bruce, *Centennial History of the Civil War,* 3 vols.
Donald, David, ed., *Why the North Won the Civil War.**
Eaton, Clement, *A History of the Southern Confederacy.**
Franklin, John Hope, *Reconstruction After the Civil War.**
McPherson, James M., *The Struggle for Equality: Abolitionists and the Negro in the Civil War and Reconstruction.**
——— *The Negro's Civil War.*
Nevins, Allan, *The War for the Union,* 4 vols.
Patrick, Rembert W., *The Reconstruction of the Nation.**
Randall, J. G., *Lincoln the President,* 4 vols.
Randall, J. G. and David Donald, *The Civil War and Reconstruction.*
Stampp, Kenneth M., *The Era of Reconstruction, 1865–1877.**
Stampp, Kenneth M. and Leon F. Litwack, eds., *Reconstruction: An Anthology of Revisionist Writings.**
Thomas, Benjamin P., *Abraham Lincoln.*

Fiction

Basso, Hamilton, *The Light Infantry Ball.*
Campbell, Marie, *A House with Stairs.*
Crane, Stephen, *The Red Badge of Courage.**

*a paperback book

UNIT FIVE

INDUSTRIAL

Americans thought about their Civil War in many different ways. But most of them agreed, North and South, that it was somehow a conservative war. Each side thought of itself as the conserving protector of an inherited social and political order. It was difficult for Americans to understand that what lay ahead was not a restoration of stability but a surprising burst of activity and change. The United States was transformed into a modern industrial nation in the last third of the nineteenth century. That transformation is the subject of Unit Five.

In an odd way, the people who could best have understood the revolutionary transformations of American society were those who had been most completely defeated by it: the American Indians. From the time of Jamestown, they had watched white society grow in size and power. Now, the forces of expansion increased dramatically. Railroads, miners, cattle ranchers, and farmers spilled out over the Great Plains to the Pacific Coast with fresh speed and energy.

One of the tribes that felt the forces of westward expansion most directly was the Sioux. By the close of the century, this

AMERICA

determined people had been reduced from proud independence to reservation captivity. The destruction of their way of life reached a symbolic climax in 1890 in the last "battle" between Indians and United States soldiers in American history—Wounded Knee. The defeat of the Sioux is the subject of Chapter 21. The following chapter discusses the larger process of white expansion that made their final conquest inevitable.

At the same time that postwar America was expanding geographically, a new economic landscape took shape. New inventions and manufacturing processes changed the ways that Americans earned their livings and made their goods. Giant factories in enormous cities with great immigrant and working-class populations arose. With them came the inevitable conflicts between rich and poor, employers and workers, immigrants and native Americans.

One of the most important examples of conflict was a series of events in Chicago in 1885 and 1886. It began with a labor strike at the McCormick Harvester Company, led to a famous bombing incident at Haymarket Square, and ended in the trial and execution of several immigrant German Americans. Chapter 23 tells this story and Chapter 24 explores the background of industrialization that made the conflict possible.

Social and economic change created strains on political parties and governmental institutions. The examination, in Chapter 25, of the career of President James A. Garfield and of his assassination in 1881 by a crazed, disappointed office-seeker introduces the climate of political tensions. Chapter 26 then traces the conditions that made political careers such as Garfield's possible. Politicians' concern with party politics and consequent neglect of the urgent needs created by change are explored. So are the beginnings of demands for reform exemplified in the Populist movement.

What emerges, then, from the late nineteenth century is a mixed picture of incredible industrial growth and geographical expansion alongside moments of crisis and bloodshed—with political leaders looking on as almost helpless and often confused spectators.

CHAPTER

21

"BATTLE" AT WOUNDED KNEE

THERE WAS A CONFUSION about names—there almost always was when Indians were involved. Most whites called the tribe the Sioux. But this name was just a French abbreviation of what some of the tribe's enemies had called them. They called themselves Dakota.

There was more than one Indian name for what the whites called Wounded Knee Creek, on the Pine Ridge Reservation in South Dakota. Also, whereas some people called what had happened at Wounded Knee Creek a battle, others called it a massacre. Even the man who rode out from reservation headquarters to Wounded Knee had two names. One was an Indian name, Ohiyesa. One was a white man's name, Charles Eastman. He was a Sioux, but he had been educated in white schools in New England. In fact, he was a doctor of medicine.

But there was no confusion about what Charles Eastman saw on that bright New Year's Day morning in 1891:

> On the day following the Wounded Knee massacre, there was a blizzard. On the third day it cleared, and the ground was covered with fresh snow. We had feared that some of the wounded Indians had been left on the field, and a number of us volunteered to go and see.
>
> Fully three miles from the scene of the massacre, we found the body of a woman completely covered with a blanket of snow, and from this point on we found them scattered along as they had been hunted down and slaughtered. When we reached the spot where the Indian camp had stood, among the fragments of burned tents and other belongings, we saw the frozen bodies lying

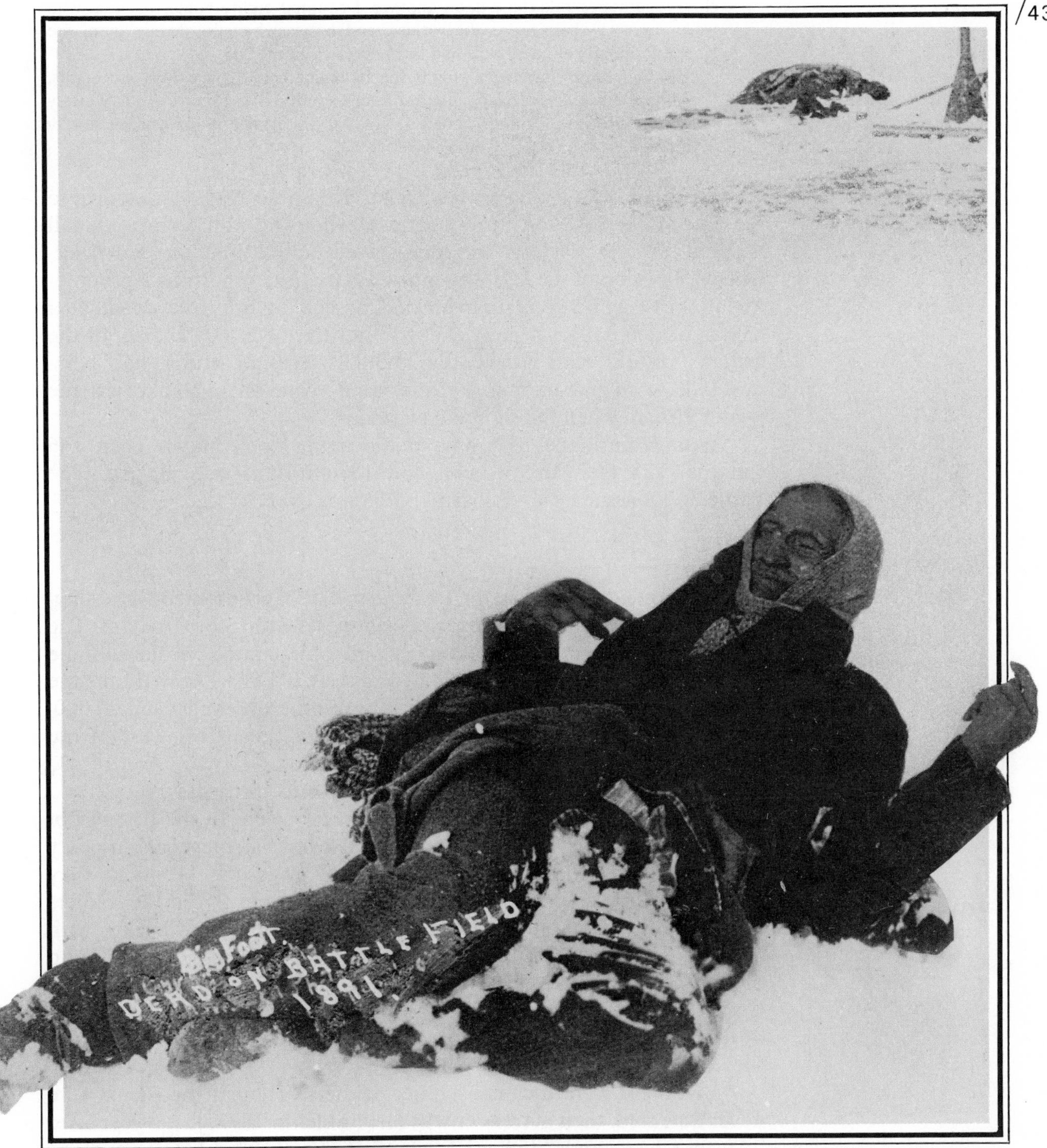

Big Foot, seventy-year-old chief of the Sioux, was one of 146 Indians killed by the U.S. Seventh Cavalry at Wounded Knee. He was found dead three days later, frozen grotesquely where he had fallen.

> close together or piled one upon another. I counted eighty bodies of men, who were almost as helpless as the women and babes when the deadly [gun] fire began, for nearly all their guns had been taken from them.
>
> Although they had been lying in the snow and cold for two days and nights, a number had survived. Among them I found a baby of about a year old, warmly wrapped and entirely unhurt. Under a wagon, I discovered an old woman, totally blind and helpless.

Eastman began to load the few survivors into wagons to return to the agency (reservation headquarters), where he had set up a small hospital. Two groups of white men stayed behind at Wounded Knee. One was a troop of the U.S. Seventh Cavalry. The other was a group of about thirty white civilians who had agreed to bury the dead, at a charge of two dollars a body. They found the body of the chief of the Indians, an old man named Big Foot, frozen half sitting, half lying down. Ill with pneumonia, he had been lying on a blanket on the winter ground when the shooting started.

It took until the next day to dig a big open grave. Then 146 Indians—128 men and women and 18 children—were buried. The battle and massacre (it was partly both) was over.

Wounded Knee was the last and most tragic moment in a long, difficult, and often ugly process: the conquest of the Sioux Indians. The conquerors were the white citizens and blue-coated soldiers of the United States. The process began before the Civil War. At that time the Sioux were a powerful tribe, probably numbering well over 20,000. They hunted on millions of square miles of the plains west of the Missouri River.

The Sioux resisted the invasion of white miners, farmers, and ranchers. They fought often, and they usually won. In the summer of 1876 they won two astonishing victories over the bluecoats, as they called the cavalry. On Rosebud Creek, in what is now Montana, they attacked a large column of cavalry and infantry and forced the soldiers into a retreat. Then, just a few days later, the Seventh Cavalry, with General George A. Custer commanding, attacked a large Sioux camp on the Little Bighorn River, just a few miles from Rosebud Creek. Custer divided his force, and the Indians killed Custer as well as most of the Seventh, one of the most experienced cavalry units operating in the West.

But there were too many other soldiers. Though the Sioux were never defeated, their surrender was inevitable. In 1877, just a year after "Custer's last stand," the great war chief Crazy Horse led many of his followers onto a reservation that had been recently set aside for the

The Sioux moved onto reservations such as this one at Pine Ridge, South Dakota, in 1877. They raised horses for hunting buffalo, which provided them with food, clothing, and skins for their portable tepees.

Sioux. Crazy Horse was murdered a short time later. Some of his people fled to Canada to join the other outstanding Sioux leader, Sitting Bull. About 2,500 Sioux then tried to survive in Canada. But hunger and cold—and the fact that white people had slain most of the buffalo—finally drove them back to the reservation. In 1881 Sitting Bull surrendered—"came in," as it was said. This was the end of a golden age for the Sioux, one that had lasted more than a century.

Originally, the Sioux inhabited the forest and lake country between Minnesota and the Great Lakes. They built permanent bark houses and lived by farming and hunting small game. About the middle of the eighteenth century the Sioux were driven westward from their forest homes onto the Great Plains by another tribe, the Chippewas. The Chippewas had come into contact with the French and had traded their furs for guns. The guns gave the Chippewas an overwhelming advantage. The Sioux had to retreat.

There were seven main divisions of the Sioux. The division that moved farthest west and became most prosperous was the Tetons. The Tetons in turn consisted of seven bands, among them the Oglalas, the Brules, and the Hunkpapas.

Plains life for the Sioux centered on the buffalo, the horse, and the rifle. These Indians became nomadic. They gave up their permanent homes for portable tepees made of buffalo hides. The tepees, and the poles over which they were stretched, could be dragged from place to place by horses. Buffalo provided meat and skins for clothing and shelter. Hunting and warfare were the primary occupations of the Sioux. A man gained prestige depending on his skill and courage at hunting and in battle.

The whites, with their cannon, railroads, and reservations, destroyed the Sioux way of life. The whites slaughtered the buffalo until there were practically none left. The whites insisted that the Sioux live in permanent log homes on the reservation. Government rations of beef, flour, and beans were substituted for the hunt. The whites disapproved of the Sioux religion and forbade the sacred Sun Dance, the Indians' most holy annual ritual. White Indian agents (those in charge of the reservations) insisted that a Sioux man have only one wife. Reservation life undercut the old Sioux society completely. The authority of warriors and chiefs collapsed with the end of a hunting economy and tribal warfare.

What was happening to the Sioux was simple and tragic. They had been defeated by a much more powerful and complex society. Some of them—the "nonprogressives"—might resist in certain ways. They might refuse to plant crops, for example, or continue to wear Indian clothing. But their defeat was still almost complete. They had long ago gladly accepted some of the white man's ways and tools: the horse, the rifle, the metal kettle that was so much better than their old buffalo-skin buckets. Such things had been useful in the old life. But the United States government had plans and hopes for the Sioux that were utterly at odds with the old Indian ways.

American policy was aimed at one long-range goal—to make the Indians into self-supporting farmers. Each family would receive its own land. Indians would cook on a stove instead of over a fire, wear white people's clothes, and, if possible, worship the white man's God instead of the old God of the Sioux, Wakan Tanka. To well-intentioned reformers in the East this meant "raising the Indian to civilization." To whites in the West it meant a final end to the Indian as a barrier to westward expansion.

For the Indians these changes meant a divided world. Even those who wanted to cooperate most—the so-called progressive Indians—lived something of a double life. An Indian man might wear a white man's clothes, plow and harvest crops, marry only one woman, send his children to white schools or even become a member of the Indian Police.[1] But the memory of the old life—a life now dead in fact—was still alive.

The deep conflict between Indian and white ways came to the surface in 1883, when a Senate investigating committee visited the

[1] The Indian police, recruited from young reservation Indians, helped the Indian agents keep order.

Sioux. Sitting Bull, who had been one of the Sioux leaders at the Battle of the Little Bighorn, came to testify. But the chairman would not recognize Sitting Bull as chief. Sitting Bull got up and left. All the Indians followed him. But several of the progressive Indians returned to plead with the committee to use its influence with the Great Father[2] to get better treatment for the Indians. Soon even Sitting Bull swallowed his hurt pride and returned to apologize.

Then Sitting Bull gave a remarkable account of what defeat had meant to the Sioux. They had been wealthy in their own terms, with land, ponies, and buffalo aplenty. In one lifetime the white man had reduced them to poverty.

> Whatever you wanted of me I have obeyed. The Great Father sent me word that whatever he had against me in the past had been forgiven and thrown aside, and I accepted his promises and came in. And he told me not to step aside from the white man's path, and I am doing my best to travel in that path. I sit here and look around me now, and I see my people starving. We want cattle to butcher. That is the way you live, and we want to live the same way. When the Great Father told me to live like his people, I told him to send me six teams of mules, because that is the way the white people make a living. I asked for a horse and buggy for my children; I was advised to follow the ways of the white man, and that is why I asked for those things.

Sitting Bull's ideas were a little confused, at least by white standards. But he summed up neatly the dilemma of the Sioux. He was still proud of himself and his tribal ways. He resented the whites' failure to understand this pride. But another side of him recognized defeat and was prepared to plead with the whites not for less civilization but for more. In Sitting Bull, and in almost all the other reservation Indians, pride, resentment, hunger, and begging were so intermixed that a meaningful pattern of life was almost impossible.

The situation was the same among all the Sioux. During the 1880s the Indians were gradually becoming "civilized." But the hunger and anger were just below the surface. Some crucial event or idea was all that was needed to bring the conflict with the whites back into the open, tip the scales one way or another, and offer the Indians a clear choice between the old life and the new.

A new idea did come, and from an unpredictable direction. In the summer of 1889—about a dozen years after Crazy Horse had surrendered his band of hostiles—the Sioux began to hear rumors of an Indian messiah (or savior) who had come to earth in the west. They

[2] Great Father, or White Father, was the title used by the Indians for the President of the United States,

had learned enough of Christianity on the reservation to understand the alien notion of a messiah. If it were true that a messiah had come to save the Indians from the whites, surely it was worth investigating, they thought.

The Messiah was said to be at the Paiute reservation at Walker Lake, Nevada. Three of the six Sioux reservations[3] selected important men to make the trip west. It was about a thousand miles away—farther than almost any of the Sioux had ever traveled. Pine Ridge Reservation sent eight men, including Kicking Bear, who was to become the most effective disciple of the new Messiah. From Rosebud went Short Bull. The Cheyenne River Reservation, smaller than either Pine Ridge or Rosebud, sent one man.

Wovoka, the Messiah, claimed to be sent by God to save his people. He preached non-violence and brotherly love. He demanded of his followers only that they dance the Ghost Dance and await the resurrection of their dead.

The eleven Sioux started west by train. Railroads had by then penetrated all the major Western areas, and Indians hopped freight cars with little or no opposition from the white railroad men. When the Sioux reached Wyoming, they found that other tribes—Cheyennes, Arapahoes, Bannocks, and Shoshonis—had also sent wise men to seek the Messiah. The whole group then traveled south to Walker Lake. There the Paiutes gave them wagons to complete the pilgrimage. Soon they were in the presence of the Messiah.

His Indian name was Wovoka, his white name Jackson Wilson. He was about thirty-five years old. He was a Paiute, but he had grown up close to a white ranching family named Wilson. (They gave him his English name.) The Wilsons were a religious family. From them Wovoka had learned in some detail how Jesus had controlled the wind and the seas, how he had promised eternal life to his followers, and how other whites had crucified him. Wovoka was apparently the son of a Paiute shaman, or medicine man.[4] One day in 1889, when he was ill (and perhaps delirious) with a high fever, there was an eclipse of the sun. This led him to believe that he had been taken up to heaven. After talking with God, he had been returned to earth to bring salvation to the Indians.

Wovoka's doctrines were a fairly straightforward Indian version of some of the basic teachings of the New Testament. In a sermon to some visiting Cheyennes he summarized his new faith:

> You must not hurt anybody, or do harm to anyone. You must not fight. Do right always.

[3] One so-called Great Sioux Reservation had been created in 1868. It consisted of about 43,000 square miles in what is now South Dakota, and it was administered from several agencies on or near the land. In 1889 the Sioux territory, much reduced in size, was broken up into six separate reservations— Pine Ridge, Rosebud, Lower Brule, Crow Creek, Cheyenne River, and Standing Rock.

[4] Almost all American Indians relied on shamans, men or women who were thought to have supernatural powers such as foretelling the future or curing the sick.

> Do not tell the white people about this. Jesus is now upon the earth. The dead are all alive again. I do not know when they will be here; maybe this fall or in the spring. When the time comes there will be no more sickness and everyone will be young again.

Ghost shirts, emblazoned with bright-colored thunderbirds and buffaloes, were supposed to protect Indians from the white man's weapons in battle.

In a simplified way Wovoka was telling his disciples that the dead would be resurrected soon. The earth would tremble; he often said that a new earth would cover the old. But true believers need not be afraid, because they would soon enjoy perfect life, youth, and health. In the meantime, the Indians should live in peace with the whites.

Wovoka gave the visiting Cheyennes some clay for making the sacred red paint of the Paiutes. Symbols drawn with it were signs of their salvation. Then he advised them: "When you get home, you must make a dance to continue five days. You must all do it in the same way."

This was the famous Ghost Dance from which Wovoka's new religion soon took its name. During the five days it lasted, men and women sang certain songs and went into hypnotic trances. It was during the dance that Indians were supposed to be able to visit their departed relatives in heaven.

After Short Bull returned to South Dakota, he gave his version of the Ghost Dance religion to his excited Sioux audience. The tone was much more militant than Wovoka's. Short Bull promised punishment for those who refused to be converted—just as the Christian missionaries promised damnation for those who rejected their Messiah. And Short Bull emphasized that the Ghost Dance would enable the Sioux to see their dead relatives. He also promised victory over the hated and feared soldiers for those who wore holy shirts into battle. The shirts were supposed to protect wearers from whites' bullets.

It was not only Short Bull who brought this interpretation back from the trip to Wovoka. A similar version of the Ghost Dance faith emerged on all the Sioux reservations during the summer of 1890. The Sioux were offered a new ritual, the Ghost Dance, and a new faith, which held that the whites would soon be buried in the earth and the Indians would once again own the plains. Nevertheless, most of the Sioux probably rejected the Ghost Dance and decided to continue along the white man's path. For many, though, the religion of Wovoka offered great hope for the return of the old life and the end of their humiliating captivity.

There is no way of knowing how sincere Short Bull was. Nor is there any way of knowing whether Sitting Bull—who soon became a disciple of the Ghost Dance—really believed in the coming resurrection. But there can be no doubt that large groups of Sioux did accept the Ghost Dance.

Agents on all the reservations tried to stop the dances, using Indian police. But, time and again, the dancing Sioux refused to be cowed. They threatened their own police with rifles, insulted the agents, and began to behave like the Sioux of the 1870s. The agents reacted in various ways. When the police failed to make the Sioux obey, some of the agents refused to issue rations to those Indians who were active Ghost Dancers. At least two of the agents asked for federal troops. One, a new agent at Pine Ridge, was so incompetent that the Indians named him Young-Man-Afraid-of-Indians. White newspapermen, always hungry for a sensational news story, began to write about "hostile" Sioux. And white settlers in the Dakotas began to demand protection from the government.

Finally, after a tug of war between the Department of the Interior and the Department of War in Washington, the government authorized the army to send infantry and cavalry onto the reservations. This move brought about the first real confrontation since 1876 between the Sioux and the dreaded bluecoats. On November 20, 1890, cavalry and infantry units occupied Pine Ridge and Rosebud. A few days later the entire Seventh Cavalry arrived at Pine Ridge. This was Custer's unit, and it included many veterans of the Little Bighorn.

The effect on the Sioux of the appearance of the troops was overpowering. Instead of retreating to the outer edges of the reservations, most of the Indians at Pine Ridge and Rosebud immediately left their cabins and camps and gathered around the agency buildings. They pitched their tepees in rambling confusion and hoped that they would not be suspected of any wrongdoing. It was as though the only

During the Ghost Dance, which went on for five days, the Sioux worked themselves into a trance. Believers thought they could visit their dead while in this state.

way to be safe from the rifles and cannon of the army was to be right under the noses of the officers and agents.

Thus the arrival of the army segregated the Indians. Those who wanted peace with the whites—those who had the good sense to be afraid—had gathered at the agencies. Only the most militant of the Ghost Dancers, led by Kicking Bear and Short Bull, decided to hold out. They were gathered along the creeks not far from the Pine Ridge Agency—at Medicine Root, Porcupine, and Wounded Knee.

Kicking Bear spread the doctrines of the Messiah to Sitting Bull and the Standing Rock Reservation. But he gave the new faith a militant interpretation that caused a white reaction.

About a week after the cavalry's arrival, several hundred of the militant Indians broke for open country. They plundered the farms of the peaceful Indians who had fled to the agencies, and they raided the agencies' cattle herd for beef. Then about 600 warriors and their families struck out for a low plateau at the northwest corner of Pine Ridge. This area was known as the Stronghold. Here the Indians had grass, water, cattle, ponies in large numbers, and plenty of guns and ammunition. They announced that they intended to stay all winter, dancing, and then see what the spring brought.

Fortunately, the officer in command at Pine Ridge decided to be cautious. He sent one messenger after another to the Stronghold, promising that there would be no punishment if the Indians surrendered and returned to the agency. In turn the Indians had to agree to give up the Ghost Dance and return the cattle and other things they had taken. The messengers were badly treated, but some of the men at the Stronghold wanted to surrender. It seemed clear that sooner or later the Indians would disagree among themselves and the threat of uprising would be broken. The situation at Pine Ridge settled into a stalemate, with neither side ready to force a confrontation.

Now the scene of the action shifted north to Standing Rock, where Sitting Bull kept his camp. The nonprogressive Indians regarded Sitting Bull almost reverently. He was probably not as great a war chief as Crazy Horse had been. But Sitting Bull had held out against the whites longer than any other Sioux leader. And his people believed that he had extraordinary powers as a medicine man.

The agent at Standing Rock was James McLaughlin, a tough, fair, and experienced agent. For years he had struggled to gain moral leadership of the Indians, and for years Sitting Bull had stood in his way. McLaughlin had been looking for a way to break Sitting Bull's strong hold over the nonprogessive Indians at Standing Rock. When Sitting Bull took up the forbidden Ghost Dance, McLaughlin decided that arresting him would be the best course. McLaughlin wanted to delay the arrest until winter, when the Indians stayed indoors to avoid the bitter cold and to rest. The agent also believed that the arrest should be made by the Sioux Indian police, not by the cavalry units stationed near the agency at Fort Yates.

In November 1890 McLaughlin began to enlarge his Indian police force. He ordered them to keep a close watch on Sitting Bull's camp and make certain that the old chief did not leave.

In mid-December McLaughlin learned that Sitting Bull had been invited to the Stronghold, where he would join the Pine Ridge and Rosebud Sioux under Short Bull and Kicking Bear. The agent was determined to stop Sitting Bull from taking his group to Pine Ridge. He knew what kind of stalemate had developed there, and he felt that Sitting Bull's presence might be enough to tip the scales toward open warfare between the Sioux and the cavalry. So McLaughlin ordered Sitting Bull's arrest. He commanded the Indian police, who were led by an experienced lieutenant, Bull Head, to sneak into Sitting Bull's camp at dawn on December 15. They were to arrest the chief and bring him into the agency.

Bull Head and the police met the command with mixed feelings. Most of them were progressives. They prayed to the white man's God before starting their mission. But the thought of Sitting Bull still brought back memories of the great days of the Sioux. One of the police, He Alone, whose white name was John Lone Man, later remembered the way he felt when the orders were read and translated to the police. (The English here is the work of an educated relative of his.)

> I'm simply expressing my viewpoint as one who had reformed from all the heathenish ways, formerly one of the loyal followers of Chief Sitting Bull. But ever since I was about ten years of age, I had participated in a good many buffalo hunts and fought under Sitting Bull. But the most important fight I took part in was the Custer fight. After this fight I still went with Sitting Bull's band to Canada. Even after Sitting Bull was returned to Standing Rock Reservation, I remained in his camp, where I tamed down somewhat. We all felt sad.

The police gathered in the early evening of December 14 and passed the night telling war stories. Then, just before dawn, Bull Head ordered He Alone and the thirty or so other police to get ready.

Sitting Bull's camp stood on the north bank of the Grand River. The police, circling from the east, crossed the river to cut off any possible escape southward toward Pine Ridge. Soon they could see Sitting Bull's log cabin. In front of it stood the very tall tepee that was the headquarters for the Ghost Dance. Sitting Bull's two wives, his son Crow Foot, and several other children and relatives lived in the cabin. Other tepees were scattered around it. The police paused for a moment, then crossed the river again. He Alone recalled:

Sitting Bull and his family accepted reservation life in 1881, five years after defeating Custer at Little Bighorn. The unsettling mixture of pride, resentment, and recognition of defeat is visible on his face. This potentially explosive mixture stirred white fears.

We rode up as if we attacked the camp. We quickly dismounted, and while our officers went inside we all scattered around the cabin. It was still dark, and everybody was asleep, and only dogs greeted us.

Bull Head knocked at the door, and the Chief answered, "*How, timahel hiyu you.*" [All right, come in.]

Bull Head said, "I come to arrest you. You are under arrest."

Sitting Bull said, "How. Let me put on my clothes and go with you."

When Sitting Bull started to go with the police, one of Sitting Bull's wives burst into a loud cry which drew attention. No sooner had this started, when several leaders were rapidly making their way toward Sitting Bull's cabin. Bear That Catches, particularly, came up close saying, "Now, here are the metal breasts [5] just as we had expected. You think you are going to take him. You shall not do it."

By now the entire camp was up and angry. The police might still have been able to arrest the sleepy Sitting Bull if Crow Foot, his seventeen-year-old son, had not intervened. Sitting Bull had been grooming Crow Foot to be a chief, filling his youthful head with tales of courage in battle. As He Alone described it, Crow Foot upset the delicate balance of fear and anger:

Just about this time, Crow Foot got up, moved by the wailing of his mother and the remarks of Bear That Catches, and said to Sitting Bull, "Well, you always called yourself a brave chief. Now you are allowing yourself to be taken by the metal breasts."

[5] "Metal breasts" was a reference to the policemen's badges.

> Sitting Bull then changed his mind, and said, "*Ho ca mni kte sni yelo.*" [Then I will not go.]
>
> Lieutenant Bull Head said to the chief, "Come now, do not listen to any one."
>
> I said to Sitting Bull, "Uncle,[6] nobody is going to harm you. Please do not let others lead you into any trouble."
>
> But the chief's mind was made up not to go, so the three head officers laid their hands on him, pulling him outside. By this time, the whole camp was in commotion. Bear That Catches pulled out a gun from under his blanket and fired into Lieutenant Bull Head, wounding him. I ran up toward where they were holding the chief, when Bear That Catches raised his gun. He pointed and fired at me, but it snapped [misfired]. I jerked the gun away from his hands and laid him out. It was about this moment that Lieutenant Bull Head fired into Sitting Bull while still holding him, and Red Tomahawk followed with another shot which finished the chief.

There was more shooting, and soon the Ghost Dancers ran for a line of trees. After a time the police took shelter in Sitting Bull's cabin. The inner walls of the cabin were unfinished but hung with strips of brightly colored sheeting, sewn together and tacked to the walls. Suddenly, one of the policemen noticed a movement in a corner, behind the sheeting. He Alone raised the curtain:

> There stood Crow Foot, and as soon as he was exposed to view, he cried out, "My uncles, do not kill me. I do not wish to die." Lieutenant Bull Head said, "Do what you like with him. He is the one that has caused this trouble." I do not remember who fired the shot that killed Crow Foot—several fired at once.

Just after Crow Foot was killed, the cavalry units from Fort Yates arrived. The remaining members of Sitting Bull's band scattered toward the south.

Four Indian policemen had died at Sitting Bull's camp. Two more, including Lieutenant Bull Head, died later from their wounds. At least eight of Sitting Bull's people had died. Their bodies were left where they fell. Only Sitting Bull was buried. A few moments after the ceremonies for the dead police, his body was put in a plain grave at the Fort Yates cemetery. The only people there were three officers as witnesses, along with the four guardhouse gravediggers who shoveled the dirt over the simple wooden coffin.

None of Sitting Bull's followers was present at his burial. Most of them—about 400—had fled south and west from the Grand River camp. The authorities at Standing Rock had a number of nightmarish

[6] Indians often used words like "Uncle" and "Father" as terms of respect.

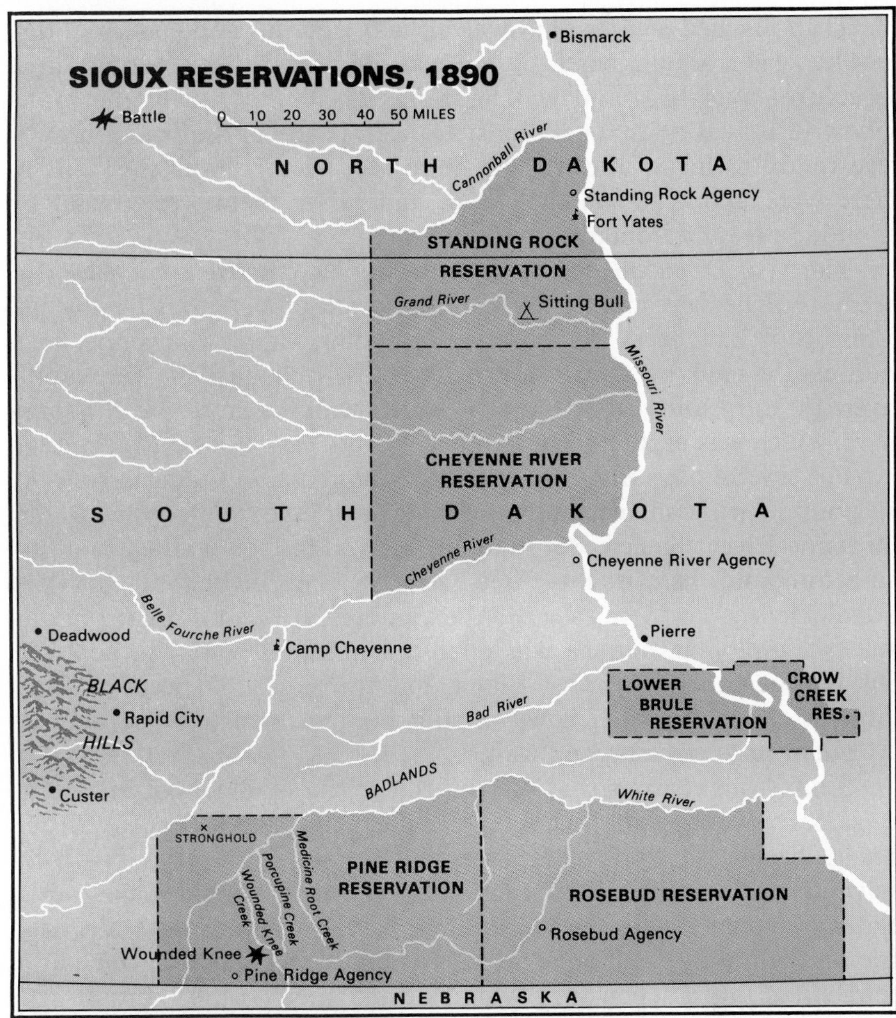

ideas about what might happen next. Most likely, the Standing Rock Ghost Dancers might join Chief Big Foot on the Cheyenne River, where the dance had been in full swing for weeks. Then, too, the frightened Sitting Bull group might strike out for the Stronghold, where Short Bull and Kicking Bear still held out. Or they might set Big Foot in motion toward the Stronghold too, with terrible results. A potential "domino" effect could ignite the entire Sioux reservation system, once the news of Sitting Bull's death spread.

Agent McLaughlin immediately sent friendly scouts to find Sitting Bull's band. Upon finding them, the scouts were able to persuade over half to return to the Standing Rock Reservation. Some of the others simply scattered and sooner or later went back to their homes around Grand River. The rest—fewer than a hundred—headed south to join Big Foot.

They reached a camp that was already nervous and confused. Big Foot had been a great chief. But he was old now, in his seventies, and his control over his band was slipping. The band's medicine man, Yellow Bird, was a fanatical Ghost Dancer. Many of the young braves were ready to bring about their hoped-for victory over the whites. There were about 200 in the band, and all of them were aware of mounting pressure from the white soldiers.

The War Department had ordered Big Foot's arrest, on the false theory that he was almost as large a source of potential trouble as Sitting Bull had been. An observation camp, Camp Cheyenne, had been established by the cavalry just a few miles up the Cheyenne River. Infantry units from the east were trying to cross the Missouri River, which was partially ice-covered.

For several days Big Foot wavered among various alternatives. At one point he was convinced by messengers from the cavalry to go to the Cheyenne River Agency. But many of his young men wanted to go to the Stronghold instead. Big Foot had also been invited by the Pine Ridge chiefs to go there to settle the troubles. He had a great reputation as a diplomat, and he was offered a hundred ponies to heal the split between the "friendly" Sioux and the Ghost Dancers at Pine Ridge. Most of the time, however, Big Foot seemed to want only to stay put at his own camp and wait.

Finally, for reasons that are difficult to guess, Big Foot made his decision. He would go to Pine Ridge, make peace, and accept the gift of ponies. What he did not realize was that leaving his reservation when the whites were so frightened of a Sioux "uprising" would make him a fugitive "hostile" in the eyes of the military. Almost immediately, new orders went out for Big Foot's arrest. His band was to be disarmed and their horses taken. Then they would be marched to the railroad and sent to Omaha—far away from their own reservation lands. Big Foot never understood that this was the army's plan. He assumed that he was going to Pine Ridge on a mission of peace.

Big Foot's band left camp on December 23, under the cover of night. As soon as the officers at Camp Cheyenne realized that the old chief had gone, a desperate series of cavalry units started patrolling the line between Big Foot's camp and the Stronghold. But the chief passed east of the patrols. The band moved very slowly, for Big Foot had caught pneumonia. He rode in a wagon without springs. Soon Big Foot was bleeding through his nose. And it was bitterly cold for the old man. At one point, in a pass through a steep wall along the Bad River, Big Foot's men had to dig out a road for the wagon. Big Foot managed to reach Porcupine Creek, only about thirty miles from the Pine Ridge Agency, without being sighted by the army. He sent men ahead to tell the Sioux he was coming.

On December 28, five days after starting south, Big Foot's band was finally "captured" by the Seventh Cavalry. When the Indians and cavalry met, there was a tense moment. The cavalry formed a skirmish line and brought up cannon. Big Foot's braves formed a battle line in front of his wagon. But then the cavalry commander came forward. He and Big Foot shook hands, and the chief accepted an "escort"—going, he thought, to Pine Ridge. Together, the cavalry and the Indians made their way to a trading post at Wounded Knee Creek.

The officer in charge had wisely not tried to disarm the Sioux, and he let them keep their horses for the trip. He even transferred Big Foot into an ambulance wagon. When the two groups reached Wounded Knee, the Indians were issued rations. The rest of the Seventh Cavalry came from Pine Ridge to join the patrol. The Indians pitched their tepees in a low hollow near a ravine that led into the creek. There were 102 men, and 230 women and children. The soldiers—a total of about 500—camped on a rise just to the north. Armed sentries surrounded the Indians, but on the whole everything seemed peaceful enough.

Soon the Indians settled down and the cavalry—except for the ring of sentries around the Indian camp—went to sleep. Only a few officers, veterans of the Little Bighorn disaster, stayed up late. They celebrated over a keg of whiskey someone had brought from the agency.

The next morning Colonel James Forsyth, commander of the Seventh Cavalry, asked all the men of Big Foot's group to gather in a council between the tepees and the cavalry encampment. The sentries remained in place. The rest of the cavalry units drew up, mounted, around the Sioux men and their camp. Forsyth asked the Indians for their weapons.

Big Foot tried diplomacy. From his ambulance bed he quietly advised his men to give up the bad guns but hide the good ones. Soon Forsyth sent twenty of the Indians to the tepees to bring the guns. Meanwhile, however, the Sioux women (who understood the value of a weapon) had hidden the rifles that the Sioux had bought, stolen, or taken in battle. The Indians returned to the council with only two old, broken cavalry carbines.

Forsyth heightened his search. He placed a line of troops between the Sioux braves and their camp and sent his own men into the tepees. But this search uncovered only thirty rifles, most of them old and useless. This left one other real possibility: the Sioux were hiding their rifles under the blankets they kept draped over their shoulders against the cold.

By now the situation was very delicate. Forsyth ordered Big Foot brought out on his blanket. The medicine man, Yellow Bird, was dancing around, chanting Ghost Dance songs, urging the young braves to be firm. In the tepees women were hastily packing, ready to run.

Suddenly, one Indian, Black Coyote, pulled a rifle from his blanket and began to shout, holding the weapon over his head. He was probably deaf and, by the Indians' own testimony, a little insane. Two soldiers grabbed him and struggled for the rifle. It went off, firing overhead. In what may have been a signal, Yellow Bird threw a handful of dust into the air. Several braves pulled rifles from their blankets and aimed at the cavalry. "By God, they have broken," an officer shouted. The Indians fired, and at about the same moment came the command "Fire! Fire on them!"

No one could stop what happened next. Big Foot was quickly killed. Cavalry carbines ripped into the group of Sioux men. The bullets that did not find a Sioux body passed on across the ravine into the tepees. Women ran this way and that, followed by children. Some of the Indians broke toward the creek, where they were cut down by waiting cavalrymen. Others ran into the ravine.

Some officers did what they could to prevent women and children from being shot down. But the Indians (at least those who still had weapons) were fast and accurate with their repeating rifles, and the soldiers sometimes fired at anything that moved. When the artillery on the hill opened up on the Indians in the ravine, the shells exploded on all without regard to age or sex. Apparently, too, some of the soldiers broke ranks and chased down fleeing Indians. These were the bodies Charles Eastman found miles away from Wounded Knee.

The actual battle lasted only a few minutes and the cavalry's mopping-up only a short time longer. About 150 braves rode out from Pine Ridge, too late and too few to help their comrades. The cavalry gathered their own dead (25) and wounded (39) and returned to the Pine Ridge Agency. They took some of the wounded Sioux with them and left the rest on the field. There were at least 146 Indian dead—about half of them men. Some bodies were probably taken away during the next two days, before Eastman's party arrived to rescue the living and bury the rest. All in all, probably 200 Sioux and whites had died.

Wounded Knee was followed by a few small skirmishes. But soon Pine Ridge was pacified. The Stronghold Indians had given up while Big Foot's band was on the march. The Ghost Dance was over. Spring came and went, but the earth did not cover the white man, as the Messiah had promised. Paul Weinert, the cannoneer at Wounded Knee, received a Congressional Medal of Honor for his action at the edge of the ravine.

The Sioux who died at Wounded Knee were buried in a mass grave. With them died the last remnants of Indian resistance on the Western plains.

A small white church was later built at the Sioux mass grave, on what came to be called Cemetery Hill. In 1903, with the help of missionaries, the Indians put up their own small monument, burying Wounded Knee in the past.

> This monument is erected by surviving relatives and other Ogalalla [Oglala] and Cheyenne River Sioux Indians in memory of the Chief Big Foot Massacre, Dec. 29, 1890. Col. Forsyth in command of U.S. troops. Big Foot was a great chief of the Sioux Indians. He often said, "I will stand in peace till my last day comes." He did many good and brave deeds for the white man and the red man. Many innocent women and children who knew no wrong died here.

CHAPTER

22

Settling the Last Frontier

THERE IS NOTHING unique about the history of the Sioux. It is true they resisted the whites longer and more ferociously than most other Indians, east or west. And they were the only tribe that, inspired by the Messiah's new religion, developed a militant resistance to reservation life. But, despite these differences, they were finally defeated in a manner typical of the way in which white Americans subdued all the Indians.

The defeat of the Sioux and the other Plains Indians was just one part of continental expansion. White Americans had begun moving west in the 1830s. In the decades after the Civil War this movement increased in speed and recklessness.

THE LAST WEST

Until the 1840s America had a clearly drawn frontier. It was possible at each census before

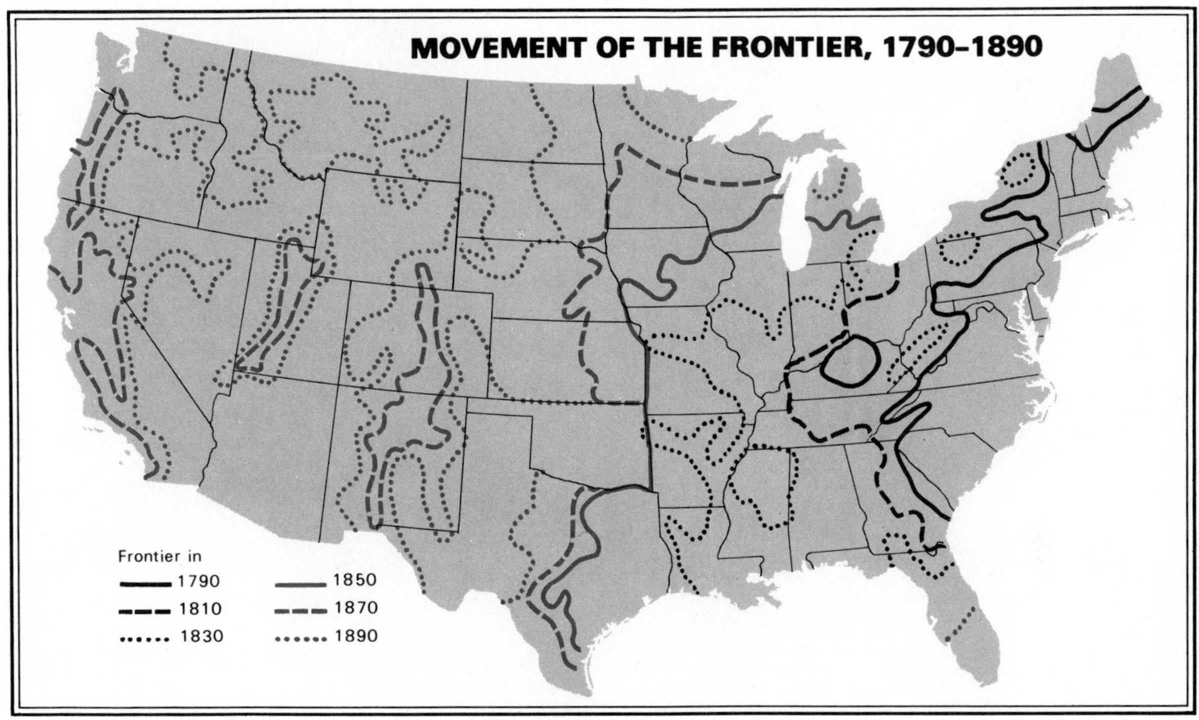

then to draw a zigzag line, north to south across the country, showing how far settlement had advanced in each decade. But after the Mexican War this was no longer true. The drift of pioneers into Oregon, the settlement of Texas and Utah, and the discovery of gold in California created isolated pockets of white settlement thousands of miles beyond the old frontier line near the Mississippi. By the early 1850s it was evident that the Pacific Coast would be settled fairly quickly, organized into territories, and carved into states. California had already been admitted to statehood as part of the Compromise of 1850. Oregon entered the Union nine years later.

Between the Pacific Coast and the old frontier in eastern Kansas and Nebraska lay a vast stretch of plains and mountains. It formed an area larger than the whole nation when Washington was President. This region was the last frontier, the last region to be settled by white Americans.

The Great Plains begin in the first tier of states west of the Mississippi River, and extend west to the Rockies. In 1836 the Senate Committee for Indian Affairs declared that the Great Plains were an "uninhabitable region." The Indians there "are on the outside of us, and in a place which will forever remain on the outside." In fact the plains were given an official name, "The Great American Desert." The weather there is dry. There is no water in many of the rivers during most of the year. The land is not covered with trees but with stubborn grass. Only the Indian and the buffalo seemed able to thrive. The Rocky Mountain region also seemed to offer little to encourage settlement. For many years its great peaks and high valleys were the home only of small Indian bands and a few American fur traders.

There were many reasons why this myth that the West could not be settled came to an end. Three of the earliest and most important factors were gold, railroads, and cattle. As min-

Virginia City, Nevada, sprang up after the discovery of silver nearby in 1859. Mark Twain described it as "the liveliest town that America ever produced" in its early years. Schools, churches, and "respectable" businesses replaced saloons and gambling halls after the initial excitement of silver fever had died down.

ers, railroad men, and ranchers moved into the region, they systematically seized Indian lands. Then came the final pioneers of the last West, the farmers. In 1890 the Census Bureau announced that the frontier no longer existed.[1]

THE MINING FRONTIER

The discovery of gold and silver had been responsible for the rapid development of California. Miners who reached the Pacific Coast too late to find gold easily soon began to drift east over the mountains, looking for new bonanzas. In 1858 prospectors found gold near Pike's Peak in Colorado. Soon people were pouring into new, ramshackle towns like Denver, Pueblo, and Boulder. Their covered wagons proclaimed "Pike's Peak or Bust!" A year after the first strike about 100,000 people—mostly men without their families—had moved into the area. Like most other Western gold and silver strikes, the Pike's Peak boom did not last. The earliest prospectors soon raked off the surface gold. The remaining precious metal was buried deep in the mountains, where it could be mined only with expensive machinery that individual miners could not afford. Within three months in 1859 the population of the Colorado gold fields dwindled to about 50,000. But enough men stayed to create a pocket of white settlement in the mountains.

A similar process was under way farther west, in what is now Nevada. Miners from California found gold near the western border of the region in the late 1850s. In 1859 they discovered the famous Comstock Lode. One of the richest

[1] The Census Bureau, of course, was referring only to the territory beyond the Mississippi River to the west coast. Alaska, which was purchased from Russia in 1867 by Andrew Johnson's Secretary of State William Seward, was still largely unsettled in 1890. That territory was really America's last frontier.

single mines in America, it produced over $200 million worth of gold and silver in the thirty years after its discovery. Thousands of men rushed over the mountains from Sacramento to build nearby Virginia City. Soon the town had five newspapers, a miniature stock exchange, and a horde of prospectors, saloonkeepers, prostitutes, and gamblers. A few men became enormously wealthy. Most of the prospectors, however, went away disappointed.

Some miners who stayed found small pockets of loose gold that could be mined with a pan or a sluice, a simple trough that runs water downhill over dirt and loose rocks, washing out the heavy gold dust. This kind of mining, called placer mining, soon washed off the free metal near the surface. The only way to make the gold fields pay off on a large scale over a long period was to invest money in machinery that could dig out hard rock below the surface. This meant that the miner's frontier quickly became a corporate frontier, exploited by mining companies owned by Eastern investors. Within a few years any successful field soon became an industrial development. And the prospectors scattered again in search of a new discovery and easy pickings elsewhere.

The California Gold Rush that had excited so many thousands of Americans in 1849 was repeated over and over again throughout the West. In the late 1850s a small strike was made in eastern Washington, but it soon petered out. Restless miners headed farther east, up the Snake and Salmon rivers into Idaho. There they built Boise, Silver City, and other new mining towns. By 1861, the start of the Civil War, there were probably 30,000 white men in Idaho.

During the Civil War—while their countrymen were battling at Bull Run and Chickamauga—white miners moved from Idaho into Montana. There they struck gold and silver at Last Chance Gulch (which later became the city of Helena) and Alder Gulch (Virginia City). By 1863 Idaho had enough citizens to organize as a territory, and Montana followed only a year later.

Open-pit mining, utilizing expensive heavy machinery to dig through the surface of hard rock to the ores below, helped turn the miner's frontier into a corporate frontier.

The Telegraph

Modern telegraphy and the name of Samuel F. B. Morse are forever linked. Morse was the inventor of the first usable telegraph in the United States. Yet the telegraph key and the code for transmitting messages that bears Morse's name were devised by others. But it was Morse's gift to see the possible use of electricity in communications. He persisted in the face of great odds to prove his ideas.

The inventor's fascination with electricity won him a university teaching post. He could then pursue his special interest. In 1836 he completed a crude apparatus consisting of a transmitter of electrical impulses and a receiver that made marks on a moving strip of paper in response. But the impulses could travel only a few feet by wire. His real breakthrough—and the basis for his status as an inventor—came from his addition of a relay device for reinforcing the electric current. This made long-distance telegraphy feasible.

In 1838 he applied for aid from Congress to continue his research but was refused. Although years of poverty and frustration followed, he did not give up. Finally, in 1843, he was granted $30,000 to build an experimental telegraph line from Washington, D.C., to Baltimore. On May 24, 1844, at the Capitol building, Morse transmitted the first formal message: "What hath God wrought?" The quotation was from the Old Testament, and the event became legendary.

At first the government decided to operate the telegraph service as a government agency, like the post office. But private companies were formed in the East, with Morse holding patent privileges. Early in 1847 Congress mistakenly concluded that the telegraph business would be unprofitable. It turned over the Washington-Baltimore line to Morse's partners. The rush to build telegraph lines began.

Lines from New York to other major cities were set up first. By 1848 Florida was the only state east of the Mississippi without telegraph service. Poor message service was common, often because of bad weather. But the popularity of the telegraph increased. Newspapers and stockbrokers were the most eager customers.

The 1850s saw the birth of many rival companies, for equipment was cheap and financing became easy. Gradually, a few giants emerged. Western Union, formed in 1856, was the leader. Its fabulous growth is shown by the increase in capital stock from $385,000 in 1858 to $41,000,000 in 1867. A few years later the company held 66,000 of the 73,000 miles of national lines.

Other landmarks in the growth of the telegraph were the spanning of the continent (1861), the invention of the stock ticker (1866), and the beginning of successful transatlantic cable service (1866). Probably more than any other invention, the telegraph knit together the nation. For his part, Samuel Morse acquired wealth and fame—and a series of costly law suits with rival inventors and telegraph companies.

This 1859 sketch shows a stage near Tucson, Arizona, on the Butterfield Overland Express route. Passengers had to endure the rough ride through desert lands on springless seats.

The last Western gold rush occurred in 1874. In the Black Hills of South Dakota, in the heart of the Great Sioux reservation, an army expedition commanded by General Custer found traces of gold. According to a treaty between the United States and the Indians, the hills belonged to the Sioux "forever." For a short time the government tried to prevent white men from entering the Black Hills. But the pressure to find gold was too great. Within two years about 7,000 whites had built Deadwood and Custer City. The Sioux lands had been decisively invaded.

TRANSPORTATION WEST

The influx of miners, together with the settlement of Oregon and California, led to demands for quick, safe, and economical land transportation between the settled East and the Far West. Every new mining town wanted to be linked to the rest of the country. People who lived on the west coast wanted an overland route as an alternate to the long sea voyage from the east coast around South America.

Trail, Stage, and Pony The Oregon Trail, Santa Fe Trail, and other routes followed by pioneers in the 1840s and early 1850s were more or less protected by army posts along the way. But they were far from being real roads. Something else seemed necessary.

In 1858 the first stage road was finally cut through the countryside for the Butterfield Overland Express. Its route ran 2,000 miles from St. Louis south through Indian Territory,[2] then across Texas, New Mexico, and Arizona. The ride was rough and usually very hot, and the trip took twenty-four days. But the road was faster than the sea voyage. Soon other stage and freighting companies were opening additional roads across Colorado and Utah to California.

In 1860 businessmen set up a mail service known as the pony express. Small, lightweight boys, like jockeys, rode big horses (not ponies) in relays between St. Joseph, Missouri, and Sacramento, California. The young riders were able to carry a message across the country in ten days. The pony express prospered for only about a year, however. In 1861 the first telegraph line was put through to the west coast. The time for sending and receiving cross-country messages was then cut to a split second.

[2] This region—corresponding roughly to the present state of Oklahoma—was set aside in 1834 for Indians removed from east of the Mississippi. Later, parts of it were reserved for Western Indians, too.

 A Transcontinental Railroad All these ways of getting people, goods, and information across the country were only preludes to the most dramatic and successful method of all, the railroad. A transcontinental railroad had been a dream since the 1840s—to move people through the West to California. The North and South, however, had not been able to agree on the western part of the route. The North wanted a line to run from Chicago to San Francisco. The South insisted on a route through Texas to southern California.

The Civil War ended this competition. By seceding, the South lost its right to participate in the decision making. In 1862 Congress settled on a route between San Francisco and Council Bluffs, Iowa. The same law provided for enormous financial support from the federal government. There would be two companies. The Central Pacific would build east from San Francisco. The Union Pacific (a patriotic name for wartime) would go west across Nebraska and Colorado. They were to meet somewhere in the middle. Each railroad would be given a right of way 400 feet wide. In addition, the government would lend the railroads up to $48,000 for each mile of track laid—less for flat country, more for mountain track. Most important, the railroads would be given 6,400 acres for every mile of track completed. In 1864 this land allowance was doubled.

The Central Pacific started building toward the east slowly. The company lacked funds, and labor was scarce. But gradually these problems were resolved. The Lincoln administration cooperated by including mountains in the flat-country category, thereby entitling the railroad to the largest possible loans. The labor problem was soon solved by importing thousands of Chinese. In all of 1864 the railroad laid only

A railroad line spanning the continent would not have been possible without the help of thousands of Chinese laborers, who did much of the work on the Central Pacific.

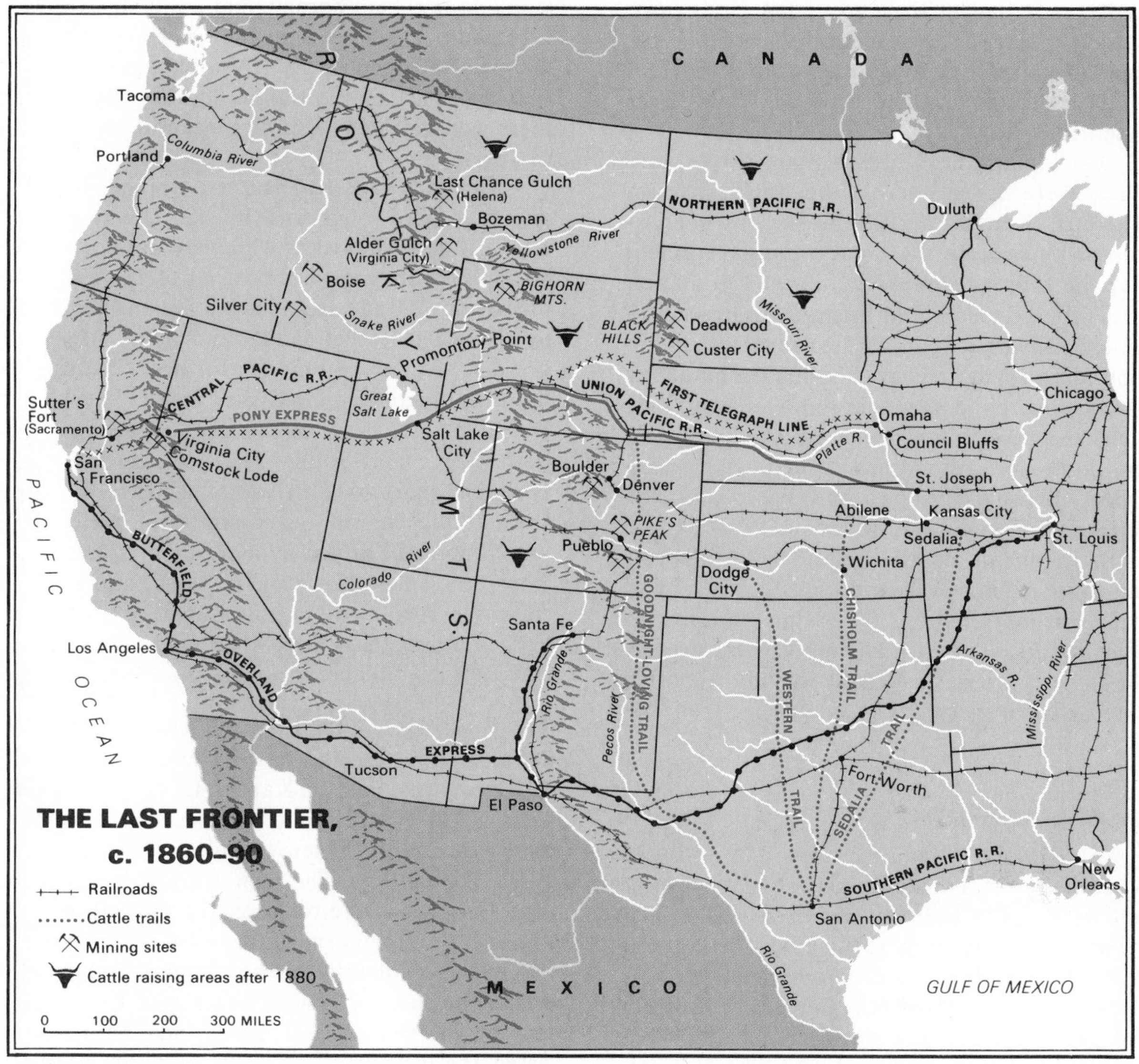

about 20 miles of track, but by 1867 the pace was up to 20 miles a month.

At the other end of the proposed route the Union Pacific also built slowly. It picked up speed by bringing in thousands of Irish immigrants to lay rails. In 1868 alone the Union Pacific laid 425 miles of track.

In May 1869, after only five years of construction, the two work gangs met at Promontory Point, Utah, just east of the Great Salt Lake. The last tie put down was coated with silver, the last spike was gold. A telegraph operator cabled east and west: "Hats off—prayer is being offered." Then there was a wait of almost fifteen minutes. Again the telegraph clicked: "We have got done praying. The spike is about to be presented." Railroad officials took turns with the hammer—the first blow was a bad miss—but the work was done. The two locomotives eased forward until they touched. The nation celebrated almost as wildly as it had at the end of the Civil War. Chicago's parade was seven miles long. The nation was joined, east to west, across a desert that an earlier generation had believed would never be settled.

During the next fifteen years three more routes were opened across the Rockies. Iowa, Missouri, Kansas, and Nebraska were crisscrossed by rails. In the process the government gave the railroad companies almost 180 million acres of public land, and it lent them over $100 million. Because of complicated regulations that allowed railroads to delay choosing the land they wanted to keep along their rights of way, they could keep great stretches of land for years. At one point the railroads controlled—at least on paper—almost all of Iowa and Wisconsin. The Northern Pacific, whose route crossed the northern tier of states between Lake Superior and the Pacific, had a strip of land larger than many European nations. The same kind of situation developed in Arizona and New Mexico. By 1885 the railroads held land totaling almost a sixth of the entire country.

FROM BUFFALO TO CATTLE

What mattered in the long run was not the paper land grants. The railroads did make millions of dollars in profits from land sales. But the real effect of the railroads was to open new avenues of profit in the plains environment. Obviously railroads benefited the corporations that were taking gold, silver, and lead from the Rockies. They also helped to create an entirely new industry— ranching. Building the railroads hastened the destruction of the plains buffalo herds. But it also made possible the exploitation of another animal, the cow.

Early in the sixteenth century the Spanish had begun importing European cattle into America. Over the years the cattle had multiplied. Some had escaped and become wild, especially in southern Texas around the Nueces River. These were the famous Texas longhorns—lanky, tough, long-horned, and too dangerous to be captured or herded on foot. They roamed at will over the open range, a huge expanse of grass that was part of the public domain. By 1860, there were probably 5 million head of longhorns in Texas.

The Mexicans had learned to rope, brand, and even herd longhorns. In fact, it was Mexicans and not Americans who were the first cowboys. They originated almost all of the tools of the cowboy's trade, from his big hat and kerchief to his tooled leather saddle and boots. Mexico, however, had no real market for beef. The situation was different in the United States.

The Civil War sent beef prices soaring in both North and South. The beef herd in the Northern states was smaller at the end of the war than at the beginning. At the same time, the population had grown by more than 20 percent. Thus the demand for beef increased, and so did the price. A man could buy a longhorn steer in Texas for as little as three dollars. The same steer in Chicago would be worth ten times as much.

The Long Drive By 1866 the Missouri Pacific Railroad had pushed its line west to Sedalia, Missouri, just east of Kansas City. That same year the first large group of Texans drove enormous herds north across Indian Territory to reach the rail line. The men ran into many difficulties. Part of the route passed through dense forests. The longhorns, unaccustomed to woods, panicked and refused to be driven through the trees. The Indians (whose treaty gave them control of any white travel across their land) harassed the cowboys. This early attempt showed, however, that it was possible to herd cattle safely over hundreds of miles to the railroad—and thus to Eastern markets.

Thus began the twenty-year era of the "long drive." As the years passed, the railroads extended farther west. New cattle towns replaced Sedalia. Among them were Abilene (probably the most successful), Wichita, and Dodge City. Between 1866 and 1888 Texans drove as many as 6 million head of cattle over the grasslands to Kansas.

For those who succeeded, the profits of the long drive were enormous. Cattlemen claimed that as much as 40 percent profit per year was not unusual. Like the miner's frontier, the cattleman's bonanza soon attracted thousands of eager Easterners. Each usually had a few hundred dollars and a dream of running a vast ranch. Like the prospectors, most of the would-be ranchers were disappointed. Many of them returned home or switched to another line of work such as running a store or saloon.

The long drive, despite the romantic myth of the cowboy it fostered, was a business. It required capital if it was to succeed on a big scale. In the end only the lucky few who had been there first (like the prospectors in California or Nevada) became "cattle barons." In the long run, it was Eastern and European investors, with enough capital to buy and move large herds, who controlled most of the industry.

The End of the Open Range The long drive had a brief existence. Gradually, people north of Texas realized that as the railroads came closer, it made sense to breed and feed cattle nearby instead of bringing them up from Texas. During the 1880s the long drive from Texas was replaced by an even wilder cattle bonanza in other plains territories to the north. In 1860 there were no cattle at all in the northwestern plains, and there were only a few in Kansas and Nebraska. By 1880 Montana, the Dakota Territory, Wyoming, and Colorado had great herds, totaling almost 4 million head.

But the days of the open range, when cattle wandered on public land from one spring to the next, could not last long. The cattle industry soon found itself in a situation faced earlier by tobacco and cotton growers—overproduction. Rapid expansion led to an overstocked range. The grass could not support so many cattle. The increased

The long drives of cattle from the rich grasslands of the Southwest to Northern markets lasted through the 1880s. They created vast fortunes for a few fortunate cattle barons and gave the country the legend of the cowboy.

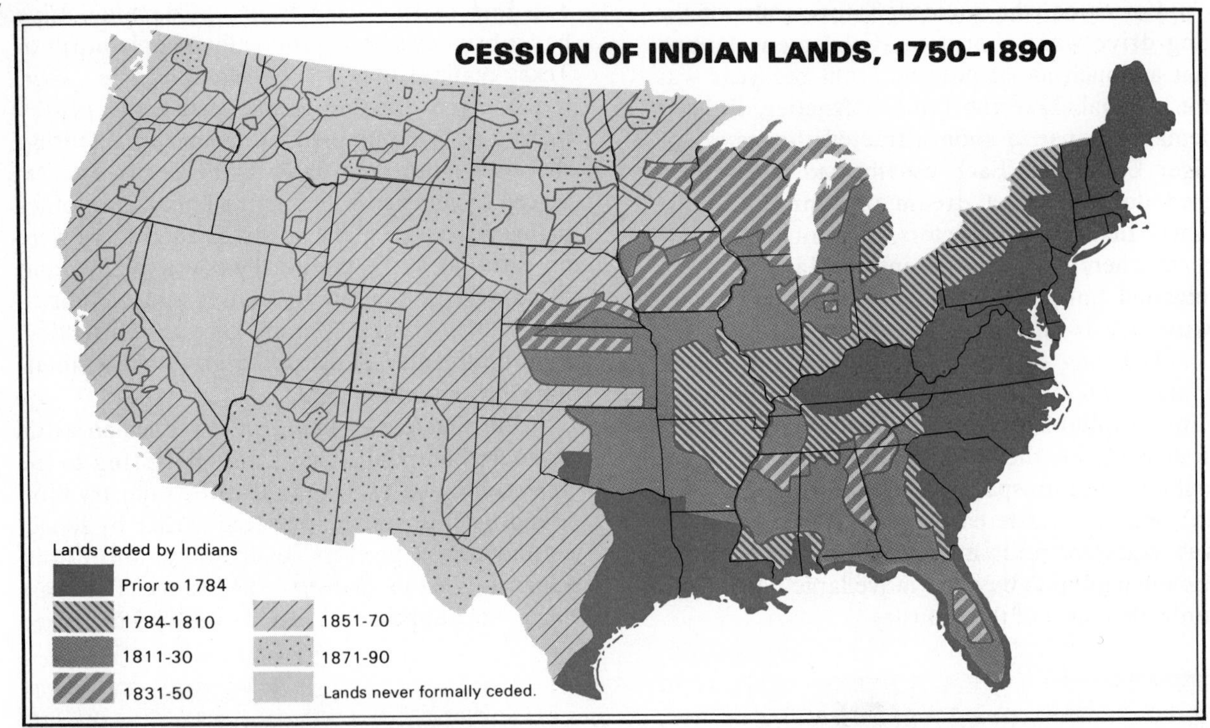

supply also caused prices to fall. Between 1885 and 1886 the price of a steer dropped from thirty dollars to ten dollars. The following winter on the plains was the bitterest in memory. Thousands of cattle starved and froze to death. The cattle bonanza was over.

THE DEFEAT OF THE WESTERN INDIANS

The miners, railroads, and cattlemen brought about the final chapter in the conflict between whites and Indians. It was a conflict older than Jamestown and as dark as any aspect of American history. The whites cloaked their actions with high-sounding expressions like "civilization against savagery" or "Manifest Destiny." But the facts were very simple: the white men came and took the Indians' lands.

White people in the New World had always regarded the Indians as a problem. For most whites—whether they were French, Spanish, or English— the Indians were seen either as a people to be exploited through trade or slavery or as a barrier to westward expansion. A few whites sympathized with the Indians and did what they could to protect them from the worst aspects of white civilization. But even to those who were sympathetic, help meant teaching the Indian to "adjust to civilization."

The Indians might be a problem for the whites but the whites meant disaster for the Indians. At stake for the whites was only the delay of continental expansion for a generation or so. The stakes were much higher for the Indians. They were in danger of losing their culture, their freedom, their identity as human beings and, in many cases, their lives. This was true from the time Cortes invaded Mexico, through Bacon's Rebellion and the removal of the Cherokee and other tribes westward,[3] down to the final conquest of the tribes of the West.

Advantages of the Whites White people's ways were overpowering to the Indians. In the first place, the whites' methods of dealing with the environment were totally unlike those of the Indians. Some Indians farmed a little. But the whites were able to cultivate vast stretches of land, first with teams of mules or oxen, then with machinery. Some Indians, like the Navajos, made ornaments out of silver or gold. But the whites came for gold and silver in droves. Big new towns and frightening machines and explosives changed the face of the mountains and valleys of the Rockies. The Indians hunted wild animals, which seemed numerous enough to last forever. But the whites killed off wild animals, fenced in the range, and raised great herds of cattle instead.

These were the main white weapons–farming, mining, and ranching. Along with these the whites brought strange powers and "medicine" that made the Indians' situation hopeless indeed–the railroad, soldiers' machine guns and cannons, and the telegraph.

Another weapon of the whites against the Indians was something they did not use on purpose–indeed, the whites feared it themselves. This was disease. Smallpox, measles, and other sicknesses may have wiped out as many as half the Western Indians before any significant number of whites even arrived in their territory. The germs traveled with traders and so preceded actual white migrations by decades. The Indians had no inherited resistance or immunity to many diseases of the whites, since the germs had been "imported" from Europe. Indians died by the band and even by the tribe from sicknesses that only made most whites uncomfortable.

Finally, the whites had an advantage that probably counted more than anything else–

These Mandan Indians survived a smallpox epidemic in 1872. Indians had no immunity to white men's diseases like smallpox and therefore died by the thousands when exposed to them.

people. They poured west by the thousands. In one change of seasons, between one Sun Dance and another, the whites seemed to b able to throw up towns like San Francisco, Denver, or Deadwood–towns larger than the whole Sioux nation.

One by one, the tribes of the Great Plains, the California-Intermountain area, and the Northwest Coast were made to realize that the whites were a force they could neither understand nor control. Some groups, like the Sioux, the Kiowas, and the Apaches, fought back. They were sustained by their myths, their magic, and their hatred of the cavalry that invaded their villages, shooting men, women, and children. But, in the end, all the tribes were defeated. Only something as unusual as the Messiah's Ghost Dance could convince the Indians–and only a few at that–that ther was any way to combat the enveloping white civilization.

[3] In the 1830s the federal government forced the so-called Five Civilized Tribes–the Cherokees, Chickasaws, Choctaws, Creeks, and Seminoles–to move from the Southeast to Indian Territory. The Indians suffered so much on the trip west that the journey became known as the trail of tears.

 Dealing with the Tribes From the beginning, United States policy toward the Indians had been contradictory. On the one hand, the government treated tribes as independent nations with whom it could make treaties. On the other hand, Indians were not citizens but wards of the government, subject to federal control. In addition, the nation was growing with incredible speed. Again and again, government aims that seemed practical in one decade were obsolete ten years later.

In California and Oregon, and in the frontier regions of the Rockies, relations between whites and Indians were poorly controlled by the government. Groups of whites simply drove the Indians out, murdering many of them in the process. The Indians of California suffered especially. They had settled around Spanish missions and learned farming and various crafts. After the Spanish missions were closed down in the 1830s, the Indians were defenseless against the greedy whites. In the ten years after the Gold Rush of 1849, some 70,000 of these mission Indians died from starvation, whites' diseases, and outright murder.

On the Great Plains whites might band together to attack Indians. But the government and its army played a much larger role there than it did farther west. After 1850 the history of Indian-white relations settled down to a fairly steady rhythm of treaties, uprisings, war, and new treaties. The Indians were always the losers. Even when they won the battles, they lost in making the treaties.

This process began in 1851 at Fort Laramie on the Oregon Trail. To protect the trail, the government called hundreds of Indian leaders together and pursuaded them to agree not to bother the wagon trains passing across their territory. Each tribe accepted boundaries to its hunting grounds. In return the government promised to leave them in peace.

These agreements left the Indians in possession of almost all the Great Plains. But accepting boundaries laid out by Washington opened the door to a new government tactic—getting each tribe to give up part of its lands in separate treaties. By 1865 the Indians had given up all of Kansas, most of Nebraska, the central half of Utah, and almost all of Texas.

The Sand Creek Massacre Much Indian land was surrendered peacefully, in return for promises of peace and annual shipments of government supplies, called annuities. But in 1861 in Colorado, a government attempt to move Cheyennes and Arapahoes onto a small reservation at Sand Creek resulted in a three-year guerrilla war by the Indians. In 1864 the leader of the warring Indians, Black Kettle, tried to make peace with the whites. The army and the territoral government refused. The unyielding commander of the Colorado militia, Colonel John Chivington, told Black Kettle: "My rule for fighting white men or Indians is to fight them until they lay down their arms and surrender."

Black Kettle led his people to a camp at Sand Creek, where he hoped to be left in peace. But the Indians woke on November 29, 1864, to find 1,000 of Chivington's militia surrounding them. The militia rushed the camp, shooting at everything that moved. When the "fight" was over, 450 Indians were dead. Only about 50 had escaped the massacre. The next year the Cheyennes and Arapahoes had to sign a new treaty. It forced them to leave their Colorado plains for a barren corner of Indian Territory.

Negotiations with the Sioux The Sioux fared better, at least for a time. Their agreement at Fort Laramie in 1851 gave them one of the largest hunting areas in the West—most of the Dakota Territory and the region around the Powder River in eastern Wyoming and southern Montana. But by 1865 miners had crowded into Montana at Bozeman, Virginia City, and Helena. These towns soon demanded a road connecting them with the Oregon Trail. This road would cross the Yellowstone River, skirt the Sioux hunting areas around the Big Horn Mountains, and cross directly over the valley of the Powder River.

In the summer of 1865 the cavalry moved into the area to construct forts and begin work

Chief Joseph

> I am tired of fighting. The old men are all dead. [My brother] who led the young men is dead. It is cold, and we have no blankets. The little children are freezing to death. My people, some of them, have run away to the hills. No one knows where they are. I want to have time to look for my children and see how many I can find. Maybe I shall find them among the dead. Hear me, my chiefs. From where the sun now stands, I will fight no more forever.

With these words Chief Joseph of the Nez Percé surrendered to American troops on October 5, 1877, in the Bearpaw mountains of Montana. The ''rebellion'' of the Nez Percé, started four months earlier, ended. It began when the Indians were forced to leave their homeland in the Wallowa Valley of Oregon. They had eluded their pursuers by a roundabout route through the rugged mountains of Idaho, Montana, and Wyoming. Hopeful of refuge in Canada, they were only thirty miles from the border when they were attacked. The Indians held out four days. Finally, after being told that his people would be sent to a reservation in Idaho, Joseph surrendered. He handed his rifle to his captors and made his solemn promise of peace. He never broke that promise.

He came from a proud and peaceful people. (The Nez Percé, French for ''pierced nose,'' were named for their habit of wearing ornamental pieces of shell.) They were buffalo hunters, cattle breeders, and superb horsemen. In 1855 they had agreed to reservation status in order to keep their land. But, in 1863, when gold was discovered there, the reserve was drastically reduced. Joseph's father refused to sign away his ancestral lands. He and some other chiefs separated from the ''treaty Indians.'' This bold move went unchallenged for years.

In 1871, at age 30, Joseph became chief When settlers began moving into the Wallowa Valley, Joseph protested. President Grant responded by declaring the area a reservation ''for the roaming Nez Percé.'' But in 1875 this policy was reversed.

Joseph's people were ordered to leave their homeland for a reservation in Idaho.

The young braves resisted at first, but Joseph convinced them that war was futile. In great sorrow the exodus began: about 250 warriors, 450 women, children, and old people, and 2,000 horses. Whites harassed the group and stole some horses. The braves retaliated, killing some whites. Although a man of peace, Joseph would not abandon his people. So, with federal troops closing in, he planned an escape to Canada. Outnumbered, he played a grim game of hide-and-seek, counterattacking only when provoked.

But Joseph was unable to help his people. They were not sent to the Idaho reservation as promised. Instead, they were placed on the plains of Oklahoma. Many died there. Joseph made several trips to Washington, to plead for relocation, but his eloquence failed. Forbidden to return to his homeland, he died in 1904. The official cause of death was described as a broken heart.

A wagon train expedition, protected by Colonel George Custer's cavalry, entered the Black Hills of South Dakota in search of gold in 1874. Within three years the Sioux were forced off their lands and onto reservations.

on the road. A Sioux chief, Red Cloud, led his people in a two-year attack on the road and the forts. And in 1868 the government made a new treaty that seemed to give the victory to Red Cloud. The road was abandoned. But the Sioux, in return, had to agree to a reservation that included only the Dakotas west of the Missouri—the so-called Great Sioux Reservation. According to the treaty, they co[illegible] Powder River country. For [illegible] ever, they had accepted a reserv[illegible] the large domain that their 185[illegible] recognized.

The same commission that made th[illegible] agreement with the Sioux dealt with other P[illegible] tribes in the same way. Reservations were creat[illegible] ed in Indian Territory for the southern groups—the Kiowa, Comanche, Arapaho, Cheyenne, Osage, and Pawnee tribes. Between 1868 and 1874 the northern tribes—Crow and Blackfoot, Shoshoni and Mandan—also accepted new, restricted reservations. By 1876 the Plains Indians had given up over three-fourths of the land they had held under the Fort Laramie Treaty.

The Battle of the Little Bighorn The policy of concentrating Indians on reservations was applied once again in the Black Hills area of South Dakota. The treaty of 1868 guaranteed the Tetons complete possession of the Black Hills. But in 1874 rumors of gold led to a reconnaissance of the area by a military column of the Seventh Cavalry under Colonel George Custer. Custer's men found gold, and the resulting rush into Deadwood and other mining towns made conflict between the Sioux and the whites inevitable.

The Grant administration tried for a time to hold the prospectors back. The army even removed some of them. But finally the government gave in and allowed the prospectors to enter the Black Hills "at their own risk." The next step was as cruel and illegal as any the government ever took against the Sioux. To prevent clashes between the miners and the Indians, Washington ordered all the Sioux to report to reservation agencies. Any who remained outside would be considered automatically "hostile" and liable to attack. Many of the Sioux obeyed the order. But about 8,000 of them defied the government and gathered in the area of the Big Horn Mountains for their annual summer encampment and Sun Dance.

In June 1876 the army launched powerful forces of infantry, cavalry, and artillery against these Indians. One column, marching north from the Platte River, met Crazy Horse at Rosebud Creek on June 17. The army was beaten back in fierce fighting. Crazy Horse returned to the Sioux camp at the Little Bighorn River, where 8,000 Teton Sioux had gathered—the most powerful single force of Indians the army would ever face. Another army column advanced from the east. On June 25 the Seventh Cavalry, again under Custer's command, rode foolishly to the attack. The Sioux killed almost all of Custer's force in the most famous (and, from the white point of view, perhaps the most stupid) Indian battle in American history.

Another cycle of treaty, war, and new treaty was about to be completed. Within a year the Sioux were forced to give up their important Black Hills area. They were now forced onto a reservation covering only the central part of South Dakota, between the Missouri River and the Black Hills. But their troubles were not over. A railroad was pushing toward the reservation, and the remaining Sioux stood in its path. Farmers and ranchers were also beginning to look longingly at the land that the Sioux still held.

A Changing Indian Policy At this time a new government policy toward Indians was beginning to take shape. Reformers—many of them missionaries and people who had never spent a day with an Indian—were promoting the change. It was not enough, they argued, to concentrate the Indians on reservations. They had to be "civilized"—converted to Christianity and white people's way of life. The best way to do this, the reformers felt, was to make the Indians into landholding farmers. Each one would receive land and be taught how to plow and plant.

When the Indians had agreed to give up land, they did so as tribes, not as individuals surrendering private property. The reformers believed that this attitude toward land ownership was harmful. To counteract it, they proposed that the Indians be given land as separate individuals. For once, Eastern reformers and Western exploiters agreed. The latter, who were anxious to break up the reservations, could do simple arithmetic. In almost every case, after individual allocations were made, there would still be reservation land left over. It, too, would become available to whites.

The new policy became law in the Dawes Act of 1887. Each Indian family head received 160 acres, each single adult 80 acres, and each dependent child 40 acres. The whites began to apply the policy immediately. In 1888, after a great deal of argument and some trickery, the Sioux were persuaded to accept the new policy.

The same policy was applied to the other Plains Indians. The resulting demoralization provided a fertile ground for the new Ghost Dance religion. No matter what the intentions of the people who wrote and supported the Dawes Act, it was a disaster for the Indians. In 1887 the Indians held about 130 million acres of land. By 1930 total Indian landholdings had been reduced to less than 50 million acres.

With the new policy came even stronger efforts to convert the Indians to white civilization—to make them "walk the white man's road," as Sitting Bull put it. These efforts hardened the conflicting attitudes of the progressive Indians, who accepted the new ways, and the nonprogressives, who clung to the old ones. The division was dramatized when Sitting Bull was arrested by Indian police from his own tribe. Even after the "reforms" of the 1880s American policy toward the Indians was a calamity. They were reduced to a condition in some ways worse than that of the freed slaves in the South.

FARMING ON THE PLAINS

Mining, railroads, and cattle ranching had created a scattered pattern of settlement on the Great Plains and in the Rockies. Miners gathered in towns that were separated by hundreds of miles. Railroads created towns but only along their rights of way. And ranchers needed only a few cowhands to handle even very large herds. The actual white settlement of the plains had to await the slower migrations of farmers away from the Mississippi and onto the dry grasslands.

The Homestead Act The pace and pattern of settlement depended very much on government encouragement. In its youth the Republican party had been the party of "free soil," which meant both agriculture without slavery and free land for any American. One of the first measures promoted by the Lincoln administration was the Homestead Act of 1862. According to this law, any citizen (or any immigrant who had taken the first step toward becoming a citizen) could claim 160 acres of public land, just by paying a fee of $10. If he "lived upon or cultivated" the land for five years, the land became his, free and forever. If the homesteader did not want to wait five years, he could pay for the land at $1.25 an acre and own it immediately.

The Homestead Act resulted in over half a million claims, totaling 80 million acres. But if its purpose was to give away most of the public lands of the West to simple farmers, it was a failure. Much more land was given to railroads and states or sold directly to speculators than was ever acquired by small farmers.

Moreover, many of the homestead claims were phony. By law it was possible to transfer ownership at any time to any other person or corporation. So for example, a rancher could have each of his hands claim a homestead and then (for a small bribe) transfer ownership to the ranch. Any land speculator could do the same, just by paying a bribe to a stranger passing through.

Other Land Acts Congress made the situation worse by passing several more laws that promoted corruption and the robbery of public land. First, in 1873, came the Timber Culture Act, which allowed a homesteader (or a rancher or speculator) to claim an additional 160 acres if he would plant trees on 40 of the acres. In 1877 Congress passed the Desert Land Act, which allowed an individual to claim 640 acres of land if he would begin irrigation. Under the law ranchers took up section after section of land, especially in the Southwest, since they needed it for grazing cattle. They had their friends swear that it was irrigated (even if they had only poured a bucket of water on it in the presence of their "witnesses").

Even more corruption resulted from the Timber and Stone Act of 1878. This law applied to forest land that could not be farmed but that was highly profitable for timber. Under this law any citizen or immigrant could purchase up to 160 acres of Western forest for $2.50 an acre. Lumbermen used the same tricks that ranchers and other speculators used. They imported sailors, prospectors, and others to buy land and then sign it over to a company for a small fee. And since one good log sold for about $2.50, every tree but the first from any acre of land was pure profit. Under these laws over 20 million more acres of potentially valuable public land fell into the hands of corporations and speculators.

Hardships and Solutions Despite the fact that many of the profits went to land speculators and big corporations, Western lands were opened to the American people. Though they might have to pay ten dollars an acre to a speculator instead of getting free homestead land from the government, farmers moved out onto the plains anyway. The majority came from the states bordering the Mississippi. Most of the rest were immigrants. Almost no workers from Eastern cities made the trip west. But the men and women who did go to the plains performed a monumental task. In the thirty years after 1870 they brought more land under cultivation than had been cleared and plowed by all the generations of farmers from the settlement of Jamestown to the Civil War.

These farmers confronted problems that they had not met farther east. They found that their old ways of plowing and planting would not work. For one thing, rainfall was scarce, rivers often ran dry, and the water table[4] was low. Farmers had to haul water from long distances or collect it in holes when it did rain. New well-digging machinery invented in the 1880s and 1890s, however, enabled people to dig

[4] The water table of an area is the supply of water within the ground.

From the 1860s through the 1880s settlers rolled across the plains in prairie schooners like these, conquering one frontier after another. Hardships endured along the way paled in comparison with those met in taming the land.

deeper wells. And steel windmills made it easier to pump the water up. Plains dwellers also developed dry farming. This technique—by which a farmer covers a plowed field with a blanket of dust—conserves the moisture in the soil.

Another problem on the plains was lack of wood. Farmers living there often made their first homes from cakes of sod. For fuel they burned old hay or dried cow dung. Fencing was a special problem until the invention of barbed wire in the 1870s.

A farm family soon learned that, while sixty acres of land could support them farther east, five times as much was needed on the plains. Plowing, planting, and harvesting extensive acreage were greatly aided, nevertheless, by the invention of mechanized farm equipment (see Chapter 24).

Nature seemed to do things on a grand scale on the plains. In the summer the wind blew hot and twice as hard as in the East. In winter blizzards howled down out of the mountains, burying homes and killing livestock. Tornadoes, dust storms, and plagues of locusts and grasshoppers were frequent.

Dry years drove thousands of farmers back east. Many of those who stayed barely survived. In the end, though, farmers turned the plains into the world's most efficient area for producing wheat, corn, and other grains. By 1880 American

Homesteaders like this Montana farmer took advantage of the government offer of cheap land in the West. Many failed, but those who mastered the harsh climate turned the Great Plains into the bread basket of America.

flour—like American beef and pork from the same area—was being exported in great quantities all over the world.

In all this the Indian was, of course, the great loser. The whites' successes on the plains did seem to prove what white Americans had always believed—that the Indians could not make "proper" use of their environment because they lived too much with it and not enough from it. White men were able to exploit even the tough plains environment, to draw from it enough food to feed not only most of the United States but part of the rest of the world, too. The Indian, in contrast, had been willing to settle for the little he needed to maintain his way of life. A full century was to pass before white Americans began to ask themselves seriously whether the Indian's way was not somehow at least as good as theirs. Only one thing was certain: in his "primitive" way the Indian had respected nature more. He had never viewed his world as an object to be owned, changed, and exploited. This, at least in part, was what the battle at Wounded Knee was all about.

REVIEW OF CHAPTERS 21 and 22

1. What present-day states make up what used to be called "The Great American Desert"? Why was the area called that?
2. Why did the mining frontier become a "corporate frontier"?
3. Why was no transcontinental railroad built before the Civil War? How did the government aid the building of a transcontinental line? Was this government policy of aid worth the cost?
4. What was the purpose of the long drive? Why did it end? To what does the phrase "open range" refer? Why did it lead to the overproduction of cattle?
5. What was the attitude of most Americans, including sympathizers, toward the Indians?
6. Describe the major weapons used by whites in overpowering Indians.
7. Cite examples to show that no matter what policy they followed—warfare or treaty-making—the Indians were always the losers.
8. Were those who were attempting to promote individual land ownership and farming among the Indians mistaken? Why or why not? Cite the Dawes Act in your answer.
9. What was the purpose of the Homestead Act? Show how it and other land acts failed to achieve this purpose.

Beyond the Text

1. Look into Frederick Jackson Turner's thesis on the meaning of the closing of the frontier and prepare a discussion defending or opposing it.
2. Discuss the cowboy in fact and in fiction. Include in the discussion the significance of the black cowboy in the development of the frontier.
3. Debate the proposition: The Culture of the Indians Was As "Good" As That of the Whites Who Tried to Eliminate It.
4. In 1972–73 Indian activities at Wounded Knee again became prominent. Check newspapers and magazines to determine what were the issues between the Indians and the government, what tactics were used, and what success these tactics had.
5. What problems did the Great Plains area present to settlers, and how did they solve these problems? Specifically investigate how the pioneers provided fencing and building materials in an area where there was no lumber, and how they acquired water in an area of low annual rainfall.

Bibliography

Nonfiction

Adams, Andy, *Trail Drive.*
Atherton, Lewis, *The Cattle Kings.**
Billington, Ray A., *Westward Expansion.*
Billington, Ray A., ed., *The Frontier Thesis.*
Brown, Dee, *Bury My Heart at Wounded Knee.**
Fee, Chester A., *Chief Joseph.*
Josephy, Alvin, Jr., *The Indian Heritage of America.**
Monaghan, Jay, *Custer.**
Robbins, Roy M., *Our Landed Heritage.**
Shannon, Fred A., *The Farmer's Last Frontier.*
Utley, Robert M., *The Last Days of the Sioux Nation.**
Webb, Walter P., *The Great Plains.**

Fiction

Allen, Henry, *No Survivors.*
Blackburn, Thomas W., *A Good Day to Die.**
Cather, Willa A., *My Antonia.**
Grey, Zane, *The U.P. Trail.**

* a paperback book

CHAPTER

23

STRIKE AND VIOLENCE IN CHICAGO

April 15, 1885

My Dear Virginia,

We have had a week of trial and anxiety on the great subject of disturbances in our main factory—the serious labor troubles we have encountered—a great "strike," and all the resulting derangement of our relations—old and pleasant as they were—with our workmen.

Trouble has come to hundreds of families in consequence; hatred and fierce passions have been aroused; and an injury has resulted to our good name.

It began with a few molders[1] and went on, one force operating on another, until 1,200 men went out, part of them by intimidation and part of them led by ignorant and blind passion. It ended by our conceding the terms demanded.

What a sore heart I have carried these days!

Your Devoted Mother

THIS LETTER was written by a bewildered woman in her early seventies to her daughter. The writer, Nettie Fowler McCormick, was the widow of Cyrus Hall McCormick. An ambitious and ingenious Virginia farm boy, McCormick had made millions of dollars from the invention and

[1] Molders are factory workers who pour molten iron into molds to make metal parts for various machines.

Workers gathered in Haymarket Square to protest police treatment of striking workers. The speakers' oratory was fiery and the police ordered the crowd's dispersal, leading to violence that was to set back the labor cause for some time.

Cyrus Hall McCormick invented the first successful reaping machine in 1834. He turned his invention into a booming business, employing new sales methods such as installment buying.

manufacture of the reaper, a machine that harvested crops mechanically. He opened his Chicago factory, the McCormick Harvester Works, in the 1840s. It was the largest producer of harvesting machines in the world.

Nettie McCormick had always paid close attention to the family business. Now, just a year after her husband's death, a stable and profitable enterprise seemed to be falling to pieces before her eyes. At first, she remembered, her husband had known all the original twenty-three workmen by name. He had worked alongside them in the little Chicago factory. Even after a few years, when there were about 200 workers making over 1,000 reapers a year, he could still name those who had been with the company for any length of time.

As the business grew, relations with the workers had become more difficult. During the Civil War, when labor had been scarce and prices jumped every week, there had been many strikes or threats of strikes. McCormick had been forced to agree to one wage increase after another. But the company had survived and continued to grow.

In 1884, the year Cyrus Hall McCormick died, it had shown a profit of 71 percent! The plant covered dozens of acres. Its modern machinery, including two huge steam engines that supplied the power, filled twelve full acres of factory floor space. About 1,300 men (depending on the season of the year) put in six ten-hour days a week at the plant. They turned 10 million feet of lumber and thousands of tons of iron into about 50,000 reapers a year. And these machines that poured out of the factory were making possible an agricultural revolution in the United States.

Most of the McCormick workers had seemed contented enough. Nine out of ten were Germans, Norwegians, or Swedes. Most lived just west of the plant in neighborhoods that Cyrus McCormick had built, little industrial suburbs with Swedish and German street names. All the McCormicks agreed that the trouble had to lie with one small group, the molders, who worked in the huge foundry. The molders were largely Irish—"fighting Irish," as one plant official called them. And they had a union, Molders Local No. 233. This union had been making trouble for the McCormicks since the Civil War, twenty years earlier.

Nettie Fowler McCormick, wife of the founder of the McCormick Works, understood little of the underlying causes of worker discontent at the plant in 1885.

There were only about ninety molders and about an equal number of semiskilled helpers in the foundry. But their work was crucial to the production of reapers. And the molders had always been well-organized. Whenever prices rose, they were the first to demand a wage increase and threaten a strike. Whenever Cyrus McCormick cut wages, the molders were always the first, and usually the only, group of workmen to fight back.

As Nettie McCormick had said, the molders were in the forefront of the recent strike. In December 1884 the company's new young president, Cyrus McCormick II, announced a 15-percent cut in pay for the molders and at least a 10-percent pay reduction throughout the factory. At first even the molders seemed to accept the cut. Actually, they were only biding their time until production reached its annual spring peak. Then, in March 1885, they demanded a restoration of wages. When McCormick refused, the molders went on strike.

McCormick was anxious to prove himself. He sent telegrams to company agents all over the Middle West asking them to send strike-breaking molders to Chicago. He hired the strikebreakers and housed them inside the plant grounds. They were actually listed on the McCormick payroll as "scabs," the union's insulting name for men who replaced striking workers. Company records referred to their barracks as "scab house."

Then came that awful day, April 14. Police were scattered throughout the city to patrol a local election. Striking union men attacked McCormick workers all around the plant. A horse-drawn bus carrying Pinkerton guards into the plant with a case of Winchester repeating rifles was set upon and burned. The rifles disappeared into the crowd, and the police captain—an Irishman named O'Donnell who was probably sympathetic to the strikers—did nothing!

Naturally enough, Cyrus McCormick went to the mayor of Chicago to demand better police protection for his plant and his scabs. But the Mayor, Carter Harrison, knew that the McCormicks were his political enemies. All he did was recommend that young Cyrus reach an agreement with the molders. The last straw came when old Philip Armour, head of a large meat-packing company in Chicago and a veteran of many labor troubles, told McCormick that he was already beaten and had no choice but to give in to the molders.

Everything seemed to run counter to young McCormick's wishes—Mayor Harrison's unwillingness to help, the obvious sympathy between the police and the strikers, and Armour's negative advice. So he gave in. He tried to hold the wage increase to 10 percent, but the molders refused to accept it. He ended by restoring the original 15 percent.

The strike confirmed the McCormicks' view of the Irish molders as troublemakers. Their attitude was shared by the Pinkerton Detective Agency, hired by McCormick as a private police force during the strike. A Pinkerton man submitted this report on the "fighting Irish":

> The assault on the Pinkerton police during the strike of last week was urged by Irishmen, who are employed at McCormick's as molders and helpers. These

> Irishmen are nearly all members of the Ancient Order of Hibernians, who have a most bitter enmity against the Agency.

To the Pinkerton Agency there seemed to be only one possible conclusion:

> The Germans who participated in McCormick's strike were merely tools, and the Irish were the real instigators both in inaugurating the strike and in the outrages which followed—and in forcing Mr. McCormick to come to terms at a 15 percent increase.

In April 1885, when Mrs. McCormick wrote to her daughter, Cyrus McCormick II was busy trying to analyze the strike. He wrote to his mother:

> The whole question of these labor troubles is vast and important and throws more new light on a department of our manufacturing interests which we have not hitherto studied with sufficient depth and understanding.

McCormick was only twenty-five at this time. Three years earlier his father had taken him out of Princeton to help run the factory. When his father died two years later, young McCormick had become president of the company. In handling the strike perhaps he had made mistakes, he thought, the mistakes of inexperience. As he mulled over the preceding weeks, McCormick came to two firm conclusions. First, he agreed with his mother and the Pinkerton report that the molders had been the chief villains. Second, he grew more and more determined to defeat their union. He felt that he and his company could not afford to be dictated to by any union, especially one composed of only a few highly skilled workers who could, at will, stop production entirely.

McCormick went to work at once to "weed out" the offending Irish molders. He focused his efforts on a daring technological gamble. During the summer of 1885, the summer following the strike, the McCormick Company bought a dozen new pneumatic molding machines. They were supposed to perform mechanically most of the foundry tasks that the skilled molders had always done by hand. The machines were expensive, and they were experimental. No one knew whether they would work. McCormick hoped that they would enable the company to rid itself once and for all of the troublesome molders.

In August the McCormick foundry was closed for two months so that the machines could be installed. The closing was not unusual, since reapers were manufactured seasonally—much like automobiles are today, with new model seasons every fall. August and September were always light months at the Harvester works. But when the foundry reopened for full production, not one molder who had participated in the spring strike was back on the payroll.

McCormick seemed to have won a complete victory. All he had done was spend a vast sum of money on the new machinery. A few months after the machines went into operation, he wrote his mother triumphantly that the machines

> are working even beyond our expectations and everybody is very much pleased with the result. Two men with one of these machines can do an average of about three days work in one. Add to this fact that we have only nine molders in the whole foundry (the rest are all laborers), and you can see what a great gain this will be to us.

McCormick was being more optimistic than he should have been—probably to reassure his anxious mother. Actually, there were troubles with the machines. In October the McCormick Company complained to the manufacturer that the castings turned out by the pneumatic molding device were too brittle to use. And in November Cyrus McCormick was called home from a trip to New York because of a crisis in the foundry. He wrote in his diary for Wednesday, November 11: "Telegram from mother urging come home at once about molding machines—probably failure. Critical situation."

The machines were fixed, but even when they worked they seemed to require an endless amount of labor to keep them functioning. Before the machines were installed, the total wage bill in the foundry was about $3,000 a week. After the machines had been in operation for about six months, the wages at the foundry totaled $8,000 a week,

Prior to the mechanization of the molding floor at the McCormick Works, much of the labor was done by unskilled and semiskilled workers. Pouring the molten metal into molds was the job of the common laborer, but working the metal into shape required more skill and was more highly paid.

more than double the old labor cost. Most of the labor was common, unskilled work. But gradually the company had to hire additional new molders to supervise the work. Economically, the machines were a complete failure.

Still, the new technology had broken the molders union at McCormick. And the union was unhappy. The leader of the molders was a veteran union man named Myles McPadden. He devised a new scheme. It was much more dangerous to the McCormicks than the old union, with only ninety members. If there was to be no molders union, then McPadden would simply organize all the other workers in the plant into one union or another. The workers were discontented, so the time was ripe. By February of 1886 he had succeeded in organizing every major group of workers in the plant. The skilled workers—blacksmiths, machinists, and so on—joined the Metalworkers Union. McPadden encouraged the others to join the Knights of Labor, a general nationwide union. Only 300 of the 1,400 McCormick workers remained nonunion. The lines of a new strike battle were shaping up clearly.

During this time McCormick was busy, too. After his frustrated attempt to get Mayor Harrison to help, McCormick had gone to some lengths to make peace with the powerful political leader of the city. In every election before 1885 the McCormicks had opposed Harrison. After that year they supported him. As a result, Captain O'Donnell, the Irish police official who had been sympathetic to the workers in the spring of 1885, was replaced. The new man in charge of the area where the works were located was Police Inspector John Bonfield.

Bonfield had a reputation as a tough antilabor cop. He had once literally beaten his way through a crowd of strikers, shouting a slogan for which he became famous: "Clubs today spare bullets tomorrow." If there was going to be trouble in 1886, McCormick could count on the police in a way impossible a year before.

In mid-February 1886 a union committee representing all three unions—the Knights of Labor, the Metalworkers, and the Molders—presented McCormick with a series of demands:

> First, that all wages of laboring men be advanced from $1.25 to $1.50 a day. Second, that all vise hands[2] be advanced to $2.00 a day, and that blacksmith helpers be advanced to $1.75. Third, that time the men spend in the water closet [the toilet] not be limited as heretofore. Fourth, that, inasmuch as the molding

[2] "Vise hands" refers to workers who used a vise, a tool for holding metal being worked. They had a skill and were, therefore, to receive higher wages than the "laboring men," who were unskilled workers.

> machines are a failure, the preference should be given the old hands. The scabs in the foundry must be discharged, and a pledge given that no man would be discharged for taking part in a strike.

The company offered to meet some of the demands, but not the fourth, which must have made Cyrus McCormick furious. The unions rejected the counteroffer and called a strike.

Before the strike was scheduled to begin, however, the company announced a complete shutdown of the plant for an indefinite period of time. Union pickets started marching near the plant, but they were kept away by 400 city policemen, now under Bonfield's command. To show its gratitude, the company served free hot meals to the police, with Cyrus McCormick sometimes personally pouring the coffee.

After two weeks the works were reopened, but only to nonunion employees. There was a loyal force of only 82 men. The company furnished them with pistols. McCormick hoped they would lead an enthusiastic rush for jobs. But only 161 men showed up the first day. The second day was not much better. Once again the company's agents scoured the region for workers. Gradually, the company's situation improved a little. McCormick was actually willing to sacrifice almost half a year's production in order to settle the union question once and for all.

For the men on strike the situation was just as important. If they lost, their future at McCormick (or any other manufacturing plant in the city) was dim. As March turned into April, stomachs grew tighter and tempers hotter. The explosion McCormick had avoided the year before by giving in to union demands now looked inevitable.

The situation at McCormick was complicated by the fact that during the spring of 1886 there were strikes all over Chicago. On May 1 all the unions in Chicago began a general stike for the eight-hour day. This was one of the largest and most heated labor actions in American history. The strike at McCormick merged with the more general agitation, involving thousands of skilled and unskilled workers from plants all over the city.

Then on May 3, two days into the strike for an eight-hour day, a lumber workers union held a mass meeting to hear an address by August Spies, a radical labor agitator. The meeting took place on Black Road, just a short distance from the McCormick factory. Some McCormick men were at the meeting, even though none was a lumber worker.

The McCormicks had been so desperate for workers that they had already granted the eight-hour day (with ten hours' pay) to their scab workers. So, at 3:30, two hours before the former 5:30 closing, the bell at the plant rang, and the strikebreaking workers left the plant. The striking union men at the meeting watched the strikebreaking workers leave the plant on their new short schedule.

The sight proved too much. Several hundred men, some of them McCormick strikers and some of them lumber workers, mobbed the scabs leaving the plant, driving them back inside the gate. The strikers began to smash windows, unleashing anger that had been building for months. About 200 policemen, under Inspector Bonfield, were there. Suddenly, they began firing their revolvers into the crowd, forgetting Bonfield's slogan about using clubs to spare bullets. When the noise died away, two workers were dead and several others were wounded.

August Spies, who had been addressing the meeting of lumber workers near the McCormick Works, followed the crowd and witnessed the violence that occurred. The next day, in the newspaper office where he worked, he heard that a mass meeting was scheduled at Haymarket Square to protest the shootings at McCormick. A circular announcing the meeting was being printed in both German and English when Spies arrived at the paper:

Courtesy Chicago Historical Society

Attention Workingmen!

GREAT

MASS-MEETING

TO-NIGHT, at 7.30 o'clock,

AT THE

HAYMARKET, Randolph St., Bet. Desplaines and Halsted.

Good Speakers will be present to denounce the latest atrocious act of the police, the shooting of our fellow-workmen yesterday afternoon.

Workingmen Arm Yourselves and Appear in Full Force!

THE EXECUTIVE COMMITTEE.

Spies agreed to address the meeting, but he insisted that the final line in the circular be omitted. About 200 of the circulars had already been printed, but the line was removed from the rest. Few of the

20,000 circulars that were finally distributed on the streets of Chicago contained the threatening reference to arms.

August Spies was not, strictly speaking, a workingman. He might best be described as a radical journalist. At the time of the Chicago troubles he was thirty years old and the editor of the *Arbeiter-Zeitung*, a German-language newspaper with a radical viewpoint. He was also the business manager of an organization called the Socialistic Publishing Society, a propaganda organization of a small political party known as the Socialist Labor Party. (This party still exists and runs candidates for national office in several states.)

From time to time Spies had been in trouble with the police. Only a year before, during the McCormick strike of 1885, he had angered the police by intervening in the case of a poor German servant girl. She had been arrested by the police and held in jail for several days. When Spies and the girl's mother went to the jail, they discovered that the girl had been molested repeatedly. Rather than keep quiet, Spies swore out a warrant for the police sergeant in charge of the jail. He lost the case for lack of evidence, but he became well-known to the Chicago police.

Spies was, in short, a politically active radical who did not hesitate to condemn people in positions of authority. He was also a committed socialist politician. Furthermore, he hoped that the rally at Haymarket would attract enough people to fill the square, which could hold about 20,000.

Spies reached Haymarket Square late, at about 8:30 on the night of May 4. He must have felt disappointed. No meeting was in progress, and there were only about a thousand people scattered around the square. The other main speaker, a socialist named Albert R. Parsons, was nowhere in sight. Spies climbed on a wagon, sent someone to look for Parsons, and began his talk. He was a good speaker, and soon the small crowd became enthusiastic:

> The fight is going on. Now is the chance to strike for the oppressed classes. The oppressors want us to be content. They will kill us. The day is not far distant when we will resort to hanging these men. [Applause, and shouts of "Hang them now" came from the crowd.] McCormick is the man who created the row on Monday, and he must be held responsible for the murder of our brothers! [More shouts of "Hang him!"]

Spies went on in the same vein for about an hour, trying to rouse his working-class audience to anger and a sense of solidarity against their "oppressors." Then someone announced that Albert R. Parsons had been found. Spies turned over his wagon rostrum to the second speaker.

The crowd had been waiting for Parsons, for he had a reputation as a spellbinder. Unlike Spies and many other Chicago socialists, he was a native American. Parsons, born in Alabama in 1848, came from a family whose ancestry went back to 1632 in New England. He was a self-trained printer in Texas before the Civil War. During the war he fought for the Confederacy in a Texas artillery company. After the war Parsons became converted to socialism. He moved to Chicago, the center of working-class politics in the United States.

Like Spies, Parsons was not a worker at all but a political journalist. He edited a radical workingmen's paper called *The Alarm.* The Haymarket rally was just one more in a long series of political speeches for him. His speech was much like Spies', with a slightly stronger tone:

> I am not here for the purpose of inciting anybody, but to speak out, to tell the facts as they exist, even though it shall cost me my life before morning. It behooves you, as you love your wife and children—if you don't want to see them perish with hunger, killed or cut down like dogs in the street—Americans, in the interest of your liberty and independence, to *arm,* to *arm* yourselves!

Here again there was applause from the crowd and shouts of "We'll do it! We're ready!"

What Parsons and Spies did not know was that the crowd was full of police detectives. Every few minutes one or another ran back to a nearby station house to report what the speakers were saying. Waiting in the station were almost 200 policemen, fully armed, and under the command of none other than John Bonfield.

Parsons and Spies probably did not notice Mayor Carter Harrison in the crowd, either. Only the mayor's presence had kept Bonfield from breaking up the meeting. As Parsons finished, the mayor left; it was obvious to him that everything was peaceful. It was almost ten o'clock and rain was in the air. Most of the crowd, too, began to drift off as the third speaker, Samuel Fielden, began to talk.

Suddenly, 180 policemen (a group almost as large as the crowd itself) marched into the square and up to the wagon where Fielden was speaking. One of the captains turned to the crowd and said: "In the name of the people of the State of Illinois, I command this meeting immediately and peaceably to disperse." After a moment the police captain repeated his order. The crowd was already starting to melt away (it was almost 10:30 by now). Fielden had stopped speaking and was climbing down from the wagon platform. "We are peaceable," Fielden said to Bonfield.

At that moment, without any warning, a dynamite bomb was thrown (it is not known from where or by whom) at the police. The fuse burned for a second or two after the bomb struck the ground. Then it went off with a deafening roar. Screams split the air as people ran in all directions. A number of policemen lay on the ground, one dead and the others wounded. Quickly, the police re-formed their ranks, and some of them began to fire into the crowd. Other policemen waded into the confusion swinging their clubs. The uproar lasted only a minute or two. Then suddenly the square was empty.

In addition to the one dead policeman there were seventy-three wounded, six of whom died later. Four civilians were killed, and the official reports listed twelve as wounded. The twelve were those who had been too badly hurt to leave the square. Probably several times as many limped or struggled home and never became official statistics.

Like most riots, the Haymarket affair had been short. And, considering what could have happened, very few people were hurt. But the incident occurred on the heels of trouble at the McCormick plant, in the midst of the eight-hour strike, with 80,000 Chicago workingmen off the job. Thus the Haymarket bomb touched off a near panic in the city and much of the rest of the nation. Thousands of respectable citizens convinced themselves that a dangerous conspiracy of anarchists, socialists, and communists was at work to overthrow the government and carry out a bloody revolution. One of the leading business magazines of the day, *Bradstreets'*, spoke for thousands of Americans when it said of the Haymarket incident:

> This week's happenings at Chicago go to show that the threats of the anarchists against the existing order are not idle. In a time of disturbance, desperate men have a power for evil out of proportion to their numbers. They are desperate fanatics who are opposed to all laws. There is no room for anarchy in the political system of the United States.

Also important was the fact that many people had been frightened and angered by a recent flood of immigration from Europe to Ameri-

Courtesy Chicago Historical Society

A contemporary sketch of what happened after a bomb exploded in Haymarket Square shows workers as well armed as police in battlelike poses. Pictures such as this fed the popular notion of union men as anarchists.

ca—and many of the "anarchists" were also foreigners. Not only in Chicago, but all over the nation, newspaper editorialists and public speakers demanded the immediate arrest and conviction of the alien radicals who had conspired to murder honest policemen and subvert law and order. The result was a swift and efficient series of illegal raids by the Chicago police. They arrested people and searched property without warrants. They imprisoned people without charging them and threatened potential witnesses. All in all, the authorities arrested and questioned about 200 "suspects"—probably none of whom had anything at all to do with the bombing.

In this heated atmosphere, fueled by journalists who whipped up unreasonable fears of an anarchist conspiracy, a jury met to determine if indictments could be brought against anyone for the violence. It decided that, although the specific person who threw the bomb could not be determined, anyone who urged violence was a "conspirator" and as guilty of murder as the bomb thrower. On the basis of this decision another jury met and indicted thirty-one persons on counts of murder. Of the thirty-one, eight were eventually tried, all of them political radicals. Most had not even been present at the Haymarket bombing.

The effect of the Haymarket Affair had now become clear. What had begun weeks before as an ordinary strike at the McCormick Works had been transformed into a crusade against political radicalism, most of which was said to be foreign in origin. Only Parsons and Samuel Fielden were not German or of German descent. The names of the other six would have been as natural in Berlin or Hamburg as in Chicago: August Spies, Michael Schwab, Adolph Fischer, George Engel, Louis Lingg, and Oscar Neebe.

In one way or another, all the defendants had some connection with the labor movement and with political agitation for revolution. Several of them were anarchists, though their ideas about anarchism as a philosophy were vague. They might as well have called themselves socialists, as several of them did at one time or another. In general, they were intellectuals. Their jobs were connected with radical journalism in either the English- or German-language press. They did not all know each other, but by the time their trial was over, most of them were probably "comrades," a word they used more and more in the months ahead.

On the other side of the battle were all the forces of law, order, and authority. True, some agreed with Mayor Harrison that the Haymarket meeting had been peaceful, that the whole idea of a conspiracy was a false and legally incorrect notion. But most of Chicago society (including even many elements of the labor movement) favored a quick conviction and the hanging of all eight defendants. The judge who tried the case, the prosecuting attorney, most business leaders, almost all the local clergymen—almost everyone who had anything to say in Chicago—were convinced before the trial that the defendants were guilty. Moreover, most of Chicago's leading citizens, and their counterparts in the rest of the country, agreed that the trial was a struggle to the death between American republicanism and foreign anarchism. The entire established order of American society, with very few exceptions, was determined to make an example of the "conspirators."

The Haymarket trial began on June 21, 1886. The first three weeks of the seven-week trial were spent selecting a jury. Under Illinois law the defense had the right to reject a total of 160 jurors on peremptory challenges—that is, without having to discuss a juror's qualifications and abide by the judge's decision. As one prospective juror after another was called, it became clear that most of them were extremely prejudiced against the defendants. The defense attorneys quickly used up their 160 challenges. They then had to show cause for turning down a juror and depend on the judge, Joseph Gary, to rule fairly. Again and again, plainly biased jurors were accepted by the judge—whose own prejudice against the defendants became apparent as the process went on. The result was a jury composed of twelve citizens who obviously wished to hang the defendants.

In his opening statement prosecuting attorney Julius Grinnell set the tone of the entire trial:

> Gentlemen, for the first time in the history of our country people are on trial for endeavoring to make anarchy the rule. I hope that while the youngest of us lives this will be the last and only time when such a trial shall take place. In the light of the 4th of May, we now know that the preachings of anarchy by these defendants, hourly and daily for years, have been sapping our institutions. Where they have cried murder, bloodshed, anarchy, and dynamite, they have meant what they said. The firing on Fort Sumter was a terrible thing to our country, but it was open warfare. I think it was nothing compared with this insidious, infamous plot to ruin our laws and our country.

It was obvious that this would not be an ordinary murder trial. The defendants would be judged by their words and beliefs. A ninth "conspirator," Rudolph Schnaubelt, had fled. The prosecution would try to prove that he had thrown the bomb. The next step would be to convict the other eight of conspiracy, which would carry the same penalty as murder itself. And they would be convicted by the fact that they had made speeches and written newspaper articles urging violent revolution. Day after day the prosecution offered evidence about the defendants' beliefs, their writings, and even pamphlets they had supposedly helped to sell.

The prosecution had weak cases against the individual defendants. They were able to prove that one of the defendants, Lingg, had actually made bombs. But Lingg was a stranger to most of the others, and he had not even been at Haymarket Square. Parsons, Spies, Fischer, and Schwab had left the square before the bomb was thrown. George Engel proved that he had been home drinking a glass of beer with his wife. In the end the prosecution's case rested on a theory of "general conspiracy to promote violence." No evidence of a single violent act was brought into court that could withstand even the mildest cross-examination by the frustrated defense attorneys.

After four weeks of testimony the jury retired. The jury members had been instructed by Judge Gary in such a way as to make conviction almost inevitable, and they needed only three hours to discuss the matter. After this short deliberation the jury filed solemnly back into the courtroom. It was ten o'clock, August 19, 1886, when the foreman read the verdict:

> We the jury find the defendants Spies, Schwab, Fielden, Parsons, Fischer, Engel, and Lingg guilty of murder in the manner and form as charged, and fix the penalty at death. We find Oscar Neebe[3] guilty of murder in the manner and form as charged, and fix the penalty at imprisonment in the penitentiary for fifteen years.

Years later Judge Gary recalled that "the verdict was received by the friends of social order with a roar of almost universal approval."

Before they were sentenced, each of the defendants made a speech to the court. Spies spoke for all of them when he said, in a German accent that he never lost:

> There was not a syllable said about anarchism at the Haymarket meeting. But "anarchism is on trial," foams Mr. Grinnell. If that is the case, your honor, very well; you may sentence me, for I am an anarchist. I believe that the state of classes—the state where one class dominates and lives upon the labor of another class—is doomed to die, to make room for a free society, voluntary association, or universal brotherhood, if you like. You may pronounce the sentence upon me, honorable judge, but let the world know that in A.D. 1886, in the state of Illinois, eight men were sentenced to death because they believed in a better future.

There were appeals, of course, first to state courts and then to the Supreme Court of the United States. One by one the appeals failed. Then there were pleas to the governor of Illinois for mercy, and the sentences of Fielden and Schwab were commuted to life. Lingg, the

[3] Oscar Neebe was the youngest defendant; almost no evidence had been presented against him. Most of the jury's three-hour deliberation was devoted to his case.

Courtesy Chicago Historical Society

Albert Parsons, August Spies, George Engel, and Adolph Fischer were hanged on November 11, 1886, after one of the most unfair trials in American history.

bomb maker, who was probably half-mad, committed suicide in jail—using dynamite set off by a fuse that he lit with his jail-cell candle. The other four condemned men—Engel, Spies, Parsons, and Fischer—were hanged on November 11.

As the four stood on the scaffold, ropes around their necks and hoods over their heads, Spies broke the deep silence of the prison yard by shouting: "There will come a time when our silence will be more powerful than the voices you strangle today!"

At the McCormick Works the situation had returned to normal months earlier. On May 7, 1886, three days after the Haymarket bombing, Cyrus McCormick was able to write in his diary: "A good force of men at the works today, and things are resuming their former appearance." Three days later, taking full advantage of the public outrage over the "devilish plot," as McCormick called it, at Haymarket Square, the McCormick Works quietly resumed the ten-hour day. On Monday, May 10, McCormick wrote: "Things going smoothly. We returned to 5:30 closing hour today, instead of 3:30."

CHAPTER

24

Factories, Cities, and Immigrants

THERE Is a popular type of nursery rhyme that tells a story by linking together a strange sequence of events—a chain of odd happenings somehow related to one another. These events build upon each other. The final result is totally unrelated to each event but quite impossible without any one of them. One of the most popular concerns "the house that Jack built." A rat (soon to suffer an unkind fate) begins the sequence: "This is the rat that ate the malt that lay in the house that Jack built." Each line of the rhyme adds something new to the series. Before long a curious group of characters enters the system, each doing his odd bit to tickle the fancy of a child:

> This is the farmer, sowing the corn,
> That kept the cock that crowed in the
> morn,
> That waked the priest all shaven and
> shorn,
> That married the man all tattered and
> torn,
> That kissed the maiden all forlorn,

That milked the cow with the crumpled
    horn,
That tossed the dog,
That worried the cat,
That killed the rat,
That ate the malt,
That lay in the house that Jack built.

Such nursery rhymes have a simple appeal apart from their quaint images and galloping rhythms: they put isolated people, animals, and things together into a system. In most cases the system only works once: the cock crows one time, and the poor rat can only die once in the house that Jack built. But still the result is a system—a whole with parts that work together to achieve some purpose.

THE INDUSTRIAL SYSTEM

This chapter examines the creation of a new system in the United States: the industrial order. Like the house that Jack built, this system involved a large number of parts that had to fit more or less together if the system was to work at all.

In some sense industry is as old as human society. People have always made things—tools, weapons, clothing, and so on. But, beginning in the eighteenth century, their ability to make goods began to increase rapidly. The so-called industrial revolution that resulted originated in England and spread quickly to the rest of Western Europe and the United States. By the time of the Civil War this revolution was well under way in North America, fed by inventions like the steam engine, the cotton gin, and the reaper. After the war, industrialization drastically altered the basic patterns of life in the United States.

Everything had to be changed, since every element in this new house that people built had to hang together. Raw materials, like coal and iron for making steel, had to be found and developed. Cheap transportation, like railroads, had to be available to bring these materials to factories and to take finished products from them. Workers had to be hired to operate the factories. And agriculture had to be improved so that fewer and fewer farmers would be needed to grow more and more food. More and more machines had to be used to feed more and more factory workers, who would in turn make still more machines. Nothing could happen at all unless everything else happened—and in the proper order, too. Just as the farmer had to sow the corn to feed the cock and so on until the rat was dead, every factory functioned as part of a chain of invention, materials, transportation, and workers.

The McCormick Harvester Company, for example, was only one part of a complicated series of events and machines. The reapers made at the McCormick Works enabled farmers on the Great Plains to produce unheard-of quantities of grain. Some of this grain was milled into flour, for bread eaten by people like McCormick's molders. Other farm products fed cattle, which were slaughtered in big cities at other factories owned by men like Philip Armour.

The new transcontinental railroads were necessary to take the reapers west and bring the flour and beef east. Since there were not enough workers to lay the new rails, Irish and Chinese were encouraged to immigrate. The McCormick plant, too, was tended by immigrants, and it was German immigrants who were the main victims of the Haymarket Riot. The city of Chicago itself was a new kind of city, built around railroads and factories, in a way that no other American city had ever been built—a great barracks for the workmen at dozens of factories like the McCormick Works.

In achieving its own industrial system, the United States was transformed. It had once been a nation in which nine out of every ten people lived on farms or in rural communities. By the end of the nineteenth century it was the world's most productive industrial nation. The landscape had been remade. (Many Americans would later decide it had been ruined by careless exploitation.) The people had been changed, too. There had always been immigrants to the United

 States. But new industries attracted different types of immigrants in great numbers. In the end the daily lives and even the language of Americans were changed. New words like "telephone," "subway," "scab," and "millionaire" became common speech. They signaled just how deep and complete the change had been and how different this new house was from the old.

TECHNOLOGICAL CHANGE

Few of the men and women who made or watched the industrial revolution understood its complexity. Most of them probably regarded it as a product of technological change—the invention of new types of machines or the improvement of existing ones. Though this was important, it was not the whole story. Certainly one of the most obvious changes of the nineteenth century was that many things that had once been done slowly by hand were now being done rapidly by machine.

An Agricultural Revolution Agriculture was a prime example of the replacement of hand labor by machine power. The most rapid and striking introduction of new agricultural technology took place on the Great Plains. On these flat and treeless expanses, plowing, planting, and harvesting could be done on a scale that would have stunned colonial settlers and even most plantation owners of the Old South. But what happened on the plains was just an exaggerated version of what went on in all phases of American agriculture: the industrialization of the farm.

At first, the new machinery was fairly simple. McCormick's earliest reapers, built before the Civil War, were small. They were drawn by one horse and worked by one or two men. Another invention—a steel plow that could cut deeper and faster than the old iron plow—was a small step. But gradually the new technology gained force and speed. Reapers were soon equipped with automatic binders that could fasten grain into bunches mechanically. The single steel plow was soon modified into a multiple, or gang, plow that could cut three or four furrows at one time.

Soon other new machines appeared. One could plow and plant at the same time. Another, the combine, added to the reaper a mechanical thresher, which could separate grain from stalks automatically. A combine could move quickly through a wheatfield, gathering wheat and leaving behind only waste to be plowed under in the spring. The machine worked without a single person's hand touching either the earth or the wheat plants.

During most of the nineteenth century new machinery was still driven primarily by animals. Some steam engines were used, but the final mechanization of farms had to await the gasoline-driven tractor in the twentieth century. Still, even before the tractor, the life of the American farmer had been fundamentally altered by technology. Farming gradually came to resemble the running of factories, in which a product for sale was processed and made ready by machinery. Nor was it just grain farmers in the West who experienced this revolution. Dairy farmers acquired milking machines and automatic separators, which could divide cream from milk in a matter of seconds. Sooner or later, almost every step in all but a few kinds of agriculture was mechanized.

The result of the mechanical changes in agriculture was to double and redouble the volume and pace of food production. In 1840 it took more than three hours of human work time to produce a bushel of wheat. In the 1890s the time had been cut to ten minutes. In 1840 a bushel of corn required almost five hours of labor, from planting to final processing. In the 1890s the time had been cut to forty minutes.

Hand in hand with the reduction of hours was a marked decrease in the number of farmers needed to produce food. Mechanization made it possible for a tiny minority of Americans to feed the large majority. Those who left farms were then free to work for the railroads and in oil fields, iron mines, factories and offices—thereby aiding the process of rapid industrialization.

The amount of land under cultivation dou-

The introduction of machines such as the combine greatly increased farm efficiency. The combine was so called because it brought together a reaper and a thresher in one machine.

bled between the Civil War and 1900. The net result of the agricultural revolution was an enormous abundance of food.

Improving Rail Transport The agricultural revolution depended not only on new technology on the farms but also on new machinery to take food from farms and bring it to cities—that is, railroads. It was railroads that brought Wyoming beef, Kansas wheat, and Louisiana rice to the table of a McCormick molder. Without the new railroad network built after the Civil War, the mechanization of agriculture would have had small effect.

Railroads, just like farms, benefited from new technological developments. The principle of the steam engine remained the same. But almost every other mechanical aspect of railroading changed drastically during the generation after Appomattox.

The old railroads had used iron rails, small and dangerous wood-burning engines, and tiny, rickety coaches and freight cars. The new lines used steel rails that would last for many years without cracking or rusting. Because they could support almost twenty times as much weight as iron rails, larger engines and cars could be built. The typical pre-Civil War engine had weighed about 20 tons. By 1900 some engines weighed as much as 300 tons. The coal-burning locomotive became a giant source of power that could pull huge freights over the most difficult grades efficiently and safely. Freight cars increased in weight from 10 tons to over 100 tons. At the same time, the length of trains grew from 20 cars to as many as 100. The new trains were also faster; by 1900 many locomotives could travel over a hundred miles an hour.

Railroad mileage increased, too. In 1870—even after the completion of the first transcontinental line—there were only about 60,000 miles of track in the United States. By 1900 there were over 250,000 miles. This total was greater than the entire railroad mileage of Europe, including Russia. Other inventions like the telegraph and the electric signal made it possible to control complicated traffic patterns and freight yards. The trains and tracks of 1900 were as dramati-

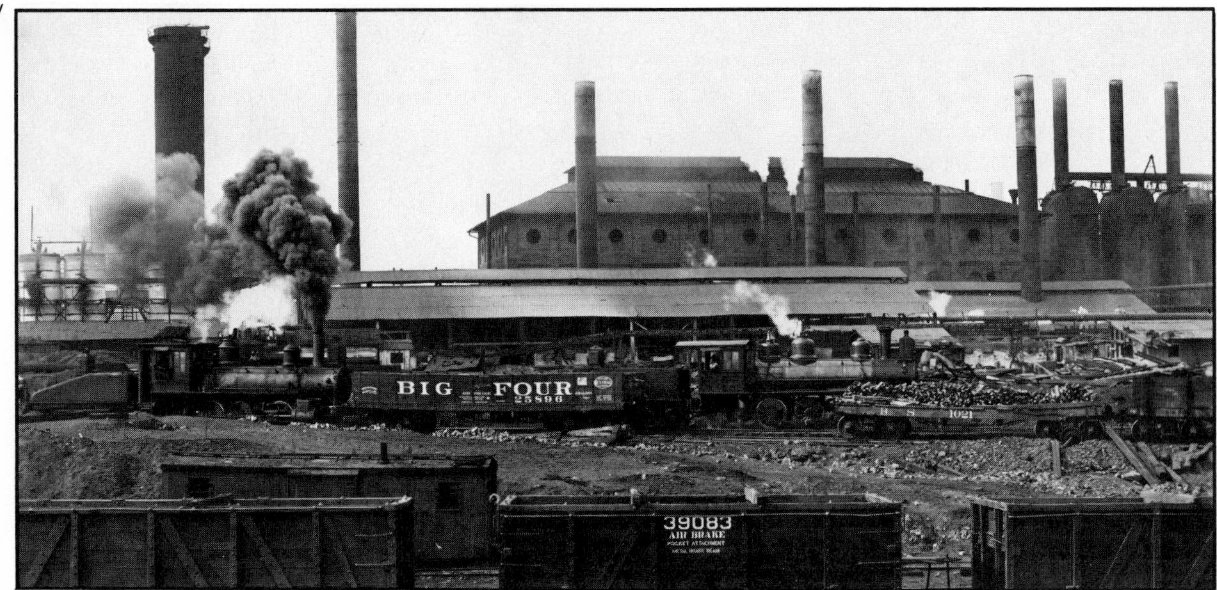

Alabama, rich in iron ore and coal, became a center of the steel industry. Steel was produced in giant blast furnaces, like these of the Tennessee Coal, Iron, and Railroad Company of Ensley, Alabama, and transported by rail to other centers.

cally different from those of 1850 as the jet airplane is from the first wobbly passenger craft of the 1920s. These new giants of the landscape transformed the nature of moving food, objects, and people from one place to another.

MANUFACTURING

Taken by themselves, the technological changes in agriculture and the railroads would have meant little. They were important only in their relation to other parts of the new industrial order. In this system it was manufacturing that was crucial.

By 1900—a little more than a century after Washington had taken the oath of office—the United States was the leading manufacturing nation in the world. Many factors made this growth possible. Americans found new beds of coal. They discovered iron ore in Michigan and Minnesota. They opened oil fields in Pennsylvania, the Ohio Valley, and the southern Great Plains. These raw materials and energy sources fed in turn the new factories of Pittsburgh, Chicago, and dozens of other cities. Mechanized agriculture made it possible for millions of people to move to cities to work in industrial plants. A high tariff kept down competition from foreign manufactured goods. Most important of all were the new machines and processes that enabled Americans to produce so much so quickly.

The Steel Industry Steel was (and still is) very close to the heart of the new economy. It is stronger than iron, more resistant to rust, and easier to shape or mold. People had been making small quantities of steel for centuries, but the process was slow and difficult, since it depended on hand labor. In the 1850s an Englishman named Henry Bessemer invented a converter that could turn iron into steel by blowing a blast of hot air through the molten iron. The process was spectacular to watch, sending a brilliant shaft of sparks and smoke toward the sky. The economic results were just as startling. For the first time it was possible to produce steel in massive quantities.

The combination of the Bessemer converter,

the demand for steel from the railroads and other industries, and the discovery of additional sources of iron ore and coal created a new industry. In 1870 the United States produced only about 77,000 tons of steel. By 1900, however, steel production had increased to over 11 million tons a year—an increase of almost 2,000 percent. Pittsburgh became the first (and is still the largest) of the steel towns. But eventually cities like Birmingham, Alabama, and Gary, Indiana—built almost entirely around the steel industry—sprang up in what had recently been open countryside.

Other Industries What happened in steel was repeated in dozens of other industries. The sewing machine and other inventions made it possible to manufacture shoes and clothing on a mass scale. Steam-powered mills using steel equipment could cut lumber or grind wheat or print newspapers with a speed and efficiency no one had dreamed of earlier (see chart, page 639).

Another new industry grew up based on electricity. The foremost American in this field was the versatile Thomas A. Edison. Throughout the late nineteenth century a stream of inventions poured from his laboratories. These included the phonograph, the first practical electric light bulb, the storage battery, the dynamo, the electric voting machine, and the motion picture.

An industry also developed rapidly around the discovery of oil and new ways of refining it. It yielded kerosene to light lamps and fuel stoves. Heavier oils lubricated the motors of the new technology. Beginning around 1900, it became important as a source of gasoline for the internal combustion engine (see Chapter 32). This vast industry had simply not existed in 1800.

A revolution in communications began in 1876, on the hundredth anniversary of the Declaration of Independence. In that year a young inventor named Alexander Graham Bell exhibited the first working model of the telephone. At first the telephone was purchased only by individuals who wanted to communicate between two specific locations, like a house and a factory or office. But soon there were enough phones in use to create the first telephone exchange. It was opened at New Haven, Connecticut, in 1878. Other cities and towns followed suit.

Soon cities began to link up with each other. The first connection linked New York and Boston in 1884. New York and Chicago were joined in 1892. By 1915, when lines connected New York and San Francisco, it was possible to place calls between any two cities in the nation.

The only way to measure the magnitude of what was happening to the United States is to use statistics. In 1869 the value of American manufactured goods was about \$1 1/2 billion. By the end of the century the figure was more than \$4 1/2 billion. In 1869 about 2 million workers ran American shops, mills, and facto-

In 1877 the telephone was the subject of a humorous song. By the turn of the century it had revolutionized communications in every major city in the United States. Just fifty years after its invention almost every middle-class American home had its own telephone.

ries. Simple arithmetic shows that the market value of the average person's yearly work was only about $940. By 1900, when almost 5 million men and women worked in industry, the average market value of their yearly efforts was almost doubled, to nearly $1,800.

Comparatively, by the 1890s the United States had more steel, more rails, more electric trolleys, more telephones, and more electric lights than any other nation in the world. To accomplish all this, Americans mined more metal, cut more lumber, dug more iron ore, and pumped more oil than any other country.

THE GROWTH OF BIG BUSINESS

Technology and manufacturing were crucial in making the United States an industrial nation. Equally vital were new methods of organizing industry and business.

The Factory System At the beginning of the Civil War the majority of Americans who worked in industry were employed in small shops and mills—a tailor shop, for example, or a blacksmith's, or harnessmaker's. In 1870, when the revolution in industry was already well under way, the average industrial plant had only 8 employees. A median plant (one halfway between the largest and the smallest) had 30 workers. By 1914 the average plant had 28 workers, and the median 270. In 1870 no factory in America employed over 1,000 workers. By 1914 several had over 10,000 workers.

What was occurring, in other words, was a change that went beyond the technology of production and the rate of manufacturing. It was nothing less than a parallel revolution. The factory was replacing the traditional small shop.

In a traditional shop (or in home manufacture of items like cloth or soap) work centers on the person. Power is supplied mainly through human toil. The same worker is involved in all stages of production, from spinning thread, for example, to weaving the final cloth.

The idea behind a factory (first introduced into England in the late eighteenth century) is very different. Work in a factory centers on a machine. Power is mechanical, not human. Parts are nearly identical, and so they are interchangeable.[1] Most important is the division of labor. Each worker specializes, performing only one step in a chain. He may never touch or see the raw material. Or he may never look at or handle the final product. The result is mass production—manufacturing large numbers of articles in standard shapes and sizes.

Changes in Organization Factories were inevitably larger than shops. They cost more money to build and equip with machinery. People needed more and more capital in order to enter and compete in almost any line of business. As the factory system grew, so did the size of companies.

Growth in turn demanded changes in the organization of business. Mass production required a sizable investment. This made it difficult for family firms and partnerships to be truly competitive. So large corporations gradually replaced companies owned by one family or a few partners.

The corporation is an old idea. The Virginia Company and the Massachusetts Bay Company were both corporations. The idea is as simple as it is old. If many people invest in an enterprise by buying stock in it, the company can grow much larger than if it is funded by only a few individuals. If the company fails, each investor has lost only the value of his stock. He cannot be held responsible for any of the corporation's debts.

Just as there had been American factories before the Civil War, so had there been corporations. But their number increased greatly after the war. The corporation became the standard way of organizing business, just as the factory became the characteristic method of organizing production.

[1] A pioneer in this field was Eli Whitney, the inventor of the cotton gin. In 1799 he developed the principle of interchangeable, machine-tooled parts for muskets he was making for the army.

Andrew Carnegie

''Welcome Carnegie, generous son'' was the message of the banners on the streets of Dunfermline, Scotland. A festive crowd gathered to welcome back Andrew Carnegie and his mother to his birthplace. It was 1877. Thirty-three years before, when Andrew was twelve, the Carnegies had fled a life of grinding poverty for a promising New World. Now they returned to receive the honorary citizenship of the city and to dedicate the first Carnegie library outside the United States. Carnegie considered it a high moment of his life.

Carnegie never lost his relish for the good life of a multimillionaire. But more important to him was the ''business' of being a philanthropist—the planning and supervision of his give-away. In a famous magazine essay in 1889 entitled ''The Gospel of Wealth,'' he declared that it was a ''disgrace'' for a rich man to die rich. His wealth was merely held in trust for the benefit of society. The rich man should spend his fortune wisely in his own lifetime. He should act as a ''trustee and agent for his poorer brethren, bringing to their service his superior wisdom, experience, and ability to administer, doing for them better than they would or could do for themselves.''

Carnegie believed in ''scientific philanthropy.'' By this he meant that wealth should not be used for charity but ''to stimulate the best and most aspiring poor of the community to further efforts for their own improvement.'' Since he was self-educated, he wished to encourage the reading habit. To Carnegie libraries were a prime field for ''investment,'' for there were few at that time. Consistent with his self-help policy, he granted support for the buildings only, very rarely for books. He expected the communities to maintain the libraries properly. At a cost of over $50 million nearly 2,800 libraries were built. A third were located outside the United States. This allowed Carnegie to boast that the sun never set on Carnegie libraries.

Carnegie's sentimental journey to Dunfermline began his career as a philanthropist. To him it was

an enjoyable hobby. He built libraries and spread his gospel of wealth. He ''collected'' honorary citizenships from fifty-four cities. To ''Dear Smoky Pittsburgh,'' as he put it, he gave a cultural center. It later became the Carnegie Institute of Technology. Only after he had sold Carnegie Steel in 1901 did he devote full time to the distribution of his fortune.

From then until his death in 1919, philanthropy was his primary concern. He worked at it with characteristic zest, scanning the growing list of his contributions as eagerly as he used to eye stock reports. Although he hobnobbed with philosophers, he appointed businessmen as executives of his funds. Most important, he broadened his base for gift giving into other areas—scientific research, colleges and universities, peacemaking. He managed to give away $350 million, 90 percent of his fortune. Almost $125 million was used to set up the Carnegie Corporation. This philanthropic trust was the largest the world had ever known. It remains a living legacy, fulfilling Carnegie's hopes ''to continue to benefit humanity for generations untold.''

Mass production required not only corporate investment. It also demanded that each firm market its product efficiently on a broad national scale, instead of selling just locally. To remain in business, a corporation had to create effective distributing and selling divisions. It had to buy raw materials on a large scale. Ideally, in fact, it would purchase its own supply of raw materials—for example, a forest for a paper company or cotton plantations for a textile mill.

In other words, mass production made it profitable for a company to invest money in all the stages of its industry, from original materials to final sales. Economists call this phenomenon vertical integration. It involves a business firm not only in manufacturing but in all the other stages and phases relating to the business. An oil company that owned wells, pipelines, and refineries and had its own sales force would be almost perfectly integrated. It would be freed from dependence on any other economic unit—except, of course, customers.

Competition and Consolidation The new industrial order brought a new kind of competition into the American economy. Before mass production small shops and mills had catered to limited territories. They competed only where one territory bordered another. But large corporations needed large markets to absorb their massive outputs. Thus a number of companies might find themselves competing for the same customers.

To win a big market, a corporation might advertise heavily. It might hire high-pressure salesmen and reward them with big commissions. But the most obvious way to win a market was to cut prices. A large company with efficient factories and lower production costs could force its competitors into bankruptcy simply by lowering prices beyond the point where the smaller firms could stay in business.

In one industry after another a few corporations gradually emerged as the leading firms. Each was too large and powerful to be driven out of business by the others. Each was too small to be able to control the whole market. Whenever this happened—and it happened sooner or later in most industries—the firms entered a period of cutthroat competition.

Most American businesses did not welcome such competition. In the 1880s and 1890s they tried to find ways to avoid it. The railroads led the way. Railroad owners had witnessed the havoc and ruin that could be created when one railroad waged a price war with another. By a process of trial and error the railroads worked out private agreements among themselves to control freight rates. Railroads also developed a system of grouping their customers in "pools"; each line was entitled to a certain share of the market. Gradually, too, the railroads had become consolidated into a few major lines, each one absorbing dozens of smaller companies. The Pennsylvania and New York Central railroads dominated the Northeast. The Southern Railway controlled much of the South. The Louisville and Nashville line was supreme in the Ohio Valley.

By agreements and consolidations the railroads had become the models for big business. Other industries soon copied what railroad leaders had learned and used the economic devices they had developed. Consolidation became the order of the day.

No matter what industry was involved, the process was the same. First, a few large competing firms would emerge. A period of intense and costly competition would follow. Then firms would consolidate as a way of avoiding competition. During its period of rapid growth the McCormick Harvester Company was competing with a handful of other large manufacturers of agricultural machinery. In the years after the Haymarket Affair, however, the McCormicks began to realize that competition was wasteful and unnecessary. Early in the twentieth century McCormick merged with its competition to form the huge International Harvester Company. Since then, it has produced practically all the harvesting machinery manufactured in the United States.

A similar development occurred in the steel industry, which was dominated for almost half a century by a Scotch immigrant, Andrew Carne-

(continued on page 497)

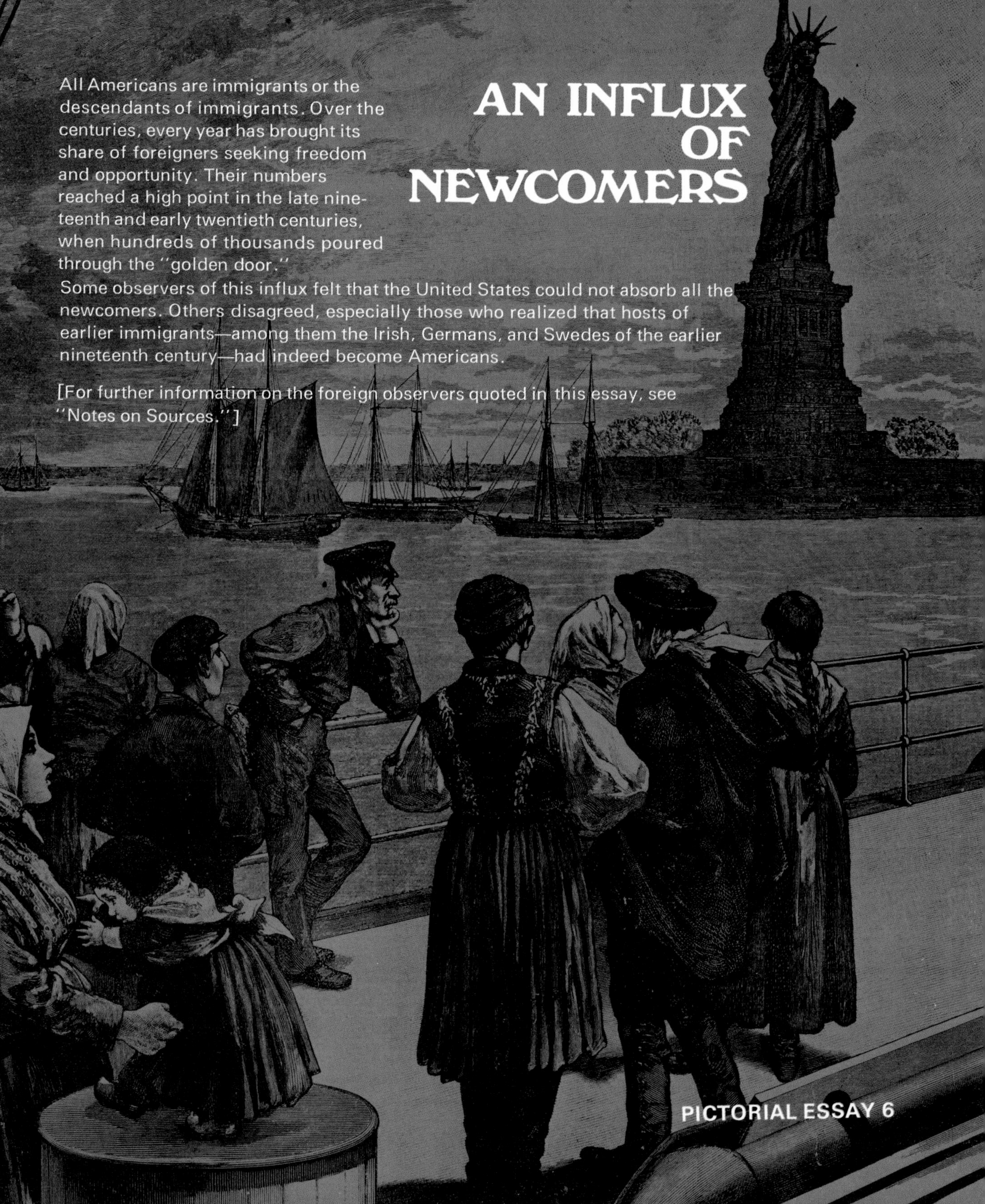

All Americans are immigrants or the descendants of immigrants. Over the centuries, every year has brought its share of foreigners seeking freedom and opportunity. Their numbers reached a high point in the late nineteenth and early twentieth centuries, when hundreds of thousands poured through the "golden door."

AN INFLUX OF NEWCOMERS

Some observers of this influx felt that the United States could not absorb all the newcomers. Others disagreed, especially those who realized that hosts of earlier immigrants—among them the Irish, Germans, and Swedes of the earlier nineteenth century—had indeed become Americans.

[For further information on the foreign observers quoted in this essay, see "Notes on Sources."]

PICTORIAL ESSAY 6

PE 6–2/ *My uncle Olaf, a seaman, used to come to us between voyages, and he was all the time talking about America; what a fine place it was to make money in. The schoolmaster told us one day about the great things that poor Swedes had done in America. A man who had lived in America once came to visit near our cottage. He said that food was cheap in America and that a man could earn nearly ten times there as in Sweden. So at last it was decided that my brother was to go to America.*

[AXEL JARLSON, 1903]

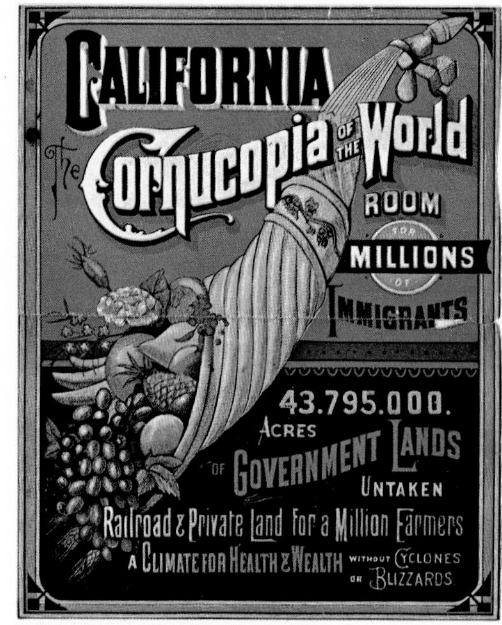

Railroad poster soliciting immigrants

The emigrants flocked into the mess-room from the four doors to twenty immense tables spread with knives and forks and toppling platters of bread. Nearly all the men came in in their hats—in black glistening ringlety sheepskin hats, in fur caps, in bowlers, in sombreros, in felt hats with high crowns, in Austrian cloth hats, in caps so green that the wearer could only be Irish. A strange gathering of seekers, despairers, wanderers, pioneers, criminals, scapegoats.

[STEPHEN GRAHAM, 1913]

Between Decks in an Emigrant Ship

We carried our luggage out at eight, and in a pushing crowd prepared to disembark. At 8:30 we were quick-marched out of the ship to the Customs Wharf and there ranged in six or seven long lines. All the officials were running and hustling, shouting out "Come on!" "Hurry!" "Move along!" and clapping their hands. Our trunks were examined and chalk-marked on the run—no delving for diamonds—and then we were quick-marched further to a waiting ferry-boat [*for Ellis Island*].

[STEPHEN GRAHAM, 1913]

Immigrants disembarking in New York City

A doctor examining boys at Ellis Island

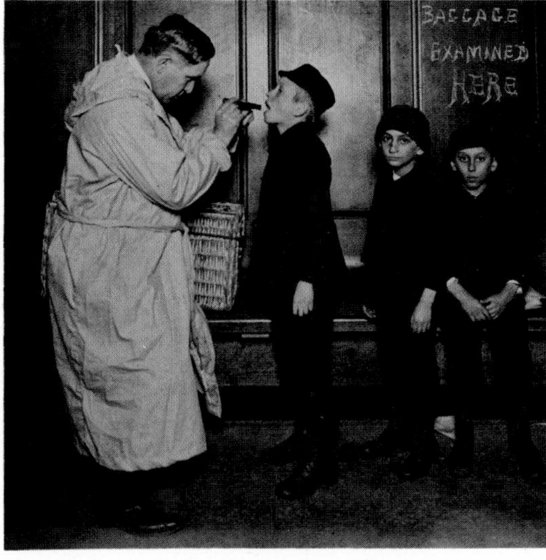

I visited Ellis Island yesterday. The central hall is the key. All day long, through an intricate series of metal pens, the long procession files, step by step, bearing bundles and trunks and boxes, past this examiner and that, past the quick, alert medical officers, the tallymen and the clerks. On they go, from this pen to that, pen by pen, toward a desk at a little metal wicket—the gate of America. Ellis Island is quietly immense. It gives one a visible image of one aspect at least of this world-large process of filling and growing and synthesis which is America.

[H. G. WELLS, 1906]

Waiting for processing at Ellis Island

We were carefully examined, and when my turn came the examining officials shook their heads and seemed to find me wanting. I confessed that I had only five cents in my pocket and had no relatives here, and that I knew of nobody in this country except Franklin, Lincoln, and Harriet Beecher Stowe, whose Uncle Tom's Cabin *I had read in a translation. One of the officials, who had one leg only and walked with a crutch, with a merry twinkle in his eye said in German: "You showed good taste when you picked your American acquaintances." I learned later that he was a Swiss who had served in the Union army during the Civil War.*

[MICHAEL PUPIN, 1874]

George Bellows, *Cliff Dwellers*

Italian saw sharpener at work on the sidewalk

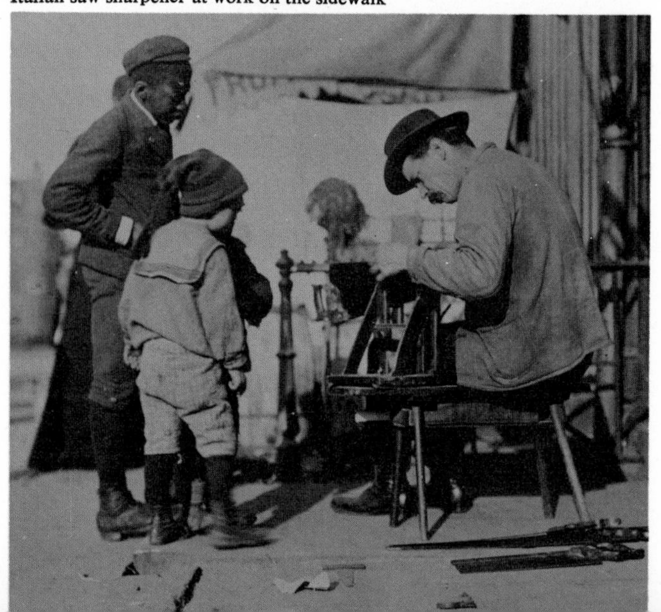

There was a bootblack named Michael on the corner. When I had time I helped him and learned the business. Francisco, too, worked for the bootblack, and we were soon able to make the best polishes. Then we thought we would go into business.

We had said that when we saved $1000 each we would go back to Italy and buy a farm, but now that the time is coming we are so busy and making so much money that we think we will stay. We meet many people and are learning new things all the time. We were very ignorant when we came here, but now we have learned much.

[ROCCO CORRESCA, 1902]

Immigrant iron workers in Pennsylvania

The work given to the new arrivals is generally of a rudimentary nature, but it teaches them to work, and the wages, although low, at least enable them to live, besides giving them the chance of joining the great labor unions of the country and taking if ever so small a part in the industrial pursuits of the people among whom they have come to live.

[COUNT VAY DE VAYA UND LUSKOD, 1908]

←*The inhabitants seem to have come from all quarters of the globe and to represent every known type. The streets, wide as they are, are yet too narrow to hold the masses of people who surge to and fro in them. Everyone is busy; everyone carries a parcel containing articles of clothing or food. Bargaining goes on in all the languages imaginable, and one hears an Italian praising his oranges as in the piazza of St. Lucia; a German discussing sausages of doubtful origin with a French urchin, who plays the part of a chef at the corner of the street; and Russian emigrants share their vodka, as a token of friendship, with Polish Jews.*

[COUNT VAY DE VAYA UND LUSKOD, 1908]

In the evening my sister and I took a walk; she went shopping and asked me to go with her. I saw a Jewish sign (in Hebrew letters) in a window reading "Kosher Butcher." I stopped and admired it very much and said to my sister, "This is the first time I see Hebrew letters in a window." In Rumania it is not allowed. Then I started to realize what anti-Semitism really meant and what an anti-Semitic country Rumania was.

[ROBERT MYERS, 1913]

Jewish hot potato vendor, New York City

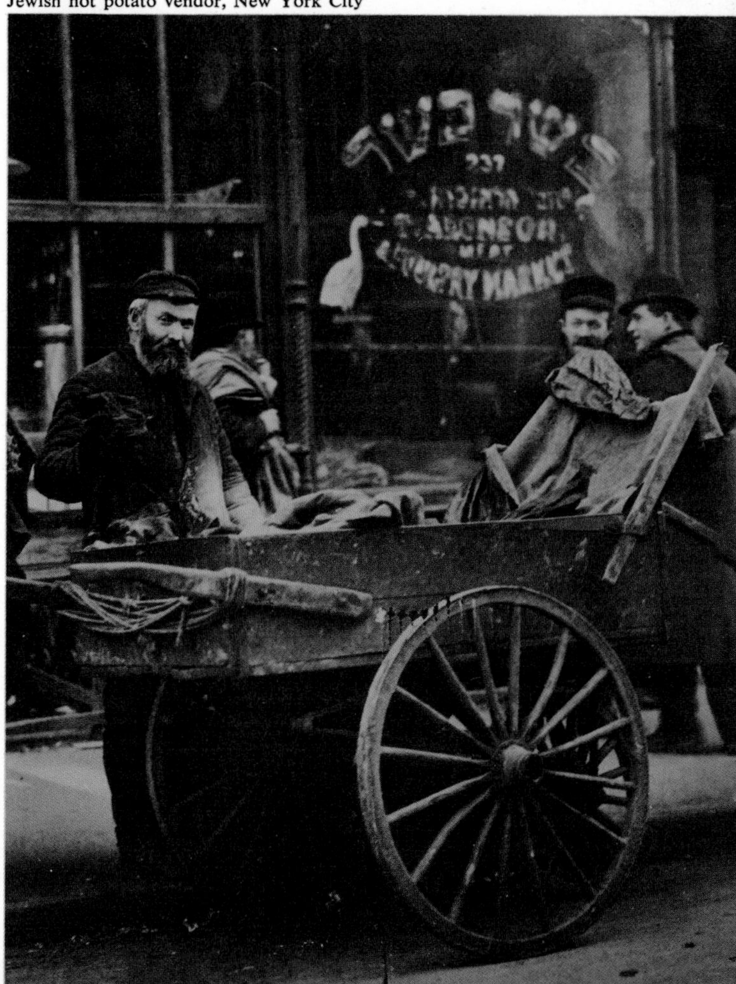

Program for festivities at a Milwaukee *Turnverein* (German social and athletic club)

German band, Cincinnati

The German in America is badly off. Where in the world can he find a wife? He has little opportunity for family life. So the young people get acquainted only in public places, in restaurants, concerts, the theater, balls. But what can they learn of each other there? Everything, except that which relates to a wife and her duties.

[KARL GRIESINGER, 1858]

Polish store, Chicago

Courtesy Chicago Historical Society

Those who are Americanized are American, and very patriotically American. Those who are not thus nationalized are not in the least internationalized. They simply continue to be themselves; the Irish are Irish; the Jews are Jewish; and all sorts of other tribes carry on the traditions of remote European valleys almost untouched. Very often these exiles bring with them not only rooted traditions, but rooted truths.

[G. K. CHESTERTON, 1921]

Returning to the log house, we spent the evening—twenty-one Swedes altogether—in games, songs, and dancing, exactly as if in Sweden. I felt myself happy in being with my countrymen, happy to find them so agreeable and so Swedish still in the midst of a foreign land.

[FREDRIKA BREMER, 1850]

Harvesting, **by the Swedish American painter Olaf Krans**

Irish politicians, Chicago

Courtesy Chicago Historical Society

I made the acquaintance of two local celebrities (Irish), namely Paddy Ryan and Michael McDonald. Paddy is a fighting man lately defeated in the twenty-four-foot ring by a compatriot, Sullivan. Michael McDonald runs a granite quarry. But his principal importance arises from his political position. He is supposed to direct and control what is called the rowdy element in Chicago—largely made up of our countrymen—and this gives him very great local influence. He is a rough diamond, with a decisive, masterful way about him, which clearly marks him out as a leader of men. His friends claim for him that he returned the present mayor of Chicago—the first Democratic mayor returned for Chicago for thirty years.

[LORD RUSSELL OF KILLOWEN, 1883]

PE 6–8 /

The Chinese have built a great part of the Northern Pacific from the Continental Divide to the Pacific. As we sped along, we came upon their encampments again and again in forest glades, by the shores of the rivers and lakes, on the outskirts of the cities—always a community apart. It is said to their credit that they insist, when they can, on being located near water for purposes of personal cleanliness.

[LORD RUSSELL OF KILLOWEN, 1883]

Chinese workmen on a Western railroad

In a place so exclusively Mexican as Monterey, you saw not only Mexican saddles but true vaquero riding—men always at the gallop up hill and down dale, and round the sharpest corner, urging their horses with cries and gesticulations and cruel spurs, checking them dead with a touch, or wheeling them right-about-face in a square yard. In dress they ran to color and bright sashes. Not even the most Americanized could always resist the temptation to stick a red rose into his hatband.

[ROBERT LOUIS STEVENSON, 1879]

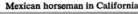

Mexican horseman in California

gie. Carnegie was a classic example of the "rags-to-riches" success story.[2] At thirteen he came to America with his family and immediately went to work. At eighteen he was a telegraph clerk for the Pennsylvania Railroad. During the quick railroad expansion of the Civil War years, Carnegie realized that iron and steel for rails and bridges were the keys to the railroads' future, and that railroads, in turn, were the key to an expanding economy. He saved every cent and invested daringly but successfully. By 1872 he was able to build his own steel plant near Pittsburgh.

Carnegie's company grew with the industry. By 1890 he was producing almost a third of a million tons of steel. By 1900 this amount had nearly tripled. At the same time, Carnegie worked to achieve vertical integration. He bought iron ore deposits, steamers to transport ore on the Great Lakes, railroad cars, and all the other facilities he needed for making steel.

In the meantime the process of competition had eliminated all but a few other steel companies. In 1892 the Carnegie Company was reorganized to combine seven other corporations in which Carnegie had acquired a controlling interest. In 1901 the largest steel concerns in the nation were all merged into one great new corporation, the United States Steel Corporation. The power behind this consolidation was another dominant figure of the period, J. Pierpont Morgan, a New York banker and financier. Morgan spent nearly a half-billion dollars to buy out Carnegie and set up this supercorporation. Like International Harvester, the giant company dominated its industry. It produced almost all of some forms of steel and three-fifths of the total steel made in the United States.

The Trust An even more stunning example of consolidation brought John D. Rockefeller into control of the oil industry. Rockefeller started out as a poor boy, like Carnegie. He too saved every cent (except for the 10 percent tithe he regularly gave to the Baptist Church). Starting with one refinery in Cleveland, Rockefeller created the Standard Oil Company in 1872. Using every means of competition, Rockefeller was able to absorb seventy-four competing firms in six years!

Rockefeller also created a new device that made it even easier to consolidate an industry—the trust. A trust in industry is an arrangement in which several companies sell themselves to a group of trustees. The companies are paid for with shares in the new trust itself. Only paper changes hands, but the result is a group of directors who control the operations of several companies.

Through the Standard Oil Trust the Rockefeller interests acquired almost total control of the oil industry. The trust could phase out unnecessary plants. It could take full advantage of mass production and distribution techniques to sell kerosene for Americans' lamps or oil to lubricate their machines. Rockefeller himself summed up adequately the reasons for the trust:

> It has revolutionized the way of doing business all over the world. The time was ripe for it. It had to come, though all we saw at the moment was the need to save ourselves from wasteful conditions [of competition]. The day of combination is here to stay. Individualism has gone, never to return.

One by one the main American industries passed from competition to consolidation. It might occur through giant corporations created by mergers, like International Harvester or United States Steel. Or it might result from the formation of trusts—which involved everything from cottonseed oil to sugar to whiskey. By 1900 a few large concerns controlled almost all the major facilities of production and distribution in the United States.

THE NEW AMERICANS

The house that Jack built needed people—a farmer, a priest, a maiden—to make the system

[2] Actually, many successful businessmen of this period came from comfortable middle-class homes. But enough had emerged from poverty to keep the success myth alive.

U.S. GROWTH OF POPULATION, 1870-1910

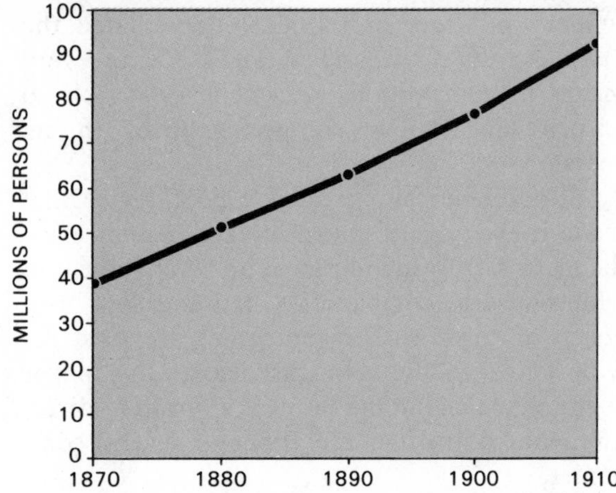

go. The new industrial order needed people to make it work, too. The growth in agriculture, railroads, and industry demanded millions of people, both as workers and consumers.

The American population kept pace with the growing industrial order. For every 100 persons living in the United States in 1870, there were 126 in 1880. In 1890 there were 158, in 1900 there were 190, and in 1910 a surprising 230! In one generation the population more than doubled, from about 40 million in 1870 to over 90 million forty years later.

These were the millions who moved into the Great Plains and the Rockies, bringing about the final collapse of the Western Indians. These were the millions that bought McCormick's harvesters, worked in his factory, and built the railroads that carried his reapers into every flat corner of the country where grain could be planted and harvested by machine.

These millions, however, were not just more of the same kinds of Americans who had lived here in Jacksonian times. They were a new people, with different languages, different religions, and different ways of life. Andrew Jackson's common man was almost certain to be a "native" American—white, and Protestant and a farmer. His parents or grandparents might have immigrated to the United States, but they would probably have come from England or Scotland. When they arrived here, they would have found the language, the way of worshiping God, and the customs familiar and comfortable.

The common man in New York in 1900 was more likely to be a Jew from Poland or a Roman Catholic from Italy. He probably lived in a city and had a job in a factory. His English might be poor, his memories of the "old country" at least as important to him as his hopes for the new. He represented a social revolution that had accompanied the revolutions in technology, industry, and business—the creation of an urban immigrant working class.

Shifting Trends in Immigration There had always been immigrants in America, at least from the time when the Indians began to cross over from Asia into Alaska. Over the years since the American Revolution the actual proportion of immigrants to the total population did not change much. Two other things happened instead: (1) the nature of the immigrant population changed; and (2) the immigrants (along with other Americans) began to congregate in urban centers. These two changes made factory cities like Chicago the gathering places for a new kind of American: the poor immigrant from a country where English was not spoken and where an Anglo-Saxon Protestant was rare.

In 1790 the United States took its first census under the new Constitution. Nine out of ten Americans (except for the black slaves in the South) had English or Scotch ancestors. This pattern changed somewhat with the "old immigration" of the 1840s and 1850s, when large numbers of Germans, Scandinavians, and Irish began to immigrate. Most of the Germans and Scandinavians, however, were Protestants, though their languages were strange to American ears. And though many "native" Americans resented the Irish because of Catholicism, these immigrants at least spoke English. In 1865 the United States had only about 200,000 inhabitants who had been born in Southern or Eastern Europe. They were easily absorbed by a total population of about 40 million.

By 1914 this picture changed dramatically.

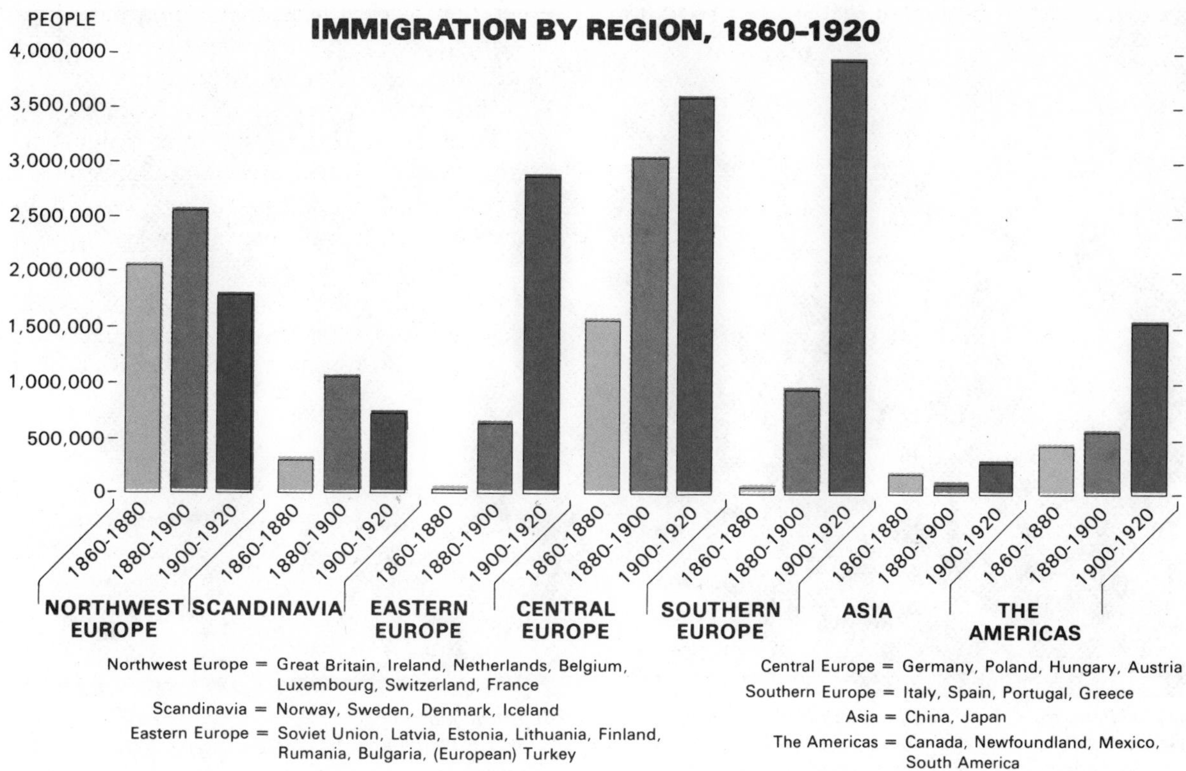

A "new immigration"—mainly from Italy, Russia, and Austria-Hungary—flooded into the United States. Poverty drove many of these people from their home countries. Some men left to avoid the military draft, which discriminated against the poor. Jews wanted to escape the official anti-Semitism of Russia and Poland. Armenians fled from persecutions carried out by the Turkish government. The new immigrants were drawn to the United States by advertisements of cheap steamship transportation, by rumors of free land and golden opportunity, and by a massive propaganda campaign conducted by railroads anxious for workers and customers to buy up their lands.

Immigration from Southern and Eastern Europe amounted to only a trickle in the 1860s and 1870s. But by the 1890s over half the immigrants to America were from Southern and Eastern Europe. In the next decade—the peak decade for all forms of immigration in the history of the United States—the proportion of new immigrants had risen to over 75 percent. In simple terms this means that over 6 million Italians, Russian Jews, Hungarians, and other immigrants from Southern and Eastern Europe came here between 1901 and 1910.

Reactions to the Newcomers The strike at McCormick and the Haymarket Affair occurred just before the peak of the new immigration burst over the United States. But prejudice had already been aroused by the Irish and Germans and by the beginnings of the influx from Eastern and Southern Europe. Both the McCormick strike and the trial of the so-called Haymarket radicals occurred in an atmosphere of fear and bigotry. The Pinkerton report on the "fighting Irish" molders and the newspaper comments on foreign "anarchists" make it clear that events would have been different in Chicago had the bewildering fact of immigration not existed.

The new immigrants were not only different in culture, language, and religion. They also be-

The new immigrants from Southern and Eastern Europe fueled the industrial machine by their labor. Forced to live in cities where the jobs were, they clustered in crowded and unsanitary ghetto areas like New York's Lower East Side.

haved in different ways. They moved into a society that was no longer predominantly agricultural and rural but urban. So they did not fan out onto farms as most of the old immigrants had done. Instead, they followed the lead of millions of other Americans and settled in cities. Two-thirds of foreign-born residents in the United States lived in towns or cities by 1900.

Bewildered and ofter victimized in America, new immigrants clustered together in their own city neighborhoods, or ghettos.[3] People from a particular province or even a particular village would move into buildings on the same block, recreating much of the culture of their Old World homes. As the new immigration increased, so did nativist, antiforeign sentiment. Ghetto dwellers earned a reputation among "native" Americans for being clannish, dirty, superstitious, and generally undesirable. They were considered strange, chattering in their odd languages, and somehow suited only for city life. Actually, of course, they were no more "natural" city dwellers than the English who came to Virginia and Massachusetts in the seventeenth century. They were simply caught in a phase of the industrial revolution—the creation of an urban society.

[3] The word "ghetto" dates back to the Middle Ages. It is Italian and may come from *borghetto,* meaning a small settlement outside the town. The term originally applied to the Jewish quarter of a city.

Becoming "American" In the era of the new immigration the goal was assimilation—taking on the traits of the new society so as to blend with it. But becoming an "American" was not an easy process for most Europeans who migrated to this country in the late nineteenth century. Foremost was the problem of language. Real assimilation meant being able to take advantage of American economic and political opportunities. And this in turn depended upon learning the language.

Since a knowledge of English brought with it an almost immediate economic advantage over those who could not speak or write the language, most immigrant groups sacrificed the income they would have received from their children's labor to send their children to the free public schools. Workers often attended special night school classes after their exhausting days in the factories. A Jewish immigrant, Mary Antin, wrote:

> Education was free. It was the one thing that my father was able to promise us when he sent for us; surer, safer than bread or shelter. On our second day in the country a little girl from across the alley came and offered to conduct us to school. We five children between us had a few words of English by this time. We knew the word "school." We understood. This child, who had never seen us till yesterday, who could not pronounce our names, who was not much better dressed than we were, still was able to offer us the freedom of the schools of Boston!

Countless immigrants must have felt similar emotions at the discovery that schooling—so restricted in Europe—was so readily available in the United States. As Mary Antin said: "No application made; no questions asked; no examinations, rulings, exclusions; no fees."

Learning English was the first step in assimilation. After that many immigrants joined some form of voluntary association that put them in contact with native-born Americans. The most available of such groups for city dwellers were the political parties. They provided favors, food, and jobs for poor and needy immigrants (see page 530). They also helped "Americanize" them.

"Boss" Richard Croker of Tammany Hall in New York described the function of his political machine as taking the city's newcomers, who "do not speak our language and do not know our laws, yet are the raw material with which we have to build up the state," and turning them into Americans. He asserted that a

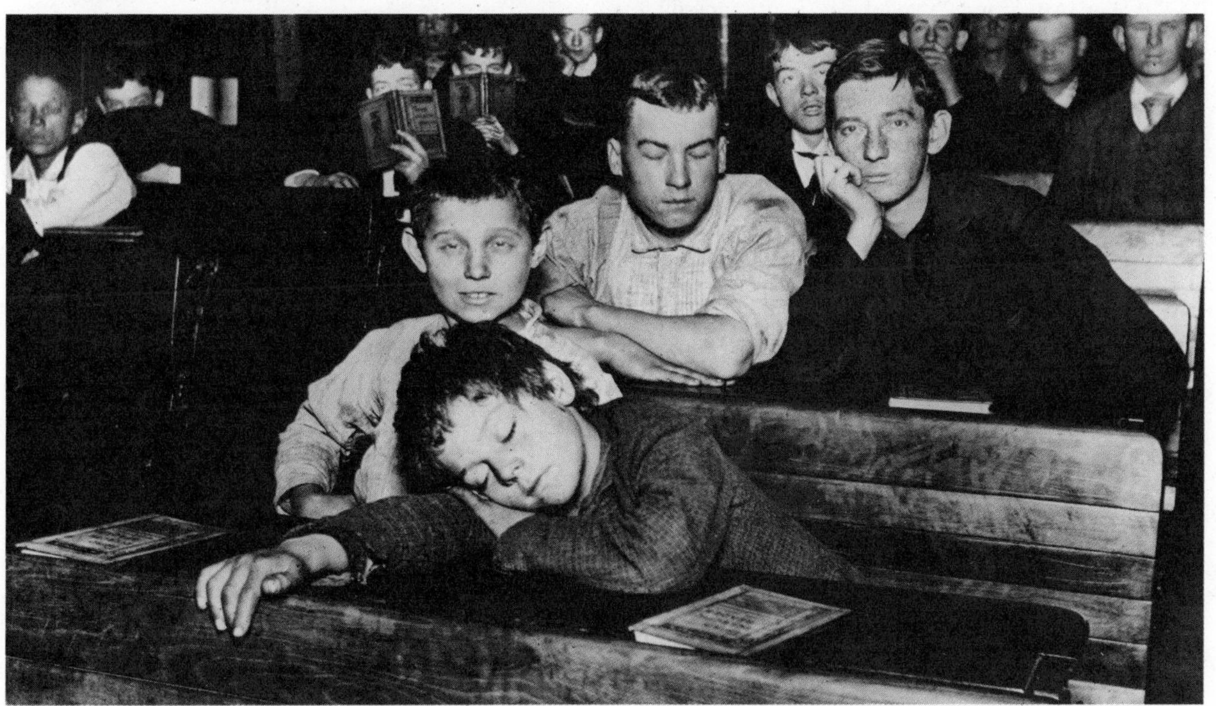

Children old enough to work in factories did so by day and attended school at night. The goal was assimilation: shedding enough of the old folkways to enter "native" American society.

World's Columbian Exposition

Chicago was the proud host for the World's Columbian Exposition of 1893. To commemorate Columbus' discovery of America (and to boost Chicago), the city invested $15 million. In two years almost 700 acres of sandy wasteland on the shore of Lake Michigan were transformed into a magnificient setting known as the White City. There, reflected in an artful landscape of canals and lagoons, stood massive exhibit buildings of gleaming white plaster. These structures, with their domes, arches, columns, and heroic statues, were, according to one commentator, ''as white and as richly ornamented as a congregation of royal brides.'' At night the buildings shone brightly, illuminated by thousands of electric bulbs. The Age of Electricity was at hand, and White City was its symbol.

The fair lasted six months, from May through October. Attendance totaled an almost incredible 27,500,000 visitors. Though the year brought hard times to many financially, this did not deter the crowds. Some people even used their life savings for a trip to Chicago. Twenty-seven nations took part in the exposition. Spain sent a full-size model of Columbus' flagship, *Santa Maria*. France built a replica of the Great Hall of Versailles. The most advanced products and processes in manufacturing, agriculture, mining, and transportation were displayed. All forty-four of the states had exhibits. Montana contributed a solid silver statue of a woman. California sent a knight in a suit of armor made entirely of prunes. The ferris wheel was invented for use at the fair. This giant device, over 250 feet high, could carry 2,160 persons. Also noteworthy was Little Egypt, the hootchy-kootchy dancer. Attempts to close her show failed.

Chicago Historical Society.

The exposition can be credited with three major achievements. First, it brought together major talents in architecture, engineering, and the fine arts. Second, the harmonious beauty of White City that resulted from its creators' innovative teamwork was itself an accomplishment. Third, the fair provided a forum for the discussion of many serious subjects—economics, labor, education, women's rights, and religion.

The architecture of White City had a widespread, long-lasting influence. Its neoclassic style was copied by banks, courthouses, and railroad stations throughout the land. To Chicago architect Louis Sullivan, designer of a modernistic exhibit building at the fair, Neoclassicism represented a step backward in the development of a truly American style. But his was a minority opinion. Most people agreed with city planner Daniel Burnham, who said: ''The American people have seen the classics on a grand scale for the first time. I can see all America constructed along the lines of the fair, in noble, dignified classic style.''

In the long run White City had even greater impact upon the American landscape. It opened peoples' eyes to the values of civic planning. A flowery tribute was paid by the Chicago *Tribune*, which saluted the fair with the words: ''This splendid fantasy of the artist and architect seemed to foreshadow some faraway time when all the earth should be as pure, as beautiful, and as joyous as the White City itself.''

political machine like Tammany "looks after them for the sake of their vote, grafts them upon the Republic, makes citizens of them, in short; and although you may not like our motives or our methods, what other agency is there by which so long a row could have been hoed so quickly or so well?"

Another strong influence on the new immigrants was a small number of immigrants who had arrived before the great influx. They had learned English and then helped recruit workers from Europe for factory labor in the United States. They often paid the newcomers' transportation and helped them settle in the ghettos of American cities.

Such men were sometimes called *padrones* (an Italian word meaning "patrons"). They might be paid by three different groups: (1) employers, for supplying cheap labor; (2) political machines, for delivering the votes of immigrants once they became citizens; and (3) the immigrants themselves, for favors received. Often the *padrones*—who existed among Jewish, Greek, Armenian, Polish, and other immigrant groups as well as among the Italians—were ward leaders in political organizations. They provided a link between the concerns of the ghetto newcomers and those of the citywide machine.

URBANIZATION

In the ancient world only two great cities—Rome and Alexandria—had populations of over half a million people. By the time George Washington was born, Rome and Alexandria had long ago declined. The only cities to have reached a comparable size since were London and Paris. At the time of the Haymarket Affair, however, Chicago had become a great city. In fact, by 1900 the United States had six cities with more than half a million inhabitants—more than had existed anywhere before 1800.

The process of urbanization was not confined to the United States. All the industrializing nations of Western Europe experienced it, too. The factory system demanded high concentrations of workers, and the agricultural revolution made it possible for millions of people to leave their farms—whether in Germany or in Maine—and move to towns.

The United States experienced three great migrations in the generation after the Civil War. One was from the East to the Great Plains and the Far West. Another was from Europe to America. The third was from the country to the city. Of the three the movement from farm to city was easily the most extensive.

In 1790 only about three Americans out of every hundred lived in towns larger than 8,000. By the end of the century this proportion had grown 1,000 percent; almost a third of the nation lived in cities of over 8,000. In 1800 there had been only six cities larger than 8,000; in 1900 there were over 400.

This increase was not gradual and smooth. Most of it came in the half century after the end of the Civil War. During this period at least 15 million "native" Americans moved out of farming areas and into cities, and their number was swelled by an almost equal number of new immigrants who settled in cities instead of on farms. Statistics tell the story. Between 1870 and 1900 the population of the United States increased by about 35 million people. During the same period the urban population increased by about 24 million. The cities, which cover such a small proportion of the land, had absorbed more than two thirds of the total increase!

Technological Factors A city is not just a collection of people in a small area. Like industry, modern cities were made possible by technological change. In the centuries before the industrial revolution the size of a city had been determined mainly by the transportation available. It could not be too big, because a person had to be able to walk or travel by wagon or carriage to a marketplace or job and back home again. After about 1880, however, cities began to experience a transportation revolution. The introduction of electricity made it possible to replace slow and awkward horse-drawn transport with fast, clean trolleys, elevated trains, and subways. These improvements meant that people could live many miles from their place of work and still be part of a vast city.

Electricity also made it possible to light city streets. Cleveland, in 1879, became the first city to have electric street lighting. Similarly, the introduction of the telephone in the 1880s meant that homes, offices, and factories could be tied together in an almost instantaneous communications network.

At first city buildings themselves were a limiting factor. Even with the thickest walls, a stone or brick building could not extend higher than fifteen stories. To build a structure even this high, builders had to make windows smaller and smaller because glass could not support the weight. A second problem was that human legs could tolerate only so many stairs. The first problem was solved by the invention of the skyscraper. This development was pioneered by a Chicago architect, Louis Sullivan. Skyscraper construction—in which walls were hung on steel frames—made possible structures as tall as a hundred stories. Thus even more people could be concentrated, level upon level, on smaller parcels of land. The second problem was solved in the 1880s by the invention of the electric elevator.

Technological change turned American cities (and European ones, too) into points at which power, innovation, and wealth came to-

A turn of the century view of a typical Midwestern city, Kansas City, Missouri, shows that the pulse of American life had quickened and taken on an increasingly urban character. The city itself was being transformed—trolleys transported people as once horses had done.

The growth of New York City depended upon improved transportation facilities like the Brooklyn Bridge. The bridge's completion in 1883 made it possible to live outside Manhattan and commute to work by steam car, carriage, or on foot.

gether with poverty, ignorance, and disease. Cities like New York and Chicago contained the factories, offices, and homes of families like the McCormicks or the Rockefellers. They were also magnets that drew people from the farms of America and Europe, people who came in search of work and success.

Problems and Contradictions In all the major American cities a new phenomenon, the tenement slum, began to appear. The new cities might tower with skyscrapers and glisten with electric lights. But they were also centers of grinding poverty and disease, especially the immigrant ghettos. In New York City certain parts of the Lower East Side became crowded with Jewish and Italian immigrants. According to statistics, more than 30,000 people were squeezed into half a dozen city blocks. The density was 986 people per acre, making this the most populous area in the entire world!

Middle-class Americans became aware of the poverty and suffering of the slum population largely through the writings of a New York police reporter named Jacob Riis. Riis, himself an immigrant, had come to America from Denmark in 1870. For years he collected information and photos of the people in New York City's various ethnic ghettos. He published his findings in 1890, in a book called *How The Other Half Lives: Studies Among the Tenements of New York*. The scenes Riis described were familiar to most city workers, wherever they lived.

> Cherry Street. Be a little careful, please! The hall is dark and you might stumble over the children pitching pennies back there. Not that it would hurt them; kicks and cuffs are their daily diet. They have little else. Here where the hall turns and dives into utter darkness is a step, and another, another. A flight of stairs. You can feel your way, if you cannot see it. Close? Yes! What would you have? All the fresh air that ever enters these stairs comes from the hall-door that is forever slamming, and from the windows of dark bedrooms that in turn receive from the stairs their sole supply of the elements God meant to be free, but man deals out with such niggardly hand.

The city, with its extremes of wealth and poverty, skyscrapers and slums, mansions and tenements, was a focus for many of the problems and contradictions of the new industrial order. The main foundations of the industrial house-that-Jack-built had been laid—in agriculture, railroads, factories, corporations, the labor force, and cities. There was much that people might proudly call progress. Indeed, Americans of the nineteenth century liked nothing better than to boast about the country's fantastic rates of growth.

But the new industrial order meant more than growth. It created new problems that Americans were slow to recognize and even slower to solve. The workers at McCormick, the McCormick family, the Chicago police, and the other actors in the Haymarket Affair—all were caught in a web of difficulties that would almost certainly lead to violence and persecution. Haymarket was not an event that can be understood simply as a local occurrence or in terms of the personalities of a McCormick or an Irish molder. The strike at McCormick and the Haymarket Affair have to be seen as the outcomes of a host of dislocations and contradictions resulting from fundamental changes in the entire social and economic system.

1. What changes occurred during the agricultural revolution? Why could there have been no agricultural revolution without a parallel revolution in transportation?
2. What factors account for the industrial supremacy of the United States at the turn of the century?
3. In what ways is the factory system different from the small shop? What factors are necessary to bring about mass production?
4. Why was cutthroat competition necessary to the new industrial order? How did pools eliminate competition? What advantages did trusts have over pools as a form of business consolidation?
5. Who were the new immigrants? Compare the reasons for their coming with those of the old immigrants. Why was resentment greater toward the former?
6. What is the meaning of assimilation? Was it preferable to letting the immigrants keep their own ways? Why or why not?
7. What groups contributed to the tremendous growth of cities? What technological developments aided that growth?

Beyond the Text

1. Were the big businessmen of this era "robber barons" or "industrial statesmen"?
2. Horatio Alger propularized the "rags to riches" myth. Report on the myth and its validity for the post–Civil War years.
3. Men like McCormick, Carnegie, and Rockefeller accumulated millions of dollars at a time when most factory workers barely made ends meet. At the same time these men spent millions on various philanthropies. How did they justify the accumulation and the distribution of their money? Do you agree with their philosophy?
4. Bigotry appears to occur in cycles in American history. Investigate the reasons for its reappearance in the 1880s and determine from which segments of the population it came at that time and why. Compare this cycle of bigotry with the Know-Nothing movement of the 1850s.

Bibliography

Nonfiction

Barnard, Harry, *Eagle Forgotten: The Life of John Peter Altgeld.*

Bremner, Robert H., *From the Depths: The Discovery of Poverty in America.**

Carnegie, Andrew, *Autobiography of Andrew Carnegie.*

Cawelti, John G., *Apostles of the Self-Made Man.**

David, Henry, *History of the Haymarket Affair.**

Ginger, Ray, *Eugene V. Debs: A Biography.**

Hays, Samuel P., *The Response to Industrialism.**

Higham, John, *Strangers in the Land.*

Hofstadter, Richard, *Social Darwinism and American Thought.**

Miller, William, ed., *Men in Business.**

Nevins, Allan, *John D. Rockefeller*, 2 vols.

Rayback, Joseph G., *A History of American Labor.**

Schlesinger, Arthur M., *The Rise of the City: 1878–1898.**

Wiebe, Robert H., *The Search for Order: 1877–1920.**

Wyllie, Irvin G., *The Myth of the Self-Made Man in America.**

Fiction

Barber, Elsie O., *Hunt for Heaven.*

Dreiser, Theodore, *Jennie Gerhardt.*

Gerdell, Alexander, *The Race and the Tiger.*

* a paperback book

CHAPTER

25

THE ASSASSINATION OF GARFIELD

ON THE MORNING OF July 2, 1881, the President of the United States, James Abram Garfield, was strolling toward a waiting train in a railroad depot in Washington. The train, scheduled to depart at 9:30 A.M., was to take him on the first leg of a trip to Williams College, his alma mater. There he was to address a class reunion and enroll his two sons. Walking alongside the President and chatting with him was the Secretary of State, James G. Blaine, a close political associate and friend. Already inside the train were Garfield's two sons and other members of his Cabinet.

The President and the Secretary of State walked toward the train platform. Neither noticed a thin, bearded figure, dressed in shabby and unpressed clothing, staring at them from a few feet away. The two men broke off their conversation for a moment and prepared to step aboard the train.

Suddenly the man who had been watching them drew a pistol from his pocket. He pointed it at the President and fired twice. Garfield fell to the ground. The President managed to cry "My God!" before he fainted. Blood spurted onto his gray traveling suit. He lay wounded and unconscious where he fell.

At the sound of the shots, Blaine had lunged toward the assassin. But when he saw the President lying on the floor, he quickly returned to his side. Along with others who had reached the scene, Blaine raised

NEW YORK HERALD, SUNDAY, JULY 3, 1881.—QUINTUPLE SHEET. 7

SHOT DOWN.

President Garfield Dangerously Wounded.

AN ASSASSIN'S WORK.

Fired at Entering the Railroad Depot at Washington.

THE SERIOUS HIP WOUND.

Carried in an Ambulance to the White House.

CHEERFUL IN THE FACE OF DEATH.

Grave Symptoms Succeeded by a More Hopeful Condition.

A STRONG MAN'S STRUGGLE

Arrest and Imprisonment of the Criminal.

CHARLES JULES GUITEAU.

An Erratic Creature of Low Antecedents—His Strange History.

MRS. GARFIELD'S SORROW

She Reaches Washington and Meets Her Husband.

INTENSE EXCITEMENT—WORLDWIDE SYMPATHY

As President James A. Garfield, accompanied by Secretary Blaine, was entering the depot of the Baltimore and Potomac Railroad at Washington yesterday morning to take the train for Long Branch, he was shot twice by a scoundrel named Charles Jules Guiteau who had been lying in wait for him. This occurred at 9:20 A. M. The first ball from the assassin's revolver struck the President near the left shoulder and passed out by the shoulder blade; the second struck him in the back over the left kidney. The President turned at the first shot and fell forward on his knees at receiving the second bullet. Postmaster General James and others of his party who had preceded him rushed to his assistance. The assassin was instantly overpowered and arrested. The President was carried to a room on the floor above, medical aid was summoned and stimulants administered. The great, strong man thus basely stricken down soon rallied from the shock and was at once borne in an ambulance to the White House, where efforts were made to ascertain the nature of the wounds. The gravest fears were entertained. The patient remained conscious, conversed cheerfully and hopefully, but his pulse was high, he was suffering some pain and internal hemorrhage was believed to be taking place. Morphine was hypodermically injected and he became easier, obtaining some sleep. The danger from shock and from internal bleeding having been, in the estimation of his physicians last evening, tided over, it was hoped the remaining danger from inflammation would be surmounted. Nothing occurred up to the hour of going to press to destroy this hope. At eleven P. M. the President was cheerful, pulse 124, temperature 99, respiration 20. All the symptoms were favorable.

The most intense excitement prevailed through the length and breadth of the country on the news becoming known.

To Mrs. Garfield, convalescing at Long Branch and awaiting her husband's return from the national capital, the news came

SCENE OF THE ASSASSINATION.

Map of Washington Showing Location of the Baltimore and Potomac Railroad Depot.

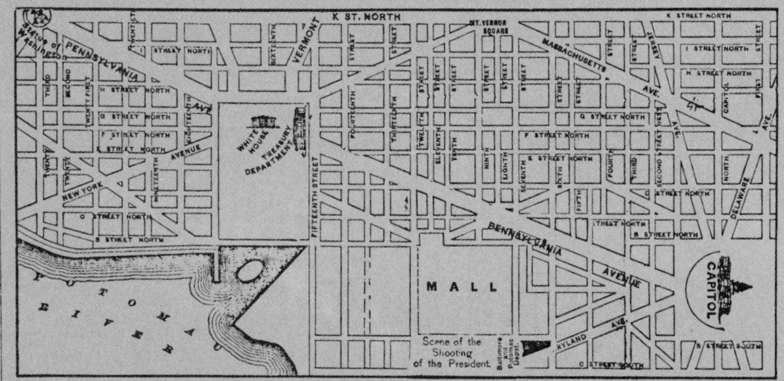

moments later the President's carriage drove in front of the depot, and the President and his only companion, Secretary Blaine, alighted and both entered the depot by the main entrance on B street. There was a slight pause on the steps, and a moment later the President and Secretary of State, side by side, were walking across the ladies' reception room, in which there was not at the time half a dozen persons. One of these was a man of short stature, a wicked expression in his face, who moved about nervously until the two statesmen had half crossed the reception room, a distance of not more than ten feet from the door. A report as of a big fire cracker challenged the attention of the policemen at the main door, who thought some boy had fired it in honor of the President's departure. Instantly another report was heard and President Garfield lay prostrate upon the floor of the reception room wounded in the right arm and in the side just above the hips. The mysterious nervous individual was Charles Guiteau, a half Frenchman, now from Chicago, about thirty years of age, who had been imploring the President to give him a Consulate in France. His excited condition had changed in the presence of his intended victim, and he stood as firm

victim by the assassin's hand, he quickly gave the order for the troops stationed at the arsenal to hold themselves for immediate orders. The same was done by the Secretary of the Navy, who directed that the marines should be held for similar orders. Meanwhile word was sent to Surgeon General Barnes, Drs. Norris, Lincoln and Woodward requiring their immediate presence at the depot. With the messengers trooping over the pavements it was not long before every part of Washington was informed of what had happened, and the fact became generally known. Then a crowd soon assembled, and in less than ten minutes Sixth street and B street were packed with people, and the news of the horrible affair flew from mouth to mouth and spread over the city like wildfire. An attempt was made to rush into the building and cries were raised to lynch the assassin, but a strong force of policemen, summoned by telephone, had arrived promptly on the scene and preserved order. In the meantime the President had been carried to a room up stairs and the physicians summoned.

POLICEMAN KEARNEY'S STORY.

Policeman Kearney, of the Island precinct, who first tried to arrest the assassin, makes the following statement of the shooting:—

House, and Messrs. Kilburn and Adams, of the newspaper press of the city, who were about to leave with their families for the North. We stood just opposite the special train which was waiting for the President. In it were some dozen people, more than half of whom were ladies, the wives, sons and daughters of Secretaries Windom and Hunt, Postmaster General James, Colonel Rockwell and others of the Presidential party. They were a merry party, laughing and joking with the numerous friends who had come down to see them off for a fortnight's holiday and frolic. Soon Secretaries Windom and Hunt came out of the car and began promenading up and down the platform, quietly smoking their cigars. Later Postmaster General James alighted from the car and joined our party.

NEWS THAT HORRIFIED.

"We began congratulating him and ourselves that we were to escape the fearfully hot weather, and were trying to joke him about the administration leaving business for pleasure, when a young man stepped up to Mr. James and said to him, excitedly, that the President had been shot.

"Mr. James turned and said, 'What! There is no joke in a thing like that.'

"His informant, almost scared to death, replied, 'I assure you it is true.'"

"Without another word Mr. James turned and ran to the depot building, and we all naturally followed him. When I reached the ladies' reception rooms the doors were being closed. There were at least

"I was standing in the ladies' room and saw the President as he entered in company with Secretary Blaine. The latter had stepped a little in advance as they entered the door, as if to give the President more room. I had noticed this man Guiteau lounging around the ladies' room for a half hour before the arrival of the President. I did not like his appearance from the first time I saw him. It is my business to see that such characters do not loaf around the ladies' room, and I thought seriously of having him pointed out to our watchman, Mr. Scott, so that he should be made stay in the gentlemen's room. When the President and Secretary Blaine entered he was standing near the entrance door. He wheeled to the left and fired, evidently aiming for the heart. It was a quick shot and struck the President in the left arm. The President did not at first seem to realize that he had been struck, although Secretary Blaine instantly stepped to one side as though dazed at this unexpected movement. The President then partly turned around and the assassin advancing two steps fired the second time—the whole thing being the work of a few moments. The President advanced one step, then fell to the floor. I ran to him at once and raised his head and held it in that position until some gentlemen came, and we remained until his son came from the car where he was seated, with the rest of the Presidential party, awaiting the arrival of his father. The entire party followed him

an uneasy, nervous man. At that time there were but few persons present and nearly all ladies. I was attracted by the report of a pistol. I immediately pressed into the ladies' room and saw the assassin, pistol in hand, standing about two feet inside of the entrance door. I saw him advance two paces and fire the second shot. The President had then advanced more than half way across the room on his way to the train, Secretary Blaine slightly in advance. The President turned around, after receiving the first wound in the shoulder, and received the second shot in the region of the thigh, toward the back. There was an interval of about four seconds between the first and second shots. Just as soon as the second shot was fired I took in the situation and ran out of the office for the purpose of securing the assassin. In the meantime Guiteau tried to make his escape by the main door on Sixth street, but being headed off he turned to make away by the exit of the ladies' room on B street, when I grappled him by the left hand and the left shoulder and held him until Officer Kearney and Depot Watchman Scott came to my assistance in a few moments, the former holding him by the right shoulder and the latter securing him by his clothing in the back. From the moment I took hold of him until he was carried to Police Headquarters he never uttered a word about Chester Arthur now being President, he was a stalwart, &c. What he did say was that this letter which he held in his hand and flourished frantically about his head was going to General Sherman and explained all. When I first laid my hand on him he made desperate efforts to release himself; but upon finding that it was useless he subsided."

THE PATIENT AT THE WHITE HOUSE.

It was evident that whatever was to be done must be done quickly, and as it would be impossible to proceed with medical and surgical treatment at the depot, it was decided to remove the wounded President to the mansion. Carefully the mattress on which he lay was taken up and borne down the long flight of stairs to the police ambulance now awaiting his coming. It was a pitiable sight to see the somewhat shabby looking ambulance which contained the prostrate form of the President driving rapidly along Pennsylvania avenue to the White House, surrounded by mounted police. When one remembered in what excellent spirits General Garfield had ridden over the same pavement scarcely an hour before, or how joyously he had ridden along to it to and from his inauguration four months ago. And by the same route, in the rear of the Treasury Building, as the President drove on the 4th of March, surrounded by the Cleveland Horse Troops, to-day drove the ambulance surrounded by the mounted police. Arrived at the mansion, the President was carried up stairs to the large chamber in the south side, and the bedside was soon surrounded by physicians and agonized friends. The regular troops shortly after arrived and all the gateways leading to the President's grounds were closed. Armed sentries took their places at the main gateway and only those having passes were permitted to enter.

It was now half-past ten. A feverish excitement added to the intense heat of the day. "Will he die?" "Is he badly wounded?" "What do the doctors say?" and a hundred similar inquiries were addressed to anybody supposed to have superior facilities in getting news from the White House. The sidewalks fronting the White House grounds, and the square opposite were packed with people peering through the iron railing at the house a hundred yards distant, as though something could be discovered in the in the atmosphere that would tell them just the condition of the President's wounds. At eleven o'clock Dr. Barnes, the Surgeon General, sent over the wire from the White House a statement that the wound in the loin would probably prove fatal, though nothing could be decided until consultation. It was not five minutes that this sad news was on the wing and the eager crowd whispered it and sent it to every part of the city. The possibility of the President's dying was realized now for the first time. There had been hope that that Providence which prepared the time of assassination had turned the bullet in a harmless direction, but too soon was it suspected that the lower wound was of a nature from which the President could scarcely recover and that death was only a question of a few hours.

DIAGNOSIS BY THE DOCTORS.

Dr. Smith Townshend, the District Health Officer, who was the first physician to reach the President, gives the following statement:—"I arrived at the depot four minutes after he was shot and found him lying upon the floor of the depot, surrounded by an immense gathering. He was then in a fainting condition. From his appearance and the pulsations at the wrist I thought he was dying. I took some of the pillows from under his head that he might rest easier. I prescribed aromatic spirits of ammonia and brandy, which revived him. I ordered the police to get the crowd back and had the President removed to an upper room. He rallied considerably, and I proceeded to examine his wounds. I found that the last bullet had entered his back about two and a half inches to the right of the vertebrae. When I placed my finger in the wound some hemorrhage followed. I then administered another dose of the stimulant, which again revived him. In the meantime Drs. Purvis and Bliss arrived. I had, however, previously asked him how he felt and where the most pain was felt, and he answered in his right leg and feet. I asked him the character of his pains and he said that it was a pricking sensation. Dr. Woodward, of the army, also came in afterward, and after a consultation we concluded to remove him to the White House. It was then about ten o'clock, and all the members of the Cabinet were present. I forgot to tell you that after I made the examination of the wounds the President looked up and asked me what I thought of it. I answered that I did not consider it serious. He continued, 'I thank you, doctor, but I am a dead man.' When we arrived at the White House, and just before he was removed from the ambulance, he asked me to call to Major Brock to clear the hall, as there might be another assassin around. Quite a number of the doctors and others went along with the ambulance. When taken from the ambulance he was in a fainting condition, and we revived him with stimulants, and upon consultation we concluded to give an hypodermic injection of morphia and allow him to rest until three o'clock. Afterward we gave him an injection of atropia and morphia, which brought his pulse up to eighty. At three o'clock, when we had another consultation, we found his pulse 102 and temperature ninety-six, or two and a half below normal. While we were in consultation he became very much nauseated

After less than six months in office President Garfield was shot by a disgruntled office seeker, Charles Guiteau, as Secretary of State James G. Blaine looked on. Though the President was in a public place, he had no Secret Service protection.

the wounded man's head from the floor. Garfield regained consciousness almost immediately.

Garfield's two sons and the Cabinet members rushed from the train to join the crowd of onlookers. Some railroad workers gently lifted the heavy-set man and placed him on a ragged mattress, brought hastily from a nearby room. The first physician to arrive was Dr. Smith Townsend, the District of Columbia health officer. The doctor assumed from Garfield's appearance that the chief executive was dying. Townsend gave the injured man aromatic spirits of ammonia and some brandy to ease his pain. Then he inspected the more serious of the two wounds Garfield had received—the one on the lower right side of his back. Garfield winced. The doctor's touch had reopened the wound. Townsend's face and manner remained grim but, somewhat mechanically, he assured Garfield that his back wound was not serious. "I thank you, doctor," replied Garfield in evident pain, "but I am a dead man."

After firing the shots, the assassin calmly returned his pistol to his pocket. Then, as anxious and curious spectators surrounded the bleeding President, he rushed toward a railway station exit. Just as he reached it, the exit's massive door burst open. The man who had shot the President found himself face to face with Patrick Kearney, a District of Columbia patrolman. Kearney had been running toward the sound of the shots. In an attempt to flee past the policeman, the slender, dark-complexioned figure mumbled in an excited voice, "I have a letter to send to General Sherman."[1]

Kearney, sensing that the agitated man was somehow connected with the earlier pistol cracks, held him for a moment. Several railroad employees raced to the exit and reported that the President had been shot. The policeman verified this by peering at Garfield's body, which still lay on the station floor. Then he rushed his prisoner away from the scene. As they left the station, the man finally spoke, saying: "I did it. I will go to jail for it; [Vice President] Arthur is President."

When Kearney reached the police station, his fellow officers would not believe that Garfield had been shot. It took a few minutes before they accepted the patrolman's story. Kearney himself, still excited over having captured the man who had tried to kill the President, did not even bother to seize the prisoner's gun until they had reached the stationhouse. For that matter, only then did the patrolman think of asking the assassin his name. The prisoner reached into his pocket,

[1] William Tecumseh Sherman was then commanding general of the American army.

withdrew a small printed calling card, and handed it to Kearney, who stared at the name and address: Charles Guiteau, Chicago, Ill.

There had been some change back at the railroad depot. Several people had carried the President onto a police ambulance, which rushed him back to the White House. There he was placed in a second-floor bedroom. Dozens of physicians, family members, government officials and well-wishers scurried about the sickroom for the remainder of the day. A horde of newspapermen also managed to reach the sickroom door. They pestered each visitor to the President's bedside for fresh news of his condition.

The physicians all agreed that Garfield's back wound was too serious to allow immediate removal of the bullet. They felt they could do nothing but give the President large, continual doses of morphine to dull his pain. Their frequent bulletins to the waiting reporters seldom varied in content: "The President's wounds were grave. He remains pale, weak, and cold. Although he is not bleeding profusely *externally,* there was every chance of massive *internal* hemorrhaging."

To doctors and reporters alike, this meant only one thing: the President was dying. Several members of Garfield's Cabinet joined his family and physicians in the sickroom. Together they waited for further developments throughout the long night. At one point the Secretary of War walked out into the corridor for a breath of air. He turned to a reporter and said: "How many hours of sorrow I have passed in this town." With this remark, Robert Todd Lincoln, Abraham Lincoln's son, reentered the sickroom.

Garfield's spirits, and his condition, improved greatly once his wife reached his bedside. She had left her New Jersey resting place hurriedly after receiving word of her husband's shooting. A special train brought her to Washington. Arriving at the White House in early evening, she spent a few minutes alone with Garfield. Then she stationed herself outside his sickroom, praying and waiting for news. The President, after being told that she had gone to bed, fell asleep himself.

An hour later Garfield awoke. He turned to the attending physician, D. W. Bliss, who had taken charge of his treatment, and asked about his chances for recovery. He told the physician, as Dr. Bliss later remembered, "that he desired a frank and full statement, that he was prepared to die and feared not to learn the worst." Dr. Bliss, somewhat less than frank, replied: "Mr. President, your injury is formidable [but] in my judgment you have a chance for recovery." Garfield smiled and, placing his hand upon the doctor's arm, answered simply: "Well, doctor, we will take that chance." The warmth, good humor, and

The public's view of Garfield as a homespun, simple man was reinforced by the fact that he was "the last of the log cabin Presidents." This painting of his birthplace in Orange, Ohio, gives us a nostalgic view of the pure and pastoral life of Garfield's youth.

optimism that had characterized James Abram Garfield throughout his rise to the presidency did not desert him during this final struggle for life.

Garfield's rise to the presidency parallels the success story of several other nineteenth-century American Presidents. He was a man of humble origins. Like Presidents William Henry Harrison and Abraham Lincoln before him, he had the good sense to be born in a log cabin. The log cabin had become the American symbol of homespun integrity and was therefore very useful to budding politicians.

Garfield, who was born in Ohio in 1831, was a seventh-generation American. His ancestors came to Massachusetts Bay with John Winthrop. His father was a pioneer Ohio farmer, who died when Garfield was two. His mother, Eliza, raised the future President and three other children in bitter rural poverty.

As a boy, Garfield worked at a variety of jobs, helping to support his mother while striving to earn an education. After graduating from a neighboring school called Western Reserve Eclectic Institute (later changed to Hiram College), Garfield worked his way through Williams

College in Massachusetts. He graduated from there in 1856. Returning to Ohio, Garfield served first as a teacher and then—though still in his twenties—as principal of Hiram Institute. In 1858 he married Lucretia Rudolph, his childhood sweetheart.

Throughout the 1850s Garfield exhibited the talents that were later to win him high political office. In 1859 he ran for, and won, the Republican seat in the Ohio senate. He made friends easily, worked furiously, displayed great tact and an ability to compromise, took few extreme positions, and—above all—sought to please. When the Civil War began, the young state legislator organized a volunteer infantry regiment composed largely of his former students. Although he had no previous military experience, he mastered the appropriate army training manuals quickly and well.

Colonel Garfield's regiment was assigned to the Union army command in Kentucky. There it defeated a much larger force of Confederate soldiers at the Battle of Middle Creek in January 1862. This victory earned Garfield the rank of brigadier general. After fighting at the Battle of Shiloh, he had to leave the field because of poor health. When he returned to active duty in 1863, he served with distinction during the important Battle of Chickamauga. Garfield left the army in December 1863 with the rank of major general. He had been elected to the House of Representatives that fall.

Garfield was then thirty-two and extremely popular in Ohio's Western Reserve district. This area returned him to Congress seven more times. His skill as a legislative leader and orator quickly made him a leading Republican in the House. So great was his personal popularity that Ohio voters reelected him despite the fact that they did not agree with him on many issues.

Garfield, like all successful officeholders, quickly learned the skill of political survival: when to speak out on an important question, when to blur an issue, and when to remain silent. During Hayes' administration Garfield's talent for bringing together different viewpoints within the Republican party led to his selection as House minority leader. Early in 1880 he was elected by the Ohio legislature to a six-year Senate term. But he never filled this seat.

It was in that year that the Republicans held their convention to nominate a presidential candidate. They were bitterly divided among three leading contenders—former President Ulysses S. Grant, Senator John Sherman of Ohio, and Senator James G. Blaine of Maine. There was a three-way deadlock on thirty-four ballots. On the thirty-fifth a break occurred. On the thirty-sixth Garfield, who had gone to the convention as Sherman's campaign manager, emerged with his party's nomination for President.

Blaine quickly became a close political ally. Sherman remained

Garfield was the ideal compromise candidate. A tireless worker and an able speaker, he rarely took a strong independent stance. Not an extremely ambitious man, he seems to have had responsibility thrust upon him rather than to have actively sought it.

cordial, if suspicious. Grant's managers (particularly the influential New York senator Roscoe Conkling) never forgave Garfield, despite the fact that Chester A. Arthur, Conkling's colleague from New York, was chosen Garfield's running mate. Garfield and Conkling did eventually smooth their differences, and the Republicans carried a close election with a popular plurality of only 10,000 votes. James Garfield, a mild-mannered and unforceful politician, became President of the United States.

During his years in Congress Garfield and his family had lived modestly. When Congress was in session, they stayed in Washington. At other times they made their home in Mentor, Ohio, a small agricultural town on Lake Erie, twenty-five miles from Cleveland. They had a farm there, which they called Lawnfield. Garfield enjoyed the farm work and rural way of life. He left Mentor for the last time in 1881, for Washington and his inauguration. The letters he wrote during his few months as Chief Executive show that he often yearned to return to the peaceful isolation of Lawnfield.

Although Garfield had been a professional politician for more than twenty years by the time he entered the White House, he retained an avid interest in cultural matters. This interest, no doubt, was a carry over from his days as a student, teacher, and college principal. Throughout his adult life he corresponded with some of the country's leading men of letters and reformers.

But Garfield himself was not a reformer. Throughout his legislative career he allied himself with railroad, industrial, and other established interests. He expressed skepticism about reforms dealing with women's suffrage, contempt for proposals to assist the Indians, and indifference toward efforts to aid blacks. Above all, Garfield was a party "regular"—a politician whose primary concern was advancing his own fortunes and those of his party.

Garfield did not know that one of the proposals he ignored would eventually mark him for an assassin's bullet. The issue was civil-service reform, which advocated filling government posts by qualifying tests rather than by political appointment. Some minor steps toward such reform were taken by Garfield's predecessor in the White House, Rutherford B. Hayes. But Garfield let the matter drop when he became the President.

Instead, he put up with the hundreds who came weekly to the Executive Mansion in search of government jobs. True, they annoyed him. Daily, as he walked through his own offices and living quarters, he was besieged by a "band of disciplined office hunters who drew papers on me as highwaymen draw pistols.'"[2] One of these constant job-seeking visitors to the White House who "drew papers on the President was a forty-year-old Chicago lawyer, bill collector, and itinerant preacher named Charles Julius Guiteau.

Charles Julius Guiteau's life was an interesting contrast to that of James Abram Garfield. Garfield had married happily and raised a family. His efforts as student, educator, soldier, and politician were all rewarded. The President remained secure in his early religious beliefs. He numbered among his friends and admirers not only the most powerful people in America but also many of its intellectuals. The road from log cabin to White House had been, by and large, a smooth one that he traveled with outer serenity and inner contentment. Garfield represented, for many of his generation, living proof of the continued American formula for achievement: personal integrity plus hard work plus trained intelligence yields success and happiness.

Both the personal life and public career of Charles Guiteau had been marked by frustration and failure. He was born the fourth of six children on September 8, 1841, in Freeport, Illinois. Jane Howe Guiteau, his mother, died when he was seven. The boy was raised by his father, Luther Wilson Guiteau, a Freeport bank official and religious disciple of John Humphrey Noyes.[3] Charles was usually cared for by his older sister, Frances, who maintained an interest in the boy's welfare even after her marriage to George Scoville, a Chicago lawyer.

Guiteau, like Garfield, worked extremely hard as a young man, helping his father at the bank and tending to family chores. Both young men were enthusiastic Republicans; both were physical- and mental-fitness buffs; and both dreamed of eventual success. Guiteau had fought many stormy quarrels with his domineering father. In 1859, the same year that Garfield became principal of Hiram Institute, Guiteau decided to leave Freeport to seek his fortune.

The first goal he set for himself was obtaining a college education. Guiteau went to the university college at Ann Arbor, Michigan, where he attempted to register. But the teachers there asked that he first train for university work by enrolling at a Michigan preparatory school. Lonely, lacking funds, and keenly feeling his lack of academic preparation, Guiteau turned to religion for solace. Not surprisingly, he became interested in his zealous father's faith, the teachings of John

[2] White House security measures were not as strict then as they are now. Visitors were free to come and go, so that they might well run into the President as he was walking elsewhere in the Executive Mansion.

[3] John Humphrey Noyes was the founder of the Oneida Community, an experimental communal colony in upstate New York.

Humphrey Noyes. In June of 1860 Guiteau left Ann Arbor to join the Oneida Community.

The Oneida Community, like other utopian settlements in mid-nineteenth-century America, was based upon religious fellowship and the principle that both work and worldly goods would be shared. Guiteau was no happier at Oneida than he had been in Ann Arbor. He was unpopular among other members of the community. Neither then, nor at any other point in Charles Guiteau's life, did he manage to keep a single close friend. A bad-tempered, solitary, and nervous figure, he often came under attack for selfishness and conceit at the community's important mutual-criticism sessions. In 1865 Guiteau left the community.

For the next fifteen years Guiteau's life consisted mainly of a series of career failures. He constantly borrowed from family members. He was always in debt and often ran away to escape arrest. He flitted between periods spent in New York City and in Chicago (where his sister lived). Hoping and expecting some great new career—which would be achieved instantly—Guiteau generally found himself teetering on the edge of despair.

Guiteau ran through a succession of jobs with alarming ease. After leaving the Oneida Community, he tried to found a religious newspaper. But he failed. He spent a short time in 1867 as a subscription and ad salesman for the Reverend Henry Ward Beecher's influential weekly paper, the *Independent*. He soon gave up the post. Then he spent a year threatening a lawsuit against Noyes and his other former brethren at the Oneida Community. He tried to blackmail them into paying him $9,000. Otherwise, he threatened to publicize the colony's controversial sexual practices.[4] Guiteau's own father denounced his son publicly for this betrayal of Oneida. Guiteau finally stopped his abusive letters to Noyes after the latter threatened to prosecute him.

Guiteau next moved to Chicago, where he apprenticed in a law office. He was admitted to the Illinois bar in 1868. He made only one appearance as a trial lawyer. Inevitably, he lost the case. After this his legal practice consisted almost entirely of bill collecting, a trade he followed with little success until 1875.

In 1869 Guiteau had married an eighteen-year-old girl, Anne Bunn. The union lasted five turbulent years, during which he often beat his wife severely and sometimes even locked her in a closet overnight. In 1874 his wife divorced him.

By then, Guiteau had acquired a reputation as a sleazy and dishonest bill collector. He served a brief jail sentence in 1875 for petty

[4] The community held that traditional marriage and family patterns bred selfishness and, thereby, many evils in society. Therefore, monogamy was banned, and children were cared for by the entire community.

fraud and abruptly that same year, shifted his career plans once more. The penniless lawyer now announced plans to raise $200,000 in order to purchase a Chicago newspaper. Attempts to borrow the money quickly failed. Guiteau retreated to his family again. During a visit to his sister Frances, he threatened her with an ax. A physician who examined Guiteau after this incident recommended that he be placed in an insane asylum. Guiteau fled.

Now Guiteau adopted yet another vocation. He became an itinerant preacher and wandered across the country, selling religious pamphlets and preaching a version of John Humphrey Noyes' theology. Apparently Guiteau earned almost no money between 1875 and 1881. Yet somehow he managed to survive on the misplaced trust of creditors.

Charles Guiteau truly believed that Garfield's death was a necessity that would unite the Republican party and save the Republic. He claimed that the idea had come to him under "divine pressure."

In 1880 a new vision of success appeared to Guiteau. This time it was a political one. He wrote an incoherent pro-Garfield essay and had it privately printed. Then he attached himself to the Republicans' New York City campaign headquarters. There he became one of the many unwanted and unused hangers-on. Though he did nothing to bring it about, Guiteau viewed Garfield's election as a personal triumph. He immediately began making plans to apply for a high post in the diplomatic corps.

Guiteau wrote several letters to Garfield and other important Republican leaders to carry out his plan. In them he asserted his importance in the party's New York victory and requested assignment to various foreign ministries. Eventually, he decided on the Paris consulship. He moved to Washington—one jump ahead of his creditors—to press this claim.

During the early months of Garfield's presidency, from March to June 1881, Guiteau became a familiar face at the White House and in the State Department corridors. He pestered Garfield and Blaine about the Paris post at every chance, by letter and even in person (when he managed to push his way through). "Never bother me again about the Paris consulship so long as you live," Blaine shouted at the pesky figure after one such May encounter. By then, Guiteau had decided that Blaine was a "wicked man," He demanded Blaine's dismissal in notes to Garfield that became increasingly intimate in tone. A new scheme for glory now began to hatch in Guiteau's crazed mind: a plan to murder the President.

Guiteau was not familar with firearms. As his obsession grew more vivid, he purchased a revolver and practiced target shooting on the banks of the Potomac. He took to following the President and observ-

Roscoe Conkling, head of the Stalwarts, was a political boss who believed that "parties were not built by deportment or gush." He ruined his political career in an attempt to thwart Garfield's policies.

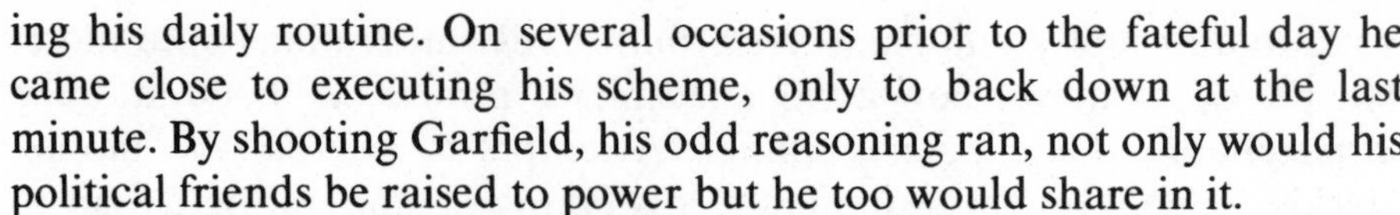

ing his daily routine. On several occasions prior to the fateful day he came close to executing his scheme, only to back down at the last minute. By shooting Garfield, his odd reasoning ran, not only would his political friends be raised to power but he too would share in it.

Finally, on July 2, 1881, Charles Julius Guiteau, a failure's failure, managed to carry out the last of his innumerable schemes. He shot the President. Guiteau later acknowledged:

> I have had an idea [since my youth] that I should be President, and it has never left me. When I left Boston for New York, in June 1880 [to campaign for Garfield], I felt that I was on my way to the White House. My idea is that I shall be nominated and elected as Lincoln and Garfield were—that is, by the act of God.

Many blamed Garfield's opponents among the Republican party's Stalwart wing[5] (somewhat unfairly) for having allowed the assassin even a minor place within their ranks in New York during the 1880 campaign. Some even blamed Vice President Arthur. Until Garfield selected him as a running mate, Arthur had been a loyal associate of the country's leading Stalwart, Senator Roscoe Conkling of New York. Arthur remained loyal to Conkling despite his new responsibilities as Vice President.

In May 1881 Garfield insisted on appointing an anti-Conkling Republican to an important patronage post—Customs Collector for the Port of New York. Conkling and his New York Stalwart colleague, Thomas C. Platt, both resigned from the Senate. Arthur supported their decision. Conkling and Platt hoped, by resigning, to put pressure on their Senate colleagues to reject the President's nominee on the grounds of "senatorial courtesy." They planned to win Senate reelection from the New York state legislature and then to return to Washington with added power. This was the dispute between Garfield and the Stalwarts that Guiteau claimed had triggered his decision to kill the President.

Senator Thomas C. Platt, a faithful political crony of Roscoe Conkling, followed his lead in resigning from the New York State legislature. Promptly dubbed "Me Too" Platt, his loyalty cost him his Senate seat.

In the end Conkling and Platt lost the struggle—and their power. The two were brought down in July 1881 by Conkling's personal arrogance and an ill-timed peek over an Albany hotel transom by a political opponent. Platt withdrew from the contest the same day that Garfield was shot in order not to hurt Conkling's chances. It was no use. Neither man gained reelection. Thus, ironically, Garfield had begun to win his struggle against Conkling for control of the Republi-

[5] The Stalwart wing was centered in New York. It actively opposed civil-service reform. Guiteau claimed to be a Stalwart, acting for the good of that faction in shooting Garfield.

can party at the very moment he was cut down by a maddened office seeker claiming to be a Stalwart.

Garfield himself never blamed his political opponents for the shooting. Garfield also forgave the political treachery of his Vice President, who had supported Conkling's reelection bid. During Garfield's struggle to recover from the shooting, Arthur remained at his New York City home, grief-stricken and withdrawn from public notice. Garfield turned the daily management of government over to his Cabinet. The rumors of a Stalwart conspiracy guiding Guiteau's hand quickly died away.

The wounded President lingered between life and death for seventy-nine days. He remained in his second-floor sickroom, only rarely writing official dispatches or dealing with government business. Doctors, medical consultants and free advice poured into the White House to assist in the President's treatment. But the bullet remained lodged in his back while physicians continued their painful probing. Nothing seemed to help.

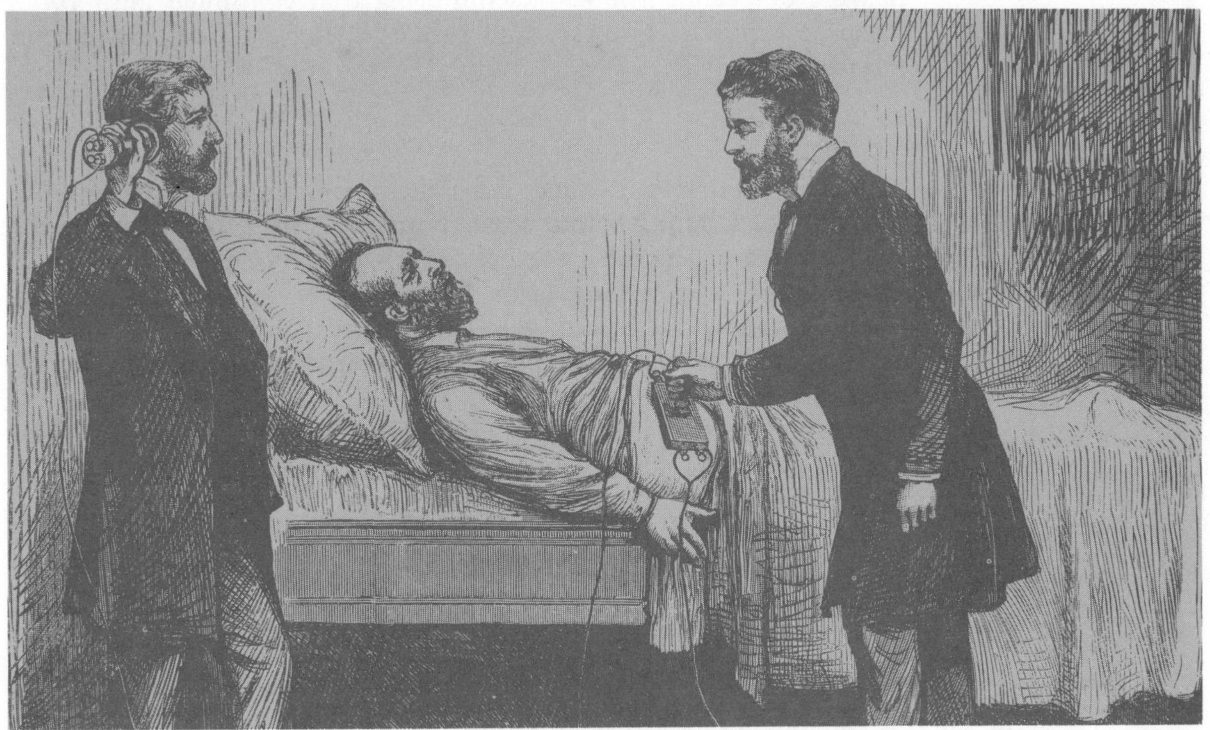

A reproduction of a contemporary sketch shows two doctors attempting to discover the location of the bullet in Garfield's body through the use of a strange telegraph-like apparatus. They never succeeded in removing the bullet.

At first the President's condition improved. But a mid-July rally turned into a late-July decline. In Washington's sweltering summer heat, Garfield ran a fever that only occasionally broke. His normally robust 200-pound frame shrank to 120 pounds by late August. When early September brought a record heat wave, the doctors decided to move Garfield to the cooler temperatures of his oceanside summer house at Elberon, New Jersey. He was carried there by special train on September 6, but his condition continued to deteriorate. Persistent job seekers continued to plague him. Still, almost to the end, his spirits remained good. He even tried to cheer those around him.

On the night of September 19, with only an old friend, Captain D. G. Swain, and one servant attending him, Garfield's final agony began. He awoke suddenly, clutched his heart, and cried out, "How it hurts here!" Swain handed the President a glass of water, but it failed to help. The President cried: "Swain, can't you stop this?" Then Garfield fell into a coma. Within moments Dr. Bliss and Mrs. Garfield entered the room. Mrs. Garfield sat down calmly and held her husband's hand. But the strain was too much, and she had to leave the room. Dr. Bliss remained with his patient for a few minutes, then walked quietly to a nearby study and wrote in his medical log: "Applying my ear over the heart, I detected an indistinct fluttering that continued until 10:35 when he expired. The brave and heroic sufferer, the nation's patient, has passed away."

The waiting had ended; the grieving began. Garfield's seventy-nine days of suffering before death, borne with stoic dignity, made the slain President a hero in the eyes of his countrymen. His body was brought back to Washington on September 21 to lie in state in the Capitol rotunda. Thousands—Southerners and Northerners, Democrats and Republicans alike—filed past to pay their last respects. The world's rulers also mourned. The President's widow received condolence messages from Queen Victoria of England; the emperors of China, Russia, and Japan; the kings of Belgium, Italy, and Spain; the Pope; and the sultan of Turkey.

American advocates of civil-service reform found an obvious moral in Garfield's assassination by a disappointed office seeker. Throughout his long death agony reformers organized countless meetings protesting the spoils system and demanding government appointments based on merit alone. "Garfield dead," one historian later wrote, "proved more valuable to reformers than Garfield alive."

The great majority of Americans, however, mourned Garfield's passing more sincerely. On September 23 a special train carried the

President's casket from Washington to Cleveland for burial. Crowds lined the entire route to honor the dead President, just as sixteen years earlier throngs had wept as Lincoln's funeral train followed a similar route from the East back to Illinois. Some 250,000 people from throughout the Middle West jammed Cleveland's streets for Garfield's funeral ceremony. Thousands of tributes—sermons, memorial leaflets, and letters—reached his widow at their Mentor home. The nation's grief seemed remarkably intense, considering the fact that Garfield, unlike Lincoln, had not been a war leader. Moreover he had held the highest office in the nation only a few months.

In New York Walt Whitman heard of the President's death. In his journal he wrote some lines that expressed the genuine sorrow of most of his less eloquent countrymen:

> The sobbing of the bells, the sudden death-news everywhere,
> The slumberers rouse, the rapport of the People,
> (Full well they know that message in the darkness,
> Full well return, respond within their breasts, their brains, the sad
> reverberations,)
> The passionate toll and clang—city to city, joining, sounding, passing,
> Those heart-beats of a Nation in the night.

Another New Yorker also recoiled at the awful news that evening. At Chester Alan Arthur's house the bell rang at midnight. A reporter informed the servant who answered the door that Garfield had died. "Oh, no, it cannot be true," cried Arthur, who overheard the news. "It cannot be. I have heard nothing." His face was pale, and he was crying. When the reporter persisted, Arthur could say only "I hope—My God, I do hope it is a mistake."

The man who had just become President turned and walked back to his study, where a small group of silent friends now waited. The bell rang again, and a messenger handed Arthur a telegram sent by a number of Garfield's Cabinet members. It confirmed the President's death and advised Arthur to take the oath of office immediately. Arthur's friends rushed out to find a judge who could administer the oath. Someone checked it for the exact wording. Within minutes a state supreme court justice, roused from his bed, administered the oath of office to the Vice President. The next morning President Chester A. Arthur left for Washington.

On September 20, two days after Garfield's death, his assassin sent a letter to Chester Arthur. He wrote, "My inspiration is a godsend to you, and I presume you appreciate it. It raises you from $8,000 to $50,000 a year. It raises you from a political cipher to President of the

This caricature of Garfield's assassin shows some of his crazed intensity of purpose. We can easily believe that he wrote: "I presume the President was a Christian, and that he will be happier in Paradise than here."

United States with all its power and honors. For the Cabinet I would suggest as follows . . . ." President Arthur never answered the letter. Instead, he ordered Guiteau tried promptly. He personally helped select the prosecuting attorneys.

Guiteau, however, still seemed convinced that the Stalwarts would somehow rescue and reward him. His confidence waned, though, as the trial date neared. He continued to deny responsibility for the killing. He insisted that divine inspiration made him pull the trigger. "I am here as God's man, and don't you forget it." No independent lawyer would touch the case, despite a newspaper appeal for such assistance. When the trial began on November 14, 1881, Guiteau's brother-in-law, George Scoville, served as defense counsel.

Lines between the defense and prosecution arguments were drawn clearly from the start. Scoville argued that his client was an insane religious fanatic and therefore could not be held legally responsible for his actions. Furthermore, the defense insisted that Garfield's wounds were not necessarily mortal. The President had died, Scoville claimed, only because of incompetent medical treatment after the shooting.

Both defense arguments had merit, although the prosecution, of course, denied them. It insisted that Guiteau, although morally evil, had killed the President while in complete possession of his faculties. He had done so for calculated political motives—namely, as a malicious and disappointed job seeker.

The case against Guiteau, then, centered on the question of his sanity. Both prosecution and defense attorneys presented "expert" medical testimony to prove their respective contentions. A majority of the doctors who had examined Guiteau found the prisoner sane within the prevailing legal definitions of sanity, which were far broader than those today. Guiteau demonstrated his unbalanced mental state by frequently interrupting the trial to shout abusive statements at everyone, including his own lawyer. He continued to claim divine inspiration.

The prosecution argued that such outbursts were merely a cynical act by Guiteau, who was trying to portray himself as mad. Apparently the jury also believed this. It took only a half-hour on January 25, 1882, to find Guiteau guilty of murder. The prisoner vented his anger by shrieking: "My blood will be upon the heads of [this] jury. God will avenge this outrage." One doctor who had observed the trial daily, George M. Beard, a noted psychologist, disagreed strongly with the jury's decision. Beard later wrote:

> The physicians called in to make a diagnosis mistook the symptoms of insanity for the symptoms of wickedness. [This] error is quite as natural for nonexperts in insanity in our time as that of the village physician of Salem, Dr. Griggs, in witchcraft times, in attributing insanity to possession by the devil.

Nevertheless, on February 3, Judge Walter Cox sentenced Guiteau to hang.

Before sentencing, Guiteau addressed the court a final time. He insisted again that Garfield's killing had been "God's act, not mine." He compared his fate to Christ's and threatened bloody divine vengeance on the United States if he hung. In the months before his execution the condemned man continued to believe that President Arthur would issue a last-minute reprieve or pardon.

Finally, Guiteau recognized the reality ahead of him. Four days before his death, while in his cell, he scrawled a "Scene between the Almighty and my murderers." In this imaginary scene God confronts Guiteau's persecutors, including President Arthur, and condemns them along with the entire American nation. A few days later, on June 30, 1882, Charles Guiteau was hung. He went to the scaffold, fighting back tears and singing a childlike hymn he had written especially for the occasion. Then he gave a final shout: "Glory hallelujah! I am with the Lord. Glory, ready, go!"

CHAPTER

26

Politics in Transition

THE ECONOMIC and social landscape of the United States in the nineteenth century underwent dramatic change. The period might best be termed a transitional one. It was characterized by the emergence of a new, industrial society. In the decades after the Civil War the preindustrial issues that dominated the ante-bellum era were overridden in importance by the realities of a rapidly maturing industrial society. New economic and social factors, some of them grim, were changing life. They included: transcontinental railroads, a truly national market for goods, a growing monopoly in oil, the factory system, and new technology in steel and other industries. In addition, there were deplorable urban living conditions, millions of new, non-English-speaking immigrants, rising labor violence, growing discontent among farmers, and brutal poverty among workers and farmers.

These factors were clearly visible. But both Republican and Democratic politicians managed to avoid confronting them. Not until a paralyzing business depression in the 1890s and the rise of a new third party, committed to reform, did politicians finally start to deal with the problems brought about by industrial development. Before then, in the 1870s and 1880s, political leaders were more concerned with traditional issues, particularly the currency and tariffs. They argued, for example, over whether the amount of currency in circulation should be expanded or reduced. And they debated whether the United States would benefit more from raised or from lowered tariffs.

Why did politicians avoid considering the problems of the new industrial society? Basically, they (and voters too) were still intensely involved with the emotional questions arising out of the Civil War and Reconstruction. But with the ending of war and the termination of Radical rule in the South, old issues had disappeared. This transitional generation of politicians was simply unprepared to face the new problems of an industrial nation.

A GENERATION OF ORDINARY MEN

Through the 1870s and 1880s politics continued along at an unhurried pace. Leaders tried to avoid difficult issues. In large part the people who entered politics during this period were ordinary men, like Garfield. They displayed little achievement beyond their ability to win votes.

In *The American Commonwealth* (1888) James Bryce, an English historian, noted that in a country where all careers are open to those having talent and where "political life is unusually keen and political ambition widely diffused," the highest positions in the land are seldom "won by men of brilliant gifts."

Why did eminent figures usually not choose to run for political office in this period? First, for talented people American politics did not seem interesting and important. This situation contrasted with that in European countries, where officeholders in national governments generally held much more power over people's lives. Thus, first-rate men were attracted to vocations in which they felt they could make a significant impact. Politics was not one such vocation.

A second reason for the lack of brilliant people in politics was that success generally required a slow rise through the party ranks. The long apprenticeship in party loyalty necessary to achieve office discouraged ambitious people who wished to move quickly into positions of prominence. Also American voters, then as today, were distrustful of anyone who seemed overly eager for political power, although he or she might have been very capable.

Finally, persons of outstanding ability may not have entered politics simply because the era seemed a quiet one, at least compared with the age preceding it. Profound ideological questions no longer separated the parties. The problems of slavery, sectional divisions, and civil war were settled. Few issues were significant enough to attract talented people into politics.

Small-Town Background Given the lure of other fields, the slowness of the process of reaching the top, and the relative quietness of the times, the quality of those who held high public

President Garfield's home in Mentor, Ohio was the kind of country setting most national politicians of this era preferred. Their living patterns represented a nostalgia for an older, simpler way of life in an increasingly complex industrial society.

office is hardly surprising. Nor is it surprising to find that those who did make politics their career shared very similar patterns of life. It was far more likely for someone like Garfield to become President than for a man like his assassin Guiteau.

In fact, most successful figures in late nineteenth-century national politics, including the great majority of congressmen and senators, had backgrounds similar to that of Garfield. They came from small towns and cities like Garfield's Mentor, Ohio, rather than from large cities or predominantly rural areas. Furthermore, most began their careers in such professions as law, business, the ministry, or teaching.

During the 1860s and 1870s the number of politicians having business interests increased. But despite this fact most politicians were nonetheless provincial in their values and outlook on life. They tended to be more comfortable with their preindustrial way of thinking. They remained aloof and sheltered from the habits and problems of urban-industrial society. They brought to national affairs a viewpoint similar to that of their pre–Civil War counterparts. Most national elected officials, in fact, had little direct personal contact with the major new realities of a changed America—cities, industries, and immigrants.

As with most of the national politicians of this period, the presidential candidates—especially the Republicans—were men with roots in small cities and towns. And all the Republican candidates but James G. Blaine in 1884 came from the Middle West. Thus, even if a man like Charles Guiteau had managed to build a successful career for himself in a city like Chicago or New York, his urban ties would probably have blocked his road to the White House.

Guiteau may have been more successful as a Democrat, however. The Democrats generally nominated presidential candidates from big cities during these years: Horatio Seymour (1868), Horace Greeley (1872), Samuel Tilden (1876), and Grover Cleveland (1884, 1888, 1892). But of this group only Cleveland succeeded in becoming President. Thus, while they controlled the big cities and even had respectable showings in congressional elections, the Democrats largely failed to take the biggest prize of all—the presidency.

Civil War Experience As important as a small-town background seemed to be in achieving political success, there was another factor at least as important in advancing a politician's career—his Civil War record. This was true at all levels in American politics but particularly in regard to seeking the presidency. Indeed, another reason why Guiteau could never have become President was that he had not served in the Union Army.

For many Northern voters Republicanism was practically a family religion, sanctified by wartime sacrifices. (Most Northerners had lost at least one family member in the fighting.) The "martyrdom" of Lincoln and Garfield practically guaranteed the presidency for the Republican party.

The Republican presidential candidates were usually Civil War generals. General Hayes succeeded General Grant in the presidency. He, in turn, was succeeded by General Garfield. As death and old age thinned out the number of high-ranking officers, Colonel Benjamin Harrison, and, finally, Major William McKinley entered the White House.

The Democrats, for their part, failed to choose nominees having a military background, at least on the national level. The single Democratic candidate who was a Union military man was General Winfield Scott Hancock. He lost to Garfield in 1880. It is understandable that Union officers were not nominated. The Democrats depended, for the most part, on Southern support for victory. In local and regional elections, of course, where Southern support was irrelevant, Democrats could play on old Civil War loyalties to win elections. But, again, the presidential prize eluded them.

Codes of Personal Conduct The victorious politicians of this period, besides sharing a small-town background and Civil War experience, were also strong believers in the strictest of

John Peter Altgeld

Chicago Historical Society

"He was a lover of his fellow man." With these words in 1902 the famous lawyer Clarence Darrow eulogized his friend the former governor of Illinois. "When John P. Altgeld died," he continued, "the poor and weak and defenseless lost their truest friend."

Indeed, John Peter Altgeld had been a friend of the unfortunate. He himself had been poor, and he never forgot how it felt. He was born in 1847 in Germany. When he was three months old, his parents brought him to Ohio. There his father, an illiterate, narrow man who scorned "book learning," struggled with little success to earn a living at farming.

Young John shared his father's long hours of grinding labor on the farm. He did not share his scorn for books, however. He attended school when he could, which was rarely. At sixteen he went to fight in the Civil War. Then he drifted for a while, doing whatever work he could find. Finally he began to study law on his own and in 1875 moved to Chicago.

By 1886 he was a successful lawyer, made prosperous by investments in real estate. He entered public life, first as a judge and then, in 1893, as the first Democratic governor of Illinois in thirty-six years.

It was a time when government did not know how to meet the pressing problems created by the country's rapid shift from agriculture to industry. Altgeld's inauguration speech showed that he had some ideas on how to deal with this new situation. He outlined his plans for reforms in health and labor conditions, the prison system, civil service, education, personal liberty, and taxation.

Altgeld was beset by crisis from the start. Long before he became governor, he had been troubled by the Haymarket Affair. The three convicted men who had not been executed were still in prison in Illinois. Many people demanded their release. Altgeld agonized for six months. He wanted to see justice done, but he knew the consequences. As he said to his friend Darrow, "If I pardon those men, it will not meet with the approval that you expect; from that day I will be a dead man politically."

Nevertheless, he pardoned the prisoners and published a detailed message stating his reasons. He used the trial records to document his conclusions that the judge and jury were prejudiced and that the evidence was insufficient to prove guilt.

Altgeld's dire prediction of political death proved correct. He was not elected to a second term. But another, happier prediction also proved true. Shortly after he became governor, he told a friend that he would soon present a broad program of reforms. All of them, he said, would one day be enacted into law. It probably took longer than he hoped, but by the 1920s virtually every one of his reforms was either the law of the state or the law of the land.

Grover Cleveland was elected President despite his failure to meet Victorian moral standards. His political incorruptibility and reform-mindedness were assets in office.

moral codes. They usually presented themselves to the public as family men, who lived their private lives according to the rigid ethical precepts of American middle-class culture. We do not know, of course, whether this was fact or sheer image building. The author of Garfield's semiofficial campaign biography wrote, for example: "No profane word, no unseemly jest is ever heard at Lawnfield [his home]. No wines sparkle on its table. The moral atmosphere is sweet, pure, and healthgiving to heart and soul. It is a Christian family—a Christian home."

Prior to the Civil War a politician's personal habits and morality had rarely influenced the success of his political career. Neither Andrew Jackson's background of frequent duels nor Henry Clay's frequent gambling prevented these men from seeking the highest prizes in American politics. During the middle of the nineteenth century, however, the American family adopted a stern moral code on such questions as sexual behavior, drinking, and gambling. Voters began to apply these standards to vote seekers as well. Thus, had Guiteau chosen to run for office, his stormy relationship with Anne Bunn would probably have been used against him.

Perhaps the only national politician of the era to successfully overcome hostility toward "loose" morality was Grover Cleveland. He won the presidency in 1884 despite the fact—brought out in the campaign—that in his youth he had fathered an illegitimate child. Ironically, voters that year were offered a choice between repudiating either Cleveland's single offense against private morality or James G. Blaine's questionable public morality. While a senator during the 1870s, Blaine had allegedly accepted money and stocks from railroad companies in return for political favors. When the returns were in, the electorate had registered its preference for a candidate with a single confessed private lapse to one probably tainted with several instances of political corruption.

ELECTING A PRESIDENT

National politics during the 1870s and 1880s was not oriented toward issues, although some of the older issues did play a part in the elections. Basically, politicians were concerned with party affiliation and moral, ethnic, and religious differences among the electorate. Three basic factors shaped presidential elections of the late nineteenth century: a close balance in voting strength between the two major parties, high voter turnout, and a stress on party regularity.

The Closeness of Contests The statistics for every presidential election of the era show clearly that the parties were evenly matched. In the disputed 1876 election Republican Rutherford B. Hayes was elected by one electoral vote, although he had received almost 250,000 fewer votes than his Democratic opponent, Samuel J. Tilden. In 1880 Garfield defeated the Democratic candidate, Winfield Scott Hancock, by a comfortable electoral majority. But his nationwide popular margin was a mere 7,368 votes. Actually, Garfield received only a plurality of the votes—48 percent; a third-party candidate, James B. Weaver of the Greenback-Labor party, cut into the major parties' totals.

Democrat Grover Cleveland's presidential election history is an interesting one, for he crossed and recrossed the narrow line between victory and defeat. In 1884 Cleveland won with less than 49 percent of the popular vote. His margin in the popular vote was only 63,000. When he was defeated by Republican Benjamin Harrison in the 1888 election, Harrison received the majority of electoral votes despite receiving 96,000 fewer popular votes. Cleveland again became President in 1892 when he received 360,000 more votes than Harrison. In this race a new third party, the Populists, received over 1 million votes. Thus a President-elect once more won with only a plurality, not a majority, of the popular vote.

The closeness of these presidential contests helps to explain the efforts usually made by both Republicans and Democrats to blur their basic differences over issues at the national level. Although the Republicans supported high protective tariffs, for example, there were many in the party, including Garfield, who favored much lower rates. Similarly, the Democrats were a low-tariff party. But Cleveland's decision to press the tariff-reduction issue during his first term cost the party support from many high-tariff Democrats and independents who might otherwise have voted for him when he ran again. In order to make its position seem close to that of the other party, and thus hopefully to gain votes, each party had to suppress its conflicting factions on issues such as the tariff.

Because of the narrow margins of victory in each presidential election, both Republicans and Democrats were essentially in competition for the support of a small group of swing voters in a few doubtful states. These voters shifted from party to party throughout this period. Business help was often invaluable in swinging the key votes and deciding the outcome of the election. Thus Garfield's election in 1880 owed much to

Election night, 1892, in New York City is typical of voter enthusiasm in this era. Despite political corruption and the lack of great issues, excitement over politics ran high.

The Tweed Ring

New York City in the mid-1800s was growing rapidly. European immigrants, as well as native-born Americans, poured into the city in search of work in the booming urban-industrial society. In 1840 the city population numbered 300,000. By 1870 it had reached 950,000 inhabitants, about 400,000 of them foreign-born.

The effects on the city were staggering. Housing, public transportation, sanitation, and health facilities became dangerously inadequate. So did the existing methods for governing the city. The old residents—the "best people"—had governed a city where their way of life was the norm. Now they found themselves surrounded by what they considered strange and threatening intruders. And they quickly made their hostility known.

Not everyone shared their view of the newcomers, however. A political club with headquarters at Tammany Hall saw them in a different light—as potential voters. As quickly as the older residents alienated the new arrivals, Tammany welcomed them with open arms.

Tammany's leader was William Marcy Tweed. He saw the immigrant as the basis for a strong constituency that would secure political power for him and his associates. So "Boss" Tweed courted the immigrant. He sent his people to meet ships bringing immigrants in. The confused and uprooted strangers soon learned who would help them get jobs, find places to stay, and become citizens.

Once they were settled in wards, or political districts, the immigrants learned that the ward leader knew of their existence. When they had a death in the family, he sent flowers. When they had trouble with the law, he used his influence. In return for these blessings new citizens were generally glad to give their votes.

Thus in 1866 the Tweed Ring, the country's first big city political organization, or "machine," was born. Ward leaders could deliver the vote to maintain the Tweed Ring in political office. Tweed's people could then levy taxes and decide on the allocation of money for projects. Tweed could in turn offer the ward leaders jobs on these projects for their voters—as well as other profitable favors.

With their power base secure, the Tweed Ring plundered New York City. Of every tax dollar, only fifteen cents went for legitimate uses. The rest went into the pockets of the ring, the overpaid builders, or bribe-welcoming officials.

Soon though, New Yorkers learned the price they were paying. Thomas Nast, a brilliant political cartoonist, began exposing Boss Tweed and his ring. The Tweed operation could not withstand the light of publicity. By the mid-1870s it was destroyed. Many of its members were imprisoned; its leader became a fugitive hiding out in Spain.

Although the Tweed Ring robbed New York City of anywhere from $30,000,000 to $200,000,000, it did leave a legacy. The way it built and maintained its support on the ward level was to remain standard practice in many American cities for nearly a hundred years.

the fact that John D. Rockefeller instructed his thousands of salesmen in various states in the Middle West to work actively for the Republican ticket. Similarly, in 1888, Harrison's victory was due in part to corporate donations that helped finance intensive drives for votes in a few key swing states.

Turnout of Voters Another basic factor in presidential elections in the late nineteenth century was a surprisingly high voter turnout. This phenomenon is somewhat more difficult to explain. There were no dramatic public issues bitterly dividing the two parties as there had been earlier—and would be in the near future. Part of the explanation, however, can be found in the popular view of elections as spectacles.

Both parties waged furious campaigns. Republicans "waved the bloody shirt"—that is, they reminded the voters of Southern Democratic disloyalty during the Civil War. Democrats, in turn, pointed to the corrupting influence of business on the Republican party.

Political campaigns were often the greatest shows in town. Huge numbers of voters marched in torchlight parades. They listened for hours to familiar but rousing partisan oratory. As participants in and spectators of such grand displays, voters reaffirmed their strong faith in their party identifications.

Importance of Party Loyalty Political loyalties among politicians and voters were clear and strong during this period. However blurred the political issues might be, this kind of loyalty strengthened the parties as institutions in American life.

Among politicians party loyalty or regularity was extremely important at the national level. Presidential power, which had reached a high point with Lincoln's wartime authority, declined after the crisis of civil war ended. Presidents were largely at the mercy of Congress in achieving their programs. The President's political task was twofold: (1) to "carry" enough congressmen of his own party into office when he was elected; and (2) to hold their loyalty once he won.

Concerning the former, Presidents were not too successful. No President during this entire era governed for his entire term with a majority of his own party in control of Congress. The Democrats, for example, won control of the House in 1874, lost it in 1880, regained it in 1882, lost it in 1888, and won it back in 1890. Although Republicans controlled the Senate throughout this period, except for the 1879–81 session, for all but two years they held no more than a slim three-vote Senate majority. There was considerable turnover in congressional membership during the 1870s and 1880s, particularly in the House.

It was even more difficult for a President to hold the party loyalty of congressmen after election. There were numerous factions in both parties. Various means of keeping the party together seemed to work, however. By the end of the era, congressional caucuses were a device used in both parties. They generally decided the legislative policies that all members were expected to, and usually did, abide by. A congressman who did not support the party could be disciplined in a number of ways. Leaders might deny him important committee assignments. They might refuse to help him in the passage of the numerous private bills that every congressman introduces yearly on behalf of his constituents. If necessary they would oppose his renomination. In these circumstances, most congressmen, of course, obeyed the dictates of their party's leaders.

Party loyalty among American voters was more easily assured. American voters adhered as firmly to their party allegiances as they did to their religious faiths. If one was raised as a Democrat or as a Republican, one usually remained a Democrat or a Republican for life.

Recent studies point to the importance of ethnic and religious backgrounds as factors in the political behavior of most Americans in the period following the Civil War. A voter's ethnic, cultural, and religious ties shaped his party loyalty as much as it did his attitudes on specific economic or political issues. For example, in order to help capture the votes of the immigrants, who badly needed employment, civil-service reformers in each party complained about the use of the spoils system by urban political machines in the other party. Although jobs were dispensed through political patronage under the spoils system, and thus recent immigrants were unlikely to get them, few of these immigrants favored introducing a merit system. This, they felt, might result in jobs being awarded mainly to native-born Americans who had had greater opportunity to receive education and training.

Religious beliefs were also a factor in determining political affiliation. Recent voting studies have shown that during this period the more an individual's religion stressed correct behavior rather than strict adherence to doctrine alone, the more likely he was to vote Republican. Some Protestant religious denominations viewed politics as a moral battleground in which state power should be used to regulate ethical behavior. For example, they supported laws prohibiting the sale of alcohol. Members of these denominations tended to support Republicans for office, whether in the 1850s or the 1890s. Certainly Republican opposition at the state level to using public funds for parochial schools (schools particularly important for many new immigrant families) and the party's support for prohibition (viewed as an assault on Democratic-voting Catholic immigrant "drinkers") attracted large numbers of native-born Episcopalian, Congregationalist, Presbyterian, and other similar voters.

This does not mean that immigrant groups and church members voted in blocs for a single party. Nonetheless, ethnic and cultural ties did indeed influence political loyalties in the period of the 1870s and 1880s.

THE REPUBLICANS IN POWER

For three decades, from 1861 to 1892, the Republicans (except for Democrat Cleveland's 1885–89 term) governed nationally, despite the close political balance between the parties. During this period, as already stated, the President was extremely dependent on Congress. In fact, more often than not, Congress—not the President—determined party policies and the legislation that emerged from Washington.

Americans did not seem to want strong Presidents during this period. Certainly they did not appear to need them because of the relative quietness of the times. So, none of the Republican Presidents—Grant, Hayes, Garfield, Arthur, or Harrison—managed to wrest control of Republican policies from the Senate and House leaders.

Men like Blaine and Conkling remained the party's most influential national spokesmen throughout the period. They largely shaped national legislation during the era. Since they were Republicans, they believed in an effective and energetic national economic policy. In general, the purpose of this policy was to encourage industrial expansion. For this they were often criticized by Democratic politicians who retained their party's traditional faith. This Democratic faith rested on the belief that government should not meddle actively in the economic lives of Americans.

But the Republican party, founded in an era when the national government had to expand its powers to preserve the Union, saw nothing wrong with continuing this trend at the war's end. To encourage economic development, party leaders aided business in every possible way. In accomplishing this purpose, they forged an informal alliance between the national government and the great majority of businessmen—bankers, industrialists, and merchants in foreign trade. While this alliance did further economic growth, it had other less fortunate consequences as well. It gave the era a reputation for corruption unparalleled in American history until then.

Corruption Under Grant It is ironic that people who lived by strict small-town moral codes in their private lives found it difficult to maintain the same kind of integrity in public affairs. Political corruption was widespread in this period. The Grant years in particular saw some of the worst offenses against honest government in the nation's history.

A series of Cabinet scandals during Grant's administration involved many people close to the President himself. His Secretary of the Navy sold work to contractors rather than take honest bids. His Secretary of War sold extremely profitable tradeships on Indian reservations. Department of Interior officials worked hand in hand with dishonest land speculators.

Some of the worst scandals involved the Department of the Treasury. Grant's Secretary of the Treasury farmed out the collection of unpaid taxes to a private contractor who kept half the collections. The President's own private secretary protected a Whiskey Ring of corrupt Treasury inspectors. These officials received millions of dollars in bribes from liquor distillers to avoid payment of government revenue taxes. Through Grant's personal bungling the Department of the Treasury cooperated with two New York stock speculators, James Fisk and Jay Gould, to manipulate government selling of bullion. The two men cornered the gold market briefly in September 1869, forcing anyone else who needed gold to pay an exorbitant price to get it. Although they caused a panic in the money market, Fisk and Gould made a fortune on the deal. Once they were exposed, Grant did little to punish the guilty parties in his administration.

The opportunities for politicians to profit through corrupt practices increased vastly as a result of the economic boom of the 1860s and 1870s. Many national leaders like Garfield had carefully watched their money while young to further their educations and careers. Suddenly they were responsible for handling billions of dollars in government funds. Politicians found themselves able to reap tidy sums (and benefit the country) simply by helping businessmen with government funds or favorable legislation.

The railroads were notorious seekers after these government favors. Railroad owners paid millions in bribes to public officials each year to secure cash subsidies, gifts of government land, and favorable legislation. Both Garfield and Blaine were linked to such transactions, although no specific criminal charges were ever made against either of them.

Elected for being a great military man, Ulysses S. Grant was not a great President. His appointees, chosen more for personal loyalty than administrative competence, blackened his administration's record with scandals.

During Grant's administration, Garfield apparently profited, along with numerous other public officials, from a shady company known as the Crédit Mobilier. This was a purchasing and construction corporation organized by a few stockholders of the Union Pacific Railroad in the late 1860s. The Union Pacific stockholders retained control of the Crédit Mobilier, to which they awarded huge and fraudulent contracts connected with building the railroad. Congressmen of both parties, including Garfield, were bribed with money and stocks in the Crédit Mobilier to avoid congressional inquiry into these transactions. Before the affair was exposed in 1873, the Crédit Mobilier (despite the Union Pacific's virtual bankruptcy) had paid yearly dividends to stockholders that often exceeded

 300 percent of the original investment. Moreover, sometimes these excessive profits went to Congressmen who paid nothing for the stock in the first place!

Although the Grant administration provides the most famous instances of scandal, governmental corruption was not limited to the national level or to Republicans alone. In fact, some of the worst instances of corruption took place at the city level, where Democrats were more likely to be in control. New York City, for instance, was run by a Democratic political organization, or "machine," known as the Tweed Ring (see page 530). Its political leader, "Boss" William Marcy Tweed, and members of his machine stole over $100 million in public revenues ($14 million in one profitable day).

Civil-Service Reform An important source of Tweed's money was from kickbacks forced from people who wanted city jobs. Once in office, the machine politicians had the power to distribute jobs. Many reformers of the era thought that this spoils system for filling political posts should be eliminated and replaced with a merit system. This system, they thought, would do away with much of the corruption in high places that had plagued the country at all levels.

Grant's successor, Rutherford B. Hayes, ordered that officeholders not be asked to make political contributions or be required to do political campaigning. But these orders were largely ignored. Garfield, as noted in the previous chapter, backed away from Hayes' civil-service commitment. With Garfield's assassination public attention focused on Guiteau not merely as an actual assassin but as a symbol of the various evils that Americans identified with the spoils system of selecting officeholders.

Although the most blatant instances of national corruption had taken place a decade or more earlier, in 1883 Congress responded to the public outcry by passing the Pendleton Act. President Arthur, himself a one-time spoilsman, had lobbied hard for the bill. The act established a bipartisan Civil Service Commission, appointed by the President. Its purpose was to conduct competitive examinations to choose officeholders on the basis of merit. Arthur appointed three solid reformers as civil-service commissioners.

The original measure did not solve the entire problem, however, for the merit system affected only about one of every ten federal jobs. The others were to be filled as political appointments. Nonetheless, the Pendleton Act gave the President the authority to expand the number of positions classified as merit jobs. By 1900 over 40 percent of federal posts had been brought under the civil-service heading. This percentage has expanded in every decade since.

CONTINUING BUSINESS INFLUENCE

The assault on the spoils system did not have much effect on business influence within the national government. Businessmen tried less often to buy favors from individual politicians. Instead, increasing numbers of them began either running for office themselves or supporting politicians committed to business policies through legal campaign contributions. Industrialists and bankers poured millions into Republican campaign treasuries.

Even more important than business involvement in presidential contests, however, was the growing importance of senators who represented large corporate interests. By 1900 such businessmen, most of them Republicans, comprised a third of the Senate. Fifteen senators were involved in railroads; fifteen in extractive industries—minerals, oil, and lumber; nine in banking and finance; six in commerce; and three in manufacturing. Wealthy members of both the House and Senate were not captives or "puppets" of the business interests with which they held close ties. But on issues affecting the national economic life their policies tended to favor businessmen and monied interests rather than farmers, laborers, and the poor. And they made only token efforts to regulate American industry or finance.

This pro-Greenback cartoon portrays a gold-nosed government octopus linking itself to big business with its tentacles while strangling labor, farmers, and small business.

Currency Expansion Favoritism toward business interests is shown clearly in the monetary programs enacted by Congress in the era. The debate involved the amount of currency in circulation. Farmers and most other debtors favored an increase in the amount of money issued by the government. Businesses, on the other hand, especially banking interests, wanted the opposite.

To understand the farmers' demands, it is important to keep in mind that this group was experiencing especially hard times during this period. The mechanization of agriculture was a mixed blessing to farmers. It greatly added to their efficiency; but it helped create vast surpluses and consequent falling prices. Wheat, for example, which sold for $2.50 a bushel in 1868 dropped to an average of 78 cents a bushel in the late 1880s.

While prices continued dropping, the cost of running farms remained high. Many farmers, for instance, were at the mercy of railroads that held a monopoly on transportation in their areas. These railroads often charged excessively high rates for carrying agricultural products to markets. Besides the cost of transportation, the cost of land, machinery, and tools was quite high.

Faced with high costs and declining prices for their own products, farmers usually went into debt by mortgaging their land and goods. In the 1880s the number of mortgages soared. Of the total number of farms in the country, over 40 percent were mortgaged. In some areas, like Kansas, the figure was closer to 60 percent. Interest rates on these mortgages were high—6 to 15 percent on land and 10 to 18 percent on goods.

Farmers felt that government could relieve their distress by pumping more money into the economy. The government had increased the amount of paper money—greenbacks—in circulation during the Civil War in order to finance the war effort. After the war the government began to withdraw these greenbacks from circulation. This cutback in currency was hitting the indebted farmer particularly hard because he had borrowed when money was "cheap" or plentiful. Now he had to pay his debts in currency worth much more than its original value.

From the bankers' point of view, of course,

the situation was ideal. They had a stake in seeing that money became scarcer. They would profit more on the repayment of loans, since the value of a dollar increases as its supply decreases. The government agreed with this viewpoint. During the Hayes administration, the Specie Resumption Act of 1875 reduced the number of greenbacks in circulation. This was a direct slap at debtor interests, particularly farmers. The act gave an even more direct favor to the financial community. It provided that bonds issued during the Civil War should be paid off in gold. The banking community, of course, held most of these bonds. The provision meant that war bonds that had been bought with greenbacks worth less than 40 cents to the dollar could now be turned in for currency worth 100 cents to the dollar.

An antitariff cartoon of the 1880s shows the spiraling bad effects of a high tariff. The tariff wall results in a glut of products on the home market, consequent cuts in production, and then widespread unemployment.

This resumption of specie payments, as it was called, so enraged some farmers that they banded together to form a third party. They were joined by many recruits from labor and became the Greenback-Labor party in 1878. In the short run the movement was unsuccessful, since it failed to win many votes or to change the government's policy in currency. In the long run, however, it was significant in laying the basis for an agrarian movement far more powerful during the 1890s.

Agitation for expanding the currency did not stop after the initial failure of the greenback movement. In fact, a new strategy was tried—a demand that silver be used to back the dollar. In 1873 the government had stopped coining silver and put the country back on the gold standard—that is, backed money with gold alone. But in the 1870s the supply of silver increased tremendously because of the discovery of new silver deposits in the West. Many charged that silver had been demonetized illegally. By the 1880s farmers and other debtor groups saw in the "remonetizing" of silver a way of getting cheaper money. This in turn would raise crop prices and secure them relief from their debts.

Those who agitated for silver were partially successful during the 1870s. The Bland-Allison Act of 1878 required the Department of the Treasury to buy not less than $2 million and not more than $4 million worth of silver each month to back the dollar. Unfortunately, the government continuously bought the lesser amount. Though the silver interests were placated, farmers did not get much relief.

The Tariff Issue Another government policy that tended to favor business interests at the expense of other segments of society involved the tariff. The tariff debate, as old as the country itself, took on new importance with the coming of the industrial age. The original justification for a tax on imports was to protect infant industries from the competition of foreign manufacturers. But long after competition from abroad ceased to be a threat, the tariff still remained high on most goods. And it was going higher.

Again those particularly hurt by the tariff were the farmers. They complained that they had to sell their goods competitively on an open world market. But they had to purchase tariff-protected manufactured and processed goods such as farm machinery and oil. In fact, consumers in general suffered from the imposition of high tariffs. Without the competition of cheaper imported goods, they paid whatever prices domestic manufacturers set. These were often determined by monopolistic practices.

Republicans were by no means the only supporters of high protective tariffs. Factions in both parties backed business interests (or farmer interests) on this matter. But it was not until a Democrat, Grover Cleveland, took office that there was a serious challenge to high tariffs. Cleveland's advocacy of a lowered tariff provided the leading issue in his reelection bid in 1888. He was defeated, as was noted earlier, partly because he had alienated the protariff faction in his own party. But his downfall came mostly because businessmen poured millions of dollars into the campaign of the Republican candidate, Benjamin Harrison.

Harrison repaid his business backers by supporting the highest tariff in the nation's history. The McKinley Tariff of 1890—named after its sponsor, William McKinley (who, with business backing, would himself become President a few years later)—aimed not just at discouraging competition but at eliminating it altogether. It raised rates from an average of 38 percent to an average of almost 50 percent. It clearly marked a triumph for American industrialists.

Token Reform Although business influence was at its height, the government could not afford to ignore the public altogether. Some steps were taken in this period to deal with elements in the changed economy. But these proved to be less than effective. Congressmen from both parties joined in passing two basically mild bills to regulate the new giant industries.

The Interstate Commerce Act in 1887 set up a federal commission (the ICC) to oversee "reasonable and just" rates on the nation's railroads. Congress did not provide the commission with any strong enforcement powers, however. Its only avenue was the courts, and these generally consisted of probusiness conservatives. Moreover, the persons who were appointed as commissioners during the 1890s were sympathetic to the railroads. This, of course, further prevented the ICC from making any serious efforts to regulate the lines in order to ensure fair and equal treatment for all shippers.

A second law, the Sherman Antitrust Act of 1890, was also supposed to curb big business. Anticipating public reaction to the high McKinley Tariff congressmen hoped that the Sherman Act would quiet agitation. Unfortunately, it provided only mild and ineffective penalties against companies that formed combinations in restraint of trade. Furthermore, it was rarely applied during the 1890s. Only five years after the law was passed, the Supreme Court handed down a decision in *U.S. v. Knight* that exempted most industries from its provision. A monopoly, according to the Court, was not itself illegal. It became so only when it served to restrain interstate trade.

The immediate effect of such token efforts was to prevent a massive public outcry. In the long run, though, they only added further grievances to the growing list of problems confronting the country. The nation had lived through more than two decades of conservative rule resulting from the informal alliance of business and government. The public was ready for reform, and pressure was mounting in various parts of society to bring that about.

THE POPULIST CRUSADE

The first sector of the population to voice the need for change and take steps in this direction were the farmers. Their lot had been difficult throughout this period. It worsened in the late 1880s with the onset of a severe farm depression

Populist conventions mixed the gaiety of a county fair with the fervor of a revivalist meeting. This one in New York in 1896 decided against running an independent slate and endorsed Democrat William Jennings Bryan, marking the end of the party.

affecting especially the South and the West. The price of farm products continued to decline while production costs skyrocketed. Angry at their political powerlessness within the existing party system, farmers decided to strike out on their own in a new third party.

They called themselves the Populist party. Although they managed to attract some support from working-class and middle-class reformers, most Populist leaders and party members came from the ranks of previous farmer protest organizations. They met in Omaha in 1892 to assemble a reform program. Ignatius Donnelly, foremost Populist writer and orator, wrote their platform. In its preamble he charged:

> The controlling influences dominating both these parties have permitted the existing dreadful conditions to develop without serious effort to prevent or restrain them. Neither do they now promise us any substantial reform. Instead, they have agreed together to drown the outcries of the people [in the campaign ahead] with the uproar of a sham battle over the tariff, so that capitalists, corporations, national banks, rings, trusts, the demonetization of silver may all be lost sight of.

The Party's Program At the convention a program was adopted that was followed in most essentials by Populist candidates throughout the 1890s. The program reflected the party's largely rural and agrarian base. Therefore, although there were planks that defended the right of unions to organize and denounced the oppression of factory workers, these were not central Populist concerns. And, although the platform also demanded a graduated federal income tax, direct election of senators, and other constitutional or political reforms, these were not central Populist concerns either.

What the new party wished, above all, was a series of reforms designed to help American farmers overcome what they felt were the unfair handicaps imposed upon agriculture in the United States by industrial growth. The most important of these demands was strict regulation or government ownership of the nation's railroads, which farmers believed discriminated against them. They also wanted an increase in the supply of money through remonetizing silver, since the Bland-Allison Act had been largely ineffective. Finally they proposed establishing a government subtreasury warehouse system, at which farmers could deposit their crops and receive loans up to 80 percent of the current market value of these crops. They would redeem the crops and sell them when open market prices had risen to acceptable levels.

The impact of the Populist crusade was felt by the two major parties as soon as the 1892 election results were in. After only six months of life the new third party had carried four states with twenty-two electoral votes. It had received over a million popular votes and elected a number of congressmen and senators.

Failure of the Movement Despite this dramatic success, just four years later the Populists aligned with the Democrats to support William Jennings Bryan for President, only to lose badly at the hands of Republican William McKinley. By 1900, although they ran a presidential candidate, they were no longer a major political force. A key factor affecting the Populist decline was the spread of the economic depression. This depression that had first hit farmers in the late 1880s soon affected other groups in the economy. Business entered a slump, and millions of workers were laid off. By 1894, at the height of the depression, probably one out of every five workers was unemployed. Four out of five were living at a subsistence level.

Strangely, the decline that had earlier spurred the nation's farmers to take active steps for their own relief had no such effect on the rest of the country's workers. They failed to join the Populist movement. Several factors help to explain this. For one, the Populists never succeeded in breaking down the traditional political loyalties of most Americans since party loyalty was extremely important to voters at this time. Even under the impact of economic depression, people remained with their parties.

It was also true that the depression occurred during a Democratic administration—Cleveland's second term. This resulted in political gains for the major opposition party even more impressive than those made by the Populists. In fact, Republicans almost doubled their number of House members in 1894—moving from 127 to 244—while the Democrats lost 113 seats. This was the most rapid major reversal of national political strength in American history, marking the first step in ending the close balance between the parties that had existed during the 1870s and 1880s.

Besides the depression working against them, there were other problems that the Populists could not overcome. The South presented the Populists with a unique set of problems that impeded their growth. There the new party attempted, for the first time since Reconstruction days, to create a biracial political coalition of black and white farmers against the business interests that still dominated most Southern state governments. For a time they made striking gains. Georgia Populist leader Tom Watson told farm audiences from both races: "You are made to hate each other, because upon that hatred is rested the keystone of the arch of financial despotism which enslaves you both." But the political opponents of Southern Populism played upon such deeply felt racial fears and hostilities so effectively that, by the end of the decade, the new party had lost almost all its influence in the South. In that region, in fact, Populism had the ironic effect by 1900 of raising the race issue to an intensity and importance that it has maintained throughout most of the twentieth century.

Populist strength was sapped, especially in the industrial states, by internal tensions among its diverse sources of support. Such tensions between utopians and pragmatists often characterize reform movements. The Populists' agrarian leaders tended to be the movement's practical figures. Their overriding concern was for specific, immediate, and achievable goals such as free coinage of silver, the subtreasury plan, and other measures that would improve the economic bargaining position of most American farmers. On the other hand, many middle-class and working-class reformers joined the Populist party in order to use it as a vehicle to overhaul American economic institutions. It was not surprising, therefore, that the latter groups, along with some of the more radical farm leaders, opposed the party's decision to support Bryan against Republican William McKinley in 1896 rather than run its own uncompromising candidate.

Bryan's Defeat All of these factors and others contributed to William McKinley's smashing defeat of Bryan in 1896. McKinley had the almost united financial support of the business community in the election. It was driven into McKinley's camp by its unbounded fears of Bryan's and Populist reform. The careful organization of McKinley's campaign by his astute manager Mark Hanna also contributed to the Republican victory.

Perhaps the most striking feature of the 1896 election, however, was the Republicans' ability to put together a national majority that cut across class lines. McKinley won the votes not only of industrialists and the middle class but also of a majority of urban workers. Bryan failed to capture the cities and the votes of most industrial laborers, despite prolabor planks in the Democratic platform. Many urban workers clearly felt that their economic interests were better protected by a probusiness Republican President than by a Democratic candidate who spoke (in the rich twang of Midwestern rural America no less) mainly about the problems of farmers.

But if Bryan failed in 1896 to create that farmer–laborer–small-businessman coalition that he believed could win national power and make needed political and economic reforms, he did lay the groundwork for such reformers, not only within the Democratic party but among Republicans as well. In the process of laying the groundwork for reform, Bryan set a precedent for active presidential campaigning that almost all subsequent major party candidates followed in the twentieth century. Within a decade Theodore Roosevelt, McKinley's Republican successor as President, would use a similar energetic personal style of campaigning to drum up public support for reform measures. In the end, therefore, the struggle for change in American society gathered momentum during the late 1890s despite Bryan's defeat, despite the disappearance of Populism, and even despite the country's return to economic prosperity.

This 1896 caricature of William Jennings Bryan denounces him for having deserted the Democratic party in 1892 to support the Populist candidate, James B. Weaver, and then returning four years later in search of the Democratic presidential nomination.

1. Was it accurate to say that "Garfield dead proved more valuable to reformers than Garfield alive"? Why or why not?
2. Why do historians refer to politicians of this era as preindustrial? Why were successful Democrats likely to come from big cities? Why was Union Army experience not an asset for a Democrat seeking national office?
3. How might the importance of swing voters in this era be explained? Why was voter turnout so high at this time?
4. Is it accurate to say that the Republican party had become the party of big business by this time?
5. For what reason were recent immigrants more likely to oppose civil-service reform than were native-born Americans? Why were Catholics more likely to be Democrats than Republicans?
6. What did reformers hope would result from civil-service reform? What steps did the Pendleton Act take to bring it about? Why was it inadequate?
7. For what reasons did farmers favor and bankers oppose an increase in the amount of money in circulation? What evidence is there to show that the government carried out the bankers' wishes?
8. What steps did the government take to regulate industry? Why are these measures regarded as "token" reform?
9. Why was the Populist party founded? How did internal dissension work against its success? Why didn't urban workers support William Jennings Bryan for President?

Beyond the Text

1. Because Garfield lingered for seventy-nine days, questions arose as to his ability to perform his duties of office. Who determines if the President is unable to perform his duty? If the Vice President takes over how can a President, once recovered, regain his powers?
2. Historians have rated American Presidents according to these categories: Great, Near Great, Average, Below Average, and Failure. Evaluate the Presidents elected between 1876 and 1900. Consult *Life Magazine* (November 1, 1948) and Thomas A. Bailey's *Presidential Greatness* in preparing an answer.
3. Ethnic and religious affiliations determined voting behavior in the 1870s and 1880s. Are they still important in present-day presidential elections?

Bibliography

Nonfiction

Faulkner, Harold U., *Politics, Reform & Expansion, 1890–1900.**
Garraty, John A., *The New Commonwealth: 1877–1890.*
Hicks, John D., *The Populist Revolt.**
Kirkland, Edward C., *Industry Comes of Age.**
Kleppner, P., *The Cross of Culture.*
Marcus, Robert D., *Grand Old Party: Political Structure in the Gilded Age.**
Morgan, H. Wayne, *From Hayes to McKinley.*
———, ed., *The Gilded Age.**
Rothman, David J., *Politics of Power: The United States Senate, 1869–1901.**
Sproat, John G., *"The Best Men": Liberal Reformers in the Gilded Age.**
Wiebe, Robert H., *The Search for Order: 1877–1920.**
Woodward, C. Vann, *The Origins of the New South: 1877–1913.**

Fiction

Adams, Henry, *Democracy.**
Dowdey, Clifford, *Sing for a Penny.*
Ford, Paul L., *The Honorable Peter Stirling.*

*a paperback book

UNIT SIX

PROGRESSIVE

The new century brought to Americans confidence in their own ability to control the nation's destiny. It also brought concern for the unresolved problems of industrial growth, urban squalor, and immigrant poverty. The business depression of the 1890s had ended by 1898, returning the country's middle and upper classes to full prosperity. A global empire had been won almost without cost or exertion. Reformers across the land increased their efforts in the early 1900s while, in the White House itself, a young new President, Theodore Roosevelt, pushed political, economic, and social reforms. Truly there seemed cause for such confidence.

The chapters that follow describe the three decades of confidence, concern, and change within American society from 1900 to the New Era of the twenties. The first of these chapters on the Triangle Fire dramatizes the lives of southern and eastern European immigrant workers in New York City garment factories. Underpaid and impoverished, they struggled to unionize the clothing industry. Only when a flash fire killed scores of young female workers

AMERICA

at the Triangle Company did their appeal for better working conditions receive a hearing.

Chapter 28 then opens with a discussion of the urban world within which most of these recent immigrants lived. The chapter explores the varieties of industrial reform efforts. Since the political life of progressive America (1900–17) often concerned the struggle for change, Chapter 28 also examines the connections between reform activities and partisan politics.

Popular confidence rose during these decades partly because of the ease with which the United States assumed a leading role in world affairs. Chapter 29 portrays one of the unhappier consequences of that new role—the unsuccessful revolt by Filipino nationalists against American takeover of their islands. The Philippine Revolt serves as the context for a general discussion in Chapter 30 of American foreign policy. The chapter traces developments from the country's brief involvement in the Spanish-American War to its costlier participation in the First World War. The connections between domestic concerns in progressive America and the nation's actions as a major global power emerge clearly.

Rounding out the unit are two chapters on the evolution of the United States as a technological society during the first third of the twentieth century. One of the most widely publicized instances of American technological superiority was Charles Lindbergh's pioneering flight across the Atlantic in 1927. His feat captured the imagination of a machine-oriented world. Lindbergh's story unfolds in Chapter 31.

In the accompanying chapter the achievements, attitudes, and patterns of the optimistic, mechanically advanced America that produced Lindbergh's flight are examined. From the vantage point of the 1970s, the United States of the progressive era may seem, whatever its problems, a less complicated and perhaps even happier society. Certainly this country's leaders—even most of its critics—looked to the future with a measure of confidence that withstood involvement in a world war and collapsed only during the 1930s under the onslaught of the Great Depression.

CHAPTER

27

THE TRIANGLE FIRE

In September 1909, 200 Jewish and Italian immigrant workers at New York City's Triangle Shirtwaist Company walked off their jobs. The previous year, Triangle's owners had organized an Employees Benevolent Association, a so-called company union, designed to head off unions organized by the workers themselves. But the tactic had not worked. Protesting miserable working conditions and poor pay, the workers at Triangle—most of them young women—sought to gain recognition of their union by their employers. They were led by officials from the recently organized International Ladies' Garment Workers' Union (ILGWU). They had also received the support of the Women's Trade Union League (WTUL).

The Triangle strikers and workers in other shirtwaist shops in the city had a number of complaints. They were forced to work in crowded, unclean factories. Fire hazards and unsanitary conditions presented a serious threat to their health. Windows and doors in the shops were often nailed shut. Rarely did the sun penetrate the factory lofts, which workers referred to as sweatshops.

Long hours and low wages added to the workers' discontent. Most employees in New York's garment factories worked a fifty-six-hour, six-day week. When a factory owner had a rush order, he could force employees to work overtime at night or on Sunday without pay. Wages in the shirtwaist industry were as low as $6 a week. Employers often

The Triangle Shirtwaist Company occupied the top three floors of the ten-story Asch Building in Lower Manhattan. A fire raged on those floors on March 25, 1911, that was ultimately to affect the working conditions of a large segment of American laborers.

deducted penalties from the workers' pay for mistakes made in sewing clothes. They charged the workers fees for "renting" the machines and using electricity. In addition, employees were subjected to a series of petty fines for talking, smoking, and singing on the job.

It was against such conditions, in the face of active opposition by the police who were openly sympathetic to the factory owners, that workers finally took a stand.

The strike dragged on into winter. Workers at nonstriking shirtwaist companies grew angrier as they watched police and hired thugs abuse the striking employees. On the evening of November 22 the city's shirtwaist workers held a mass meeting at Cooper Union to discuss the situation. Among the reformers and union leaders asked to speak were Samuel Gompers, president of the American Federation of Labor (AFL); Abraham Cahan, editor of the *Jewish Daily Forward;* and Mary Dreier, president of the Women's Trade Union League. Gompers, a moderate in labor disputes, surprised the audience by stating that "there comes a time when not to strike is but to rivet the chains of slavery upon our wrists."

Within a few days between 10,000 and 20,000 workers, mainly young women, had walked off their jobs. The strike affected over 500 shirtwaist and dressmaking companies, including all the smaller shops and most of the big companies in the city. "The Uprising of the Twenty Thousand," as the ILGWU called the walkout, was the first industry-wide strike of immigrant workers in New York City. It was also the largest strike by women ever held in the United States to that time.

The shirtwaist[1] industry was a relatively recent one. The 1900 federal census described it as a "branch of the garment industry that has developed during the last decade." Before 1900 many of the garments produced in New York City and elsewhere came from workshops in ghetto slum apartments. Families were paid according to the number of garments produced. This piecework system proved inefficient. Clothing production gradually shifted to new loft buildings constructed especially for the trade.

By 1910 New York had become the national center for the garment industry. The city's 600 shirtwaist and dress factories employed over 30,000 workers. They sold more than $50 million worth of clothing annually. In the new shops skilled machine operators, usually men, supervised crews of young women who performed simple, unskilled tasks in preparing shirtwaists and dresses. At large factories such as

[1] The shirtwaist was a tailored blouse for women that was styled somewhat like a man's shirt. It was usually made of sheer cotton to give it a "feminine" look.

Triangle the machine operators, called contractors, were paid by the owners not only for their own work but for the labor of their crews as well. The contractors, in turn, paid weekly salaries to their female assistants. This system was often abused by dishonest contractors, who cheated young women workers out of their proper wages.

Four out of every five workers in the garment trades were women. In the Uprising of the Twenty Thousand 75 percent of the strikers were young women between the ages of sixteen and twenty-five. Almost all had been born abroad or to recently arrived immigrant families. Most of the workers were either Jewish or Italian. Most of the factory owners were Jews.

The 1909 garment trade's strike marked the first time that many of these immigrant workers managed to set aside their mutual fears and suspicions to work for common economic interests. The strike brought Jewish and Italian women together on the picket line and in the union. Thus it set a pattern for future cooperation in the labor movement among the city's ethnic communities. Jewish union organ-

Sweatshops like the one shown were common in the garment industry. Unskilled women laborers usually worked under skilled male machine operators in crowded, poorly ventilated, and unsafe shops.

izers learned a smattering of Italian, while Italian leaders acquired enough Yiddish to make themselves understood. Political and community leaders from each ethnic group also worked together on behalf of the strikers. Meyer London, a socialist lawyer who later became the country's first Jewish congressman, cooperated with Fiorello LaGuardia, a young state legislator who later became the country's first Italian congressman. LaGuardia, the son of a Jewish mother and an Italian father, symbolized the alliance then being forged by the two groups.

Several hundred black workers who were frequently hired as scabs in the garment factories joined the Uprising of the Twenty Thousand. One black shirtwaist striker—a "real born American," as she described herself—kept a diary of the events. In it she recorded her shop's reaction to the November 22 call for a general strike:

> It's a good thing, this strike is. It makes you feel like a real grown-up person. I simply can't get over the way little Ray Goldousky jumped on a chair and suddenly, without a minute's notice, stopped the electricity [in the shop]. Why, we were simply stunned. Before you could say Jack Robinson, we all rose, slipped on our duds, and marched down the stairs, shouting, yelling, and giggling about our walkout, as they called it.

Similar incidents in New York's garment factories shocked the industry's manufacturers into taking action against the strikers. Several weeks before the general walkout, the Triangle Company's owners, Blanck and Harris, proposed to other employers that an employers' mutual protective association be founded to counter efforts by workers to organize unions. Not until their own shops began striking, however, did other manufacturers agree to the idea. Then they joined together to form the Associated Waist and Dress Manufacturers. It directed anti-strike activities. These activities ranged from encouraging police brutality against strikers to organizing company unions among the minority of workers who did not support the strike.

Employers also tried using "carrot-and-stick" tactics. They offered incentives to those who remained on the job and hired hoodlums to beat up workers on the picket line. The anonymous shirtwaist striker noted in her diary that the Triangle Company promised nonstrikers "from fifteen to twenty dollars weekly, free lunch, and dancing during the noon hour."

These tactics, however, failed to break the morale and unity of the shirtwaist strikers. The Uprising of the Twenty Thousand continued throughout the bitterly cold winter of 1909–10. Reformers, labor unions, and other sympathizers contributed over $60,000 to aid the striking workers. But the strike fund supplied only a fraction of the money that the workers and their families needed for food, clothing, rent, medical care, and other expenses. "As the days go by," one striker wrote in her diary on December 1, "the girls suffer more and more. During the tedious picket duty they get frozen, catch colds, go without food until they're nothing but shadows of their former selves–it's real disheartening." On December 27, she noted proudly that "girls with sore throats and girls with broken noses, girls with wet, torn shoes and girls without hats or coats, shivering from cold and faint with hunger [all voted] to stay on strike."

The Triangle strike was an important event not only for women garment workers but also for women's suffrage reformers, ghetto community leaders, labor officials, and socialist politicians. All these groups donated time and money to make the strike a success.

Members of New York's economic and social elite posted bail bonds for arrested strikers. Wealthy New York socialites such as Mrs. Henry Morgenthau, Mrs. O. H. P. Belmont, Anne Morgan, and Mrs. J. B. Harriman raised funds for strike benefits and worked to secure the release of jailed employees. Mrs. Belmont even offered her Madison Avenue mansion as security for an $800 bail bond. When a judge asked sarcastically whether the mansion was adequate security, Mrs.

Strikers in the shirtwaist strike of 1909–10 sold copies of the Call, *a New York socialist daily, in order to publicize their demands and raise money for their living expenses while on strike.*

Belmont replied: "I think it is. It is valued at $400,000. There is a mortgage of $100,000 on it, which I raised to help the cause of the shirtwaist makers and the women's suffrage movement."

These "uptown" supporters were joined by several of the city's most active reform groups: The Women's Trade Union League, the National Women's Suffrage Association, the Political Equality Association, and the National Civic Federation. The WTUL raised 20 percent of the strike benefit fund and joined the picketers in support of the walkout. Early in December the WTUL, which led a march on City Hall to plead the strikers' cause, had organized many marches on behalf of women's suffrage legislation.

A host of muckraking reporters,[2] academics, social workers, and other professionals also worked on behalf of the strikers. Many of these middle- and upper-class reformers were German Jews whose ancestors had come to the United States during the mid-nineteenth century. The strike gave them an opportunity to display their solidarity with poorer Jews from the Lower East Side, most of whom had recently left Eastern Europe for the United States.

Everywhere on the Lower East Side community leaders and organizations worked in support of the strike. They included union officials from the United Hebrew Trades, Socialist party orators from both the Jewish and Italian communities, sympathetic rabbis and priests, and editors of Jewish newspapers. A number of other New York newspapers supported the striking workers, as did many of the city's residents. An open meeting held on December 5 drew over 8,000 pro-strike demonstrators. Pressure mounted on the garment trade employers to resolve the dispute.

A settlement was finally reached in February 1910. The agreement came in two stages. It represented a victory for the union, though not a total triumph. At first the shirtwaist workers rejected several compromise offers arranged by arbitrators who brought the two sides together. Then a number of smaller manufacturers began settling privately with the ILGWU. They agreed to hire only union members and not to deal with contractors who employed nonunion help. But larger manufacturers such as Triangle continued to insist on the right to maintain an open (or nonunion) shop, as opposed to a closed (or union) shop. Eventually, some of the larger firms agreed to a settlement, promising workers higher wages and better working conditions. In the agreements, however, neither the union nor the union shop was recognized.

By February 15, 1910, only 1,100 workers, from 13 shops, were

[2] Muckraking reporters were writers of the late nineteenth and early twentieth centuries who exposed corrupt conditions in business and government.

still away from their jobs. The ILGWU officially declared the strike over. Over 300 firms had accepted the union's terms completely, and 19 shops (including Triangle and other large firms) had agreed to open-shop compromises. The garment workers made several important gains in the settlements: reduction of the workweek to 52 hours, a two-hour limit on night work, wage increases of 12 to 15 percent, and a promise by employers to end the contractor system of payment.

Later that year, prominent Jewish citizens of New York City helped to arrange a second agreement between employers and workers. Louis Brandeis, a Boston lawyer, served as chief arbitrator between union and management. Brandeis skillfully played on the common Jewish background of garment employees and garment employers. Many of the employers themselves had begun as poor workers.

On Labor Day evening both sides agreed to a "Protocol of Peace," which became a milestone in American industrial relations. Its provisions included the end of the contractor system and the charges levied against workers for materials and electricity. There was also an agreement by employers to give preference to union workers in hiring. Garment employees were guaranteed a six-day, 54-hour week in all shops, an end to night work after 8:30 P.M., and limits on the amount of overtime an employer could require. The agreement also called for the creation of a board of arbitration to settle major disputes between workers and bosses. A Joint Board of Sanitary Control—representing union, management, and the public—was set up to oversee health and safety conditions in garment factories. Although the agreement eventually broke down, the Protocol represented a significant victory for the ILGWU. Its membership skyrocketed from 400 to 60,000 workers in the months following the "Uprising."

At the Triangle Company, however, the union remained unrecognized. Many strikers were not rehired, and most of the strikebreakers who had worked during the walkout were kept on the payroll. Some workers complained that the major effect of the settlement was to end the phonograph music and dancing contests that had been provided for nonstriking employees. Otherwise work returned to normal at the country's largest shirtwaist shop, at least until the afternoon of March 25, 1911.

The Triangle Shirtwaist Company occupied the top three floors of a new loft structure, the Asch Building, in lower Manhattan. The ten-story building, constructed in 1901, was located on the northwest corner of Green Street and Washington Place. It stood next to New

York University and a block east of Washington Square. Since the turn of the century, over $150 million had been spent on the construction of loft factories in lower Manhattan. The new buildings, made of brick or stone, were supposed to be fireproof, but they had wooden frame interiors that could easily catch fire. Few of the buildings had adequate fire escapes or staircases.

Using such buildings, manufacturers took advantage of cheap insurance rates, low operating costs, and a concentrated labor supply. State law required employers to allow 250 cubic feet of air per worker. But the law did not specify where the air space should be. Loft buildings, with their ten-foot-high ceilings, enabled owners to crowd hundreds of employees onto a floor and still meet the space requirements. (The extra space was above the worker's heads; it was not distributed among employees.) At Triangle about 500 people jammed the Asch Building's top three floors.

The Triangle employees never had a fire drill. Even though several small fires had occurred on the premises in 1909, no improved safety measures had been taken. There were only two narrow staircases leading down from the Triangle's three floors. All but one of the doors leading to the stairways were kept closed (often bolted) to prevent employees from loitering or stealing fabric. The single fire escape in the building went down only to the second floor, so that it was difficult to reach the street in case of emergencies. The only other means of descent were two small freight elevators, each about five feet square. Huge piles of cloth, tissue paper, rags, and cuttings covered the company's tables, shelves, and floors. The floors and machines were soaked with oil, and barrels of machine oil lined the walls. All these factors made the Triangle factory highly flammable.

As the day's work drew to a close on Saturday, March 25, 500 Triangle workers finished their chores and prepared to leave the building by the one open door on the eighth floor. A company guard stationed at the exit checked the women's handbags for cloth fragments. The time was 4:30 P.M. Saturday's weather was brisk and sunny—a perfect early spring afternoon.

Hardly had the guard rung the closing bell when a young woman employee on the eighth floor ran up to Samuel Bernstein, the company's production manager, and cried: "There is a fire, Mr. Bernstein." The manager and several other men, who had battled a small fire on the floor two weeks earlier, tried to put out the blaze with pails of water. But the flames shot up even higher. One of the men later remembered: "It was like there was kerosene in the water; it just seemed to spread it." Bernstein quickly realized that it would be impossible to stop the fast-spreading flames. He shouted to an assistant: "You can't do anything here. Try to get the girls out!" Bernstein and a few others tried to lead the stunned workers out in orderly fashion. But screams of "Fire!" soon filled the eighth floor.

Panic and confusion spread with the inferno. The 225 eighth-floor workers scurried across the smoke-filled room toward the various exits. As they ran, many called out the names of relatives—sisters and brothers, fathers and mothers—who also worked for Triangle. A young bookkeeper on the floor, Diana Lipschitz, sent an urgent message by interoffice teletype to the tenth floor: "The place is on fire. Run for your lives." The bookkeeper who received the message at first thought that Diana was joking. But the flames soon spurted through the tenth-floor windows, igniting bundles of cloth. Employees on that floor spread the alarm and hurried toward the exits. Because the Asch Building was supposedly fireproof, the blaze could not damage the walls or floors. But the flames curved in a swirling mass through the eighth-floor windows and engulfed the ninth and tenth floors within minutes.

On every floor workers pressed against one another in a desperate effort to reach the exits. The intense heat from the surrounding flames seared their bodies. Those on the eighth floor who had pushed their way down the congested stairway collapsed on lower floors, where firemen later found them.

Employees on the ninth floor, meanwhile, had not received even a teletype warning of the blaze. They learned of the danger only when the fire darted through the windows, bursting into pockets of flame. Most of the women dashed frantically toward exits. Others froze in fear and remained at their machines. When they discovered that the door next to the freight elevators was locked, the women rushed toward the other stairway. Over 150 workers fought for access to the twenty-inch passageway that led to the open stairway.

A fireman looks on helplessly as the fire in the Asch Building rages out of control just fifteen minutes after its start. Rescue efforts had to be abandoned.

On the tenth floor those who did not escape via the roof crowded into the two freight elevators. Jammed with fleeing workers, the cars began their descent to the ground floor. Then, some workers still trapped on the top floors started jumping into the elevator shafts to land on top of the descending elevators. One elevator operator, Joseph Zito, recalled that so many girls hit the top of his car that it would not work: "It was jammed by the bodies." Nineteen bodies were later found wedged into one of the elevator shafts. The other elevator broke down when its power circuit became waterlogged by the spray of the fire hoses.

By 4:45 P.M. the top three floors of the Asch Building were engulfed in flames. Escape was no longer possible.

By this time, the fire on the top floors of the Asch Building was visible in the street below. Within minutes a crowd gathered around the building to watch the blaze. One policeman watching the scene observed: "It's mighty hard work burning one of those fireproof buildings, but I guess it's lucky it's Saturday afternoon. It looks as if everyone is out of the place." Suddenly, an object that looked like a bale of dress material dropped from an eighth-floor window. A reporter from the *New York World,* who had joined the bystanders, described what followed:

> "Somebody's in there all right," exclaimed a spectator. "He's trying to save the best cloth."
>
> Another seeming bundle of cloth came hurtling through the same window, but this time a breeze tossed open the cloth, and from the crowd of 500 persons there came a cry of horror.
>
> The breeze had disclosed the form of a girl shooting down to instant death on the stone pavement beneath.
>
> Before the crowd could realize the full meaning of the horror, another girl sprang upon another window ledge. It seemed that she had broken open the window with her fists. Her hair, streaming down her back, was all ablaze, and her clothing was on fire.
>
> She stood poised for a moment with her arms extended, and then down she came. Three other girls at the same moment threw themselves from various windows, and other girls could be seen clinging to the window frames, struggling for breath and trying to decide between the death within the factory room and the death on the stone pavement and sidewalk below.

The firemen's nets caught only a few of those who jumped. More often, as Fire Captain Howard C. Ruch recalled, the bodies—which struck the ground with a force almost a thousand times their actual

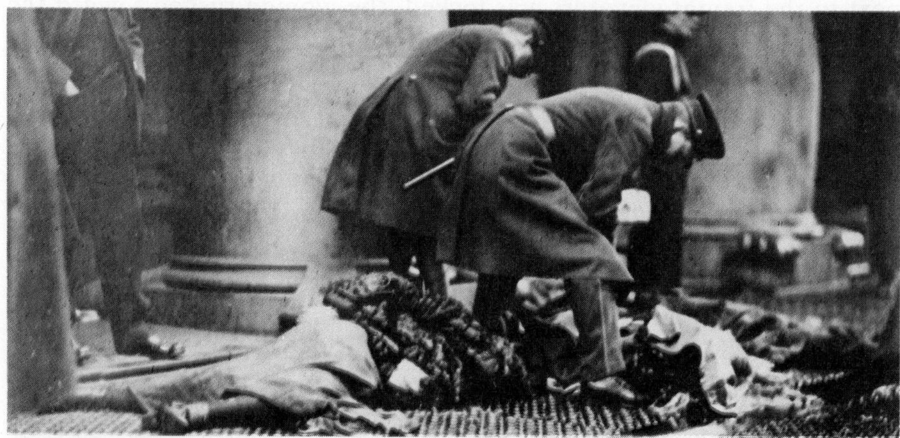

The sidewalk in front of the Triangle Company was strewn with the bodies of those who had jumped to their death at the height of the blaze. The fire department's safety nets were too weak to break the victims' fall.

weight—"didn't break through the nets; they just carried them to the sidewalk. The force was so great it took the men off their feet; they turned somersaults over onto the bodies." Sometimes, a group of girls would join hands before jumping from the ledge, soothing their fears in a joint death fall.

Fifteen minutes after the firemen arrived the fire was brought under control. In those few minutes 46 people jumped to their deaths. The charred remains of 100 workers were later recovered from inside the building. Most of those who perished were Jewish. All but 21 of the victims were women, and a dozen were so badly burned or disfigured that they were almost unrecognizable. In fact, 7 were never identified.

Hundreds of workers had managed to escape the flames. Those injured, stunned, and weeping survivors soon filled the hospitals and ghetto apartments of the Lower East Side. Police officials hurriedly tried to find coffins for the dead. On East 26th Street a huge, enclosed pier was converted into a temporary morgue. The Triangle dead were piled up on sidewalks near the Asch Building while firemen watered down the smoldering building.

Police Department "death wagons" rode throughout the evening, bringing the dead to the temporary morgue. Policemen searched through personal belongings in an effort to identify victims. Fourteen engagement rings were later found on one floor of the Triangle factory alone. These and other rings collected at the morgue testified to one particularly bitter aspect of the tragedy. Some of the victims had stuffed their skimpy pay envelopes inside their clothing. Others still had their wages clutched in their hands.

Many of the Jewish families on the Lower East Side had relatives or friends working at Triangle, and the community's grief was almost unbearable. Tens of thousands rushed to the East 26th Street pier searching for missing friends or relatives. They were joined by numerous Italian and other immigrant familes. The police finally let the frantic throng file through the pier a few dozen at a time. Inside the temporary morgue the bodies of the Triangle victims had been laid out in coffins in neat rows.

Heartbreaking scenes of recognition filled the night. A mother, discovering her daughter's body, would break down into uncontrollable wailing and have to be escorted out. A young woman, finding her sister's charred body, would simply faint. Some women completely lost control and tried to kill themselves, either by swallowing poison or by jumping off the pier. Police and onlookers stopped at least a dozen such attempts.

Thousands of mourning relatives and friends filed through the temporary morgue on the East 26th Street pier to identify the victims. Some were never identified.

In the days following the fire the Triangle victims were buried quietly by their families. Friends and relatives from the Lower East Side attended the funerals. They poured out their grief and sorrow. Reformers and community leaders arranged a series of memorial meetings to honor the victims. A fund-raising appeal conducted by the Red Cross, Jewish community groups, and the WTUL collected over $120,000 to assist needy families. Several of the victims had been the sole support of their families, in either New York or "the old country." Half a dozen families had lost two sisters (one a widow with five children); another had lost two brothers. In one Italian family a mother and two daughters were killed in the fire.

On April 5 a symbolic mass funeral was held in lower Manhattan. Over 100,000 people—mainly women who lived and worked on the Lower East Side—marched silently in the rain for five hours to honor the Triangle dead. The memorial service was the climax of a week of mourning and protest. The march had been organized by the garment unions to demonstrate labor solidarity. "Come and pay your respects to our dead," intoned the *Forward,* "every union man with his trade, with his union." Most of the marchers wore armbands that read simply: "We mourn our loss." One group of women garment workers carried a banner that said: "We demand fire protection."

In the streets of Manhattan over 400,000 spectators watched as the mourners marched toward Washington Square to the beat of muffled drums. Almost all the Triangle survivors marched. The procession was led by an empty hearse draped in black and drawn by six white horses. "The skies wept," began the *World's* story on the event.

Later that afternoon the seven unidentified victims—coffin numbers 46, 50, 61, 95, 103, 115, and 127 in the police records—were buried. Catholic, Protestant, and Jewish clerics read brief prayers before the coffins were lowered. The mourners, meanwhile, continued their march to Washington Square Park, where they were to proceed up Fifth Avenue to 34th Street. As they approached the Asch Building, the women who marched gave way completely to their emotions. As one paper reported, they uttered "one long-drawn-out, heart-piercing cry, the mingling of thousands of voices, a cry that was perhaps the most impressive expression of human grief ever heard in this city."

Who was to blame for the tragedy? This question haunted New Yorkers in the weeks that followed the Triangle disaster. "That a terrible mistake was made by somebody," *The New York Times* observed, "is easier to say now than to point out just where the blame for this destruction of human life may be placed."

The city's fire department bore a share of the responsibility, despite the bravery of those who fought the blaze. The department had failed to enforce even those few mild safety laws that were on the books. Moreover, its equipment was inadequate for fighting fires in the city's new loft buildings. The tallest fire ladders reached only the sixth floor, although half the city's factory workers worked in lofts above this floor. Some of the department's safety nets were so weak that they broke under the force of falling bodies.

The City Buildings Department too had to accept a measure of the blame. The Asch Building, like most of New York City's garment shops, lacked adequate safety features. Several months earlier, a factory inspector had warned the owners of the Asch Building of such violations as insufficient exits and locked stairway doors. But the department made no effort to ensure that these conditions were corrected. There were only 47 inspectors in Manhattan to check over 50,000 buildings. Of these buildings 13,600 had been listed as dangerous by the fire department the previous month. Inspectors managed to visit 2,000 buildings in March, but the Asch Building was not among them.

Nor were the fire insurance companies innocent of blame. Insurance brokers in New York suffered heavy losses from the numerous fires that occurred in the city's loft buildings. Yet the insurance industry failed to insist on safety standards that might have reduced fire hazards. Rather, they preferred to pay off after a fire and then raise a company's premium costs. Higher policy rates also meant higher commissions for insurance brokers. During the 1890s a group of insurance companies attempted to offer cheaper rates to manufacturers who installed sprinkler systems in their factories. These companies were soon driven out of business by the city's powerful insurance industry. It was simply easier and more profitable to leave the "fireproof" firetraps alone and to settle afterward.

At the time of the fire the Triangle Shirtwaist Company carried insurance policies totaling $199,750. The Triangle owners eventually collected full repayment for their losses in equipment and property damage. They were also given an extra indemnity of $64,925, or $445 for each worker killed. The company's owners defended themselves against charges of responsibility for the fire by pointing out that building inspectors had never entered a complaint against the firm and that an employee carelessly dropping a cigarette might well have started the fire.

On April 11, a week after the public funeral for the Triangle victims, Isaac Harris and Max Blanck were indicted by a grand jury and charged with manslaughter. Their trial began in New York eight months later on December 4. Crowds of women gathered outside the courtroom each day screaming "Murderers! Murderers!" A heavy police guard was called in to protect the defendants. Harris and Blanck—"the shirtwaist kings"—engaged as their defense counsel a well-known Jewish lawyer, Max D. Steuer.

In order to simplify the case, the state decided to try the pair only for responsibility in the death of a single worker, Margaret Schwartz, who died in the fire because of the locked ninth-floor door. Most testimony centered on three questions. (1) Was the ninth-floor door kept locked regularly? (2) Was it locked at the time of the fire? (3) Most importantly, did Blanck and Harris know it was locked?

The prosecutor called a number of Triangle employees. They testified that the ninth-floor door had been locked regularly and was locked when the fire began. Defense attorney Steuer then called other Triangle workers and supervisors. They testified not only that a key was always kept in the door but that the door was always left open. Steuer tried to persuade the jurors that prosecution witnesses had been coached before coming to the witness stand. But the state offered convincing rebuttal evidence that defense witnesses had lied, that they actually knew the door was kept locked.

In instructing the jury members, the judge pointed out that unless they believed Blanck and Harris were aware of the locked doors "beyond a reasonable doubt," they would have to acquit the defendants. The jury took less than two hours to find the shirtwaist kings not

Not much remained of the "fireproof" Asch Building after the fire had run its course. The Triangle owners collected insurance money for losses in equipment and property damages though their company had inadequate safety features.

guilty. As one jury member later told a newsman: "I believed that the [door] was locked at the time of the fire. But I could not make myself feel certain that Harris and Blanck knew that it was locked."

One interesting sidelight to the tragedy emerged during the trial. The Triangle owners kept their exit doors locked for fear that employees would steal garments or pieces of fabric. At one point the prosecutor asked Isaac Harris: "How much in all the instances would you say was the value of all the goods that you found had been taken by these employees? You would say it was not over $25, wouldn't you?" Harris turned pale before responding: "No, it would not exceed that much."

If Harris and Blanck had been convicted, the Triangle fire might have been forgotten more easily. The public might have been satisfied that justice had been done. As it turned out, the acquittal of Blanck and Harris sparked a new effort to improve the conditions under which New York City's laborers worked. Responding to public pressure, the state legislature created the New York Factory Investigating Commission in June 1911 to study working conditions in the state.

Among the commission's most active members were two politically powerful New York City Democrats, State Assembly Majority Leader Alfred E. Smith and State Senate Majority Leader Robert F. Wagner, Sr. They helped throw the Tammany machine's full support behind the commission's many proposals for reform. Other members included Samuel Gompers of the AFL and Mary Dreier of the WTUL. Many experts on factory safety and working conditions assisted the commission. Among them were progressive reformers such as Belle and Henry Moskowitz, and young social workers such as Frances Perkins, who later became the nation's first woman Cabinet member as Secretary of Labor.

The Triangle Commission went far beyond an investigation of fire hazards alone. It studied almost every type of labor problem in New York. In 1911 the group held public hearings in the state's major manufacturing cities and heard 222 witnesses. Staff field inspectors visited 1,836 factories in 20 industries. Smith, Wagner, and their associates talked with factory workers who had lost limbs because of unsafe machinery. They examined the "doctored" records kept by many companies on employees' wages and hours. Commission inves-

By 1900 at least 1,700,000 children under sixteen were in the labor market. One result of the Triangle fire was the passage of laws limiting child labor and improving working conditions for women and children.

tigators watched hundreds of women leaving ten-hour shifts at 5 A.M. They studied the horrible conditions in the disease-ridden tenements where workers lived.

On farms in upstate New York, commission members observed migrant women working alongside their children for eighteen hours a day or more. In canneries across the state they saw children of five working full time. The conditions wore no party label; the worst offenders among New York's manufacturers included both Republicans and Democrats. In the factory of a leading upstate Democratic progressive, for example, Smith and Wagner found "the vilest and most uncivilized conditions of labor in the state."

During the four years that commission members and staff toured the state, they gathered material for thirteen volumes of reports. These were submitted to the state legislature. The reports did not gather dust. Between 1911 and 1915, Smith and Wagner introduced over sixty bills based on their investigations. Despite much conservative opposition in the legislature, the two Tammany Democrats managed to pass fifty-six of their proposals by fusing the votes of Democratic regulars and antimachine reformers. The bills they passed called for the creation of a Bureau of Fire Prevention and the enforcement of strict fire safety codes (including compulsory fire drills and the installation of sprinklers in factories). Two other major bills provided for an increase in the number of factory inspectors and a strengthening of the supervisory authority of the state's Department of Labor.

One of the most hard-fought proposals in the legislature was a bill calling for a 54-hour workweek for women and minors. When cannery owners objected to the measure, Smith replied sarcastically that they wished to revise the Bible to read "Remember the Sabbath to keep it holy—except in canneries." The bill passed. Other laws forbade night factory work for women, prohibited smoking in factories, and called for better ventilation and sanitary facilities. Child labor was outlawed in tenement manufacturing and canneries. Sunday work was forbidden ("one day's rest in seven"), and insurance (workmen's compensation) was provided for employees injured in accidents. Other laws forbade employment of children under fourteen and required improved working facilities, rest periods, and minimum wages for women and children.

In the Triangle Commission's four years of existence Smith and Wagner helped to pass the most enlightened code of industrial reform in the country. Their work served as a model for legislators in other states and foreshadowed many of the federal laws enacted under the New Deal. Out of the ashes of tragedy had come new hope for workingmen.

CHAPTER

28

New Waves of Reform

THE MISERABLE working conditions that provoked the great shirtwaist industry strike of 1909 were typical of American manufacturing in the half-century of industrial growth that followed the Civil War. Workers in manufacturing plants toiled an average of 59 hours each week. They earned less than $10 per week for their back-breaking labor.

By contrast their employers—the manufacturers, bankers, and merchants who directed the course of economic development in the United States—profited handsomely from the workers' long hours and low wage rates. Between 1860 and 1900 the country rose from fourth to first place among the world's industrial nations, producing more in 1900 than Britain, France, and Germany combined.

The rewards for business success during this period were high indeed. In 1890 an estimated 200,000 people owned 70 percent of the country's wealth. A survey taken in 1892 showed that close to 4,000 people had become millionaires since the Civil War. Almost all these individuals made their fortunes in manufacturing, railroads, trade, or finance. This great concentration of wealth in America's upper classes only added to the discontent of the nation's industrial laborers.

Union organization seemed to hold the only promise of changing the working conditions of American workers. But despite the efforts of union leaders and rank-and-file organizers throughout the period, no strong, united workingman's association emerged among the industrial labor force of the United States. Instead, in this era of economic growth industry-wide unions like the ILGWU came and went. Several unions also attempted, with varying degrees of success, to organize American workers. The ILGWU, for example, was only the latest in a line of unions attempting to organize the garment industry, the earlier ones having failed at the task.

At the turn of the century 10 million men and women, over a third of the entire labor force, worked in factories. Yet the union movement had succeeded in organizing less than 4 percent of America's industrial workers. What was this union tradition? Why had it failed to mobilize the country's underpaid, overworked, and poorly treated laboring masses?

THE RISE OF ORGANIZED LABOR

Those who led and took part in the Uprising of the Twenty Thousand inherited a tradition of industrial union activity more than a half-century old. In Jacksonian America factory workers and craftsmen attempted to form their own unions. Few of these trade organizations lasted beyond the Civil War. In the half-century after the war a number of major unions were formed. Almost all these unions employed the strike weapon, though rarely with complete success. During the 1880s, for example, over 24,000 strikes occurred in the United States, involving over 6 1/2 million workers.

During the turbulent depression years of the 1890s, 3 million people were thrown out of work, perhaps 15 to 20 percent of the country's work force. Over 7,000 strikes were called during this period. Between 1894 and 1896 numerous small armies of the unemployed marched on Washington demanding federal relief assistance.

By the early twentieth century the infant ILGWU, which was to lead the great shirtwaist strike of 1909, had counterparts in every other industry in the country. Like the garment union, most of these organizations were small and had to struggle for existence. The experience of the 1909 garment workers' strike demonstrates many of the difficulties unions encountered in organizing.

Difficulties in Union Organization For one thing, few unions were as successful as the ILGWU in persuading workers from different ethnic backgrounds to put aside their fierce hatreds and work for common goals. Indeed, the 1909–10 strike was the first time that most of New York City's Jewish and Italian workers had joined together in one union. More often, tensions among nationality groups, differences in language, and racial hostilities within the working class hampered union organization.

Employers skillfully exploited these ethnic and national hostilities to divide workers. When Jews went on strike, Italians would work, and vice versa. When both groups went on strike, blacks were called in to scab. Furthermore, the influx of southern and eastern European immigrants in the late nineteenth and early twentieth centuries kept wage rates down in most industries. More often than not, the labor supply greatly exceeded demand. Employers had little difficulty filling the unskilled and semiskilled positions at their plants.

Employers resorted to a variety of tactics to defeat the efforts of union organizers. These included the use of strikebreakers (such as the hoodlums who attacked ILGWU picketers), and the hiring of scabs (another tactic employed by Harris and Blanck). Employers also used blacklisting—the denial of work to union officials by all the firms in an industry—and lockouts of striking workers. Firms like the Triangle Company sometimes enlisted the aid of sympathetic policemen and judges who harassed strikers with arrests and court action. Another important weapon of management was the yellow-dog contract, in which new workers agreed not to join a union as a condition of their employment.

Attempts at Union Organization At the national level the union movement faced a number of difficulties in the half-century after the Civil War. Several national unions rose and fell because of unsuccessful strikes, the opposition of the middle class, and the inability of unions to hold the loyalty of most workers. The National Labor Union played a prominent role briefly during the depression of the 1870s. The Knights of Labor, under the leadership of Terence V. Powderly, became a major force in the labor movement in the following decade. These unions favored improvement of the American worker's economic state and a broad program of reform within American society.

The Knights had many self-employed or salaried middle-class Americans in its membership. During the 1880s it tried unsuccessfully to organize a series of strikes and to set up cooperative factories and stores—owned by the workers themselves—as an alternative to the privately run corporations. Leaders of the Knights were blamed for the Haymarket Affair of 1886 and were attacked as "anarchists." Actually, they had played no part in the bombing. Membership in the Knights of Labor nevertheless declined from 700,000 in 1886 to 74,000 by 1893. The union played an insignificant role in the labor movement during the 1890s, joining finally with the agrarian-led Populist party. By 1900 it had lapsed into obscurity.

The leading force within American unionization during this period was the American Federation of Labor (AFL). It was a loose confederation of independent craft unions and semi-industrial affiliates such as the ILGWU. The AFL was formed in 1881 under the leadership of Samuel Gompers. A one-time socialist, Gompers criticized earlier union organizations such as the Knights for stressing general reforms in American society.

The labor movement, Gompers believed, should concentrate exclusively on winning economic gains for the working class. It should leave the tasks of reform to others. Union leaders should devote all their time and energy to raising workers' wages, reducing hours, and improving

Samuel Gompers, shown here at a meeting to organize the 1909 garment workers' strike, founded the American Federation of Labor around such craft unions. Using both the strike and collective bargaining, he forged a powerful national labor organization.

working conditions. Gompers also believed that unions should avoid independent political action, such as the affiliation of the Knights with the Populist party in the 1890s. Instead, labor should support its political friends and oppose its enemies, regardless of party. When asked at a congressional hearing what the unions wanted, Gompers replied simply: "More!"

By the time of the New York garment industry strike the AFL, under Gompers' leadership, had become the country's dominant national labor organization. It was also the most powerful union politically and economically up to that time.

REFORMERS IN THE LATE NINETEENTH CENTURY

Union leaders were not the only people concerned about the conditions of American workers. Socialists, middle- and upper-class reformers, and city politicians all worked to improve conditions for American laborers. Their suggested solutions to the problems posed by industrial society, though, were as different as the backgrounds out of which these reformers emerged.

The Socialist Vision In the late nineteenth century a group of socialist writers became the first generation of critics to tackle the dilemmas of urban-industrial America. They were grouped as socialists because they held in common the belief that ownership and control of industry, land, and so forth should be shared by the community as a whole. These writers put forth a series of proposals for a complete overhaul of American institutions. In *Progress and Poverty* (1877–79) Henry George attacked the inequities of the American economic system. Edward Bellamy's *Looking Backward* (1888) presents a vision of a socialist Utopia. His book became a best-seller in the 1880s and 1890s. Henry Demarest Lloyd's *Wealth Against Commonwealth* (1894) attacked the corrupt business practices of the Standard Oil Company. Other influential critics of American industrial life included economist Richard Ely, "social gospel" minister Washington Gladden, and utopian writers Ignatius Donnelly and William Dean Howells.

Uppermost in the minds of these late nineteenth-century reformers was the notion that, if conditions in the nation's slums, factories, and farms were not improved quickly and drastically, the United States would explode into class warfare. Surely, they reasoned, abused workers would not tolerate such conditions indefinitely. They believed that a social catastrophe was close at hand. It could be prevented only by an immediate and total alteration in the nation's social and economic structure.

They offered no single remedy. Some, like Lloyd, Bellamy, and Howells, believed in a socialist commonwealth. They argued, though, over the details of Utopia and how to achieve it. Others, like George and Ely, felt that a single tax on unearned income from land would somehow provide enough money to solve the nation's problems. All these reformers were united in their belief that a single problem underlay all the social ills of the United States. Find and correct this overriding problem–"the root of our social difficulty" as George put it–and Americans could begin moving toward an era of moral and social perfection.

In this utopian vision of the United States these late nineteenth-century reformers resembled their pre-Civil War, preindustrial counterparts. Garrison, Emerson, and Fuller had also walked a thin line between social criticism and religious prophecy. However "practical" their remedies, therefore, people like George and Bellamy were basically seers. They preached a gospel of total reform, without which total catastrophe would result.

The Settlement House Movement The struggle to improve the lives of the immigrant poor, both in the factories and in the ghettos, was aided by a number of middle-class reformers and socially conscious members of the American upper class. Women like Mrs. Belmont and other affluent leaders of the Women's Trade Union League who were active in the shirtwaist strike are representative of this trend.

During the 1880s and 1890s many college-educated women became concerned especially with the slum conditions under which immigrant workers lived. They helped to organize settlement houses in the ghettos of east coast and Middle Western cities. There, foreign-born workers received food and shelter, and learned how to speak English. They were given help in understanding and exercising their rights as Americans. In 1889 Lillian Wald founded the Henry Street Settlement in New York City. Jane Addams and Ellen Gates Starr founded Chicago's Hull-House that same year.

By 1910 over 400 settlement houses had been established in the country's slum districts. On New York's Lower East Side settlement workers assisted the victims of the Triangle fire and their families. In the previous year they had provided money and support for the striking garment workers. As valuable instruments for Americanizing immigrant communities, the settlement houses helped immigrants to improve their working and living conditions at a time when most middle-class Americans remained indifferent or even hostile toward the foreign-born poor.

Municipal Reorganization For some reformers, the settlement house movement seemed an inadequate response to the many problems of America's enlarged industrial cities. It was somewhat like putting bandages over a festering infection without treating the infection itself first. For such reformers the roots of the infection seemed clear: the inefficiency and corruption of urban political machines in alliance with equally corrupt business interests. Democratic politicians such as Al Smith and Robert Wagner, Sr., viewed New York's Tammany machine as the logical friend of the immigrants. But reformers such as Henry George and, later, Fiorello LaGuardia believed that the machines merely exploited the immigrants, using their trust and votes to line the pockets of ward heelers, city officials, and local businessmen.

Reform groups such as the National Civic Association (which later helped to organize the Triangle Fire Commission investigation) sparked a concern among voters for driving the political machines from office. These groups sought to run urban government more efficiently and less corruptly than the machines.

Municipal reformers then, as today, came largely from middle-class or upper-class backgrounds. They included businessmen, lawyers, ministers, and journalists—professionals concerned with the concentration of power in the hands of working-class-supported political machines and giant corporations. Many were native-born Protestants. Most had little direct contact with foreign-born, largely Catholic and Jewish immigrants until they began a career of reform.

Quite often, these basic cultural differences among immigrants and reformers made it difficult, it not impossible, for the two groups to join successfully. Their interests were also often in direct conflict. New immigrants depended on the very political favors—jobs and other assistance from local political bosses—that the reformers wanted to eliminate. Moreover, the immigrant culture was more tolerant of gambling and drinking than the reformer's tradition of stern Protestant moralism. These differences over values certainly diluted the effect of municipal reformers in curing urban ills.

A NEW GENERATION OF REFORMERS

Many of those who had opposed unions and other reform movements prior to the 1890s gradually became convinced of the need for basic reforms in American society. They had been deeply affected by the tumultuous events of the '90s: the depression, the social unrest on farms and in factories, the deepening class conflict.

By the turn of the century many middle-class Americans saw the dangers. Conservative journalists such as William Allen White, "big business" lawyers such as Clarence Darrow and

Jane Addams

''Even as a little child, she seemed inclined toward special work of some sort. In fact, she was anxious for a career.'' This is how, with some dismay, Mrs. John H. Addams described her stepdaughter Jane. After all, a girl born to a prosperous family in Cedarville, Illinois, in 1860 was not supposed to have such ambitions. She was expected to attend a ladies' seminary, travel in Europe in search of culture, and then return home to marry.

Jane fulfilled the first two expectations. But instead of marrying, she worried over what that ''special work'' could be. She knew that it was not missionary work or teaching. For eight years she traveled, read, and attended the social functions that suited Mrs. Addams' plans for her. It was a period of frustration, nervousness, and unhappiness. ''I am filled with shame that with all my apparent leisure, I do nothing at all,'' she wrote.

At long last, during a European trip, an idea began to take shape in her mind. She told her friend and traveling companion, Ellen Gates Starr, about it. Jane wanted to move into a large house in a poor neighborhood. There she and other educated young people who wanted to do something important could live among the poor. They could share the problems of poverty and help to improve the neighborhood. In no way would this be an attempt to ''uplift the masses.'' Instead it would be a learning experience for all concerned.

Jane Addams and Ellen Starr soon returned to the United States to put the plan into effect. They located a house, formerly owned by a man named Hull, in a poor area in Chicago. They unpacked their things, invited the neighbors to stop in, and waited.

Before long two things happened. First, neighbors, most of them immigrants, started coming—to attend lectures and form clubs. Second, a number of talented and energetic men and women moved into Hull-House. They saw the social settlement as a place where they could enjoy stimulating intellectual company and at the same time do something about growing urban problems.

Chicago Historical Society

Soon Hull-House was truly the neighborhood center. Here working mothers brought their children for day care. Here newly formed labor unions met. People of all ages came to attend classes in music, art, homemaking, and handicrafts. Residents and neighbors joined in community betterment projects.

Under Jane Addams' leadership Hull-House took on another, more far-reaching task. It became a clearing house for several reform movements. The residents researched urban problems and then tried to convince those in power to do something about them. They pressured legislators to act on such matters as child labor, factory inspection, recognition of labor unions, protection of immigrants, and industrial safety.

By the time of Jane Addams' death in 1935, Hull-House stood as a monument to her philosophy: ''Without the advance and improvement of the whole, no man can hope for any lasting improvement in his own moral or material condition.''

George Norris, and middle-of-the-road Republicans such as Theodore Roosevelt had all concluded that the future political and social health of the American republic depended on a variety of reforms. They sought improvements in the conditions under which the urban poor lived. They also wanted to bring giant trusts under governmental supervision in the public interest. These various reform interests came together in a movement that historians have labeled "progressivism."

The Progressive Movement However different progressive reformers were in their social and economic concerns, most shared certain fundamental beliefs. For one thing, unlike the Bellamys and Georges of the previous generation, they did not believe in imminent social catastrophe. Rather, they were highly nationalistic and optimistic about the future of the United States. Herbert Croly, one of their most influential writers, argued that this "promise of American life" consisted of "an improving popular economic condition, guaranteed by democratic political institutions, and resulting in moral and social [improvement]."

Nationalism and reform, then, went hand in hand. Both impulses were based on an idealistic faith in American potential. Most progressives believed that a decent society for all Americans could be created through gradual reform, rather than through revolutionary changes. The reformers of the previous generation had not been so confident.

Progressive reformers harnessed their optimism about domestic affairs to a firm belief in the value of Christian morality. It was within this "ethical climate" that much reform legislation of the era took shape. To Frances Perkins the new climate was dominated by "the idea that poverty is preventable, that poverty is destructive, wasteful, demoralizing, and that poverty in the midst of potential plenty is morally unacceptable in a Christian and democratic society." An end to poverty, injustice, and unregulated economic power, the preservation of the nation's natural resources, a return to honest government—all this, the progressives believed, would follow from applying Christian ethics to reshaping the social environment.

Another belief shared by progressive thinkers was a confidence in the use of "experts" to manage public affairs. Professional advisers such as those who had assisted the Triangle Commission would provide rational, "scientific" measurement of the country's problems; they would also suggest efficient means for tackling social ills.

Progressive reformers called for the establishment of legislative investigating bodies at all levels of government, and the use of expert advisers—brain trusts—to help city and state governments develop programs of reform. They wanted to create regulatory agencies to supervise business practices. Progressives also favored the establishment of nonpartisan commissions or councils to eliminate machine corruption in city government. The independent commission form of city government originated in Galveston, Texas, in 1900. By 1914 it had spread to over 400 American cities, although not to most larger ones.

Finally, most reformers of the era believed strongly in the value of publicizing social problems as a first step toward solving them. As early as 1898 Congress had established a commission to study the giant business trusts. The commission eventually published nineteen volumes on American social and economic problems. In addition, many states set up investigatory groups to study business corruption. This technique of exposure was carried out most systematically under the reform governorship of Robert M. LaFollette in Wisconsin from 1901 to 1906. LaFollette's efforts to uncover business abuses and press for needed social legislation set a pattern for reform administrations in other states.

Newspapers and magazines provided a forum for investigations of social problems by muckraking journalists. Ida Tarbell wrote an explosive expose of the Standard Oil Company. Lincoln Steffens studied corrupt city political machines. David Graham Phillips examined Senate corruption. Magazines such as *McClure's* and *Harper's Weekly* increased their circulation to the hundreds of thousands by becoming champions of reform.

New Politics for the Cities Nowhere was the belief in rational government stronger than at the local level. Here progressives were as appalled by corrupt city politics as they were by dirty tenements and unsafe factories. All three conditions came under the attack of municipal reformers. Beginning in the 1890s, reform groups won control of a number of cities and began dealing with slum and factory conditions. In New York City, for example, after driving Tammany Hall from power in 1901, Mayor Seth Low worked closely with reformers to improve parks and playgrounds, tighten housing laws, and strengthen the city's health services to the poor. But, despite his efforts, much remained to be done, as conditions in the city at the time of the Triangle fire demonstrated.

In other cities too the concern for social reform proved strong. During the 1890s and 1900s three remarkable Middle Western businessmen—all self-made millionaires—became pioneers in urban reform. Their cities served as models for social reformers throughout the country.

Hazen Pingree, mayor of Detroit, Michigan, from 1889 to 1896 and then governor of the state, fought corruption by politicians and local industrial groups, especially street railways and gas companies. Pingree authorized the construction of a city-owned electric lighting plant and urged public ownership of other such utilities. In Toledo, Ohio, Samuel M. "Golden Rule" Jones, mayor of the city from 1897 to 1904, established free kindergarten day-care facilities for working mothers, pressed for a minimum hourly wage and other social legislation, and supported public ownership of utilities.

Thomas Johnson, Cleveland's mayor from 1901 to 1909, became a social reformer after reading Henry George's *Progress and Poverty*. He too fought the private utility interests and urged public ownership. Johnson sponsored a number of social welfare projects, including the

Ida M. Tarbell's stunning exposés revealed the way giant corporations gained advantage over competitors by securing special rates—rebates—from railroads. Her landmark study of the oil industry appeared in McClure's *magazine, which established it as the leading muckraking periodical.*

Lincoln Steffens, one of the leading reformer journalists, wrote numerous articles exposing political corruption in city government. His autobiography gives an accurate account of the development of the muckraking movement.

Upton Sinclair is best remembered for his novel, The Jungle, *that told of the brutal and unsanitary conditions in Chicago's stockyards. The public revulsion it aroused resulted in the passage of the Meat Inspection Act of 1906.*

Tom Johnson, Cleveland's reform mayor, instituted reforms, including city planning, that made that city one of America's best-governed. He had his own political machine, observing, "It all depends on whether a boss is a good one or a bad one."

construction of municipal bathhouses (a crucial urban health measure, since many tenement houses did not have adequate bathroom facilities) and careful inspection of consumer meat and dairy products.

All three Middle Western mayors ran nonpartisan governments, dominated by professional administrators and reformers who took over the jobs that had formerly been filled by appointees. Unfortunately, driving political machines from office did not always produce improvements in ghetto or factory conditions. Many municipal reformers were less interested in improving slum conditions than in eliminating the power and corruption of immigrant-supported political machines. In Pittsburgh, for example, two-thirds of those involved in trying to revise the city's charter came from upper-class backgrounds and were closely tied to the city's leading banks and industries.

Changes at the State Level Many of the major reforms of this period were achieved at the state level. In a number of states progressive reformers were elected governors. Among them were Robert LaFollette in Wisconsin, Charles Evans Hughes in New York, Hoke Smith in Georgia, Hiram Johnson in California, and the transplanted Southern-born president of Princeton University, Woodrow Wilson, in New Jersey. Each state had its special problems, each its particular group of "entrenched interests." In Massachusetts, the railroads and insurance companies dominated; in California it was the powerful and corrupt labor unions.

Almost all reform governors fought for stricter regulation of railroads, public utilities, and industries within their states. They tried to force corporations to pay a fair share of taxes and conserve natural resources like forests and mines, which provided raw materials for industry. Finally, they fought to make state government more democratic through such reforms as the initiative, the referendum, and the recall.[1]

During the first two decades of the century many states enacted broad programs of social legislation dealing with the wages and hours of factory workers, the employment of women and children, and safety conditions in tenements and factories. Maryland adopted the first state workmen's compensation law in 1902. A year later Oregon passed a law restricting women's industrial work to ten hours per day. Illinois adopted the first measure providing public assistance to mothers with dependent children in 1911. And Massachusetts passed the first minimum wage law (applying to women and children) in 1912. All these measures were landmarks in the struggle of progressive reformers to achieve economic and social justice for all Americans.

Amending the Constitution Suffrage—the right to vote—had been a central concern of the women's rights movement for several decades. In

[1] The initiative is a device by which a small number of citizens, sometimes as little as 5 percent, can bypass the legislature and vote upon measures at general elections. The referendum forces legislatures to return proposed laws to the electorate, who then approve or reject the proposals. The recall, perhaps the most controversial device, allows the electorate to remove an elected official from office. It requires a special election, called after a certain number of voters have signed a petition asking for the official's removal.

1910 the American labor force employed over 8 million women, including a number of college-educated women who had entered the professions. During this period 36 percent of all professional jobs were held by women. Yet, prior to World War I only eleven states had granted women the right to vote.

Between 1914 and 1919 women's rights advocates gave the suffrage issue national importance by conducting a massive campaign of petitions, lobbying, picketing, and nonviolent demonstrations. The campaign was sponsored by the National American Women Suffrage Association, led by Carrie Chapman Catt and Anna Howard Shaw. The picketing and demonstrations that had brought public sympathy for the demands of shirtwaist employees during the Triangle strike worked with similar effect for the Suffragists. The involvement of women in war work during World War I brought the movement increased public support. In June 1919 Congress responded by passing the Nineteenth Amendment, giving women the right to vote. The amendment received final state ratification in August 1920. Later that year, for the first time, American women in every state voted in a presidential election.

Another progressive interest, the temperance movement, had been a concern of reformers since before the Civil War. Municipal reformers joined the anti-alcohol drive for two major reasons. First, there was much political corruption associated with urban liquor dealers. Secondly, reformers felt that alcoholism was destroying the moral fiber and social well-being of many Americans.

The prohibitionists made their first gains at the local and state levels. A number of Southern and Western states voted themselves "dry." During World War I many of the same groups that later pushed the women's rights amendment through Congress secured passage of the Eight-

Women concentrated on making political gains in the early twentieth century. An intense campaign, and their increasing importance in the labor market, finally gained them full suffrage on a nationwide basis by constitutional amendment—the Nineteenth.

 eenth Amendment, which forbade the sale and distribution of alcoholic beverages. Ratified by the states in January 1919, the amendment took effect the next year. It was considered the most impressive yet the most debatable triumph of progressive moralism.

In 1913 progressive reformers won two other important victories. The Sixteenth Amendment instituted a federal income tax. And the Seventeenth Amendment provided for direct election of senators. An amendment prohibiting child labor passed Congress under intense reform pressure. It met strong opposition from the business community, however, and failed to win ratification by the states.

PROGRESSIVISM IN THE WHITE HOUSE

With the death of William McKinley on September 14, 1901, Theodore Roosevelt became the third man in less than forty years to succeed to the presidency because of an assassin's bullet. At forty-three he was the nation's youngest President. Roosevelt came to the White House with a distinguished career in public service. He had served as state legislator, federal official, city police chief, army colonel, governor of New York, and Vice President. An energetic and impulsive man, Roosevelt responded candidly to McKinley's death: "It is a dreadful thing to come into the presidency this way; but it would be a far worse thing to be morbid about it."

Roosevelt's Square Deal for America Roosevelt moved cautiously during the next few years to take control of the Republican national machinery from McKinley's close friend Senator Mark Hanna of Ohio. In his first term he made few reform proposals. He did, however, publicize reform more and more, especially as his second term drew to a close. During this period no other American did as much as Theodore Roosevelt to educate his fellow citizens to the need for political and social change. He called the presidency "a bully pulpit." He often mounted its steps to criticize "malefactors of great wealth" and others—trusts, political bosses, destroyers of natural resources—who endangered his vision of a "square deal" for all Americans.

But Roosevelt did far more than simply publicize reform. Despite his strong party loyalties and keen appreciation of political patronage, he brought into government service a remarkable number of reformers. Roosevelt appointed William Howard Taft as Secretary of War, conservationist Gifford Pinchot as chief of the Forest Service, James R. Garfield (the son of the former President and a dedicated conservationist) as Secretary of the Interior, and the great jurist Oliver Wendell Holmes, Jr., as Supreme Court justice. Unlike his Republican predecessors in the White House, Roosevelt worked for the support of the black community. He consulted Booker T. Washington, president of the Tuskegee Institute in Alabama, as his chief adviser on Southern Republican appointments.

Underlying Roosevelt's actions and policies during his administration were certain firm beliefs shared by other progressives as well. Among them was the belief that government must begin intervening in the economy to bring unregulated businesses under control. It was argued that such a move would reduce class tensions in American society as well. Toward this end Roosevelt lobbied actively to push several important reform measures through Congress. The Elkins Act of 1903 forbade railroads to give rebates[2] to large industrial companies. The Hepburn Act of 1906 strengthened the powers of the Interstate Commerce Commission (ICC) to regulate the nation's railroads.

In these and other regulatory measures Roosevelt received the support of several members of the business community. For many business leaders, federal action seemed the most rational response to the country's growing industrial problems. Thus the railroads favored tighter federal regulation to eliminate the rebate system

[2] Rebates were special rates, lower than the published ones, granted secretly to users who accounted for a large share of freight traffic. Farmers felt especially cheated by these special rates, usually granted to industries.

Theodore Roosevelt surrounded himself with conservationists like John Muir who believed that the natural environment must be protected. Through Roosevelt's influence 148,000,000 acres of forests were set aside for national parks like Yosemite, seen in the background.

and avoid even more rigid state regulation. Similarly, giant lumber corporations endorsed federal intervention to enforce a rational set of guidelines for the industry.

An energetic outdoorsman, Roosevelt did much to educate the American public to the need for environmental protection. The Newlands Act, passed in 1902, authorized federal funds for the construction of dams and reclamation projects in the West. In 1907 he signed an executive order converting over 17 million acres of forest land in Western states to national reserves. Roosevelt also withdrew from private sale many valuable natural resources, including coal and mineral lands, oil reserves, and water-power sites. In 1908 he summoned the nation's conservation experts to a White House National Conservation Congress. Its purpose was to plan future policies for the protection of natural resources.

Busting the Trusts In 1902 Roosevelt began a policy of "trust busting." He moved to break up many of the giant corporations that had been organized by industry mergers during the previous decade. At first Roosevelt sought only to

The Bull Moose Convention

"We stand at Armageddon, and we battle for the Lord!"

Theodore Roosevelt shouted this rallying cry to Progressives at the Republican convention in June 1912. He was a man with a mission. He wanted to regain the presidency because he had a Progressive program, his "New Nationalism," that he wanted to see enacted into law. In his characteristic way he was ready to do battle. "I feel as fit as a bull moose," he told reporters.

When he lost the nomination, the Progressives would not accept the end of their dream. On August 5, 1912, they met as the newly formed Progressive, or "Bull Moose," party. Here in Chicago they would nominate Roosevelt as their presidential candidate.

The religious note that Roosevelt had sounded at the Republican convention seemed to find its real audience here. One historian has described the delegates as "a group of well-dressed, serious citizens with the respectability of Sunday School superintendents." The gathering seemed more like a religious revival meeting than a political convention. Speaker after speaker took the podium to deliver rousing, emotion-packed sermons on social justice. An already converted audience listened intently and often tearfully. Occasionally they would be moved to respond with hymns, feet stomping, and quotes from the Bible.

These were the men and women who for years had sought reforms in their own communities. They were frequently isolated from the rest of society because of their beliefs. One writer described them as "men of character who had fought against local grafting politicians. College professors, social workers, businessmen of vision and independence, farmers tired of seeing agriculture on the cross—[all] were enlisting in a cause they loved for unselfish service."

On the second day of the convention Roosevelt rose to present his "Confession of Faith" in political and economic reform. Before he could speak, 15,000 people came to their feet to welcome him. They poured out all of the emotions that had been building in them since he was denied the Republican nomination.

Roosevelt did not disappoint them. His mood matched theirs. When it came time for him to accept their nomination, he launched the crusade in fervent, enthusiastic terms:

> Six weeks ago here in Chicago, I spoke to the honest representatives of a convention which was not dominated by honest men; a convention wherein sat, alas! a majority of men who, with sneering indifference to every principle of right, acted so as to bring to a shameful end a party which had been founded over half a century ago by men in whose souls burned the fire of lofty endeavor. Now to you men who, in your turn, have come together to spend and be spent in the endless crusade against wrong, to you who face the future resolute and confident, to you who strive in a spirit of brotherhood for the betterment of our nation, to you who gird yourselves for this great new fight in the never-ending warfare for the good of mankind, I say in closing what I said in that speech in closing: We stand at Armageddon, and we battle for the Lord.

regulate the trusts through appropriate legislative channels. He asked Congress to pass legislation authorizing the federal licensing of corporations, full disclosure of company earnings and profits, and other supervisory measures. But the conservative majority in Congress rejected these proposals. So Roosevelt took on the trusts himself, using the powers given to the President by the 1890 Sherman Antitrust Act.

The President's first target was the National Securities Company. This was a consolidation of three major railroad systems: the Northern Pacific, the Great Northern, and the Chicago, Burlington, and Quincy. New York banking houses, led by Rockefeller and J. P. Morgan, had organized the merger to put an end to damaging competition among the three lines. Roosevelt ordered his Attorney General, Philander C. Knox, to file suit against the Northern Securities Company for violating the Sherman Act. In 1903 the Supreme Court declared the merger illegal and ordered the Northern Securities Company dissolved.

Roosevelt brought similar antitrust actions against several other giant corporations. These included Standard Oil, the American Tobacco Company, and DuPont. In this policy, which proved highly popular politically, Roosevelt asserted the supremacy of federal authority over private economic interests.

In his antitrust compaign Roosevelt insisted that he opposed not large corporations as such but corporate action against the public interest. The exact nature of that interest, Roosevelt felt, was something the President must judge. He wrote: "Our objection to a given corporation must be not that it is big, but that it behaves badly." In 1902 Roosevelt used his authority to force the settlement of a coal strike that threatened to deprive residents of the east coast of fuel during the winter months. With the aid of Wall Street banker J. P. Morgan he forced coal company executives to accept a settlement favorable to the United Mine Workers. It was the first time that an American President had intervened in a labor dispute on behalf of the striking workers.

Roosevelt's actions toward big business were not always consistent, however. He came to private arrangements with U. S. Steel and other giant corporations to avoid invoking antitrust action. In some labor disputes though, he called in federal troops as strikebreakers. Perhaps he believed that the federal government had to play the role of a neutral third party in resolving major disputes on industrial relations.

When Roosevelt left the White House in 1909, he bequeathed to his hand-picked successor, William Howard Taft, a well-formulated set of reform proposals for congressional action. These proposals included thorough governmental regulation of business, federal supervision of the stock market, a federal workmen's compensation law, and compulsory arbitration of labor disputes.

Taft and the Old Guard The new President showed little interest in carrying out Roosevelt's proposals. Not that Taft opposed reform completely. During his four years as President he supported constitutional amendments providing for an income tax and for direct election of senators. In addition, Taft initiated twice as many antitrust actions as Roosevelt. But unlike his predecessor, he never acquired an image as a trust buster. Under Taft's administration Congress established the eight-hour day for government workers, widened the ICC's authority to include interstate communications systems, and extended a tax on corporate profits. Taft also gave genuine and vigorous support to the conservation movement.

In other areas, however, Taft remained a conservative, politically allied to the Republican Old Guard. In 1910 Taft's Interior Secretary Richard Ballinger made an agreement with private firms allowing them to develop valuable coal and water-power sites in Alaska. Chief Forester Gifford Pinchot objected to this decision, but Taft supported Ballinger and fired Pinchot. This move infuriated Roosevelt and marked the beginning of a political break between the two men.

Taft also supported Republican conservatives in their battle for control of Congress against a coalition of reform Democrats and Republicans. He worked actively for the defeat of leading Republican insurgents in the 1910 congressional election. Again Taft's actions angered Republican reformers, among them Senator Robert LaFollette, the party's most prominent progressive. Later that year Taft cooperated with the Republican Old Guard in helping to pass the Payne-Aldrich Tariff, a high-tariff measure beneficial to big business. The battle over the Payne bill split congressional Republicans into conservative and progressive wings. Long before the close of his term in office, Taft had lost the support of most Republican reformers. They turned again to Teddy Roosevelt for leadership.

The Election of 1912 Roosevelt did not disappoint them. Beginning in 1910, he toured the country, supporting party insurgents against Taft, and denouncing the Ballinger-Pinchot affair. He made it evident that he wished the Republican party's nomination for an unprecedented third term in the White House. Roosevelt's active campaigning helped him to capture the presidential primaries in six states. But in most states presidential nominations were made by party conventions rather than by primary elections. Taft had gained control of the party machinery during his four years in office. Thus in June 1912 the Republican national convention nominated Taft for a second term.

Republican progressives led by Roosevelt and LaFollette then split from party ranks. In August 1912 they organized the Progressive (or Bull Moose) party, which nominated Roosevelt for the presidency. The new party attracted the attention of the country's leading reformers. Its 1912 convention, held in Chicago, was attended by such figures as Jane Addams, William Allen White, and George W. Perkins—all activists in the era's various reform movements (see page 574).

The Progressive party platform reflected a broad concern for major reforms in American life. It called for tighter governmental regulation of giant industries and financial companies, national presidential primaries, women's suffrage, and the initiative, referendum, and recall. Progressives also favored the prohibition of child labor, minimum wage standards for women, workmen's compensation, and a variety of banking and currency reforms.

On July 2, the Democrats nominated for the presidency a moderate reform candidate, Governor Woodrow Wilson of New Jersey. The Democratic platform favored collective bargaining for unions and revisions in the country's banking system. Unlike the Progressives, the Democrats sought the abolition of giant corporations rather than their regulation. Wilson called his program the New Freedom.

The Republicans, too, ran on a platform of moderate reform. They favored, among other legislation, tighter regulation of trusts and banking and currency changes. Thus, although Taft was more conservative than either Roosevelt or Wilson, he could hardly be considered an opponent of reform. A fourth candidate, Socialist Eugene V. Debs, ran on the most radical platform of all. In this curious election of 1912 all four candidates were committed in varying degrees to reform.

In the end the Republican split sent Wilson to the White House. Roosevelt received 4,126,000 votes and Taft 3,483,000. Had these votes been combined, the Republicans could have retained control of the presidency. Wilson received 6,286,000 popular votes, less than 45 percent of the total. But he won enough state pluralities to capture a majority of electoral votes. For the first time since the depression of the 1890s, the presidency returned to Democratic hands. In the election the Democrats gained control of both houses of Congress. Thus the new President had a working majority to pass his legislative program.

Wilson and the New Freedom During his first term in office Wilson proceeded to enact his programs. Though he applied stern moral standards to the conduct of foreign relations, Wilson was a skillful realist about domestic affairs. He quickly tossed the notion of breaking up the trusts into the political ashcan. Instead, adopting Roosevelt's more moderate idea of regulating giant corporations, he helped push several bills through Congress to achieve this purpose.

The Federal Trade Commission Act of 1914 established a bipartisan body to supervise industry and prevent unfair methods of competition in interstate commerce. The Clayton Antitrust Act, passed that same year, strengthened the 1890 Sherman Act by spelling out specific business practices that violated the antitrust laws. The Clayton Act also restrained the government from using court injunctions against striking unions.[3] Though on paper the new law seemed a powerful weapon, it actually did little to regulate the behavior of giant corporations or aid organized labor. In 1913 Wilson helped to steer through Congress the Underwood Tariff, the first downward revision in tariff rates since before the Civil War.

In December 1913 Congress passed the Federal Reserve Act, which created the present American banking system. The new law established twelve regional Federal Reserve banks, which were to serve member banks in their various geographic districts across the country. The Federal Reserve banks issued paper currency, supervised bank credit, and controlled other banking practices. The act also required existing national banks to become members of the Federal Reserve.

Wilson was supported in all these measures by his close associations with Southern Democrats. Some historians have called his election "the revolution of 1912" because, for the first time since the Civil War, Southerners regained a large measure of national influence. Born and raised in the South, Wilson felt most comfortable with those from his native region, many of whom became his closest advisers. He appointed a number of Southerners ambassadors and awarded some with other high-level government jobs. Several of his Cabinet members came from the South; others, like Wilson himself, were of Southern background ("the South in exile," as some called it).

The Senate Majority Leader, Thomas Martin of Virginia, and the House Majority Leader, Oscar Underwood of Alabama, worked closely with the new President. During Wilson's administration fifteen out of seventeen Senate committees were led by Southern chairmen. These senators helped to formulate Wilson's domestic program and steer it through Congress. The Federal Reserve Act was largely the work of three Southerners, including Wilson's Secretary of the Treasury, Carter Glass of Virginia. The Clayton Antitrust Act was sponsored by Henry Clayton of Alabama and House Majority Leader Underwood led the fight for the tariff-revision bill.

Protest and Progress Wilson's Southern background had less fortunate consequences, however. Segregation officially came to Washington under Wilson's regime. Governmental offices and other public facilities in the city were ordered segregated by race. In doing this, Wilson was only following a practice that had become common after Reconstruction. In the late nineteenth century "Jim Crow" laws[4]—that is, laws keeping blacks and whites apart in all public places—were enacted throughout the South (with little protest from the North). In 1896, in the case of *Plessy* v. *Ferguson,* the Supreme Court ruled that "separate but equal" facilities were constitutional. The decision was based to some extent on pseudoscientific assumptions of the day shared by many middle-class progressives in both the North and South. They believed that blacks (as well as southern and eastern Europeans) were essentially inferior. With the approval of the court, white supremacy asserted itself in segregated railroad cars, restaurants, schools, and other public facilities and institutions.

In the early twentieth century the problems of black Americans were brought to the nation's attention by a group of young black businessmen and professionals under the leadership of the

[3] An injunction is a court order requiring or forbidding certain activities. Business and government have sometimes used the injunction as an antiunion weapon to prevent strikes.

[4] The laws got their name from a song sung by Thomas Rice in a Negro minstrel show.

W. E. B. DuBois, the first black to receive a Ph.D. from Harvard, founded the NAACP to agitate for black political rights. When he died in 1963, his goals were beginning to be realized, though he himself, disheartened, had moved to Africa.

great scholar W. E. B. DuBois. In 1905 they founded the militant Niagara Movement to press for an end to Booker T. Washington's policy of "accommodation" with whites.[5] The leaders of the Niagara group sought a return to active agitation for complete political and civil equality of blacks with whites—the earlier goals of Radical Reconstruction.

Four years later, members of the Niagara Movement and white supporters of black civil rights formed the National Association for the Advancement of Colored People (NAACP). DuBois was appointed editor of the NAACP's journal, *The Crisis*. Active in the new organization were several reformers who would support the garment workers' strike that same year: Lillian Wald, Jane Addams, and publisher Oswald Garrison Villard (William Lloyd Garrison's grandson). The NAACP grew rapidly in the next decade. It quickly took the lead in opposing the segregationist policies of the Wilson administration.

Wilson found himself under growing pressure from other groups of reformers as his first term drew to a close. There seemed little chance that he could again slip into the White House through a split in Republican ranks. Roosevelt had rejoined his party, and most Progressives were unhappy with Wilson's refusal to support social welfare legislation. Concerned over the political situation, Wilson began a determined campaign to win over reform-minded voters by pushing several progressive measures through Congress.

The Federal Farm Loan Act, passed in May 1916, aided domestic agriculture by expanding the credit resources of American farmers. The Adamson Act, passed the same year, provided an eight-hour day for workers in interstate commerce. The Kern-McGillicudy Act created a model workmen's compensation program for federal employees. In August of 1916 Congress attempted to deal with the problems of child labor by passing the Keating-Owen Act, which outlawed the interstate shipment of products manufactured by children under fourteen. (Two years later the law was declared unconstitutional.) Wilson nominated progressive lawyer Louis Brandeis to the Supreme Court and fought for his confirmation in Congress against conservative opposition. Brandeis became the first Jewish Supreme Court justice.

During the election of 1916 Democrats stressed Wilson's skill at maintaining American neutrality in the growing war in Europe (see Chapter 30). But it was the President's energetic sponsorship of reform measures that won him the support of the labor movement and most middle-class reformers. In a hard-fought campaign against Republican Charles Evans Hughes, Wilson won reelection by narrow popular and electoral margins. In his second term he devoted most of his attention to the problems of fighting a war and winning the peace. Domestic reform took a back seat to world affairs during Woodrow Wilson's last four years in office.

[5] Washington believed that it was more important for blacks to achieve economic gains than political ones. He preached patience, conservatism, and the primacy of education in achieving material prosperity to his black followers.

1. Why has the "Protocol of Peace" come to be regarded as a milestone in American industrial relations?
2. Why were unions largely unsuccessful in organizing workers in the early years of the twentieth century?
3. Was the membership of large numbers of self-employed workingmen in the Knights of Labor a hindrance to its effectiveness? Why or why not? Why did Samuel Gompers believe that reform activity and independent political action by unions hindered their effectiveness?
4. Why did many reformers of the late nineteenth century believe that a social catastrophe was imminent? How did men like Edward Bellamy and William Dean Howells propose to avoid it?
5. Why did some reformers believe that settlement houses were inadequate responses to urban problems? What was their solution?
6. Who were the progressives and what beliefs did they share? What were some of their accomplishments at the city and state levels?
7. Did Theodore Roosevelt want to break up all trusts? Why did he believe it necessary to move against the Northern Securities Company?
8. Was President Taft a progressive? For what reasons did he and Roosevelt have a falling-out? How did that falling-out affect the election in 1912?
9. Why did Wilson begin to press for social welfare legislation at the end of his first term? Cite some examples of this legislation.

Beyond the Text

1. Compare and contrast the Knights of Labor and the AFL with regard to (1) structure, (2) membership, and (3) attitudes toward the strike.
2. Compare Theodore Roosevelt and Woodrow Wilson in terms of their aims, their accomplishments, and their influence on history.
3. Booker T. Washington and W. E. B. DuBois represented two different approaches to black advancement in American society. Describe their differences and indicate which you think more correct.

Bibliography

Nonfiction

Aaron, Daniel, *Men of Good Hope: A Story of American Progressives.**

Davis, Allen F., *Spearheads for Reform: The Social Settlements & the Progressive Movement, 1890–1914.**

Flexner, Eleanor, *Century of Struggle: The Women's Rights Movement in the United States.**

Grob, Gerald N., *Workers and Utopia.**

Hays, Samuel P., *Conservatism and the Gospel of Efficiency.**

Hofstadter, Richard, *The Age of Reform.**

Kolko, Gabriel, *The Triumph of Conservatism.**

Lasch, Christopher, *The New Radicalism in America, 1889–1963.**

Link, Arthur S., *Woodrow Wilson and the Progessive Era, 1910–1917.**

McKelvey, Blake, *The Urbanization of America, 1860–1915.*

Mowry, George E., *The Era of Theodore Roosevelt, 1900–1912.**

———, *Theodore Roosevelt & the Progressive Movement.**

Taft, Philip, *The A. F. of L. in the Time of Gompers.*

Fiction

Sinclair, Upton, *The Jungle.**

Smith, Chard P., *Ladies Day.*

Stone, Irving, *Adversary in the House.**

*a paperback book

CHAPTER

29

The Philippines Revolt

AT AGE THIRTY, Emiliano Aguinaldo was a seasoned revolutionary. The son of a prosperous farmer from the island of Luzon, he was a member of the Katipunan, the Filipino movement for independence. In August 1896 Aguinaldo joined a revolt against Spain, which had held the Philippines as a colony since the sixteenth century. Two months later the rebels proclaimed the existence of the Tagal Republic. When the first president of the republic died, Aguinaldo became president and commander in chief of the insurgent forces.

But revolutionary organization and high-sounding titles alone could not defeat the Spanish in the field. Nor could Spain's colonial power crush the rebels. In December 1897, after more than a year of seesaw guerrilla warfare, both sides recognized the stalemate and signed a treaty.

Spain, apprehensive over the threats posed to its Caribbean empire by rebellion in Cuba and political unrest in Puerto Rico, agreed to consider reforms in the Philippines. In turn, Aguinaldo and other leaders of the rebellion agreed to leave their country for three years. They went to Hong Kong, a British colony on the southern coast of China. Meanwhile, the Spanish deposited 400,000 pesetas in a Hong Kong bank in the rebels' name. If Spain enacted the promised reforms, this trust fund would be used to educate Filipinos abroad. If Spain failed, the insurgents could use the money to buy arms and resume the war.

The American fleet's destruction of the Spanish fleet in Manila Bay on May 1, 1898 brought the United States into an era of overseas expansion. Gaining the Philippines from Spain proved easier than winning the loyalties of the Filipino people, as events of the next four years would show.

The Filipinos soon became convinced that they had been tricked. Spanish Governor-General Miguel Primo de Rivera did not declare a general amnesty, as expected. Reforms acceptable to the rebels did not come to pass. The trust fund that rested in Hong Kong now seemed to the rebels to be no more than hush money, a bribe to silence Filipino leaders. From their headquarters in the British colony, the insurgents began planning for future campaigns.

During this period rebellion in Cuba brought on a crisis in Spanish-American relations. (Americans and their government were sympathetic to freedom movements in Latin America.) As Spain and the United States moved closer to war, the Filipino rebels thought about an alliance with the United States. Then, in April 1898, Aguinaldo was told that the American consul in Singapore, W. Spencer Pratt, wanted to discuss important matters of interest to both countries. The Filipino agreed to meet with Pratt in Singapore.

The Aguinaldo-Pratt talks took place in the Raffles Hotel, legendary center of "East Asian intrigue" and British colonial power at the turn of the century. Pratt claimed that Spain had broken the terms of the truce. He urged Aguinaldo to resume the rebellion. The consul added some important news: "As of the other day, Spain and America have been at war. Now is the time for you to strike. Ally yourselves with America, and you will surely defeat the Spaniards!"

Aguinaldo was clearly interested in this proposal, but he remained cautious: "What can we expect to gain from helping America?" Pratt assured him: "America will give you much greater liberty and many more material benefits than the Spanish ever promised you."

When Aguinaldo asked whether such an arrangement could be put in writing, Pratt sidestepped. He obviously had no authority to speak for Washington. Yet he continued to offer verbal assurances: "The American Congress and President have just made a solemn declaration disclaiming any desire to possess Cuba and promising to leave the country to the Cubans after having driven away the Spanish and pacified the country. Cuba is at our door while the Philippines are 10,000 miles away." In short, Pratt suggested, there was no chance that the United States would occupy the Philippines.

Consul Pratt also told Aguinaldo that he would try to arrange for the rebels to be transported to Manila on American ships. Pratt contacted Commodore George Dewey, commander of the United States Pacific fleet in Hong Kong. The cable to Dewey read: "Aguinaldo, insurgent leader, here. Will come Hong Kong. Arrange with Commodore for general cooperation insurgents Manila if desired." The Yankee sailor answered quickly and tersely: "Tell Aguinaldo come as soon as possible." When informed of Dewey's okay, Aguinaldo promised that if his forces obtained sufficient arms the rest of the Filipino people would rise against the Spanish. Pratt, seldom at a loss for reassuring words, added that Dewey felt that "the United States would at least recognize the independence of the Philippines under the protection of the United States Navy."

But Commodore Dewey never met with Aguinaldo before the United States Pacific squadron sailed for Manila. A few years later he denied all knowledge of a political deal. By then Commodore Dewey had been promoted to admiral, a rank created especially for him by Congress: he had become a national hero. Dewey dismissed Consul Pratt as a "busybody interfering with other people's business," a man whose letters he simply filed and ignored. Toward the Filipinos Dewey adopted a paternal and disapproving stance. "They seemed to be all very young, earnest boys," he recalled. "I did not attach much importance to what they said or to themselves."

Commodore George Dewey created the conditions for United States involvement in protracted guerrilla warfare in the Philippines. He needed Filipino help to defeat Spain but did not reckon with Filipino nationalist feelings after the conflict.

Certainly Dewey did not believe the rebels' boasts that they already had 30,000 armed men in the Philippines, with many more available. Why then did Dewey agree to take Aguinaldo and other Filipino leaders to Manila? By his own account, to get rid of them. "They were bothering me. I was very busy getting my squadron ready for battle, and these little men were coming aboard my ship at Hong Kong and taking a good deal of my time." So he consented to transport the rebels, though in the end only one Filipino went along.

Despite his denials, Dewey did want something from the Filipinos. He needed troops to occupy Manila and other parts of the Philippines if and when he defeated the Spanish navy. Aguinaldo and his followers might help Dewey accomplish the job.

On May 1, 1898, American forces defeated the Spanish navy in Manila Bay. The spectacular victory reaffirmed the rise of American military power on the world scene. The United States squadron blew the remnants of the decaying Spanish navy out of the water. (Some of Spain's ships were hulks, rotting at dockside, with guns that would not function.) Within a few hours it was over. Spain no longer ruled the Philippines. Yet Manila remained to be captured and occupied. The Spanish army had not been routed, nor had its commander indicated a willingness to surrender.

The victory at Manila Bay reopened the question of Dewey's need for Filipino support. From his ships Dewey could do nothing. Spanish artillerymen had allowed Dewey to anchor close to Manila's shore, but the commodore knew that opening fire would expose the city to prolonged bombardment. Moreover, his small Marine battalion was an

Emilio Aguinaldo was evaluated differently by his enemies and his own people. To Dewey he was at first a nuisance and later an "Oriental despot." To the Filipinos, however, he symbolized their hope for independence.

insufficient landing force. The commodore felt that with 5,000 troops he could end the war in one day. But he did not have 5,000 troops. Insurgent Filipinos comprised the only immediately available source of military manpower.

Early in May Dewey sent for the rebel leader. Aguinaldo and a dozen of his associates in Hong Kong arrived in Manila on a United States Navy auxiliary vessel. Within a few days Dewey and Aguinaldo met for the first time. Their versions of the encounter are as different as the men themselves.

According to Aguinaldo, the American commander repeated the familiar promises about American disdain for acquiring colonies and its support of Filipino independence. Dewey also requested that the insurgents resume fighting. He supplied them with sixty-two rifles and some abandoned Spanish naval guns. The United States commander stressed that all promises were guaranteed "by the word of honor of Americans." Finally, Aguinaldo claimed that Dewey instructed him to have a Filipino national flag prepared. It would be hoisted as soon as Spain surrendered.

Dewey presented an equally questionable account of the events. Shortly after meeting with Aguinaldo, Dewey claimed, the Secretary of the Navy instructed him to avoid entangling the United States in alliances with the Filipino insurgents. Dewey complied because he was bound by obedience and because he did not like the insurgents. He had little faith in their cause. He considered the soft-spoken Aguinaldo an "unimpressive little man," though he recognized the Filipino's enormous prestige among his people.

Dewey admitted that the insurgents might be of service in clearing the shoreline from the naval base of Cavite to Manila City. Thus he allowed the rebels to enter the Cavite arsenal. But he warned that the Filipinos and the Americans should keep their distance. The United States commander continued to maintain that Aguinaldo had been forced on him by the barrage of pleas from the American consuls in Hong Kong and Singapore. Dewey also insisted that he never believed the Filipinos wanted independence. How could they? Aguinaldo "considered me as his liberator, as his friend."

Friend would soon become foe, and Aguinaldo himself bore some of the blame for his later disillusionment with the United States. During his months of exile in Hong Kong and his first few weeks back in the Philippines, Aguinaldo seemed to accept everything the Americans promised. His proclamations and public letters of the time praised the United States in lavish terms.

The distance that Dewey sought to create between himself and Aguinaldo was quickly established. American officers began complaining about the many Filipinos inside the Cavite naval base. These "natives," they argued, might be friends or foes. So Dewey told Aguinaldo that he and his men must leave the arsenal but could remain in the town of Cavite. From this headquarters the Aguinaldo movement grew. Enlistees poured in, many of them armed with captured Spanish rifles.

On May 21 Aguinaldo felt militarily strong enough to issue a proclamation outlining his ultimate aims: "Everything appears favorable for attaining independence. The hour has arrived for the Philippines to belong to her sons." Aguinaldo advised his men to fight a "civilized" war, warning that "if we do not conduct ourselves thus, the Americans will decide to sell us or else divide up our territory, as they will hold us incapable of governing our land." Like it or not, Aguinaldo knew, the Filipinos would have to deal with the United States. Neither Japan nor the European powers had demonstrated a willingness to confront America over the fate of the Philippines.

Throughout May Manila remained in Spanish hands. The Americans had made no commitments to the rebels, but United States troops were on the way. In June the Filipino insurgents announced the establishment of a provisional government and issued a declaration of independence.

The declaration also recognized the dictatorship of Emilio Aguinaldo. On June 23 Aguinaldo dissolved the dictatorship and declared himself president of the revolutionary government. In an effort to win support from the United States and other nations, the Filipinos promised to work for two primary goals: independence and the establishment of a representative, republican government.

By the time Aguinaldo formally declared independence, he and his forces controlled most of Cavite province and almost surrounded Manila. From the panic-stricken city, Dewey received requests from Spanish officials to help evacuate foreign and Spanish civilians, as well as wounded soldiers. Some were placed aboard foreign ships in the harbor. Aguinaldo, mindful of the need to wage war in a manner approved by Europeans, allowed civilians and wounded soldiers to pass through his lines. His cooperative spirit reached its height in mid-July when he helped pick the spot for a landing of United States soldiers. Thanks to the insurgents' advice, admitted Dewey, "we were able to land our troops within easy striking distance of their objective," a position more than halfway between Cavite and Manila.

But American gratitude did not mean acceptance of the Filipino forces as a political entity. According to Dewey, in fighting their way up the coast and surrounding Manila, the insurgents had merely prepared "a foothold for our troops when they should arrive." American Army units, under General Wesley Merritt, entered Manila on June 30. From then on, the war against Spain became an exclusively American affair.

American soldiers quickly moved to replace the Filipinos in the trenches dug near the Manila fortifications. One of General Merritt's officers tried to convince the insurgents to pull out of the line and turn their trenches over to the Americans. In return he offered to supply the rebels with cannon and other artillery. The local Filipino commander consulted Aguinaldo. Aguinaldo would comply, but only if the request and the offer were put in writing. This concession demonstrated the Filipino leader's desperate desire for legal recognition of his government's standing. Pull out first—then we will furnish the paper, answered the Americans. Aguinaldo ordered his troops out of the trenches. But they never saw the cannon, nor did their commander receive written confirmation. Once again, as in Cavite, Aguinaldo yielded to an American request under American pressure. This decision proved extremely costly to the rebel cause.

With insurgent forces neutralized and Aguinaldo's political status in doubt, the American capture of Manila proceeded swiftly and with little bloodshed. On August 13 the city capitulated. The United States now ruled the Philippines. A War Department dispatch dated August 17 declared that Filipino insurgents would not form part of the occupation forces:

> The United States, in possession of Manila City, Manila Bay and harbor, must preserve the peace and protect persons and property within the territory occupied by the military and naval forces. The insurgents and all others must recognize the military occupation and authority of the United States.

What was in store for the Philippines beyond the period of military occupation? In Washington President McKinley began the process of reconciling the facts of conquest with the arguments of territorial expansionists. At first McKinley opposed taking all the Philippines, though he held open the possibility that conditions might change. The President favored keeping Luzon, the large island in the northern part of the archipelago, and establishing a United States naval base at Manila. McKinley wished to show Europe that "a lofty spirit" guided American actions. But he also supported the "general principle of holding on to what we get."

These statements reflect McKinley's personality and his tactical approach to political decision making. The President worked hard to create the impression that he was forced to act. He wanted to make it appear that public opinion and the pressure of events directed the outcome of the Philippine conflict. In reality, as McKinley surely realized, the decision to take Manila made full-scale American involvement in the Philippines unavoidable.

In October 1898 Spanish and American negotiators met at the bargaining table in Paris, to write a peace treaty. When the American delegates left for France, McKinley still appeared to be uncertain about how to deal with the Philippines. But he later wrote the head of the delegation: "There is a very general feeling that, whatever it might prefer as to the Philippines, the United States is in a situation where it cannot let go." McKinley argued that the islands were too interconnected by history and commercial ties, too dependent on Luzon, for a selective policy of partition to work. The United States could not ignore the moral obligations imposed by its victory. But neither could it overlook Spain's inability to rule the islands. Finally, the United States would not allow their transfer to another foreign power. It became the responsibility of Secretary of State John Hay to work out the details of an arrangement.

The Treaty of Paris, which ended the Spanish-American War, was signed on December 10. Spain agreed to grant Cuba independence and to cede to the United States Puerto Rico and the tiny Pacific island of Guam. The United States also received the Philippine Islands, for which it paid Spain $20 million. "A goodly estate indeed!" crowed the head of the American delegation. He wrote President McKinley: "Perhaps the treaty may be an acceptable Christmas offering to you from the American commission."

During the negotiations between the United States and Spain, Aguinaldo tried desperately to gain legal standing for his revolutionary government. On August 6, shortly before Manila capitulated, he issued a memorandum to all foreign powers. It asked recognition of the belligerent status of the insurgents, a first step toward full diplomatic recognition. It also asked support for their ultimate aim of independence. But other countries refused to recognize the rebels. Nor did the United States indicate a willingness to consider Philippine independence seriously. Filipino insurgents were not America's allies, stated a directive from Washington. They had merely cooperated with Americans "against a common enemy."

Under these circumstances tension between Americans and Filipinos mounted. In December 1898 President McKinley sent a message to the new military commander in the Philippines, General Elwell S. Otis. The President assured Otis that the United States wished to pursue a policy of "benevolent assimilation" in the islands and bestow the "blessings of good and stable government." But he warned Otis that all obstacles to achieving these ends were to be removed. Before publishing McKinley's message, General Otis cut out several sections critical of the Filipino rebels. When a junior United States officer in the city of Iloilo mistakenly printed the entire text, Filipino resentment grew.

The insurgents' reactions in January 1899 were firm but still friendly. Aguinaldo rejected the American claim to rule his country and accused the United States of betraying a loyal ally. In the United States another Filipino leader, Felipe Agconcillo, tried to reason with the new colonial power in terms of its own declared ideals: "I cannot believe that in any possible action on the part of the American republic toward my country there is an intention to ignore, as to the ten millions of human beings I represent, the right of free government." He concluded his memo with the warning that the accidental or impetuous act of one Filipino or American soldier might trigger a full-scale war.

On February 4, 1899, the situation changed radically. An American soldier on guard duty near Manila challenged a Filipino to halt. When the Filipino disobeyed, the sentry shot and killed him. Fighting between Americans and Filipinos, confined during the previous six months to isolated incidents, broke out all along the outskirts of Manila. The war was on. And as even Dewey had to admit: "Perhaps the insurrection was bound to break out."

Inevitably, each side circulated conflicting reports about the incident. The Filipinos accused the Americans of deliberate provocation, adding that they were unprepared to launch attacks and that several of their leaders were on leave. They also asserted that Aguinaldo had believed the initial exchange of shots to be accidental. The day after the incident, the rebels claimed, one of their generals proposed an immediate cease-fire to General Otis. But Otis rejected the offer, and ordered the fighting to continue "to the grim end."

McKinley responded with an equally one-sided account. First, he brushed off the cease-fire claim: "There appears to have been no such application." Second, McKinley claimed, no American officer had promised the rebels independence. The most that Aguinaldo could have hoped for when he returned to Manila was the ouster of Spain. Their ambitions had led the Filipinos to launch an "unprovoked attack" on American troops.

Throughout the war American military leaders tried to downgrade the enemy. American officials viewed Aguinaldo as a bandit, who robbed his own people and lived in luxury on the proceeds of his looting. Whatever Aguinaldo's shortcomings, he remained the leading

Filipino insurgent for two years, the chief symbol of resistance to colonial power and of hope for independence.

General Otis, who predicted a quick and easy suppression of the rebellion, failed at the job. Otis boasted that his 21,000 troops would crush the insurgents in a few weeks. He repeated this promise with depressing regularity for the next twelve months. The gap between Otis' fantasies and the realities of the Philippine war can be measured by the increased number of troops the General soon demanded. Shortly after the outbreak he asked for 35,000. A year later he had 70,000 and wanted 30,000 more.

In the spring of 1899 the United States Army drove northward from Manila to occupy—or pacify, as the government called it—the island of Luzon, center of Tagal resistance. In April American forces captured the insurgent capital of Malolos. Aguinaldo and his followers fled farther north. But in mid-May they had to give up their provisional capital at San Isidro. Then, instead of mounting an all-out American attack, General Otis halted the advance. The rainy season had just begun, and many of the troops were scheduled for immediate return

home. So Otis, a cautious field commander, suspended military operations.

Back in the White House McKinley remained optimistic. He assured Theodore Roosevelt that "Otis had things entirely in hand and that the insurrection would be speedily put down certainly after the opening of the dry season."

In the meantime, the Schurman Commission, a mixed civilian-military commission headed by the president of Cornell University, Jacob Schurman, was formed to investigate conditions in the Philippine Islands. A preliminary report, issued in the fall of 1899, found much to praise in the Filipinos. It expressed great interest in the islands' natural resources and potential for economic growth. But the report stressed that immediate self-government was out of the question and that the American presence must continue to assure peace and order. The commissioners concluded: "Whatever the future of the Philippines may be, there is no course open to us now except the prosecution of the war

Combat in the Philippines was perhaps the most grueling experienced to that time. Fought in jungle terrain against twin unseen enemies—the guerrilla insurgents and disease—the war produced over 7,000 American casualties.

until the insurgents are reduced to submission." The report delighted McKinley.

Most Americans agreed that Filipinos were unprepared for self-government. Some, like Republican Senator George F. Hoar of Massachusetts, protested that Filipinos should be left to govern themselves, whatever the results. But the majority felt otherwise. They predicted that an American pullout would quickly produce internal wars and anarchy. This they were sure would be followed just as quickly by the intervention of other foreign powers. Theodore Roosevelt hoped that Filipinos might be able to govern themselves at some future, undetermined date. But he warned that the "consent-of-the-governed doctrine must not be pushed to an extent that would restore savagery."

William Howard Taft, at the time a federal judge, went to the Philippines as the first American governor. He expounded on the theory of Filipino inferiority. In 1902 the Senate committee investigating the war asked Taft whether Filipinos were in fact so ignorant that a few leaders could easily misguide them. Taft replied: "That is quite possible, and that is one of the chief reasons why the Filipino people are utterly unfit for self-government." Americans had to lead the way, Taft asserted, for the Filipinos lacked any knowledge of how to carry on a government. The United States could not remain "blind to their serious defects, many of which are due to the environment, social and political, which has been presented by their history of three hundred years."

General Robert P. Hughes spoke more bluntly. In referring to one of the Filipino ethnic groups, he testified: "These people do not know what independence means. They probably think it is something to eat. They have no more idea what it means than a shepherd dog."

The suspension of American offensive operations in the spring of 1899 gave Aguinaldo and his followers time to regroup—and make a key decision. The insurgents knew they could not defeat the rapidly growing United States forces in conventional warfare. From then on, Aguinaldo and his staff decided, Filipino rebels would engage in guerrilla tactics. In order to succeed, they would have to depend on their own countrymen's support, voluntary or forced, and on their ability to blend in with the civilian population.

Aguinaldo's tactical switch posed new and serious problems for the United States Army. When General Arthur MacArthur resumed his northward advance in Luzon in October 1899, his men had trouble distinguishing friend from foe among the Filipinos. The guerrillas tried to wear down the enemy by ambushing American

War atrocities committed by Americans, such as the burning of the native district of Manila in 1899, caused divisions of popular sentiment at home. Mark Twain suggested bitterly that the field of stars on the flag be "replaced by a skull and crossbones."

patrols and firing at night into towns occupied by United States troops. Along the trails between villages Filipino rebels set up booby traps—pits lined with sharpened bamboo spears and covered with foliage. General Hughes complained: "As to actual engagements, there were very few. It was very hard to get an engagement of any kind. You could get what we would call a little skirmish, and probably there would be ten or twelve killed."

Though Americans denied that the Filipino army had any legal standing, guerrilla prisoners were not automatically executed as rebels. Instead, a generous American amnesty policy for the insurgents allowed for a decent gap between the official United States position and the actual treatment of those Filipinos who wished to surrender.

Many insurgents did surrender and swear allegiance to the United States. Some even joined American troops to crush the rebels. Combat reports often mentioned the Macabebe soldiers. They were Filipinos who fought with and supported the United States throughout the war. But American officials in the Philippines rejected the idea of forming an all-Filipino regiment. "To put in command of a Filipino a thousand men with a thousand rifles would not be wise," warned Taft. Still, many Filipinos cooperated with the Americans, and, as in most wars, the majority of the population remained uninvolved. These facts bolstered the American argument that Aguinaldo and his forces actually hurt the Filipinos more than anyone else.

Filipinos who continued to resist and rejected the American offer of amnesty received rough treatment. Captured insurgent leaders were shipped to Guam, and "enlisted men" were imprisoned. For a short while Americans even set up security camps for Filipino civilians. This same tactic, when employed by Spain in Cuba, had enraged the American public. In the insurrectionary province of Batangas American officials ordered a ban on all trade, hoping that wealthy Filipinos who supported the insurgents would yield to the pressure.

In the field, United States soldiers routinely burned Filipino villages. Sergeant Leroy Hallock testified that he had participated in the burning of a village of over 3,000 people. He claimed that he had heard of other burnings, including a town of 10,000 inhabitants. Another enlisted man recalled: "If a column was marching along and was fired upon, it was the practice to burn the buildings in that neighborhood. That impressed the natives with the fact that they could not fire upon us with impunity, although they did not often do very great damage."

No specific orders had been issued authorizing such indiscriminate reprisals, but they continued. Colonel Arthur L. Wagner defended the policy on practical and religious grounds:

> It is not always possible to discriminate between those who are active enemies and those who are not. We know that a certain community has been conducting itself badly. In such a case it would be justifiable to destroy the town, although we might burn the property of inoffensive people, if the town were notoriously a nest of *ladrones*—that is, [thieves, insurgents]. The Almighty destroyed Sodom, notwithstanding the fact that there were a few just people in that community—less than ten.

Early in 1900 the superior military strength of the United States forces began to make itself felt. In May General Otis resigned rather than work under the all-civilian Taft Commission, which had been sent to Manila to set up a civil government. Otis' replacement, General Arthur MacArthur, harried the Filipino guerrillas whenever and wherever he could find them.

The biggest setback for the insurgents' cause came with the capture of Aguinaldo himself. During late 1900 and early 1901 Aguinaldo's whereabouts remained a mystery. Some American military men and journalists began circulating rumors of his death. MacArthur knew better. In February 1901 United States troops captured an insurgent soldier carrying dispatches from Aguinaldo to rebel officers in the field. The messages did not pinpoint the location of rebel headquarters, but they indicated that the captive knew where to find Aguinaldo. Interrogation began, and before long the courier talked: Aguinaldo could be found in the village of Palanan, in the mountains of Luzon near the northeast coast.

But how could the Americans get to Aguinaldo? Thirty-six-year-old Brigadier General Frederick Funston, head of a volunteer regiment from Kansas, had a plan. The intercepted messages called for the movement of small groups of rebel reinforcements toward Aguinaldo's headquarters. Funston decided to use eighty Macabebe scouts pretending to be rebel reinforcements. He and four other American officers would go along, supposedly as prisoners. One additional and crucial element remained: several Tagals loyal to the United States would be needed to pose as leaders of the expedition. Funston found three such men, plus the messenger who had been captured. General MacArthur gave his approval but with misgivings. Instead of wishing Funston well, he remarked: "I fear I shall never see you again."

The march to Palanan proved more difficult than the capture itself. The expeditionary force landed by gunboat on the east coast of Luzon, about a hundred miles from its objective. The men had to struggle for several days through rough terrain near the shoreline, heavy rains, and dense jungle. It had been decided, for reasons Funston never made clear, that the Tagal officers and the Macabebes would enter the village about an hour before the Americans.

On March 23, 1901, the Macabebes arrived in the rebel camp.

Filipino guerrillas were not highly regarded as soldiers by the American military. General Arthur MacArthur claimed that they "could not hit a stack of barns" with their guns. But it took 70,000 American troops three years to defeat them.

They were relieved to find only a handful of insurgent soldiers to greet them. The Tagal officers entered rebel headquarters to confer with Aguinaldo and his staff. As the conversation wore on, all but two of the insurgent officers drifted out of the room. An expedition officer leaned out the window to give the Macabebes the signal to open fire. Aguinaldo, thinking that his own men were firing in the air to welcome the fresh troops, rushed to the window to tell them to stop wasting ammunition. At that point one of the Tagal officers seized Aguinaldo. The others opened fire on the insurgent guards.

Frederick Funston reaped most of the acclaim for the capture of Aguinaldo, including a Medal of Honor. But it was the Tagals and the Macabebes who actually captured the Filipino rebel leader.

It was all over before Funston and his American companions arrived. Funston rushed to the headquarters, and Aguinaldo asked if the "capture" was some kind of joke. When Funston identified himself, Aguinaldo let his shoulders drop in resignation and defeat. On March 28 the group returned to Manila. Aguinaldo was imprisoned in the governor's mansion. When General MacArthur arrived, ever skeptical, he asked Funston: "Where is Aguinaldo?" Funston had the triumphant pleasure of replying: "Right in this house."

Aguinaldo had sworn many times that he would never be taken alive. For several weeks American officers pressured him to swear an oath of allegiance to the United States. On April 19 he agreed to take the oath. He promised to issue a proclamation calling on Filipinos to lay down their arms in order to avoid further bloodshed. Aguinaldo's declaration suddenly made him a hero in American eyes. *The New York Times,* which had once described Aguinaldo as an "enslaver" and a "criminal aggressor," now found him to be "honest and sincere," a "natural leader of men with considerable shrewdness and ability."

On July 4, 1901, Taft took over as the civil governor of the Philippines. He left a revealing account of his reception in Manila: "The populace that we expected to welcome us was not there, and I cannot describe the coldness of the army officers and the army men who received us any better than by saying that it somewhat exceeded the coldness of the populace." By the end of the year President Roosevelt reported to Congress with a mixture of satisfaction and exasperation: "The insurrection has become an affair of local banditti and marauders. Encouragement, direct or indirect, to these insurrectos stands on the same footing as encouragement to hostile Indians in the days when we still had Indian wars."

Still, the rebellion—the ill-fated and barely understood war of national liberation—continued. Its center shifted southward to the island of Mindanao. The inhabitants of the island were Moros. They

More than 20,000 Filipino insurgents died in the three-year conflict—and independence was not achieved.

were Moslems who opposed the American presence but who had never accepted the authority of the Tagals in Manila. Fire fights and armed conflict broke out. One fire fight in northern Mindanao left ten Americans dead and forty wounded. Fighting between American troops and Moro rebels continued off and on for another twelve years.

In the meantime, the "unfriendly" island of Samar exploded. Company C of the regular Ninth United States Infantry was stationed on the island in the fishing village of Balangiga. Hundreds of Filipino workmen, supposedly loyal to the United States, fell on the Americans with knives, bolos (machetes), and bare hands. A few soldiers escaped in a boat to another island. They were the only survivors. The massacre at Balangiga would not be forgotten. For the next six months American troops called for revenge, in the same way that a previous generation of American soldiers had sought to avenge Custer's defeat at the Little Bighorn.

Major Littleton Waller of the Marines received the punitive assignment. The area commander, General Jacob ("Hell Roaring Jake") Smith, told Waller that he wanted the Samar rebellion ended quickly. Smith ordered Waller to remove all Filipino civilians from the island's interior and place them in stockades. Those who resisted, especially those capable of bearing arms, were to be considered enemies and shot. Waller asked what the cutoff point was. Anyone more than ten years old, replied Smith. Waller and his men did as they were told.

The pacification of Batangas province followed the same script. Miguel Malavar, head of the revolutionary government there, had

5,000 men and was better organized than the rebels on Samar. The American general, J. Franklin Bell, an ambitious young man who only three years before had been a lieutenant, saw his chance and took it. He waged an intense campaign, herding thousands of civilians into security camps. In April 1902, after several months of dodging and fighting on the run, Malvar surrendered. The last sustained pocket of armed Filipino resistance had been eliminated.

The war between American troops and Filipino rebels had lasted more than three years. Countless Filipinos lost their homes in the burning of towns and villages. Thousands of rebel soldiers were killed or wounded in the fighting. The United States had not gained an easy victory. Almost as many Americans died in the Filipino conflict as in the war with Spain. And the rebellion had cost the United States $160 million, or eight times the "indemnity" paid to Spain for the islands.

On July 4, 1902, the United States government declared the Philippine insurrection officially over. President Roosevelt, who had become President after McKinley's assassination, sent a special message to the Army. The President praised American soldiers for the rapid accomplishment of their mission, despite great hardships in more than 2,000 skirmishes and battles. Teddy Roosevelt was still mentally fighting Indians, for he went on to say: "Utilizing the lessons of the Indian wars [the army] relentlessly followed the guerrilla bands to their footholds in mountains and jungle and crushed them." With surprisingly few exceptions, the President maintained, American troops had been humane and kind to both prisoners and civilians. They had fought bravely against "a general system of guerrilla warfare conducted among a people speaking unknown tongues, from whom it was almost impossible to obtain the information necessary for successful pursuit or to guard against surprise and ambush." The Army, declared Roosevelt, had added honor to the flag.

CHAPTER

30

Becoming a World Power

BY 1900 MANY AMERICANS came to question the presence of American soldiers in the Philippines. Wasn't the war with Spain fought to liberate Cuba, an island ninety miles off the coast of Florida? Then why was the United States involved in places halfway round the globe? Whose interests were served by such overseas commitments? Answers to these questions lay tangled in the history of late nineteenth-century America and in the international power struggles of an imperialist age.

For most of the nineteenth century Americans had been more than content to search for and use the wealth of their own country. America was their Garden of Eden. And although many of its products were sold overseas (much cotton went to Britain, for example), the United States had avoided foreign political ties. America had allied itself with a foreign power only once in its history–during the Revolutionary War, when it signed an alliance with France. Concerned with domestic problems and opportunities, Americans had concentrated on developing their own continent.

GAINING AN OVERSEAS EMPIRE

Two major factors helped to change this attitude and promote American interests overseas. First, domestic industry grew at an astounding rate during the second half of the nineteenth century. A massive and efficient transportation network was constructed across the American continent. Much of the country's agriculture was mechanized, and heavy industries were established. By 1900 the United States was the world's leading economic power, one that could play an influential role beyond its own territorial borders.

Second, the major nations of Europe had been scrambling for empire in Asia and Africa. They were carving up these two continents into colonial dependencies, much as Spain had done three centuries earlier in the New World. As the nineteenth century ended Americans entered into the same race. American power was to expand not only into the Caribbean and the rest of Latin America but into the Far East as well.

Arguments for Empire Basically, the United States shunned overseas political involvement. But many Americans argued for commercial

In this illustration Uncle Sam looks longingly over the sea and says, "The world is my market; my customers are all mankind." Industrial and agricultural growth encouraged the late nineteenth-century belief in the necessity of overseas outlets to absorb American surpluses.

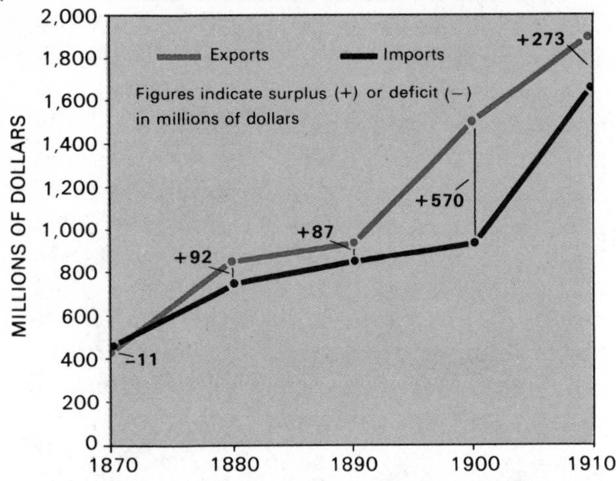

expansion during the late nineteenth century. Why shouldn't the United States seek additional markets for its agricultural products and manufactured goods? The periodic recessions and depressions in the decades following the Civil War reinforced the argument for commercial expansion. Many business leaders had begun to feel that domestic markets were saturated. The new industrial complex seemed to be producing more goods than Americans could buy. Substantial cuts in production were out of the question. They would only put large numbers of American workers and farmers out of work. In turn, unemployment might cause political unrest and social instability. Perhaps the surplus from American factories and farms could be channeled into enlarged and more profitable markets overseas.

Other expansionists argued for American imperialism on strategic grounds. The chief spokesman for this point of view was Alfred T. Mahan, a naval officer and instructor at the Naval War College. In 1890 Mahan advanced his theory in a series of lectures, which he later published as *The Influence of Sea Power on World History*. Mahan asserted that through the ages naval power had been primarily responsible for national or imperial power. He also held that no country could maintain commercial expansion without a strong navy and overseas ports (bases, for example, such as the Philippines and other Pacific islands).

Mahan's ideas quickly gained favor with imperialists in every major European country. More important, they also influenced several American foreign policy makers at the turn of the century. Chief among the American advocates of a strong navy were Roosevelt, McKinley's Assistant Secretary of the Navy, and John Hay, who served as Secretary of State under McKinley and later under Roosevelt himself.

Expansionism also had its defenders outside the business and military communities. Many Americans prided themselves on the myth of Anglo-Saxon racial superiority and the dominance of Western culture. For both selfish and humanitarian reasons they argued that the United States had a moral duty to uplift and enlighten its less civilized neighbors. The culture and religion of the Anglo-Saxons should be exported to "heathen" lands for everyone's good. This spirit was captured in 1899 by the British poet of imperialism, Rudyard Kipling. His "White Man's Burden" was written and first published in the United States. It reflected the mood of many Americans who were then debating the virtues of keeping the Philippines.

Current theories of evolution seemed to support the claims of Anglo-Saxonists. In his book *Origin of Species* (1859) Charles Darwin argued that through the process of natural selection only the "fittest" would survive. Individual animal species might adapt and prosper while others declined and perhaps disappeared. So-called social Darwinists extended these generalizations to the domains of the social scientist, businessman, and politician. That is, individual nations and empires might attain greatness at the expense of their less fit neighbors. These ideas were powerfully "scientific" supports for the missionary zeal of the expansionists.

Extending the Monroe Doctrine Although the United States moved cautiously and with uncertainty at first, it soon began to behave like a world power. Its debut on the world scene as a leading economic power provoked a great deal of controversy. But as the nineteenth century drew to a close, the prospect of increasing commercial activity abroad became highly attractive to American businessmen and politicians alike.

Even Grover Cleveland, who opposed acquiring new territories, supported commercial expansion. The severe depression that began during his second administration (1893–97) gave the President added reason to seek foreign markets. Commercial expansion might cure some of America's economic ills. It might help the nation start its slow climb back to prosperity. But a drastic change would be needed in the pattern of America's overseas trading. Historically, farm products—not manufactured goods—had been the country's main export and source of foreign exchange. American business leaders began arguing for expanding the sale of industrial goods to nonindustrialized countries such as China, the Philippines, and Latin American nations.

As early as 1889 Benjamin Harrison's Secretary of State, James G. Blaine, had organized the first Pan American Congress to promote American commerce in the Western Hemisphere and increase United States influence in Latin American affairs. During the 1890s a significant number of American businessmen responded to this opportunity by investing in Latin America. The United States thus began the process of replacing Britain as Latin America's major foreign investor. Both Harrison and Cleveland supported these efforts.

Cleveland's Latin American policy received a major test in 1895 when a crisis arose between Britain and Venezuela. The two nations disagreed over the boundary line between Venezuela and British Guiana. When the British threatened to use force against Venezuela, some Americans demanded that President Cleveland step in and apply the Monroe Doctrine to curb the European power. Stung by accusations of cowardice and beset by domestic problems, Cleveland decided to force a confrontation. He insisted that Britain submit to arbitration of the boundary dispute. Sensing that Cleveland was not bluffing, the British agreed.

The President's actions led to an important extension of the Monroe Doctrine: European powers could no longer resolve conflicts in the Western Hemisphere by military means. In a note to the British government Secretary of State Richard Olney declared that the United States considered itself "practically sovereign" in this hemisphere. The will of the United States, Olney boasted, "is law." American industrial power and growing military and naval power made these phrases more than empty words.

The Problem of Cuba Another incidence of American expansionism concerned Cuba, the island ninety miles south of Florida. Americans have always been interested in Cuba. From the early decades of the republic American politicians eyed the island with interest and greed. By the beginning of the nineteenth century Spain had lost most of its overseas empire. The remnants of that empire—Cuba, Puerto Rico, and the Philippines—became all the more valuable to the Spanish as their power waned. During the second half of the nineteenth century substantial American trade developed with the Spanish islands of the Caribbean. The situation appeared stable. But periodically groups of Americans called for absorbing Cuba, either by purchase or force.

Cubans resented Spanish rule, which was repressive and corrupt. They had revolted unsuccessfully in the 1860s. By the 1890s they had had enough. At that time, the economic crisis in the United States had reduced the American sugar trade with Cuba. The Spanish island colony suffered sharply from the effects of the American depression. In 1895 a Cuban revolutionary movement called Cuba Libre ("Free Cuba") moved for independence. The Cuban rebels embarked on a new war of national liberation, a war similar to the revolution then under way against Spanish rule in the Philippines.

Neither Cuba Libre nor the Katipunan in the Philippines had sufficient strength to push out the Spanish without outside help. Cuban rebels engaged in guerrilla warfare to wear down Spanish soldiers. The Cubans also burned sugar plantations and anything else of value, hoping to drive out Spanish landowners. In response, Spanish officials set up *reconcentrados*, or "detention camps," for civilians suspected of helping the rebels. Thousands of Cubans died in the camps because of poor food, inadequate sanitation, and lack of medical attention.

The United States had been sympathetic but strictly neutral during the earlier Cuban revolution. But in the 1890s Americans gave increasing support to the Cuban rebels. A variety of factors led Americans toward direct intervention in Cuba. First, Americans had little sympathy for Spain and its culture. Many still believed in the "Black Legend."[1] Second, Spanish troops were committing atrocities. Little did most Americans think that their own soldiers would shortly be acting in a similar manner to suppress the Filipino revolt. Third, many American businessmen had investments in Cuba, though these investments were small. Finally, Americans' new determination to become the dominant Caribbean power made events in Cuba of vital concern to Washington.

The Cuban question soon became a leading issue in United States politics. During the 1896 presidential election year Congress passed a resolution calling for recognition of the belligerent status of the Cuban rebels. President Cleveland, a Democrat who opposed territorial expansion, rejected the resolution. Cleveland's successor in the White House, Republican William McKinley, also opposed intervention in Cuba. McKinley was apparently less eager for expansion than most other members of his party. The Republican platform of 1896 was openly proexpansionist and favored involvement in the Caribbean. McKinley remained firm.

But events in Cuba and America's desire to impose its will in the Caribbean won over McKinley's promises. "Jingoism"—boastful patriotism—soon took hold of the nation. Two sensationalist New York City papers, William Randolph Hearst's *Journal* and Joseph Pulitzer's *World*, helped to stir up the interventionist frenzy. Both Hearst and Pulitzer ran stories, some of them deliberate lies, attacking Spanish cruelty in Cuba and praising the rebels. The stories spread to other newspapers across the country. By early 1898 it had become clear that Spain could not put down the Cuban rebellion. Nor would the United States allow the stalemate to continue much longer.

On the night of February 15, 1898 an explosion aboard the U.S.S. *Maine* in Havana harbor settled the issue of United States intervention. The battleship had been sent to Cuba to demonstrate American concern for the Cuban situation. The explosion killed 260 American sailors. Spain, which had the most to lose from American intervention in Cuba, hastily sent notes of regret to Washington. The cause of the explosion was never determined. But public opinion in the United States placed the blame squarely on the Spanish. "Remember the Maine!" became the slogan of American interventionists. The United States government began to pressure Spain to grant Cuba independence. But Madrid would not accept the loss of its Cuban colony.

On April 11, 1898, McKinley sent a message to Congress, asking for authority to use armed forces in Cuba. The President described Americans as "a Christian, peace-loving people" who still hoped to achieve a just solution through diplomacy rather than war. But Spain would not modify its position, even with the certainty of American armed intervention. By late April both nations were at war.

War with Spain The Spanish-American War of 1898 was over within a few months. American forces dominated Spanish military and naval power. Spanish soldiers and sailors fought bravely, but they were hopelessly ill-equipped for war. Spain won no battles and suffered heavy losses. American casualities were light. Many more soldiers died from disease than from combat.

[1] This was the English notion—dating back to the days of Queen Elizabeth and the defeat of the Spanish Armada—that the Spanish were a particularly cruel and treacherous people.

Walter Reed

The year 1900 had been called the yellow-fever year in Cuba. The Spanish-American War had brought thousands of American troops there. Hundreds of them lay near death from the disease in Columbia Barracks in Havana. Doctors and nurses worked untiringly to try to save them, too often with no effect.

Early that year a tall slender officer, very military in appearance, with a serious but kind face strode into the office of the Surgeon General of the Army in Washington, D.C. He was Major Walter Reed, an army doctor who had just arrived from Cuba. He had come to ask that he be sent back there with equipment and personnel. With these he would study the permanently damaging and often fatal yellow fever.

As a practicing doctor and a scientist, Reed was well suited to the job he sought. In 1869 he had earned a medical degree from the University of Virginia in his home state. He was eighteen at the time. From there he went to New York City, where he earned a second medical degree. As an army doctor he specialized in the new science of bacteriology, studying the causes and transmission of diphtheria and typhoid fever.

Now he urgently wanted to discover how yellow fever was transmitted. The theory then accepted was that a person caught it upon coming into contact with the clothing or bedding of an infected person. Reed did not agree. He thought that a certain kind of mosquito carried the disease and infected people with its bite. He was determined to discover which theory was correct.

Soon his orders came through. He was to return to Cuba to organize and direct the work of three doctors "for the purpose of pursuing scientific investigation of yellow fever." The dry wording of his orders did not hint at the danger involved. Only humans contracted yellow fever Therefore humans, not animals, would be subjected to experiments.

Reed and his group set up the experimental situation. In one building volunteers slept on bedding used by yellow-fever victims. In another volunteers lived in uncontaminated surroundings but were exposed to the suspected mosquitoes.

It was not long before the results were clear. None of the persons who slept on soiled bedding was infected. But those bitten by the mosquitoes did contract yellow fever; in fact one of them died as a result, as did one of the three doctors. The discovery was credited with being "worth more than the cost of the Spanish-American War, including lives lost and money expended."

Armed with the knowledge that the mosquito was indeed the culprit, United States sanitary engineers went out to clean up the filth in which the mosquitoes bred. They were so successful that by 1902 there was not one case of yellow fever in Cuba. It was also eradicated from the United States, where epidemics had periodically struck cities on the eastern seaboard. And when work began on the Panama Canal, mosquito-control measures were taken. These removed the workers from the peril of yellow fever. Walter Reed's persistence had paid off.

When the fighting ended in the summer of 1898, United States forces had won Cuba and occupied Puerto Rico. In the Philippines Dewey's squadron held Manila Bay while awaiting the arrival of American troops. Spanish officials reluctantly agreed to meet with American negotiators to hammer out a treaty that would end Spain's status as an imperial power.

During the short struggle American expansionists achieved their longstanding wish of an-

Military action in the Spanish–American War of 1898 occurred on two fronts: the Philippines and Cuba. Hostilities commenced in the Pacific. The United States Asiatic Squadron under Commodore George Dewey sailed from Hong Kong in late April to attack the Spanish Philippines. On May 1 Dewey destroyed the Spanish naval force in Manila Bay with no loss of American lives.

In the Caribbean theater the Spanish fleet under Admiral Pascual Cervera arrived in Santiago harbor in May and was blockaded there by an American naval squadron. The blockade was reinforced June 1 under the command of Rear Admiral William T. Sampson. In late June United States troops under General William R. Shafter landed in Cuba at Daiquiri and Siboney and marched on Santiago. This force included the Rough Riders, a volunteer cavalry regiment under Colonel Leonard Wood and Lieutenant Colonel Theodore Roosevelt. On July 1 the troops captured the heights north and east of Santiago in the battles of El Caney and San Juan Hill. They then began an artillery bombardment of Santiago.

On July 3 Admiral Cervera attempted to run the United States blockade and escape from Santiago harbor. But Sampson's force destroyed the entire Spanish fleet in a four-hour battle along the coast. The Spanish garrison of Santiago soon surrendered (July 17). Hostilities were ended in the Caribbean by July 25.

In the Pacific Dewey's naval squadron was reinforced in July by the arrival of American troops under General Wesley Merritt. On August 13 United States troops and Filipino guerrillas occupied the city of Manila.

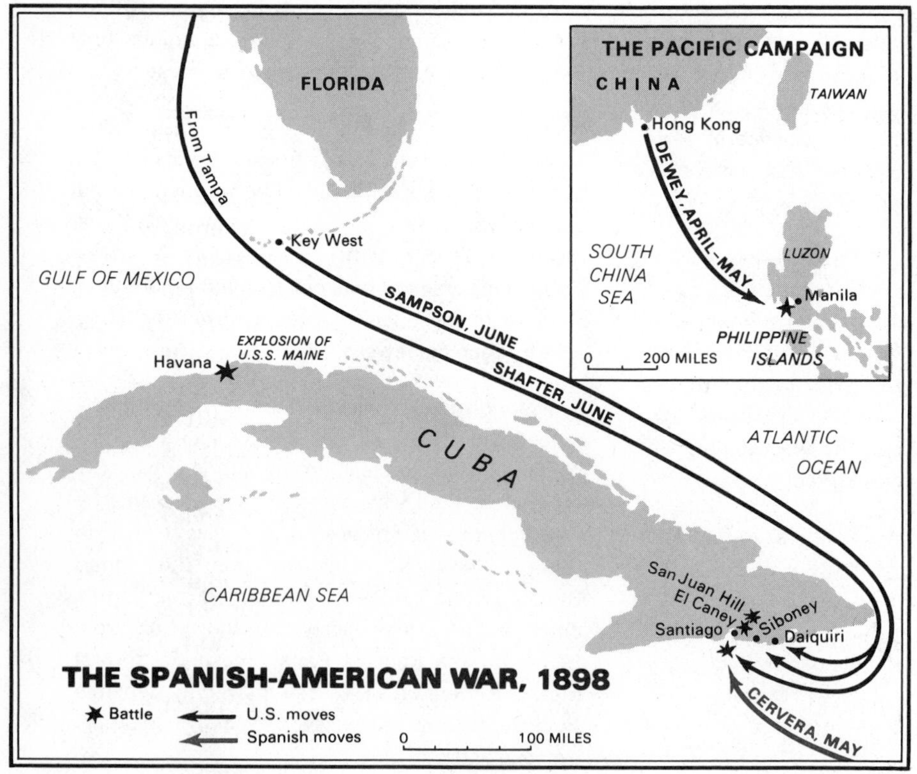

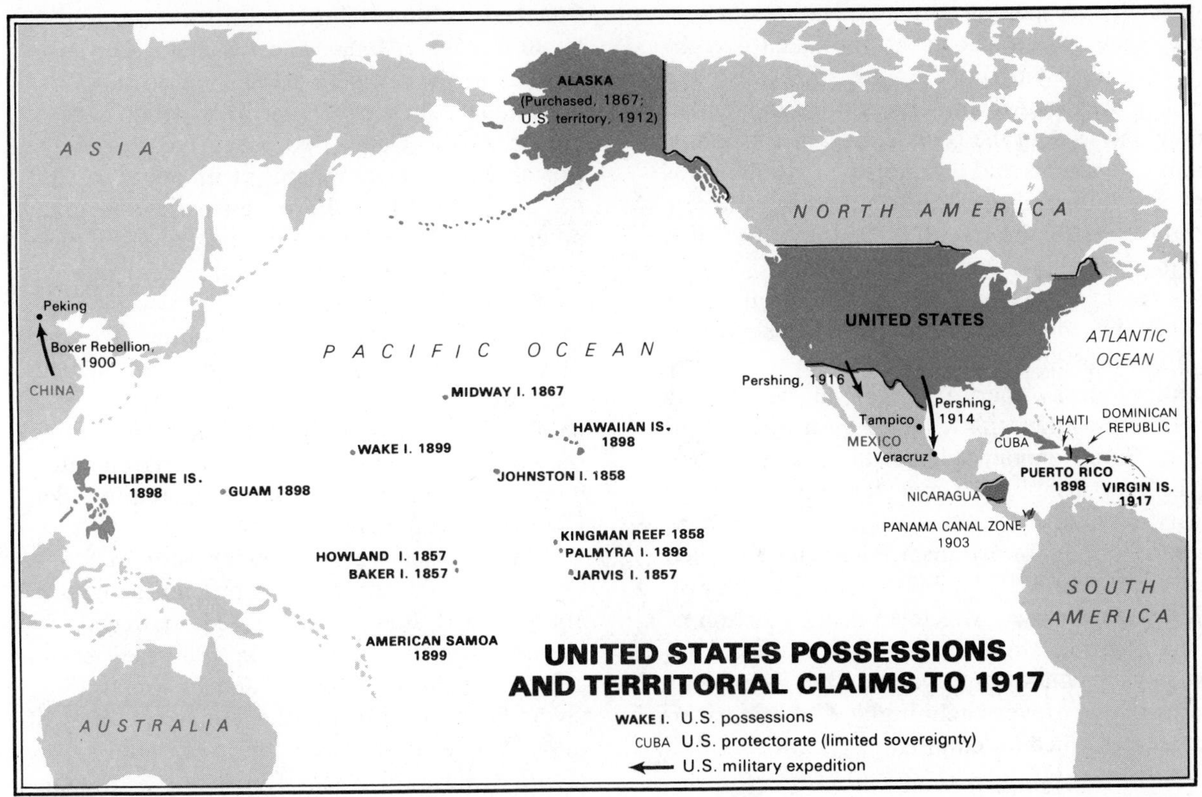

nexing Hawaii. In 1893 a revolutionary movement backed by American businessmen successfully overthrew the Hawaiian monarchy and sought annexation to the United States. But like Texas between 1836 and 1845, Hawaii had to sit out a period of uneasy independence—five years—until United States politics entered into an expansionist phase. By mid-1898 annexationist forces had gained a majority in the House and the Senate. Congress passed a joint resolution declaring Hawaii a territory of the United States.

When Spanish and American negotiators met in Paris to work out the terms of a peace, the fate of the Philippines had not yet been established. But all signs pointed to a continued American presence on the islands. President McKinley's stance of indecision fooled few people—least of all Emilio Aguinaldo and other Filipino leaders. The President had clearly been drawn into the expansionist camp. For several months McKinley played a waiting game while expansionist forces in the Senate gathered support for a Spanish-American treaty.

In the end, McKinley demanded what he perhaps had in mind all along. Determined to "educate the Filipinos, and uplift and civilize and Christianize them," McKinley asked Spain to give up all the Philippines. The Spanish had to agree. The Treaty of Paris was signed in December 1898. The United States gained control of Cuba, the Philippine Islands, and Guam.

Most Americans had supported the war with Spain. But the Treaty of Paris, which proposed immediate acquisition of an American overseas empire, ran into stiff opposition. Many Americans feared that imperialism would endanger American democracy. Others objected to imperialism on moral grounds. Nations or cultures, they argued, should not be taken over by larger nations merely because they were too weak to resist. An anti-imperialist movement organized to fight the peace treaty. In the Senate many Democrats and a minority of Republicans opposed imperialism. William Jennings Bryan, the Democratic presidential candidate of 1896, led the antitreaty forces.

But at the last minute Bryan changed his course. The day before the vote on the treaty, fighting broke out between American troops and Filipino rebels. Americans regarded the uprising as a show of ingratitude on the part of the Filipinos. Bryan announced that the challenge had to be met firmly. He threw his support to the treaty, though he declared that he would continue to oppose imperialism. The Senate ratified the Treaty of Paris in February 1899. Bryan, who again opposed McKinley in the election of 1900, attempted to make imperialism the central issue of the campaign. Bryan and the Democrats were defeated overwhelmingly. The American people had voted for empire.

The Search for Asian Markets Early in the nineteenth century a few American businessmen had entered into a prosperous trade with China. But even with the "opening" of Japan in the 1850s, the volume of United States trade in Asia never reached the proportions anticipated by American business leaders. By the end of the century overproduction in America's factories generated new and powerful pressures for foreign trade. The lure of the China market made itself felt again.

But participation in the China market could not be accomplished without political involvement in Asia. The European powers had already carved up China into "economic spheres of influence."[2] American businessmen believed they could compete successfully in China if they were given a fair opportunity. In September 1899 Secretary of State John Hay sent a series of diplomatic notes to Japan and the major European powers. In the notes he asked them to support a new trade policy in China. This policy became known as the Open Door. Hay recognized the existence of foreign spheres of influence in China, but he asked the European nations to grant other countries free-trade privileges within these spheres—thus keeping the Chinese door open to all who wanted to trade there. Hay also called on the European powers to guarantee Chinese "territorial integrity"—that is, to avoid outright political partition of the country. The European nations did not formally reject Hay's proposals, though some grumbled about American interference. Hay announced boldly that the Open Door was accepted by all.

While America was seeking support for its Open Door policies, a group of Chinese nationalists, called Boxers, organized to drive foreigners from their country. In 1900 they began killing foreign missionaries and diplomats. Survivors fled to Peking and the temporary safety of the British legation. There, they withstood a two-month siege until troops from their own countries relieved them. The United States participated by rushing in troops from bases in the Philippine Islands. The Boxer Rebellion was ended. Within a few months peace—and imperialism—were reestablished. In July Hay issued a second series of diplomatic notes. In them he asked the victorious European powers to preserve Chinese territorial integrity. Hay reaffirmed America's desire to "safeguard for the world the principle of equal and impartial trade with all parts of the Chinese Empire." Not wishing to risk a major war, the imperialist powers agreed not to divide up China. They accepted instead a sum of money from the Chinese in payment for their losses.

In comparison with other powers, the United States had acted as a friend and protector of China. But did the Open Door represent an American willingness to guarantee Chinese territorial integrity? The United States had not signed a formal agreement with China, or with any other foreign nation, to enact its Open Door

[2] A nation often established with other nations a world area where it would hold a dominant economic position. Once other countries agreed to accept this arrangement, the area in question would be free from the competition of other nations.

policy. Hay quickly admitted that his country would not go to war to enforce the Open Door—not in 1900 at any rate. European imperialistic powers had battled to a draw in China with the creation of economic spheres of influence. Hay's Open Door declarations filled the partial vacuum created by this stalemate. The Open Door would work to America's advantage only as long as no other major power embarked on an all-out push to dominate China.

This Chinese Boxer, a member of the society whose official title was the Fist of Righteous Harmony, believed that his country's survival depended upon expulsion of foreign powers threatening to divide China for economic profit. The Boxer Rebellion nearly led to the extinction of China as a national entity.

INTERVENTION IN LATIN AMERICA

The growth of United States industrial and military power, combined with America's interest in the Caribbean, meant that Britain's position as the leading Caribbean power would not last long. In 1895, during the first Venezuelan crisis, the Cleveland administration had asserted America's new role in the Western Hemisphere. The events of the next decade confirmed this role.

Building a Canal to the Pacific Britain proved very cooperative in the building of a canal across Central America. A fifty-year-old treaty between Britain and the United States became an early casualty of America's new attitude of expansion. The 1850 treaty called for participation by both nations in the construction of any transoceanic canal. In February 1900 Secretary Hay negotiated another accord with the British ambassador, Lord Pauncefote. Under the Hay-Pauncefote Treaty Britain granted the United States exclusive rights to build a canal. But the American government was prohibited from fortifying it. This compromise did not satisfy the United States Senate. The treaty was quickly rejected. Hay returned to the negotiating table, pulled a few teeth from the reluctant British lion, and produced a second agreement. The revised treaty placed no limitations on military fortification of the canal. The United States had only to promise that during peacetime all nations could use the canal on equal terms.

Americans next turned their attention to the question of where the Central American canal should be built. The shortest route was across the Isthmus of Panama, a province owned by Colombia. The Colombian government had sold the rights to the Panama site to a French company, headed by Ferdinand DeLesseps (builder of Egypt's Suez Canal). After several unsuccessful attempts to build a canal, the French offered to sell their rights for $109 million. Another proposed site, in Nicaragua, was a much longer route. But it was less expensive and free of foreign entanglements.

President Roosevelt and Congress argued the relative merits of both routes and initially favored the Nicaraguan site. Then, early in 1902, the French company lowered the price for sale of its rights to $40 million. Roosevelt quickly changed his mind in favor of the Panama site. Permission also had to be gotten from Colombia. In January 1903 Secretary Hay signed a treaty with Colombia agreeing to pay $10 million and an annual rent of $250,000 for a hundred-year-lease on a canal zone in Panama.

But the Colombian senate, in a burst of patriotic pride and financial self-interest, rejected the canal treaty. President Roosevelt complained about the "bandits" of Colombia and their insistence on national honor. Roosevelt considered intervening in Panama under the terms of an 1846 treaty with Colombia. This granted the United States the right to maintain "free transit" across the isthmus. But United States troops were then busy fighting in the Philippines. Besides, the 1846 treaty required the agreement of Colombian authorities for the use of force in Panama.

In November 1903 a revolt in Panama settled the canal question. The revolt was organized by Phillipe Bunau-Varilla, an agent of the French canal company. The Panamanian rebels received immediate United States aid. American ships were sent in to prevent Colombian forces from landing on the isthmus. Within a few days the new Panamanian government declared independence. Bunau-Varilla was appointed its chief representative to the United States. Bunau-Varilla and Secretary Hay quickly came to an agreement on an American-operated canal. Under the treaty the United States granted diplomatic recognition to Panama and obtained a perpetual lease on a canal zone.

Roosevelt's famous boast that "I took the canal zone and let Congress debate" is caricatured here. Roosevelt is seen heaving his shovelful of Panamanian soil on Bogota, capital of Colombia, the country from which Panama was detached.

Roosevelt's "big stick" diplomacy in Panama received sharp criticism from some Democrats in Congress. But the majority of Americans approved of the deeds and the bluster of their President. Some years later Roosevelt acknowledged with few apologies: "I took the canal zone and let Congress debate, and while the debate goes on, the canal does also."

In 1914 the Panama Canal opened to merchant shipping. The canal was acclaimed as a marvel of American engineering. It also put the finishing touch on a program for United States domination of the Caribbean and economic penetration of Latin America.

Policing the Caribbean While negotiations were being carried on in Panama, a second international crisis erupted in Venezuela. The dispute involved an attempt by European powers to collect debts owed their citizens by Venezuela. In December 1902 Britain, Germany, and Italy sent warships to blockade the Venezuelan port of LaGuaira. An international court decided that the three nations that had blockaded Venezuela should be given priority in collecting their debts.

Roosevelt contested this decision. America could not permit European powers to use force to settle disputes in the Western Hemisphere. When a similar financial crisis arose in 1905 in the Dominican Republic, another Caribbean country, Roosevelt moved quickly to avoid European intervention. American officials took over the government and the financial affairs of the Dominicans.

In 1904 Roosevelt announced to Congress that the United States would not tolerate "chronic wrongdoing" by any Latin American country. If political or economic developments in

Latin America invited the danger of European intervention, the United States would intervene first. The President's message, which became known as the Roosevelt Corollary to the Monroe Doctrine, asserted the role of the United States as an "international police power" in the Caribbean. The statement was actually a broad departure from the earlier doctrine.

Dollar Diplomacy Theodore Roosevelt's successor, William Howard Taft, pursued Roosevelt's policies in Latin America. He favored economic penetration of foreign nations, a policy that became known as dollar diplomacy. Taft urged American capitalists to invest millions of dollars in overseas ventures, especially in the Caribbean. Such investments, he said, would bring Wall Street handsome profits. More important, they would serve the interests of American security. Also, American guardianship of the Western Hemisphere would benefit the people of Latin America. It would ensure them political stability and economic growth.

Nicaragua mounted the most serious challenge to the new American policy. Nicaraguan president José Zelaya, a strong opponent of the United States, tried to avoid the snares of dollar diplomacy. In 1909 he canceled special economic privileges granted to an American mining company. Zelaya's downfall came quickly. A revolutionary movement, supported by American businessmen, overthrew the Nicaraguan president. The United States granted diplomatic recognition to the new regime, took over the government's finances, and sent in the marines to protect American interests. The pattern for implementing dollar diplomacy had been clearly established.

Idealism Versus Intervention in Mexico In 1913 Woodrow Wilson, a Democrat, moved into the White House. In his campaign Wilson promised a more liberal internationalism. He wanted a new foreign policy to curb the growing imperialist impulse. Wilson's choice for Secretary of State, the anti-imperialist William Jennings Bryan, gave some indication that Republican policies would be modified or abandoned. Wilson stated that his aim in Latin America was to support "the orderly processes of just government based upon law, and not upon arbitrary or irregular force, and to cultivate the friendship of our sister republics of Central and South America."

But idealistic aims proved no match for big-power politics. As President, Wilson used military force in Latin America even more than his Republican predecessors. Seeking to bring peace and "constitutional liberty" to the unstable governments of Latin America, he sent troops into the Caribbean to put down a rebellion in Haiti. A year later, in 1916, the President ordered United States Marines into the Dominican Republic. There a military government was established under the Department of the Navy. Troops remained in both countries throughout Wilson's administration.

Wilson played his strongest and most controversial role as a moralist when he intervened in the Mexican revolution that had begun in 1910. The President at first refused to recognize the government of General Victoriano Huerta, who had risen to power in 1913. An unsavory politician, Huerta had ordered the murder of his predecessor, Francisco Madero, Mexico's first freely elected president in decades. Wilson wanted Huerta to resign and permit free elections in Mexico. Though such goals might have been welcomed by the Mexican people, they could hardly be imposed from outside by persuasion alone.

Huerta refused to budge from the presidential palace in Mexico City. But Wilson remained determined to "teach the South American republics to elect good men." Early in 1914 the President allowed ships to supply arms to Huerta's foes. In April Huerta's forces arrested a group of American sailors who had landed at the port of Tampico. Washington demanded formal apologies. Huerta agreed but only on the condition that the United States support his government. Wilson and Bryan refused. When the President learned that an arms shipment from Germany—intended for Huerta's forces—was

General John J. Pershing and his hastily mobilized American troops invaded Mexico in 1916 in pursuit of "Pancho" Villa. The mission was a failure and may even have convinced Germany of America's military unpreparedness.

nearing the Mexican port of Veracruz, he decided to act.

In the meantime, Congress had granted Wilson permission to use armed forces against Huerta. A message went out to the United States naval commander in the Caribbean: "Take Veracruz at once." American forces quickly seized Veracruz. Mexican opposition rose within a few days. Fighting broke out, and both sides suffered heavy casualities. Wilson, who had not anticipated bloodshed, found himself in an embarrassing position. Americans protested the involvement—and the death of United States soldiers. Withdrawal of troops had to be arranged by a mediating commission of three South American countries.

Wilson's problems regarding Mexico were not over, however. Huerta was overthrown in July 1914 by the Constitutionalist forces of Venustiano Carranza. As the new president tried to consolidate power, civil war again broke out in Mexico. In November 1915 Wilson gave unofficial support to Carranza's government. This move angered other pretenders to the Mexican presidency, particularly "Pancho" Villa. Operating in northern Mexico, Villa decided to teach the "gringos" a lesson. Early in 1916 Villa's forces stopped a train and killed sixteen American engineering students. Villa then crossed the border to raid the New Mexico town of Columbus, an act of revenge that cost seventeen American lives. The calculating and cold-blooded Villa hoped to lead America into military intervention in Mexico. Then, as the leading opponent of the United States, he would gain support from those people who supported Carranza.

Villa guessed correctly about United States intervention. But he misjudged its political consequences. Americans were enraged by Villa's actions. General John J. Pershing—soon to gain fame and glory as commander of the United States Army in France—led a "punitive" expedition deep into Mexico. Villa could not be found. Instead, American troops fought a bloody skirmish with Carranza forces. The battle was unwanted by both sides. The incident threatened another Veracruz. But anti-interventionists in Congress won out over those who wanted war. Early in 1917 Pershing's forces were withdrawn from Mexico. For most Americans it had become clear that Wilson's Mexican policy meant continuous trouble. By this time, too, the American people had become far more concerned with developments in Europe, where a destructive war had been raging since 1914.

THE UNITED STATES AND WORLD WAR I

Europe had enjoyed a period of relative peace during the century after Napoleon's defeat in 1815. International rivalries did not die down, and many short but limited wars broke out. Yet Europeans had managed to avoid a general war. European leaders relied on the balance of power to maintain peace and political stability. Two powerful blocs kept each other in check: the Central powers (Germany, Austria-Hungary, and Turkey) and the Allies (Britain, France, and Russia). But a buildup of arms on both sides foreshadowed trouble. In 1914 the assassination of Archduke Franz Ferdinand, heir to the Austro-Hungarian throne, set off a chain reaction that resulted in World War I.

The United States tried to stay out of the war. Whatever their personal opinions or sympathies, most Americans preferred neutrality. In 1914 Wilson issued a proclamation calling on all Americans to remain impartial "in thought as well as in action." But over the next three years a combination of factors edged the United States closer and closer to the side of the Allies and involvement in the European war.

The Road to War European powers violated America's rights as a neutral nation. American shippers tried to continue, and even expand, commerce with both sides. As in the case of the Napoleonic Wars a century before, American interests quickly clashed with those of Britain, the world's leading sea power. The British declared the North Sea a military zone. Before a neutral ship could pass through British waters, it had to enter a British port. There the ship's cargo was examined for contraband (war materials). British escorts would then lead the neutral ship through minefields to safety. Many Americans protested, and Wilson publicly condemned the British practice. But the United States clearly was not going to make the issue a cause for war. No American lives were lost as a result of the British

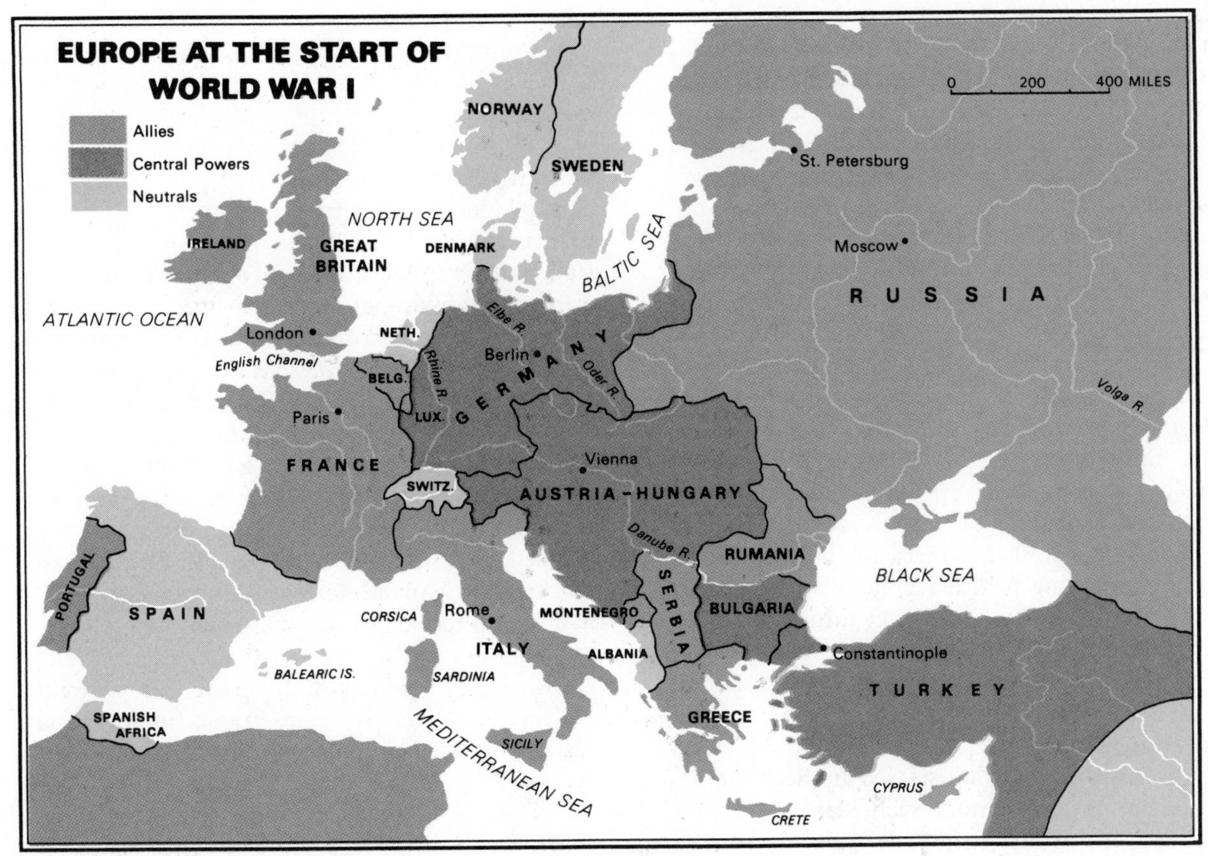

regulations. No American seamen were impressed into the British navy, as in the War of 1812.

The Germans knew that their navy was no match for British sea power. For the most part German battleships and cruisers remained at anchor in home ports. Instead, the Germans turned to the submarine as a means of crippling their enemies. The British blockade of Continental Europe, launched soon after the war, threatened the German people with starvation. Germany fought back by declaring all-out submarine warfare. The Germans announced that any ships found in the waters surrounding the British Isles would be torpedoed without warning. Loss of life in such cases usually ran high.

Wilson denounced the German declaration as a violation of American neutral rights. Many Americans condemned submarine warfare as immoral. In the spring of 1915 the British passenger liner *Lusitania* was torpedoed by a German submarine off the Irish coast. Over 1,000 people died, including 128 Americans. Germany refused to accept responsibility for the incident or pay indemnities for American losses. The Germans pointed out that Americans had been publicly warned not to sail on British ships. Besides, the *Lusitania* carried arms as well as passengers. But Wilson drafted a strongly worded note to the Germans insisting that they end their surprise attacks.

Economic factors also contributed to American intervention on the side of the Allies. The United States had always traded more with Britain than with Continental Europe. The onset of world war, combined with British domination of the seas, ensured an expanded trade with Britain and its allies. Americans might have to endure annoying British regulations, but at least most American ships could get through to Britain. Between 1914 and 1916 Allied purchases in America quadrupled. It soon became apparent that Britain and France would need loans in order to continue trading. Wall Street stood ready. Anti-interventionists, led by Secretary of State Bryan, argued that such loans were contraband and would inevitably drag the United States into the war. Again Wilson proclaimed strict neutrality. He did not move to prohibit credit to the Allies, however. The loans were, after all, big business, and the United States economy was booming.

Another important factor influencing American involvement in the war was close cultural and political ties with Britain. Since the end of the nineteenth century relations between Britain and America had improved dramatically, though the two nations had not entered into a formal alliance. Most Americans sympathized with Britain and its allies. German Americans, as well as Irish Americans who opposed Britain's policies in Ireland, were notable exceptions. Perhaps the strongest supporter of Britain was Wilson himself. The President admired British culture and the parliamentary form of government. In contrast, Germany's image in America had suffered a complete change during the nineteenth century. Americans once viewed Germany as a country of poets and philosophers but came to see it as a stark and frightening nation of militarists.

Within the context of these three factors—neutral rights, economic interdependence, and cultural ties—Wilson tried to maintain a course of neutrality. By 1916 the war had become a stalemate. Neither side seemed capable of gathering enough strength to defeat the other. Hundreds of thousands of soldiers died in a series of brutal, inconclusive battles. Wilson attempted to use American prestige and the threat of use of power to negotiate a European peace. His trusted adviser, Colonel Edward M. House, crossed the Atlantic several times to confer with foreign ministers and heads of state. European statesmen listened to House—America was too powerful to ignore—but they did not heed his message. They had fought too long and suffered too many losses to accept Wilson's "peace without victory." The British and French skillfully played along with Wilson and House, banking ultimately on American intervention to bring an Allied victory.

The war dragged on indecisively for three years. Early in 1917 Germany renewed unrestricted submarine warfare, cutting off food and supplies to the French and British. Germans also launched a massive land offensive that threatened to destroy the Allies. Germany knew that this action would bring the United States into the war. But Berlin hoped to smash the Allies before a large American force could be mobilized and sent to Europe.

Wilson acted. Early in 1917 Washington received news of a revolution in Russia and the establishment of a constitutional government. The overthrow of the Russian czar removed many of the moral problems that Wilson faced in seeking support for American involvement on the side of the Allies. In April the President asked Congress to declare war on Germany. Wilson called upon Americans to embark on a great crusade, a "war to end all wars" and to make the world safe for democracy. In his message to Congress Wilson noted: "It is a fearful thing to lead this great peaceful people into war. But right is more precious than peace."

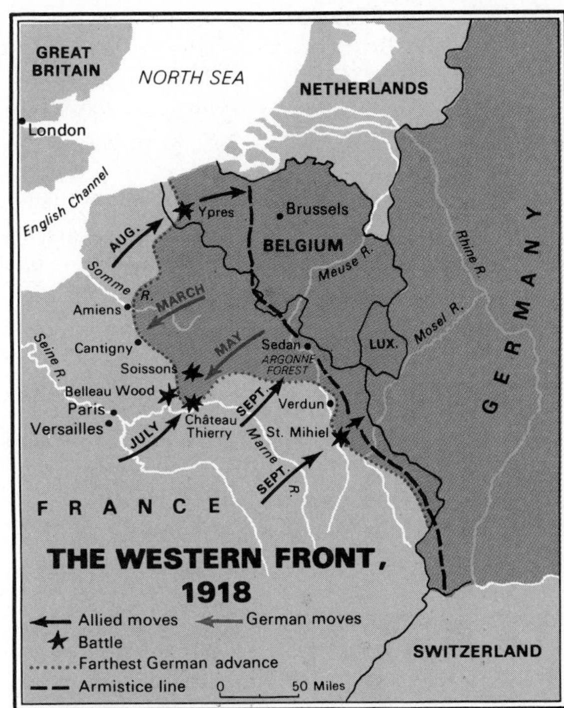

War broke out in July 1914, one month after Serbian nationalists had assassinated Archduke Franz Ferdinand of Austria. Although the United States was a neutral for the first three years of the conflict, its ships were at times seized by the British and some were sunk by the Germans. In early 1917, after the Germans renewed unrestricted submarine warfare against all shipping, the United States broke off diplomatic relations with Germany. Provoked by continued German submarine attacks, the United States declared war on Germany in April of that year. The United States entered the war on the side of the Allies as an associated power. In June an American Expeditionary Force under General John J. Pershing arrived in France.

In March 1918, after years of trench warfare, the Germans began an offensive with the Second Battle of the Somme, intending to reach the English Channel. The Allies (including the United States) later set up a unified command for the Western Front under French General Ferdinand Foch. In May the German armies approached to within fifty miles of Paris. The turning point of the war came in July–August, when the German advance was stopped at the Second Battle of the Marne. Allied advances in the second half of 1918 were marked by major offensives at Belleau Wood in June–July, Ypres in August, St. Mihiel in September, and the Meuse-Argonne Forest drive of September–November.

The military position of the Central Powers deteriorated rapidly during the summer of 1918. On November 11, an armistice was signed, putting an end to the war.

The Great Crusade When the United States entered World War I, the major European powers were nearly exhausted. On both sides men previously considered too old or too young for combat were pressed into military service. But after April 1917 the Allies suddenly had a great new reservoir of manpower to draw upon—the young manhood of the United States. The regular American army was small. Close to a million soldiers had to be recruited. But America prepared willingly to meet the demands of Wilson's crusade. Military conscription was accepted by most Americans with far fewer objections than during the Civil War or during the war in Vietnam.

The German submarine campaign achieved startling success during the first six months of 1917. The Allied navies soon devised an effective countermeasure: the convoy system. A single ship crossing the Atlantic had little chance against the German submarine fleet. But a large group of troop ships and freighters traveling together could reach Europe in relative security. The rate of sinkings by German submarines fell

The Fight Over the League of Nations

On July 19, 1919, Woodrow Wilson submitted the Treaty of Versailles with its League of Nations covenant to the United States Senate. A poll taken earlier in the year showed that sixty-four senators—the necessary two-thirds majority—favored ratification. But time and events had reduced that figure. Everyone knew that trouble lay ahead.

One source of the trouble was Wilson himself. He had created hostility by neglecting to ask any leading Republican to accompany him on the peacemaking mission. Then, too, he was a stubborn man. Once he made a decision, he was certain that it was right. He refused to compromise.

Another source of trouble lay in the diverse reactions of the senators to the treaty and the League. Some thought the treaty dealt unfairly with various nations, but they favored the League of Nations. Others had no trouble with the treaty itself but feared that the League would take away American independence and possibly lead the United States into war again. And there were those who thought the treaty provisions were unjust and that the League would only uphold these injustices. Several Republicans objected to the League simply because they thought that members of both parties should have had a stake in its creation.

Isolationist Senators Borah, Lodge, and Johnson refuse to give a lady—Peace—a seat.

Battle lines were being drawn. There were forty-seven Democrats and forty-nine Republicans in the Senate, divided into three discernible groups. First there were those who were willing to ratify the treaty immediately—forty-three Democrats. Then there were the "reservationists"—about thirty-five Republicans and one Democrat—who wanted some of the provisions changed before they would agree to vote for ratification. Finally there were the "irreconcilables"—the remaining Republicans, including three Democrats. This last group vowed never to sign the treaty under any circumstance.

At the center of this controversy was Senator Henry Cabot Lodge of Massachusetts, the new chairman of the Foreign Relations Committee. Lodge disliked Wilson and objected to the treaty, which he thought was too easy on Germany. He was therefore, at heart, an irreconcilable. But he thought he knew a better way of defeating the treaty. As he said to one senatorial colleague, "I do not propose to beat it by direct frontal attack, but by the indirect method of reservations."

Before the treaty went to the Senate for a vote, it was stalled for two months in the unfriendly Foreign Relations Committee. When it emerged, forty-nine revisions and amendments were attached to it. The disheartened Wilson was adamant. Democratic senators were not to vote for it with these "Lodge reservations." "Never! Never!" said Wilson. "I'll never consent to accept any policy with which that impossible name is so prominently identified."

He kept his word, and enough Senate Democrats stayed loyal to him to defeat the treaty with reservations. On November 19 it was all over. The Senate adjourned and the treaty that Wilson thought would be his crowning achievement would not be considered again. The United States would never join the League of Nations.

The Meuse-Argonne offensive in World War I was noted for its vastness—1,200,000 American troops—and its human costliness—over 120,000 casualties. Sergeant Alvin York, the prewar conscientious objector, became famous here for his single-handed capture of 132 Germans.

rapidly. Most important, nearly all American soldiers completed the passage to France safely.

The large but still untested American army–General John J. Pershing's American Expeditionary Force–went into action late in 1917. French generals, hungry for more manpower, had originally called for small-sized American units, which they wished to integrate into their own commands. Pershing worked cooperatively with the French commanders and with the Allied commander in chief, Marshal Ferdinand Foch. But he and other senior American officers insisted that the Americans operate as an independent army.

American soldiers soon received their own piece of the Western front to defend. American troops helped the Allies hold their positions. Then they joined the Allied counteroffensive in the summer and fall of 1918. By November Germany was beaten. The Kaiser fled into exile in Holland. Worn out by four years of brutal warfare and beset by unrest at home, Germany asked for peace.

At home America organized its wartime economy as quickly and effectively as it had mobilized its soldiers. The United States had begun to prepare for war as early as 1916. In that year Congress created the Council of National Defense, a mixed governmental and business commission. During the war the council supervised a network of agencies that controlled every aspect of the American economy. Under Bernard Baruch the War Industries Board supervised the allocation of raw materials and set production goals. The Food Administration controlled prices, and a War Trade Board regulated imports and exports. Congress established at least half a dozen other agencies, all of which reported to the President.

Wilson used his presidential war powers to the limit in waging a battle against dissent. Most Americans supported the war. But sizable minorities did not. German Americans opposed United States support of the Allies for ethnic reasons. Socialists and radicals condemned the war as a "capitalist" venture for profit. During the first months of American participation German Americans suffered the abuse (and sometimes the assaults) of their fellow citizens. But when it became certain that Germany would have to yield to the Allies, radicalism came to be regarded as the prime threat to Wilsonian peace. In November 1917 communist forces in Russia overthrew the new constitutional government and withdrew their nation from the war. With the new "red scare" radical dissenters replaced German Americans as the nation's principal outcasts.

A government propaganda machine, the Committee on Public Information, was set up to publicize war efforts and to censor information or newspaper opinions unfavorable to the Allied cause. Congress enlarged the war against dissent by passing strict laws against treason. By the time the war ended, almost all Americans had been enlisted in the crusade.

Wilson the Peacemaker At the war's end Wilson turned his energies and ideals to the formidable task of obtaining a fair and lasting peace. The President had outlined his proposals for peace—the Fourteen Points—even before the armistice. The Germans surrendered in November 1918, hoping that Wilson's peace program would guide Allied policy.

The American President called for a new world order. It would help to eliminate worldwide political and economic rivalries. He sought to substitute international cooperation for the unstable and dangerous balance-of-power politics that had led the world to war. Wilson also proposed national self-determination for ethnic groups in the decaying European empires. Finally, Wilson called for a "general association of nations," a league of all the countries in the world. The league's members would cooperate actively to avoid future international conflicts.

In January 1919 Allied negotiators met at Versailles, a city outside of Paris. The peace conference was attended by Wilson and other Allied heads of state: Premier Georges Clemenceau of France, Prime Minister David Lloyd George of Britain, and Premier Vittorio Orlando of Italy. Clemenceau's overconcern with French security, though understandable, gave Wilson the most trouble. Lloyd George sought a middle ground, though he always kept the interests of the British Empire in mind. Orlando, junior partner of the Allies, did not participate in most of the "summit" deliberations.

The treaty that emerged from Versailles was a compromise. But it was surprisingly in tune with Wilsonian goals. The President was defeated overwhelmingly on several issues. Despite Wilson's call for "open convenants of peace, openly arrived at," most of the treaty negotiations took shape in secret conferences among the Allied "Big Three"—Wilson, Lloyd George, and Clemenceau. Wilson compromised on national self-determination, allowing European leaders to redraw the political map of Europe. He agreed that Germany and its allies should pay staggering amounts in war damages. Allied powers greedily divided up Germany's colonies, ignoring the wishes of the inhabitants of those areas. Nonetheless, most of the Fourteen Points were incorporated into the treaty. Perhaps most important for Wilson, the Treaty of Versailles called for the establishment of an international peacekeeping body, the League of Nations.

But dedication to ideals does not ensure success in politics, as Wilson quickly found out. Wilson brought the treaty and the League home to debate and disaster (see page 614). A small group of isolationists in the Senate were opposed to any American participation in an international league. They feared that a headlong rush into internationalism would curb essential American rights and hurt American interests. Other American senators wanted to be convinced. If Wilson had confided in these senators and attempted to work out a compromise with them, the treaty and the League of Nations might have been saved.

Wilson, however, saw all opposition as betrayal of the highest trust, the cause of world peace. He cracked the whip of party discipline over Democratic senators and went on the campaign trail seeking public support for his treaty. The trip ended tragically when Wilson suffered a stroke, which left him partially paralyzed. During 1919 the Senate rejected several versions of the treaty.

Wilson began looking ahead to the presidential election of 1920, which he hoped to turn into a "solemn referendum" on the League. The election became instead a referendum on Wilsonian politics. Republican Warren G. Harding, who promised Americans a retreat from internationalism and a return to "normalcy," won a landslide victory. All hope for American participation in the League of Nations vanished.

1. Why did Aguinaldo and the Filipino insurgents go to war against the American occupation troops?
2. Why didn't the insurrection come to an end when Aguinaldo swore an oath of allegiance to the United States? When did it end?
3. Explain the connection between mounting interest in overseas expansion and industrial growth in the United States.
4. How did Captain Mahan, Kipling, and the Social Darwinists justify the need for expansion?
5. Why did the United States support Cuban independence? What events led to the Spanish-American War.
6. Why did American businessmen expect to benefit from the Open Door Policy? Was the policy harmful or beneficial to the Chinese?
7. Describe some of the efforts of the United States to police the Caribbean during Roosevelt's administration. How did the Roosevelt Corollary to the Monroe Doctrine justify such intervention?
8. In what way did Woodrow Wilson claim he was going to change American foreign policy? Was the Mexican intervention consistent with this claim? Explain.
9. Could the United States have avoided intervening in World War I? In what ways was the American contribution to the Allied victory a major one?
10. What was the purpose of Wilson's Fourteen Points? Was the Treaty of Versailles in line with them? Why or why not? Why did the United States reject the treaty?

Beyond the Text

1. Since newspapers played such a significant role in bringing on the Spanish-American War, discuss the questions: Is public opinion too easily swayed to serve as a guide for setting national policy? Should newspapers be limited in the kinds of news they report?
2. Compare Roosevelt's actions in taking the Canal Zone with those of President Nixon in sending troops into Cambodia without congressional consent. Should presidential power in foreign affairs be curbed?
3. Who was responsible for the defeat of the League of Nations—Wilson or the Senate?

Bibliography

Nonfiction

Bailey, Thomas A., *Woodrow Wilson and the Great Betrayal.**
———, Woodrow Wilson and the Lost Peace.*
Beale, Howard K., *Theodore Roosevelt and the Rise of America to World Power.**
Beisner, Robert L., *Twelve Against Empire: The Anti-Imperialists, 1898–1900.**
Friedel, Frank, *The Splendid Little War.*
LaFeber, Walter, *The New Empire: An Interpretation of American Expansion, 1860–1898.**
Levin, N. Gordon, Jr., *Woodrow Wilson and World Politics.**
Link, Arthur S., *Wilson the Diplomatist.**
May, Ernest R., *Imperial Democracy.**
———, *The World War & American Isolation, 1914–1917.**
Mayer, Arno J., *Politics & Diplomacy of Peacemaking.**
Morgan, Howard W., *America's Road to Empire.**
Murray, Robert K., *The Red Scare.**
Williams, William A., *The Tragedy of American Diplomacy.**
Wolff, Leon, *Little Brown Brother.*

Fiction

Castor, Henry, *The Year of the Spaniard.*
Cummings, E. E., *The Enormous Room.**
Dos Passos, John, *Three Soldiers.**

*a paperback book

CHAPTER

31

LINDBERGH'S FLIGHT

THE CAPTAIN was a little man, dapper and very French. But he sought a big prize: $25,000 for the first man to fly an airplane from New York to Paris. His name might sound somewhat strange—even funny—to American ears: René Fonck. But his reputation was incredible. He had been the youngest French air ace in the Great War of 1914 (as World War I was known until World War II). Without being seriously injured himself, he had shot down at least seventy-five German planes. In a war that had turned the new aviators into overnight heroes, Fonck's reputation for skill, courage, and "dash" was probably greater than that of any other pilot. Now, in the summer of 1926, he was preparing for a flight that could make him an even greater hero, both in France and in the United States.

Compared with any of the planes Fonck had flown during the war, his new silver-colored craft was huge. Like most of the other large aircraft of the day, it had three engines and two wings—a biplane, it was called. Its large cabin was equipped for a crew of four: a pilot, a copilot, a mechanic, and a radio operator. The problem that Fonck faced was simply getting the plane off the ground with enough fuel to fly the 3,600 miles to Paris. All summer he tested the plane in New York, gradually increasing the gasoline load for each test.

At daybreak on September 21 Fonck's plane was pulled onto the east-west runway at Roosevelt Field, a small airport on Long Island. The wind was blowing from the west, as it almost always does after

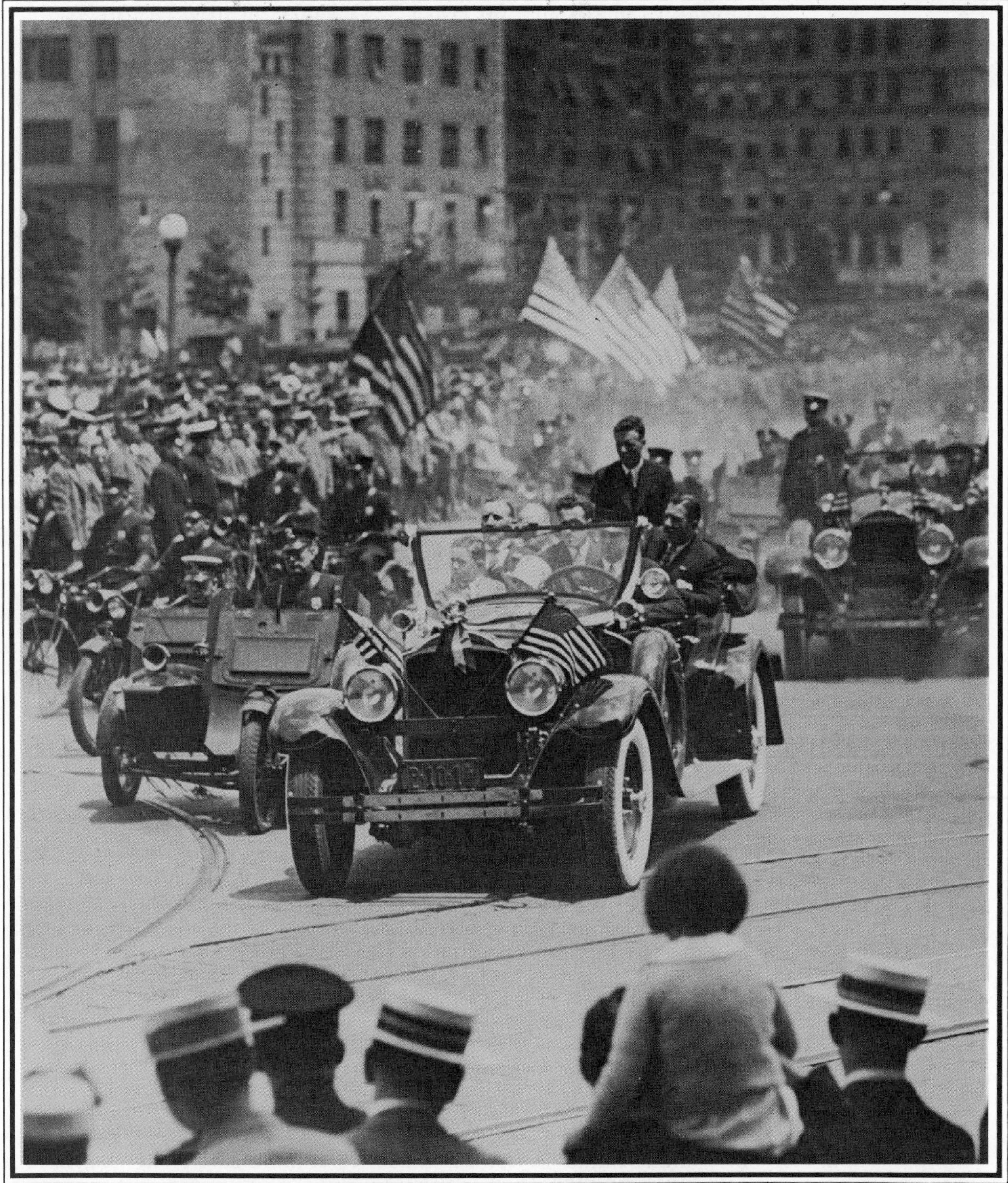

The American public was intoxicated by Lindbergh's adventure, a solo flight across the Atlantic. He was honored as a national hero in cities throughout the country—here in a parade in New York City.

dawn on Long Island. So Fonck would take off from east to west. To get the plane off the ground he and his crew would have to attain a speed of eighty miles an hour. One by one, the engines were turned up to their maximum power. After blocks were pulled away from the wheels, the plane began to move. It lurched slightly, having over 2,000 gallons of gasoline aboard, and chased its own awkward shadow down the dirt runway.

When the plane passed the halfway point on the small airstrip, it did not have the speed needed for takeoff. The small crowd of onlookers waited for Fonck to cut power. But something had gone wrong, either with the pilot or with his controls. The plane simply roared on. The runway ended. The plane took a sharp, short drop into a gully, then exploded and burst into flames. Somehow Fonck got out, and so did his navigator. But the copilot and the radio operator burned to death.

Despite the crash, the man who had offered the $25,000 prize—Raymond Orteig, a Frenchman who managed two hotels in New York—announced that his offer still stood. For a while Fonck's crash made headlines and kept alive the idea of a New York–Paris flight. Late in February 1927 others began to announce that they would make the flight. It was soon obvious that a real contest was developing. It would not be merely a battle between one airplane and the ocean but a race among several aviators and their planes. The stage was set for what the public began to sense would be the greatest thrill of the decade.

By the end of March 1927 there were four serious contenders. One was the *America*, a plane piloted by Admiral Richard E. Byrd, who had gained fame as the first man to fly to the North Pole. Byrd was backed with over $100,000 from a wealthy New York merchant. His three-engined plane, with a wingspread of over seventy feet, was huge by the standards of the day. It seemed to have the best chance.

A second entry was another trimotored craft, the *American Legion,* named after and supported by the veterans' organization. It too was backed with $100,000. Unlike Fonck's plane and Byrd's *America* the *American Legion* carried only two men. A third entry was a plane known as the *Columbia,* a single-winged, single-engined craft. The *Columbia* would soon set the world endurance record by flying for over fifty hours. Finally, there was a French entry, a single-engined biplane called the *White Bird.* Its pilot and copilot, a pair of French aces from the Great War, planned to make the flight in reverse—from Paris to

New York. The *White Bird* was said to have the most powerful gasoline engine ever put into an airplane.

By mid-April the weather had warmed up enough to make flight over the North Atlantic seem possible. On April 16 Commander Byrd took his *America* up from a New Jersey airport for its first test flight. Byrd and three crewmen tested the plane for a few hours and then brought it down for its first landing. The heavy landing gear touched ground smoothly. But almost at once there was a sound of splintering wood and wrenched metal. The *America* flipped over and skidded to a halt on its back. All four men managed to escape. Byrd had a broken wrist, and two of the other crewmen were badly hurt. They would not be able to fly again for weeks.

Ten days later the *American Legion* was in Langley Field, Virginia, undergoing its last test flight. The plane had flown well in earlier attempts. But both its designers and pilot knew it was too heavy. To find out whether the plane could make the Paris flight, the pilot and copilot decided to fly it from Virginia to New York with a full load of gasoline. The takeoff was slower than usual. For a moment it seemed as if the plane would not clear a line of trees at the end of the runway. To avoid them, the pilot banked to the right a few degrees. The slight turn was too much. It upset the delicate balance of the plane. The *American Legion* slid downward into a wet marsh and turned over. The pilot and copilot were trapped inside the cabin that filled first with gasoline fumes and then with water. By the time rescuers came wading through the marsh, the two men were dead.

Four men had been killed and three others hurt, and the race over the Atlantic had not yet begun. On both sides of the ocean, in America and in France, newspapers brought public excitement to a high pitch. Surely one of the planes would make it, sooner or later. But no one knew what might happen next or who might be injured or killed. The race to Paris had the competitive excitement of a World Series or a heavyweight championship fight. And it had the danger and drama of war. In the United States the race was almost as important as the war of 1898, the sinking of the *Lusitania,* or the declaration of war in 1917. And in France the excitement was heightened by the memory of Fonck's crash. Moreover, two other young ace pilots from the Great War, Charles Nungesser and Francis Coli, held great promise. Both had been wounded a total of twenty-six times in air combat. Between them they had won almost every medal that their government could award.

At dawn on May 8 Nungesser and Coli took off for New York from Le Bourget airport near Paris. A great crowd gathered to watch the two heroes and their *White Bird.* Nungesser got the wheels off but too soon. The *White Bird* dropped back down on the runway with a thud. Finally, it gathered speed and left the ground almost two-thirds of a mile down the long strip.

The next morning American newspapers reported that the plane had been sighted over Newfoundland. Paris celebrated with an excitement that almost matched that on the day of the armistice. Nungesser and Coli had dropped their landing gear over the ocean to save weight and lessen wind resistance. New Yorkers watched the harbor where the Frenchmen hoped to land and float until they could be reached by waiting boats. But the *White Bird* was never seen again. In France the celebrations quickly came to a shocked end.

The death toll of the New York–Paris race had reached six in less than a year. The world's most experienced pilots—backed by large sums of money, flying the best airplanes that modern technology could provide, with the most powerful motors ever developed—had all failed.

The man who was finally going to win the race to Paris had been reading every newspaper report he could find on all the airplane tests, takeoffs, and crashes. When Fonck's plane burned, Charles Lindbergh was flying air mail between Chicago and St. Louis. When Byrd and the others announced that they would enter the competition, Lindbergh was in San Diego supervising the construction of a new plane for himself. When Nungesser and Coli took off from Paris, he was waiting in San Diego for the weather to clear over the Rocky Mountains and the Great Plains, so he could fly east to St. Louis. From there he would go on to New York to make his attempt.

Lindbergh had only $2,000 of his own money, carefully kept for him by his mother in Detroit. He was only twenty-five years old. He looked even younger, so that almost everyone called him a boy. Worst of all, he decided on what struck everyone as a suicidal idea: to make the flight in a single-engine plane with only himself in the cockpit. He had been able to persuade some St. Louis businessmen to back him to the extent of $15,000. But this was a small sum compared to the support that Byrd's group and the *American Legion* had. Still, late in the summer of 1926, just before Fonck's crash, Lindbergh had come to an almost religious conviction that he could make the Paris flight.

At first Lindbergh tried to negotiate with several large aircraft companies. He was turned down. No one wanted to risk a company's reputation on an insane stunt like flying from New York to Paris alone. Then Lindbergh sent a plain but daring telegram to Ryan Airlines, a small, little known factory in California:

RYAN AIRLINES, INC. FEB. 3, 1927

SAN DIEGO, CALIFORNIA

CAN YOU CONSTRUCT WHIRLWIND ENGINE PLANE CAPABLE FLYING NONSTOP BETWEEN NEW YORK AND PARIS. IF SO PLEASE STATE COST AND DELIVERY DATE.

Surprisingly, the answer came quickly. The small company could build the plane, and it could do so for the amount of money Lindbergh had at his disposal. But it would take three months, the telegram said. Lindbergh answered:

RYAN AIRLINES FEB. 5, 1927

SAN DIEGO, CALIFORNIA

COMPETITION MAKES TIME ESSENTIAL. CAN YOU CONSTRUCT PLANE IN LESS THAN THREE MONTHS. PLEASE WIRE GENERAL SPECIFICATIONS.

This drawing shows the plane Ryan airlines built for Lindbergh. Although the goal of the design was simplicity, sacrificing safety to the need for carrying as much gasoline as possible, the plane was quite a sophisticated piece of machinery.

Again the company answered quickly, making as much of a guess as a calculation. It could build a plane capable of carrying 380 gallons of gasoline at a cruising speed of 100 miles per hour, with an engine rated at only 200 horsepower. (This was less than half the power of the big engine that had taken the *White Bird* out over the Atlantic. It was much less than the power supplied by the three engines of Byrd's great *America* as well.) Most important, the company promised to have the plane ready in time.

By the last week in February Lindbergh was in San Diego working out the details on his plane. Neither Lindbergh nor the engineer who designed the plane knew how far it was to Paris. They drove to the San Diego public library to measure off the distance on a globe with a piece of string. Lindbergh remembered it this way:

> "It's 3,600 miles." The bit of white grocery string under my fingers stretches taut along the coast of North America, bends down over a faded blue ocean, and strikes the land mass of Europe. It isn't a very scientific way of finding the exact distance between two points on the earth's surface, but the answer is accurate enough for our first calculations. The designer was making quick calculations in pencil on the back of an envelope. "Maybe we'd better put in 400 gallons of gasoline instead of 380," he concludes.

Lindbergh's project was simple, almost amateurish: quick telegrams, bits of string stretched across a public-library globe, figures on the back of an envelope, and "maybe" calculations. But with no more detailed or expert plans, he decided to go ahead.

The mechanics and carpenters at Ryan started work at once on the plane that Lindbergh would call the *Spirit of St. Louis.* They built it almost literally around the pilot. The narrow, simple cockpit was just large enough to hold Lindbergh's tall, skinny body (and then only if the overhead ribs were hollowed out a little to make room for his head). In the end the plane would be only about three feet taller than Lindbergh himself. Moreover, it would have a smaller engine that any of the other planes in the race. But this was the secret of Lindbergh's plane—simplicity. He would build the smallest, simplest plane possible, a machine designed with only one purpose: to carry enough gasoline for the trip. Everything else—comfort, safety, complicated navigating equipment—would be sacrificed to save weight, weight that could be turned into gallons of gasoline.

On April 26, the day the two pilots of the *American Legion* were killed in Virginia, the *Spirit of St. Louis* was finished. Two days later Lindbergh was ready for his first test flight. He shoved himself into his

(continued on page 625)

The Maturing of American Culture

Generations of foreigners, while admiring American achievements in other fields, criticized the nation's artistic backwardness. Even Americans who patronized the arts—like this eager visitor in Frank Waller's 1881 painting of the Metropolitan Museum—were said to appreciate money more than merit. Such views were exaggerated, yet held some truth. Until the late nineteenth century, a distinctive American culture was slow to emerge. But the situation changed in the next few decades. By the 1920s foreigners were admiring American literature, painting, architecture, and music. The United States had found a cultural voice of its own.

[For further information on the foreign observers quoted in this essay, see "Notes on Sources."]

PICTORIAL ESSAY 7

PE 7–2 / American art is still in a stage of evolution; the painters of today are the precursors of those who shall adorn the Golden Age which is to come. Though there have been, and are, individual artists of distinguished merit and ability, art itself is not yet fully developed nor understood. The nation has had hitherto neither time, opportunity, nor inclination to interest itself intelligently in the fine arts.

[COUNT VAY DE VAYA UND LUSKOD, 1908]

Behold! Mark Twain had curled himself up in the big armchair, and I was smoking reverently, as befits one in the presence of his superior. The thing that struck me first was that he was an elderly man; yet, after a minute's thought, I perceived that it was otherwise, and in five minutes, the eyes looking at me, I saw that the gray hair was an accident of the most trivial. He was quite young. I was shaking his hand, I was smoking his cigar, and I was hearing him talk—this man I had learned to love and admire fourteen thousand miles away.

[RUDYARD KIPLING, 1889]

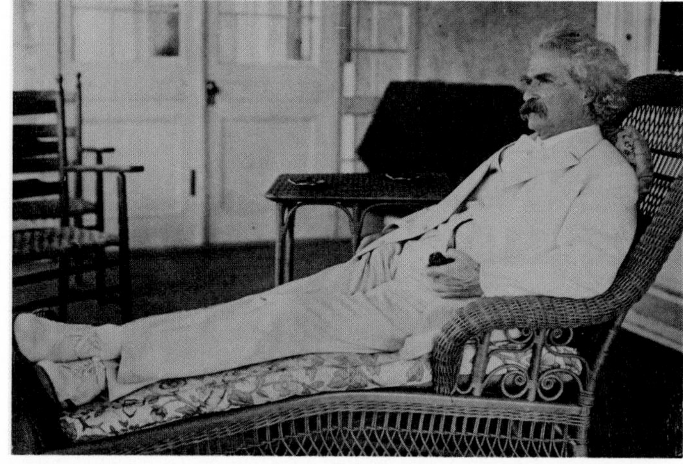

Mark Twain in 1907. By this time the writer had gained world-wide acclaim for such books as *The Adventures of Tom Sawyer* (1876), *Life on the Mississippi* (1883), and *The Adventures of Huckleberry Finn* (1885).

American paintings are no longer strange to Europe. In the art division of the last Paris Exposition, Americans took their share of the honors, and they are highly appreciated at most of the Berlin and Munich picture shows. Sargent and Whistler are the best known. Sargent, as the painter of elegant ladies, prosperous men, and interesting children, has undoubtedly the surest and most refined gift with his brush of any son of the New World. Whistler is doubtless the greater, the real sovereign. He fathoms each human riddle, and expresses it intangibly, mysteriously. Everything is mood and suggestion, the dull and heavy is lightened, the whole is rendered in rich twilight zones.

[HUGO MÜNSTERBERG, 1904]

The Last of Old Westminster, painted by James Abbott McNeill Whistler in 1862. The scene is London, where Whistler lived for much of his life. This work was followed by a number of outstanding portraits, including the famous one of his mother (which he actually titled *An Arrangement in Grey and Black*).

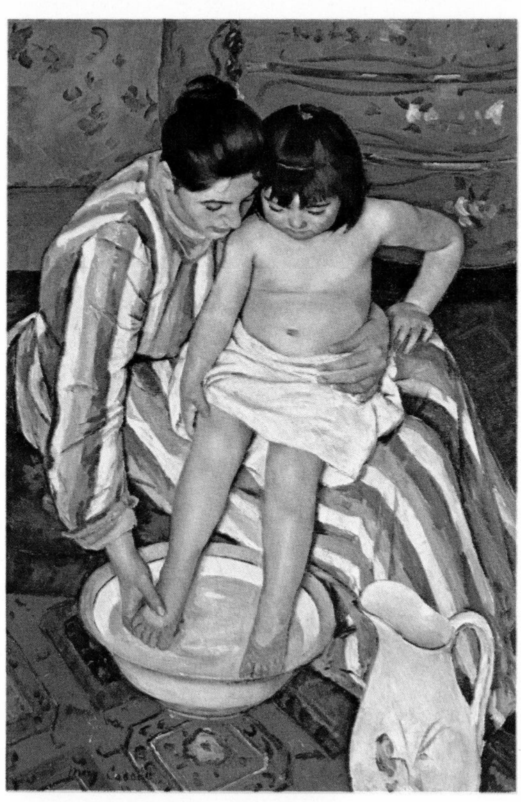

Miss Cassatt is a true phenomenon. In more than one of her canvases she is on the verge of becoming a notable artist with unparalleled natural feeling, penetrating observation, and a welcome subjection before the model which is the accomplishment of peerless artists.

[ALBERT WOLFF, 1881]

The Bath, by Mary Cassatt, dates from about 1891. The artist—who lived most of her adult life in Paris—liked to paint mothers and children. She communicated feelings of warmth and tenderness without sentimentality.

The taste for plastic art [in the United States] has slowly worked upward. Recent movements have left many beautiful examples of sculpture. Cities are jealously watchful now that only real works of art shall be erected, and that monuments which are to be seen by millions of people shall be really characteristic examples of good art. More than anything else, sculpture has at length come into a closer sympathy with architecture than perhaps it has in any other country. Such a work as Saint-Gaudens' Shaw Memorial in Boston is among the most beautiful examples of modern sculpture. Vigorous and mature is the American, in plastic art as well as in poetry.

[HUGO MÜNSTERBERG, 1904]

This work, showing Augustus Saint-Gaudens in his studio, was painted by Kenyon Cox in 1908. The sculptor was known for his public statuary, including Lincoln, in Lincoln Park, Chicago; General Sherman, near Central Park in New York City; and the Shaw Memorial on Boston Common.

Mr. and Mrs. Isaac Newton Phelps Stokes, portrayed by John Singer Sargent in 1897. These prominent New Yorkers, though pictured in informal dress, epitomize the wealth and refinement typical of Sargent's subjects.

PE 7–4 / People are inclined to smile at me when I suggest that you in America are at the commencement of a period of fine and vigorous art. The signs, they say, are all the other way. Of course you ought to know best. All the same, I stick to my opinion with British obstinacy, and believe I shall see it justified.

[JOHN GALSWORTHY, 1919]

Willa Cather builds her imagined world almost as solidly as our five senses build the universe around us. She has within herself a sensitivity that constantly presents her with a body of material which would overwhelm most of us. She has also a quality of mountain-pony sturdiness that makes her push on unfatigued under her load and give an accurate account of every part of it.

[REBECCA WEST, 1927]

On the threshold of her career, in 1902, Willa Cather had yet to gain a name for herself. She became noted for such novels as *O Pioneers!* (1913) and *My Antonia* (1918).

Sloan's canvas of girls under the elevated has more of New York in it than anything else I know.

[DIEGO RIVERA, 1942]

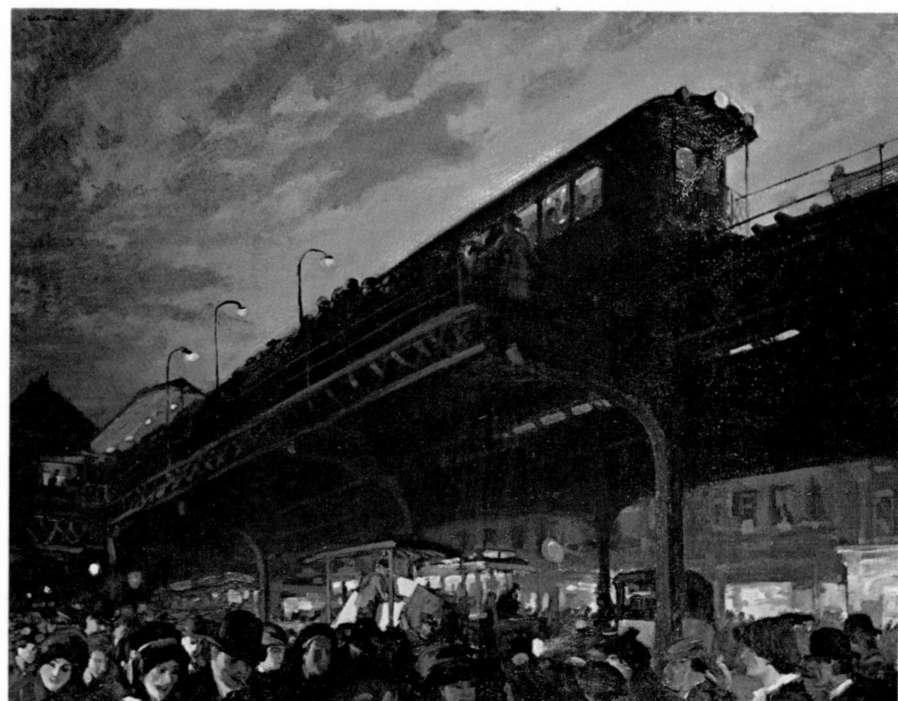

Six O'Clock was painted by John Sloan in 1912. He was one of a group called The Eight. They were known more familiarly as the Ashcan School because they depicted scenes of everyday city life rather than the more formal and traditional subjects favored by academic artists.

Characteristic of Frank Lloyd Wright's so-called "prairie houses" is this home in River Forest, Illinois. It was built in 1908. Wright's later works, noted for their daring innovation, included the Imperial Hotel in Tokyo, the Johnson administration building in Racine, Wisconsin, and the Guggenheim Museum in New York City.

Most of Wright's country houses, fitted into the oceanlike endlessness of the prairie, are very low, joined with, indeed pressed down toward, the earth. As a consequence the interior rooms spread out horizontally from one another. Therefore these houses do not seem like some grotesque thing which has grown out of the earth; they appear native to the soil and fitted to it, like the farmhouse.

[LUDWIG HILBERSHEIMER AND UDO RUKSER, 1920]

The chances are that Robert Frost will become a national figure, a sage, a Yankee sage. He has personal thought; he has wisdom; he has a basic conception from which he can speak. He likes the nation, every nation, and he dislikes the state, every state. He is a puritan, but he goes by the dictates of the heart.

[PADRAIC COLUM, 1936]

Robert Frost, as seen by artist James Chapin in 1929. The New England writer had by this time published some of his best-known poems, among them "Mending Wall," "Birches," and "Stopping by Woods on a Snowy Evening."

PE 7–6 / The mission which this land has, like all others, is to discover its own being, to fulfill its task of representing itself. And if one puts his ear to the ground, then one hears millions of forces at work to forge and shape this individual being.

[ANTON ERKELENZ, 1927]

Eugene O'Neill is one of the really great figures in modern drama. O'Neill is an example of what I mean when I say America is producing, and will produce in ever greater quantities, an art I feel is indigenous; it belongs to the American soil. No European dramatist could possibly have written those plays. The drama, under him, has found a new type of artistic expression.

[GERHART HAUPTMANN, 1932]

Eugene O'Neill in 1921, at the start of his career. His greatest plays came later: *Desire Under the Elms* (1924), *Mourning Becomes Electra* (1931), and *The Iceman Cometh* (1946). In 1936 he became the first American playwright to win the Nobel prize.

A scene from *Beyond the Horizon,* by O'Neill. Produced in 1920, it was the first full-length play by the dramatist to be acted.

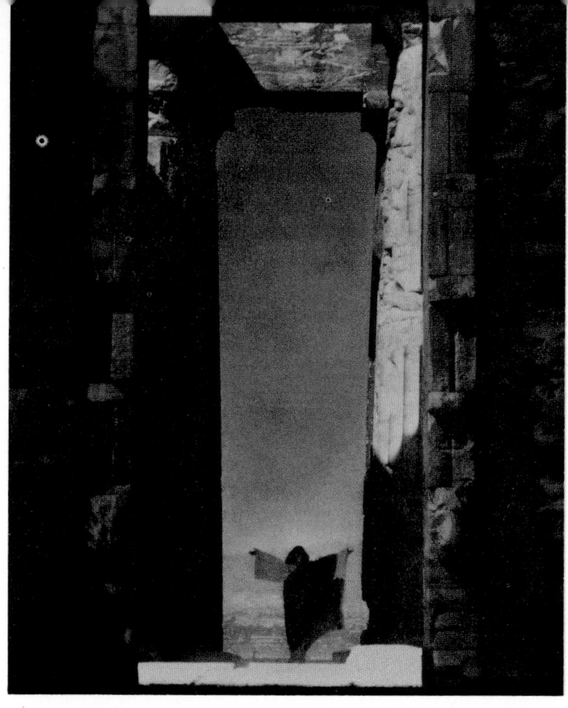

What she gives us is a sort of sculpture in transition. Imagine a dozen statues expressive, say, of the cardinal phases of despair—the poses and gestures and facial expressions of the moment in which each of these phases reaches its maximum of intensity. Then imagine some hundreds of statues that represent, in faultless beauty, every one of the moments of slow transition between these cardinal phases, and you get the art of Isadora Duncan.

[ERNEST NEWMAN, 1921]

The great American photographer Edward Steichen captured some of the magic of dancer Isadora Duncan in this 1921 photo, taken at the Parthenon. Her flowing Grecian costumes and striking interpretive power transformed modern dance.

Gershwin's Rhapsody [in Blue] is by far the most interesting thing of its kind I have yet met with. It really has ideas and they work themselves out in a way that interests the musical hearer. Perhaps it is better not to prophesy. What is at present certain is that Gershwin has written something for a jazz orchestra that is really music, not a mechanical box of tricks.

[ERNEST NEWMAN, 1924]

Mexican artist David Siqueiros painted this *Portrait in a Concert Hall* (George Gershwin) in 1936. The composer, who died the following year, had followed his *Rhapsody in Blue* (1923) with *An American in Paris* (1928) and *Porgy and Bess* (1935).

The young Ernest Hemingway was painted by Henry Strater in 1922. His best work, yet to come, included ***The Sun Also Rises*** (1926), ***A Farewell to Arms*** (1929), and ***For Whom the Bell Tolls*** (1940).

The outstanding achievement of American literature is the swiftness with which it strode from provincialism to half-acknowledged universality. Before 1800 there is nothing, save in the field of politics, which could command, or even deserve to command, a European audience; by 1900 it is true to say that there were few forms of creative effort in which Americans had not done work of the highest quality. America had moved to the very front of the cosmic stage. Henceforth it might be disliked; it could not be neglected.

[HAROLD LASKI, 1948]

It is hardly an exaggeration to say that Ernest Hemingway, more than any of his American colleagues, makes us feel we are confronted by a still young nation which seeks and finds its exact form of expression.

[NOBEL PRIZE CITATION, 1954]

Lunched with Sinclair Lewis. He is full of imagination. He tells me he wrote four or five novels before he wrote Main Street, *but they were not successes. I asked him why that had not discouraged him. He laughed, he said it was no use being discouraged, that writing novels was all he could do, he might starve at it, but he was incapable of any other form of work. (Truly an artist!)*

[CLARE SHERIDAN, 1921]

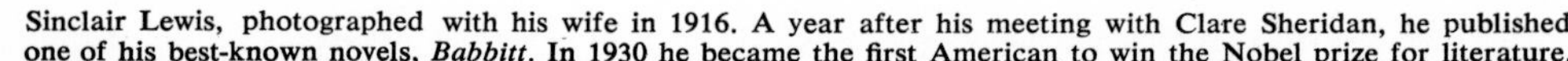

Sinclair Lewis, photographed with his wife in 1916. A year after his meeting with Clare Sheridan, he published one of his best-known novels, *Babbitt*. In 1930 he became the first American to win the Nobel prize for literature.

The cockpit of the Spirit of St. Louis *was a model of stripped-down efficiency. The wicker seat was probably uncomfortable but lightweight. Only side windows were thought necessary since there was not much to see in flight. Leg room was limited by the controls.*

seat in the cockpit. He could touch both sides of the fuselage with his elbows. To the front the cockpit was blind. Shiny metal sloped all the way up from the engine to the top of the wing. There were only two side windows and a glassed-in skylight overhead. For takeoffs and landings he had to lean out one of the side windows. But the plane was designed for only one important takeoff and landing. The rest of the time, over the Atlantic, there would be nothing to see but ocean, clouds, sun, and stars.

Directly in front of Lindbergh's face was a small cluster of instruments—an air-speed indicator, a turn-and-bank indicator, a fuel-flow meter, a compass, and one or two others. The plane carried a pitifully small survival kit containing a rubber raft, a flashlight, a canteen of water, some matches, and string. Surrounding the cockpit were nothing but gasoline tanks. One tank rested in the nose between the pilot and the engine. Another lay behind the cockpit in the fuselage. And there were more tanks in the wings overhead. There was no radio, no heater to provide warmth at freezing altitudes, no sextant for navigational sightings, not even a parachute. The *Spirit of St. Louis* was built to carry only gasoline—over a ton of it, as it turned out, weighing more than the plane and the pilot put together.

To Lindbergh, as he walked onto the sunny runway in San Diego, the *Spirit of St. Louis* was a thing of beauty and awe:

> What a beautiful machine it is, resting there on the field in front of the hangar, trim and slender, gleaming in its silver coat! All our ideas, all our calculations, all our hopes, lie there before me, waiting to undergo the acid test of flight. For me, it seems to contain the whole future of aviation.
>
> "Off! Throttle closed."
>
> I'm in the cockpit. The chief mechanic turns the propeller over several times.
>
> "Contact!"
>
> He swings his body away from the blade as he pulls it through. The engine catches, every cylinder hitting. This is different from any other cockpit I've been in before. The big fuel tank in front of me seems doubly large, now that I'm actually to fly behind it.
>
> I signal the chocks [blocks in front of the wheels of the plane] away. The *Spirit of St. Louis* rolls lightly over the baked-mud surface of the field.

The *Spirit of St. Louis* moved very quickly. Its tanks were almost empty for this first test flight.

> The tires are off the ground before they roll a hundred yards. The plane climbs quickly, even though I hold its nose down. There's a huge reserve of power. I spiral cautiously upward. I straighten out and check my instruments. I circle over the factory, watching little figures run outdoors to see the machine built actually flying overhead. I rock my wings and head across the bay.

During the next week Lindbergh tested the *Spirit of St. Louis* for speed, control, and, most important, takeoff under load. More and more gasoline was filtered by hand into the tanks for each run. With a load of slightly over 300 gallons the plane took off easily. But continued landings with large loads were dangerous. Lindbergh decided to stop the tests.

The *Spirit of St. Louis* had needed a little more than 1,000 feet of runway to take off with 300 gallons. From this and other data, the Ryan designers made a theoretical calculation that, fully loaded with 400 gallons, the plane would need 2,500 feet of hard runway. Rather than tempt fate, as the crew of the *American Legion* had done by testing with a full load, Lindbergh decided to trust the plane and the designer's arithmetic. He was ready. And he knew Byrd's *America* had been repaired and was undergoing final tests. The *Columbia* too was ready. Both planes were poised on Long Island. Time counted more than tests.

But time seemed to work against Lindbergh. A big storm blanketed the western United States, moving with painful slowness eastward. Lindbergh had to wait several days until the rain and clouds had moved east. On the evening of May 10 he began the first leg of his trip, from San Diego to St. Louis. He flew the 1,500 miles in record time. It was the longest nonstop solo flight ever made. Then, after a night's sleep, he headed for New York.

Lindbergh arrived on Long Island on May 12. He had set another record for the fastest transcontinental flight in history. The crews of Byrd's *America* and the *Columbia* came over to shake his hand and wish him luck. There was a crowd. Newspaper photographers and reporters pushed and shoved their way to Lindbergh, shouting for pictures and answers to their questions. A crowd of people climbed to the roof of a small building next to the hangar where Lindbergh parked the plane. Their weight caused a wall to collapse. Something new and strange was happening to Lindbergh. The newspapers and the public were making him into a hero, almost a myth.

Even without Lindbergh, the New York–Paris contest had all the elements of an exciting publicity event: death, drama, and competition. But Lindbergh added new elements. He was going alone, so he could become an object of hero worship in ways that the crews of the other planes could not. Moreover, he was young, and along with his youth went other personality traits that soon endeared him to the newspapers. He was tall, thin, blue-eyed, handsome in a boyish way. Above all, he was modest, shy, and simple.

All these traits combined presented a picture of an innocent young man ready to dare the impossible, alone. Lindbergh was the honest, plain-spoken, cowboy-like young man from the West. He was a modern David challenging the Eastern Goliaths, with their money, their experience, their financial backers, and their head start. In short, he was an underdog. The *Spirit of St. Louis,* too, was simple and seemingly innocent compared with the other planes in the race. It was a sentimental favorite as well.

What attracted the public to Lindbergh, besides his boyish good looks, was the power he had of symbolizing what was best about the country: not just daring, but moral courage and independence of spirit.

Lindbergh could not leave his hotel room without being mobbed by people anxious to touch him "just for luck." And the newspapers played his story for all it was worth. They nicknamed him "Lucky," "The Flyin' Fool," or just "Lindy." (He had always been "Slim" to his friends.) All the hero worship that the Americans of the 1920s usually reserved for baseball players like Babe Ruth or movie stars like Rudolf Valentino was now showered on the twenty-five-year-old airmail pilot. The worship was made more serious by the fact that "The

Flyin' Fool'' was doing something real and dangerous, not merely hitting baseballs or posing for motion picture cameras.

In most ways this public personality created for the new celebrity was only a myth. Lindbergh may not have had Byrd's $100,000, but he had finally obtained solid backing from St. Louis businessmen. And even if the *Spirit of St. Louis* was smaller than the other planes, it was still a sophisticated piece of machinery, created by advanced technology. It was a little silly for newspapers to write of Lindbergh and his plane as though they were a cowboy hero and his beloved horse.

Nor was Lindbergh's background as simple as the newspapers tried to make it appear. He came from a well-to-do and educated family. His father had been a congressman. Lindbergh had been to college for a time and held a commission as captain in the Army Air Service Reserve and the Missouri National Guard. He had been chief pilot for the air-mail company in St. Louis. He was, despite his youth, an experienced professional pilot, flying an advanced aircraft.

But there was just enough truth to the mythical picture to make it stick. It probably infected Lindbergh somewhat, too. He had always been a bit wild, even though he was shy. Cars, motorcycles, ice boats—anything that involved speed—had always fascinated him. When he was just twenty he dropped out of college to learn to fly. This had started him on a short and dangerous career. He bought his first craft, a war-surplus plane, even before he had made a solo flight, and he almost crashed it on his first takeoff.

Lindbergh had barnstormed all over the West, crashing regularly and surviving only with luck. He had walked on airplane wings while in flight and done dangerous parachute jumps for one aerial circus after another. Four times he had been forced to parachute for his life from planes that had collided, run out of gas, or gotten lost at night.

All this—combined with Lindbergh's shyness and boyishness, his faith in himself and his plane—did smack of something religious and mythical. So the hero worship that began almost as soon as he reached Long Island was probably inevitable. At times the publicity and the public attention irritated Lindbergh. Reporters went so far as to burst into his hotel room without knocking to discover what kind of pajamas, if any, he wore to bed. But the irritation could not overcome the excitement. Lindbergh was becoming, even before takeoff, a national hero.

The *Columbia* was scheduled to take off on May 13, the day after Lindbergh reached Long Island. But the weather was closed in over New York and the North Atlantic. The same storm that had delayed

Lindbergh in San Diego was making its slow progress north and east. So the *Columbia* had to wait. Lindbergh was able to test and tune his engine, to check and recheck every instrument. A noisy crowd that sometimes numbered over a thousand gathered around the hangar to watch him. By May 16 he was ready. As far as he could tell, Byrd was ready too. The weather was suitable for all three planes to take off. In the *Columbia* organization there was a legal quarrel over who would be the pilot. One of the men who had trained for the flight had secured a court order preventing the plane from taking off without him. But the court order could be lifted at any minute. So there seemed to be a real chance that two or possibly even three planes would take off from Roosevelt Field on the same morning.

The storm persisted for three more days. Then, on the evening of May 19, the forecast called for clearing skies. Though it was not clearing rapidly, Lindbergh made his decision. He would fly the next morning. This would mean taking off into a rainy sky from a muddy field. He bought five sandwiches "to go." A few hours later the *Spirit of St. Louis* was towed to the west end of the Roosevelt Field runway. Lindbergh had decided to take off at night instead, when the wind was east to west. This was the opposite direction from the one Fonck had taken the preceding autumn. Not far behind the *Spirit of St. Louis* was the scorched area, marked by a bent propeller stuck into the ground as a tribute, where Fonck's plane had burned.

Slowly, carefully, mechanics strained five-gallon cans of gasoline into Lindbergh's plane. The tanks were oversized. They had a capacity of 450 gallons instead of the 400 that the designers had planned earlier. Lindbergh decided to fill them to the brim, even though it meant a dangerous overload for the takeoff. In the hangers of the *America* and the *Columbia,* there was only darkness and silence. No one else was going to fly.

As he looked over the situation, Lindbergh wondered whether he should go. He was overloaded with gasoline. The field was muddy. The wheels of the *Spirit of St. Louis* sank into the earth as though warning him that flight was out of the question. The wet weather affected the engine, which turned about thirty revolutions per minute slower than it should have at full power. Worst of all, the process of getting ready took so long that Lindbergh lost the night wind. By the time he was ready to fly, the breeze had shifted to his back, creating a tailwind of five or six miles per hour. This meant he would need even more speed on takeoff.

Lindbergh's only guidelines were the San Diego tests. They had demonstrated theoretically that he should be able to take off in 2,500 feet on a hard runway with no wind and with full engine power. At the

Moments before the takeoff, Lindbergh readied himself for the flight, while policemen guarded and his backers inspected the plane that would carry him to Paris.

end of the Roosevelt Field runway were a ditch, a tractor, some telephone wires and then a hill with a line of trees. He had to clear them all. He considered towing the *Spirit of St. Louis* through the misty rain and mud to the other end of the runway to get the help of the wind. He thought about postponing the flight altogether. But he decided to go.

Lindbergh looked around at the crowd that had gathered to watch. Nearby there were the mechanics, the engineers, several policemen, all looking into the dark cockpit at his pale face.

> Their eyes are intently on mine. They've seen the planes crash before. I lean against the side of the cockpit and look ahead, through the idling blades of the propeller, over the runway's glistening surface. I study the telephone wires and the shallow pools of water through which my wheels must pass. A curtain of mist shuts off all trace of the horizon. Sitting in the cockpit, in seconds, minutes long, the conviction surges through me that the wheels *will* leave the ground, that the wings *will* rise above the wires, that it *is* time to start the flight.
>
> I buckle my safety belt, pull goggles down over my eyes, turn to the men at the blocks, and nod. Frozen figures leap to action. I brace myself against the left side of the cockpit and ease the throttle wide open.

The *Spirit of St. Louis* feels more like an overloaded truck than an airplane. The tires rut through mud as though they really were on truck wheels. Even the breath of wind is pressing me down. The engine's snarl sounds inadequate and weak.

A hundred yards of runway passes. How long can the landing gear stand such strain? I keep my eyes fixed on the runway's edge. I *must* hold the plane straight. Pace quickens—the tail skid lifts off ground—I feel the load shifting from wheels to wings. The halfway mark is just ahead, and I have nothing like flying speed.

The halfway mark streaks past. Seconds now to decide. I pull the stick back firmly, and—*the wheels leave the ground!* The wheels touch again. I ease the stick forward. Almost flying speed and nearly 2,000 feet ahead. The entire plane trembles. Off again—right wing low—pull it up—ease back onto the runway. Another pool, water drumming on the fabric [covering the fuselage]. The next hop's longer. I could probably stay in the air, but I let the wheels touch once more.

The *Spirit of St. Louis* takes herself off next time. Full flying speed. The controls taut, alive, straining—and still a thousand feet to the telephone wires. If the engine can hold out one more minute. Five feet, twenty, forty. Wires flash by underneath. Twenty feet to spare!

Green grass below—a golf links. People looking up. A low, tree-covered hill ahead. The *Spirit of St. Louis* seems balanced on a pinpoint, as though the slightest movement of controls would cause it to topple over and fall. Five thousand pounds suspended from those little wings. Five thousand pounds on a blast of air.

Now I'm high enough to steal glances at the instrument board. The earth inductor compass needle leans steeply to the right. I bank cautiously northward until it rises to the center line—65 degrees—the compass heading for the first 100-mile segment of my great-circle route to France and Paris. It's 7:54 A.M. Eastern daylight time.

Back in San Diego, when Lindbergh and the designer of the *Spirit of St. Louis* had measured the distance of the flight across a library globe, the string had made a straight line between New York and Paris. But on a flat map, where the lines of latitude are straightened out into parallels, the route had to bend into an arc known as a great circle. The route Lindbergh would take curved north and east from New York, up the east coast over Cape Cod, then out over the ocean to Nova Scotia. Lindbergh planned to change his course every hundred miles (about one hour's flying time in the *Spirit of St. Louis*). He would head a few degrees farther south and east across the southern coast of Newfoundland and out over the North Atlantic.

As Lindbergh flew up the coast on this route, people waited on streets and housetops to watch him pass. Despite the fact that his navigating equipment was primitive, he managed to reach the Nova Scotia coast only a few miles off course. Every hour excited messages were telephoned to New York giving details of his progress. In the twelfth hour of his flight, Lindbergh passed over St. John's, Newfoundland, then out over the ocean:

> I come upon it suddenly—the little city of St. John's, after skimming over the top of a granite summit. Farther ahead, the entrance to the harbor is a narrow gap with sides running up to the crest of a low coastal range. Twilight deepens as I plunge down into the valley. It takes only a moment, stick forward, engine throttled, to dive down over the wharves (men stop their after-supper chores to look upward) and out through the gap. North America and its islands are behind. Ireland is 2,000 miles ahead.

Throughout the flight Lindbergh faced the ever-present dangers of engine failure, storms, and the possibility of a structural weakness in the *Spirit of St. Louis* itself. But between Newfoundland and Ireland there were two additional dangers. The first was sleep. Lindbergh had not slept at all the night before his takeoff. During the next night and the day after, as he flew over the ocean, he fought back the terrible temptation to close his eyes for just a few seconds of rest. Despite its virtues, the *Spirit of St. Louis* was not a very stable plane. Lindbergh knew that if he relaxed his hold on it for more than a moment, he might crash. He had to hold his eyes open with his hands. Once he even had to hit himself full force in the face to keep awake.

The second danger was ice. This hazard hit Lindbergh suddenly after he had climbed over 10,000 feet, trying to clear a bank of clouds about 200 miles east of Newfoundland. He was suddenly aware of being cold himself. (He had left the glass out of the side windows of the *Spirit of St. Louis*, hoping that the fresh air and engine noise would keep him alert.) Cold? He jerked himself wide awake. If *he* was cold, what about his plane?

> Good Lord! There are things to be considered outside the cockpit! How could I forget! I jerk off a leather mitten and thrust my arm out the window. My palm is covered with stinging pinpricks. I pull the flashlight from my pocket and throw its beam on a strut. The entering edge is irregular and shiny! *Ice*!
>
> I've got to turn around, get back to clear air—quickly!

Lindbergh fought the urge to turn quickly. He knew that if he did, the ice on the wings might cause the plane to go out of control. Instead, he eased the *Spirit of St. Louis* around in a long, slow curve back toward Newfoundland.

> I throw my flashlight [beam] onto the wing strut. Ice is thicker! Steady the plane. Everything depends on the turn indicator working till I get outside the cloud. Just two or three more minutes.
>
> My eyes sense a change in the blackness of my cockpit. I look out through the window. How bright! What safety have I reached! I was in the thunderhead for ten minutes at most, but it's one of those incidents that can't be measured by minutes. Such periods stand out like islands in a sea of time.

After this brief but dangerous encounter with the night sky, Lindbergh picked his way cautiously toward Ireland and dawn. (Since he was flying west to east, into the sunrise, he was experiencing the shortest night of any man before him in history.) He sipped cautiously at the quart canteen of water. For the rest of the time he just flew his plane, waiting for moonrise, then sunrise, then land fall. He later recalled the twenty-eighth hour of his flight.

> I keep scanning the horizon through breaks between squalls. Is that a cloud on the northeastern horizon, or a strip of low fog—or—*can it possibly be land*? It looks like land, but I don't intend to be tricked by another mirage. I'm only sixteen hours out of Newfoundland. I allowed eighteen and one-half hours to strike the Irish coast.
>
> But my mind is clear. I'm no longer half asleep. The temptation is too great. I can't hold my course any longer. The *Spirit of St. Louis* banks over toward the nearest point of land.
>
> I stare at it intently, not daring to believe my eyes, watching the shades and contours unfold into a coastline. Now I'm flying above the foam-lined coast, searching for prominent features to fit the chart on my knee. I've climbed to 2,000 feet so I can see the contours of the country better. Yes, there's a place on the chart where it all fits—Valentia and Dingle Bay, *on the southwestern coast of Ireland*! I can hardly believe it's true. I'm almost exactly on my route, closer than I hoped to come in my wildest dreams back in San Diego. What happened to all those detours of the night around the thunderheads? Where has the swinging compass error gone?
>
> Intuition must have been more accurate than reasoned navigation.
>
> The southern tip of Ireland! Of course, over two hours ahead of schedule; the sun still well up in the sky, the weather clearing!

Now it was easy. So easy that Lindbergh himself fell into the temptation of making a myth out of his own achievement:

> I'm angling slowly back onto my great-circle route. I must have been within three miles of it when I sighted Ireland. An error of fifty miles would have been good dead reckoning under the most perfect conditions. Three miles was—well, what was it? Before I made this flight, I would have said carelessly that it was luck. Now, luck seems far too trivial a word, a term to be used only by those who've never seen the curtain drawn or looked on life from far away.

After Ireland the landmarks appeared rapidly—a lighthouse, the coast of England and the coast of France, "like an outstretched hand to meet me." For the first time Lindbergh felt hungry. He ate one of the sandwiches, stale and dry now, that he had bought in New York. He picked up a series of beacon lights marking the route between London and Paris. Then the city arose before him. He circled the brightly lit Eiffel Tower and then turned northeast to look at Le Bourget. "You can't miss it," he had been told. He was like a tourist.

It was almost ten o'clock at night in Paris. Lindbergh was confused by an incredible number of lights around the dark spot where the airport ought to be. A factory, he thought. He did not know that he had suddenly become the most famous man in the world. Thousands of Parisians had rushed out to the airport to greet the American flyer. The little roads toward Le Bourget were jammed with cars with headlights blazing.

Finally, Lindbergh was able to pick out floodlights showing the edge of a runway. He dragged the field once, flying low over it to check for obstructions—a tractor or maybe some sheep let out to crop the

As the clock struck 10 P.M. *the* Spirit of St. Louis *came to rest on the runway at Le Bourget airport. To the French, who had gathered by the thousands to celebrate the "Flying Fool's" success, Lindbergh was the epitome of "a real American."*

grass, he thought. He brought the plane in as carefully as possible, as though he were teaching a student to fly. The plane felt sluggish. By his own guess he still carried a lot of gasoline. His own reflexes seemed slow. Lindbergh had never landed the *Spirit of St. Louis* at night. He glided in at an angle so he could peer out his side window.

> It's only a hundred yards to the hangars now. I'm too high, too fast. Drop wing. Left rudder. Careful. Still too high. I push the stick over. Below the hangar roofs now. Straighten out. A short burst of the engine. Over the lighted areas. Sod coming up to meet me. Careful. Easy to bounce when you're tired. Still too fast. Tail too high. Hold off. Hold off. But the lights are far behind. Ahead, there's nothing but night. Give her the gun and climb for another try?
>
> The wheels touch gently. Off again. No, I'll keep contact. Ease the stick forward. Back on the ground. Off. Back, the tail skid too. Not a bad landing, but I'm beyond the light. Can't see anything ahead. The field *must* be clear. Uncomfortable, though, jolting into blackness. Wish I had a wing light, but too heavy on the takeoff. Slower now, slow enough to ground-loop safely. Left rudder. Reverse it. The *Spirit of St. Louis* swings around and stops rolling, resting on the solidness of earth, in the center of Le Bourget.
>
> I start to taxi back to the floodlights and hangars. But the entire field ahead is covered with running figures!

About 100,000 Frenchmen had broken through police lines to rush onto the field. They were almost hysterical over the new American hero. All day—and all the previous day—the transatlantic cables, the radios, and the newspapers had been full of news about the flight. As soon as Lindbergh taxied back to the hanger, the crowd rushed his plane. He was afraid (as he would be for months whenever he landed at a crowded airport) that people would run into his spinning propeller. And when he tried to climb out of the *Spirit of St. Louis*, the crowd grabbed him. For a long time he could not touch French soil but was passed from shoulder to shoulder. He shouted for a mechanic to take care of his plane. No one could hear or understand him.

In the log he kept of the flights of the *Spirit of St. Louis* Lindbergh made this brief, slightly bitter entry: "May 20. Roosevelt Field, Long Island, New York, to Le Bourget Aerodrome, Paris, France. 33 hours. 20 min. Fuselage fabric badly torn by souvenir hunters."

The first part of the log entry, the flight, was what seemed significant to Lindbergh. But the second part—the half-crazy hero worship of the "souvenir hunters"—is just as important in understanding Lindbergh's achievement. Not just in Paris but even more in dozens of American cities, Lindbergh was adored. People crowded around wherever he went. They grabbed his hats in restaurants. Even his shirts and underwear were stolen by laundry employees for souvenirs. From the time Lindbergh landed at Le Bourget, his life was not his own. He had become a public hero.

CHAPTER

32

A "New Era"

OCCASIONALLY, some particular event or act (like John Brown's raid or, more recently, the assassination of President Kennedy in 1963) causes masses of people to undergo a great excitement. At such times most people are not really interested in facts about the event. Instead, they project significance into the event. They see historical actors as demons or heroes, usually in unrealistic ways. By doing so, they make some new sense out of their own lives.

So it was that Charles Lindbergh became a hero and a symbol to the American people. More than any other individual of his generation, Lindbergh captured the imagination, the admiration, and the hopes of his contemporaries.

On the surface, there was no solid reason to make Lindbergh into a hero. His flight had proven nothing except that a superb pilot with an airplane built especially for the purpose could fly 3,600 miles. The *Spirit of St. Louis* could not carry any cargo or passengers. (In fact, Lindbergh refused to carry even one pound of mail for an offer of $1,000.) Even more important, Lindbergh had not even been the first man to fly the Atlantic.[1] But, in 1927, when Lindbergh made his famous trip, almost no one could remember these earlier pilots, while Lindbergh's name became a household word.

A number of extraordinary changes in American society had prepared the way for Lindbergh's fantastic reputation. And the ways Americans chose to celebrate Lindbergh as their hero suggests a great deal about the nature of the new society that was beginning to emerge in the period after World War I.

REACHING A MASS AUDIENCE

One of the reasons for Lindbergh's rapid rise to fame was the publicity he received from the press and the radio. Since the 1890s the newspapers of the United States had been increasing in number and circulation. They competed fiercely for the attention of the public. This expansion of newspapers was only part of an important revolution in communications that began in the nineteenth century and still continues today.

One by one, new inventions brought people's lives closer together. These included the telegraph, the telephone, the phonograph, the camera, the radio, and the motion picture. They created a world in which whole nations and continents could share almost simultaneously in distant events. Lindbergh's flight was "covered" intensely by the press, which transmitted its stories over telegraph and telephone lines. Lindbergh was also photographed mercilessly. His activities were recorded both in newspaper photographs and in the newsreels that accompanied the early silent motion pictures. Hour-by-hour reports of his famous flight were transmitted on the radio—an invention that had come into use only a few years before. As soon as Lindbergh landed in Paris, the news was flashed back to the United States by transatlantic telegraph cable.

[1] Before 1919, a British dirigible (a balloon powered by propeller engines) had crossed from New York to England twice. An American seaplane had made the flight, landing several times on the ocean, in 1919. That same year, two pilots had made it *nonstop* from Newfoundland to Ireland, to win a prize of $50,000, more than twice the prize Lindbergh won.

In many ways Lindbergh the hero was the creation of mass communications. He was the first celebrity to have the full advantage of every modern form of communication except television. (Television did not come into wide use until after World War II.)

The Communications Revolution The revolution in communications began with the telegraph, which linked California and New York more than half a century before Lindbergh's flight. During the same period newspapers began to attract a mass audience. The telephone, too, contributed to the rapid and widespread circulation of information. In the first part of the twentieth century the number of telephones in use skyrocketed, from a little over 1 million in 1900 to more than 10 million in 1915. By the time Lindbergh took off for Paris, practically every middle-class American home had its own telephone.

But the communications revolution did not gather full speed until the invention of the radio. The principle of wireless transmission of sound was almost as old as the telephone. In 1887 a German scientist proved the existence of electrical waves in space. He speculated that they might be turned into signals. An Italian inventor, Guglielmo Marconi, applied the theory to wireless transmission of telegraph signals in 1896. From then on it was only a matter of assembling the appropriate tubes, transmitters, and receivers.

In 1920 Americans heard their first commercial radio broadcast. The station was KDKA in Pittsburgh, and the program was a news report on the 1920 presidential election. Soon after that the winner of the election, Warren G. Harding, installed a radio set in the White House. Gradually Marconi's invention was transformed from a toy into a commercial reality. By the time Lindbergh made his flight to Paris, an estimated 10 million sets were in use in the United States, almost one for every telephone.

Two other inventions, the phonograph and the camera, furthered the revolution in mass communications. Thomas A. Edison found a way

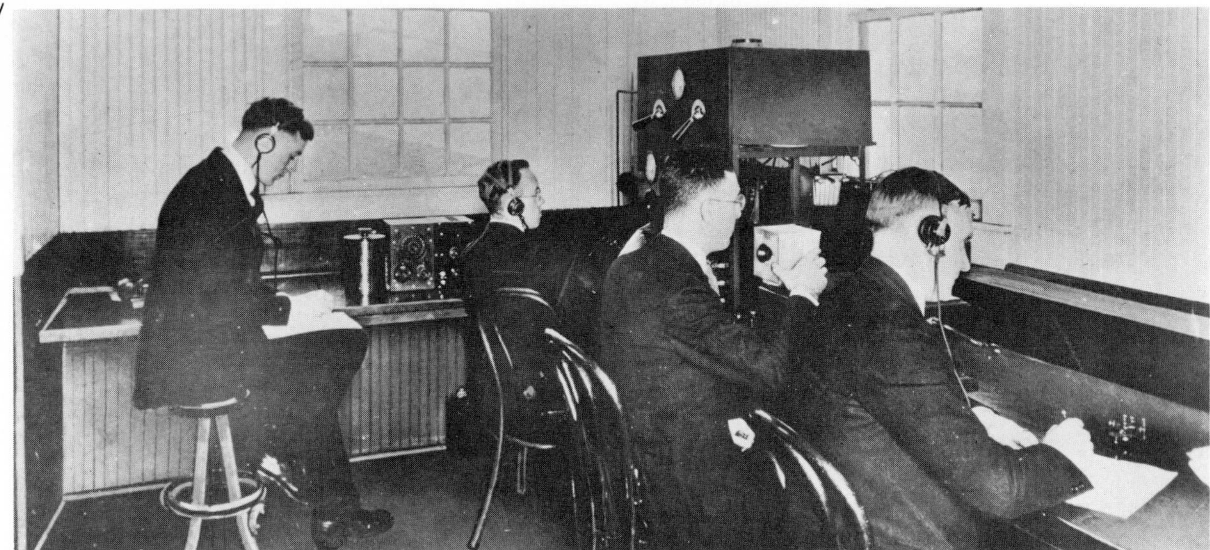

With the broadcast of the Harding-Cox election returns in November 1920, KDKA in Pittsburgh gave birth to commercial radio. The broadcast opened a new era in communications.

of capturing and recreating sound that was to make music available to millions at an instant. George Eastman's perfection of the camera made it possible for newspapers to include pictures on their pages.

All these changes allowed millions of people to participate indirectly in events that they were not present to witness. In other words, these developing communications facilities had created a potential public that could take part in any happening, frown at any villain, worship any hero.

A Middle-Class Public The new public to which Lindbergh was such a hero was overwhelmingly white and well-to-do. Despite a growing literacy in America, newspapers still appealed primarily to a middle-class audience. Radios and telephones too were almost exclusively middle-class conveniences. In 1927 millions of Americans still regarded the phonograph and the camera as strange novelties. Blacks, poor farmers, and poor immigrants in the cities were largely excluded from the new prosperity.

Thus, if Lindbergh represented values, they were not necessarily the values of all Americans. Rather they were primarily the beliefs and hopes of white middle-class citizens. It was easy to confuse these citizens with the whole nation. The American ambassador to France proclaimed at the time that Lindbergh was the best possible representative "of the spirit of our people." The *New Republic* magazine said that "he is US personified." But the "people" and "US" were primarily the middle-class public defined by the communications network.

THE MACHINE AND THE MAVERICK IN A TECHNOLOGICAL SOCIETY

Americans were fond of calling the period after World War I the New Era. Much of what they meant by the phrase was summed up symbolically in Lindbergh's airplane. The New Era was above all a machine age, a triumph of advanced technology. Compared with a modern jet or a moon rocket, the *Spirit of St. Louis* was a very primitive machine. But to millions of Americans of the 1920s it was the final and glistening outcome of the industrial and technological revolution that had begun in the preceding century. It symbolized what they believed was happening in the United States: the creation of a new kind of

DEVELOPMENTS IN TECHNOLOGY, 1865–1930

(DATES REFER TO PATENT OR FIRST SUCCESSFUL USE)

YEAR	INVENTOR	CONTRIBUTION	IMPORTANCE/DESCRIPTION
1869	George Westinghouse	AIR BRAKE	Provided smoother and quicker braking action for railroad cars.
1874	Joseph Glidden	BARBED WIRE MANUFACTURE	Speeded the end of open grazing of cattle.
1876	Alexander Graham Bell	TELEPHONE	Made out of a cigar box, wire, and two toy magnets; revolutionized communication.
1877	Thomas Alva Edison	PHONOGRAPH	Extended availability of music to millions.
1879	Thomas Alva Edison	INCANDESCENT BULB	Made possible electric lighting.
1880	W. E. Sawyer	PRINCIPLE OF SCANNING	Established the possibility of using only a single wire or channel for transmission of a picture, thereby making television possible.
1888	George Eastman	HAND CAMERA	Revolutionized newspaper journalism.
1888	Nikola Tesla	FIRST MOTOR TO BE RUN BY ALTERNATING CURRENT	Made the transmission of electrical power over long distances possible.
1892	John Froelich	MOTORIZED TRACTOR	Powered by a 20-hp., single-cylinder gasoline engine; greatly increased agricultural efficiency.
1895	George B. Selden	INTERNAL COMBUSTION AUTOMOBILE ENGINE	Initiated a new mode of transportation.
1896	Guglielmo Marconi	WIRELESS TELEGRAPH	Formed the basis for radio transmissions.
1903	Orville & Wilbur Wright	FIRST FLIGHT OF A HEAVIER-THAN-AIR CRAFT	Marked the beginning of the air age.
1904	Thomas Alva Edison	SOUND MOTION PICTURE	Inaugurated a new entertainment/information medium.
1913	William M. Burton	CRACKING OIL-REFINING PROCESS	Made possible production of gasoline from kerosene.
1917	Ernst F. W. Alexanderson	HIGH-FREQUENCY ALTERNATOR	Made worldwide wireless transmission possible.
1918	Peter C. Hewitt F. B. Crocker	HELICOPTER	First helicopter to rise successfully from the ground.
1922	Herbert T. Kalmus	TECHNICOLOR PROCESS	Made possible color film.
1926	Robert Hutchings Goddard	ROCKET	First liquid-propellant rocket.

 civilization, a miracle of progress in which every barrier to human comfort and achievement would be broken by industry and invention.

The United States of the mid-1920s was much more thoroughly industrialized than it had been at the turn of the century. Total steel production, for example, quadrupled during the period between the death of McKinley and Lindbergh's flight to Paris. The total value of all manufactured goods increased almost eight times in the same period. The number of people engaged in agriculture declined to about one-fourth of the total population. American cities grew at an astounding pace. By 1930, three years after Lindbergh's flight, 40 percent of the total population of the United States lived in twenty-five large metropolitan centers. In short, Lindbergh appealed to a society that was overwhelmingly industrial and urban and fundamentally dependent on machines and factories.

Electric Power and Assembly Lines In some ways the New Era was an extension of the revolution in industry that had occurred after the Civil War (see Chapter 24). The factory system had continued to expand. New and more complex forms of machinery were developed to produce more and more goods. But if the basic trends were the same, there were some new elements too. The New Era, much more than the old, was driven by electricity and organized around assembly lines.

In 1870, when the industrial revolution was making its first powerful impact, steam power and water wheels were used equally to drive industry. Steam continued to be the main form of motor energy in industry until about 1917. But steam had its drawbacks, and the introduction of electricity made possible extraordinary advances in industry.

Again, the basic inventions belonged to the nineteenth century. Within the ten-year period from 1877 to 1887 the dynamo for generating electricity and the motor for converting it into motion were both perfected. This was largely the work of Thomas Edison. During these same years Edison introduced his incandescent light into homes and streets. In 1882 the first commercial electric-power station, the Edison Illuminating Company, was built in New York.

While electric lighting brightened life in offices, houses, and streets, the electric motor helped transform industrial production. In 1900 electric motors provided only one-twentieth of the power used in American industrial plants. By World War I this figure had increased to about one-third. When Lindbergh flew to France, just ten years later, electricity provided almost two-thirds of the total industrial power in American factories and mills. Between 1870 and 1920 the amount of raw energy used by American industry, measured in horsepower, increased by well over 1,000 percent!

The development of the moving-belt assembly line also had far-reaching effects on industrial production. Assembly lines were first introduced on a large scale by Henry Ford at his automobile plant in Michigan in 1913. The principle was a simple one. Workers were placed in a row in the order of their jobs. The product

This photograph of a day's production of car chassis at a Detroit Ford plant vividly illustrates the increase in output possible by the use of the assembly line. Mass-production methods cut assembly time from 12½ to 1½ hours.

Henry Ford

As much as any other single factor, automobiles caused the dramatic change in American life in the twentieth century. Yet the man who did the most to put the nation on wheels, Henry Ford, disliked the change. The older he grew, the more fondly he looked back on the America of his youth. He valued its rural base, Puritan work ethic, and simple pleasures.

Life began for Henry Ford on a farm near Dearborn, Michigan, on July 30, 1863. Early in his life two traits became apparent: he loved machinery, and he hated farming. He was a born tinkerer. By the time he was thirteen, he could disassemble and reconstruct a watch. He was forever fixing his father's farm machinery and his mother's household appliances. When he ran out of repairs at home, he repaired neighbors' watches, clocks, and machinery.

As soon as he could, he left the farm for Detroit to become a machinist. He quickly learned his trade and was soon a well-paid, highly skilled workman. In his spare time he worked on a gasoline buggy in an old brick shed behind his home. By 1896 he was able to drive it through a hole knocked out of the shed wall. Mounted on four bicycle wheels was a two-cylinder, four-horsepower engine. Mounted on that was a buggy seat. To steer it he used a curved stick like the tiller on a boat.

From this awkward beginning he built a billion-dollar industry over the next fifty years. But as he grew from home-shop tinkerer to industrial tycoon, he never really changed his boyhood attitudes. They remained those of an agrarian Populist of the 1880s and 1890s.

As a result, Henry Ford was a mass of contradictions. While he professed a firm belief in the value of the individual workman and of hard and useful work, he developed an assembly-line process that was truly dehumanizing. He broke down each of the jobs involved in making a car into its tiniest steps. Consequently, a workman did only one thing—like tightening a single bolt—all day long. Ford was even proud of the fact that 43 percent of the jobs in his factories could be mastered in no more than one day.

While he was an expert businessman, as shown by his development of an enormous personal fortune and a vastly profitable corporation, Ford disliked many aspects of capitalism. He had an abiding mistrust of bankers and moneymen.

And while he continued to turn out millions of cars, making Americans a highly mobile and rootless society, he romanticized the stable, well-rooted small-town life. He so loved nineteenth-century rural America that he spent twenty years constructing a reproduction of the community he grew up in—Greenfield Village. There skilled artisans worked at jobs that had long since been taken over by assembly lines.

Henry Ford died an old man of eighty-four, puzzled and unhappy with the people and the world he had done so much to transform.

 (in this case the automobile) was then moved past them while each man performed an assigned task. The idea might be simple, but the savings in time and motion were dramatic. Each worker, using a specialized tool to perform a small task, could now produce much more in a given day. Ford's assembly line was copied by dozens of other industries. By the middle of the 1920s it was a standard technique.

Effects of Mechanization The industrial revolution continued. The changes brought about by the electric motor and the assembly line made the lives of most Americans in 1927 very different from their lives a generation or two earlier. More and more, the ways people lived and worked were determined by machines and technological innovations. More and more, mechanical devices replaced human energy and skill.

This process of mechanization had two deep effects on American society. First, it made modern Americans more conscious of the efficient use of time and effort than any other people in the history of the world. Second, it threatened to standardize life by reducing the area of imagination and individuality in peoples' daily working environment. The celebration of Lindbergh was connected to both these consequences.

In planning his flight, Lindbergh was almost ruthlessly efficient. The *Spirit of St. Louis* was a nearly perfect machine. It was designed to perform one simple task in the most effective way, with a minimum of wasted energy. Like a machine in a modern factory, the plane represented the harnessing of energy to a carefully designed instrument for the performance of a rigidly defined task. Much of what Americans admired in Lindbergh was precisely what they admired in their own society—his technological achievement.

But there was another side to Lindbergh. He was a maverick. Some of the pet names the newspapers gave him, like "The Flyin' Fool" and "Lucky," made his daring seem more important than his technical skill. Lindbergh seemed to go against the trend toward standardization of life in the New Era. He represented individual imagination, as well as engineering and piloting skill. A large part of Lindbergh's fame probably rested on this contradiction. His flight was both a triumph of technology and a victory for individual daring.

WHEELS AND WINGS: THE MOTOR AGE

The development of electricity had a powerful effect not only on industry but also on American home life. New inventions like the electric washing machine and refrigerator (which utilized small, inexpensive motors) changed the working and eating habits of American families. And a dozen other smaller electric appliances—from toasters to thermostats for home furnaces—helped usher in American consumers' vision of a New Era.

Perfecting the Automobile The largest change in American social life was brought about by the gasoline engine. The basic principle of the internal combustion engine was understood by the middle of the nineteenth century. The principle was simple. Instead of burning fuel externally to convert water into steam, the internal combustion engine burned fuel in an explosive way inside a chamber. The force of the explosion was then used to drive a piston or a rotor. The first internal combustion engine was built and operated in the 1860s in France. Power for the new engine was available in the form of gasoline, a "waste" product in the making of kerosene, the basic fuel oil of the nineteenth century.

It was only a matter of time, then, until someone perfected the engine, mounted it on a "horseless carriage," and so created the automobile. No one, however, could have begun to guess at the end of the nineteenth century just how rapid the development of the automobile would be. Nor could they foresee the surprising range of consequences it would have on the ways Americans lived.

The first man in the United States to build a workable automobile powered by a gasoline en-

The automobile early became a symbol of the "good life." Here a family picnics on the grass with their Model T Ford parked behind them.

gine was probably Ransom E. Olds. (His rickety machine was the forerunner of the present-day Oldsmobile.) Five years later, in 1895, Henry Ford put together his first car. The new machine was noisy, unreliable, and expensive. Still, a few Americans were willing to pay the price and stop their ears against the noise. By 1900 there were about 8,000 of the curious new machines operating in the country.

But Ford was not so much an inventor of the automobile as the inventor of a style and a method of production. In the early years of the century Ford began simplifying the automobile. He cut away every fancy decoration and convenience that had been adapted from the luxurious carriages of the day. Moreover, he reduced costs by turning out standardized, mass-produced machines. The results were astonishing. In 1907 the average price of an automobile was over $2,000. The next year Ford introduced a model selling at only $850. By 1914 he was able to cut the price to a little over $500. By the mid-1920s Ford was selling his assembly-line Model T for less than $300. The car was similar in many ways to the *Spirit of St. Louis.* It was the simplest machine possible, designed to do a plain task in the most efficient way.

Other automobile makers began to imitate and compete with Ford. The result was an exploding new industry. By the 1920s the manufacture of automobiles was by far the largest consumer products industry in the United States. It employed tens of thousands of workers at large and growing factories centered in Detroit. The automobile had a remarkable impact on other industries, especially steel and rubber, which provided the raw products for the assembly lines. The oil industry also underwent a major expan-

The prosperity in the 1920s that enabled millions of Americans to purchase automobiles gave rise to that most modern phenomenon—the traffic jam.

sion. The automobile turned gasoline into the main stock-in-trade of the petroleum companies.

Life in the Motor Age The most obvious impact of the automobile was not on industry but on American social life. By 1927 Ford had made 15 million cars. About 20 million American families owned an automobile. The immediate result was that horses and other draft animals disappeared from the landscape and the streets.

But the automobile had less obvious and predictable effects. First, the automobile encouraged Americans to move farther and farther away from cities, out into the suburbs. From about the time of Lindbergh's trip to Paris, the "lure of the suburbs" attracted more and more middle-class Americans. Second, cars and buses transformed American education, especially in small towns and farm areas. The school bus made it possible to consolidate school districts into larger units. Gradually the simple one-room schoolhouse, with one or two teachers for all the grades, disappeared.

Finally, the automobile, the truck, and the bus almost destroyed the principal industry of the late nineteenth century, the railroad. By the early 1930s the railroads had lost most of their passenger traffic to the car and the bus. The trucking industry took away most of the railroads' valuable freight traffic. The train, with its mighty steam engine, had been the great symbol of the early industrial revolution. By the middle of the twentieth century much of the railroad industry was sick and unprofitable.

In the long run the automobile proved to have unwanted as well as unpredicted consequences. Among these the modern decay of central cities was the most serious. Gradually large sections of cities like New York, Boston, and Chicago became the slums of the poor, who could not afford suburban homes. Also, although no one in Lindbergh's day could have predicted it, the automobile caused a major problem of air pollution. Smog resulted from the exhausts of millions of cars and trucks burning hundreds of millions of gallons of gasoline every year.

To most Americans, though, the automobile was an unquestioned miracle. To those who could afford it, it meant freedom to move at will through the city or the countryside. It also gave status, as manufacturers introduced more elaborate models, some costing ten times as much as

Ford's Model T. And the automobile meant adventure. Middle-class Americans could get behind the wheel of a powerful, complicated piece of machinery—just as Lindbergh climbed into the cockpit of his machine—and be off on an exciting journey of motion and speed every day. Like Lindbergh, too, Americans went beyond a concern with efficiency and practicality to a romantic affection for their machines. They polished them, paraded them, and gave them pet names like the "old bus," the "flivver," the "tin Lizzie," and the "merry Oldsmobile." Despite its defects, Americans loved the car.

Development of Air Transportation For the first quarter of the twentieth century the automobile had the greatest social and economic impact on America. The development of the aircraft industry and airline passenger service did not become truly important until years after Lindbergh's flight. But the airplane was in many ways more thrilling than the automobile. (This was why Lindbergh and other pilots could make a living in the 1920s barnstorming across America in their aerial circuses.) Like the automobile, the airplane depended on the small, powerful, and efficient gasoline engine.

The first men in history to fly a heavier-than-air craft were Orville and Wilbur Wright. Their primitive biplane had no engine and no cockpit: the pilot simply lay down on the lower wing. They managed to get the flimsy craft into the air for a few seconds at Kitty Hawk, North Carolina, in 1903. The development of airplanes was slow after that. The advent of World War I brought about a quick jump in design, engine power, and reliability. The war also romanticized flight by creating a new kind of celebrity, the flying ace.

The main civilian use of the airplane was shipping mail. The government began service in 1918. Later private companies (like the one Lindbergh worked for in St. Louis) took over the service. The operation was dangerous. A majority of the pilots were killed in crashes during the early years. But by the mid-1920s there was regular, all-weather air-mail service between most major cities in America.

Lindbergh's flight, combined with the introduction of larger airplanes like Byrd's *America,* did more than any other single event to encourage the growth of air transportation. Lindbergh had faith in the future of aviation. Soon after his return to America in 1927, he began a flying tour of the country to promote air mail and air transportation. By 1930, just three years after his solo transatlantic flight, there were 43 domestic airline companies, operating over 30,000 miles of flying routes.

NEW MANNERS AND MORALS

All these changes—the development of mass communications, the expansion of industry, the introduction of a new technology—brought about another revolution. This revolution marked a dramatic difference in the manners and morals of the American people. Americans of the 1920s knew they were living in a time when the world was undergoing rapid change. They coined new words and phrases—like the "roaring twenties," the "lost generation," and "flaming youth,"—to describe what was happening to them. Americans were adopting habits and moral standards that their parents found shocking and offensive.

A Revolution for Women At the center of the revolution in manners were women. The revolution that would change women's lives did not begin in the 1920s. During the first two decades of the twentieth century, many middle- and upper-class women had adopted new patterns of behavior (including divorce) that broke with the traditions of nineteenth-century Victorian America. But because of the impact of World War I and the influence of books, radio, and advertising, the trend started at the turn of the century began to affect ever-widening circles of women. By the 1920s the revolution was in full bloom.

Politically, women were new creatures. After

decades of agitation, they finally won the right to vote with the passage of the Nineteenth Amendment in 1920. But this new political role was only a small part of the emancipation of women. The new woman of the 1920s wanted to do everything. "Everything" included more opportunities than her mother had had.

She was much more likely than her mother to attend college. She might go to work, too. By 1930, 10 million women were employed in the American labor force. This new experience of education and work made women more likely to remain single, or, if they did marry, to get divorces. The divorce rate in 1930 was twice what it had been before the war. This did not mean that marriages were more unhappy. It meant, instead, that women were less likely to put up with a bad marital situation. They would demand their freedom instead.

The new woman dressed differently, too. The fashionable woman that gradually emerged in the decade of Lindbergh's flight was the flapper. She wore her hemlines shorter—above the knee rather than at the ankle. And her dresses were made of thin material, designed to move with her body as she walked or danced.

The flapper symbolized the new woman's daring—her flouting of traditional social and moral restraints. Short, bobbed hairdos, knee-length skirts, and sheer silk stockings identify these four women as flappers, as does their surroundings—a nightclub.

The flapper took off the corsets that had constrained women of an earlier generation. She put on more make-up and perfume and jangled with more jewelry on her wrists and around her neck. In advertisements or movies (and more and more in real life) she was likely to have a cocktail in one hand and a cigarette holder in the other—the ultimate in the new sophistication of the 1920s.

The Jazz Age The new woman was part of a changing culture. A freedom of action and belief unheard of before seemed to go hand in hand with the triumph of industrial technology, with its prosperity and sense of unlimited possibilities for life. Both men and women listened to new music—jazz—and danced new steps. Instead of formal waltzes and other Victorian dances, they moved to the fast Charleston and the Black Bottom. They also danced close together in the slow fox trot. Many older Americans were shocked by these changes. But these dances became part of the new culture, sweeping their way through high-school gymnasiums and college campuses across the country.

The sexual ideas of Americans were changing, too. The ideas of the Austrian psychologist Sigmund Freud on sex began to be discussed at the dinner table and in the polite magazines of the middle class. Words like "bitch" appeared in novels published by respectable publishers and read by respectable people. "Petting" and "necking" became part of the everyday vocabulary of magazine readers and even ministers. In the movies sex became a major box-office attraction. Stars like Theda Bara and Clara Bow appeared on the screen in thin clothing, locked in long, passionate embraces with their leading men. When Clara Bow was advertised as the "It" girl, hardly anyone needed to ask what "It" meant.

Americans drank more too. Despite prohibition (see page 651) liquor was easy to obtain. And since liquor was illegal, millions of Americans became technically criminals on an almost daily basis. Probably half the respectable, middle-class families in the nation had their regular

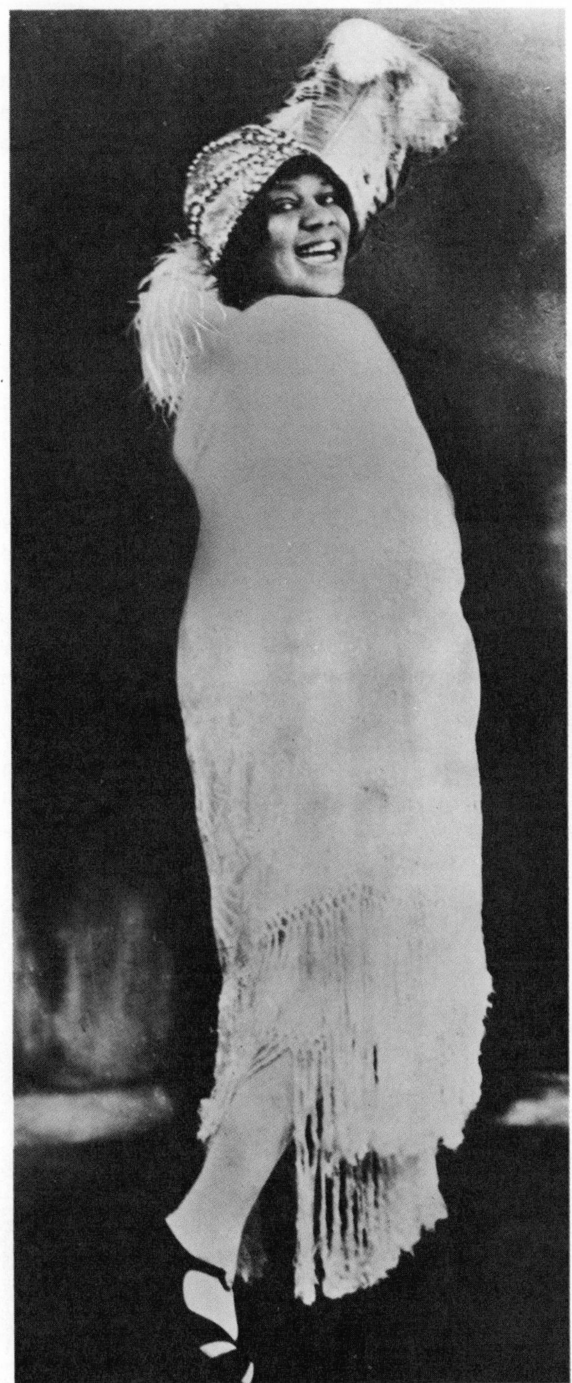

The "Jazz Age" gave birth to the blues, an especially plaintive, bittersweet music of black American origin. Bessie Smith, one of the best American jazz artists, made the singing of the blues uniquely her own.

Movie Stars as Public Idols

In its earliest years the American film industry had no movie stars. Instead, each studio had a number of anonymous "players" who were used over and over again in "the pictures." As time went on, moviegoers began to single out certain favorite players. They gave them names so that they could discuss them. There was the "Biograph girl," so named because she worked for Biograph Studios. There were "the little girl with the golden curls" and "the little fellow." All were anonymous, and all were loved by their fans.

Before long the public was clamoring to know who these players were. Letters poured into the studios demanding their real names. The studios did not want to comply. Once their players became famous, it was feared they would want higher salaries. For a time the public was infuriated. But the studios held firm.

Then an industry maverick, Carl Laemmle, recognized that there was money to be made in revealing players' names. If the public knew the names of their favorites, they would know in what films they were appearing. This, in turn, would ensure these films success at the box office. Laemmle began by luring the popular "Biograph girl" to his studio. He told the world she was Florence Lawrence and featured her in movies under her own name.

The "star system" was born. The public created it, and the studios exploited it. And Hollywood did not always wait for movie fans to find their own favorites. Through clever and imaginative press agentry, the studios could create, package, and distribute stars.

One such press-agent creation was the "vamp," Theda Bara. Born to an Egyptian mother and a French father, she grew up learning the secrets of the Orient. She possessed an evil power over men, and she had a name that could be respelled "Arab Death." At least that was what the fans were told about her. She thrilled them when she looked up from her tiger-skin rug, turned her hypnotic eyes on her leading man, and said, "Kiss me, my fool." Actually, she was Theodosia Goodman, a tailor's daughter who grew up in Cincinnati. But that was not the kind of background that sold tickets.

Stardom was not a job—it was a way of life. As one student of the film culture has put it:

> Stars lived like stars, larger than life. Clara Bow, the original 'It' girl, queen of the 'Jazz Babies,' received 100,000 fan letters a year, gave parties for whole football squads, owned a Kissel roadster (colored red to match her hair) with two red Irish setters trained to ride on the running boards, earned $4,000 a week and spent it all.

Hollywood gave people what they wanted—idols whose tastes, fashions, and manners they could imitate, whose luxurious lives seemed so much more adventurous and exciting than their own. Above all, Hollywood epitomized America's rags-to-riches dream: a tailor's daughter could indeed become a highly paid, glamorous, and adored celebrity.

bootlegger. Terms like "bathtub gin" and "speakeasy" became part of the national language. Especially in colleges, drinking became a regular pastime of the "flaming youth" of the decade.

The Search for Innocence As their own lives became more and more confused, Americans began to celebrate innocence. In their movies and sports they created simple, naïve heroes who were guided by straightforward codes of justice and virtue. The most popular type of movie hero of the decade was the cowboy, a symbol of innocent, preindustrial man. And the most popular movie star of the period, Rudolf Valentino, played roles that put him on horseback in a country far removed from Fords and factories and modernity. It was no accident too that the greatest sports hero of the decade, George Herman Ruth, was innocently nicknamed "Babe."

Lindbergh stirred the deep urge of people to believe in innocence. His youth, honesty, and simple determination made him seem much purer than the public that worshiped him. Lindbergh did not smoke or drink. He displayed no interest in women, at least at the time of his flight. And his boyish face looked out at the world through clear blue eyes. They seemed to say that everything was still the same, that the world had not lost its innocence after all.

A CONSERVATIVE TIDE

For millions of Americans the continuing atmosphere of change that dominated the period after World War I seemed threatening. In national politics, the 1920s was a decade of sharp reaction against all the reforms of the progressive period. But the reaction went much deeper than politics. Not every American participated, but a large and active segment of society believed that dramatic action was necessary to save their country from the dangers of "foreign" political ideas, from alcohol, from new ideas like evolution, and from the influence of Catholic and Jewish immigration.

Many of the people who made Lindbergh into a hero in 1927 did so because he seemed so clean, so morally upright, so much a product of middle-class standards and morals. As much as anything else, this conservative reaction, with its simple values and direct methods, gave the period its peculiar tone and color.

The Red Scare The conservative reaction focused sharply on radicalism. The Russian Revolution, which had brought the communist government of the Bolsheviks to power, was followed by communist uprisings in Germany and Hungary. These developments created an atmosphere of fear in the United States. Many people, including a number of powerful leaders in federal and state governments, believed that a communist conspiracy was at work among them, ready to "radicalize" the country.

In 1919 a series of spectacular strikes and the outbreak of political sabotage fed the fear. In the spring of that year two small groups of anarchists attempted to bomb the homes and offices of a number of government officials and businessmen. The bombs, sent through the mails, were probably the work of mentally unstable persons. Certainly they had nothing to do with the tiny organized Socialist and Communist parties of the country.

In fact, the bombers were incompetent. One large package of bombs was never delivered because it did not have enough postage. Another bomb only damaged the house of its intended victim, but it blew the bomber himself—an Italian anarchist—to bits. A third, addressed to a Georgia politician, was opened by his maid (a black worker, not a capitalist). She lost her hands as a result. But the bombings did convince many people that revolution was at hand.

One of the people who was most convinced was Woodrow Wilson's Attorney General, A. Mitchell Palmer. Like Wilson, Palmer was a liberal and a strong antiradical. The Attorney General also had his eye on the Democratic nomination of 1920. So he used the "red scare" to make his department the center of the action. He obtained an extra appropriation for hunting

Nicola Sacco and Bartolomeo Vanzetti entered a courthouse to make their final appeal in 1927. They were convicted essentially because they were Italians at a time when hatred of aliens ran high, and anarchists in a politically conservative era.

down radicals. With the money he formed a new antisubversive division of the Justice Department, headed by J. Edgar Hoover.

Beginning in November of 1919 the Justice Department conducted a series of raids against radical groups, seeking out suspected communists at union meetings, at Communist party headquarters, and in their homes. The most spectacular of the raids, which came on New Year's Day 1920, resulted in the arrest of 6,000 people. In the end the Palmer raids led to the conviction of only a handful of citizens, most of them for minor crimes. Immigrant aliens, who were Palmer's main targets, suffered more. About 600 were eventually deported, mostly to the Soviet Union.

Palmer's campaign created an atmosphere of near hysteria among many Americans. It led to one tragedy that did more than any other single event of the 1920s to divide Americans of different political beliefs. In 1920 two Italian anarchists were arrested in Boston on a charge of robbing a shoe company and murdering two of its employees. Their trial soon became a political event, a test of the established authority against political radicalism. The trial was unfair. Even the judge privately referred to the defendants, Nicola Sacco and Bartolomeo Vanzetti, as anarchists.

But in the political air of the red scare Sacco and Vanzetti were convicted and sentenced to death. The process of appeals was long and unsuccessful. Finally, in 1927, the year of Lindbergh's flight, both men were executed in the electric chair. To the small number of American liberals and radicals of the 1920s, Sacco and Vanzetti were the century's greatest martyrs. They were modern counterparts of the victims of the Salem witch trials and the Haymarket Affair. But to most Americans, they were just Italian radicals who had been properly punished.

The red scare also made it possible for those Americans who feared immigrants and their ethnic and religious differences to restrict immigration. In February 1921 (over the veto of President Wilson) Congress passed a law that limited immigration, especially from countries in southern and eastern Europe. According to the law, the number of immigrants from a country in any given year could not exceed 3 percent of the number of people of that nationality who were already in the United States in 1910. In 1924 the law was made even more restrictive. Quotas would now be based on resident population in 1890, immigration limited to 150,000 a year after 1927, and Asians totally excluded. The effect of the laws was to end, almost at once, the flow of immigration.

Prohibition and Reaction Like the red scare and the movement for immigration restriction, the prohibition of alcohol in the 1920s had roots in the progressive period. In 1919 the states had passed the Eighteenth Amendment, which empowered Congress to prohibit the sale of alcoholic beverages. The amendment marked the victory of a long campaign of temperance. It provided another rallying point for conservative, small-town Americans. They divided society into the "drys" and the "wets" and opposed any politician who did not favor prohibition.

The prohibition movement failed to stop Americans from drinking. In most cities people continued to drink whiskey in speakeasies. The sale of bootleg whiskey was controlled largely by organized gangs of criminals. Gangs like the one led by Al Capone in Chicago bribed public officials and policemen to cover up their operations. But for most conservative Americans prohibition was above all a moral crusade. It was an issue they could use to split their countrymen into two camps: one composed of decent people, the other of riffraff.

Another conservative campaign of the 1920s was the attempt of many Protestant Americans—again, especially in the South and the Middle West—to prevent schools from teaching dangerous or un-American ideas. In several Southern states this crusade aimed mainly at the idea of evolution. The notion of biological evolution was an old one. It became scientifically respected in the nineteenth century through the work of Charles Darwin. By the 1920s practically every scientist in the world believed that animals, including man, had evolved over a long period of time. But this seemed to many people to go against the fundamentals of their religion. They saw it as a challenge to the biblical story of creation.

Several state legislatures forbade their schools to teach the doctrine of evolution. In 1925 John Scopes, a schoolteacher in Dayton, Tennessee, decided to challenge the law. He was arrested, and his trial became almost as much a spectacle as the trial of Sacco and Vanzetti.

Scopes was defended by the most famous criminal lawyer in the United States, Clarence Darrow of Chicago. William Jennings Bryan led the prosecution. Bryan, an aging but still powerful leader of millions of fundamentalists, stood ready to smite the forces of modernism. He was humiliated on the witness stand by Darrow. Reporters from every major American newspaper—and several European papers—covered the events.

Scopes lost the trial and was fined $100. The Tennessee law stayed on the books. But after the Scopes trial the direction of education in the South and elsewhere shifted away from Bryan's intellectual conservatism toward the acceptance of modern science. Bryan's crusade, like many other conservative movements of the 1920s, was only a temporary victory over twentieth-century ideas and social habits.

Extremism: The Klan The most spectacular popular conservative movement of the period was the revitalization of the Ku Klux Klan. The Klan, which had died after Reconstruction, was reorganized in Georgia in 1916. Its membership grew slowly until the early 1920s. Then, like other conservative movements, the Klan gained a large following. By the middle of the decade it had about 5 million members, most of them from the South and Southwest. But the Klan also had supporters in the Middle West. It was strongest of all in Indiana, where for a few years it controlled the state government.

The Ku Klux Klan was an extremist organization. It usually attracted only the most violently conservative Americans. With its white hoods, burning crosses, the use of violence, and intense prejudices, the Klan represented the worst aspects of American life. Secrecy, rituals, and bizarre offices ("Dragons," "Kleegals," and so on) characterized the Klan. It provided many Americans with a way of expressing anger at the way "their" country had been "taken over" by foreigners, Jews, Catholics, liberal intellectuals, blacks, and gangsters.

The Klan was not so much typical of American conservatism in the 1920s as it was a symbol. Millions of conservative Americans were deeply troubled by the direction their country had taken during the preceding generation—and by worries about the future. Like the prohibition movement and Protestant fundamentalism, the Klan, even at the height of its power, seemed destined to lose in the long run.

The country was running headlong and at breakneck speed into the future. Technology had brought prosperity, and prosperity had fostered change. Nothing but a catastrophe was likely to slow the pace. Americans in the 1920s could foresee no such event. But by 1929 the event was upon them. The stock market crash of that year signaled the end of the New Era and the beginning of much bleaker times.

The lunatic fringe of the 1920s had considerable strength, as this parade of Klansmen in the nation's capital in 1925 indicates. Terror was the Klan's chief method of warding off members' own fears of a rapidly changing America.

1. Why might it be said that Lindbergh was a hero created by the mass media? Why was his public essentially a white and well-to-do one? Explain whether this makes any difference in the significance of his feat.
2. Which technological developments do you think were most basic in bringing about the New Era? Defend your selections.
3. In what ways was it possible for Lindbergh to be both an embodiment of the New Era and a maverick?
4. How was Henry Ford able to lower the cost of his cars so sharply between 1900 and the mid-1920s?
5. What were the effects of the invention of the automobile on the city, education, and the transportation industry? Were these effects advantageous?
6. In what ways may it be said that there was a "new woman" emerging in the 1920s? Could she have appeared without other changes occurring in the New Era? Why or why not?
7. Why was there a conservative reaction in the United States during the 1920s? To what evidence would the conservatives have pointed to prove the existence of a "radical" plot? Would the evidence have convinced you?
8. How did the immigration law of 1921 practically end the flow of "new" immigration?
9. Who were the religious fundamentalists? Why did they believe that the theory of evolution conflicted with the Bible?

Beyond the Text

1. Discuss the effects of mass-production techniques on individuality in America, considering the following questions: (1) How does the assembly line affect a worker's pride? (2) What is the effect of mass-produced products on consumers?
2. Compare the Sacco-Vanzetti case with the trial of those involved in the Haymarket Affair as to the attitudes of the judges, the bias of the jurors, the nature of the evidence, and the general intolerance of the times.
3. By the 1920s America had definitely become an urban nation. Investigate and report on the conflict between urban and rural values as shown in: (1) prohibition, (2) fundamentalism, and (3) the revival of the Ku Klux Klan. Davis' *The Social and Cultural Life of the 1920s* is a useful reference.

Bibliography

Nonfiction

Allen, Frederick L., *Only Yesterday.**
Chalmers, David, *Hooded Americanism.**
Cohen, Stanley, *A. Mitchell Palmer.*
Furniss, Norman F., *The Fundamentalist Controversy, 1918–1931.*
Jacobs, Lewis, *The Rise of the American Film.**
Kazin, Alfred, *On Native Grounds.**
Leighton, Isabel, ed., *The Aspirin Age: 1919–1941.**
Leuchtenburg, William E., *The Perils of Prosperity, 1914–1932.**
Morris, Lloyd, *Not So Long Ago.*
Murray, Robert K., *Red Scare: A Study in National Hysteria, 1919–1920.**
Nevins, Allan and Frank Hill, *Ford.*
Prothro, James W., *Dollar Decade: Business Ideas in the 1920s.*
Ross, Walter S., *The Last Hero: Charles A. Lindbergh.*
Sinclair, Andrew, *The Era of Excess.**

Fiction

Anderson, Sherwood, *Kit Brandon.*
Dos Passos, John, *U.S.A.**
Fitzgerald, F. Scott, *The Great Gatsby.**

*a paperback book

UNIT SEVEN

MODERN

Fifteen million Americans were unemployed on March 4, 1933, when the new President, Franklin Delano Roosevelt, was inaugurated. Roosevelt stirred his audience when he told his stricken countrymen: "Let me assert my firm belief that the only thing we have to fear is fear itself." A despairing nation responded eagerly to Roosevelt's determination to act quickly and boldly in confronting the emergency.

Twenty-eight years later another new President, John Fitzgerald Kennedy, also used his inaugural speech to proclaim new energy in national affairs. "Let the word go out," Kennedy intoned, "that the torch has been passed to a new generation of Americans [willing] to pay any price, bear any burden, to assure the survival and the success of liberty."

Roosevelt's address rallied Americans to begin the process of economic recovery. Kennedy's speech summoned Americans to leadership of the Western world. The three decades between these two orations saw the United States emerge from economic catastrophe to become the strongest and most prosperous country in

AMERICA

world history. The following chapters trace the steps in this evolution.

The defeat of the Bonus Marchers in 1932, narrated in Chapter 33, symbolized the old order's inability to respond effectively to the vast human suffering of the times. Most of the marchers were unemployed World War I veterans who had come to Washington seeking aid. It took the New Deal to provide such assistance. The accompanying chapter discusses both the discredited political assumptions of the 1920s and the experimental world of Roosevelt's New Deal. It also portrays the Great Depression's impact upon American social practices.

The attack on Pearl Harbor, dramatized in Chapter 35, highlights the beginning of a shift in national attention from domestic to foreign concerns. Roosevelt and his successors, determined to avoid future "Pearl Harbors," led the country in a search for collective security through treaty alliances. The wartime "Grand Alliance" of the United States, Great Britain, and the Soviet Union rapidly deteriorated after World War II. A new era of Cold War between the Western allies and the Soviet communist camp began. Pearl Harbor thus vaulted the United States into a position of world leadership. Chapter 36 traces the development of that role from the 1930s to the Kennedy administration.

Running parallel to Cold War developments in foreign affairs were anticommunist rumblings at home. The Alger Hiss case figured prominently in this. Hiss was a former high government official who was convicted in 1950 of having lied about involvement with Russian agents. His case came to symbolize for many the threat of communism to American society. The Red Scare that the incident touched off was central to many of the political, social, and economic developments that the next chapter discusses. Among those developments the nation's return to affluence, the rise of a "military-industrial complex," and the beginnings of certain social problems that would haunt the next decade are discussed. The dramatic flare-up of some of those problems during the Kennedy-Johnson-Nixon years is the subject of the Epilogue.

CHAPTER

33

Defeat of the Bonus Marchers

THE WITNESS shifted nervously but stood his ground. Having waited a long time to testify, he was not going to be put off. Without formally addressing the committee or saying so much as a polite "Gentlemen," he began: "My comrade and I hiked here from nine o'clock Sunday morning, when we left Camden. I done it all by my feet—shoe leather. I come to show you people that we need our bonus. We wouldn't want it if we didn't need it."

The witness was Joseph T. Angelo, veteran of World War I. He was addressing a committee of the House of Representatives of the United States Congress in 1931. The committee was hearing witnesses testify about a controversial matter: the immediate payment of a "bonus" to all the veterans of the war. The country was in the third year of a depression, and the bonus would pay about $1,000 each to over 3 million veterans and their families.[1] It would, in fact, be the greatest program of direct relief for the poor ever undertaken by the federal government.

For six days officials of the Republican administration testified. President Herbert Hoover was opposed to the bonus. The testimony of government officials reflected this opposition. A few congressmen, and one or two officials of veterans' organizations, spoke out for the bonus. But they were outnumbered by a long string of bank vice presidents, insurance executives, and other businessmen. The testimony was dull.

[1] Congress had set up the bonus (a combination of life insurance and a pension) in 1924. It was not due to be paid until 1945, except to heirs of veterans who died earlier.

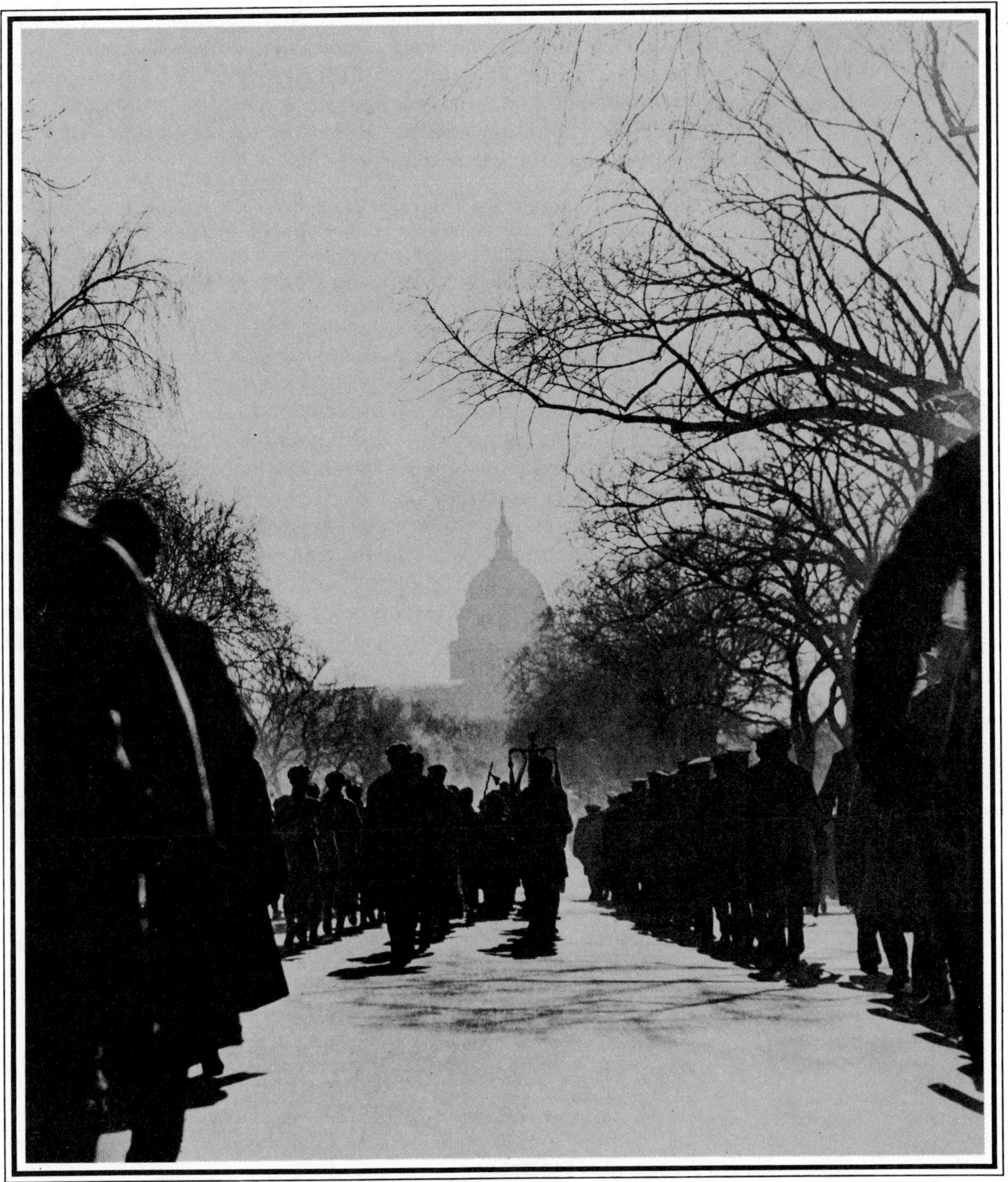

Disciplined regiments of World War I veterans marched silently and gravely to the Capitol in June 1932. This was a veterans' parade with a difference—the men did not want the people's gratitude now, but a bonus that would help them through hard times.

It was full of statistics designed to prove that the bonus would bankrupt the federal treasury and bring about a dangerous inflation.

But now for the first time an ordinary veteran, with no job, a hungry family, and a plain man's English, was testifying. Before Angelo finished, the committee and the audience were stirred into a mixture of laughter, admiration, and stunned confusion.

> I have got a little home back there [in Camden, New Jersey] that I built with my own hands after I came home from France. Now, I expect to lose that little place. Last week I went to our town committee and they gave me $4 for rations. That is to keep my wife and child and myself and clothe us; and also I cannot put no coal in my cellar.

Here, in the poor grammar and tired face of the witness, was the whole meaning of the depression that had begun in 1929. Angelo said he spoke for hundreds like himself in New Jersey. But he spoke, too, for millions all over the country who had not worked for a long time, who stood in bread lines, and who built the shacks in the shabby little towns they wryly called Hoovervilles.

But Angelo was also a veteran. So he spoke from his experience of the two most important events in his time—the war that people still called the Great War and the depression they were beginning to call the Great Depression. There was no economic theory or political philosophy in his testimony. He was just a hungry man who had fought in France.

> All I ask of you, brothers, is to help us. We helped you, now you help us. My partner here has a wife and five children, and he is just the same as I am. He hiked down here at the same time with me, and our feet are blistered. That is all I have to say. And I hope you folks can help us and that we can go through with the bonus. We don't want charity; we don't need it. All we ask for is what belongs to us, and that is all we want.

Some of the congressmen were confused. Others were curious. Following the custom of congressional committees, they began to question the witness:

> MR. FREAR: What is your business?
>
> MR. ANGELO: Nothing. I am nothing but a bum.
>
> MR. FREAR: You say you have not worked for two years?
>
> MR. ANGELO: I have not worked for a year and a half. But there is no work in my home town.
>
> MR. RAINEY: You are wearing some medal. What is it?
>
> MR. ANGELO: I carry the highest medal in America for enlisted men, the Distinguished Service Cross.
>
> MR. RAINEY: You have a Distinguished Service Cross? What is that for?
>
> MR. ANGELO: That is for saving Colonel Patton.

George S. Patton was already a well-known army officer. (In World War II he would become one of the most famous and controversial of America's generals.) Congressman Rainey continued the questioning and pressed Angelo for details. Angelo responded with a startling tale. He had been part of a 305-man unit attacked by German machine guns in the Argonne Forest in 1918. When the battle was over, he said, most of the men were dead. Colonel Patton was wounded, and only he—Angelo—was left standing. Then Angelo showed the committee a tie-pin made from a bullet he said was taken from Patton's leg in France. Neither the watch nor the medal had ever gone to "Uncle," Angelo's pet name for the pawnshop that had swallowed up his other possessions.

The afternoon was wearing on, but Angelo had roused the attention of the committee members and the audience as none of the other witnesses had. So the congressmen began to ask about his life. As Angelo answered, the audience sometimes laughed, sometimes applauded. He told them of working in a DuPont plant, making munitions for the British before the United States entered the war. When Congress declared war in 1917, he enlisted at once. But he was almost rejected because he weighed a mere 107 pounds. Only after ten doctors had poked at him and a general had watched him do a handspring and jump a table was he accepted.

Then, obviously agitated, Angelo wound up with another statement:

> I can make money. I can make lots of money. Now, I could go bootlegging. It is just the same way I could have went to France and I could have run out on my outfit. Which is the best, to be a live coward or a dead hero?
>
> When this was put on me, brothers, I wasn't worried when I went through. I don't have nothing to worry about. I wasn't married, and I got a wonderful send-off when I went to France. My father throwed me out. [Laughter.] And when I came back, I went home to my father. I saw a big, fat woman sitting in the seat. I knowed her from next door. I said, "She is the last woman you want on earth. Pop, what is she doing here?" He says, "That is my wife." I says, "Oh, My God!" She says, "Get out of here," and that was my welcome home, and I got out. [Laughter.]
>
> So, folks, I tell you all I will say to you is, help us through with the bonus. That is the best answer for you folks to give to the fellow at home. Don't forget me for a job. [Applause.]

Joe Angelo was three things: a veteran, a bum, and a victim of the most serious economic depression in American history. In each of these roles he was not just an individual grappling with purely personal problems. He represented over 4 1/2 million soldiers (about half of whom had actually been sent to Europe) suddenly discharged into civilian life in 1918 and 1919. These veterans organized—like other veterans in America's previous wars. More than a million joined the new American Legion and the Veterans of Foreign Wars. They thought of themselves as a special type of citizen, with a special claim on their country's gratitude.

As a bum, Angelo also spoke for countless people, many of them veterans, who had worked unsuccessfully at one job or another but mostly drifted through the 1920s. Naturally, the depression added millions of new "bums." Angelo, who had not been able to find work for a year and a half, was only one of a great, restless mass of unemployed. When he appeared before the congressional committee, at least 5 million men and women were classed as unemployed. Probably another 5 million were able to find only part-time work. Almost every other worker in America had his wages cut after the stock market crash of 1929. Few people could doubt in 1931 that unemployment was one of the most serious problems the United States had ever faced.

Joe Angelo's instinct was to turn to Washington for help. On his walk from Camden he had met other small groups of veterans with the same idea. The unemployed, the veterans, and the bums (often one man was all three) were looking more and more to the federal gov-

A group of New York veterans gathered in the yards of the Baltimore and Ohio Railroad at Jersey City, New Jersey, on June 4, 1932. These angry, frustrated men were hoping to seize a train for Washington where they could demand payment of their bonus.

ernment for relief. They had one fairly good chance of getting help from a reluctant Congress and a stubborn President—payment of the bonus. This, in Angelo's words, was "the best answer for you folks to give."

Angelo wanted $1,000 immediately, instead of waiting until 1945 to collect a larger amount. This was the heart of an issue that was about to create the most dramatic crisis of the depression—the massing in Washington of a "Bonus Army." Behind the crisis lay the old task of writing a final chapter to the World War and the new, complicated task of dealing with the depression. But for the marchers in the Bonus Army, the problem was quite simple: When and how would they be able to collect their bonus in full?

Veterans could already borrow money against the promise of the government to pay. Over 2 million had taken out loans that averaged $100 each—just enough to pay a back grocery bill, buy some coal for winter, or meet a medical emergency. But veterans everywhere were beginning to ask for ten times more, the payment of the entire bonus. And they found some sympathetic ears in Congress. Representative Wright Patman of Texas introduced a bill to authorize printing almost $2 1/2 billion in new paper money to pay the bonus. As time passed there was more and more talk of the bonus, not only in Washington but wherever knots of hungry veterans gathered.

In November 1931 a group of veterans left Seattle to ride freights to the capital. All over the country others were doing likewise. A movement began that would shake the Hoover administration.

For two years the President had been telling the nation that the depression was not so serious and would soon end. Administration officials had always played down unemployment statistics. They portrayed the crisis as a temporary economic slump that would cure itself. Meanwhile, Hoover kept to his principle that the federal government should not provide direct relief to poor individuals. The veterans who were hitchhiking and jumping freight trains headed toward the capital were not so sure of their principles. Certainly they lacked the President's political experience and skills. But they knew that they needed the bonus.

By May 1932, 300 more men from Portland, Oregon, left for Washington in a group. They called themselves the Bonus Expeditionary Force—a play on the name of the American army in France, the American Expeditionary Force. They elected a leader, Walter F. Waters, once an army sergeant, now an unemployed foreman in a fruit cannery. They rode freight cars east and, by late May, reached East St.

Louis, Illinois. There they tried to hop new trains going farther east. When railroad police told them to leave, they began to break up trains by uncoupling cars. They also soaped the rails in some places, making it impossible for engines to move.

The state called for its national guard to drive the veterans away. A scuffle occurred, but no one was hurt badly. The marchers were soon on their way again—in national guard trucks Illinois provided them in return for their promise to leave the state peacefully. But, most important, for the first time, the newspapers and the public heard in a notable way about the Bonus Army. Other veterans soon followed suit.

The scene was repeated everywhere. Merchants and mayors, railroad officials and governors, found that it was easier to supply trucks or boxcars than to stop the veterans. Thus a steady stream of bonus marchers was emptying into Washington. Each group had a leader or two, and their purpose was the same. They were in Washington to demand their bonus, even if they had to wait there until 1945 to get it.

One man deeply interested in the veterans' cause was Pelham D. Glassford, a West Point graduate and the youngest American in the World War to become a brigadier general. In 1931 Hoover appointed Glassford superintendent of Washington's police force. So he would have to deal with the Bonus Expeditionary Force in the capital.

Glassford hoped that the Bonus Army either would not come or would go home quickly. But as the marchers arrived, he became sympathetic and helpful. He regarded them as "his boys." He assigned them quarters in abandoned buildings on Pennsylvania Avenue. The location was at the heart of official Washington, between the White House and the Capitol.

At Glassford's suggestion, also, the marchers made a "muster," or list of their groups, to make it easier to track down criminals and keep out the "Reds" and radicals. Gradually the marchers formed companies and then regiments. They elected Walter Waters, leader of the Portland group, commander of the Bonus Expeditionary Force. He appointed junior officers and divided the men into companies named after states. Soon, the Bonus Army had a structure of command like the regular army.

Glassford's original decision to let the marchers camp along Pennsylvania Avenue was based on his hope that few would come. Soon it was obvious that the Bonus Army was much too large and dangerous (and embarrassing to the administration) to be in the center of things. Glassford sent most of the marchers to a new campsite a few miles southeast of Capitol Hill. The place was Anacostia Flats, a muddy land-fill near the forks of the Potomac and Anacostia rivers. There, about 6,000 veterans built a shabby but orderly camp, with shacks and tents arranged in winding rows.

At Anacostia Flats the veterans tried to re-create their old army life. They woke to bugles, conducted roll calls, and had inspections. A company of men was assigned every day to "KP." Waters exercised strict discipline.

Other aspects of camp life were more relaxed. Some men had brought their wives and children. The Salvation Army set up a post office, a library, and a recreation room. Glassford managed to borrow some field kitchens and other equipment. He supervised the distribution of food donated by Washington citizens, American Legion posts, and others. At one point Glassford gave several hundred dollars of his own money to buy food. There was even a newspaper to keep the veterans informed about the progress of bonus legislation in Congress.

General Pelham D. Glassford here watches some men at Anacostia Flats prepare a stew for their dinner. Although as chief of police he was responsible for dealing with the alarming number of veterans arriving in the capital, Glassford was not unsympathetic to the Bonus Marchers' cause.

By June 6, 1932, the veterans were ready for their first direct action. About 7,000 left their separate camps around the city and lined up neatly in six "regiments" to parade through Washington. The men felt fairly hopeful as they moved along. The Patman bill, which was in the House, seemed as if it would pass soon. The rumors that they were controlled by communists, spread by some politicians to smear the Bonus Army, were not given much credit. Best of all, their parade had drawn a crowd of about 100,000, mostly Washington clerical workers. Every time another company with its American flag passed, the crowd applauded.

Shortly after dark the long line of march reached a monument circle near the Capitol. (They were forbidden to pass the White House or go to the Capitol itself.) Orders were given to fall out, and the marchers broke ranks to walk quietly back to Anacostia. They had heard that in less than a week the House would vote on the bonus bill. If it passed both the House and the Senate and was signed by Hoover, most of the veterans could collect the thousand dollars needed to get their hungry families through another depression year.

The parade was simply a beginning. Veterans kept coming to Washington—the police estimated a hundred every hour. On June 15, when the House passed the bill, there were probably 15,000 veterans, plus some of their wives and children, scattered around Washington. Anacostia Flats was crowded, but new shacks kept going up. By now the ex-soldiers had stripped half the city of every stray board or door, every spare piece of tin or canvas. One man moved a burial vault onto the flats and took up residence in it. The camp was about level with the river, and had to be protected by a levee. When it rained, mud was a foot deep. But the Bonus Army kept building.

Obviously some kind of crisis might soon develop. Health officials predicted a typhoid epidemic. Waters predicted victory when 100,000 more veterans arrived. Hoover's advisers predicted that communists would take over the Bonus Force.

The Bonus Army and the administration were both waiting for the Senate to vote on the Patman bill. Hoover was sure he would win. The House elected in 1930 was Democratic. Since it was the first body of politicians to graduate from the depression, it was full of representatives who had recently promised their constituents direct action. But only a third of the Senate had been elected in 1930. The majority were still firmly Republican and loyal to the President. Both houses were striving for a July adjournment. (It was an election year, and everyone wanted to get home to campaign.) The administration hoped that the Bonus Army would simply disappear after the Senate voted and Congress adjourned.

On June 17 the Senate would debate and vote on the bonus. Waters commanded his marchers to go to the Capitol and fill the galleries, steps, and grounds. By noon, there were 10,000 marchers in and around the Capitol.

Inside, the Senate debated. Men would leave the galleries every few minutes to report to the marchers out on the steps. The opponents of the bill argued Hoover's position on what should be done about the depression: the government ought to cut spending, not spend more. Direct relief to individuals was not a federal responsibility. Recovery would come as large banks, businesses, and railroads regained their health. Then jobs would become available, and the economy would escape from radical tinkering.

Many senators supporting the bill argued that since the veterans were hungry and would be able to collect the bonus in thirteen years anyway, they should have it now. But one or two senators gave a more complicated justification for the bonus. In a depression, they insisted, the government should spend money, not save it. If the government printed 2 1/2 billion new dollars for the bonus, the money would swiftly circulate. The veterans would be only the first to gain. Then the stores where they spent their payments would get the money. These stores, in turn, would order more goods from wholesalers and manufacturers. So every bonus dollar would become a dollar in motion, moving through the economy and stimulating all business. Naturally, when the depression was cured, the government would stop deficit spending—that is, spending more than it raised in taxes. The economy would return to normal. The government would only "prime the

Thousands of veterans waited tensely on the steps of the Capitol, as the Senate debated the fate of their bonus. The eventual defeat of the Patman bill that would have made their dream a reality nearly triggered a violent confrontation between them and the marines.

pump" with its paper dollars. The happy results would then be automatic.

Though the argument went on, it soon became clear that only a political miracle could save the bonus. The Senate was much too conservative to experiment with such legislation. Even some of the liberal senators who usually opposed Hoover questioned the bill. What was needed, they said, was a general bill for relief of all the unemployed. Veterans should receive no special favors.

Finally, after eight o'clock, someone came from the galleries and whispered to Waters. The bill had lost decisively, 62 to 18. Waters climbed the steps and turned to face the largest body ever gathered in Washington to demonstrate for a cause. The marchers had been waiting for hours, and for a moment it seemed as if they might riot. Marines were stationed nearby, just in case. Members of the administration wanted to ready machine guns, but Glassford persuaded them not to. Waters shouted: "Comrades![2] I have bad news. Let us show them we can take it on the chin. Let us show them we are patriotic Americans." There was a muttering from the crowd. Then a gigantic roar came from 10,000 throats. Waters pleaded for calm:

> We are not telling you to go home. Go back to your camps. We are going to stay in Washington until we get the bonus, no matter how long it takes. And we are one hundred times as good Americans as those men in there who voted against it. But there is nothing more to be done tonight.

[2] This was an old term from the war, not a communist greeting.

The situation was tenser than any in the capital since the Civil War. Ten thousand disappointed people, who had kept good discipline for weeks, were ready to break and mob the Senate. Waters played a final card to keep order: "I call on you to sing 'America,' he shouted. After a few false starts, the men obeyed. Gradually, the song gathered strength.

The emergency was over, at least for the moment. The singing died out, and bugles sounded assembly. The men milled about, looking for their outfits for the march back to camp. It was dark now, and the nervous men waiting in the White House and the Capitol could take a deep breath. The bonus was dead, at least until Congress reconvened in December, after the presidential elections.

But the Bonus Army did not disappear. The government issued reports that the men were leaving. The Bonus Force and the police reported, however, that new recruits were arriving about as fast as old ones left. Estimates of the size of the force issued by the government, police, newspapers, and the Bonus Army itself varied widely. At its largest the Bonus Army probably numbered just under 20,000 men. Membership shifted constantly; perhaps as many as 50,000 veterans

Veterans inhabited eye-sores such as these, located on government property close to the Capitol. In an election year the government felt especially threatened by their well-publicized presence.

were in Washington at one time or another during June and July of 1932.

The government offered to lend the marchers train fare or gas money to leave town, plus seventy-five cents a day for other expenses. Many veterans simply took the money and stayed in town. Others used it to recruit new members. Thus, a month after the Senate defeated the Patman bill, there were about as many marchers as ever. The police estimated 15,000 people, two-thirds of them now crowded into Anacostia Flats.

By July, with no hope of a bonus from Congress, the veterans' mood soured. Their newspaper published more militant calls for action. Waters began to allow the small group of about 150 communists to eat occasionally at the Anacostia mess. (He had always thrown them out before.) He even began to talk about a permanent organization of veterans in politics, which he would call "Khaki Shirts," in imitation of the "Brown Shirts" that Adolf Hitler had organized.

In the White House, too, opinions were getting stronger. After the Senate defeated the bonus, the President decided the marchers had no business squatting on government land. He also decided they were not truly patriotic veterans asking for relief. Instead he believed they had been

> organized and promoted by the communists, and included a large number of hoodlums and ex-convicts determined to raise a public disturbance. They were frequently addressed by Democratic congressmen, seeking to inflame them against me.

The differences grew sharper, the summer hotter, and tempers shorter. On July 16 the most serious incident so far broke out at the Capitol. Congress was about to adjourn. Waters order his men to make one last symbolic demonstration. By midday nearly 7,000 Bonus Marchers were at the Capitol. Their mood was much uglier than a month before. Senators and congressmen crowded near every window to watch. Even Glassford lost his nerve.

Glassford ordered Waters taken into custody and moved to the basement of the Capitol. When the veterans saw what was happening, they stopped cheering Glassford and began to boo and jeer. "Waters! Waters!" they shouted. Glassford was forced to bring the Bonus Army's commander onto the platform. After a short, harsh exchange with Glassford, Waters tried to calm his people. Then he ordered them to move to the middle: "Use the center steps. But I want you to keep a lane open for the white-collared birds, so they won't rub into us lousy rats. We're going to stay here until I see Hoover!"

The demonstration was clearly dangerous. Several congressmen came out of the Capitol to speak to the demonstrators, trying to cool them off. Finally the Speaker of the House, John Nance Garner, agreed to meet with Waters and a committee of his aides inside the building. Garner handled the situation well. He made a few empty promises of help and was photographed with Waters. When the conference was over, Waters went back outside and ordered his followers to their camps. For a second time an extremely touchy and potentially violent situation had been controlled.

In the White House, however, tempers were also growing shorter. Hoover had just been renominated by the Republicans to run for a second term. The Democrats would meet soon to nominate Franklin D. Roosevelt, then governor of New York. Hoover knew the campaign would be rough. But he knew he would win if he overcame the widespread idea that he was responsible for the depression. A favorite tactic of Hoover's closest associates was to picture him as the firm opponent of all kinds of radicalism.

Unfortunately, the Bonus Army was the most visible kind of radicalism. Hoover had always opposed the bonus. Now he and his advisers decided to move firmly against the veterans. Some even hoped for an incident. Then it would appear that the government had to defend its very life against a radical insurrection.

A few days after Congress adjourned, the administration decided to move. The tensest point in Washington was the two square blocks on the south side of Pennsylvania Avenue, just a block from the Capitol and a mile from the White House. The buildings here were part of a triangle of structures that had been condemned to make way for a government building program. All over the triangle veterans camped in and around vacant and half-demolished structures, eye-sores that embarrassed the administration. On July 21, on instructions from the Treasury Department, the commissioners who governed the District of Columbia (and were directly responsible to the administration) ordered the veterans to evacuate the two blocks. For various reasons the order was not carried out at once. But Waters told his people to be ready to leave. Glassford was locating another site farther away, where they could take their few possessions and settle again.

Finally, at about 10 A.M. on July 28, Treasury officials accompanied by Glassford and his police entered the area. The veterans began to evacuate the buildings and vacant lots, leaving behind everything that they could not carry or push along in small carts or baby carriages. Everything went peacefully, though a few veterans had to be taken out under arrest. Before noon the first building was empty. In the mean-

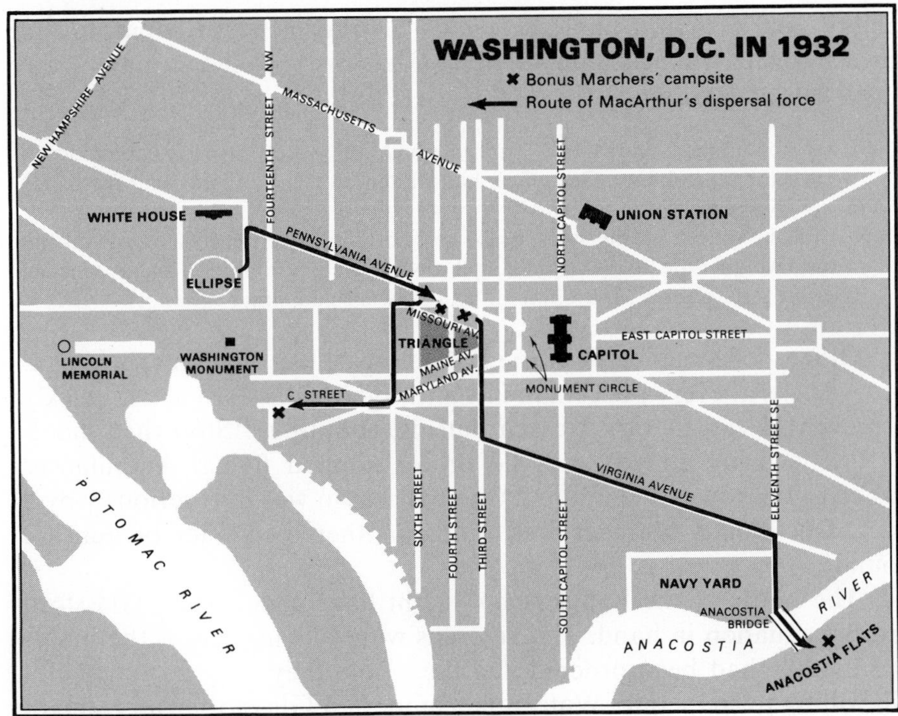

time, a large crowd of Washington citizens gathered to watch. Their sympathies were divided between the police and the veterans.

Then, a little past noon veterans from other camps filtered into the area, mixing with the crowd. One group came to stage a formal demonstration. Paul Anderson, a journalist, watched what happened next:

> At noon, three bonus men, one carrying a large American flag, started across the block, followed by several hundred. When the leaders encountered a policeman, he grabbed the flag. There was a scuffle, and one of the marchers was hit on the head with a night stick. He wrested it from the officer and struck the cop, and there was a shower of bricks from the buddies in the rear. It looked like an ugly mess, but the cops kept their heads, and no shots were fired.
>
> Glassford dashed into the heart of the melee, smiled when a brickbat hit him on the chest, and stopped the fighting. Within two minutes, the veterans were cheering Glassford.

For another half-hour the police continued their work. The veterans were leaving the buildings, but they stood around outside, many on big piles of bricks. No one is certain what happened next. Some witnesses said a policeman tried to clear veterans out of a building that had not even been ordered vacated. They resisted. Another observer said that a policeman started climbing some makeshift stairs, lost his balance, and fell. In a panic he pulled his revolver and began to fire wildly into a crowd near him. General Glassford gave what may be the most accurate account:

> I was about twenty yards away from the building when I heard a commotion. I went to the second floor. One officer had started up the steps, and near the rear, I heard some say, "Let's get him!"
>
> As he started up the steps, bricks started falling on him [Glassford was not certain whether the bricks were being thrown or were just falling], and as I leaned over the railing above, I saw him fall and draw his gun, firing two shots.

Other policemen also started shooting. Then veterans began to throw bricks at every policeman in sight. Again Glassford acted quickly to prevent a vicious riot. He ran outside, shouting, "Stop that shooting!" The firing ended, and the bricks stopped flying. Ambulances rushed to take away the injured. One policeman was hurt seriously by a brick. One Bonus Marcher was dead; another died later of gunshot wounds.

The battle of the Bonus Army might have ended here. Glassford had the situation in hand. The veterans were moving out of the buildings as they had been ordered. On the whole they were reluctant but still willing to cooperate. Waters had supported Glassford every step of the way. Within another hour or two the evacuation of the two blocks

When the Bonus Marchers were ordered to clear the federal property on which they had been squatting, fights broke out between them and the police that led to a larger battle.

would have been complete. But the administration also had decided to act. Hoover ordered the Chief of Staff of the Army, General MacArthur, to bring troops into the city to restore civil peace.

The troops—about 500 at first, then later over 1,000—formed up behind the White House. They came armed with bayoneted rifles and heavy blue canisters of tear gas. There were cavalry with sabers, a machine-gun squadron, several infantry companies, and even a half-dozen tanks. MacArthur put the troops under the command of General Perry L. Miles. But he later wrote, "In accordance with the President's request, I accompanied General Miles." With MacArthur was his aide, Major Dwight David Eisenhower. And in the cavalry was George S. Patton (who had no way of knowing that Joe Angelo had come back to Washington and was out in the troubled city with about 12,000 of his buddies, waiting).

General Douglas MacArthur with his aide, Dwight David Eisenhower, led the forces that finally cleared Washington of Bonus Marchers. MacArthur later claimed that if the situation had continued the institutions of government would have been threatened.

At about four o'clock the cavalry led the way, the iron shoes of their horses clattering on the asphalt of Pennsylvania Avenue. Then came tanks, more cavalry, the infantry, and the mounted machine gunners. They rode, walked, and rumbled up to the triangle, pushing the crowds back and surrounding the buildings. Without any conference or hesitation the troops (who wore gas masks and carried fixed bayonets) began to throw tear-gas bombs into the buildings. They were going to clear the entire area.

The veterans did not resist. A few hung back, and had to be jabbed at with bayonets. Mostly they stumbled out of the area and toward Anacostia. MacArthur, who also had tears streaming down his face from the tear gas, ordered most of his men to herd the veterans south. Another detachment moved west, to attack the small, separate camp of the communist group.[3] Suddenly, it became clear that the general intended to clear the entire District. In the triangle, smoke began to rise. There, the troops had set fire to the shacks, tents, and scattered belongings of the Bonus Army.

MacArthur's forces kept pushing the straggling veterans before them with bayonets and sabers. The sun was going down behind them. Ahead lay the drawbridge to Anacostia. The Bonus Army's rear guard hurried across the bridge at about sunset. Waters had already given the order to evacuate Anacostia and had sent word to MacArthur asking for time to move women and children out of the camp. On the flats about 7,000 men were scurrying around, trying to keep order in a forced retreat.

From the time the troops first appeared, the bonus marchers gave

[3] Communists in this camp included James Ford, their candidate for Vice President. On July 31 the New York *Times* ran a front-page article quoting the communists. "We agitated for the bonus and led the demonstration of the veterans in Washington." However, the communists were never the Bonus Force's prime movers.

Troopers used tear gas in a final effort to clear the Bonus Marchers out of Washington. The veterans were forced to retreat and in the main did not resist.

no resistance. They hung back, they booed, they swore—but they moved. MacArthur left his tanks north of the river and paused before Anacostia Flats for an hour before sending the infantry. But when they went onto the flats, the soldiers threw tear gas everywhere. Stragglers were treated very roughly. The soldiers then set fire to the camp. (Many of the veterans has already put matches to their borrowed army tents.) Next they moved out of the camp to the nearby area where many of the veterans still stood watching their shacks burn. As the troops rushed up the hill which was not federal property, they continued to throw tear gas. One woman, whose baby had actually been born since the Bonus Army's arrival, told this story:

> The troops came up the hill, driving the people ahead of them. As they passed by the house [where the woman was staying], one of them threw a tear-gas bomb over the fence into the front yard. The house was filled with gas, and we all began to cry. We got wet towels and put them over the faces of the children. About a half an hour later, my baby began to vomit. I took her outside in the air and she vomited again. Next day, she began to turn black and blue.

A few days later the baby died—the third and last fatality of the battle of the Bonus Army.

The day after the action was a time for summing-up. The White House and other administration officials issued statements. MacArthur gave his version in a press conference:

> That mob was a bad-looking mob. It was animated by the essence of revolution. They had come to the conclusion, beyond the shadow of a doubt, that they were about to take over either the direct control of the government, or else to control it by indirect methods. It is my belief that had the President not acted today, he would have been faced with a grave situation. Had he let it go on another week, I believe that the institutions of our government would have been severely threatened.

To this version of the threat posed by the Bonus Force, MacArthur added a simple lie—that it was the veterans who had burned their shacks in the triangle.

Another kind of summing-up came from Joe Angelo, who told a newspaper reporter his story. He was at Anacostia Flats, watching a group of infantrymen in gas masks overrun the shack he had been living in. They were urged on by a tough, confident cavalry officer. Angelo blinked the burning tear gas out of his eyes and recognized George S. Patton. Then like the rest of the Bonus Army, he ran. Soon he was back home in Camden, from where he had started his long hike to Washington a year and a half before.

On July 29, 1932, in a blazing finale that brought the battle of the Bonus Army to an end, the camps at Anacostia Flats went up in flames.

CHAPTER

34

Prosperity and Depression

MOST OF THE Bonus March veterans who went to Washington were as politically innocent as Joe Angelo. Some of their leaders had a little political knowledge—and the tiny fraction who were communists thought they understood the basic problems of American society and sought a revolutionary solution. But the great rank and file of the marchers were simply caught in a web of circumstances they did not understand or want.

These people had been affected deeply by all the technological and social changes of the 1920s. But when they came to Washington in 1932 to demand their bonus, the veterans faced a much more frightening challenge. The 1920s had been difficult times in many ways; life grew more and more unsettled and confused. But in 1929 every problem of living in a modern society came to a head in an economic depression. Millions of Americans—not just Bonus Marchers—came to realize that their government had grown too rigid to deal effectively with the realities of unemployment, hunger, and economic collapse.

The Bonus Marchers asked the federal government to take an unusual step to meet an unusual difficulty. The Hoover administration's refusal to pay the bonus was part of the political reality of inflexibility and conservatism that had developed in the 1920s. But, soon after the marchers were driven out, an election swept Hoover out, too. Franklin Delano Roosevelt became President, promising a New Deal that would end the depression and cure some of the economic ailments of the preceding decade. A generation that had already lived through sweeping technological and social changes now was to experience equally vast changes in the American economy and government—changes that the Bonus Army experienced and, in a small way at least, helped to bring about.

HARDING'S CONSERVATIVE REVIVAL

With the end of World War I the Republicans sensed a mood in the country of relaxation from the demands of reform and war on which the Wilson administration had built its policies. They met full of hope at their national convention in Chicago in 1920. They were still the majority party. President Wilson's illness had disorganized the Democrats.

Still, the party was split into two factions. The convention deadlocked for six ballots because no candidate could get a majority. Then a few party leaders huddled in the most famous "smoke-filled room" in American history and chose a presidential candidate—Warren Gamaliel Harding.

Harding was a small-town newspaper publisher and politician. He had risen through the ranks of Ohio Republicans to become a senator. A handsome but simple man, he was puzzled by complicated issues like taxation, the tariff, and foreign affairs. He was "one of the boys," who enjoyed a night of whiskey and poker with his cronies. He had never proposed an important law or policy, nor made an important speech, in his whole career. But he had a face that voters wanted to trust. And the people who ran the party knew they could trust him, too. He was a party regular. He would not have any strange ideas about regulating business or supporting labor unions or propose any odd reforms. He was, in a word, conservative.

For Vice President, the Republicans nominated Calvin Coolidge, another small-town politician who had become governor of Massachusetts. Coolidge was less a party regular than Harding, but he was just as conservative. And no one imagined, anyway, that he would ever be anything but Vice President.

The Democrats nominated a lackluster candidate, James M. Cox. They did try to spice up the ticket with a dashing young New Yorker, Franklin D. Roosevelt. Roosevelt had served as assistant secretary of the navy under Wilson. The

Warren Harding, who won the presidency by being one of the boys, was aware of his limitations. About his search for a capable economic advisor he said: "I don't know where to find him and haven't the sense to trust him when I find him." His candor was winning but, unfortunately, prophetic.

convention hoped the Roosevelt name would attract voters who remembered his cousin Theodore. But probably no Democratic ticket could have won in 1920. The voters wanted a change. Sixty percent of them voted for Harding. They also sent large Republican majorities to both the House and Senate, making it one of the most complete victories in the history of American national politics. Harding carried every state outside the Democrats' solid South and cracked even that by winning Tennessee. The repudiation of Wilson's New Freedom seemed complete.

Return to Normalcy Harding took office with a slogan that coined a new word. He said the country needed a "return to normalcy." No dictionary defined "normalcy," but almost every American probably knew what the President meant. Harding believed that there had been too much experimentation, too many attempts to regulate the economy and the working lives of Americans, too much speculation about new diplomatic arrangements such as the League of Nations. Normalcy meant letting things take their natural course—not interfering in the decisions of businessmen or in the complex affairs of other nations. Normalcy meant, in short, a return to simpler times and uncomplicated politics.

Harding's relaxed conservatism was not actually a well-defined policy. Rather it was a wish for fewer policies and less activity by the government. For his Cabinet the President chose people sympathetic to the practices of industrial and business leaders. His most important appointment, in fact, was Secretary of the Treasury Andrew Mellon, a Pennsylvania industrialist who owned the only important company then making aluminum in the United States.

Mellon helped to shape the small amount of legislation that the Harding administration presented to Congress. His pet bill was one cutting the income tax on the wealthy from a maximum of 65 percent to 25 percent. (Congress at first reduced the limit to only 50 percent, but Mellon later got most of what he wanted.) He also proposed, and got from Congress, much higher tariffs on imports, a policy that benefited American business and industry by limiting foreign competition.

The Ohio Gang Specific legislation was less important in Harding's conservative administration than its general relaxation of federal controls over business. Harding did not try to tear down the established regulatory agencies, like the Interstate Commerce Commission or Federal Reserve Board. Instead, he merely appointed persons to these agencies who were so friendly toward corporations that they administered the law gently or not at all. And Harding named as his Secretary of Commerce Herbert Hoover, who had made a fortune as a mining engineer and investor. Hoover used the Commerce Department to help, not hinder, the activities of American businessmen. His approach typified the triumphant conservatism of Harding's administration.

Unfortunately, Harding also brought to Washington a group of friends who soon became known as the Ohio Gang. Some held seemingly harmless positions, like Old Doc Sawyer, a doctor in less than good standing with the medical profession. Old Doc became the White House physician, with the rank of army brigadier general. Other Ohio Gang members took more important positions such as Attorney General and Secretary of the Interior.

After two years in office, Harding, who was personally honest about money, began to realize that his appointees were stealing and peddling influence. In the spring and summer of 1923 two administration officials committed suicide while being investigated. In June Harding began a long vacation in the West. As he left, he complained to a journalist, "My God, this is a hell of a job. I have no trouble with my enemies. But my friends! They're the ones that keep me walking the floor nights!"

Two months later, in California after a trip to Alaska, Harding suffered from what Old Doc Sawyer called food poisoning. Harding now had to pay in person for this political appointment, for Sawyer was wrong. The President had suffered a heart attack instead; on August 2 he died.

In a way, Harding was lucky. He was mourned by his countrymen almost as much as Lincoln had been. He was spared the knowledge of a new scandal that would later become almost synonymous with his name.

Albert Fall, Harding's Secretary of the Interior, had finagled Interior Department control of oil reserves set aside for the navy. There were two large reserves, at Elk Hill in California and at Teapot Dome in Wyoming. Private oil interests were willing to pay almost any price to drill the land. They did.

Two oil company executives, Edward L. Doheny and Harry F. Sinclair, gave and "lent" Fall almost a half million dollars in return for secret leases allowing them to drill on the reserves. The secret leaked out faster than the oil. The Government managed to cancel the leases, but Fall went to prison for a year. He was the first Cabinet officer in American history to be put behind bars.

When the Teapot Dome scandal, involving the bribing of Republican officials, broke, a Memphis newspaper published this cartoon entitled, "Assuming Definite Shape."

COOLIDGE AND BUSINESS

When Harding died, Vice President Calvin Coolidge became President. Though privately a talkative man, "Silent Cal," as Coolidge was called, spoke very little in public. He kept most of Harding's appointees, and basically followed his predecessor's policies for the rest of the term. As the 1924 election approached, there was little doubt about what the Republicans would do. Their convention enthusiastically nominated Coolidge.

The Democrats experienced a struggle between two wings of their party. One represented the rural South and West, the old Bryan supporters. They were at least as conservative as the Republicans. The other wing was newer and based in the Northern cities. It was made up mostly of "wets" (opponents of prohibition) and depended heavily on the support of immigrants (many of them Catholics or Jews). After 103 ballots the convention settled on a compromise candidate, John W. Davis.

Coolidge was conservative. But so was Davis, who was associated with the firm of J. P. Morgan. Once more the time seemed right, as in 1912, to try a third party. The Progressive candidate was Robert La Follette, now nearly seventy but still a fiery opponent of business interests. He did well. Coolidge won the election easily, though, with 15 million votes. But La Follette managed to get almost 5 million votes, and to carry Wisconsin's electoral vote. Davis and his badly split party could muster only 8 1/2 million votes, less than a third of the total.

Coolidge's second term in office was a continuation of the conservative policies of the earlier years, but without the scandals of 1921–23. Mellon and Hoover still exercised great influence. The new administration went on supporting high tariffs, low taxes on corporations and the wealthy, and a hands-off policy on trusts. It had an essentially do-nothing approach to farm problems and a negative attitude toward labor as well. The entire conservative politics of the 1920s was summed up in Coolidge's most famous sentence: "The business of America is business."

Still, the President was popular, and doubtless he could have been nominated for a second full term and won. But his second most famous sentence was: "I do not choose to run." Coolidge may have meant simply that he would accept a draft. Still, for once, "Silent Cal" had spoken too soon and said too much. The Republicans took him literally and turned to Herbert Hoover, the most prestigious official in the administration.

The Democratic Challenge of 1928 The Democrats partially healed their old split, hoping for victory. Governor Alfred E. Smith of New York won the nomination easily. Smith and Hoover were almost perfect contrasts. Hoover was conservative, even gloomy. He dressed in neat blue suits and was the perfect representative of stability and efficiency. Above all he opposed any extension of federal power over private enterprise (unless, as with tariffs, federal power could be used to help business).

Smith, on the other hand, was a happy, talkative, cigar-chomping Irish American politician. He wore a brown derby and checked suits and talked with an urban twang. His Catholicism and the fact that he was a "wet" disturbed rural voters, especially in the South. During the campaign Hoover accused Smith of socialism because the New Yorker favored federal ownership of electric power generating facilities.

But Smith did not really differ much from Hoover on economic policies. The contest was actually between two political styles. And Hoover won. He came close to Harding's record with 58 percent of the vote. In doing so, he cut deeply into the South, where he carried Virginia, Tennessee, North Carolina, Florida, Arkansas, and Texas. Hoover amassed 21 million popular votes, more than Coolidge and La Follette combined in 1924.

Plainly, the Republican regime was still in full swing. Hoover could look to the future with even more confidence than Harding or Coolidge. Surely a strong industrial system—watched over at a distance by a friendly government—would now move the nation into unheard-of prosperity.

BOOM AND BUST

On the surface, at least, the 1920s was a decade of great prosperity. Progress seemed inevitable as more and more cars, radios, washing machines, and other goods poured off assembly

One of every four farms was sold for debt or taxes from 1920 to 1932. Farm machinery proved costly not only in purchase price but in the overproduction and falling prices it caused. Dust storms on the plains in the thirties proved the final blow to many more farms like the one pictured.

lines. More workers were producing more goods than ever before. The United States seemed to have created an economic miracle.

American buyers and investors were confident. The New York Stock Exchange, where the economy's pulse seemed most vital, enjoyed an amazing boom period after 1923. Sales on the Exchange quadrupled between 1923 and 1930. As sales increased, so did the prices of stocks. Americans were on an investment binge. The total amount of money they kept in stocks and bonds increased faster than any other economic factor during the period (much faster, for example, than actual production or sales of goods).

Much of the new investment was made on credit. According to the rules of the New York Stock Exchange, investors could buy stock by putting some money down and owing the rest to their brokers. These "brokers' loans" showed how little of the investment rush was real money and how much was pure speculation. By 1927 almost $4 billion was still owed on such loans. The whole structure of the stock market was rickety.

Such investment was really a form of gambling. If a stock cost $10 a share and an investor expected it to go up, he could buy a share and wait for the price to rise. But he could also buy ten shares, one for cash and the other nine on loan. When the stock went up, he could then sell his shares at the new price, pay off his broker, and pocket the difference in cash. There would be a problem though if the stock went down. Then, when the broker's loan was due, the investor might have to sell not only his ten shares of stock but other assets as well. If the stock market fell too low, he could be ruined.

Year after year, the gambles paid off. More and more ordinary people with only small amounts of money began to play the market. The prospering economy appeared to justify their confidence.

A Warped Economy But this prosperity was very unevenly distributed through the population. There were many large pockets of people throughout the country who did not share it at all. Blacks in both the South and the North did not benefit much. Nor did most farmers, whose lives had long been difficult.

The problem of farmers was an especially hard one to solve. During the war they had been relatively prosperous, producing both for the home front and the battle front overseas. But after the war, the demand in both markets decreased. Complicating the picture, farmers greedily bought up new farm machinery, such as new gasoline-powered tractors. Mechanization increased production. But since the market was smaller than it had been, the effect was overproduction and a sharp drop in prices.

The position of laborers was better. Except for "sick" industries such as coal mining and textiles, conditions of labor had improved and living standards had risen. The progress occurred despite the fact that the union movement was not growing. The lack of growth resulted from the cautious and conservative policies of the leading union movement, the AFL, and a campaign by manufacturers to win acceptance of the open (that is, nonunion) shop. Perhaps because wages seemed to be rising, labor was not militant in organizing. But, a dangerous trend was developing in the economy: the power of people to buy goods was not keeping pace with the volume of goods being produced.

This problem did not result from conscious decisions by any group. The new technology let factories turn out more and more goods. So the total output of products for sale increased much faster than the population. This increase should have meant that almost everyone could have more of life's comforts and conveniences. For this to happen, manufacturers would have to raise wages or lower prices, or both, as production became cheaper. Then the people who actually made the goods could afford to buy them.

But businessmen generally raised wages less than they should have. They also kept prices high. In the short run, their measures meant higher profits—and higher profits for corporations meant the price of their stock rose. They could either invest the profits in still larger factories to produce still more goods. Or they could invest them in stock, to heat up the stock market even more. Many corporations did both.

The result was a warped economy. The amount of goods that could be produced ran far ahead of the people's power to purchase them. Sooner or later, an adjustment had to be made. Otherwise factories would have to close until the surplus cars, clothes, tools, and other items could be bought. For a time the problem could be avoided in two ways. The surplus products could be sold, on credit, to people who could not really afford them. A family could pay for a car, for example, over two or three years. Or, the surplus could be exported to foreign countries. But both credit and exporting could help a warped economic system only briefly.

The Stock Market Crash These facts were difficult to see. On the surface, the economy had never looked better, and Americans continued to bet on the future by speculating in stocks. In 1928 the average price of industrial stocks increased by about 25 percent. An investor who bought, say, $1,000 worth of stock in January could sell it in December for $1,250. Or he could take the extra $250 and invest it in some new gamble. Most speculators did the latter.

Then, after a few rumblings and warnings, the bubble burst. The stock market was not a sure indicator of economic health or disease. In 1929 reality finally caught up with it.

In September the most popular index of stock prices stood at 452. Two months later it was 234. What this meant, in plain terms, was that the market value of stocks on the Exchange had been halved. Most of the holders of the $4 billion in brokers' loans were ruined. So were many of the brokers. On the worst day of all, "Black Tuesday," October 29, the market index fell 43 points. Other days were almost as bleak and ruinous. Stock prices continued to slide. They reached bottom in 1932. Then most stocks were worth little more than a tenth of their cost in September 1929. The Great Depression had begun.

It was difficult then, and still is, for people to understand why the panic on Wall Street should have had any effect on the real economy. The factories were still there, ready to roll out goods. The farms were still there, ready to produce food. All the hands willing to work before Black Tuesday were still there, still willing to work.

But, month by month, the entire economic machine ground down. The stock market crash was the crucial link in the chain of events leading to this breakdown. It caused people to make some grim decisions: not to buy or invest. Many foreclosed on loans made to others because they needed money to pay off their own loans. So storekeepers sold less. And factories made less or closed down altogether.

Farmers behind on their payments lost their farms as banks desperately tried to collect hard cash. The banks needed cash because millions of people with savings accounts, frightened now, lined up at tellers' windows to withdraw their money. The banks often could not produce the cash because they had invested or lent it. So even the banks began to fail.

Builders of houses or offices stopped construction because they could not borrow money to continue. Down at the bottom of this tangle were plain workers who, by the millions, received notices that they need not come to work anymore. Their jobs disappeared. Since they could not work, they could not buy; since they could not buy, others could not sell or make goods.

The jobless were not just the old-line poor. Many had been solid, middle-class citizens, bank tellers or factory foremen. Others were farmers, who had barely managed to survive throughout the decade. Now they had lost their farms forever. They came to cities, looking for food and work, or they began to drift, looking for migrant workers' jobs. People combed garbage heaps for food for their families. They made soup from dandelions. Mostly, however, they waited in a cold, gloomy fog of despair for something to happen.

Hoover's Optimism The question posed by the depression and symbolized by the Bonus March was simple. Could the federal government be

Amid the bright lights of Times Square hundreds of New York's hungry formed bread lines in 1932. Ironically, scarcity was not the problem. As Socialist Norman Thomas remarked: "It remained for us to invent bread lines knee-deep in wheat."

used as a tool for dealing with economic disaster? In the past the answer had been no. Other depressions had been allowed to run their course without any federal attempt to bring early recovery or relieve human suffering. But the Great Depression was by far the worst ever. Now the industrial economy was so large and complicated that its collapse affected people far more. Countless millions were jobless, banks were failing by the thousands, and tens of thousands needed food. Something had to be done.

At first the Hoover administration was optimistic. The stock market crash was called a needed adjustment. The economy, Hoover announced, was fundamentally sound. Recovery would be natural and would come soon. Meanwhile, no federal action of any kind was needed.

Surprisingly, most Democrats agreed. In the congressional elections of 1930, the Democrats made prohibition as big an issue as the depression. Nor did the voters heavily punish the administration for its failure to bring about recovery. The Democrats won the House but the Senate stayed Republican. Hoover was still predicting that a return to prosperity was just around the corner.

But things kept getting worse. In 1929, over 600 banks shut down; in 1930, over 1,000; in 1931, 2,000. For farmers there seemed to be no bottom. Wheat in 1931 sold for $.36 a bushel compared to $1.03 in 1929. No one even knew how many people were unemployed by 1932, but guesses ran as high as 15 million. For those who still had jobs, pay envelopes grew smaller. By 1932 wages in industry were less than half what they had been in 1928.

As he faced all these facts—or, sometimes, tried not to face them—the President grew gloomy and confused. He tried to stay optimistic in public, believing business confidence was crucial to recovery. In private, however, he was trapped between two different beliefs. A humane man, he did not like to see people suffer. But he still thought that government should not interfere in the economy. Free enterprise would bring the nation back to its feet.

Most important, Hoover believed that the federal government must never give direct relief to the poor, unemployed, and hungry. Direct federal welfare, he thought, would destroy people's moral character. It would make them dependent instead of healthy, strong personalities. This set of attitudes, which he referred to as individualism made Hoover seem insensitive and cruel. He became the target of bitter jokes. People named their shantytowns Hoovervilles and called an empty pocket, turned inside out, a Hoover flag. Reluctantly, Hoover decided that the government must act.

New Federal Powers Early in 1932 Hoover signed a law creating a new federal agency, the Reconstruction Finance Corporation (RFC). It could lend up to $2 billion to banks, insurance companies, and railroads. These loans, the administration believed, would be used especially by the banks to make other loans to businesses. Businesses would in turn use the money for new construction or to reopen factories. Their moves would create new jobs and save old ones. Thus, eventually RFC loans would end up in the pockets of workers, who would then spend the money and create new demand, resulting in more new production, and so on, in a circle of recovery.

The President also went against his own beliefs by signing another law empowering the RFC to lend relief money to state governments. But the amount of the loans was too small to help much. Pennsylvania, for example, could borrow only enough to provide three cents a day to its unemployed workers. Also, the RFC loans to business were far too small to aid the economy effectively. Compared to previous government activity, Hoover's actions were bold experiments in the use of federal power. But, measured against what was actually needed, they were too little too late as the Bonus Marchers recognized.

The Election of 1932 This state of affairs led to the dramatic election of 1932. When the Democrats met, they could smell victory. The Republicans had renominated Hoover, and, against him, almost any Democrat seemed sure to win. The tide was running toward Franklin Roosevelt, who had been working diligently for the nomination for months.

In contrast to Hoover, the nominee was a cheerful, brash man who was an experienced politician. In 1921 Roosevelt was crippled by polio. But he fought back with energy and could stand with the help of braces and canes. He brought a spirit of energy and experimentation lacking in the Hoover administration. He even broke a long tradition by going to the convention to accept the nomination in person (flying there, to symbolize his modernity). Standing before the cheering delegates, he announced that he would be different:

> Let it be symbolic that I broke tradition [by coming to the convention].
>
> Republican leaders not only have failed in material things, they have failed in national vision, because in disaster, they have held out no hope. I pledge you, I pledge myself to a new deal for the American people.

In the campaign no one quite knew what this "new deal" would be. Roosevelt was vague, but promised that the government would relieve suffering, provide jobs, and stabilize the economy. This promise, plus the fact the country blamed Hoover for causing the depression, was enough to give FDR, as he was often called, a smashing victory.

Roosevelt received almost 23 million votes to Hoover's 15 million. Just as important, the Democrats, for the first time in modern history, won large majorities in both the House and Senate. On inauguration day, March 4, 1933, Roosevelt expressed his optimistic belief that the government could and should act to heal the

After the stock market crash people lost confidence and began to withdraw their money from banks. As a result banks, like this one in New York City, failed or were closed by state order.

nation: "Let me assert my firm belief that the only thing we have to fear is fear itself. This nation asks for action, and action *now.*"

ROOSEVELT'S NEW DEAL

The words were brave. They had to be, for the crisis had reached panic proportions. A growing sense of despair had spread throughout the country. Millions roamed the country in search of food, shelter, and employment. Some even returned to Europe in search of work. As radios blared popular songs such as "Brother, Can You Spare a Dime?" bread lines and Hoovervilles were set up in every major city. Private, local, and state relief funds were proving insufficient for the emergency. Never had the majority of Americans been so pessimistic about the country's future.

Of immediate concern to Roosevelt was keeping the entire banking system from collapsing. Many banks were failing. A bank "holiday" closing all banks to protect them from bankruptcy, was declared in Michigan. Hoover, the night before he left office, said, "We are at the end of our rope." Roosevelt simply stretched his constitutional powers and declared a national bank holiday until further notice. Then, only five days after the inauguration, he sent to Congress an Emergency Banking Relief Act, which allowed the RFC to buy stock in banks. The law would allow the government to save a failing bank by providing cash to pay its depositors. Amazingly, the act passed both houses of Congress in eight hours! The New Deal was under way.

The Debate Over Meaning Ever since the 1930s Americans have debated almost endlessly

MAJOR NEW DEAL DOMESTIC LEGISLATION

YEAR	ACT/ADMINISTRATION	PURPOSE
BANKING, CURRENCY, SECURITIES		
1933	EMERGENCY BANKING RELIEF ACT	To save failing banks by providing them with cash to pay their depositors.
	GLASS-STEAGALL ACT	To curb speculation by banks; set up the Federal Deposit Insurance Corporation to "insure" savings deposits up to $10,000.
	"TRUTH IN SECURITIES" ACT	To require corporations floating new securities to register them with the Federal Trade Commission.
1934	GOLD RESERVE ACT	To enable the President to fix the gold content of the dollar.
	SECURITIES EXCHANGE ACT	Set up the Securities and Exchange Commission to regulate the Stock Market.
1935	BANKING ACT	To reform and strengthen the Federal Reserve System by directing interest rates.
DIRECT RELIEF		
1933	FARM CREDIT ADMINISTRATION	To provide emergency relief to farmers in the form of mortgages.
	FEDERAL EMERGENCY RELIEF ACT	Set up the Federal Emergency Relief Administration to provide grants in aid to the states; also set up the Civil Works Administration to relieve unemployment by a temporary work relief program.
	FRAZIER-LEMKE FARM BANKRUPTCY ACT	To enable some farmers to regain their farms even after the foreclosure of mortgages.
	HOME OWNERS REFINANCING ACT	Set up the Home Owners' Loan Corporation to provide emergency relief to home owners in the form of government financed mortgage loans.
	NATIONAL INDUSTRIAL RECOVERY ACT	Set up the Public Works Administration to contract for heavy construction projects in order to increase emloyment.
	UNEMPLOYMENT RELIEF ACT	Set up the Civilian Conservation Corps to provide jobs for the unemployed on conservation projects.
1934	NATIONAL HOUSING ACT	Set up the Federal Housing Administration to insure mortgages for new construction and home repairs.
1935	WORKS PROGRESS ADMINISTRATION	To relieve unemployment by light public works projects.
1937	FARM SECURITY ADMINISTRATION	To make short-term loans for rehabilitation of farms, and long-term loans for purchase of farms.

MAJOR NEW DEAL DOMESTIC LEGISLATION

YEAR	ACT / ADMINISTRATION	PURPOSE
REGULATION OF INDUSTRY AND AGRICULTURE		
1933	AGRICULTURAL ADJUSTMENT ACT	Set up the Agricultural Adjustment Administration to encourage stability in agriculture by attempting to control agricultural production.
	NATIONAL INDUSTRIAL RECOVERY ACT	Set up the National Recovery Administration to encourage corporations to create associations for planning production and controlling prices; created a blanket code of minimum wages and maximum hours.
1935	CONNALLY ACT	To prevent overproduction of oil.
	GUFFEY ACT	To control the coal industry.
	NATIONAL LABOR RELATIONS ACT (WAGNER ACT)	To give federal protection to the labor movement by making it illegal for an employer to refuse to recognize a labor union.
	PUBLIC UTILITIES HOLDING COMPANY ACT	To limit the development of holding companies and discourage financial concentration in public utilities.
1936	ROBINSON-PATMAN ACT	To prohibit wholesalers or manufacturers from giving preferential discounts or rebates to large buyers.
	WALSH-HEALY ACT	To set minimum wages and maximum hours for work done on federal contracts (enacted after NRA declared unconstitutional).
1938	AGRICULTURAL ADJUSTMENT ACT	To cut back farm production through marketing quotas, soil conservation payments, export subsidies, and crop loans. It began storage of surpluses.
	FAIR LABOR STANDARDS ACT	To establish minimum wages and maximum hours; forbade child labor.
REFORM		
1933	TENNESSEE VALLEY AUTHORITY	Set up the Tennessee Valley Authority to develop the nation's water resources and, therefore, provide cheap electric power.
1935	SOCIAL SECURITY ACT	To create a system of old-age insurance for Americans.
	WEALTH TAX ACT	To make the federal income tax more equitable.
MISCELLANEOUS		
1934	RECIPROCAL TRADE AGREEMENTS ACT	To lower tariff barriers in order to improve foreign trade.
1939	HATCH ACT	To remedy corrupt campaign practices by prohibiting active political campaigning and soliciting by federal officials.
	REORGANIZATION ACT	To reorganize the executive branch for greater efficiency.

To inspire the American people with a new sense of confidence, Franklin Roosevelt initiated a series of radio broadcasts when he took office. During these "fireside chats" he explained his proposals simply and reassuringly. They won him needed support.

and sometimes angrily about the basic nature and meaning of the New Deal. For some the New Deal was a revolution. They argue that it departed from the normal patterns of American politics to institute new and radical habits of federal regulation of economic and social life. But many other Americans believe that the New Deal produced few really fundamental changes. Roosevelt's programs, according to this view, left both the Constitution and the capitalist economy more or less intact. In fact, Roosevelt's only real purpose was to preserve the American social, economic, and political system from the kinds of revolution that were occurring in some European nations.

There is truth on both sides, depending on what comparisons are made. Compared with previous peacetime Presidents, Roosevelt looks quite revolutionary. The New Deal did take some drastic steps toward federal regulation, control, and planning of the economy. But when compared to the wartime presidencies of Lincoln or Wilson, Roosevelt's response to the depression appears to be less unusual. Also, when the New Deal is seen as part of the progressive tradition that spans the twentieth century, Roosevelt's "revolution" looks tame indeed.

Those who argue the question often assume that the New Deal was a systematic program based on a coherent political theory. It was not. The New Deal was, instead, a series of laws and executive orders that were designed to meet the problems at hand. There was only one basic idea behind these acts: federal power should be used to cure the depression and, if possible, prevent future collapses of the economy. What held the New Deal together was not ideas, really, but the personality of Roosevelt himself. And that personality was itself confused and contradictory.

The Man Behind the Program Roosevelt was forty-seven when the stock market collapsed, fifty-one when he became President. His ideas about the world were already formed. There is no evidence that the depression changed them significantly.

He was in many ways a tradition-minded man. He was a wealthy aristocrat, educated in the country's most exclusive private schools, and a graduate of Harvard. He owned a great estate, where he liked to play at being a gentleman farmer. An Episcopalian in religion, he was a commonplace capitalist in private life. He came naturally to his career in regular Democratic party politics because of his family background. Unlike other great American Presidents, he was not a scholar or writer. All in all, Roosevelt was a suave, smiling, confident man who seemed to take the institutions and beliefs of his nation very much for granted. A more unlikely candidate for leader of a revolution is hard to imagine.

On the other hand, Roosevelt's confidence opened his mind to experiments. Because he had no serious doubts about American values and institutions, he could accept almost any concrete suggestion for reform. Above all, he often said, the country demanded action. As long as the action was limited in its scope and possible consequences, he was willing to try almost any-

Eleanor Roosevelt

"About the only value the story of my life may have is to show that one can, without any particular gifts, overcome obstacles that seem insurmountable; that, in spite of timidity and fear, in spite of a lack of special talents, one can find a way to live widely and fully." With these words Eleanor Roosevelt modestly introduced her autobiography in 1960.

Indeed, timidity and fear seemed to be the dominant personality traits of the first half of Eleanor's life. She was born in 1884 to a beautiful mother, a society belle, and a handsome and charming father, the brother of Theodore Roosevelt. But it soon became obvious that she had inherited neither her mother's looks nor her father's ease with people. "I was a shy, solemn child even at the age of two, and I am sure that even when I danced I never smiled." Her mother, somewhat ashamed of her plain daughter, told a visitor in Eleanor's presence, "She is such a funny child, so old-fashioned that we always call her 'Granny.'"

It was an agonizing childhood. "Looking back I see that I was always afraid of something: of the dark, of displeasing people, of failure. Anything I accomplished had to be done across a barrier of fear." By the time she was eight, her mother was dead. Just before her tenth birthday she lost her father too.

Such unhappiness could have resulted in great bitterness. In Eleanor Roosevelt, however, it developed instead into a deep compassion for all human beings and their sufferings. At first it showed itself in the charity work she did. This was in keeping with the young society matron she became after her marriage to her distant cousin Franklin Delano Roosevelt in 1903. But as her horizons expanded, she channeled her compassion into a lifelong crusade for human rights.

In the 1920s she allied herself with the causes of better working conditions and greater political participation for women. With the coming of the

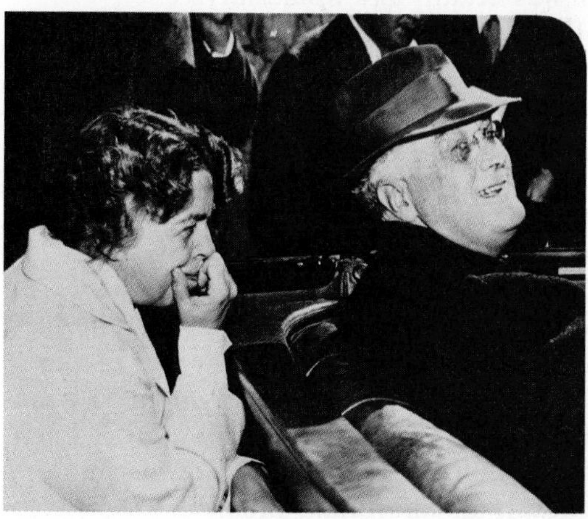

depression she concerned herself with helping hungry, jobless workers.

When her husband became President at the height of the depression, she became his eyes and ears in the field of social conditions. She crossed the country visiting farms, factories, even coal mines. Then she reported her findings to him—what people were thinking, what they needed, how they were bearing up. She became his unofficial ambassador to blacks, and she worked tirelessly to have equal rights extended to them.

In the 1940s Mrs. Roosevelt moved her crusade onto the world scene. She became a delegate to the United Nations and served as chairman of the commission to draft the Universal Declaration of Human Rights. Through her work for that body's Educational, Scientific, and Cultural Organization (UNESCO), she became an international symbol of the eternal struggle for the rights of man.

After her death in 1962, a saddened United Nations listened to United States Ambassador Adlai E. Stevenson eulogize her: "Yesterday I said I lost more than a friend; I lost an inspiration. She would rather light candles than curse the darkness, and her glow has warmed the world."

 thing. If his first try did not work, he could easily try something different because he believed the nation was healthy and would survive.

Roosevelt knew that the depression was serious and that the stakes were high. But he was sure, too, that sooner or later limited reforms would revive the economy. Then all that would be needed was a gentle system of laws and regulations to prevent the worst mistakes of the 1920s and to protect against future disasters.

No wonder, then, that Roosevelt was secretive, even coy, whenever anyone asked him during the 1932 campaign just what he had in mind. The New Deal was never a systematic plan but a loosely connected series of "programs." Each was designed to attack what FDR or his advisers thought was an unfortunate problem.

These advisers—most of them academic economists or social scientists or old law school friends—became known as the "Brain Trust." Some members of the Brain Trust did have well-thought-out schemes of social reform in mind. Also, dozens of minor officials who came to Washington to work in the administration had much more radical ideas than Roosevelt.

But the President himself thought in very specific terms. As a result he sent to Congress a confused stream of proposals for new governmental agencies. Many of them were known by their initials, so that the government soon resembled what one jokester called an "alphabet soup." FDR's first few months in office, called the "hundred days," saw intense but helter-skelter activity and experiment that resulted in many new laws.

Relief and Stabilization Measures Part of the New Deal was aimed at one simple goal: to relieve the hunger and disaster brought to millions by the depression. At first, direct relief was felt needed. The Federal Emergency Relief Act of 1933 answered that need by distributing billions of dollars to the states, which then doled out the money to millions of needy families.

But charity in the form of direct relief was thought to be degrading by many unemployed.

The WPA's immediate goal was to provide relief for the unemployed. But in its six-year life span it compiled a remarkable record of public construction, including more than 600,000 miles of road, like this one in Tennessee. Moreover, it introduced the notion of government aid to the arts. This mural in a Madison, Wisconsin, auditorium is a product of that aid.

Thus a Public Works Administration (PWA) was established in 1933. It eventually spent over $4 billion, placing people in government jobs constructing roads, public buildings, and other such projects. In 1935 a similar program, the Works Progress Administration (WPA), was set up that extended the definition of public works to include everything from light construction projects to the production of plays, concerts, and other works of art. Between 1935 and 1941 more than 8 million Americans were employed by the WPA, which spent over $11 billion on 250,000 such projects. Both the PWA and the WPA were created to give only temporary work relief until the private economy could provide jobs. They represented the kind of direct federal intervention in the economic lives of citizens that Hoover most feared. But Roosevelt, seeing the need, plunged ahead.

Other important New Deal laws were designed to give immediate emergency relief to farmers and ordinary homeowners. Under this legislation, the federal government began to make mortgage loans to families in danger of losing their homes to banks. These laws saved thousands of farms and homes. But they also helped the banks, which were paid in full instead of being saddled with practically worthless property.

This direct relief—while it might mean most to those who benefited from it—was not the most important part of the New Deal. The cornerstone of Roosevelt's program, from the hundred days to the end of the New Deal, were laws aimed at stabilization rather than recovery. Roosevelt believed that the basic economic institutions were sound. But he thought that the economy was subject to unpredictable ups and downs. These wild motions of the economy were what caused businessmen, bankers, farmers, and consumers to lose confidence. Depressions and delayed recoveries resulted. By planning and controls the important parts of the economy could be stabilized. Federal power would be used wherever needed to prevent businesses and farms from failing.

Banks, for example, had proved to be one of the most fragile economic institutions. Roosevelt had already used the powers of the federal government to rescue them. Later, he persuaded a willing Congress to go further.

A new Federal Deposit Insurance Corporation (FDIC) was given the power to insure savings deposits up to $10,000. This plan would make it almost impossible for a bank to fail, thereby wiping out a family's savings. The effect was to create enough confidence in the banks that people were willing to deposit money in them once more. Banks not only survived but began to make the loans necessary to recovery.

A smiliar logic guided the two programs that were closest to the heart of the New Deal: the National Industrial Recovery Act and the Agricultural Adjustment Act, both passed in 1933. The two laws sought to regulate the basic units of the economy—privately owned farms and business corporations—without altering their private, capitalistic character.

The National Industrial Recovery Act was, in essence, a repeal of parts of the old Sherman Antitrust Act (see page 537). Under a federal agency known as the National Recovery Administration (NRA), corporations were encouraged to create associations for planning production and controlling prices. Such a step was in many ways an abandonment of competition, but the administration was prepared during the depression to sacrifice competition to stability.

For workers, the act also proposed that employers agree on uniform standards for labor practices, wages, and hours. When some companies were slow to cooperate, the NRA created a blanket code of minimum wages and maximum hours. Companies that cooperated were awarded a flag with the NRA symbol, a blue eagle, to fly as evidence of their public spirit. Up to a point it worked. Some workers—those who had jobs to begin with—began to work shorter days and take home larger salaries.

The Agricultural Adjustment Act was a similar but more radical attempt to alter the economics of agriculture. It recognized that the farmer had a peculiar problem. When prices fell, manufacturers could cut back production. This reduction in supply would, sooner or later, raise prices. But farmers had always met falling prices by trying to grow more, not less.

The Agricultural Adjustment Act created an Agricultural Adjustment Administration (AAA) with the power to pay farmers not to plant and harvest crops. It could also buy up agricultural products such as cotton or wheat and store them. This scheme would reduce supply and raise prices. In other words, a government agency, with the voluntary cooperation of farmers, would try to control agricultural production. The goal was to enable farmers to earn as much as they had during the prosperous years 1909–14, a standard known as parity.

The AAA worked better than the NRA. Using its new powers, the government plowed under about 10 million acres of cotton. It also killed about 5 million pigs—a controversial act, when many people did not have enough to eat. But these drastic measures worked—helped along by a drought in 1933 and 1934 that destroyed much of the wheat and corn crops. In 1933 farm prices reached 55 percent of parity; by 1936, 90 percent.

Attempts at Reform The relief and stabilization programs made up the bulk of New Deal legislation. But Roosevelt also attempted a more fundamental (occasionally, even revolutionary) remodeling of American society. These measures appear quite small when compared to more recent exercises of federal power. But at the time they seemed to many people to hint at radical and permanent changes in the ways Americans lived and worked.

The Tennessee Valley Authority (TVA) was an attempt to change the basic social and economic structure of an entire region (see page 691). The Civilian Conservation Corps (CCC) hired thousands of young men to plant trees, improve parks, and clean up streams. Roosevelt even tried (without success) to revive the old practice of homesteading, to lure people from the city into agriculture.

More important to most citizens, however, were two laws of 1935 that lasted well beyond the depression. Both were designed to give protection to groups of people that Roosevelt felt were always at an economic disadvantage: workers and the elderly. The first, the National Labor Relations Act (popularly known as the Wagner Act), made it illegal for an employer to refuse to recognize a labor union. The law also contained a list of "unfair labor practices" forbidden employers. It was clearly the most powerful piece of prolabor legislation ever signed into law by an American President.

As a result of the act labor unionism tripled in membership, from a low of 3 million members in the early 1930s to about 9 1/2 million by 1941. This rapid growth in unionism was not gained without strife though. The AFL, a crafts union movement, was challenged by the Congress of Industrial Organizations (CIO), which stressed organization of workers by industry. In general most businessmen opposed all unions, but many opted for negotiation with one group rather than the numerous craft unions. Sit-down strikes at General Motors plants in 1936 and near warfare a year later in the steel industry forced industrialists to accept the CIO formula for organizing labor.

Older people had suffered more in the depression than any other group of people, except perhaps for farmers in the South and Southwest. The Social Security Act of 1935 was an attempt to create a system of insurance for Americans. (The system was modeled on programs already common in many European countries and even some American states.) The law provided that workers and their employers would each contribute a small part of each year's earnings to a common fund. When a person reached retirement age (or could no longer work because of illness), he or she would receive a small pension from the fund. If a worker died, the survivors would receive benefits. The law, though modest, was the biggest step the federal government had ever taken toward becoming what Roosevelt's critics called a "welfare state."

Taken together, TVA, Social Security, the Wagner Act, and others were a definite though incomplete move in the direction of federal planning, welfare, and control of the economy

The Tennessee Valley Authority

Though the Great Depression was severe throughout America, it was nowhere felt more keenly than in the Tennessee River Valley. This 40,000 square miles of territory spanned seven states. Loggers had long since come, chopped down its forest, and left. Each year fifty-two inches of rain fell, swelling its rivers to flood stage and washing out the meager crops. There was little industry and less hope for more. Income was not even half the national average. The extreme poverty resulted in poor schools, government, and health conditions.

Shortly after becoming President, Franklin D. Roosevelt announced a far-reaching plan for the area. It was by far the most creative experiment to date in American history. He wanted Congress to set up the Tennessee Valley Authority, a regional planning agency that would revive the area by taking full advantage of its natural resources. The TVA would direct the building of a series of dams for flood control and thus make successful farming possible. It would construct hydroelectric plants along the rivers and make these rivers navigable. The cheap power and easy water transport would make the area appealing to industry.

The TVA would also be charged with reforesting the area, making proper use of marginal lands, and in general planning for the economic and social well-being of the people in the region. Adult education, improved health conditions, and greater recreational opportunities were included in the planning.

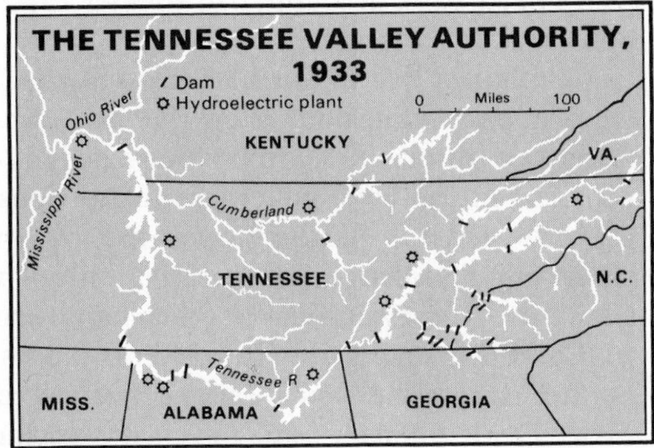

Objections to the plan came from owners of the power plants already in the area. They objected to competing with the government in producing and selling electric power. Also, there were those who objected to the idea of "social planning." Somehow it seemed communistic to them; according to Representative Joe Martin of Massachusetts, the TVA was "patterned closely after one of the Soviet dreams. I think I can accurately predict than no one in this generation will see materialize the industrial-empire dream of the Tennessee Valley."

Martin could not have been less accurate. Congress authorized the TVA and work began. Soon the valley began to develop as agricultural methods improved, industry moved in, education renewed itself, and new recreational areas emerged. Historian Arthur M. Schlesinger, Jr., has outlined the physical successes of the TVA experiment and then concluded that

> there was something less tangible yet even more penetrating: the release of moral and human energy as the people of the Valley saw new vistas open up for themselves and for their children. The jagged river, flowing uselessly past worn-out fields, overcut forests, ramshackle huts, its muddy waters reflecting the dull poverty of the life around—all this was giving way to a shimmering network of green meadows, blue lakes, and white dams.

The Tennessee river, which was once the destroyer, was becoming man's servant. There was new hope stirring in the land. The project was an apt symbol of the time. It represented man's capacity through the use of political and technical intelligence to change the conditions of life and transform defeat into victory.

 and the environment. They did *not* attempt any change in the political system as previous American reform movements had done. There was no important civil rights legislation and no use of taxation to cause a significant change in class structure. If attempting to stabilize the inherited system was revolutionary, then Roosevelt was a radical. But if failing to demand deep changes in politics, race relations, and class structure was conservative, then he was a conservative. In his own curious way, he was both.

THE END OF THE NEW DEAL

Roosevelt did everything possible to make the 1936 election a test of the voters' response to the New Deal. The result was the greatest victory in the history of American elections until then. Roosevelt surpassed even Harding's triumph of 1920, winning 61 percent of the popular vote. His Republican opponent, Alfred Landon of Kansas, carried only Maine and Vermont. A third-party candidate, Congressman William Lemke, polled less than 1 million votes. Lemke's Union party attracted the followers of three leading extreme opponents of the New Deal: Senator Huey Long of Louisiana, Dr. Francis Townsend, and Father Charles Coughlin.

Long's populistic "Share Our Wealth" program had urged, among other things, increased federal taxation of wealthy individuals and corporations. Some of Long's ideas on taxation were included in the 1935 Wealth Tax Act—though the act did practically nothing to redistribute wealth. Dr. Townsend's income-grant plan for the elderly, supported by millions of senior citizens organized into Townsend clubs, was undercut by passage of the 1935 Social Security Act. And Father Coughlin, a Catholic priest who drew an audience of millions with his radio programs, lost much of this following by attacking the New Deal in increasingly intemperate and anti-Semitic terms. By the election of 1936 none of these extremist elements threatened Roosevelt's hold on the American voter.

With his New Deal programs as tools, Roosevelt succeeded in forging from the depression a new political coalition of farmers and urban working people. The Democratic party, for the first time in a century, became the majority party in the nation, a position it still holds.

Despite this political success the economic and social problems of the depression had not been solved. In 1936 the gross national product (the total volume of all money transactions in any given year) had reached only the level of 1931. Unemployment remained high since many factories were still closed. There was measurable improvement in the lives of American farmers, but they were a distinct minority of the population. For everyone else, the depression remained a stubborn fact.

Offsetting this inability to achieve economic recovery was the New Deal's undeniable success in restoring political and social stability to American life. The relatively small vote for extremist candidates in 1936 reflected a general faith among most Americans that, whatever their failings, the two major parties would somehow guide the country through the economic crisis. The millions of poor citizens who worked on federal projects such as the WPA and the additional millions who received direct relief assistance now had more reason for hope than during the dark winter of 1932–33. Similarly, the large number of citizens whose houses had been saved by federally guaranteed mortgages and who now left their money safely in federally guaranteed bank accounts had greater cause for optimism than earlier.

Catholics, Jews, and blacks owed the New Deal a particular debt. For the first time in American history these groups were heavily represented in top-level government positions. Of the 214 federal judges appointed by the 3 preceding Presidents, for example, only 8 were Catholics. Roosevelt, on the other hand, named 51 Catholics among the 196 federal judges appointed during the New Deal era. The roll call of New Deal officials and advisors—including names such as Corcoran and Cohen, Frankfurter

Father Charles Coughlin, whose national radio broadcasts mixed calls for the nationalization of banks, utilities, and natural resources with a persistent antisemitism, drew his support from the right.

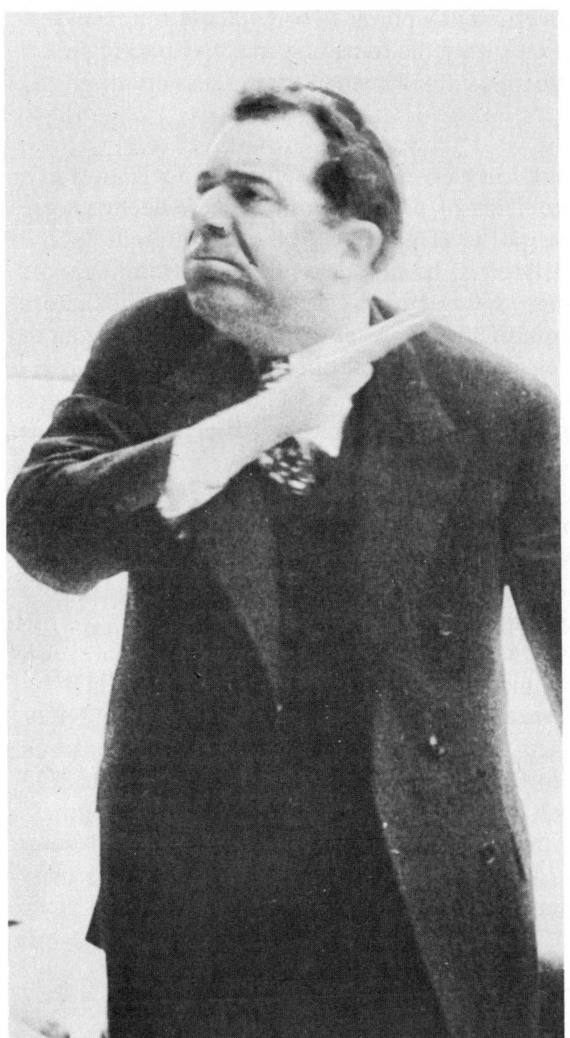

The most prominent of FDR's critics on the left was Huey Long. To secure the presidency by stirring up resentment over the maldistribution of wealth, he proposed heavy taxation of the rich and large handouts for the poor.

and Farley, Kennedy and Bunche—symbolized this change for ethnic Americans. To these men, and to lesser-known Americans from immigrant backgrounds, Roosevelt offered opportunities for public service and influence on a scale undreamed of during previous periods.

For all this, the New Deal never managed to achieve economic recovery from the depression itself. Even the limited recovery that was achieved before 1936 was soon wiped out. After the election, instead of pushing ahead Roosevelt announced that he would begin phasing out parts of the New Deal because the country was on the way back to prosperity. Partially as a result of this move, a depression within a depression began in 1937. The resulting new decline in business was even steeper that in 1929–30. Millions of people began to lose faith in the government's power to bring about full recovery. In fact, only the transition to a wartime economy after 1939 finally ended the depression for good.

Post-Election Reaction Adding to Roosevelt's problems of dealing with the new decline were the political problems he encountered. In the early days, he had depended on strong support from Democratic congressmen and senators from the South. After 1936 this support began to weaken. A new coalition in Congress of conservative Southerners and Northern Republicans made it almost impossible to enact significant new legislation, even if Roosevelt had wanted it. FDR's appeal to blacks in the South, plus his pro-labor policies, had turned many Southern white supporters against him. Roosevelt was soon deprived of his working majorities in both the House and the Senate.

A second difficulty that affected Roosevelt's popularity was the Supreme Court's rulings on several important New Deal laws. The NRA, parts of the AAA, and several other Roosevelt programs were declared unconstitutional in 1935 and 1936. The President believed that, unless something were done the Court would soon strike down other laws, like the Social Security Act or the Wagner Act.

Roosevelt grew increasingly restless. He publicly complained that the Court was behind the times. He grumbled that "nine old men" were defying the people's will as it had been expressed in the election victory of 1936. Then, in the first year of his second term, Roosevelt proposed a scheme to "pack" the Court. For every justice over seventy, he argued, the President should be empowered to appoint one additional justice to the Court. This, he said with obvious insincerity, would ease the heavy work load of the judiciary.

The battle that followed in Congress and in the press had two curious effects. First, it seems to have frightened some of the justices into a friendlier attitude toward New Deal legislation. Within weeks of the court-packing announcement, the Court ruled favorably on two such laws. One wit remarked that "a switch in time saved nine."

Second, and more important, public opinion shifted against Roosevelt. The public disliked his tampering with the Constitution and pressured Congress to reject the plan. Afterward, the administration proposed little new legislation on social and economic questions. The New Deal was over. Soon the attention of both the President and the people would turn more urgently to events in Europe and Asia.

1. Why did President Hoover refuse to support the Bonus bill for veterans? Why was the bill able to pass the House but not the Senate?
2. What did Harding mean when he urged a return to "normalcy"?
3. What did Coolidge mean by his famous statement, "The business of America is business"?
4. Would it be fair to call Al Smith a conservative Democrat? Why or why not?
5. What danger was there in having so many Americans buying stock and using credit at this time?
6. Why did the stock market crash help bring on the Great Depression?
7. Why did Hoover believe that the government should do nothing directly to bring the nation out of a depression? In what way did the government provide some indirect relief?
8. What steps did the New Deal take to provide direct relief to the needy?
9. How did the National Industrial Recovery Act and the Agricultural Adjustment Act attempt to protect the economy from unpredictable ups and downs? Why did the AAA prove to be more successful than the NIRA?
10. Why is the Wagner Act regarded as the most significant labor law in American history? Was the Social Security Act a radical governmental measure?
11. Why can it be said that the New Deal ended in 1937?

Beyond the Text

1. Using the Statistical Abstract of the United States, compare the economic status of the American farmer of the 1920s and 1930s with farmers today as to the (1) number engaged in farming, (2) percentage of the population this represents, (3) average income, and (4) relations with the government. On the basis of this information, are farmers better or worse off today?
2. "Hoover's limitations lay in the inadequacy of his philosophy; Roosevelt's strength lay in his lack of philosophy." Investigate the validity of this assertion. You may want to consult the essays on the two men in Hofstadter's *The American Political Tradition.*
3. Have a panel discussion to look into the reasons why the New Deal was unable to end the depression.
4. Prepare a report on Father Coughlin, Huey Long, and Dr. Francis Townshend. Focus on the kinds of programs they offered, the credibility of the programs, and the sources of their support.

Bibliography

Nonfiction

Galbraith, John K., *The Great Crash, 1929.**
Handlin, Oscar, *Al Smith and His America.**
Hicks, John D., *Republican Ascendancy, 1921–1933.**
Leuchtenburg, William E., *Franklin D. Roosevelt and the New Deal.**
MacArthur, Douglas, *Reminiscences.*
Mitchell, Broadus, *Depression Decade.*
Romasco, Albert U., *The Poverty of Abundance: Hoover, the Nation, the Depression.**
Schlesinger, Arthur M., Jr., *The Age of Roosevelt, 3 vols.**
Soule, George, *Prosperity Decade.**
White, William Allen, *A Puritan in Babylon.*
Williams, T. Harry, *Huey Long.**

Fiction

Steinbeck, John, *The Grapes of Wrath.**
Warren, Robert Penn, *All the King's Men.**
Wright, Richard, *Native Son.**

*a paperback book

CHAPTER

35

"Remember Pearl Harbor"

ON DECEMBER 7, 1941, while negotiations to avoid war between the United States and Japan were proceeding in Washington, 353 Japanese planes attacked Pearl Harbor. This massive, audacious, and extremely successful attack on the Americans' principal—and supposedly impregnable—naval base in Hawaii came before Japan had even declared war. Grim-faced and resolved, President Roosevelt went before Congress to call it "unprovoked and dastardly" and "a day which will live in infamy."

Until this assault Congress, like the country as a whole, had been sharply split between interventionists and isolationists. Now Congress and most Americans were furious at this shrewdly planned, superbly executed, and deadly raid. It dealt a staggering blow to American power in the Pacific. Congress swiftly and overwhelmingly voted to enter World War II. During the rest of the long, terrible conflict the single slogan that most readily aroused Americans to action was: "Remember Pearl Harbor!"

The attack on Pearl, referred to as Operation Z by the Japanese, had a history. A key figure in planning the attack was Admiral Isoruko Yamamoto, head of the Japanese Imperial Navy. If Japan's national

Battleship Row, Pearl Harbor, is seen here from a Japanese bomber during the surprise attack. The Japanese commander of the air strike said of the sight: "Below me lay the U.S. Pacific Fleet in a formation which I would never have dared to imagine. A fleet should always be on alert since surprise attacks can never be discounted."

Isoroku Yamamoto, commander-in-chief of the Japanese Imperial Fleet, was a strong advocate of the navy's use of air power. Responsible for planning naval operations, he was the mastermind of the audacious attack on Pearl Harbor.

interest called for war with the United States, the admiral reasoned, why not strike directly at the enemy fleet's Pacific home base? No mere "battleship admiral," the air-minded Yamamoto knew the possibilities of carrier-based warfare.

When the admiral took command in 1939, war plans still called for letting the American fleet plow west to meet the Japanese fleet near Iwo Jima or Saipan, fairly close to Japanese bases. Yamamoto extended the battle line far to the east shortly after reviewing some impressive results achieved by carrier-based planes in maneuvers. He also never forgot the example of his own personal hero, Admiral Heihachiro Togo, who in 1904 had battered the Russian fleet in Port Arthur in a surprise attack. Yamamoto had served under Togo and been wounded in the stunning Japanese victory over the Russian navy a year later.

Yamamoto was neither a visionary nor overly optimistic. He was quite dubious about defeating the United States in war. He knew the country, having studied at Harvard and worked at the Japanese embassy in Washington during the 1920s. He returned to Japan sobered by American industrial might. He harbored no illusions about conquering the United States. An invasion of the continental United States never figured seriously in Japanese war plans. "If I am told to fight regardless of the consequences," Yamamoto told the Japanese premier in 1940, " I shall run wild for the first six months, but I have utterly no confidence for the second or third years."

Others in the Japanese military shared Yamamoto's fears over the probable consequences of war with the United States. Then why venture such a dangerous policy, such a desperate gamble? By 1940 Japan was an authoritarian society ruled by a civilian-military government. Its leaders agreed that the country needed to gain most of its basic objectives. Most important was access to the raw materials vital for a modern industrial nation. Without them heavily populated Japan would become a third- or fourth-rate power. Without expansion the Japanese would be forced to tighten their belts even to stay alive.

So Japan decided to expand. In 1931 it took Manchuria from a helpless China. America and Western Europe objected strongly but ineffectively. In 1937 Japan launched a full-scale invasion of the rest of China. Despite Western protests the Japanese captured the coastal portions and overran much of the Chinese interior. By mid-1940 Japan's ally Hitler had conquered the French, the Dutch, and much of Europe, isolating Great Britain. Therefore, Tokyo figured it could now expand Japanese control into Southeast Asia. It planned to establish a massive sphere of influence, "the Greater East Asia Co-Prosperity Sphere."

The Japanese asked: Why should Britain reap the benefits of

Malaya's tin reserves? Why should the Dutch exploit and profit from the oil of the East Indies? Why should France have the rubber and other raw materials of Indochina? And why should America, thousands of miles from Asia, take such a high-and-mighty tone about China? "Asia for the Asians!" proclaimed the Japanese. They did not add that Japan would simply take over the role of the exploiter. If Tokyo could win this huge area without force, so much the better. But if not, it was prepared to wage war.

Thus, by early 1941, Admiral Yamamoto was contemplating his strategy. Success hinged on two factors: the attackers must achieve total surprise; and, the bulk of the American fleet, especially the capital ships (battleships and carriers), would have to be at their moorings the day of attack.

While Japanese and American diplomats in Washington continued their negotiations, naval aviators began months of intensive practice. When Yamamoto caught wind of grumbling and possible foot-dragging, he threatened to resign if the plan was scrapped. Objections ceased. Yamamoto became for the moment the symbol of the Japanese navy. Under no condition would his fellow officers accept his resignation. Operation Z (named for the signal flag that Admiral Togo hoisted before trouncing the Russians) became a reality. If diplomacy failed, only the date of the attack on America remained to be fixed.

Meanwhile, political developments ominously paralleled the course of these military preparations. After France had fallen to Germany, Japan grabbed the northern half of French Indochina. It held back from the southern half—as well as from British Malaya and the Dutch East Indies (present-day Indonesia)—after the United States warned that action in these areas would have grave consequences. Roosevelt banned shipments of aviation gasoline and scrap metal to Japan, and increased American support to China. The American ambassador to Japan, Joseph C. Grew, noted: "We are getting ready, steadily, for the ultimate showdown."

By summer 1941 matters were even more tense. Hitler invaded Russia; Japan could now pursue its Asian policy without fear of Stalin. Japan advanced, occupying southern Indochina in late July. The Americans, British, and Dutch responded by seizing all Japanese financial assets in their jurisdiction. They also ended Japan's access to their raw materials. The United States also gave an official warning that, if Japan took any further steps "by force or threat of force," the Americans would defend their "legitimate rights and interests."

In diplomacy's stilted language, these were strong words. The Japanese premier suggested that he and President Roosevelt hold a summit meeting, possibly in Hawaii. This could not be arranged. On October 16 a new premier, General Hideki Tojo, came to power. He was an all-out militarist.

Yet the national interests of both countries favored more negotiations. Further talks would hide Japanese war preparations—especially Operation Z, now in high gear. Washington would also benefit. It could use the extra time to reinforce its Pacific bases, particularly in the Philippines. In November 1941 Japan sent a veteran diplomat, Saburo Kurusu, to Washington to head a negotiating team. Diplomatic exchanges would obviously continue for at least a few more weeks.

At the same time, table-top maneuvers at the Japanese Naval War College demonstrated the most effective route for the Pearl attack force. The fleet would sail in a wide arc across the nearly deserted waters of the North Central Pacific. Then it would turn sharply south on reaching a point 500 miles north of Hawaii. Yamamoto thought that this route would give the best chance for surprise.

On November 5, while the Japanese and Americans negotiated in Washington, Yamamoto issued a secret order outlining the first phase of the Japanese offensive against Hawaii. The twenty-three attack ships included six carriers and two battleships under Admiral Chuichi Nagumo. He disliked the plan and still hoped the madcap attack would somehow be canceled.

The Japanese strike force sailed on November 26. The attack date had been set for December 7 (Sunday morning) in Hawaii. The American navy—even though on military alert because of the dangerous diplomatic situation—had weekends off. So its ships usually anchored in the harbor on Friday and stayed there until Monday. Nagumo's orders did contain one escape clause. If the Washington negotiations succeeded, the attack was off. The fleet would then wait in the North Pacific for new orders.

Yet any chance that diplomacy could ease the crisis was now vanishing. On November 20 the negotiator Kurusu made Tokyo's final offer: Japan would leave southern Indochina but remain in the northern part, as well as in China. The United States must not only lift its ban on oil but also cut off aid to China. Secretary of State Cordell Hull immediately rejected these terms. Fearful of being called appeasers, Roosevelt and Hull would make no concessions. The American note of November 26—the very day the strike force set sail—stated that America's embargo would continue until Japan abandoned both Indochina and China.

If Admiral Kimmel had initiated air reconnaissance of the seas around Pearl Harbor, Operation Z might have been discovered and foiled. But neither he nor anyone else in authority expected Japanese hostilities to begin there.

Roosevelt and Hull, along with their top civilian and military colleagues, had good reason to distrust the sincerity of Japanese negotiations. Operation Magic of American naval intelligence had cracked Japan's diplomatic codes. On November 22—two days after Kurusu's final offer and four days before the formal American reply to it—a cable intercepted from Tokyo read: "THIS TIME WE MEAN IT, THAT THE DEADLINE [November 29] CANNOT BE CHANGED! AFTER THAT THINGS ARE AUTOMATICALLY GOING TO HAPPEN."

What things? Most likely, reasoned the leaders in Washington, the Japanese planned to attack the Philippines and British and Dutch holdings in Asia. But Hawaii seemed beyond the range of effective Japanese assault. So American short-sightedness was beginning to aid the future success of Operation Z. Knowledge of Magic was restricted to Washington's inner circle. This kept Tokyo from realizing its code had been broken. Thus American brass in Hawaii had no notion of Magic.

Hawaiian military commanders received some warning on November 27 to expect a hostile move by Japan. But Washington took no action during the next ten days. Only four Magic decoding machines existed then: two in Washington, one in the Philippines, and another in London. There were none in Hawaii. The commanders there, Admiral Husband E. Kimmel and General Walter C. Short, were not even told about Magic.

Admiral Kimmel had seriously considered, but then rejected, the idea of taking his fleet out of Pearl Harbor. In open water, he felt, the ships would be too vulnerable. His four carriers were not then available to provide air cover. (Three were bringing warplanes to American-held Pacific islands; the fourth was in San Diego for repairs.) Besides, moored safely in Pearl, his ships could be protected by the several hundred army planes stationed at Hawaiian bases. Still, Kimmel might well have sent most of the battleships out with the carriers to the other Pacific islands.

General Short reacted to the war warning by increasing the army's antisabotage defenses. Sabotage, he apparently thought, might come from Hawaii's large Japanese-American community. Instead of widely spacing his aircraft or protecting them in concrete shelters already constructed on the major fields, Short ordered the planes bunched together, wing tip to wing tip. True, fewer soldiers could then protect them against saboteurs. But Japanese Americans in Hawaii never aided Japan, although some Japanese diplomats were spies.

Premier Tojo is shown in a respectful posture before Emperor Hirohito at a ceremony celebrating the Japanese Empire's 2,600th anniversary. Tojo's rise to power helped determine Japan's course toward war. Hirohito's role was largely symbolic, but he supported Tojo's militarism and anti-Americanism.

In short, Magic had been botched. Hawaiian commanders never received copies of important decoded messages. These messages piled up at the few overworked decoding centers. As far back as September, and with increasing frequency thereafter, Tokyo asked the Japanese consulate in Honolulu for details on the location of American warships in the harbor. By November such naval maps were being transmitted to Tokyo twice a week. Some of these Magic intercepts were not deciphered and translated for many days after reception. Especially revealing Japanese messages of November 29, for example, waited until December 5 to be deciphered. Even then, they received little attention.

Even key Washington officials, including Roosevelt and Hull, apparently did not take the Magic decodings very seriously.[1] For in Tokyo the die had been cast. Hull's note of November 26 refusing to lift the American embargo infuriated Premier Tojo. He thought it proved beyond all doubt American insincerity in the negotiations. Tojo persuaded Emperor Hirohito to let Operation Z proceed. A palace meeting ratified the decision for war. Hirohito did not attempt to intervene. He believed, as he later told an aide, that the United States was looking for nothing less than Japan's humiliation.

[1] On November 25 Roosevelt told Secretary of War Henry L. Stimson of his fears that Japan would strike on December 1 without declaring war, "for the Japanese are notorious for making an attack without warning." Stimson wanted to bomb Japanese convoys if they moved farther south. Roosevelt rejected the notion because "we are a democracy."

One point remained unsettled. Japan had signed the Hague Convention. It required a formal declaration of war before a nation could start hostilities. But could this "paper" commitment override the need for surprise in attacking Hawaii? Absolutely not, insisted Yamamoto. Any kind of advance warning would endanger the Japanese fleet. Yet several ministers, including Tojo, argued initially for avoiding the dishonor of a sneak attack by some advance warning.

But the argument was useless: the nature of Operation Z made all such talk pointless. In the end Tokyo instructed Kurusu to present the final note—not a declaration of war—at 1 P.M. on Sunday, December 7. The first wave of Japanese planes would start bombing at the same time. Should Kurusu continue negotiating or at least pretend to? Of course he should, Tojo decided; it would facilitate operations. In Washington Kurusu asked a Japanese newspaperman rhetorically, "Am I being used as a smoke screen?" Indeed he was.

Kurusu had to help screen the task force then steaming across the North Pacific. After leaving on November 26, the fleet enjoyed seven days of uneventful sailing. The weather cooperated. Light winds made refueling at sea relatively easy. Cloudiness and generally poor visibility decreased chances of detection. Security precautions were rigidly enforced. No radio contact was made except within the fleet. At night a blackout was enforced. Most ships communicated by signal flags and blinkers. They did not even discard garbage, to avoid leaving a trail.

The fleet's passage north of the American base at Midway provided cause for some real concern. No American planes or ships spotted them, however. On December 6 there was the final fueling. Japanese intelligence from Hawaii reported the presence of many American warships but no carriers or heavy cruisers. It was decided that the force would strike and destroy whatever was at hand.

A little past noon on December 6 all hands were summoned on deck. Their officers read them the emperor's war message. Yamamoto had also sent a statement: "The moment has arrived. The rise or fall of our empire is at stake." Then Admiral Togo's flag, the signal flag that gave its name to Operation Z, went up above the attack fleet's flagship. The crews shouted *"Banzai!"*—their battle cry— and turned the ships south toward Hawaii. All was ready for the great moment.

The launch itself was almost perfect. Pilots and flight crewmen were aroused at 3:30 A.M. The news that the Americans apparently had not adequately protected their ships encouraged the Japanese airmen. At zero hour (6 A.M.) the carriers were 200 miles from Oahu. As the ships rolled and pitched, the lead pilots waited eagerly for the order to take off. When it came, the first wave of 183 planes left the 6 carriers in 15 minutes, bettering their fastest practice runs. With Commander Mitsuo Fuchida in command, flying one of the high-level bombers, the air fleet headed for its target.

Fuchida led the attack planes in. He listened meanwhile to Honolulu radio which obligingly gave a fine weather report for the assault. The forecast was for cloudiness over the mountains. This cloud cover would hide the planes until just before they attacked.

The first wave passed over the northern coast of Oahu at 7:40 A.M. It was almost exactly the time Kurusu was scheduled to give Secretary Hull the note breaking off negotiations. The sight of all their unsuspecting targets delighted and amazed the Japanese pilots. Fuchida later recalled his own surprise at seeing ships of the American fleet anchored less than a thousand yards apart from one another. They would be an easy target for a surprise attack.

Overconfidence and negligence had made Americans complacent. Many viewed the Japanese as a society adept in imitating Western ways but with little creativity. Informed Americans knew that the Japanese had a history of attacking first and declaring war later. But most thought they would not dare attack the United States. In 1932 the American navy itself had successfully "attacked" the harbor during a mock raid. The event was quickly forgotten. The Navy Department filed the report in its archives as just another war-games exploit.

There were certainly some warnings during 1941. In January a Peruvian diplomat in Tokyo reported that a drunken Japanese official had boasted about Japan's plan to sink the American fleet and knock out Pearl Harbor. Ambassador Grew passed the "fantastic" rumor along to Washington. A few months later Grew noted that Japan was "capable of sudden and surprise action" with "a determination to risk all."

The shortcomings of American defensive reactions were considerable, in view of what was known about Japanese intentions and how much could have been learned if the data from Magic had been properly exploited. One man who worried a great deal was Admiral Kimmel. After November 27—the day Kimmel received the war warning from Washington—naval intelligence lost track of the Japanese fleet. Kimmel asked the head of his intelligence section at Pearl where the fleet was. The officer admitted he did not know. Not entirely in jest, Kimmel asked: "You mean to say that it could appear rounding

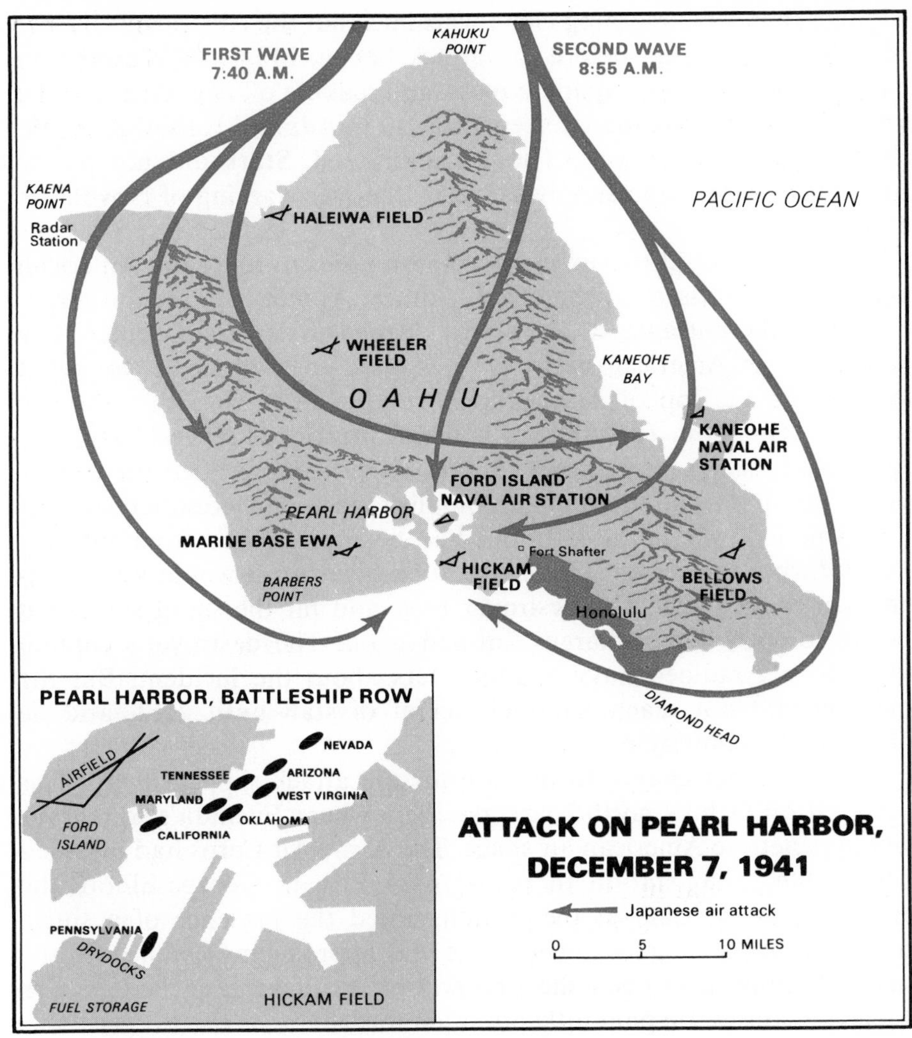

Diamond Head [a famous high point close to Pearl Harbor] without our knowing it?" The intelligence officer answered: "I hope that it would be spotted before that."

Yamamoto had no intention of parading his ships past Diamond Head, impressive though the sight would have been. Instead, his planes crossed over Oahu's northern coast. At 7:49 A.M. Fuchida broke radio silence to signal Nagumo (and Yamamoto also, since Japan picked up the message). Attack by the first wave had begun, blessed with the key element of surprise. Fuchida's first signal was "*To-To-To,*" repeating the opening syllable of the Japanese word for "charge." Soon he sent an even more welcome message: "*Tora* [Tiger], *Tora, Tora,*" which meant that the Americans were almost completely unprepared.

A special Japanese invention, the midget submarine operated by a crew of two, was used in the advance attack upon American battleships. The submarines failed in their mission that day and were not widely used in the war.

Yet that same morning came warnings that the Americans did not heed. Five full hours before the attack began, Magic in Washington had decoded the final Japanese message breaking off negotiations. The officer in charge took the intercept straight to Admiral Harold R. Stark, chief of naval operations. Though impressed, Stark did not phone Admiral Kimmel, who simply stood by the war warning of November 27.

In Hawaii itself two excellent opportunities to rouse the American garrison were missed just before the attack. At 6:30 A.M. the antitorpedo net at the entrance to Pearl was opened to let a ship enter. The captain of an American destroyer was watching. When he saw what looked like the top of a submarine coming in behind the ship, he sounded the alarm. The unidentified craft was one of several "midget" Japanese subs. (A large Japanese submarine fleet preceded the Operation Z task force, but it did not accomplish much on December 7.)

American submarine captains had been prohibited from entering Pearl Harbor underwater. Thus any submerged craft would be considered an enemy ship. The destroyer fired and hit the small sub. As it began to sink, depth charges finished it off. The destroyer's captain immediately radioed navy headquarters about the incident. But the message did not reach Kimmel's chief of staff until 7:12, and he discounted its importance.

Yet another chance to prepare for the attack slipped away. This occurred on Oahu's north coast, precisely where Fuchida's squadrons would penetrate American air space. The Army Air Corps had installed a movable radar station there. At 6:45 Private George Elliott, the enlisted man on duty at the station, noted the presence of a single plane on the radar screen. The plane was approaching Oahu from the north. It may have been the observation seaplane launched from a Japanese cruiser. He paid little attention to it.

But at 7:06 Elliott noted much larger blips on the screen, again moving toward Oahu from the north, and rapidly growing larger. He asked the advice of another soldier. They decided to call signal headquarters at Fort Shafter. But the only officer on duty there, a pilot, told them to forget about it. He knew that a dozen American planes were scheduled to arrive from California that morning. A group of B-17s—called Flying Fortresses—was indeed in the air, very close to Hawaii. Again the Japanese had benefited from a stroke of luck. Fuchida's first wave was confused with reinforcements from the States.

After sending the signal "*Tora, Tora, Tora,*" Fuchida fired a blue flare from his bomber. It informed pilots in planes without radios that surprise had been achieved. It would produce a prearranged pattern of attack, with the slow-flying but deadly torpedo bombers going in first.

But apparently one group of pilots, their vision obscured by the cloud cover, had not seen the luminous signal. At least they did not wiggle their planes' wings in response. Fuchida then committed one of the few Japanese mistakes of the day. He fired a second flare.

This changed the flight plan. Two flares meant that dive bombers would attack first. Fighters and some dive bombers were to concentrate on American airfields and antiaircraft installations rather than on the fleet. Happily for the Japanese, the commander of the torpedo bomber wing ignored the second flare. His forty heavy but superbly piloted aircraft peeled off and glided down to the prescribed low altitudes, heading straight for their principal targets, the battleships.

Meanwhile, in answer to the second signal, the faster planes went hunting for American aircraft at Wheeler, Hickam, Haleiwa, Bellows, and other fields. Wheeler housed most of the American fighter planes. These planes, already tested in combat, could hold their own against the more maneuverable Japanese fighters. But, owing to General Short's fear of ground sabotage, Wheeler's planes had been crowded together like sheep in a pen. The attackers quickly destroyed a third of the planes and damaged many more. Fires broke out in the hangars and storage buildings. One of them contained ammunition that exploded, causing additional losses.

American military aviation tried to respond but it was useless. At Wheeler, for instance, most of the pilots were still sleeping. But Lieutenants George Welch and Ken Taylor, who were breakfasting at the officers' club, saw the dive bombers swoop. They rushed for a car and speeded at a hundred miles an hour to an auxiliary airstrip unknown to the Japanese. There they took off, headed for a Japanese squadron, and shot down three planes before landing to refuel. During the dogfight

The devastation on the ground after the attack was extensive. By 10 A.M. Hickam Naval Air Station was in chaos and a smoking ruin.

one of the three machine guns in Welch's plane jammed. Taylor was wounded twice.

At Kaneohe Naval Air Station the commanding officer was drinking his morning coffee. When he heard planes, he glanced up. To his anger several V formations of planes—all flying lower than regulations allowed—were turning toward the right into the bay where most of his thirty-three new flying boats were at anchor. He leapt to his feet shouting, "Those fools know there is a strict rule against making a right turn!" His young son who was with him answered, "Look, red circles on the wings!" Realizing it was the Japanese rising-sun symbol, the commander rushed to his headquarters and set up a fierce antiaircraft fire against the invaders.

At the moment of attack only a fourth of the antiaircraft guns on the ships moored in the harbor were manned. Land-based antiaircraft guns could not respond immediately because ammunition had been stored to prevent deterioration. Their effectiveness increased as the morning wore on, however. Unluckily, the B-17s arrived from California about then. Weary after fourteen hours in the air, the American bomber pilots and crews thought they had flown into a nightmare. Columns of smoke rose from the ground. Airfields were ablaze, including the one the B-17s were supposed to use on Ford Island. Incredibly, not one Flying Fortress was shot out of the air. All landed at various fields, though some were shot at and destroyed after landing.

Ironically, Admiral Kimmel and General Short had scheduled a golf match with each other that morning. Kimmel rose early. At about 7:30 he received a phone call from a staff officer. The destroyer *Ward* had sighted a submerged submarine and dropped depth charges. Kimmel headed for his office. Just as he was leaving, he received another call adding some details about the *Ward* incident. Suddenly, the officer at the other end shouted that Japanese planes were attacking. Kimmel ran out to his garden, which overlooked the harbor. What he saw astonished him. The carnage was under way. The sky over the bay seemed alive with attack planes. Kimmel knew that his ships were doomed.

Kimmel got to his headquarters at 8:10, during the height of the first-wave attack. There was nothing he could do but stand at the window and watch his fleet and men under attack. A spent Japanese bullet crashed through the window and bounced off Kimmel's chest. He felt that "it would have been merciful had it killed me."

Fuchida's pilots were not concerned with Kimmel. They wanted to destroy the American fleet. Disappointed over not finding carriers in port, they concentrated on the battleships. Seven of the eight were lined up on Battleship Row in the harbor. Five were moored to the docks, and two were on an "outside" parallel column. Thus two of the inside battleships could not be attacked by torpedoes. The dive bombers went after them. Soon every battleship had been hit.

On the *Nevada,* at one end of the row, Bandmaster Oden McMillan stood with his musicians, ready to play morning colors at 8 A.M. As they began "The Star-Spangled Banner," a Japanese plane dropped its deadly burden on the nearby *Arizona,* then peeled off just feet above the band. The *Nevada's* deck officer, Ensign Joe Taussig, shouted over the public-address system: "All hands, general quarters. Air raid!" The *Nevada,* though damaged, tried to steam out to sea. The Japanese bore in, hoping to sink her at Pearl Harbor's mouth and thus close the port indefinitely. The *Nevada* took six bomb hits but made it to the other side of the bay, keeping the channel clear.

The *Oklahoma* took four torpedoes within one minute and began to capsize. The *California* sustained hits that caused her to settle slowly and finally sink. And so on down the row: *Tennessee, West Virginia, Maryland, Pennsylvania.* Fuchida, who was supervising the attack in his bomber overhead, frowned in slight puzzlement as his pilots raced in. They were bunched up in their assault, instead of diving in stages as first arranged. But their formation no longer really mattered—every enemy ship was a sitting duck.

The worst blow for the Americans came when the *Arizona* blew apart and sank, trapping more than a thousand men inside. Later, it was claimed that a bomb had gone straight down her stack. But the probable cause of the disaster was the detonation of the ship's ammunition store. Whatever the cause, a gigantic pillar of fire and smoke rose 500 feet. The shock was so tremendous that, far above, Fuchida could feel his bomber tremble. Miraculously, many survived this searing blast. Some of these survivors tried to swim to shore and safety, but burning oil engulfed most of them.

The second wave, 170 additional planes, came in at 8:55. Fuchida and his pilots had taken more time than planned because of additional bomb runs. The fresh attackers went to work shortly after the first wave pulled out. They encountered considerably more opposition from heavy antiaircraft fire and lost twenty-one planes. Towering columns of smoke cut visibility. Still, the second wave of bombers did considerable damage in its one-hour attack, knocking out some ships not previously hit. They withdrew at 9:45 to return to their carriers.

On Battleship Row the rescue effort began at once. Most of the giant ships were ablaze. One had overturned, while another had settled

The Japanese victory would have been more complete and would have had more serious consequences for the United States if American aircraft carriers had been in port. As it was, the Japanese had to be satisfied with destroying American battleships.

straight down into the mud. In the plotting room of the heavily damaged *West Virginia* Ensign Victor Delano watched smoke and oily water seep in. He and several others headed forward to another compartment. Just before closing a watertight door, they heard frantic calls from six seamen, blown from the deck above them by the explosions, but had to go on. Delano then returned to the plotting room, risking his life to help a wounded sailor. Neither he nor his companions could get their footing on the oil-slick deck. The ship's angle compounded the problem.

Luckily, one compartment wall was a switchboard. By grabbing its knobs, they were at last able to reach the door. As the men moved forward, they could hear the shouts and pleas of others, sealed off by the watertight doors in flooding compartments. The damage-control officer had ordered the doors closed. He knew that this order condemned many men to death. But opening the doors would merely cause the ship to sink quickly and doubtless drown even more men. Many, however, did make their way to the upper decks or swam to the surface by escaping through portholes. The harbor was filled with boats and launches busily rescuing survivors.

The overturned *Oklahoma* posed special problems. Dozens of men, perhaps hundreds, were still alive in a crazy house where floors had become ceilings. Partial flooding meant that air pockets existed in most compartments. There, survivors could exist for awhile, if they treaded water or grasped whatever protruded from walls. About thirty men trapped in the dispensary waited an hour. Noting with alarm the decreasing amount of oxygen in the air, they decided to move. But where?

Diving into the water that covered most of the dispensary, they found a porthole. Though no one knew where it led, staying in the dispensary meant sure death. Those who were thin enough to squeeze through the porthole swam clear of the ship and were rescued. Others tried but could not squeeze through the porthole. They died in the dispensary.

Another group of sailors trapped near the *Oklahoma's* center seemed doomed beyond any hope. Amazingly, one of them dove downward through a funnel. He emerged directly under the capsized ship, reached topside, then swam clear of the wreckage and reached the surface. He led rescuers to his mates.

The rescue crews relied on this kind of information. Without it, they had no way of locating the living. Rescuers banged on ship hulls, and survivors lost no time in signaling back. Yet the sounds seemed to come from everywhere and nowhere. Several times crews laboriously cut holes in hulls, then found nobody.

When they did, they had sometimes unwittingly added to the tragedy. Acetylene torches consumed the oxygen in the air pockets once the hull had been punctured. Slower working pneumatic drills allowed the precious air to escape as the water rose in the compartments. Despite these dangers inaction would surely spell doom for the trapped. So people worked through the night. They had surprisingly good results in the number of men saved.

Japanese airmen fashioned a striking yet limited victory at Pearl Harbor. The casualty figures were all in their favor.[2] But, in the long run, Operation Z failed to cripple American power. First, no American carrier was in port; the war that followed conclusively showed that

[2] All 8 battleships in Pearl on December 7 were either sunk, capsized, or were badly damaged. Ten other ships, including 3 cruisers and 3 destroyers, were also casualties. In military aviation 188 American planes were destroyed, and nearly all the others were damaged. About 100 civilians and 2,403 men in uniform died. Japan lost only 29 planes, 5 two-man submarines, and a total of 54 lives.

carriers were more vital than battleships. Second, American plane losses would soon be dwarfed by the huge air armadas that were already beginning to roll out of American factories. Third, the naval base itself had not suffered severe damage. Fourth, and probably most significant of all, the Japanese—concentrating on ships and planes—ignored the oil storage tanks. If Hawaii's fuel supply had been destroyed (as it easily could have been), Japan might have: (1) driven the carriers and other ships still functioning back to California for oil; (2) made Pearl useless as a base for several months and perhaps a year; and (3) thus given Japan freedom to expand in the Pacific without worrying about counterattacks. Instead, Pearl began to function right after December 7 as the staging area for a massive American build-up of military power.

By bombing the harbor, Japan gained some time—but little more. Even some of the sunken battleships came back to haunt their attackers. All but two were put back in service. But these consequences lay in the future. December 7 was Japan's day. The assault on Hawaii was only part of a mighty Japanese drive. Simultaneous attacks took place on the Philippines and on British and Dutch colonies.

Some diplomatic strings remained to be tied. The final Japanese note to Secretary Hull was supposed to be delivered at 1 P.M. But delay in decoding and typing the long document kept the Japanese diplomats from arriving at Hull's office until 2 P.M. In the meantime, Hull had read the Magic intercept of the note. Roosevelt got the news of the attack at 1:47 from Secretary of the Navy Knox.

Roosevelt called Hull at 2:05. The Japanese diplomats had just arrived and were in the waiting room. Roosevelt instructed Hull to receive them but say nothing about the attack. The Japanese ambassador, by way of apology, said he had been told by his government to hand over the note at 1 P.M. Hull pretended to read it (he knew its contents already) and handed it back saying it was "crowded with infamous falsehoods and distortions." With a disgusted shrug Hull dismissed the envoys.

In Tokyo Ambassador Grew still hoped to achieve something positive. The day before the attack, Roosevelt had sent a personal appeal for peace to Emperor Hirohito. Grew asked for an audience with the emperor. At 7 A.M. Grew was awakened and told that the foreign minister wished to see him. Hoping to see Hirohito, Grew rushed to the ministry, only to be handed the note breaking off negotiations. Two hours later he heard that Japan had declared war on the United States and its European allies.

Japan greeted the news of war and the victory at Pearl Harbor jubilantly. Newspaper extras appeared on the streets, and the radio

Secretary of State Cordell Hull and Japanese negotiators met several times to prevent a direct confrontation. But both sides took hard-line stands, so that the course of events was determined weeks before the final meeting at 2:00 P.M. on December 7.

alternated between martial music and patriotic slogans. At the end of December the fleet returned to Japan, and the government and people welcomed the heroes of Operation Z with celebrations and medals. Hirohito granted an audience to Nagumo, Fuchida, and several other task force leaders. The rising sun reached its zenith. But as usual the clearheaded Yamamoto warned that "this war will give us many headaches in the future."

Roosevelt and most Americans never doubted this. On December 8, when the President asked Congress to declare war on Japan, he assured his listeners that, whatever the cost, Japan would be vanquished. He was right.

CHAPTER

36

The United States as a Superpower

AFTER PEARL HARBOR anything seemed possible for the Japanese. Their plan for domination of Asia (the Greater East Asia Co-Prosperity Sphere) became a reality, at least temporarily. Japan had signed a mutual security treaty with Nazi Germany, and Hitler hastily declared war on the United States just after Pearl Harbor.

Only twenty-three years had elapsed since the end of World War I. Now another generation of American youth would have to fight overseas. Ironically, America's entry into the war came after a decade of intense isolationist feeling.

In the late 1920s and the 1930s isolationism gathered strength in America while dictatorships flourished overseas. In Japan the emperor continued to reign, but the role of the military greatly increased. In Europe new regimes emerged. A fascist dictator, Benito Mussolini, seized power in Italy in 1922. In Germany Nazi party chief Adolf Hitler became chancellor in 1933. When he started to rearm Germany, the peace settlement of 1919 began to collapse in Europe.

Most Americans heartily disliked the new

fascist regimes, which denied liberty and worshipped dictators. Worse still was the deadly anti-Semitism of the Nazis. But Americans also disliked the idea of war with the dictatorships (including Soviet Russia, where Joseph Stalin had made himself a communist dictator).

A profound disillusionment with World War I had spread throughout the United States. It no longer seemed a clean-cut crusade to "make the world safe for democracy." Instead, some regarded it as a capitalist war that the United States supposedly fought to protect loans made to European Allies by American bankers. This in turn had benefited the arms manufacturers, the "merchants of death." Republican Senator Gerald P. Nye of North Dakota developed these themes in sensational congressional hearings during the early 1930s. Nye's claims helped pressure Americans into favoring isolationism as a foreign policy.

Charles A. Lindbergh and Senator Gerald P. Nye stirred popular sentiment for isolationism. Nye's munitions industry investigations uncovered less noble reasons for this country's entrance into World War I, which led Lindbergh to campaign for nonintervention in future world power struggles.

THE NEUTRALITY ACTS

President Roosevelt quickly recognized the fascist threat to American interests and security. But he could do little. In domestic matters Congress followed his lead. In foreign affairs, however, things were different. Congress concentrated specifically on the causes of American involvement in World War I. Billions of dollars in war loans remained unpaid. So in 1934 Congress banned further loans to countries that had not paid their debts. Then the Neutrality Act of 1935 limited Roosevelt's ability to respond effectively to overseas aggression, even if American interests were endangered.

This law attempted to close the gap between a President's control of foreign relations and Congress' right to declare war. Henceforth, if war broke out anywhere, the President had to issue a proclamation of neutrality. More important, the law forbade shipping arms to any nation at war, whether victim or aggressor. Roosevelt sought power to ban or "embargo" shipments to unfriendly or aggressor nations while permitting arms to go to the victims of aggression. Congress refused this request. It also rejected Wilson's internationalism by ordering Roosevelt to warn Americans that in wartime they traveled on belligerent ships at their own risk. Congress wished no repetition of the "mistakes" of 1917.

Yet isolationist hopes proved no match for events in the later 1930s. Italy invaded Ethiopia in October 1935. Roosevelt invoked the Neutrality Act, this time willingly, since an arms embargo would hinder Italy more than Ethiopia. He also asked American oil producers for a "moral embargo" on shipments to Italy, limiting amounts to prewar levels. Ethiopia fell to the Italian invaders. Italy then quit the League, following the example of Japan and Germany. The foundations for the Axis alliance had been laid.

Further Triumphs for the Dictators The menace to the Western democracies increased in 1936. Hitler armed the Rhineland, which had been demilitarized after World War I. General

 Francisco Franco, leader of Spain's fascists, led a revolt—which was ultimately successful—against the Spanish government. France and Britain declared a noninterventionist policy toward Spain. This clearly favored the fascists, for Italy and Germany had intervened by sending planes and some troops to help Franco. Congress reacted by passing a second Neutrality Act, tightening the isolationist provisions of the first law.

So the first series of fascist moves, instead of weakening isolationism, strengthened it. Believing the Atlantic and Pacific oceans gave the United States ample security, isolationists argued that America should be a fortress prepared for any outside attack. But the United States should not meddle in foreign politics or wars.

Isolationists were not pacifists. They favored American rearmament, particularly a larger, two-ocean navy. As for Britain and France, most isolationists wished both countries well. Still, they did not think that the United States should or could guarantee the security of other Western powers. Europeans would have to fight their own wars.

Rise of the Interventionists In October 1937 Roosevelt sent up an anti-isolationist trial balloon, only to see it shot down quickly. In his "Quarantine Speech" he noted that an "epidemic of world lawlessness is spreading." Thus it was foolish to assume "that America will escape, that America may expect mercy, that this Western Hemisphere will not be attacked." To counter the threat, Roosevelt called for a quarantine of aggressor nations. Though some Americans agreed, the massive and negative outcry afterward caused Roosevelt to abandon his proposal.

A small but growing number of interventionists insisted, however, that the fascist Axis powers—if left unchecked—would eventually attack America. They saw Hitler as a madman whose ravings against "decadent" Western civilization showed what policies he would pursue. Isolationism was unworkable because not even wide oceans or great industrial power could make the United States secure if it stood alone.

Thus whatever aid America gave fascism's opponents would help the nation itself. Like the isolationists, interventionists saw a world moving toward war. But they also foresaw United States involvement—sooner or later. Better sooner, they thought, while Americans still had some overseas friends.

Events in 1938 and 1939 emphasized the failure of appeasement—the policy of buying off dictators with compromises. Compromises only brought new demands. France and Britain sold out part of Czechoslovakia to Germany at Munich in September 1938. Not satisfied yet, Hitler merely kept on expanding. He absorbed Austria as part of the German Third Reich. In March 1939 he occupied all of Czechoslovakia. Then he threatened Poland.

Roosevelt had approved of appeasement at Munich, but by 1939 he realized his mistake. He began a long campaign to repeal, or at least soften, the neutrality laws. He spoke of "many methods short of war" that might discourage aggression. But Congress would have to allow some presidential flexibility. Congress did not budge. No one can say to what extent American inertia and isolationism helped Hitler decide on war. Nevertheless, the American attitude surely encouraged him. On September 1, 1939, Germany invaded Poland. Britain and France declared war on Germany two days later, and World War II was underway.

GLOBAL CONFLICT

The start of World War II put American views on neutrality to a real test. Hitler quickly conquered Poland and divided it with Russia. Roosevelt was legally bound to issue a proclamation of neutrality. He was far from neutral, however. Nor did he try to hide his pro-Allied sentiments.

Defeat of the Axis was basic in Roosevelt's mind. If American isolation meant defeat for Britain and France, American security would be disastrously, perhaps fatally, damaged. Thus, Roosevelt would go to war before letting the other Western democracies perish.

Since 1900 American foreign policy had

increasingly involved British-American cooperation. Roosevelt developed a close friendship with Winston Churchill, Britain's prime minister.[1] Still, neither sentiment nor deep concern for the fate of democracy elsewhere in the world provided Roosevelt's chief motivation. He saw the savagery of dictators, especially Hitler. He concluded that, once Europe and Asia had been overrun by these "New Barbarians," America's turn would come.

Although Roosevelt accepted the risk of war, Congress would probably never have declared war prior to Pearl Harbor. Thus, Roosevelt's carefully worded pro-Allied efforts had to be made bit by bit. First, he asked Congress to repeal the arms embargo so that the United States might sell war goods to other Western powers. This passed with surprising ease. Now Britain and France might buy American arms but only on a "cash-and-carry" basis. Many Americans still hoped Hitler would be defeated without the necessity of making war loans to the Allies or placing American ships in Atlantic war zones.

These unreal hopes evaporated in the spring of 1940. Hitler launched a series of spectacular and successful campaigns that conquered much of Continental Europe. By May five countries had been overrun—Denmark, Norway, Luxembourg, the Netherlands, and Belgium. In June the "impossible" happened: France collapsed before the Nazi onslaught and agreed to German occupation of half its territory, including Paris. This left Britain the only effective Axis opponent.

Steps Toward Intervention These events profoundly disturbed Americans and shifted the isolationist-interventionist balance. Americans were shocked by the well-publicized sight of Hitler inspecting his new toy—the city of Paris—and dancing a little victory jig. What would come next? Americans might accept Allied defeats in limited wars, but this war seemed to have no limit.

[1] The Roosevelt-Churchill correspondence consisted chiefly of long, candid cables between the two men. Roosevelt ended one such message: "It is fun to be in the same decade as you."

Interventionists, who wanted massive aid for the battered Allies, grew bolder and better organized. Heroic British resistance to a German air assault on their homeland armed these interventionists with plenty of effective propaganda. The Committee to Defend America First, however, fought against any American involvement in the war. The America Firsters, like Charles Lindbergh, hero of the 1920s, argued that the war was simply none of our business. Many felt that a seemingly invincible Germany should not be stirred up unnecessarily.

Roosevelt moved shrewdly (1) to rearm America and (2) to aid Britain to the extent

This photo of Hitler, now known to have been doctored to make a little leap into a grotesque victory "jig," proved effective in turning American sentiment toward war.

legally permissible and politically possible. Since 1940 was also a presidential election year, he had to be cautious. Meanwhile, Roosevelt broke the traditional ban on third-term Presidents by running again. Significantly, Republican isolationists could not nominate their man, Senator Robert A. Taft of Ohio. An internationalist named Wendell Willkie, a utilities executive with little political experience, won the nomination.

In the midst of the campaign Roosevelt made a daringly unneutral move. He transferred fifty World War I destroyers to the British navy. In exchange the United States received a dozen British air and naval bases in the Western Hemisphere. Churchill said of this: "It marked the passage of the United States from being neutral to being nonbelligerent [but involved]." Roosevelt won the election by a narrower margin than in 1936. Republican gains meant that Roosevelt had to take the views of the opposition party into greater account in facing the world crisis.

Every President who wins reelection usually regards it as a mandate for his policies. Now Roosevelt went even further than the destroyers-for-bases swap. He asked Congress for a Lend-Lease program. Under this law, passed in March 1941, the President could "lend" war material to countries whose security was deemed vital to American interests. The United States would become the "arsenal of democracy." By the end of World War II over $50 billion in Lend-Lease equipment and supplies had been distributed to America's allies.

Undeclared Naval Hostilities Further support for Britain soon materialized. The American navy patrolled the western half of the North Atlantic, freeing British ships for duty nearer Europe. American ships and planes fed data on Nazi submarines to the Royal Navy. British ships used American ports freely, while this country kept sixty-five Axis ships tied in its harbors. Some Americans joined the British or Canadian air forces, and British pilots trained at American airfields. The situation, as Germany knew, was not at all neutral. But Hitler was not yet ready to declare war on America; in the summer of 1941 he had attacked his Russian "ally."

But American "nonbelligerence" soon provoked German countermeasures. When American warships began escorting Allied shipping halfway across the Atlantic, German submarines (or U-boats) responded. Several American destroyers were fired on; several merchant ships went down. In October a German submarine sank an American destroyer near Iceland. Congress then removed the last restriction of the neutrality laws: armed American ships could take war supplies directly to Britain. An undeclared naval war raged in the Atlantic.

Some members of the Roosevelt Cabinet wanted an immediate declaration of war against Germany. But Roosevelt preferred to continue active nonbelligerence. He would arm those fighting the Axis (including Soviet Russia). He would cement relations with Britain, as in the meeting with Churchill that produced the Atlantic Charter.[2] He would also let the Axis powers decide when to declare war.

THE UNITED STATES AT WAR

Japan, not Germany, made the decisive move. The assault on Pearl Harbor and other bases in the Pacific on December 7, 1941, ended the isolationist-interventionist debate. It also united the nation. Roosevelt's critics, including Lindbergh of America First, now pledged their hearty support for the war. One major isolationist, Michigan's Republican Senator Arthur H. Vandenberg, conceded that Pearl Harbor opened his eyes: "That day ended isolationism for any realist."

Could the war with Japan have been avoided? Not unless one of the two nations, Japan or the United States, had changed its basic policy. Japan intended to expand in China and South-

[2] The Atlantic Charter stated common British and American beliefs: The right of people to choose their own form of government and the need for world-wide economic cooperation and an international security system to prevent future wars.

east Asia. The United States would never recognize Japan's partial conquest of China. It would equally oppose any Japanese moves against Allied colonies, such as British Malaya or the Dutch East Indies. Neither side would budge. Japan's decision to expand by force made conflict with America almost inevitable. An attack on only British, French, and Dutch holdings would have been wiser for Tokyo, nevertheless. Had American territory remained untouched, Congress might well have refused to declare war.

Americans had a long job ahead. It was made even longer just after Pearl Harbor when Germany and Italy honored their Axis commitments by declaring war on the United States. In one way, however, this step simplified matters. American leaders believed that Hitler, the greatest threat to democracy, should be defeated first. Japan could not be ignored—Americans would indeed "Remember Pearl Harbor"—but the war in Europe against Germany, Italy, and their Axis allies received top priority. Hitler, then at the height of his power, relished the idea of smashing Franklin "Rosenfeld." (Hitler had the strange notion that Roosevelt, an Episcopalian since birth, was Jewish.)

Whatever his motives, Hitler's actions caused the creation of the Grand Alliance, a coalition of all nations fighting the Axis. America, Britain, and Russia were senior partners. Starting with a declaration by "United Nations," signed in January 1942 by twenty-six countries, the alliance grew to forty-seven members by 1945. This provided the basis for the United Nations (UN). Technically, all were equal. But in reality the great powers ran the war largely to suit themselves.

Joining the Allies was a new step for the United States. Even in World War I, America was only an "associated power" rather than an "ally." The difference went beyond hairsplitting over the meaning of words. World War II was unique; Americans felt their own security threatened. The world had indeed changed.

Big Three Relations Within the Grand Alliance, or United Nations, the closest cooperation existed between Britain and the United States. Churchill and Roosevelt met almost a dozen times to develop the partnership and sometimes to prepare a united front against Russia, the other major ally. It was not that the Soviet Union was an uncooperative ally. After withstanding the first German offensive of 1941 (a surprise attack by a former ally), the Russians fought the Germans tenaciously. The Nazi army was spending itself in Russia, winning many battles but nothing decisive. Churchill and Roosevelt hastened to assure Stalin, the Soviet dictator, of their esteem. They promised military aid as soon as possible.

But Stalin wanted immediate action by his allies in the West. Specifically, he called for an Anglo-American invasion of Western Europe launched across the English Channel in 1942. But instead of a dangerous, and probably disastrous, cross-channel invasion of occupied France that year, Western leaders settled for landings in North Africa. This move took little pressure off Russia. Stalin angrily rejected suggestions that this weak move represented a so-called second front against Germany.

Further friction developed during preliminary discussions of the postwar political settlements. Stalin, like Roosevelt and Churchill, never doubted his side would win. He wanted a hand in carving national boundaries after the war. Roosevelt conceded on this point, but Churchill usually tried to pacify but contain Stalin. Roosevelt often urged the postponement of political decisions until later in the war.

Events in Asia and the Pacific The war was fought on many fronts. After the Japanese struck Pearl Harbor, they took over most of Southeast Asia. First they conquered the rest of French Indochina (Vietnam, Laos, and Cambodia). Then Malaya, Singapore, and Burma—all British colonies—fell. The Dutch East Indies came next. Australia was so sure its turn had come that it almost withdrew its troops from North Africa for a last-ditch homeland defense.

Meanwhile, the Japanese occupied most of America's colony, the Philippines. General

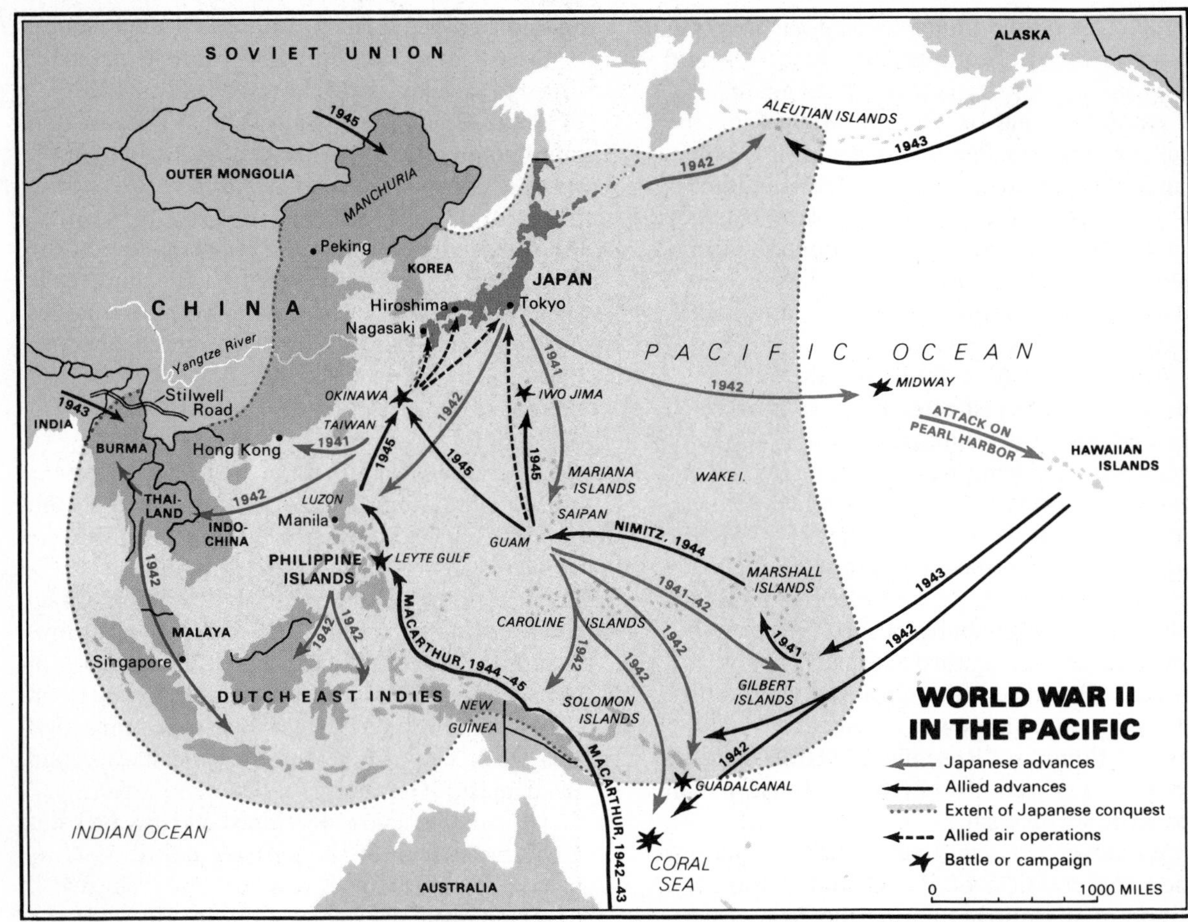

The day after the Japanese surprise attack on Pearl Harbor on December 7, 1941, the United States declared war on Japan. On that same day, the Japanese invaded Thailand and Malaya. By late December they had captured Guam, Hong Kong, and Wake Island. The Japanese invasion of the Philippines began December 10; they took Manila on January 2, 1942. General Douglas MacArthur retreated to Australia.

In February 1942 the Japanese took Singapore and by early March, most of the Dutch East Indies. In June they seized two of the Aleutian Islands. The Battle of the Coral Sea was fought between Japanese and Allied forces on May 7–8, which stopped Japan's advance on Australia. The air and naval battle of Midway (June 3–6) was a turning point in the Pacific war, and within two months the United States was for the first time on the offensive.

The first major Allied offensive, beginning in August 1942, was fought at Guadalcanal. The Japanese were driven from it in February 1943. During March–August the Japanese were driven from the Aleutians. In the second half of 1943 the South Pacific offensive took place. It gave the Allies control of the waters adjacent to the Solomon Islands. A Central Pacific offensive was launched in November under Admiral Chester Nimitz, during which the Allies took the Solomons, Gilberts, Marshalls, and Marianas. In December General Joseph W. Stilwell began a campaign in Burma; Burma was not completely retaken, however, until May 1945.

In June 1944 air attacks were opened against cities on the Japanese home islands. The Philippines campaign of June–December saw General MacArthur's return there. The naval Battle of Leyte Gulf (October 23–25) was a decisive defeat for Japan. It destroyed most of its remaining sea power. The Philippines campaign ended after the taking of Manila.

After heavy fighting, United States Marines took Iwo Jima in March 1945 and conquered Okinawa by late June. In May–August the greatest air offensive in the Pacific was launched against the Japanese home islands, culminating in the dropping of atomic bombs on Hiroshima (August 6) and Nagasaki (August 9). On August 8, the Soviet Union declared war on Japan and invaded Manchuria.

Japan surrendered and sued for peace on August 10. President Harry Truman announced August 14 as V-J Day. Japan's formal surrender took place September 2 in Tokyo Bay aboard the United States battleship *Missouri*.

(continued on page 721)

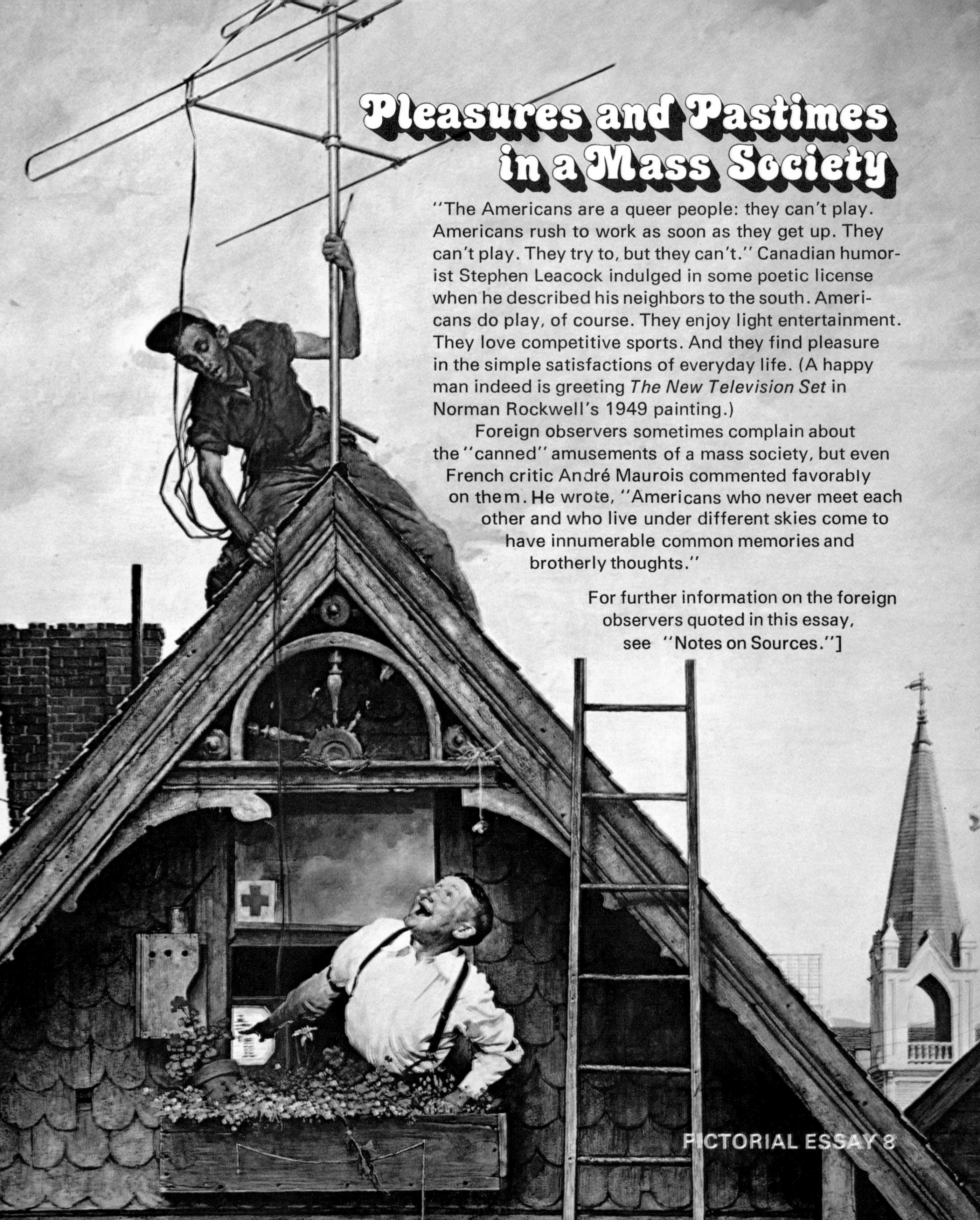

Pleasures and Pastimes in a Mass Society

"The Americans are a queer people: they can't play. Americans rush to work as soon as they get up. They can't play. They try to, but they can't." Canadian humorist Stephen Leacock indulged in some poetic license when he described his neighbors to the south. Americans do play, of course. They enjoy light entertainment. They love competitive sports. And they find pleasure in the simple satisfactions of everyday life. (A happy man indeed is greeting *The New Television Set* in Norman Rockwell's 1949 painting.)

Foreign observers sometimes complain about the "canned" amusements of a mass society, but even French critic André Maurois commented favorably on them. He wrote, "Americans who never meet each other and who live under different skies come to have innumerable common memories and brotherly thoughts."

[For further information on the foreign observers quoted in this essay, see "Notes on Sources."]

PE 8–2 / *Stronger than in various other countries, and perhaps also than in Turkey, seems to be the predilection in America for the lighter types of musical and theatrical entertainment—for jazz and operettas, or for comedies and thrillers rather than plays that have a pessimistic note or are centered around philosophical and social themes.*

[ÖMER CELÂL SARC, 1959]

Broadcasting a radio drama, 1934

Scene from *Oklahoma!* (original production, 1943)

I could not agree that the creation of films is not an art at all, only an industry. It is actually a curiously mixed activity, coming into a new category, needing all the resources and organization of a large industry, but by no means devoid of genuine artistic impulses. The public looked to films for general entertainment, on a scale hitherto unknown, and accepted the moving pictures as a substitute for theaters, books, gossip, and dreams.

[J. B. PRIESTLEY, 1935-36]

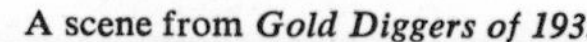

A scene from *Gold Diggers of 1933*

Let's listen to Louis Armstrong on Broadway, the black Titan of the cry, of the apostrophe, of the burst of laughter, of thunder. An imperial figure, Armstrong makes his entrance. His voice is as deep as an abyss, it is a black cave. He bursts out laughing, he roars and puts the trumpet to his mouth. With it he is in turn demoniac, playful, and massive, from one second to another, in accordance with an astounding fantasy. The man is extravagantly skillful; he is a king.

[LE CORBUSIER, 1947]

Louis Armstrong

Elvis Presley and fans

Female teenagers are in the habit of greeting their heroes, the young crooners—the one best known being Elvis Presley, of the writhing hips and thighs—with a shrill yell that seems to issue from a single throat. The picture of young and well-dressed girls comporting themselves in this fashion is enough to send cold shivers down an adult's spine. Significantly, however, it has been observed that only the girls in the rows lit up by the stage lights break out in this yell; that is, only those who can be seen by the others. Moreover, they are looking not so much at the singer as at the other members of their own group.

[HERBERT VON BORCH, 1962]

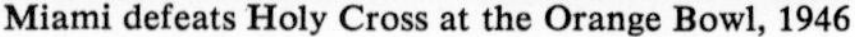
Miami defeats Holy Cross at the Orange Bowl, 1946

Willie Mays at second base, 1957

I do not pretend to understand even the coarser of the finer points of American college football, which must have been originally devised during an early revolutionary phase of American life, for like a revolution it is an odd mixture of secret plotting, with so many heads motionless and close together, and sudden violent action. When either side pressed towards goal, we all stood up. The danger over or the prize lost, we sat down again. The enormous clock ran off the seconds when the ball was actually in play. It stopped when the game stopped. And the game was always stopping.

[J. B. PRIESTLEY AND JACQUETTA HAWKES, 1954]

I have studied hundreds of photos of Louis in his big fights, of Louis preparing for his big fights, of Louis just after his big fights. His face almost never changes. The man is dignified, *in the toughest sport in the world, whether he's giving a licking or taking one. You cannot get away from this impression of the man being so superbly equipped to fight that he didn't need the window-dressing of a big grin of confidence, or glib phrases by the publicity boys. Louis wasn't just a great fighter. He was an admirable man.*

[HARRY CARPENTER, 1964]

The Brown Bomber, Louis and Schmeling Fight, by Robert Riggs

Robinson's character was the key. A fierce competitor, Jackie had in the early days to curb his angry pride. He ignored insults, and won recognition as a baseball player, on equal terms with others, whether white or black. Today ability is the key, not pigmentation. Some day Jackie's greatest honor will come when he is simply a name in a record book, when, because there was a Jackie Robinson and others like him, future generations have forgotten there was ever a need for a Jackie Robinson.

[CANADIAN SPORTSWRITER]

Cheerleaders at a high-school basketball game

To observe the North American in a large crowd within the United States—at a World Series game or a popular football game—is one of the most cheering spectacles in the world. Here we have an enormous mass of people, well balanced, attractive, determined to enjoy to the utmost an afternoon of relaxation, applauding their favorite team but wihout ill will or malevolence toward the adversary, on the contrary always disposed to recognize and applaud the courage and skill of the opposition.

[DANIEL COSÍO VILLEGAS, 1959]

We went into a bowling alley. It is the old game of skittles which the dwarfs of Rip Van Winkle played, but it has been brought up to date. Instead of a wild gully, I found a bar with tables and chairs: the bowling alleys, set side by side, are of varnished wood, and when the bowling ball has knocked over the ninepins, it falls through a trap door and is returned by an automatic device to the player. The game is so popular that the alleys are booked for days in advance. It is monotonous to watch.

[SIMONE DE BEAUVOIR, 1947]

Bowling at a fifty-six-lane alley, California

PE 8–6 /

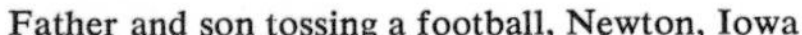

Father and son tossing a football, Newton, Iowa

Woman playing bingo in Muncie, Indiana

America is a modern land where technical ingenuity is apparent at every point, in the equipment of a kitchen as well as of a car, but at the same time a land of gardens, of flowers, of home activities, where a man, away from his office or his work-place, enjoys tinkering at his bench, making a piece of furniture, repainting his house, repairing a fence, or mowing his lawn. A land of luxury but also of simple pleasures. There is an America that strolls in the parks in its suburban Sunday clothes, or cavorts on the beaches, and plays base-ball everywhere.

[JACQUES FREYMOND, 1959]

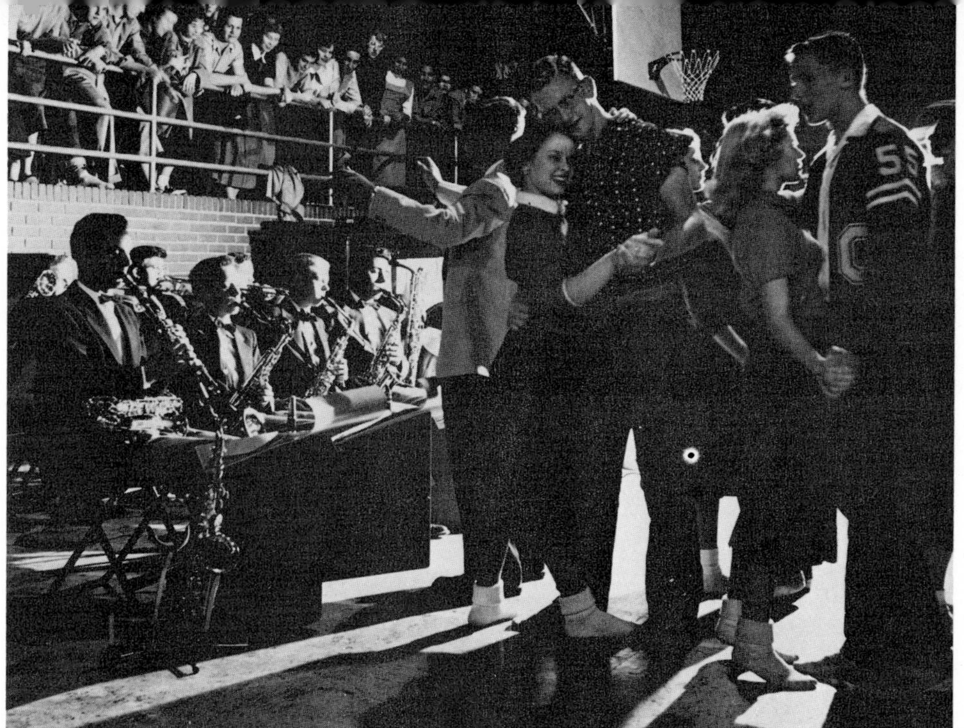

Teenagers at a "sock hop," Carlsbad, New Mexico

Wisconsin Farm Auction, by Joan Arend Kickbush

PE 8–8 /

Girls jumping rope, Cleveland

The American smile, which has been so ridiculed by those who believe the intelligent thing is to know everything already—without, of course, knowing much of anything at all—seems to me to be the expression of love for one's fellow man, of the basic fact that in the United States it is firmly believed that living together is a blessing. This is derived, in my opinion, from the historical makeup of the United States and from the American spirit, from its loneliness and the fact that for so long the presence of other men was an occasion for joy.

[JULIAN MARIAS, 1959]

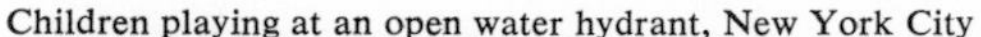

Children playing at an open water hydrant, New York City

Douglas MacArthur, the commander there when the Philippines were attacked (on the same day as Pearl Harbor), was ordered to Australia. What remained of the American army—including Filipino units—held out bravely for several months on the Bataan peninsula near Manila until overwhelmed by superior force. Most Filipinos opposed the Japanese invasion. The islands had been promised independence; the war upset this time table, forcing a postponement until 1946.

The Japanese drive of 1941–42 was soon halted. Though a naval battle in the Coral Sea in May 1942 brought neither side victory, it removed the threat of a Japanese invasion of Australia. In June a key naval battle took place near Midway. Japanese strategy called for capture of Midway, then a move against Hawaii. Japan probably should have made these two attacks right after Pearl Harbor. By mid-1942, however, things had changed. American aircraft carrier strength, though limited, was undamaged. Also, because Magic had broken the Japanese code, the American navy knew where to concentrate.

Midway signaled the end of traditional naval warfare. Planes replaced guns and torpedoes as the most important offensive weapons. Enemy aircraft carriers were therefore the main target. Four Japanese carriers were sunk but only one American flat-top.[3] More important, the troop transports turned back toward Japan. The Japanese never again made a serious thrust in the mid-Pacific.

Coral Sea and Midway set the stage for Allied offensive operations. In August 1942 Americans landed on Guadalcanal in the Solomon Islands. The battle there was long and fierce—a warning of what lay ahead. This "island hopping" followed a bloody course from Guadalcanal in 1942 to Okinawa in 1945. In a series of landings on the various islands in between

The war in the Pacific was fought by island-hopping—retaking island by island territory captured by the Japanese. This Marine landing in the Solomons in 1943 helped save Australia from conquest.

[3] All four carriers Japan lost at Midway had been used to attack Pearl Harbor. Likewise lost at Midway—or during the harsh fighting that followed in the Solomon Islands—were nearly all the daring Japanese pilots of December 7. Neither the flat-tops nor the aviators were ever properly replaced. Admiral Nagumo, who led the victory at Pearl and the defeat at Midway, survived until 1944. Then he died, evidently by suicide, during the American capture of Saipan.

 United States troops fought for every bit of territory, notably the first few yards of each beachhead. Japanese resistance never let up. Even losing battle after battle did not diminish the enemy's will to fight.

After Midway Americans had sea and air superiority. The American fleet, especially the number of carriers, grew enormously. Even when the Japanese navy or air force came out in full force (as when the United States recaptured the Philippines in 1944), Japan suffered staggering losses. On one day American pilots shot down nearly 500 Japanese planes. At Leyte Gulf Japan's navy was almost destroyed.

American submarines (though less publicized than German U-boats) sank hundreds of Japanese ships. Many of them were carrying raw materials from Southeast Asia to Japan's factories. By early 1945 Japan had no hope for victory. The war in China ground on inconclusively. The Pacific, which three years before had seemed to be Japan's, was now an American lake. The only way left to preserve Japanese martial honor or punish the American invaders was suicide assaults by *Kamikaze* pilots.[4]

Events in Europe and the Mediterranean The Allies mounted an equally relentless (and equally successful) effort in Europe and the Mediterranean. American and British forces overran North Africa and routed German General Erwin Rommel's *Afrika Korps*. In 1943 the Allies invaded Sicily and then mainland Italy. Meanwhile, massive preparations for invading France went on, with Britain as the staging area.

On another front the Russians took terrible losses. Yet they stopped the farthest German penetration at the Volga River in the Battle of Stalingrad. For the next two years the "Eastern Front" repeatedly saw Russian advances and German retreats.

The invasion of France on June 6, 1944, put Hitler's neck in the noose. Despite strong resistance Allied invaders stormed Normandy beaches. Happily, Hitler insisted that the Normandy invasion was unimportant. He refused to concentrate his available forces there. After several nerve-racking weeks American tank columns led by General George S. Patton pushed beyond Normandy and raced across France.

But the Nazi army could not be crushed in 1944. It withdrew toward the Rhine. Germany, as helpless now as Japan, was the target of massive air attacks. (Over 1,000 Allied planes participated in a single raid on Berlin.) Hitler still dreamed of victory, though he mistakenly believed his own people were betraying him. He forbade his generals to retreat. He hastened the murder of millions in concentration camps. Yet neither ravings nor cruelty produced military victories. Early in 1945 the Allies pushed ahead on all fronts.

The Big Three leaders—Roosevelt, Stalin, and Churchill—had long been preparing for victory. Stalin and Churchill met in Moscow in October 1944. There they began carving out spheres of influence. Roosevelt wanted to end the war first and then make such decisions. The Axis must accept defeat and unconditional surrender; the Allies should not squabble until they had won. Thus the 1943 Big Three meeting at Teheran, Iran, dealt mainly with wartime strategy.

By early 1945 territorial questions could not be postponed. Germany would surely surrender that year; Japan was next in line. Russian participation in the invasion of Japan could mean a shorter campaign, with fewer Western casualties. What price would Stalin demand, though, to bring Russia into the Pacific war? The answer emerged at the Yalta Conference of February 1945, a Big Three meeting at a Russian resort in the Crimea.

Stalin set a high though not outlandish price. He wanted Russian power in the Far East to equal its extent in 1904, before his country lost the Russo-Japanese War. Russia was to receive the northernmost islands of the Japanese chain, plus territorial and commercial rights in Manchuria and northern China. In return, Stalin would declare war against Japan within three months of the end of the war in Europe.

Roosevelt's military advisers warned that

[4] *Kamikaze* pilots crashed their planes, loaded with bombs, into ships.

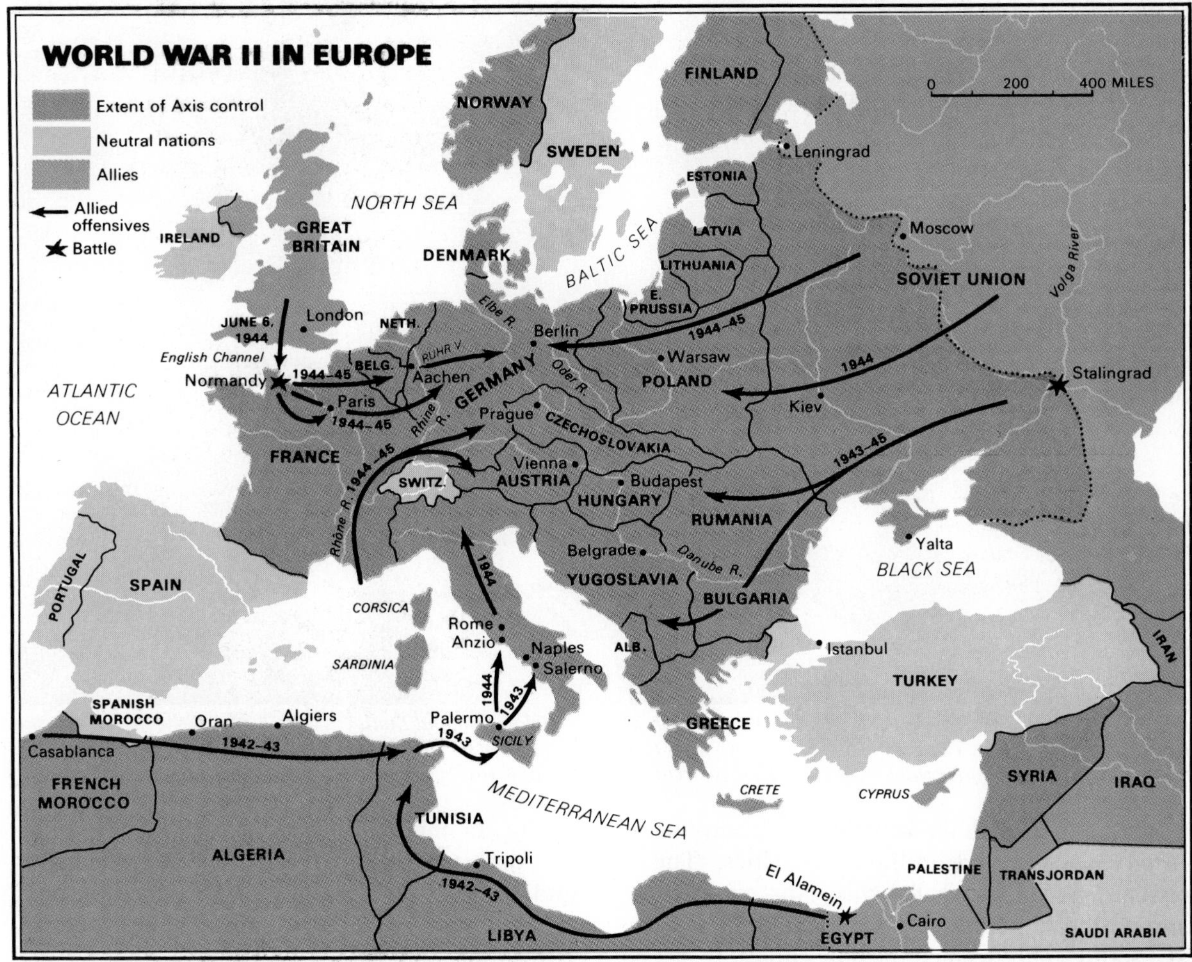

When Germany was at the height of its power, its armies had overrun much of European Russia, defeated France, occupied Norway and Denmark, and held much of North Africa. In December 1941 England and the Soviet Union were the only Allies in Europe still undefeated by Germany.

The first United States troops for the European theater of the war arrived in northern Ireland in January 1942. Six months later in North Africa, the British checked the Axis advance at El Alamein. In November General Eisenhower's Allied forces landed in North Africa. By May 1943 the Germans had been defeated there. In Europe the Russians defeated the German armies, attacking Stalingrad in December 1942 after a four-month siege—a major turning point. Thereafter the Russians began to take the offensive.

The Allied invasion of Italy began in July 1943. Italy's unconditional surrender to the Allies in September was followed by stiff German resistance in northern Italy. The Germans were not finally defeated there until 1945.

The air offensive against Germany began in January 1944 in preparation for an Allied invasion. On June 6, D-Day, Allied armies invaded Normandy in northern France in a surprise attack. By August 10 this offensive was concluded and a second front in southern France was opened that began a drive up the Rhone Valley. All of France, Belgium, and Luxembourg was liberated by September. By this time the Russians had driven the Germans out of the Soviet Union and into Eastern Europe.

The battle for Germany began in September 1944. The first large German city to fall, Aachen, was taken in October. Within five months Belgrade, Budapest, and Warsaw had fallen.

A German counteroffensive in the west was launched in December 1944. The Germans almost succeeded in breaking through the American line in the Battle of the Bulge, but they were repulsed. Then a British offensive was launched in the Netherlands. By March United States troops had penetrated the Ruhr Valley and crossed the Rhine; a month later, they reached the Elbe. The Russians entered Berlin late in April. Berlin fell on May 2. The formal end of the war in Europe occurred on May 8. Germany surrendered unconditionally to the Allies.

The strain of war was visible on FDR's face as he met with his allies, Churchill and Stalin, for the last time at Yalta. The concessions made to Stalin there to secure Russia's entrance into the Pacific war were denounced by some postwar critics as "appeasement."

invading Japan without Russia might cost the United States a half-million casualties. The President had no wish for this. Nor could he count on the still untested atom bomb to end the war. Stalin's offer seemed the only choice.

Yalta also planned for the dismemberment of Germany. The Allied powers (the Big Three and France) would each occupy a section. Germany must also pay reparations for the wartime destruction it had caused. Stalin wanted to weaken Germany so that the Germans might never attack Russia again. Reparations would keep Germany feeble. Moreover, splitting Germany into occupation zones assured Stalin that the eastern zone would remain firmly in Soviet control.

A HOT WAR TURNED COLD

Within a half year of Yalta, the Axis was subdued. In April 1945 Hitler committed suicide in Berlin as the Allies overran Germany. Four months later the Pacific war ended spectacularly and ominously. On August 6 an American atom bomb largely obliterated the Japanese city of Hiroshima, killing over 70,000 (see page 726). Three days later Nagasaki suffered a similar fate. Japan surrendered, though many Japanese wished to fight to the death.

History's greatest war ended with unconditional surrender by the Axis. Yet victory found the Grand Alliance anything but united. Differences over postwar policy produced visible strains, with the possibility of a new and dangerous confrontation. The United States and Russia were now superpowers. Their growing disagreements would soon be called a Cold War.

Soviet-American cooperation broke down completely after World War II. Eastern and central Europe came under Russian domination. The Baltic countries of Latvia, Lithuania, and Estonia ceased being independent nations. Finland avoided the same fate by curbing its foreign policy in a treaty with Russia. The countries between Western-occupied Germany and Russia, plus the Balkan nations, became Soviet satellites. (Yugoslavia would later break away.) A Russian Soviet empire emerged. Countries on its borders (Greece, Turkey, and Iran, for example) all felt the pressure of the new superpower.

The United States had hoped for cooperation, not conflict, among the major powers after the war. The status quo and isolationism of earlier periods were dead. Americans could not pull back as in 1919 and expect to maintain their interests in a vacuum. World War II had exhausted Britain and France. If North Atlantic leadership of the world were to continue, the United States had to step in. Thus Washington pushed for a new world organization, despite the League of Nations' failure and America's own sorry role in that failure.

Roosevelt wanted a league. Unlike Wilson, though, he made sure that Republicans participated in sessions that preceded the founding of the United Nations in 1945 (soon after Roosevelt's death). The UN differed from the League in various ways. It was located in New York, not Geneva. More important, the great powers established a Security Council whose permanent members (the United States, Britain, France, Russia, and China) could defeat any proposal with a single negative vote. This big-power veto, a recognition of both national sovereignty and great-power interests, gravely limited UN effectiveness in crisis situations. Yet the veto was desired by all the large powers.

Containment in the Mediterranean American hopes for postwar stability suffered as a result of Roosevelt's death. The late President did not possess a precise blueprint for peacetime policy. He had become increasingly disillusioned over Russian behavior. But he did possess enormous prestige. This was not true of Vice President Harry S Truman, a man without experience in either high-level administration or foreign policy. President Truman's baptism of fire in summit diplomacy—direct meetings by heads of government—came in July 1945. He, Stalin, and Britain's new prime minister, Clement Attlee, met at Potsdam, Germany. Full agreement proved impossible. With Japan still undefeated, Truman accepted postponement of various pending issues.

Russia's expansionism and the weakness of America's allies soon ruled out further delay. By 1947 Western Europe seemed ready to collapse. Britain, France, Italy, and West Germany (not yet a separate country) were sliding downward, perhaps toward a chaos that could only benefit Russia. Britain had to give up its empire. The British move that most affected the United States was its decision to end aid to Greece and Turkey, Britain's anticommunist Mediterranean allies. The Russians and Turks had been at odds for centuries. The post–World War II period proved no exception. The Soviets tried to gain parts of eastern Turkey and establish bases at the Dardanelles, Turkey's (and Russia's) gateway to the Mediterranean.

The Greeks (unfriendly toward the Turks but now allied with them as another target of Russian expansionism) also needed help. A communist guerrilla movement was fighting the Greek government. Only active American intervention could keep Greece and Turkey out of the Soviet sphere. In March 1947 the President enunciated the Truman Doctrine "to help free peoples to maintain their free institutions" against the threat of "subjugation by armed minorities or by outside pressures." Congress appropriated $400 million to aid Greece and Turkey.

The congressional action and Truman's strong words were highly significant. They proved the Cold War had truly begun. The United States would, by threat of a third world war, contain Russia within the areas the Soviets had occupied or dominated by 1947. The support Truman received from Republicans in Congress signaled that the policy of containment had bipartisan support as well.

Containment in Western Europe After containing the Russian advance in the eastern Med-

Hiroshima

The silence in the skies above Hiroshima was broken only by the sound of two approaching B-29s. There had already been one alert on that warm morning of August 6, 1945. But now the all clear had sounded. The people of Hiroshima were used to a weather plane flying overhead at this hour—around 8:00 A.M.—so they did not pay much attention to the sky.

But these were not weather planes. One of them was the *Enola Gay*. Its mission was to drop the first atomic bomb on enemy territory. At about 31,000 feet the bomb-bay doors opened. The bombardier released "Little Boy," a weapon that had twenty times the power of a ton of TNT. At 2,000 feet the bomb detonated.

A young Hiroshima girl who was riding a trolley gave this account:

> At that moment my eyes were suddenly blinded by a flash of piercing light and the neighborhood was enveloped in dense smoke of a yellow color like poison gas. Instantly everything became pitch dark, and you couldn't see an inch ahead. Then a heavy and tremendously loud roar. The inside of my mouth was gritty as though I had eaten sand, and my throat hurt. I looked toward the east, and I saw an enormous black pillar of cloud billowing upward. 'It's all over now,' I thought.

As the plane made a sharp turn to avoid the blast, the tail gunner looked down at the falling bomb. Within seconds he was looking directly into the center of the atomic detonation. He watched the shock wave approach the plane like a shimmering heat wave. The mushroom cloud started forming immediately. He described it as "a bubbling mass of purple-gray smoke, and you could see it had a red core to it and everything was burning inside."

Within an instant 70,000 people died. Another 30,000 would later die of radiation burns and a strange new disease, radiation sickness. Approximately 75 percent of the buildings in Hiroshima were destroyed. As another eyewitness said of those first few seconds, "Everything had crumbled away in that one moment and changed into streets of rubble, street after street of ruins."

What caused the decision to use this devastating weapon? President Truman had been told that if the Japanese fought to the end of their own islands, as they vowed to do, the war would last more than another year, and a half million American lives would be lost. He thought a quick one-two punch—one atomic bomb dropped, followed swiftly by a second on another target—would force Japan to surrender.

Historians have conjectured that there may also have been other reasons. Soviet-American relations were strained. Truman may have wanted to show the Russians that American strength was superior. Or he may have wanted to end the war before the Soviet Union could occupy Asia as it had Europe.

The atomic bomb did end the war. Three days after Hiroshima was bombed, Nagasaki suffered the same fate. The next day the Japanese asked for peace terms.

iterranean, the United States turned to Western Europe. Secretary of State George C. Marshall (see page 731) announced in mid-1947 American willingness to contribute huge sums toward European reconstruction. All Europe was included; even Russia sent envoys to a preliminary conference. But the Russians quickly withdrew and kept their satellites from joining the European Recovery Program (ERP), better known as the Marshall plan.

Congress moved more cautiously than on Greece and Turkey. But a communist takeover of Czechoslovakia in 1948 spurred it on. Billions of dollars flooded into Western Europe, stimulating the area's economic recovery. This also ended any early possibility that European communist parties would reach power through elections.

The Western allies took an added step in containing communist advances in Europe by creating a formal military alliance in 1949. The North Atlantic Treaty Organization (NATO) included a dozen North Atlantic nations (see page 729). They pledged to take any action necessary "including the use of armed force, to restore and maintain the security of the North Atlantic area." To implement the promise to defend any NATO country attacked by an outside power, large numbers of United States troops went to Germany. The American navy took over from Britain in the Mediterranean.

Through NATO the United States in effect became the policeman for the Western world, a break with American tradition. Not since the French alliance of 1778 had the United States allied itself formally with another power. NATO made the containment policy a firm one. Though the Soviets exploded their first nuclear weapon in 1949, they knew further expansion to the west was unthinkable. NATO was soon functioning effectively, with General Dwight D. Eisenhower (Supreme Allied Commander in Europe during World War II) heading NATO's forces. Obviously Washington would not allow a Russian "iron curtain" to fall over Western Europe.

The Struggle for Mainland China Unsettling events in Asia contrasted sharply with the success of containment in Europe. Postwar China was particularly disappointing for Americans. Civil war broke out there between the communists under Mao Tse-tung and the Nationalists under Chiang Kai-shek. Mao had fought for control of China long before the Japanese invasion. War with Japan temporarily united the two sides, but afterward, they returned to civil war.

By 1948 it became clear the Nationalists would lose. The next year Chiang fled to the island of Taiwan, while on the mainland Mao proclaimed his communist government, the People's Republic of China (often referred to as Red China). Massive American military intervention might have prevented the communist takeover. A few American leaders thought so, though even fewer recommended it. But later large-scale American involvement in Vietnam casts grave doubt on that course. In any case, two certainties remain: by 1949 Red China possessed considerable power, and this power would increase.

The Korean Conflict The United States refused diplomatic recognition to Red China. Yet soon after the Chinese civil war ended, Americans were forced to recognize the Red Chinese army in combat. The scene was Korea, which had regained independence from Japan in 1945. But now Korea had been divided into communist-occupied North Korea and American-occupied South Korea. The communist North invaded the South in June 1950, perhaps because Washington had declared Korea outside the zone of American vital interest.

When South Korea asked for American help, Truman quickly provided it. Available combat forces (two American divisions stationed in Japan) went at once to Korea. Also, a Soviet mistake let Truman make the American response a United Nations venture. In June 1950 Russia was boycotting all UN meetings. The Security Council promptly branded North Korea an aggressor and authorized a UN military force to repel the attack. General Douglas MacArthur, occupation leader of Japan, also headed the UN army (mostly American soldiers) in Korea.

The Korean conflict was a success and a failure for the United States. Two Koreas still exist. Thus the 1950–53 military effort there did prevent a communist takeover. But this venture became a political liability for Democrats and a lasting frustration for all Americans. After a year of seesaw campaigns up and down the Korean peninsula, fighting settled close to the original dividing line.

Total victory became unattainable because the war had limited aims. Washington too permitted only limited means to achieve them. MacArthur, a great soldier and a great egotist, was especially frustrated. He had sent his troops to within sight of China's border in 1950, provoking full-scale Chinese intervention in Korea and an American retreat. Despite this–and the risk of bringing Russia into combat also–MacArthur wanted to bomb China and fight the war more vigorously. Truman refused. When MacArthur aired his contrary views in public, Truman fired him.

Warfare in Korea was conventional in employing large numbers of men with standard weaponry in set battles. But since it was fought for limited aims—containing rather than destroying the enemy—it foreshadowed recent combat in Vietnam.

U.S. POSTWAR ALLIANCES

YEAR ESTABLISHED	ALLIANCE	MEMBERS	PURPOSE
1948	ORGANIZATION OF AMERICAN STATES (OAS)	Argentina, Barbados, Bolivia, Brazil, Chile, Colombia, Costa Rica, Cuba, Dominican Republic, Ecuador, El Salvador, Guatemala, Haiti, Honduras, Jamaica, Mexico, Nicaragua, Panama, Paraguay, Peru, Trinidad-Tobago, United States, Uruguay, Venezuela	To provide for the common defense of the Western Hemisphere and settle economic and political hemispheric problems.
1949	NORTH ATLANTIC TREATY ORGANIZATION (NATO)	Belgium, Canada, Denmark, France, Great Britain, Iceland, Italy, Luxembourg, the Netherlands, Norway, Portugal, United States Greece, Turkey (1952) West Germany (1955)	To coordinate military defense (under a central military command) against external communist aggression. An armed attack on one member is an attack on all.
1951	ANZUS PACT	Australia, New Zealand, United States	To provide security against external attack in the southern Pacific region.
1951–60	BILATERAL MUTUAL-DEFENSE TREATIES		To provide specific commitments to the military defense of the Far East.
1951		Philippines, United States	
1954		Taiwan, United States	
1954		South Korea, United States	
1960		Japan, United States	
1954	SOUTHEAST ASIA TREATY ORGANIZATION (SEATO)	Australia, France, Great Britain, New Zealand, Pakistan, Philippines, Thailand, United States	To build up Southeast Asia economically and militarily against possible communist aggression. Joint resistance to external attack is not required.
1955	BAGHDAD PACT; Reorganized in 1959 as CENTRAL TREATY ORGANIZATION (CENTO)	Iran, Pakistan, Turkey, United Kingdom Iraq (1955–59)	To provide economic and military assistance to the Middle East. The United States is a nonmember but gives extensive aid, primarily military, and is represented on some of the organization's councils.

REPUBLICANS BACK IN POWER

Truman fought the war his way; he and his party then paid the political price. Though Korea did not decide the election of 1952, it figured prominently. In promising to go to Korea if elected, the Republican candidate, Eisenhower ("Ike"), implied that he could end the conflict. This he did. Yet the truce signed in 1953 resulted less from Ike's tour of Korea than from exhaustion on both sides. Americans were happy to see the war end, though quite unhappy about the war itself. In this sense Korea was a prelude to the Vietnam nightmare.

When Republicans regained the presidency in 1952, after twenty years, they promised changes in foreign policy. Something beyond containment, something active, seemed possible to President Eisenhower and John Foster Dulles, his Secretary of State. Dulles quickly established himself as second in command in Eisenhower's administration. In foreign affairs he was first. Dulles talked tough about communism. He called Russian satellites captive nations, hinting that

John Foster Dulles is the protective nurse guarding the "children" of Asia from the lure of the "Red Piper of Peking" by herding them around the SEATO carriage.

their liberation was near. He warned that major communist wrongdoing could bring "massive retaliation" from the United States. Finally, Dulles stated he would go to "the brink of war" (including nuclear war) in pursuing his policies.

To back up his words, Dulles lined up more allies. In the Far East, the Southeast Asia Treaty Organization (SEATO) was organized in 1954. Although similar in many ways to NATO, the new alliance had some vital differences. Dulles limited his country's commitment by promising an American response to communist aggression only. Nor did the treaty set up a joint military command among the signers. Several important Asian nations (India and Indonesia, among others) would not join SEATO.

In the Middle East Dulles' initiative produced yet another anticommunist alliance, the Baghdad Pact of 1955. It included Pakistan, Iraq, Turkey, and Iran. Britain obligingly helped organize this group for Dulles, while the United States poured military and economic aid into its member nations.

Problems from Vietnam to Suez Almost at once these Dulles moves began to go awry. In French Indochina communism could not be contained. After World War II France hoped to carry on the business of her empire as usual there. But a nationalist guerrilla movement erupted under Ho Chi Minh. By 1954 the communists had all but driven the French army from North Vietnam. The United States had been supplying the French with arms. When France, its NATO ally, started losing, Washington considered intervening directly. Instead, Dulles tried to salvage half a country.

The Geneva accords of 1954 (not signed by the United States, though Dulles was present as an observer) temporarily divided Vietnam into northern and southern sectors. The communists expected to win a promised nationwide election that was never held. Instead, Dulles helped install a pro-American Catholic, Ngo Diem, as head of South Vietnam. The United States thus acquired problems and responsibilities that would later haunt Americans.

War there would not come until the Democrats took office. But the Eisenhower-Dulles foreign policy quickly suffered other setbacks. In the fall of 1956 the ideas of "liberating" Eastern Europe and "containing" Russia's growing influence in the Arab world went up in the smoke of two crises: Hungary and Suez. The Soviets ruthlessly crushed Hungary's attempt to establish a government more responsive to its own needs. Washington deplored the events in Hungary but took no action.

Suez proved equally embarrassing for the United States. In Egypt a nationalist government under Gamal Abdel Nasser took over the Suez Canal. When Israel, Britain, and France invaded Egypt simultaneously, Nasser sought help from Russia. The threat of Russian intervention convinced the United States that the invaders should withdraw. Foreign troops did leave Egypt, though this humiliation of its NATO allies embarrassed the United States.

Further embarrassment came when Russia sent up the world's first space satellite in 1957. This Soviet scientific achievement shocked Americans. In response, Washington accelerated its space program and began pumping money into scientific education.

America "Moving Again" The Eisenhower foreign policy was less activist after Dulles, dying of cancer, retired in 1959. Eisenhower made

George C. Marshall

One of George C. Marshall's biographers has described him as "the least typical of generals." He notes that what is remarkable in him is a "beautifully balanced mind thinking in terms of the dignity and integrity of the country which gave him birth."

Marshall was a soldier-statesman in the tradition of George Washington and Andrew Jackson. He was a military genius who turned diplomat, Secretary of State, and Secretary of Defense after the close of his career as a professional soldier. His actions in war caused President Harry Truman to state in 1945: "In a war unparalleled in magnitude and horror, millions of American gave their country outstanding service. General of the Army George C. Marshall gave it victory." His actions in peace won him the Nobel Peace Prize in 1953. He was the first soldier ever to receive it.

Marshall was an absolute master of organization and military strategy. But he sometimes considered this talent a liability, for although his army career involved two world wars, he was never to lead troops in battle. He was considered too valuable a planner to be risked in field command.

In the 1930s Marshall had a tedious job as an instructor in the Illinois National Guard. But by 1936 his star began to rise. He was promoted to Chief of Staff of the Army on September 1, 1939, the opening day of World War II in Europe. Between that day and the end of the war Marshall built up the army and air corps from fewer than 200,000 men to over 8 million. Without his planning it has been estimated that the invasion of Europe would have come a full year later than it did in 1944.

At war's end Marshall wished to retire. But President Truman asked him to undertake a diplomatic mission to China to try to bring the warring Nationalist and communist forces together in a coalition government. The soldier hero's second career as a controversial statesman began.

After China Marshall was named Secretary of State. He found himself in a new war—the Cold War with the Soviet Union. He helped to hammer out the Truman Doctrine and, of course, the Marshall Plan. Then he tried to retire again. This time, however, Truman wanted him to become Secretary of Defense.

In 1951 Senator Joseph McCarthy, whose crusade against communism became a witch hunt, lashed out at Marshall. He published a speech attacking Marshall's wartime strategy, his mission to China, and his actions as Secretary of State. McCarthy accused this public servant of being "a man steeped in falsehood," who was guilty of "invariably serving the world policy of the Kremlin."

Marshall resigned soon after this vicious attack, because his effectiveness in office had been greatly reduced. It was a melancholy ending to a frequently brilliant and selfless career in the service of the nation. He was remembered by one of his colleagues in the State Department as "the image of the American gentleman at his best—honorable, courteous, devoid of arrogance, exacting of others but even more of himself, intolerant only of cowardice, deviousness, and cynicism."

The Khrushchev-Eisenhower meeting at Camp David, Maryland, in 1959 produced a temporary thaw in the Cold War. Khrushchev's new policy of peaceful coexistence with the West provided economic competition as an alternative to direct military confrontation in the world.

some personally satisfying overseas tours. He even hosted Russia's new dictator, Nikita Khrushchev, on an American visit. But attempts at more summit diplomacy failed miserably. A summit conference, slated for Paris in 1960, collapsed largely because an American spy plane, piloted by an agent of the Central Intelligence Agency, was shot down over Russia just before the conference.

Eisenhower was not active in the presidential campaign of 1960, even though his foreign policy came under attack. Eisenhower and Dulles, despite some reforms, had maintained the basic postwar policy of containment. But in the President's final term the United States frequently seemed not to be acting but reacting, often too late, to Soviet initiatives. Democratic candidate John F. Kennedy made shrewd use of this issue in his campaign against Republican Vice President Richard M. Nixon. During the famous Nixon-Kennedy television debates, Kennedy stated:

> I want people in Latin America and Africa and Asia to start to look to America, not [to] Khrushchev or the Chinese Communists. Can freedom be maintained under the most severe attack it has ever known? I think it can be, and I think in the final analysis it depends upon what we do here. I think it's time America started moving again.

Kennedy's promise to get the country "moving again" won him a narrow election victory. Americans looked forward to the 1960s, keenly anticipating his fulfillment of that pledge. But when the turbulent sixties had become history, many looked back with nostalgia to the eight quiet years of the Eisenhower era.

1. Why is the attack on Pearl Harbor now regarded as "a striking yet limited victory" for the Japanese?
2. What factors contributed to American disillusionment with world politics after World War I?
3. How did Congress try to avoid what it believed had been the "mistakes" of 1917? How did Roosevelt get around these laws in his cash-and-carry, destroyers-for-bases, and lend-lease programs?
4. Could the war with Japan have been avoided? Why or why not?
5. What was the significance of the Battle of Stalingrad? Of the battles of the Coral Sea and Midway?
6. What was the "high but not outlandish" price Stalin demanded for Russian participation in the war against Japan? Why was the United States willing to pay the price?
7. What was the meaning of the "containment" policy? Why was it adopted? What steps were taken in Europe to implement it?
8. Why was Russia unable to prevent the UN from acting in South Korea? Why is the Korean conflict considered both a success and a failure for the United States?
9. Was Eisenhower's foreign policy more active against communism than Truman's had been? Why or why not?

Beyond the Text

1. Roosevelt's policy of unconditional surrender, adopted at the Casablanca Conference in 1943, has been attacked by many who believe it prolonged the war. Why has this charge been made?
2. The decision to drop the atomic bomb has been much debated. What alternate strategies were proposed and rejected? Was there any possibility that the bomb need not have been dropped?
3. Debate the proposition: The United States, More Than Russia, Bears the Responsibility for Bringing on the Cold War.

Bibliography

Nonfiction

Alperovitz, Gar, *Atomic Diplomacy: Hiroshima & Potsdam.**

Barnet, Richard J., *Roots of War.**

Buchanan, A. Russell, ed., *The United States & World War Two,* 2 vols.*

Burns, James M., *Roosevelt: The Soldier of Freedom.**

Divine, Robert A., *Roosevelt & World War Two.**

Feis, Herbert, *From Trust to Terror: The Onset of the Cold War, 1945–1950.**

FitzGerald, Frances, *Fire in the Lake.**

Gaddis, John L., *The United States & the Origins of the Cold War.**

Kolko, Joyce and Gabriel, *The Limits of Power.**

LaFeber, Walter, *America, Russia and the Cold War, 1945–1971.**

Maddox, Robert J., *The New Left & the Origins of the Cold War.*

Smith, Gaddis, *American Diplomacy During the Second World War.**

Ulam, Adam B., *The Rivals: America & Russia Since World War Two.**

Walton, Richard J., *Cold War & Counterrevolution.**

Wiltz, John E., *From Isolation to War, 1931–1941.**

Fiction

Buck, Pearl S., *Command the Morning.**

Heller, Joseph, *Catch-22.**

Hersey, John, *Hiroshima.**

*a paperback book

CHAPTER

37

THE ALGER HISS CASE

WHITTAKER CHAMBERS, star witness in the Hiss case, reflected on the importance of the case some years later and wrote to his children:

> Beloved Children,
>
> I am sitting in the kitchen of [our Maryland farm] writing a book. In it I am speaking to you. But I am also speaking to the world. To both I owe an accounting.
>
> It is a terrible book—terrible in what it tells about men, more terrible in what it tells about the world in which you live. It is about what the world calls the Hiss-Chambers case, or even more simply, the Hiss case. It is about a spy case. All the props of an espionage case are there—foreign agents, household traitors, stolen documents, microfilm, furtive meetings, secret hideaways, phony names, an informer, investigations, trials, official justice.
>
> But if the Hiss case were only this, it would not be worth my writing about or your reading about. It would not be what, at the very beginning, I was moved to call it: "a tragedy of history."
>
> For it was more than human tragedy. Much more than Alger Hiss or Whittaker Chambers was on trial in the trials of Alger Hiss. Two faiths were on trial. Human societies, like human beings, live by faith and die when faith dies. At heart, the Great Case was this critical conflict of faiths; that is why it was a great case. On a scale personal enough to be felt by all, but big enough to be symbolic, the two irreconcilable faiths of our time—communism and freedom—came to grips in the persons of two conscious and resolute men. Both had been schooled in the same view of history (the Marxist view). Both were trained by the same party in the same selfless, semisoldierly discipline. Neither would nor could yield without betraying, not himself, but his faith [and] both knew, almost from the beginning, that the Great Case could end only in the destruction of one or both of the contending figures.

Alger Hiss and Whittaker Chambers silently confront each other before the House Un-American Activities Committee in August 1948. The hearings touched off a Red scare that was to have widespread effects in the fifties.

My children, as long as you live, the shadow of the Hiss case will brush you. In time you will ask yourselves the question: What was my father?

I will give you an answer: I was a witness. A witness, in the sense that I am using the word, is a man whose life and faith are so completely one that when the challenge comes to step out and testify for his faith, he does so, disregarding all risks, accepting all consequences.

Alger Hiss, chief among those high government officials accused of communist connections, related the circumstances surrounding his involvement in the investigation:

In August 1948 I was living in New York City. For the preceding year and a half I had been president of the Carnegie Endowment for International Peace. To accept that position I had resigned from the State Department, where I was director of the office responsible for proposing and carrying out our policies in the United Nations.

My new work was closely related to what I had been doing in Washington, for the Endowment had decided to concentrate its activities on support of the United Nations as the appropriate means of furthering Andrew Carnegie's aim "to hasten the abolition of international war, the foulest blot upon our civilization."

On Monday, August 2, 1948 a reporter reached me by telephone at my apartment. He told me that, according to information coming from the Committee on Un-American Activities of the House of Representatives, a man named Chambers was going to appear before the committee the next morning and call me a communist. The reporter asked whether I had any comment.

I did not. The untruthful charge of communism had been the lot of many who had been New Deal officials in the Washington of the 1930s and the early 1940s. I had not taken such charges seriously when made against others, and I saw no reason why I or anyone else should pay much attention to a similar fanciful charge that might now be made against me.

The next morning a witness named Whittaker Chambers appeared before the committee and said that years before he had been "attached" to "an underground organization of the United States Communist party" in Washington. He said that I had been a member of that group.

As I knew no one named Whittaker Chambers I chose to make my denials not only to the newspapers but in the same setting where the charges had been made. Therefore, I sent a telegram to the committee that same afternoon saying that I wanted to appear to deny Chambers's charges under oath.

Richard Nixon, then an obscure congressman from California, considered the case the first major crisis he would face while in public life:

My name, my reputation, and my career were ever to be linked with the decisions I made and the actions I took in that case, as a thirty-five-year-old freshman congressman in 1948. Yet, when I was telling my fifteen-year-old daughter, Tricia, one day about the [subject], she interrupted me to ask, "What was the Hiss case?"

I realized for the first time that a whole new generation of Americans was now growing up who had not even heard of the Hiss case. And now, in retrospect, I wonder how many of my own generation really knew the facts and implications of that emotional controversy that rocked the nation. I experienced [the case] not only as an acute personal crisis but as a vivid case study of the continuing crisis of our times, a crisis with which we shall be confronted as long as aggressive international communism is on the loose in the world.

The Hiss case began for me personally when David Whittaker Chambers appeared before the House Committee on Un-American Activities to testify on communist infiltration into the federal government. Never in the stormy history of the committee was a more sensational investigation started by a less impressive witness.

Chambers did not ask to come before the committee so that he could single out and attack Alger Hiss. The committee had subpoenaed him. Both in appearance and in what he had to say, he made very little impression on me or the other committee members. None of us thought his testimony was going to be especially important.

AUGUST 3, 1948. Six congressmen took their seats in a near empty House committee hearing room: Karl E. Mundt (South Dakota), John McDowell (New Jersey), John E. Rankin (Mississippi), J. Hardin Peterson (Florida), F. Edward Hebert (Lousiana), and Richard M. Nixon (California). Robert E. Stripling, chief investigator of the House Un-American Activities committee (HUAC), called the sole witness waiting to testify—David Whittaker Chambers. Chambers, not an impressive-looking witness, still had quite good credentials. He had combined two public careers over the previous twenty years as a journalist and a gifted translator. Educated at Columbia College, he was fluent in several languages and had translated into English such popular works as the children's book *Bambi.*

Chambers had been subpoenaed the previous day. In answer to Stripling's questions Chambers said that in the 1920s and 1930s he had been a Communist party member "and a paid functionary of the party." He added:

In 1937 I repudiated Marx's doctrines and Lenin's tactics. For a number of years I had served in the underground, chiefly in Washington, D.C. The underground group [included] Alger Hiss. The purpose of this group at that time was not primarily espionage. Its original purpose was the communist infiltration of the American government. But espionage was one of its eventual objectives.

The committee members questioned Chambers at length about his charges. He pointed out that on several previous occasions in the past decade, he had given similar testimony to high State Department

On his role as star witness in the case against Alger Hiss, Chambers said, "I have testified against him with remorse and pity, but in the moment of history in which this nation now stands, so help me God, I could not do otherwise."

officials and to the FBI. No action, however, had ever been taken against any officials he had named as communists. The witness went on to suggest that he and Hiss had been particularly close:

> MR. STRIPLING: When you left the Communist party in 1937, did you approach any of these seven [alleged underground members] to break with you?
>
> MR. CHAMBERS: No. The only one of those people whom I approached was Alger Hiss. I went to the Hiss home one evening at what I considered considerable risk to myself and found Mrs. Hiss at home. Mrs. Hiss is also a member of the Communist party. Mr. Hiss came in shortly afterward, and we talked and I tried to break him away from the party. As a matter of fact, he cried when we separated; but when I left him, he absolutely refused to break. I was very fond of Mr. Hiss.

Despite repeated questions by committee members, Chambers stood by his charges and pointedly denied that the alleged communist underground group within the New Deal had ever committed espionage:

> These people were specifically not wanted to act as sources of information. These people were an elite group, which it was believed would rise to positions—as, indeed, some of them did—notably Mr. Hiss—in the government. Their position in the government would be of much more service to the Communist party.

Newsmen present promptly reported the hottest news item in the morning's testimony: a senior editor of *Time* magazine had accused the president of the Carnegie Endowment of being a secret Soviet agent!

August 5, 1948. It was now Alger Hiss' turn to appear before the committee. He offered a striking contrast to his stout and untidy accuser. His handsome face seemed cool and relaxed. His tall, lean body was fitted with elegant, carefully pressed clothes. Furthermore, he displayed none of Chambers' evident nervousness under questioning. Hiss began his testimony with a prepared statement.

> I am not and never have been a member of the Communist party. I do not and never have adhered to the tenets of the Communist party. I am not and never have been a member of any communist-front organization. I have never followed the Communist party line, directly or indirectly. To the best of my knowledge, none of my friends is a communist. To the best of my knowledge I never heard of Whittaker Chambers until 1947, when two representatives of the Federal Bureau of Investigation asked me if I knew him and various other people. I said I did not know Chambers. So far as I know, I have never laid eyes on him, and the statements made about me by Mr. Chambers are complete fabrications. I think my record in the government service speaks for itself.

Committee members questioned Hiss at length about his impressive government career. It included being secretary to the great Chief

Justice Oliver Wendell Holmes and assistant counsel to the Senate's Nye Committee (see Chapter 36). He also served with the Solicitor General of the United States and then held high posts in the State Department until he left in 1947 to head the Carnegie Endowment.

Then HUAC members and Stripling questioned Hiss about Chambers' accusations:

> MR. MUNDT: I wonder what possible motive a man who edits *Time* magazine would have for mentioning Alger Hiss in connection with [communist involvement].
>
> MR. HISS: So do I, Mr. Chairman. I have no possible understanding of what could have motivated him.

The committee members recognized by this time that, in Stripling's words, there was "very sharp contradiction" between Hiss and Chambers. One of the two men was a monumental liar. Yet according to Mundt, both men were "witnesses whom normally one would assume to be perfectly reliable. They have high positions in American business or organizational work. They both appear to be honest. They both testify under oath [yet their] stories fail to jibe."

At this point Congressman Nixon suggested that Hiss and Chambers "be allowed to confront each other so that any possibility of a mistake in identity may be cleared up." The other HUAC members ignored Nixon's suggestion, and the questioning continued. After Hiss concluded his testimony, a large crowd of spectators and reporters rushed up to congratulate him. Nixon later expressed the feelings of most of them—and of most members of HUAC—when he said that a terrible mistake had been made. The committee, he thought, owed an apology to Hiss. It should not have allowed Chambers to testify without first checking into the possibility of such a mistake.

A journalist confirmed this reaction when he asked Hiss: "How is the committee going to dig itself out of this hole?" HUAC was already being criticized widely for its careless handling of hearings. There was even a strong possibility that President Truman, if he won the upcoming 1948 election, would ask Congress to disband the committee. That same morning, while Hiss was denying Chambers' charges before the committee, Truman denounced HUAC's current spy investigation. He called it a red herring organized by the Republican-dominated committee to distract the public from the party's failure to pass an effective domestic economic program.

Thus, from the beginning, the Hiss-Chambers testimony was an issue in national politics, threatening Republican chances in the fall elections. "This case is going to kill the committee," one reporter told Nixon after the morning session had ended, "unless you can prove

Chambers' story." The reporter did not know that this was exactly what Nixon intended to do.

Richard Milhous Nixon was then a freshman representative from Southern California. His family, like millions of others, had suffered during the depression. He had worked hard from his earliest years. After largely supporting himself through college and law school, Nixon worked briefly in Washington and then served as a naval officer during World War II. Returning to California, he ran for Congress. In his campaign he charged his Democratic opponent with being a radical and procommunist. The tactic was successful, and he won the election. During his first year and a half in Congress, he had not acquired any wide reputation beyond his home district. Soon this would change.

Nixon later wrote that when HUAC met privately after Hiss testified, "it was in a virtual state of shock." For his part Nixon argued:

> While it would be virtually impossible to prove that Hiss was or was not a communist—for that would simply be his word against Chambers'—we should be able to establish whether or not the two men knew each other. If Hiss were lying about not knowing Chambers, then he might also be lying about whether or not he was a communist.

Nixon managed to persuade the acting committee chairman, Karl Mundt, to appoint him head of a subcommittee to question Chambers again. This time the session was to be private, with no spectators or press present.

Alger and Priscilla Hiss at first denied any knowledge of Chambers, then conceded that they knew him under another name when he exposed numerous details of their personal lives to the committee.

August 7, 1948. The HUAC subcommittee headed by Nixon questioned Chambers secretly in New York City. Nixon asked in what period Chambers had known Hiss as a communist. The witness answered "roughly, between the years 1935 and 1937." Chambers said Hiss knew him not by his real name but "by the party name of Carl." He also asserted that he collected Communist party membership dues from Mr. and Mrs. Hiss. According to Chambers, therefore, Hiss was a member of the communist underground infiltrating the government. Moreover, he was also a dues-paying member of the party itself. At this point Nixon plunged into a detailed, rapid-fire series of questions testing whether Hiss had known Chambers. Specifically, Nixon noted, he wanted to know "What should one man know about another if he knew him as well as Chambers claimed to know Hiss?"

Chambers apparently remembered a great deal about the Hisses, although as Nixon later admitted: "All of this information might have been obtained by studying Hiss' life without actually knowing him. But some of the answers had a personal ring of truth about them beyond the bare facts themselves." Chambers claimed he had seen the Hisses on numerous occasions. He had been a guest at their home several times. He also seemed to recall a great many details about the Hisses' private lives: nicknames for one another, eating and drinking habits, pets, personal mannerisms, relatives, the exteriors and furniture of their various homes.

Perhaps the most damaging details that Chambers provided about Hiss during the questioning concerned two episodes. One was the transfer of a car Hiss owned to another communist. The other impressed Nixon because it had a "personal ring of truth." It concerned a hobby the Hisses had in common. Both were amateur ornithologists, bird watchers. Chambers testified, "I recall once they saw, to their great excitement, a prothonotary warbler." At this point Congressman McDowell, also a bird lover, interrupted to ask, "A very rare specimen?" Chambers replied, "I never saw one. I am also fond of birds."

The mass of detail concerning the Hisses' lives—birds, cars, homes, nicknames, and the like—restored a faith in Chambers' honesty among committee members.

August 16, 1948. At this closed session of HUAC Hiss seemed under severe strain. The cool composure of his earlier appearance before the committee had given way to a mixture of nervousness and anger. Nixon showed Hiss two pictures of Chambers and asked again whether he knew the man "either as Whittaker Chambers or as Carl or as any other individual." Hiss began to waver, admitting that "the face has a certain familiarity." Chief counsel Stripling and the committee members confronted Hiss with Chambers' detailed claims concerning their friendship. They probed for evidence confirming the *Time* editor's account.

Hiss repeatedly protested the committee's refusal to provide him with a transcript of Chambers' earlier testimony. He became increasingly hostile. He was angry that the committee found it difficult to decide whether truth was on the side of Chambers—"a confessed former communist" and "self-confessed traitor"—or himself, a highly respected man. Stripling, in turn, snapped back sharply that Chambers had "sat there and testified for hours. He said he spent a week in your house, and he just rattled off details like that. He has either made a study of your life in great detail or he knows you."

Moments after this exchange Hiss announced: "I have written a name on this pad in front of me of a person whom I knew in 1933 and 1934 who not only spent some time in my house but sublet my apartment." Hiss was not sure this person—a free-lance writer named

Alger Hiss lived in this apartment house in Washington, D.C., from 1934-35. He admitted that he let Chambers sublet his apartment for a time in 1935.

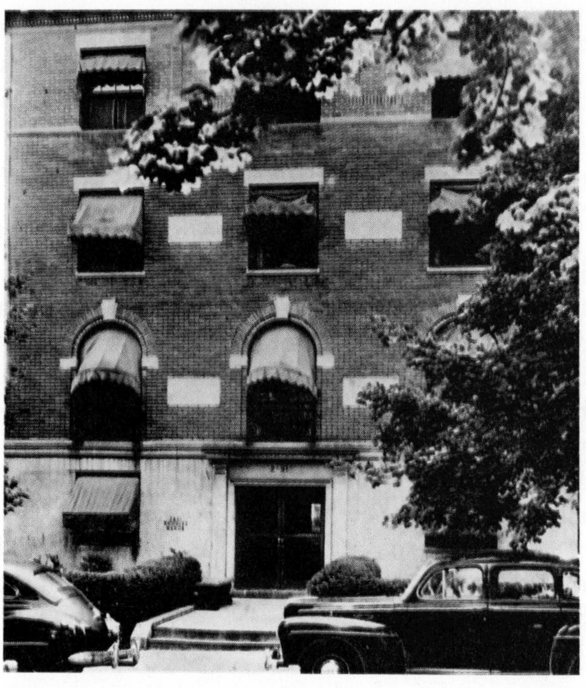

George Crosley—was Chambers. He insisted that he had not seen Crosley since 1934. Hiss gave a detailed account of this relationship, claiming to have met Crosley while he was legal counsel to the Nye Committee in 1933.

Crosley, he said, wished to write several magazine articles about the Nye Committee's munitions-industry investigation. Hiss added that he took a liking to the young journalist. When moving his family to a new apartment, Hiss briefly sublet his old apartment to Crosley and his family. At the same time he gave the journalist "an old Ford we had kept for sentimental reasons." Crosley never paid the rent money, according to Hiss. As for the car, "I threw it in along with the rent" because of a desire to "get rid of it." Deciding that he "had been a sucker and [Crosley] was a sort of deadbeat using me for a soft touch," Hiss said he never saw the man again after 1935. (He later changed the date to mid-1936.)

Hiss also remembered taking several drives with Crosley and giving him "loans [he] never paid back." Once Crosley gave him "a rug he said some wealthy patron gave him. I have still got the damned thing." At one point Nixon asked Hiss about his hobbies. When the witness mentioned bird watching, Congressman McDowell asked: "Did you ever see a prothonotary warbler?" "I have right here on the Potomac," Hiss replied, unaware of Chambers' earlier testimony.

Several members of HUAC remarked during Hiss' testimony that either he or Chambers was obviously committing perjury. "Whichever one of you is lying is the greatest actor that America has ever produced," exclaimed Congressman Hebert. Before adjourning the bitterly tense executive session, the committee decided to have Chambers and Hiss testify publicly, together, nine days later on August 25. Actually, the pair confronted one another the following day at a hurriedly arranged HUAC meeting in New York City.

August 17, 1948. The session was moved up, according to Nixon, to prevent Hiss from gaining "nine more days to make his story fit the facts." In fact there may have been another motive. The committee was uneasy over the death of Harry Dexter White, a former high Treasury Department official. He had died of a heart attack. White had appeared before a HUAC public hearing a few days earlier to deny charges leveled by Chambers that he had been either a party member or procommunist. He had asked for a postponement because of his bad heart but was refused. White had proved a good witness in his own defense despite the committee's attempt to browbeat him. Nixon and the other HUAC subcommittee members obviously hoped to divert public outrage over White's untimely death following this grueling interrogation. They would shift attention to the still active Hiss-Chambers investigation.

Throughout the session, Hiss was extremely irritable, angry, and defensive. He observed that Harry Dexter White's death had upset him greatly, so that testifying would be difficult. He also protested that the committee (despite promises to the contrary) had leaked portions of his previous day's testimony to the press. (Both Nixon and Stripling denied this charge.) Finally Chambers, who had been waiting in an adjoining room, was brought in.

> MR. NIXON: Sit over here, Mr. Chambers. Mr. Chambers, will you please stand? And will you please stand, Mr. Hiss? Mr. Hiss, the man standing here is Mr. Whittaker Chambers. I ask you now if you have ever known that man before.
>
> MR. HISS: May I ask him to speak? Will you ask him to say something?
>
> MR. NIXON: Yes. Mr. Chambers, will you tell us your name and your business?
>
> MR. CHAMBERS: My name is Whittaker Chambers. [At this point, Hiss walked toward Chambers.] I am senior editor of *Time* magazine.
>
> MR. HISS: Are you George Crosley?
>
> MR. CHAMBERS: Not to my knowledge. You are Alger Hiss, I believe.
>
> MR. HISS: I certainly am.
>
> MR. CHAMBERS: That was my recollection. [Chambers read from a magazine so that Hiss could test his voice pattern.]

Hiss then announced that Chambers was probably the man he knew as Crosley. Nixon and Stripling began a lengthy series of questions comparing Hiss' version of the relationship with Crosley—apartment rental, car transfer, gift of a rug, and other details—with the facts previously supplied by Chambers. Hiss of course denied that Crosley had been more than a casual acquaintance, saying, "He meant nothing to me." Chambers again stressed their common bond, stating, "I was a communist, and you were a communist." At last Hiss acknowledged, "I am perfectly prepared to identify this man as George Crosley." But he denied knowing whether "Crosley" had ever been a communist and pointed out that "it was a quite different atmosphere in Washington then than today." He insisted he had known Crosley only as a journalist.

August 25, 1948. The hearing room was clogged with reporters and spectators. The hearing lasted nine hours. (Hiss testified for six, Chambers for three.) Not only Hiss but all seven other alleged members of the communist cell whom Chambers had named had meanwhile testified before HUAC. Except for Hiss' brother, Donald, who joined Alger in specifically denying any communist associations, the others refused to say whether they had been communists. In their refusals all cited the Fifth Amendment, which provides protection from possible self-incrimination.

From the start Hiss, accompanied by his lawyer, treated the occasion as a kind of trial. He was convinced that HUAC believed Chambers and wished mainly to prepare evidence for a perjury charge against him. Therefore, Hiss was extremely guarded in responding. He qualified his answers with phrases such as "to the best of my recollection" more than 200 times. On several occasions he accused HUAC of believing Chambers largely for political reasons. The Republican-controlled committee, he claimed, wanted to expose a top civil servant closely identified with Democratic-sponsored programs like the New Deal, the Yalta agreements, and the United Nations.

The day went badly for Hiss. At the start both Hiss and Chambers were directed to stand. Hiss again identified the *Time* editor as Crosley. Chambers again claimed to have known Hiss in the communist underground. Some of the most damaging passages for Hiss involved the Ford car. He had previously testified turning it over to Crosley along with his apartment.

> MR. NIXON: Did you give Crosley a car?
>
> MR. HISS: I gave Crosley, according to my best recollection . . .
>
> MR. NIXON: You certainly can testify yes or no as to whether you gave Crosley a car. How many cars have you given away in your life, Mr. Hiss?
>
> MR. HISS: I have had only one old car of a financial value of $25 in my life. That is the car I let Crosley use.

A smiling Alger Hiss shakes hands with President Truman at a conference to establish the United Nations. Because Hiss was a New Deal liberal, his fall from grace carried the implication that the government was permeated with communists.

MR. NIXON: My point now is, is your present testimony that you did or did not give Crosley a car?

MR. HISS: Whether I transferred title to him in a legal, formal sense; whether I gave him the car outright; whether the car came back—I don't know.

Unfortunately for Hiss, a title search by HUAC agents produced evidence that Hiss had transferred the car on July 23, 1936, to William Rosen, the alleged communist about whom Chambers had testified earlier. The Hiss signature on the document had been notarized by W. Marvin Smith. He was a lawyer with the Justice Department. Smith told HUAC that he knew Hiss and that Hiss had personally signed the transfer in his presence. (Strangely, Smith fell, jumped, or was pushed to his death soon after he testified.)

Hiss now counterattacked. He denounced HUAC's investigation as a political attack on liberal Democrats. He reviewed his fifteen years of impressive public service and named as references for his achievements, personal character, and loyalty thirty-four prominent public figures. Nixon termed this an effort by Hiss to prove his "innocence by association," an ironic reference considering HUAC's past reputation for trying to show a witness' guilt by association.

During this day's testimony the two major witnesses reversed their previous roles completely. Chambers was now a cool, placid witness, calmly answering every question put to him. Hiss testified nervously and emotionally. But Hiss emphasized that a number of Chambers' most obvious statements about him were incorrect. Thus Hiss was not deaf in one ear, the Hisses were not teetotalers, their stepson was not a "puny little boy," and Hiss did attend church. Despite these and other important errors about the Hisses, Chambers still displayed remarkable familiarity with their private life.

Hiss offered some explanation for this apparent familiarity. He claimed that Chambers, with access to *Time*'s excellent research records, could have discovered most of the personal material on Hiss in such publications as *Who's Who*. Congressman Hebert retorted: "Nobody could have read in *Who's Who* that you found a rare bird [the prothonotary warbler]." Hiss responded that he had "told many, many people." But this did not persuade the committee.

For his part, Chambers denied that he harbored any secret reason for wishing to ruin Hiss, as the latter charged. He went so far as to call Alger Hiss "the closest friend I ever had in the Communist party." Fighting back tears, he said softly:

> I am [not] working out some old grudge, or motives of revenge or hatred. I do not hate Mr. Hiss. We were close friends, but we are caught in a tragedy of history. Mr. Hiss represents the concealed enemy against which we are all fighting, and I am fighting.

By the time HUAC finally adjourned its August 25th session at 8 P.M., Alger Hiss had been placed on the defensive. Three days later HUAC issued an interim report. It called Hiss' testimony "vague and evasive," Chambers' "forthright and emphatic." In the committee's opinion "the verifiable portions of Chambers' testimony have stood up strongly; the verifiable portions of Hiss' testimony have been badly shaken."

The next act in this "tragedy of history" took place on a national radio show, *Meet the Press*. There, Chambers charged that "Alger Hiss was a communist and may be now." Several weeks passed without Hiss responding. His supporters grew impatient. "Mr. Hiss has created a situation," complained the liberal Washington *Post*, "in which he is obliged to put up or shut up." Finally, on September 27, Hiss brought suit against Chambers for libel. By then the election campaign was in full swing. HUAC members (including Nixon) had returned to their various states. An exciting four-way battle for the presidency crowded "the Hiss-Chambers case" off the front pages.

Nixon himself faced no reelection problem. He had won his district's Democratic *and* Republican nominations, then possible under California's cross-filing system that allowed candidates to enter both primaries. He did campaign for other Republicans, however, regaling crowds with a dramatic account of the Hiss investigation.

In the presidential election Truman ran against Governor Thomas E. Dewey of New York, who avoided the anticommunist issue because he believed no case could be made against Truman as "soft" on communism. After a hard-fought campaign Truman won a startling reelection victory. The Democrats, moreover, regained control of Congress.

Prospects for continuing the Hiss-Chambers inquiry looked bleak, since Truman still considered it a political red herring directed against his administration. After the election many in Washington thought the President would try to abolish HUAC. The Hiss case itself dropped from public attention and went into its legal phase—a libel suit.

Deeply depressed by Truman's victory, Chambers even contemplated suicide (an action he considered at other critical points in the case). He also fretted at the possibility that a Justice Department controlled by Democrats might indict him, not Hiss, for perjury. Pressed for written proof of his charges and under severe emotional strain, Chambers (according to his own account) took a mid-November trip to Brooklyn. There he visited a nephew with whom, he claimed, he had left a package ten years earlier. The nephew drew from a disused dumbwaiter shaft the "proof" Chambers needed—a dusty envelope containing papers that (Chambers later insisted) he had forgotten about until the libel suit jogged his memory.

The papers were dated from early 1937 through April 1938. If genuine, they indicated that Hiss had lied in claiming not to have seen "Crosley" or Chambers after mid-1936. Furthermore, the papers had apparently been typed on an old Woodstock typewriter that belonged to the Hisses until 1937 or 1938. (The exact date that the Hisses got rid of the machine would later become a major point at issue.) Chambers hurried back to his farm with this evidence and hid the microfilms. On November 17, he submitted some of the material to Hiss' attorneys at a pretrial hearing—sixty-five pages of copied State Department documents, four memos in Alger Hiss' handwriting, and the envelope in which they had been hidden for a decade.

Chambers now claimed that he had tried until then to "shield" Alger and Priscilla Hiss from exposure as Soviet spies. But because of the pressures imposed by Hiss' libel suit, he had to reveal "that Alger Hiss had also committed espionage." Chambers then testified to Hiss' attorneys about a new claim. He allegedly was a courier for Hiss while the latter stole secret State Department documents. Some of these Mrs. Hiss had retyped while others Chambers had microfilmed. The *Time* editor now asserted that he had actually left the party in April 1938 rather than in 1937, since some of the stolen documents dated from the later period. Hiss vigorously denied this new charge. His lawyers grilled both Chambers and his wife sharply about the numerous contradictions between his previous and his new testimony.

The typed documents were explosive evidence. The Hiss and Chambers lawyers immediately turned them over to Alex Campbell, the head of the Justice Department's Criminal Division. Campbell warned both parties to the libel suit not to discuss the envelope's

Under pressure to provide HUAC with all the evidence against Hiss in his possession, Chambers led two HUAC investigators to the pumpkin patch on his farm (an arrow identifies the patch) and retrieved the microfilms from a hollowed-out pumpkin.

contents (neither Campbell nor Hiss then knew of the microfilms) until the material had been investigated. But then a story in the pro-Hiss Washington *Post* indicating that the Justice Department might drop its investigation of Hiss spurred Nixon into action. Before leaving for a Caribbean vacation, Nixon signed a subpoena ordering Chambers to provide HUAC with any further evidence he had relating to his charges against Hiss.

On the night of December 4 HUAC staff members served the subpoena. A few hours earlier, because of rumors that Hiss investigators were prowling around his farm, Chambers had taken the microfilms from his bedroom and hidden them in his pumpkin patch. Now he went to the hollowed-out pumpkin, removed the microfilms inside, and handed them to the HUAC representatives. "I think this is what you are looking for," he said. Within hours the press began headlining Chambers' mysterious "pumpkin papers" (actually not papers but microfilms). That same day Hiss confirmed the existence of the typed stolen documents produced on November 17.

The Justice Department finally swung into action. Both Chambers and Hiss were called several times, beginning on December 6, to testify before a New York federal grand jury. After a hurried and well-publicized return from his Caribbean vacation, Nixon led HUAC in a new series of hearings. At one of these new sessions Assistant Secretary of State John Peurifoy (in charge of security matters) testified. He declared that the Soviet Union or any other foreign country possessing these microfilmed documents would have been able to break all the secret State Department codes then in use.

Clearly, the Republican-controlled HUAC, which had no legal authority to put Hiss on trial, was competing with the Democratic-controlled Justice Department for jurisdiction in what was now a criminal case. Nixon frankly stated that his committee "did not trust the Justice Department to prosecute the case with the vigor it deserved." On December 9 Truman again labeled the case a red herring. On December 10 Chambers resigned from *Time*.

On December 13 the FBI produced for the grand jury several old letters typed by Priscilla Hiss on the same machine that had typed the State Department documents. That day, Alger Hiss left the Carnegie Endowment on a three-month paid leave of absence. He never returned. The New York grand jury indicted Hiss on two counts of perjury on December 15. The first was for claiming he had not stolen State Department records and given them to Chambers. The second was for swearing he had not seen Chambers after January 1, 1937.

Only the statute of limitations and the absence of witnesses who could back up the charge kept the grand jury from charging Hiss with espionage.

The former State Department official underwent two trials. The first ended on July 8, 1949, with a deadlocked jury that had voted 8 to 4 to convict Hiss. The prosecutor at both trials, Thomas Murphy, presented several types of evidence to prove the government's perjury charges. These included evidence that the two men knew one another more intimately (after 1936) than Hiss admitted, that Hiss had been a communist, and that Hiss had stolen the State Department documents. The weakest link in the government's case concerned Hiss' alleged communism. Only one witness, a professional ex-communist named Hede Massing, confirmed Chambers' claim that Hiss had been a party member. Her testimony was effectively challenged, however, by a reputable defense witness who swore that Mrs. Massing had told him an entirely different (and more innocent) story about Hiss.

At both trials Chambers repeated the story he first told to Hiss' attorneys in November 1948 during pretrial hearings involving the libel suit. According to this story, Hiss had been recruited for espionage by Chambers' communist superior during the fall of 1937. Chambers changed the date to January 1937 at the first trial, which made it possible for Hiss to have stolen all of the documents in question. Chambers said he served as Hiss' courier until April 1938. Then he broke from the party. (He previously testified to leaving the party months earlier.) At this point he turned the final batch of stolen documents over to his nephew in Brooklyn for safekeeping.

The microfilms and retyped State Department messages were at the heart of the case against Hiss. Prosecutor Murphy called them "immutable" witnesses, therefore presumably reliable ones. At neither trial did Hiss' attorneys challenge an FBI expert. He testified that a comparison of typing on the documents with other letters written by Mrs. Hiss on the same machine established her as the typist. Nor did they challenge the argument that the documents had been typed on a Woodstock machine belonging to Hiss. Hiss did claim he had given the machine away sometime before the material was typed. But this claim was never proved conclusively in court, one way or the other.

The jury at the second trial convicted Hiss of perjury on both counts. After that Hiss' lawyers began arguing that the typewriter itself was a false piece of evidence constructed by either Chambers or the FBI. They also argued that the typed documents had been prepared only to implicate Hiss. (This argument, of course, did not affect the microfilmed documents or the handwritten Hiss memos.) Since the defense had actually located the typewriter in question prior to the first

A withdrawn and beaten Alger Hiss sits on a New York subway trying to ignore headlines telling of his indictment the day before on perjury charges. He was eventually convicted but on highly disputed evidence.

trial, Hiss' supporters began arguing that the FBI somehow gained possession of the machine earlier, then "planted" it on the defense. This remains unproven even today, though those who argue that Alger Hiss was innocent tend to assume some degree of FBI involvement.

Another troubling point about Chambers' story concerns his claim to have broken with the Communist party as late as April 1938, in time to have received from Hiss the last of the secret documents. A mass of documentary evidence—too extensive to reprint here—indicates that Chambers actually broke with the party earlier that year, probably in February, when he began working as a free-lance translator. If this was true, or course, Chambers could not possibly have collected the last few months' worth of stolen government papers from Hiss. This would cast grave doubt on the authenticity of *all* the secret documents.

Thus two sets of "immutable witnesses" exist in this confusing case. The first involves Chambers' break with communism sometime

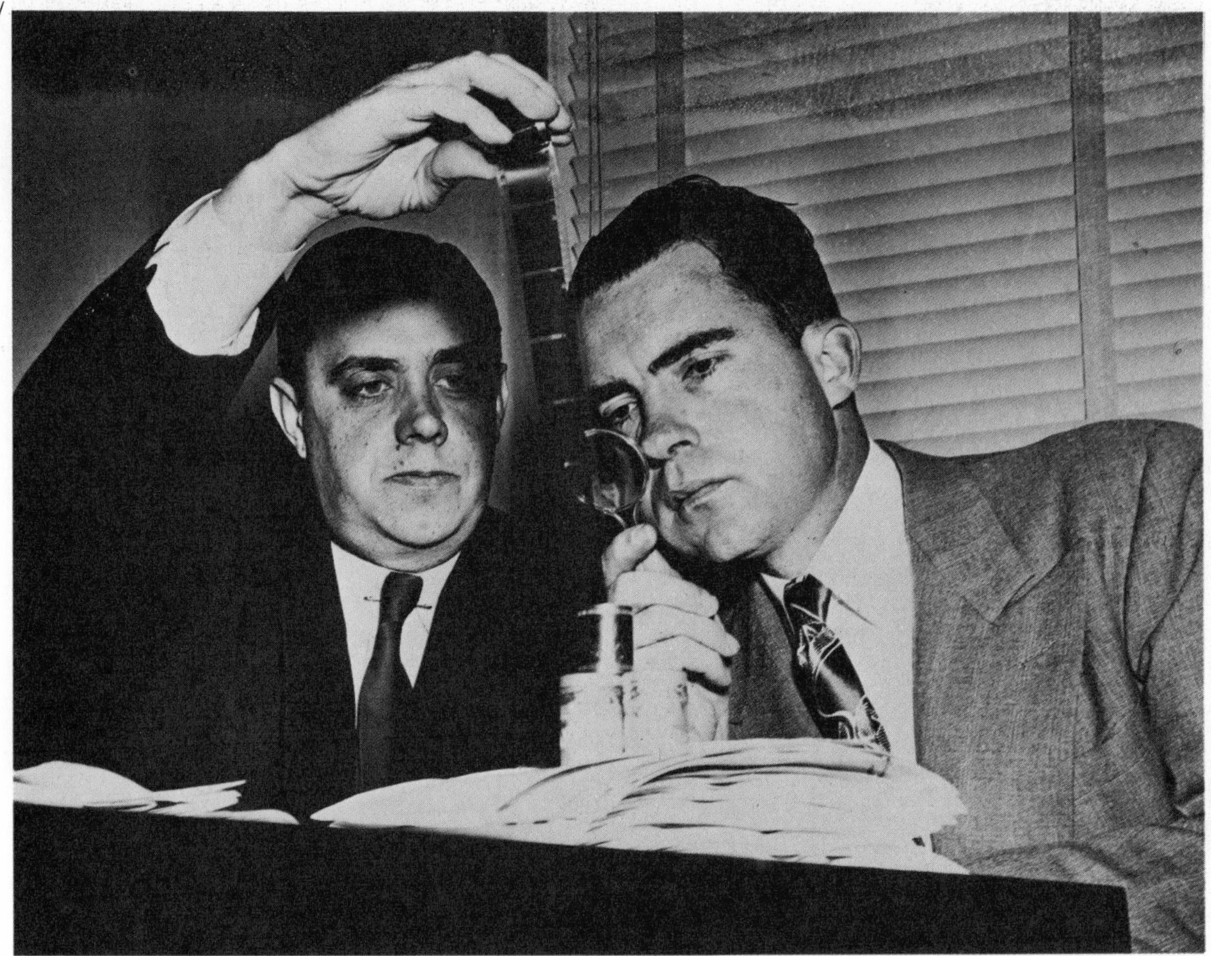

Richard Nixon and chief investigator Robert Stripling are shown examining microfilms of secret State Department documents, the most damaging evidence against Hiss, though their authenticity has been challenged.

before March 1938. The second concerns a collection of State Department documents allegedly stolen by Hiss but dating through April 1, 1938. The essential mystery of this episode centers on the difficulty in resolving these two facts.

Unfortunately for Hiss, the defense did not stress this point at either of his trials. Instead, they paraded a distinguished group of Americans before the jury to testify to Hiss' excellent career and good character. At the same time, they tried to throw doubt on Chambers' reliability. They placed a psychiatrist on the stand who labeled Chambers "a psychopathic personality" with irrational hostilities.

Prosecutor Murphy ridiculed these defense efforts at both trials. He pointed repeatedly to the evidence that Hiss' lawyers could never adequately explain—the stolen government documents. The twelve jurors at the second trial, overlooking Chambers' inconsistencies, all believed Murphy. On January 21, 1950, they found Hiss guilty. Later appeals to overturn the verdict were rejected, and Hiss served forty-four months in prison. He emerged in November 1954, still proclaiming his innocence.

Hiss, now a convicted perjurer, did not return to the Carnegie Endowment, of course. He has had a series of obscure and ill-paying business jobs. He has written his version of the episode and worked continuously to revive public interest in the case. Chambers returned to his Maryland farm, did special assignments as a journalist, and wrote his memoirs. In 1961, he died from a heart attack.

Nixon won a Senate seat in 1950, largely because of his efforts in the Hiss case. He went on to become Vice President in 1953. The House Committee on Un-American Activities temporarily regained its public prestige as a result of Hiss' conviction. Truman abandoned his effort to abolish it.

Less than three weeks after Hiss' conviction, a then obscure Wisconsin senator announced: "I have here in my hand a list of 205 known to be members of the Communist party and who, nevertheless are still working and shaping the policy of the State Department." With Joseph R. McCarthy's speech a new era of anticommunist politics in the United States acquired its leader—and its name.

CHAPTER

38

Affluence and Anticommunism

THE DEPRESSION ENDED—with a bang, not a whimper—when Japan attacked Pearl Harbor. The war years changed the lives of the two key figures in the Hiss case very little. Alger Hiss remained a top official of the State Department, while Whittaker Chambers rose in importance on *Time* magazine. But Richard Nixon saw his life altered dramatically. Although reared as a Quaker, Nixon yearned for some role in the war effort. He first joined a new government agency, the Office of Price Administration (OPA), created to regulate wartime price levels. Then the young lawyer joined the Navy and served on various Pacific islands, handling duties as a supply officer.

Nixon returned to a restless year of private practice in California before winning his first race for Congress in 1946. The war had clearly opened up significant career possibilities for Nixon, as it did for millions of his contemporaries. A nation still climbing uncertainly out of the depression in 1941 had regained, by war's end, most of its pre-1930 affluence and self-confidence.

THE WORLD WAR II HOME FRONT

Almost 4 million Americans were still unemployed on the eve of Pearl Harbor. They were receiving relief assistance from New Deal welfare and Social Security programs. Other millions still labored at government-sponsored jobs for agencies such as the WPA. Some 40 percent of America's families lived below the $1,500 annual minimum income needed for a family of four. (This amounted to only $30 a week to cover food, housing, clothing, and everything else!) Over 7 1/2 million workers earned salaries below the legal minimum wage of 40 cents an hour.

Still, there were many signs of change in 1941. The economy, thanks largely to $8 billion spent on defense production, was now strong, almost booming. Of the country's 134 million people, 56 million held civilian jobs. A tenth of them worked on defense contracts at top wages. Farm prices reached a new high in 1940, as did average hourly wages in the two dozen major defense-oriented industries.

Moreover, on the eve of war, most Americans supported the pro-Allied policies of the Roosevelt administration. A 1941 Gallup poll revealed that 85 percent believed that the United States would eventually enter the war against Hitler. Still, Americans did not expect a war to improve their condition much. Twelve years of depression had left the country somewhat doubtful of future prospects and skeptical of idealistic visions. Another poll released the week Pearl Harbor was attacked showed that many thought they would have to "work harder after the war." Only a small number felt that the chances for success after a war would be better than before it.

Bolstering Morale The government went to great lengths to counteract pessimism and ensure the cooperative involvement of most Americans in the war effort. The Office of Civilian Defense (OCD) sponsored various programs to stimulate patriotism. These included "town meetings" throughout the country. Their basic objective was "that of awakening all the elements of the community to their responsibilities for total participation for victory." Patriotic sentiments were also aroused by stage, screen, and radio productions. They tried to bolster national morale, particularly in the first year, when news from the fronts was often grim.

Usually such entertainment aimed at stirring up hatred toward the enemy, Germans and Japanese. Seldom did it assert any positive American war goals. Movie heroes such as John Wayne and radio idols like Jack Armstrong ("the all-American boy") battled tirelessly against Japan's fanatical "yellow hordes" or Nazi saboteurs. American advertising encouraged sales of government war bonds or warned defense workers and soldiers to beware of possible spies in their midst. ("Loose lips sink ships!") Such efforts were remarkably successful in achieving greater homefront efforts.

Mobilizing the Economy Conversion to military preparedness had preceded Pearl Harbor. Total mobilization of both the American people and their economy, however, advanced swiftly after December 1941. An army of 1,600,000 existed then. By war's end the number of troops who had served or were serving in the army, navy, marines, air corps (then still part of the army) and coast guard exceeded 15 million—including 200,000 women.

The home front resembled a big factory. A few statistics tell much of the story. Many Americans felt that Roosevelt was being unrealistic when in 1942 he called for an output of 60,000 planes, 45,000 tanks, and 8 million tons of shipping. Yet in 1944 the nation's factory workers—keeping plants open 24 hours daily on continuous shifts—produced over 96,000 planes. By 1945 the country's naval yards had turned out over 55 million tons of merchant shipping and 71,000 warships. Federal purchases grew from $6 billion in 1940 to $89 billion by 1944.

Total federal spending during the three and a half years of war amounted to over $320 billion, an amount twice as large as the total of all previous spending from 1789 to 1941! The government financed this vast increase through higher taxes on both corporations and individuals. Even after taxes, though, corporate profits doubled from 1939 to 1944 (reaching $10 billion that year). Much of the government's revenues came from taxes or public borrowing through war bonds. A still higher percentage came from running huge budget deficits throughout the war. The American national debt grew to $247 billion by 1945, nearly six times that of 1941.

Meanwhile, prosperity returned to the United States, and unemployment vanished. Many women took full-time factory jobs to meet the shortage of labor created by the armed forces' need for men. Public confidence in the business community increased after the widespread hostility apparent during the depression decade.

Rationing and Inflation Full employment during the war gave millions of Americans bigger bank accounts. It put more money in their pockets, though they had less to spend it on. "Disposable income" (income after taxes) increased from $67 billion in 1939 to $140 billion by 1945. Consumer spending alone rose from $62 billion in 1939 to $106 billion by 1945. Wartime rationing and shortages of consumer goods led to an increase in prices for available products or services. Higher wages and profits led, in turn, to higher inflationary prices for most consumer goods when they were available.

When gas and tires were rationed during the war, Whittaker Chambers remembered walking long distances to catch public transportation. Most Americans used gas sparingly and only on special occasions. The great majority, despite the inevitable complaining, accepted the need for such rationing with good humor. But many less honest individuals profited from selling goods at inflated prices illegally on the "black market."

Significant numbers of women belonged to the labor force that produced the winning margin in World War II, a continuous flow of planes from American factories.

The government tried to control inflation and regulate prices—which rose an average of 2 percent monthly during the war—by establishing official wage and price levels. It set ceilings on legal prices through OPA. Richard Nixon remembered his experiences in this agency as a time when he "became more conservative [and] greatly disillusioned about bureaucracy." Yet OPA did succeed in holding down runaway inflation throughout the war years, despite an enormous increase in the disposable income of most Americans.

On the farms conditions improved at this time, too. Farm income doubled during the war because of the insatiable demand for agricultural products by the armed forces and civilians alike. Despite a decline in the number of farm laborers, increased mechanization helped double farm output from 1941 to 1945. During the war legislation by powerful farm bloc Democrats brought farmers' incomes to an all-time high.

Average weekly earnings among industrial workers also increased by 100 percent during the war years. Both the AFL and CIO made "no-strike" pledges. But the number of strikes increased as prices and profits continued rising at a level greater than wage increases. Union membership increased from 10 to 15 million. The demand for factory workers led to a reduction of total unemployment from 5.6 percent of the work force in 1941 to 1 percent by war's end. More important, the war guaranteed the future of industrial unionism, which had grown with New Deal encouragement during the depression.

The Atomic Bomb The period's single most significant scientific and military achievement, which would notably affect postwar American policy, was the development of the atomic bomb. Wartime scientific research was placed in the hands of an Office of Scientific Research and Development (OSRD), headed by Vannevar Bush and James Conant. The United States benefited greatly from the work of refugee scientists, many of them Jews who had fled Nazi Germany or fascist Italy. Albert Einstein, Leo Szilard, and Enrico Fermi led this intellectual migration. It affected not only science but many other aspects of American life and culture.

Because of fears for his Jewish wife, Enrico Fermi fled Fascist Italy in 1938 for the United States. He and his refugee colleagues created the weapon that could have given the Axis powers victory—the atomic bomb.

At a cost of billions a massively organized project was undertaken to develop an atomic bomb before the Germans, who were working on a similar project. The secret program, known as the Manhattan Project, involved scientists, technicians, and industrial workers. It included design laboratories at Columbia University, the University of Chicago, the University of California at Berkeley, and—most important—at a central headquarters near Los Alamos, New Mexico. There, under the leadership of physicist J. Robert Oppenheimer, the first device was assembled. It was detonated on July 16, 1945, at Alamorgordo, New Mexico.

The bombs dropped subsequently at Hiroshima and Nagasaki led directly to Japan's defeat in August 1945. By then the United States had spent over $350 billion to achieve victory in World War II at a tremendous cost in American casualties.

The Relocation Policy The country paid not only a high cost in human life but also a certain

Japanese American children are shown saluting the flag in their San Francisco elementary school two days before their relocation to internment camps.

moral cost for its victory. For the Japanese attack on Pearl Harbor led to what the American Civil Liberties Union called "the worst single invasion of citizens' liberties" during the war. This was the confining in relocation centers of 112,000 Japanese Americans (more than half of them born in the United States). After Pearl Harbor white residents of west coast states feared an internal threat from the Japanese Americans. They appealed to President Roosevelt to remove the entire community from the west coast.

Actually, there was no evidence whatsoever of sabotage. But officials such as California's attorney general Earl Warren (later a great civil libertarian as the Chief Justice of the United States) urged their evacuation to protect the region's civil defense. Bowing to these pressures, President Roosevelt signed an executive order in February 1942 authorizing the relocation of Japanese Americans to nine inland centers. Driven from their homes into these American versions of concentration camps, these loyal Japanese Americans needlessly suffered loss of their freedom, homes, land, and dignity. This unfair treatment did not deter over 33,000 Japanese Americans from enlisting and fighting bravely for the United States. Although the Supreme Court upheld the relocation policy, the government later paid compensation to the displaced for their property losses.

THE TRUMAN YEARS

Franklin D. Roosevelt, reelected for an unprecedented fourth term in 1944, died in April 1945. He left to Vice President Truman the responsibility for governing the world's most militarily powerful and economically properous nation. On learning of Roosevelt's death, Truman quite understandably felt "as though the moon and all the stars and all the planets have fallen on me." Confronted with the galaxy of postwar domestic and foreign problems that existed, Truman had excellent reasons for such feelings.

Harry Truman was an accidental President. Roosevelt had chosen him for the vice-presidential nomination in 1944 almost as an afterthought. Truman had little formal preparation for holding the office. While Vice President, for example, he was not even told about the atomic bomb. Less than four months after taking office, he had to make the fateful decision to drop it on Japan.

A Missouri farm boy who served in World War I, Truman entered politics as a member of the notorious Pendergast machine that ran Kansas City politics. Although personally honest, he served this corrupt political machine loyally. Truman rose through its ranks and was first elected to the Senate in 1934.

Several facts helped Truman secure the vice presidency in 1944. Hard-working and extremely liberal (by Missouri's border-state standards), he had fought the Ku Klux Klan in his home state, battled loyally for New Deal programs, and served with distinction as chairman of a Senate committee that investigated national defense spending. He first seemed understandably insecure as President. ("Boys, if you ever pray," he said to newsmen, "pray for me now.") But he quickly caught on.

Many of Truman's most pressing concerns

during his first months in office were vitally important decisions on war policy and postwar settlements (see Chapter 36). Of immediate concern to the new President, once Japan surrendered, was the fact that the men overseas wanted to come home quickly. ("No Boats, No Votes," was the gist of GI mail.) Congress and President Truman responded by rapidly demobilizing (releasing from duty) the great bulk of American armed forces. By mid-1946 an army and air force of over 8 million troops the previous year was reduced to less than 2 million. A navy of almost 4 million was cut back to less than 1 million. Total military strength fell to 1 1/2 million by mid-1947, and Congress had ordered even this number reduced to under 1 million by January 1948.

Postwar Economic Policy Congress allowed the 1940 draft to expire in mid-1947. Cold War military planning focused more and more on the defense shield provided by America's monopoly of nuclear weapons. Furthermore, the discharged servicemen found that Congress had provided more generously for them than for the Bonus Marchers. Under the Servicemen's Readjustment Act (which most people called the GI Bill of Rights) more than $13.5 billion was spent on veterans in the next decade. This money went not only for college educations and vocational training, but also for special unemployment insurance (for a year) to smooth the return to civilian life. Funds were spent as well on medical help at veterans' hospitals and rehabilitation programs for the wounded. Finally, low-interest loans were available to veterans to start businesses and buy or build homes. This was particularly helpful because of the dire housing shortage at war's end.

The 1944 Democratic platform also promised to guarantee full postwar employment. There was widespread fear among the public, and many economists too, that without war spending the country would suffer a major postwar recession. A Council of Economic Advisers, created by Truman's Maximum Employment Act, committed Washington for the first time to using the nation's resources to ensure "maximum employment, production, and purchasing power." By mid-1946 Congress had also ended most wartime price and wage controls, cut taxes over $6 billion, and begun to tackle the massive problems of reconversion to a peacetime economy. These efforts were hindered by a wave of strikes and runaway inflation.

Auto workers struck for 113 days beginning in November 1945, and miners for a shorter period in mid-1946. Truman's decision to have the soft coal mines run by the government (control that continued until June 1947) lost him much support from businessmen. A railroad strike was settled the same month the mines were seized (May 1946) only when Truman threatened to take over the railroads, too. More strikes occurred in 1946 than in any other single year in American history. Over 4,750,000 workers were involved.

Truman also faced a hostile congressional coalition of Republicans and antiadministration Southern Democrats in every area of his domestic program. This coalition responded to the strikes and general unrest among American unions with a tough law (passed over Truman's veto) regulating the labor movement. The Taft-Hartley Act of 1947 limited the President to seeking an eighty-day injunction to stop any strike that endangered "national health or safety" (rather than taking an extreme step like running an industry under government supervision). The new law also (1) required unions to accept a sixty-day "cooling-off" period before striking, (2) outlawed the closed shop, (3) restricted union involvement in political campaigns, and (4) required that union officials (but not company officers) take an oath that they were not communists.

The Taft-Hartley Act did not succeed in limiting the gains of already existing unions. However, it did impede union activity in industries, such as Southern textiles, that were not yet fully organized. Congress also passed the Twenty-second Amendment to the Constitution limiting future Presidents (although not Truman) to two full terms. This was a direct slap at FDR's four-term success. In various ways the Eightieth Congress prevented Truman from getting his own legislative program.

The Fair Deal The President called his program the Fair Deal. He viewed it essentially as an effort to continue the social welfare policies of Roosevelt's New Deal. Thus, soon after he took office, Truman had proposed to Congress legislation that would guarantee full employment, vastly expand public housing, and raise farm price supports. Other proposals were to continue a permanent Fair Employment Practices Committee to block discrimination against blacks and other minorities, nationalize atomic energy, and increase the minimum wage. A few parts of the program passed quickly. Congress approved a civilian Atomic Energy Commission in mid-1946 that took control of peaceful uses of atomic energy. Most of the program, however, was blocked by the same Republican–Southern Democratic coalition that opposed Truman on so many issues.

Truman went on the offensive in 1948. He proposed not only the enactment of his entire Fair Deal program but also a set of civil rights proposals to guarantee first-class citizenship for black Americans. These proposals included a permanent FEPC, measures against lynching and the poll tax, plus other laws that would ensure blacks full federal protection of their civil and political rights. After his renomination by a divided Democratic convention in 1948, Truman called Congress into special session to dramatize its opposition to his programs. He requested repeal of the Taft-Hartley Act and passage of civil rights, housing, health, and Social Security programs. Congress rejected it all.

This rejection allowed Truman to conduct his successful "whistle-stop" campaign (see Chapter 37) against what he called the "do-nothing Eightieth Congress." The public liked Truman's new stance as an aggressive, "give-em-hell" fighter. The Man from Independence scored the most smashing upset in American presidential history. The Democrats also recaptured both houses of Congress.

Still dominated in large measure by the

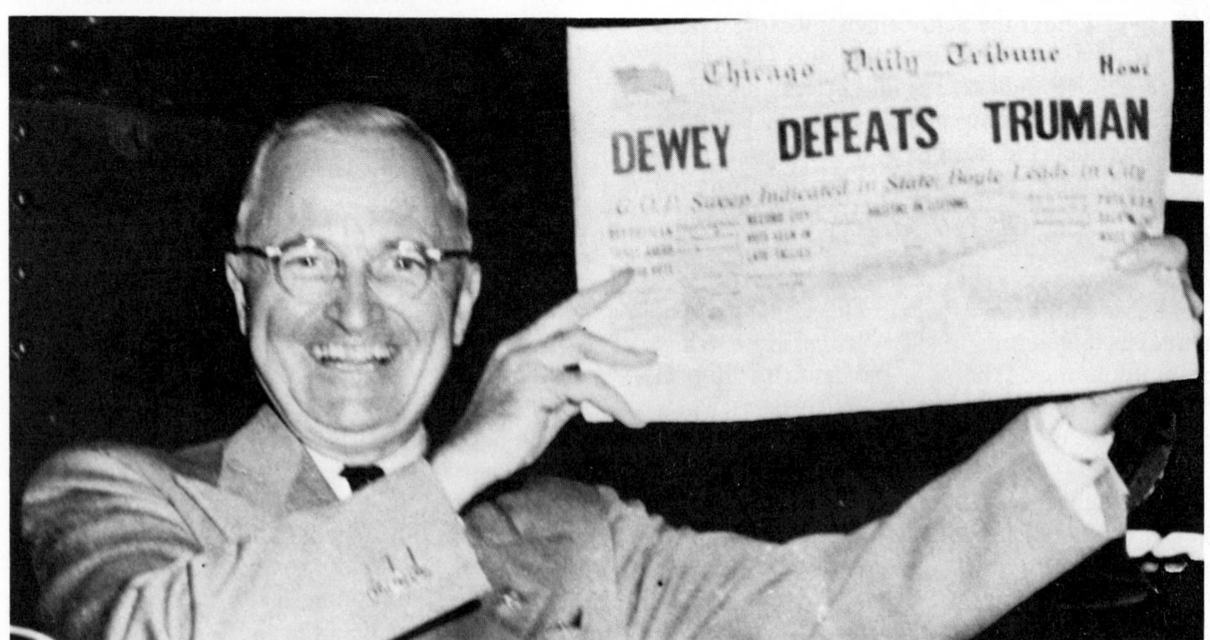

The culmination of Harry Truman's 1948 whistle-stop campaign was this triumphant pose before a crowd at St. Louis' Union Station. He called the headline "one for the books."

Republican–Southern Democratic coalition, the new Eighty-first Congress blocked Truman's farm program and his request for a permanent FEPC. But it did pass a major low-income housing and urban-renewal program, raised the minimum wage, abolished segregation in the armed forces, and enlarged existing conservation programs. All in all, it enacted more liberal legislation than any Congress since that of 1937–38.

The onset of the Korean War in June 1950, however, diverted the primary attention of Congress and the Administration from home-front reforms to foreign policy. Little important domestic legislation passed in Truman's final two years in office. His energy between 1950 and 1952 was spent primarily fighting the Korean War and improving American security against communism abroad. Ironically, he also had to defend his administration against its alleged "softness" towards communism at home.

McCARTHYISM: "THE SECOND RED SCARE"

Truman reacted angrily whenever Republicans charged that his and Roosevelt's administration had "sold out" Eastern Europe and China to communist control. To Republican cries of "Twenty Years of Treason," Truman replied that he had welded the free nations of Western Europe into military and political alliances against the Soviet Union's expansionism. The Truman Doctrine, the Marshall Plan, and NATO had largely restored European stability. China had been lost–not for lack of American help–but through Chiang Kai-shek's political and military weakness.

Elsewhere, American troops (along with UN forces) defended South Korea against communist attack. Further, the Seventh Fleet prevented communist invasion of the Chinese Nationalists' last stronghold, the island of Taiwan. To achieve this global strategy of containment, the Truman administration had increased defense expenditures from $13 billion in 1949 to $22.5 billion the next year and $44 billion by 1951. Military expenses absorbed two-thirds of the federal budget in 1952, up from only one-third in 1950. In the process of increasing defense spending so swiftly and enormously, the country's gross national product rose from $264 billion in 1950 to $339 billion by 1952. A continued high level of economic prosperity was almost assured.

None of these facts, however, silenced Republican critics. They continued to attack Truman and Secretary of State Dean Acheson. Nor were Republican anticommunist investigators like those on HUAC happy with Truman's efforts to rid the federal government of suspected subversives. The President, despite assurances from the FBI that the problem was under adequate control, had issued an executive order in May 1947, setting up a Loyalty Review Board. Its purpose was to check every federal employee and dismiss any found questionable "on reasonable grounds for belief in disloyalty." Over the next five years, such loyalty boards checked out over 6 1/2 million government employees and their families. Of this number only 490 were dismissed on loyalty grounds. The boards uncovered no cases of espionage, but the investigations wrecked the careers of many loyal government officials accused without proof.

Prosecution of Leading Communists Under mounting pressure from Congress after Alger Hiss' indictment, Truman prosecuted the eleven leaders of the American Communist party under the 1940 Smith Act. They were prosecuted for organizing a group advocating the overthrow of the American government by force. The Communist party leaders were convicted in 1949, and other prosecutions of communists began. The Supreme Court upheld the convictions in 1951. Through such actions Truman contributed to a growing climate of American fear over communism.

No single episode did more to spread this Red scare than the indictment and eventual conviction of Alger Hiss. The fact that Dean Acheson and other high administration officials testified on behalf of Hiss lent a touch of credibility to charges that the Democrats, under Roosevelt and Truman, were soft on left-wingers.

At this point Senator Joseph McCarthy began a series of speeches. It mattered little that McCarthy's figures for "known communists" in the State Department varied from speech to speech. Britain had just arrested communist Klaus Fuchs for atomic espionage; the new communist government had full control of the Chinese mainland; and Americans were jittery over possible new Russian moves against Berlin. Accordingly, many people were prepared to believe that something dire was about to befall the United States.

McCarthy's charges offended several Republicans in Congress, including Senators Margaret Chase Smith of Maine and Ralph Flanders of Vermont, who both denounced him publicly. Yet he was extremely useful to his party, despite his wild charges of disloyalty and communist activity in government. A significant number of Americans approved of McCarthy's relentless attacks. McCarthy's method, like that of most successful demagogues, was simple. He used "the multiple untruth," a statement so complex and many-sided that it was extremely difficult to deny intelligently.

A Flow of Political Melodrama Among those McCarthy tried to smear were George Marshall (author of the Marshall Plan), Philip Jessup (later chief UN delegate under President Nixon), Secretary of State Dean Acheson, and even President Truman himself. Truman had helped establish the credibility of politicians like McCarthy with his loyalty program. Other Truman administration activities did lend some support to the widespread popular belief that (in the words of Truman's own Attorney General) "many communists in America [were] everywhere—in factories, offices, butcher stores, on street corners." McCarthy turned this tactic of "Red-baiting" against the Democrats themselves. For a time, he had remarkable success. Little about his methods was new. He used the tactics of HUAC and even borrowed Nixon's files on the subject. From these he wrung a constant flow of political melodrama out of the noisy pursuit of "secret conspirators" and (occasionally) admitted communists. There were, after all, some American communists, even a few who had reached middle-level posts in the Roosevelt years.

The onset of the Korean War in June 1950 gave McCarthy and other Republican opponents of Truman additional ammunition. If communists were killing our soldiers in Korea, many Americans reasoned, why give possible Reds the benefit of any doubt in this country? Loyalty oaths and security investigations soon involved millions of people in industries and labor unions, public schools and universities, as well as in government jobs at every level.

There is much irony in the fact that Truman spent his last two years in office using American and UN forces against communist aggression in Korea while trying to prove that he was not a dupe or agent of communism at home. Truman's attorney general carried on a vigorous prosecution of alleged communist agents. In April 1951 Julius and Ethel Rosenberg were convicted of having directed a spy ring that transmitted to the Russians diagrams and other data on the firing mechanism and internal structure of the atomic bomb. According to the Rosenbergs' accusers, this information speeded up by years completion of the Soviet atomic bomb, first exploded in 1949. The Rosenbergs received the death sentence, while their accomplices were sentenced to long prison terms.

Such episodes persuaded Congress that tighter laws were needed to protect the country against domestic communists. So it passed the McCarran Internal Security Act in 1950. This law established a Subversive Activities Control Board to keep track of communist activities in America. The act made membership in the Communist party illegal and also ordered communist organizations to register with the Attorney General. Other provisions barred former members of totalitarian groups from the United States and forbade communists to hold federal office or receive passports. Many of these provisions have since been declared unconstitu-

To Senator Joseph McCarthy communism was a nationwide threat. He accused the Democrats of communist sympathies and also charged that the Protestant clergy had been infiltrated.

tional by the Supreme Court. But the act passed by a two-thirds majority over Truman's veto, which showed how politically potent the anti-communist issue had become.

"Korea, Communism, and Corruption" The Democratic administration was very unpopular by 1952. Many voters accepted McCarthy's reckless charges against Truman and his associates, despite the Democrats' strong commitment to Cold War foreign policies. Truman's decision to seize the steel industry to prevent a nationwide strike in April 1952 (declared unconstitutional by the courts two months later) reminded Americans of his earlier troubles with labor and management. Several scandals involving big businessmen and Truman's associates had also come to light. So Republicans raised the issue of widespread government corruption. The Korean War dragged on, with American casualties mounting in the most unpopular war fought by the nation until the Vietnamese conflict.

The issues of "Korea, communism, and corruption" that Republicans stressed in 1952 would probably have brought about the election of any candidate after twenty years of Democratic rule. Still, the out-of-power party took no chances. At their 1952 convention the Republicans rejected the candidacy of the able conservative Senator Robert A. Taft of Ohio because they were not sure he could win. They nominated General Dwight David Eisenhower—World War II hero, university president, commander of American NATO forces, and easily the most popular public figure in the country. The party then reaffirmed its concern for the anticommunist issue by nominating Richard Nixon as Vice President.

The Democrats drafted Governor Adlai Stevenson of Illinois, a man who, though able, was assailed by Republicans as an "egghead" because of the intellectual quality of his campaigning. Stevenson's efforts to defend Democratic achievements and promise a continuation of Fair Deal reform fell flat. Many voters were tired after two decades of depression, reform, world war, and Cold War. The public voted to make its grandfatherly first citizen, Dwight Eisenhower, President by an overwhelming 33 to 27 million popular margin and a 442 to 89 electoral majority. After two decades in the political wilderness the Republican party returned to full national power, winning not only the White House but also Congress.

THE EISENHOWER YEARS

With Eisenhower's inauguration in 1953, control of the federal government returned essentially—for the first time since Herbert Hoover—to businessmen. The new President's Cabinet officers were either corporation executives or closely allied to the business community. Eisenhower was determined to run a less activist presidency than either Truman or Roosevelt and was suspicious of the federal bureaucracy and New Deal–Fair Deal social welfare programs. He set himself the task of keeping the nation calm. Wall Street lawyers such as Herbert Brownell (Attorney General) and John Foster Dulles (Secretary of State), corporation presidents George M. Humphrey (Secretary of the Treasury) and Charles E. Wilson (Secretary of Defense) typified Eisenhower's advisers.

Eisenhower interfered less often than Roosevelt or Truman with his various department heads. Instead, he allowed each to make his own decisions with minimal overall supervision. Frequently, for example, Dulles and not Eisenhower made essential foreign policy decisions. Similarly George Humphrey slashed departmental budgets throughout the government—except for the military. Here the Joint Chiefs of Staff generally got programs they wanted. The chain of command under Eisenhower thus resembled that of a loosely organized corporation. Each department head exercised considerable independence under a President who acted like a genial chairman of the board.

The Republican party's right-wingers became a real problem for Eisenhower. McCarthy, by his actions as head of the Senate's Government Operations Committee, posed a serious threat to Eisenhower's ability to rule. He publicly led the successful opposition to Eisenhower's nomination of career diplomat Charles E. Bohlen as ambassador to Russia because Bohlen had been Roosevelt's interpreter at Yalta! McCarthy also sent his committee's chief counsel, Roy M. Cohn, to tour Europe. Cohn proceeded to berate American diplomats for being "soft" on communism and to demand that allegedly "radical" books, including those of Mark Twain, be taken from the shelves of United States Information Agency libraries.

McCarthy's Fall Until 1954 the administration had tried to compromise with the senator. In that year, however, McCarthy opened an investigation of subversion in an army base at Fort Monmouth, New Jersey. This attack on the military and Eisenhower's army secretary, Robert Stevens, for "coddling" communists proved to be the last straw. It forced a reluctant Eisenhower to take a public stand against McCarthy and his tactics.

Senate hearings considered McCarthy's charges against the army. They reviewed the army's countercharges that the senator had sought special favors for an aide, David Schine, drafted into the service. The hearings were watched on television by over 20 million Americans. McCarthy proved an adept television performer. But even more adept was the army counsel, Joseph N. Welch. He baited McCarthy into losing his temper, thus widely exposing the browbeating tactics that McCarthy had used so effectively against unfriendly witnesses before his committee in the past. McCarthy's influence began to decline.

In December 1954 the Senate (supported by the Eisenhower administration) "condemned" Senator McCarthy for "conduct unbecoming a member." After this censure he lost his remaining political influence. He died in May 1957. But "McCarthyism" lingered on.

The reckless hunt for possible communist

Jonas Salk

Polio is a disease of civilization that strikes hardest where sanitation is highest. It is also a disease that most frequently strikes children. It can keep a victim bedridden for weeks, but much worse it can cause severe paralysis or even death. Since 1894 when the first cases of polio appeared in the Green Mountains of Vermont, epidemics of the disease had been a common and dreaded occurrence. And nothing could be done to prevent them until in 1953 a young researcher, Dr. Jonas Salk, announced the development of a polio vaccine.

Jonas Salk's discovery was not one of medicine's happy accidents but rather the result of years of intensive research. Salk himself is said to have worked sixteen hours a day, six days a week over a long period of time before succeeding. His background had prepared him for such a test of endurance. The son of an immigrant garment worker, he largely put himself through school by part-time jobs and scholarships. The promise he had shown while earning his medical degree led to the offer of a research post that would start him on his career in immunology.

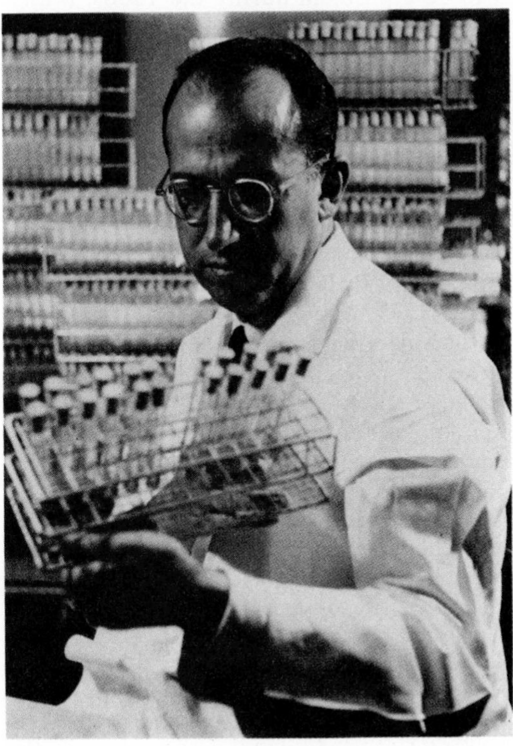

The polio vaccine that Salk finally developed was made by growing a representative strain of each of three types of polio virus in a broth made with monkey kidney. The viruses were then killed with formaldehyde, which rendered them incapable of causing the disease. However, they did not lose the power to stimulate the human body to produce antibodies. These antibodies would give a person at least limited immunity to polio.

Salk, his wife, and their three sons were among the first to receive his vaccine. Then in the Fall of 1954 a massive twelve-state test, sponsored by the National Foundation for Infantile Paralysis, was held. Almost 2 million schoolchildren in the primary grades participated. Half the children received the vaccine; the other half did not. The results were conclusive: in April 1955 the vaccine was pronounced safe and effective in preventing polio.

Salk's discovery catapulted him to instant, and largely unwanted, fame. He became a public figure deluged with offers to lecture and even to make his life into a movie. Finally, in 1955 he was awarded a congressional gold medal for "great achievement in the field of medicine." Salk, however, was more concerned with the common good and science than with public praise. He refused to accept any cash awards and eagerly returned to his laboratory at the University of Pittsburgh to continue his research.

Thanks to the dedication and perseverance of Dr. Salk, the scourge of polio is today largely a thing of the past. In 1952, before the vaccine was available, nearly 58,000 cases of polio were reported in the United States. By 1960, after the vaccine was used, that number was reduced to 3,000.

 subversives in American society, without proof of guilt or adequate safeguards for defense, continued to be a problem during the 1950s. Many thousands of Americans lost their jobs, suffered ruined careers because of blacklisting in their professions, and went to jail or even into exile because of it. The list of victims is long. It includes industrial workers, labor union officials, as well as prominent editors, broadcasters, and others in the arts. Screenwriter Dalton Trumbo went to jail for refusing to admit having once been a communist. He said of the era in 1970:

> It will do no good to search for villains or heroes or saints or devils because there were none; there were only victims. In the final tally, we were *all* victims because almost without exception each of us felt compelled to say things he did not want to say, to do things he did not want to do, to deliver and receive wounds he truly did not want to exchange. That is why none of us—right, left, or center—emerged from that long nightmare without sin.

"Peace, Progress, and Prosperity" The Eisenhower years signified far more than simply the tail end of McCarthyism. Eisenhower avoided tampering with New Deal–Fair Deal programs, even presiding over some extensions for them. He created the Department of Health, Education, and Welfare, approved a measure that added 7 million people to the Social Security rolls, signed another that raised the minimum wage, and supported a housing act that greatly increased urban-renewal projects. The country prospered. Few Americans worried much until the 1960s about the decline of public facilities such as schools, hospitals, and public transport systems. These received little federal attention in the 1950s.

Furthermore, Eisenhower avoided the type of scandal that had rocked Truman's second administration. His relations with the Democratic leaders who ran Congress were generally amicable, unlike Truman's with congressional Republicans. Eisenhower regularly consulted House Majority Leader Sam Rayburn and Senate Majority Leader Lyndon Johnson, the two Texans who dominated Congress during the 1950s.

When the President decided to run for reelection in 1956, despite a serious heart attack in 1955, there were no issues that the Democrats could exploit. Eisenhower had negotiated peace in Korea, run a basically budget-conscious and honest administration, and toned down McCarthyism. Also, he had flown to Geneva in 1955 for a summit meeting on peaceful coexistence with Russia's post-Stalin leaders (the first such meeting since Potsdam). He kept the country out of major foreign involvements in the Indochina crisis of 1953 and the Hungarian and Suez crises of 1956. Not surprisingly, Eisenhower again whipped Adlai E. Stevenson, winning a landslide 58 percent of the popular vote.

There seemed little public interest during the 1950s in rocking a very prosperous national boat. Eisenhower provided an image of safe, solid leadership that appealed even to many Democrats. Some Americans, though—particularly writers and intellectuals—worried out loud about the cheapening of America. They saw supermarkets, suburbs, and superhighways as the products of a spiritually bankrupt society. They feared that their countrymen had betrayed American ideals in the name of material prosperity. For most Americans, however, the facts spoke in more positive and glowing terms.

Farm income had almost doubled by 1960, netting more for farmers than even the thriving war years. Moreover, the much larger pie had to be divided among a smaller farm population. Median family income rose from $4,293 in 1950 to $5,904 in 1960. By 1956 white-collar workers outnumbered those in blue-collar jobs. Even for those in the latter group (particularly those unionized) real spendable income increased by 60 percent between 1940 and 1960. Much of this prosperity came in new industries—dealing with military weapons systems and space technology. These greatly expanded after the Russians sent the world's first missile, Sputnik I, into space in 1957. Suddenly, Americans found they had a lot of catching up to do if they were to equal the Russians in scientific pursuits. Many people re-

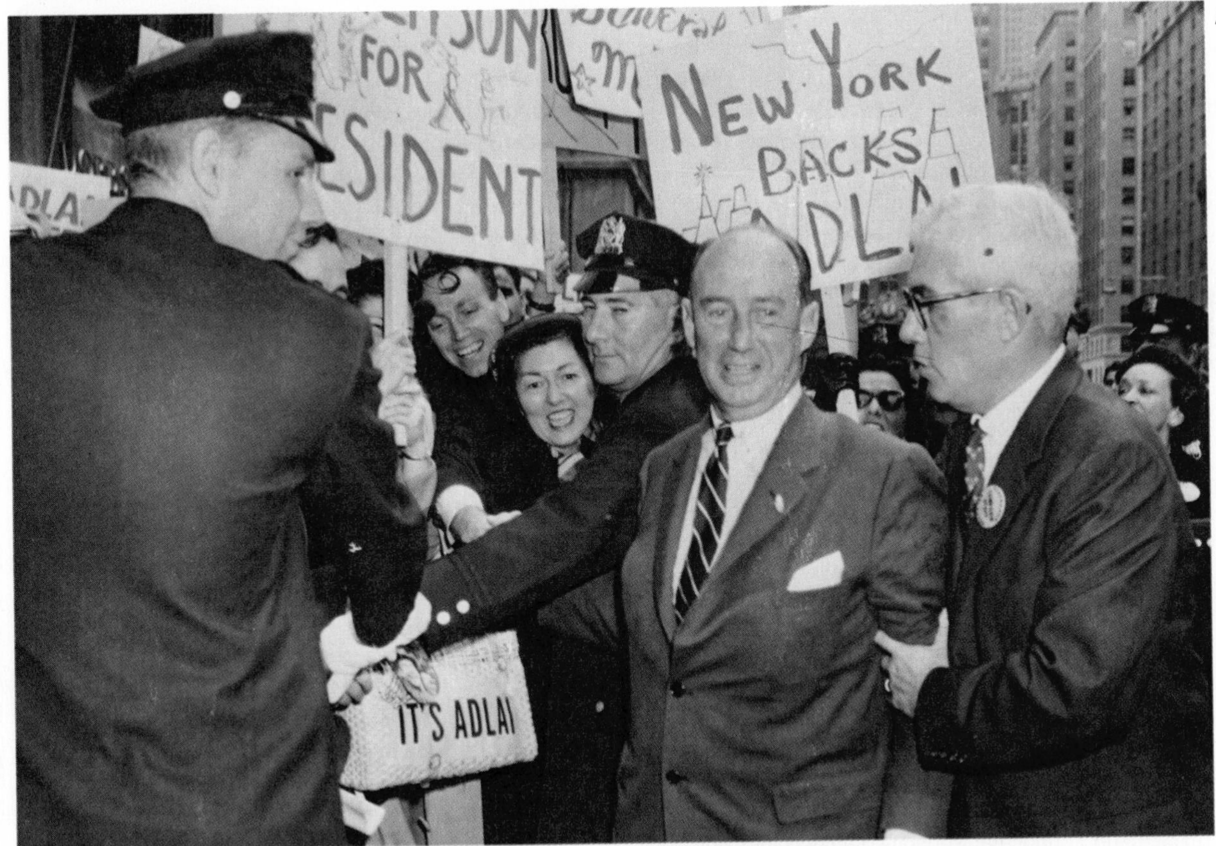

Adlai Stevenson, twice the Democratic nominee for President, was an eloquent and witty campaigner. But Eisenhower's image as a war hero and elder statesman proved unbeatable.

alized that education had been lacking and government funds were quickly demanded to inject the schools and universities with new monies for expansion and updating of their facilities.

UNSETTLED PROBLEMS

Yet various social and economic problems of enormous scope remained during the Eisenhower era. These would haunt Americans in the 1960s. For one thing, the affluent society remained a myth in 1960 for the 42 million people (almost a third of America's families) with annual family income levels of less than $4,000. The "invisible poor," as Michael Harrington described them, were not "invisible" by their own choice. They were not so much unseen as ignored by those who had made dramatic economic gains.

"Making it" often involved drawing firm barriers between oneself and those left behind. Groups heavily represented among the poor were the elderly, unskilled or nonunion workers, migrant farm laborers, blacks and Spanish Americans. The average black family income in 1960, for example, was $3,838 compared with $6,508 for white families.

The wartime FEPC had opened thousands of jobs in Northern industries to blacks. President Truman's 1950 executive order desegregated the armed forces and barred discrimination in federal employment. The next great civil rights advance for blacks came in 1954. The Supreme Court, in the famous case of *Brown v. Board of Education of Topeka, Kansas*,

Brown v. Board of Education of Topeka

Linda Brown held her father's hand tightly as they walked along one spring morning in Topeka, Kansas. He was taking her to school. But she was not going where she usually went, to Monroe Elementary, twenty blocks from her home. Instead she was going to enroll at Sumner Elementary, four blocks away. Nine-year-old Linda was mystified by the change in routine.

Reverend Oliver Brown was not mystified. He knew exactly what he was doing. He wanted to enroll his daughter in the elementary school nearest their home. His request for a transfer had been denied. Sumner was a school for white children, he was told, and Linda was black.

The school officials were well within the law in denying Linda entrance. It was 1951. If a community chose, it could segregate the races in any public facilities—schools, buses, restrooms, and so on. These segregation policies had been judged constitutional by the Supreme Court in the *Plessy* v. *Ferguson* decision in 1896. At that time the Court found that separate facilities did not deny anyone "the equal protection of the laws" promised by the Fourteenth Amendment, as long as these facilities were "equal."

But Reverend Brown did not believe that his daughter was receiving equal school facilities. So he brought suit against the Topeka Board of Education. The three-man federal court that heard the case found Topeka's schools to be equal and so decided against him. He then appealed. The Supreme Court agreed to hear his case, along with several others also based on school segregation and the Fourteenth Amendment.

The case came before the Court on December 9, 1953. It continued for over a year. The decision the Court handed down on May 17, 1954, presents the question the justices faced: "Does segregation of children in public schools solely on the basis of race, even though the physical facilities and other 'tangible' factors may be equal, deprive children of the minority group of equal educational opportunities?"

They answered this question with a firm, "We believe that it does." Among the reasons they gave was the effect of such segregation on black students: "To separate them from others of similar age and qualifications solely because of race generates a feeling of inferiority as to their status in the community that may affect their hearts and minds in a way unlikely ever to be undone."

Then they stated their final decision: "We conclude that in the field of public education the doctrine of 'separate but equal' has no place. Separate educational facilities are inherently unequal." These words, in effect, gave legal backing to Oliver Brown's belief. His daughter, and millions of blacks like her, had been deprived of their Fourteenth Amendment right to equal protection under the law.

Later, the Supreme Court instructed schools to move "with all deliberate speed" to desegregate their facilities. In the years since the decision segregated schools have not disappeared from the American scene. But the decision signified that segregation can no longer be considered the law of the land.

ruled unanimously that segregation in public-school education was illegal.

Although 792 of 2,985 biracial school districts had been integrated by 1959, none were in the Deep South or Virginia. There massive resistance from leading politicians and local White Citizens Councils raised the level of racial tension to dangerous heights. In 1956 a hundred Southern congressmen promised to overturn the *Brown* decision by "all lawful means." Then in 1957 at Little Rock, Arkansas—with white parents threatening violence against court-ordered desegregation—Governor Orval Faubus called out the National Guard to bar nine black students from a high school. After a court order removed the guard, a riot broke out. Eisenhower, himself a moderate on the segregation issue, sent federal paratroopers to help escort the nine children into the school.

Elsewhere, one Virginia county even closed its public schools to avoid integration. The University of Alabama, after a riot on the campus, expelled a black student admitted under Supreme Court order. Meanwhile, blacks in Montgomery, Alabama, led by an eloquent young minister, the Reverend Martin Luther King, Jr., organized a boycott against segregation on local buses in December 1956. Segregation on interstate buses had been banned the previous month. King's "direct action" tactics spread to other Southern cities. Soon he and other Southern black ministers formed the Southern Christian Leadership Conference (SCLC) to fight discrimination and all forms of bigotry.

In February 1960 a student wing of the SCLC held the first sit-in at a Greensboro, North Carolina, lunch counter to protest segregation in public eating places. Two mild civil rights acts in 1957 and 1960 somewhat strengthened federal authority against efforts to keep blacks from voting or exercising other rights. But as the sixties began, Americans knew the major battles to secure full equality for blacks were still ahead.

Other critical problems faced the nation as Eisenhower's second term ended. He himself emphasized a major one in a January 17, 1961, farewell speech.

> The conjunction of an immense military establishment and a permanent armaments industry of vast proportions is new in the American experience. The total influence—economic, political, even spiritual—is felt in every city, every state house, every office of the federal government. We must guard against the acquisition of unwarranted influence, whether sought or unsought, by the military-industrial complex. We must never let the weight of this combination endanger our liberties or democratic processes.

A fair warning, but Eisenhower himself had speeded the growth of the "military-industrial complex." Militarists and industrialists became more powerful during the ten years following. Still, the checks of the American system have kept them from getting complete control of the nation's political or economic structure.

Return of the Democrats America faced still other unsolved problems, but it entered the 1960s in a confident mood, sure of its purposes and powers. This confidence would not long remain. Still both 1960 presidential candidates reflected this basic assurance about the American future.

Richard Nixon, while defending the Eisenhower record, promised progressive and dynamic new policies. John Kennedy urged Democrats to rally behind him for similarly vigorous leadership. Little separated the two candidates in terms of issues, domestic or foreign. Kennedy did attack a presumed decline of American prestige abroad under Eisenhower and an alleged missile gap that threatened to make the Soviet Union dominant.

Kennedy benefited from a united party. His Texas Protestant running mate, Lyndon Johnson, helped keep much of the South Democratic for the Catholic Kennedy. He also profited from television debates with Nixon, which helped undercut the Republican charge of inexperience and youth. (Kennedy was forty-three, the youngest man ever elected President.) Most of

In his inaugural address John Kennedy challenged a complacent citizenry with the words: "Ask not what your country can do for you; ask what you can do for your country."

all, his election resulted from the strong support he received among Catholics and blacks—over 70 percent. Nixon received only mild backing from Eisenhower. Nixon's earlier career as a "Red hunter" haunted him and hurt him severely among Democratic and independent voters in 1960. Still Kennedy won by a tiny popular margin of only 113,000 votes out of 68,800,000 cast.

In his inaugural address Kennedy promised to lead the United States toward a New Frontier headed by young people: "The torch has been passed to a new generation of Americans, born in this century, tempered by war, [and] disciplined by a hard and bitter peace." The sense of promise and hope was strong among Americans that day, as the youthful new chief executive issued "a call to bear the burden of a long twilight struggle, year in and year out against the common enemies of man: tyranny, poverty, disease, and war itself." Few Americans doubted in 1961 that the country felt itself adequate to these great tasks.

1. In what way did the Hiss case help Nixon become President?
2. How did the war in Europe help bring the United States out of the depression? Why did higher wages and profits lead to inflationary prices? How was the government able to keep this inflation under control?
3. Which character traits did Truman bring to the Presidency that would make his terms of office successful? Which hindered him?
4. In what ways was the Fair Deal a continuation of the New Deal? Why was labor unhappy with the Taft-Hartley Act?
5. Why was Truman himself in part responsible for McCarthy's credibility?
6. In what ways did the Eisenhower administration extend some New Deal–Fair Deal legislation?
7. Why did many artists and writers believe that America in the 1950s had become spiritually bankrupt? Do you agree with them?
8. What is the significance of the *Brown* decision? To what does the phrase "massive resistance" refer? How did blacks like Martin Luther King deal with this resistance.

Beyond the Text

1. Discuss the reasons for the decision to evacuate the Japanese Americans from the West Coast of the United States. Consider in your discussion the following questions: How did the government justify the move? Why was similar action not taken against the Japanese in Hawaii or against the German Americans and Italian Americans? On what grounds did the Supreme Court uphold the action? Do you consider the relocation justified?
2. Truman's election victory confounded the experts. Why were all the pollsters wrong? Why did a three-way split in the Democratic party aid rather than jeopardize his victory?
3. Using Michael Harrington's *The Other America,* investigate and then hold a panel discussion on poverty in America in the 1950s and beyond. Consider such questions as why it was (or is) so widespread, why most Americans in the 1950s were not aware of its extent, and what approaches might be considered in the elimination of poverty.

Bibliography

Nonfiction

Brooks, John, *The Great Leap: The Past Twenty-Five Years in America.**
Commoner, Barry, *The Closing Circle.**
Galbraith, John K., *The Affluent Society.**
———, *The New Industrial State.**
Goldman, Eric F., *The Crucial Decade & After: America, 1945–1960.**
Latham, Earl, *The Communist Controversy in Washington: From the New Deal to McCarthy.**
Lubell, Samuel, *The Hidden Crisis in American Politics.**
Murphy, Paul L., *The Constitution in Crisis Times, 1918–1969.**
Parmet, Herbert S., *Eisenhower & the American Crusades.*
Polenberg, Richard, *War & Society: The United States, 1941–1945.**
Revel, Jean-François, *Without Marx or Jesus.**
Silberman, Charles E., *Crisis in Black & White.**
White, Theodore H., *The Making of the President, 1960.**
Yarmolinsky, Adam, *The Military Establishment.**

Fiction

Frankel, Ernest, *Tongue of Fire.**
Graham, Lorenz B., *North Town.*
King, Larry L., *The One-Eyed Man.*

*a paperback book

EPILOGUE

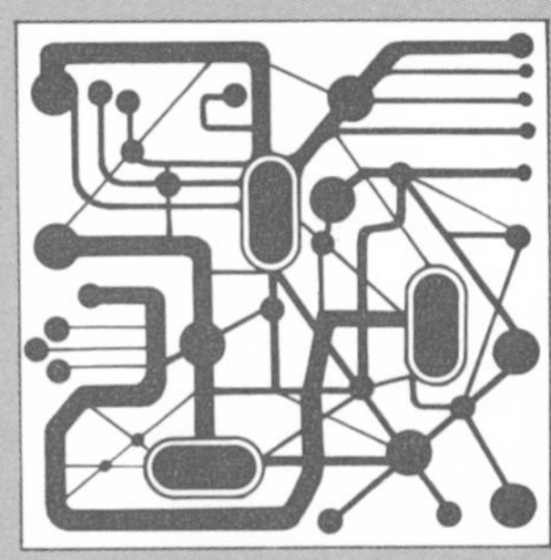

Recent American History

Episode 1	The Cuban Missile Crisis Superpower Politics
Episode 2	The "Battle of Chicago," 1968 Politics at Home
Episode 3	The Moonshot New Directions in the Economy
Episode 4	A Man and His Dream Social Dreams and Realities

The Cuban Missile Crisis

When the Soviet Union began supplying Cuba with missiles, the Cold War reached crisis proportions. As the nation watched, President Kennedy announced a counteraction that brought the world perilously close to nuclear confrontation.

ON OCTOBER 22, 1962, President John F. Kennedy appeared on television to deliver a speech his press secretary had described earlier as one of extreme urgency. The President was grave. His voice was tense, his face drawn. The Soviet Union, he announced, was placing offensive nuclear missiles on the island of Cuba. The United States would not tolerate this threat to its security. Therefore, he said, he had ordered a "difficult and dangerous effort." Beginning the next morning, the United States would place a "quarantine" on all offensive weapons being shipped to Cuba. (The President called it a quarantine instead of a blockade because a blockade would be an act of war.)

Kennedy also announced that other steps would be taken. But the quarantine was the most important and dangerous. Intelligence reports indicated that about twenty Russian ships were in the Atlantic, headed for Cuba. A dozen of them probably contained missiles or missile components. Thus what Kennedy had announced was a very dangerous confrontation between the two great nuclear powers. It was one that he and some of his advisers believed might lead to the terrible war that had been a nightmare for the world since 1945.

The President's speech was part of a crisis that had long been building. In 1958 a Cuban revolutionary, Fidel Castro, had overthrown the dictator Fulgencio Batista. Castro then began to take over American property in Cuba, establish a communist government, and build close diplomatic and military connections with the Soviet Union.

In response the Eisenhower administration attempted to isolate Cuba economically and diplomatically. But, very early in his presidency, Kennedy approved a more direct and, as it turned out, much less sensible tactic. He financed and supported an attempted invasion of Cuba at the Bay of Pigs. The invasion, mounted in 1961 by 1,200 anti-Castro Cuban exiles, was based on completely false intelligence reports that the Cuban people would rise up to welcome their "liberators" once a foothold on Cuba was established. There was no uprising. The invaders were beaten quickly and with almost ridiculous ease by the Cuban defenders, the second largest armed force in the hemisphere.

Then, the next year brought the Soviet military build-up. At first it seemed to involve only antiaircraft missiles and bombers, with Russian crews and advisers. But by September, the Soviet Union began to send offensive missiles as well. American planes with sophisticated photographic equipment kept surveying Cuba. On October 15 one plane brought home the first photographs of missile bases being constructed just ninety miles from Florida.

For the next three days Kennedy presided over long, tense meetings with advisers. Some, mostly military people, urged an immediate air attack on the missile bases and other targets. Perhaps, they argued, this might even result in the overthrow of Castro's government. Others

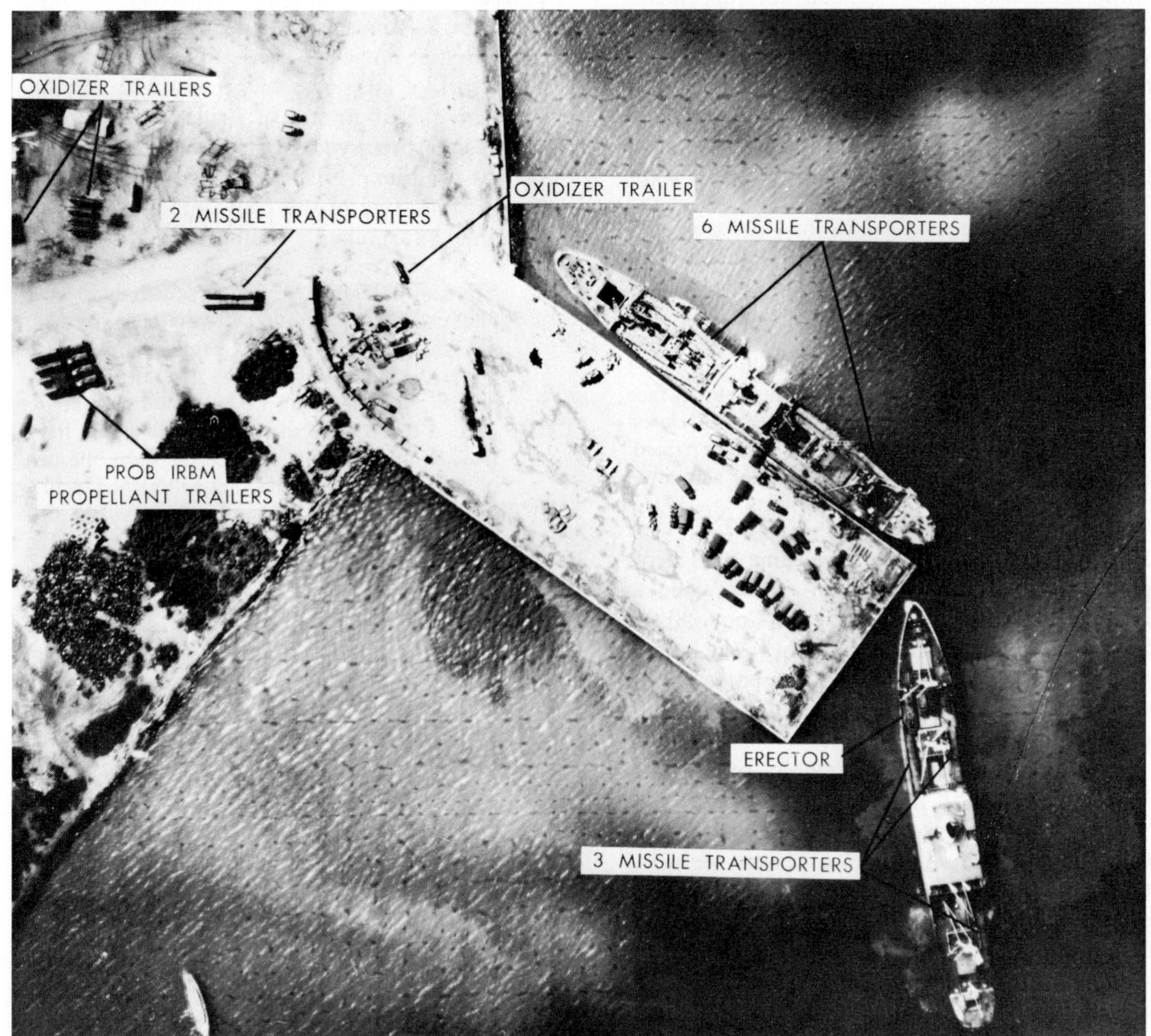

An American reconnaissance plane photographed Soviet freighters, loaded with intermediate-range ballistic missile parts, in a Cuban port.

wanted more cautious steps, such as the quarantine (dangerous though it was). After all, they pointed out, air attacks could kill hundreds of Russians in Cuba and thus provoke immediate retaliation on the United States. Finally Attorney General Robert F. Kennedy, the President's brother, pointed out that an air attack would kill many thousands of Cubans and look suspiciously like the Japanese attack on Pearl Harbor.

The President finally decided on the quarantine and made his television announcement. The next morning he sat with his brother and waited while Russian ships approached the 500-mile quarantine limit. American ships and planes were ready to stop them and turn them back—with force, if necessary. Robert Kennedy later wrote this description of the agonizing wait:

> This was the moment we had prepared for, which we hoped would never come. I think these few minutes were the time of gravest concern for the President. Was the world on the brink of a holocaust? Was it our error? A mistake? Was there something further that should have been done? Or not done? His hand went up to his face and covered his mouth. He opened and closed his fist. His face seemed drawn, his eyes pained, almost gray. We stared at each other across the table.

Just before 10:30 a messenger came in. He reported that two of the Russian ships seemed to have stopped abruptly in the water. Soon, all the Soviet ships near the quarantine line either stopped or turned back. The immediate crisis was over. The Russians had decided to play a careful game.

There was an enormous sigh of relief in the White House. But the relief was short-lived. Some Russian vessels resumed their course toward Cuba. Possibly these vessels were oil tankers containing no weapons. But, to make the quarantine effective, sooner or later a ship must be stopped, boarded, and searched. The President waited two days for the right moment. Then he carefully chose a ship that he felt carried only oil. The ship flew a Panamanian flag and was working on contract for the Soviet Union. It had no Russian crewmen. Two American destroyers pulled alongside, ordered it to stop engines, and sent armed search parties aboard. There was no resistance.

Soviet restraint and the President's cautious procedures had avoided a direct military confrontation. But, all week Russians in Cuba had continued work on the existing missile sites. In fact, they had speeded up their work. So the fundamental issue still remained. Would the United States tolerate missiles already there, or would the Russians remove them?

The first Soviet response to quarantine had been warlike language but restrained actions. Then, on the afternoon of Friday, October 26, the President received a personal letter from the Soviet premier, Nikita Khrushchev, which changed the tone of the confrontation and also contained a formula for ending it:

> You can be calm. We are of sound mind, and understand perfectly that if we attack you, you will respond the same way. I think that you also understand this. If you have not lost your self-control, Mr. President, we and you ought not to pull on the ends of the rope in which you have tied the knot of war, because the more the two of us pull, the tighter the knot will be tied. And a moment may come when that knot will be tied so tight that even he who tied it will not have the strength to untie it. Then let us not only relax the forces pulling on the ends of the rope, let us take measures to untie that knot. We are ready for this.

In this remarkable letter, which marked a definite turning point in the Cold War, Khrushchev suggested a way to resolve the specific issue of the missiles in Cuba. If the United States would end the quarantine and publicly proclaim it would never again support any kind of invasion of Cuba, then the Soviet Union would remove the missiles already in place and send no more.

The very next day Kennedy accepted the proposal. Khrushchev replied with more warmth than had been shown since the start of the Cold War: "I express my satisfaction and thank you for the sense of proportion you have displayed."

Superpower Politics

THE CUBAN missile crisis contained two separate elements. One was obvious, the other ignored by most people at the time. Both were at the core of the history of American relations with the rest of the world in the years after Kennedy's inauguration. The first and obvious element was the confrontation and then relaxation between the two nuclear superpowers. The missile crisis was not merely the closest approach to nuclear war since World War II. It was also the beginning of a process of easing tensions (or "detente," as it is often called), which eventually ended the Cold War. The second, less obvious element in the missile crisis, however, was that it represented a definite American intervention in Cuban affairs. The United States, in effect, modified the old Monroe Doctrine once more, asserting again its right to control the foreign affairs of smaller nations in the Western Hemisphere.

Both of these elements—more peaceful relations with the world's other great powers and continued intervention in the affairs of smaller nations—ran clearly through the policies of Presidents Kennedy, Johnson, and Nixon. The combination was a bit baffling. While the United States moved toward peaceful relations with the Soviet Union and China, it frequently took more forceful action in smaller countries. It was almost as though Theodore Roosevelt's foreign policy slogan—"speak softly and carry a big stick"—had been split up. The soft words would be reserved for the world's other great powers, the big sticks for smaller nations.

The trend toward soft words and relaxed tensions with the Soviet Union (and, under Nixon, with China) began to be implemented the very next year after the missile crisis. At that time the United States and the Soviet Union came to their most significant agreement since World War II—a treaty banning any further testing of nuclear weapons in the atmosphere. Eventually almost every nation (except France, Cuba, and China) also signed this agreement. But the Kennedy administration thought of the test-ban treaty as only a first step in a long process of negotiated disarmament that might take decades to complete.

"CLIENT" NATIONS

The happy ending of the missile crisis and the signing of the test-ban treaty appeared, in 1962 and 1963, very small steps toward ending the Cold War. There were still many powerful obstacles to the relaxation of conflicts between what American politicians liked to call the free West and the communist East. NATO continued to be a cornerstone of United States policy. The Warsaw Pact represented the Russian counterpart to NATO in Eastern Europe. Germany remained a divided nation. The British, French, and American occupation zones were united into "Free" West Germany facing the communist East Germany. The city of Berlin was still split politically and physically, with the western part of the city completely dependent on outside help.

Beyond Europe both the United States and the Soviet Union cultivated close relationships with "client" nations and political movements. Each gave massive military and economic support to friendly governments. Each helped finance and provide weapons for revolutionary movements in unfriendly countries throughout Asia, Latin America, and Africa. In fact, this "Third World,"—the underdeveloped nations outside Europe and North America—was the main East-West battleground of the 1960s. As a result, the United States and the Soviet Union seemed to be creating dozens of potential areas of confrontation in nations where neither country's deepest interests were at stake.

In the Middle East, for example, the Soviet Union grew closer and closer to Egypt and some other Arab nations. The United States (which also supported some pro-Western Arab governments) provided economic and military aid for Israel. Thus when war broke out in 1967 between Israel and the Arabs, Americans and Russians found themselves involved in a potential conflict over which they had no real control. The 1967 war was short (and a smashing victory for Israel). So the two nuclear superpowers avoided a crisis. But the threat continued into the 1970s.

In October 1973 fighting broke out once more in the Middle East. Egypt and Syria—aided by other Arab nations—attacked Israel, attempting to recover territory lost in 1967. This time, Israel was not able to win such a quick military victory. It did turn back the Egyptian and Syrian attacks and did capture new territory in both Arab countries. But once more the United States and the Soviet Union found themselves rushing huge shipments of planes, tanks, and other equipment to the opposing sides, trying to maintain the balance of power there.

On the Chinese-American front of the Cold War, an even more obvious source of danger was American support for the Taiwan regime of Chiang Kai-shek, one of the most powerful American client states. The survival of this Nationalist Chinese republic remained the greatest barrier to American recognition of the mainland government of Communist China. The United States Seventh Fleet still patrolled the narrow straits between China and Taiwan. Both President Kennedy and his successor, Lyndon Johnson, reaffirmed the old American pledge to protect Chiang Kai-shek's government. By the mid-1960s almost no spot on the globe seemed free from the potential for setting off nuclear war.

CHANGING WORLD CONDITIONS

Certain conditions taken together, however, made it possible for the Cold War opponents to begin settling differences. First, the cost of building advanced weapon systems and maintaining huge armies and navies was more difficult to bear each year. Obviously, the economies of both nations could not continue to support vast military budgets and at the same time produce the consumer goods their civilian populations demanded.

Second, and more important in the long

run, the world of the 1960s was different from that of the 1950s. Since World War II the United States and the Soviet Union had been the unchallenged superpowers. But by the late 1950s, and even more rapidly in the 1960s, other power centers emerged to compete with the two nuclear giants. Greatly helped by the Marshall Plan, the Western European nations recovered from the war completely. Then they developed their industrial systems to capacities undreamed of before World War II. France and Great Britain both developed modest nuclear arms of their own.

At the same time the cornerstone of American defense policy in the 1950s, NATO, grew steadily weaker. One of the most important members, France, dropped out of the organization altogether and also ordered all NATO troops out of France. The nations that did remain as members were much less dependent on NATO in the 1960s than they had been during the more critical years of the Cold War.

As economic competitors, too, the countries of Western Europe became a third great power by uniting in the European Common Market. West Germany and Japan, after being overpowered and occupied in 1945, recovered with almost miraculous speed. Neither was permitted to rearm (and neither seemed to want to become a military force). Yet in every other way the two former enemies of the United States assumed the role of great powers.

Third, and most important of all, both the United States and the Soviet Union experienced difficulties with their allies that compelled them to approach the Cold War in new ways. Nations like France, Great Britain, and Germany were no longer unquestioning friends in the conflict with the Soviet Union. For Moscow relations were even more strained. Under the leadership of Mao Tse-tung and Chou En-lai, China developed rapidly both economically and militarily. With this came a serious split between the two great communist powers.

The conflict began in propaganda, with Mao and Khrushchev firing words back and forth across their border. Soon both countries heavily fortified this border. In 1969 a dangerous but brief shooting skirmish occurred between Russian and Chinese soldiers. At the same time, the Russians were having great difficulty controlling their client states in Eastern Europe. Gradually, American political leaders realized that "international communism" was not a united movement but was instead badly divided.

To a limited extent under Lyndon Johnson—and far more rapidly under his successor, Richard Nixon—the United States actively pursued a detente with both China and the Soviet Union. By the early 1970s it was possible for Americans

The foreign and economic ministers of Western Europe are shown conferring at a Common Market meeting in 1961. Since then, with its growing economic power, that bloc of nations has become an influential third force in world politics.

During President Nixon's visit to China in February 1972, he and Premier Chou En-lai reviewed the Chinese Red Guard. Televised scenes like this startled the American public, long accustomed to thinking in Cold War terms.

to speak of the end of the Cold War. In 1972 Nixon visited China, and the United States finally accepted Chinese membership in the United Nations. Many hours of the President's trip to Peking were telecast back to the United States. Americans watched with some amazement as Nixon and the Chinese leaders exchanged hearty toasts and warm words. In 1972–73 Nixon and Soviet leader Leonid Brezhnev exchanged cordial visits to each other's capitals.

In October 1973, at a critical point in the new war between Israel and its Arab neighbors, the detente was put to an important practical test. Brezhnev flew to Cairo to talk to Arab leaders; Henry Kissinger, who had become Secretary of State, then flew to Moscow to see Brezhnev and went from there to Israel. Quickly the United States and the Soviet Union called a meeting of the UN Security Council to vote a cease-fire proposal. China, now a full member of the council, went along and did not exercise its veto power.

After a shaky beginning the cease-fire was effective. Apparently, the superpowers had been able to work together to stop the war, though it remained to be seen whether they could impose real peace in the Middle East—or anywhere else. Still, there could be little doubt that detente was becoming one of the basic goals of foreign policy for all three major parties to the Cold War.

GLOBAL INTERVENTION

The habit of aggressive intervention was harder to break than the habit of Cold War, however. The 1960s had begun with American sponsorship of the Bay of Pigs invasion—a direct military attempt to overthrow a foreign government. At the same time, the Kennedy administration was pouring millions of dollars into the small new nation of Laos (part of the old French colony of Indochina) to support a pro-West government against forces that the United States claimed were communist.

The oldest theater for American intervention is Latin America. For decades the United States had had a contradictory policy of combining military intervention and economic assistance. Early in his administration President Kennedy announced an impressive sounding Alliance for Progress for Latin America. The alliance was a program of loans, grants in aid, and technical assistance. It was designed to attack the problem of poverty that made life in most of Latin America miserable for the poor and uncertain for the well-to-do.

Confidently, Kennedy said that the alliance would not be used to support military governments just because they happened to be anticommunist. But in the ten years after the alliance was formed, military leaders overthrew republics in several important Latin American nations. The United States recognized these new military governments—and in some cases probably helped them seize power. And so, whether American leaders planned it that way or not the

With the defeat of the French at Dienbienphu in 1954, Vietnam was, in effect, divided into two countries: North Vietnam with its capital at Hanoi, and South Vietnam with its capital at Saigon. Soon Communists and nationalists began guerrilla and terrorist activity against the Saigon government, which received support and increasing amounts of military aid from the United States. These guerrilla forces, formally titled the National Liberation Army, came to be known as the Viet Cong.

In August 1964 North Vietnamese torpedo boats reportedly fired on United States ships in the Gulf of Tonkin. President Johnson ordered the bombing of North Vietnamese naval bases in retaliation. The United States was soon bombing North Vietnam regularly and also areas in South Vietnam held by the Viet Cong. In turn, United States naval bases, such as the one at Danang, were attacked. American bombers then attacked eastern Laos in an attempt to stop the flow of men and supplies from North Vietnam over the Ho Chi Minh trails. United States military involvement increased until nearly 540,000 American troops were in Vietnam.

In early 1968 the Vietcong launched their Tet Offensive—simultaneous attacks on the major cities of South Vietnam. During an American counterattack, a massacre of Vietnamese civilians by American soldiers occurred at My Lai. In the same year President Johnson called a limited halt to the bombing of North Vietnam on March 31 and a full bombing halt on November 1. In 1970 occasional air attacks were resumed.

United States and South Vietnamese forces drove deep into Cambodia in April 1970 in an effort to locate and destroy Vietcong bases there. In February 1971 South Vietnamese troops, with United States air support, crossed the border into Laos in an unsuccessful attempt to cut the Ho Chi Minh trails.

In March of 1972 the Vietcong and North Vietnam launched a massive offensive, capturing the provincial capital of Quang Tri and scoring other successes; in May the United States began systematic bombing of all North Vietnam and mined North Vietnamese rivers, canals, and ports—including Haiphong Harbor.

Under President Nixon the number of American troops in Vietnam was drastically reduced—down to 65,000 in May 1972—and combat duties were transferred to South Vietnamese forces under a policy of "Vietnamization." In 1973 a cease-fire was concluded in Vietnam.

alliance helped to stabilize governments that were neither democratic nor economically progressive. In 1964 Lyndon Johnson followed a more traditional path of intervention when he sent 20,000 American soldiers and marines into the Dominican Republic to prevent establishment of a new government believed to be friendly to Castro's Cuba.

These interventions paled in size and importance beside the American involvement in a confused guerrilla war in two artificial nations in Indochina, North and South Vietnam. The country had been divided when the French withdrew from the region in 1954 (see Chapter 36). A northern capital was set up in Hanoi and a southern one in Saigon. When elections to unite the country were not held, a National Liberation Front, composed of local communists and supported by the North, tried to bring down the Saigon government.

The Eisenhower administration had supported the South Vietnamese government with money, military equipment, and a few military advisers. Kennedy deepened this commitment by sending more American advisers and more weapons. But apparently no amount of money, arms, or advice would enable Saigon to hold out against the National Liberation Front (or "Vietcong," as they were also called). In 1965, after an alleged incident with North Vietnam involving American ships in the Tonkin Gulf, President Johnson committed American forces to battle. With congressional approval—but without a declaration of war—Johnson bombed North Vietnam with more force than had been used against Germany during World War II. He eventually sent more than 500,000 American troops to Indochina.

American involvement in Vietnam began with a limited commitment of military advisers, like this Green Beret soldier. American advisers remained in 1973, though combat troops had been withdrawn.

The war went badly for the Americans. The Vietcong and their strong supporters from the North matched the huge military concentration of American troops, machines, and weapons. If anything, the military position in the South kept growing worse. At home the war became the most divisive and heated political issue in decades. It led to a powerful peace movement that first centered on college campuses, but then spread with astonishing strength.

Under domestic political pressure Johnson announced in the spring of 1968 that he was seeking negotiations with the National Liberation Front and North Vietnam. In the election that followed, Hubert Humphrey and Richard Nixon both campaigned for the presidency on a promise to end the war. Still, somehow, the conflict lasted four more long years. Finally, just before election day in 1972, Nixon's foreign-policy expert Henry Kissinger announced that "peace is at hand." But at Christmas the United States resumed the bombing of North Vietnam while battles continued in the South. Finally, a peace agreement was signed early in 1973, involving all four parties to the struggle—the United States, North Vietnam, South Vietnam, and the National Liberation Front.

Even with international supervision, this peace settlement seemed almost impossible to enforce. True, the United States withdrew all its combat forces from South Vietnam and stopped bombing the North. But, as the year wore on, American planes were still bombing Cambodia heavily to try to prevent the collapse of the pro-West government there.

Finally, on August 15, 1973, under severe pressure from a Democratic Congress determined to end American military involvement in Indochina, Nixon stopped bombing Cambodia. The United States had spent billions of dollars on the longest air war in history. But, when the warplanes were all finally grounded, there was little assurance that any part of Indochina would soon see true peace.

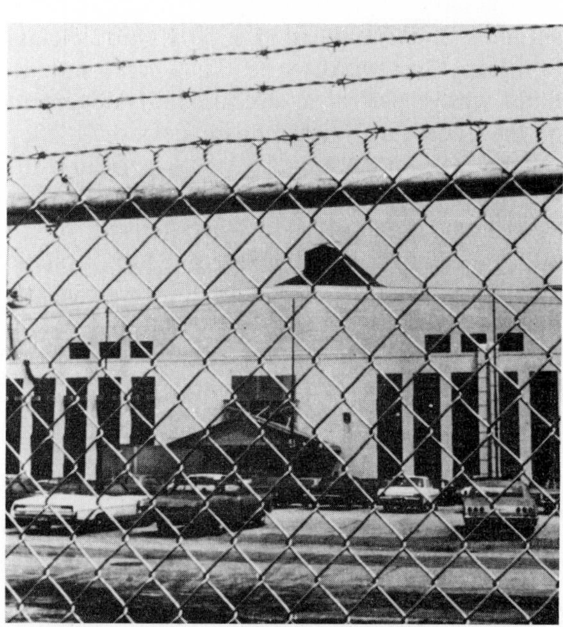

As though in preparation for a siege, workmen erected this cyclone fence topped with barbed wire around the Democratic convention hall in Chicago.

"The Battle of Chicago," 1968

In The Summer of 1968, the city of Chicago prepared to serve as host for the Democratic convention. The preparations included an unusual preoccupation with security. The area around the International Amphitheater, where the convention would meet, began to resemble a fortress under siege. Around the amphitheater workers erected a cyclone fence topped with barbed wire. They also set up rolls of barbed wire at crucial points outside the fence. For blocks around they sealed manhole covers to prevent any underground attack on the amphitheater. The Democratic mayor of Chicago, Richard J. Daley, often met with his own police officials and representatives of the state government. They laid plans to summon the National Guard, and even federal troops if necessary.

The barbed wire, the sealed manholes, and the other preparations took place in a dense atmosphere of rumor. The Chicago police heard, and sometimes believed, that black militants were planning to assassinate white leaders. Groups of "hippies"—a term then used for young persons with long hair or unusual clothing—were supposedly going to add LSD to the Chicago water supply. Other "radicals"—a term even more vague than "hippie"—were supposedly planning to mix ground glass into the food served in downtown Chicago restaurants.

Meanwhile, thousands of people, most of them young, were coming into Chicago. They came not to attend the convention as such but to protest the Johnson administration's domestic and foreign policy. By the time the convention opened, perhaps as many as 10,000 young men and women were camping in Chicago's parks, making and hearing speeches, trying to organize a coherent movement. Some practiced judo and karate. Some listened to music or read poetry. Some smoked marijuana or used other drugs. Some were earnest, even prayerful. But for the most part the young people just lounged or drifted in small groups.

Chicago city officials, some newsmen, and many other Americans simply grouped the young people under the fuzzy label "demonstrators." Actually, it is difficult to generalize about them. Most were under thirty. Many were college students and members of solidly middle-class families. Most were white. They were not, in other words, part of a revolutionary movement of the poor and downtrodden. Politically, they ranged from moderate critics of American military involvement in Indochina to revolutionaries determined to "bring down the system."

Their mood was a curious mixture of picnic gaiety and deep anger at what they regarded as the American government's betrayal of freedom and democracy. They wanted the convention to do two things (neither of them likely). First, they wanted the Democrats to condemn the long war in Indochina. Second, they wanted the party to nominate someone other than the man they considered the "regular" candidate, Vice President Hubert Humphrey. But these two wishes were drowned in a more general conviction: the party would fail them; the entire political system was hopelessly unresponsive; and all they could do was to make their presence felt by going outside politics, into the streets.

Out of this frustration a tactic developed. One group of demonstrators, calling themselves Yippies (for Youth International party), ceremoniously named a pig Pigasus and nominated him for President. The Yippies, in particular, became steadily more strident. They searched for profanities to shout at the police and other officials, profanities harsh enough to convey their anger. Soon, too, the demonstrators decided that if they could provoke the police or National Guard into violence, the whole world would see just how brutal, just how "fascist," the system had become.

For their part, Mayor Daley and other officials also developed a tactic. Again and again, they expressed their fear that the demonstrators had come to Chicago to create violence. The city, the mayor announced, would stand firm. There would be no permits for parades. The demonstrators would not be allowed to approach the amphitheater. Nor could they use the city's parks as campgrounds at night. The police would be in the streets, fully armed and ready.

Thus, on both sides, the stage was set for a violent, dramatic encounter—the "battle of Chicago." The trouble began the night before the convention was to open. All that day demonstrators had crowded into Lincoln Park, which lies along the shore of Lake Michigan, about two miles north of the amphitheater. By 11 P.M., according to a curfew announced by the city, the park was supposed to be cleared. But about a thousand young people remained, apparently determined to resist the curfew. Their spirits were fed by mimeographed sheets circulated by the Yippie organization. One of these read:

> Laugh at professors; disobey your parents; burn your money; you know life is a dream and all of our institutions are man-made illusions. Break down the family, church, nation, city, economy. What's needed is a generation of people who are freaky, crazy, irrational, sexy, angry, irreligious, childish, and mad; people who burn draft cards, burn high-school and college degrees; people who lure the youth with music, pot, and acid. The white youth of America have more in common with Indians plundered than they do with their own parents. Burn their houses down, and you will be free.

At 10:30 the police ordered Lincoln Park cleared. The immediate result was confusion. Many in the crowd simply melted away. Others stayed and shouted slogans like "The streets belong to the people." After a long pause the police began to "sweep" the park. Most Chicago police simply tried to keep order on this first night's encounter with the demonstrators. But an official report later described the ways some police behaved:

> Police followed another group of persons who had sought [refuge in an apartment building nearby] and hit one member of the group on the head with a baton [a night stick]. As the student raised his hand to feel his head, he was hit again, and two fingers were broken. Other officers ran up the exterior staircase of an apartment building and used their shotguns to force downstairs six or seven persons who had sought refuge there.
>
> The crowd surged up and down Clark Street. More tear gas canisters exploded, sending people on the run, grabbing handkerchiefs, and

(continued on page 785)

The Land Americans Have Shaped

How to describe the United States of today? Travelers use words like "size," "diversity," "achievement," "efficiency," "wealth." All are valid. But all seem somewhat abstract without a sense of the people who have worked to make America what it is. Their monuments may be as modest as a tiny New England village—this one in Vermont—or as vast as Boulder Dam. Clearly, they have transformed the land first explored by Europeans over 450 years ago. Wrote Mohamed Mehdevi of Iran: "My imagination could not keep pace with the trials and labors that must have gone into this spanning and building of a continent, an achievement of man. And it had been done not by heroes and great warriors, but everyone."

[For further information on the foreign observers quoted in this essay, see "Notes on Sources."]

PICTORIAL ESSAY 9

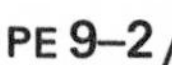

PE 9–2 /

Skyscrapers, New York City

New York is a vertical city. It is a catastrophe with which a too hasty destiny has overwhelmed courageous and confident people, though a beautiful and worthy catastrophe. Nothing is lost. Faced with difficulties, New York falters. Still streaming with sweat from its exertions, wiping off its forehead, it sees what it has done and suddenly realizes: "Well, we didn't get it done properly. Let's start over again!" New York has such courage and enthusiasm that everything can be begun again, sent back to the building yard and made into something still greater, something mastered!

[LE CORBUSIER, 1947]

Levittown, Pennsylvania

Already, three out of every five American families own homes. The horizontal trend which has replaced the vertical trend of the skyscrapers is covering the great green spaces around the cities with the individual houses of suburbia. Suburbia is a way of life. In the family-centered society which America has become in recent years, suburbia is regarded as the ideal place to rear children. In this world of carefully mowed lawns there already lives one-third of the nation.

[HERBERT VON BORCH, 1962]

South Carolina plantation

On the banks of the Mississippi stands a stately home with pillared porch, dappled oak alley and a spacious lawn, on which magnolias shed their heavy-lidded blossoms. The home is open to visitors on Sundays, though a family is in residence. There is a guide in the shape of an overpowering lady who waits until the number of visitors meets her approval. The lady praises the past in a voice that echoes in the marble halls.

[JAN DE HARTOG, 1961]

The Americans are proud of their Lincoln and Jefferson Memorials, and they enjoy showing visitors their National Art Gallery, a splendid white Tennessee marble building which looks pink after a rain. Next we visited the Library of Congress. As we walked around the city this evening in the warm moist air filled with swirling leaves, we saw the dome of the Capitol illuminated against the dark sky. Washington is not a provincial city but a melting pot for people from every state who come to do business, petition, or simply visit.

[NIKOLAI MIKHAILOV AND ZINAIDA KOSSENKO, 1960]

Joint session of Congress

The Capitol, Washington, D.C.

Assembly line workers, Detroit

I became aware of the pace of work in North America, a pace that was not the international one but that of Uncle Sam. During the eight-hour day people really attended to their job, and it was taken for granted that the chiefs would set an example of punctuality and dedication. Among us Chileans, and I believe also in all the Latin countries, the boss enjoys the privilege of arriving late at the office and staying away whenever he feels like it, and the employees, by the same token, can refrain from showing too much devotion to their work. Compared with us, the North Americans strike me as a much more powerful and better run machine.

[AMANDA LABARCA H., 1959]

Steel works, Gary, Indiana

University of Chicago Law Library, designed by Eero Saarinen

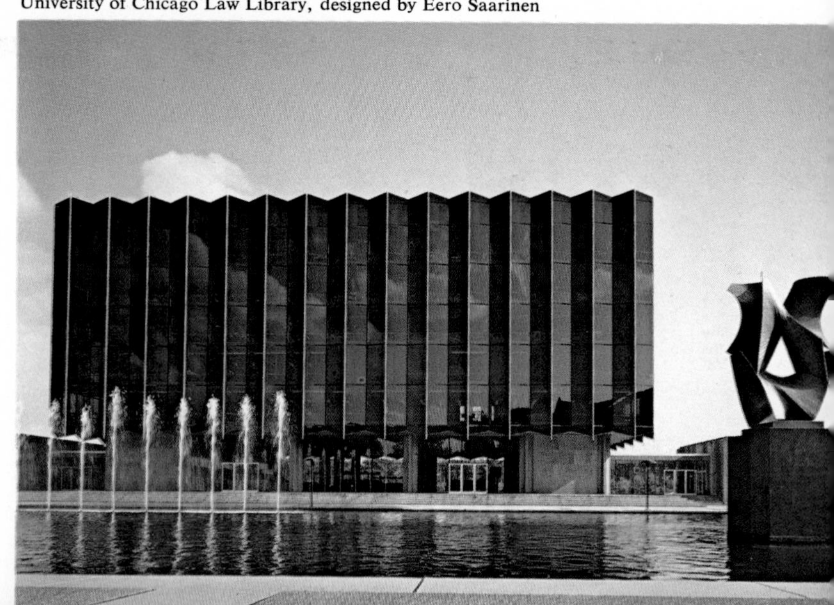

American architecture has beauty, audacity, and a superb sense of scale, absorbing what is best in modern architecture in Western Europe, adapting itself to American needs, scenery, and wide horizons, and yet presenting what is exciting, new, and vital. The architect works in freedom and according to the needs he must satisfy and the function his building must perform.

[MORRIS BROUGHTON, 1959]

Then there are the cities, and especially those small towns that hold the secret of the United States—with their frame houses, their adjoining gardens always open to the view, their grass of a succulent and hospitable green, their tall, powerful trees, their modest and silent intimacy, softened in the whiteness of the snow or expressed passionately in the floral effusion of the springtime; their hospitable and secluded churches, their bustling schools, their solitary streets along which there shine at night, among the trees, the lights of so many open windows; and the business streets with the bank, the gasoline station, the tempting and ingeniously arranged shop windows.

[JULIAN MARIAS, 1959]

Parade at Taylor, Wisconsin

Wheat farm on the Great Plains

If you come from the Eastern states, or farther east still, from Europe, going west is a continuous journey of suspense, from the moment you are over the Appalachians and know that the Atlantic has gone for good. In the Midwest, the sky is a little wider, and the prairie is a kind of sea all its own; so much so that in the wheatlands of Kansas you get the illusion of great heaving yellow swells, and the silos float by like battleships on the horizon.

[ALISTAIR COOKE, 1968]

PE 9–6/

Taos Pueblo, New Mexico

Taos is the most characteristic of all the reservations. We were struck at once by its beauty. On two sides of an open space, traversed by a stream, are enormous blocks of buildings, as high as they are long, in which adobe houses are encrusted and superimposed one above the other. The dominant color is a dull yellow, but red and violet cloths, hung up to dry on the flat roofs and fluttering in the breeze, light up the sombre background.

[SIMONE DE BEAUVOIR, 1947]

Hoover Dam (Boulder Dam), on the Arizona-Nevada border

Boulder Dam is something more than a vast utilitarian device, a super-gadget. Enchanted by its clean functional lines and at the same time awed by its colossal size, you might be tempted to call it a work of art; as if something that began with utility and civil engineering ended somewhere in the neighborhood of Beethoven's Ninth Symphony.

[J. B. PRIESTLEY, 1935-36]

Street signs, Las Vegas

A feature of Las Vegas hotels is that there are no windows or clocks. Gamblers must not be reminded to go to bed. The less expensive gambling avenue caters for a poorer class of tourist and is known as Glitter Gulch. Its electric signs made it as bright as day. It is ridiculous to sneer at the lighted advertisements of the U.S. Romantic historians are always saying how wonderful Elizabethan London must have been "with all those painted inn signs swinging in the wind." Well, here you have it still alive. Why sneer? It is living, it is folk art, it is exquisite from an aircraft, and I personally like *to be saluted by an electric cowboy a hundred feet high who waves his arm in a gesture of Hi!*

[T. H. WHITE, 1964]

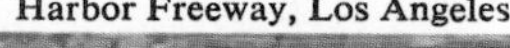

Harbor Freeway, Los Angeles

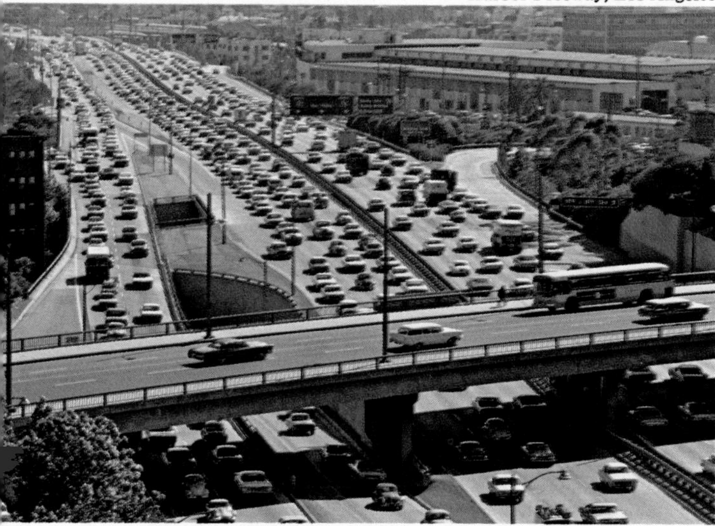

Just leaving my hotel [*in Los Angeles*] *I feel lost —the distance to the nearest drugstore is the same as between two villages in France. One's helplessness in such vastness is paralyzing. In a car with a girl I said: "Let's go somewhere out of town. . . ." "But where?" she asked. "Oh, no matter where . . .," I smiled, ". . . where the city ends." "Los Angeles never ends," she said firmly.*

[LEOPOLD TYRMAND, 1966]

We sped toward the Mark Hopkins [*and went to*] *the top floor. The walls were of glass, and we walked slowly around the room, looking at the myriad lights below; it was far more beautiful than Los Angeles at night, than even New York itself, because of the bay traced out in shining lines against a background of dark water and also those fiery ladders rising from the sea. We looked for a long time. There are, in such travels, moments which are promises and others which are only memories: this one was complete in itself.*

[SIMONE DE BEAUVOIR, 1947]

San Francisco at night

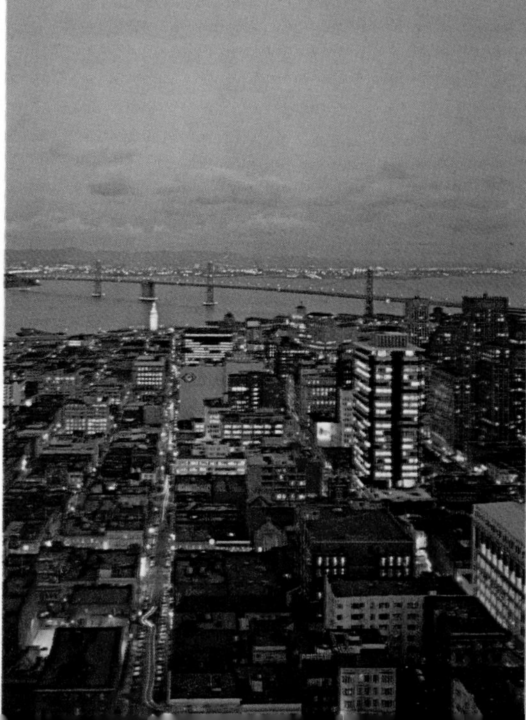

PE 9–8/

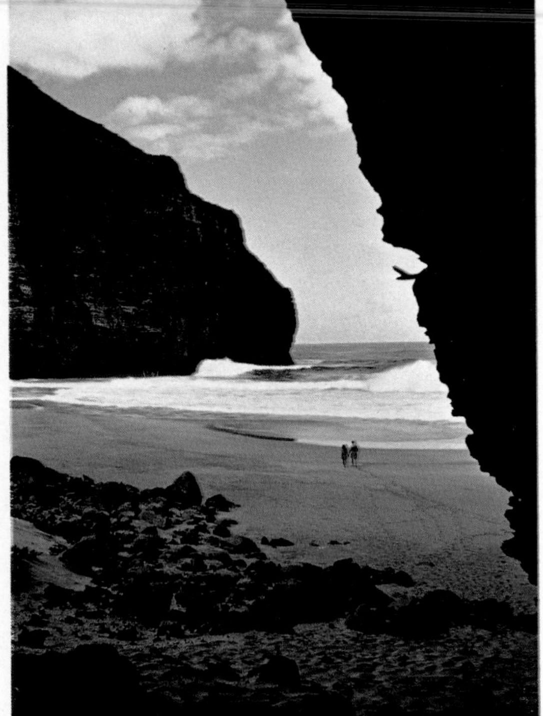

Beach and cliffs, Kauai Island, Hawaii

There is enough wilderness in the world to increase very greatly the number of national parks and to see to it that some of them are preserved in their original condition with access kept so strenuous that the solitary walker is most unlikely to be crowded out.

And this perhaps is the ultimate meaning of the wilderness and its preservation—to remind an increasingly urbanized humanity of the delicacy and vulnerability of all the living species—of tree and plant, of animal and insect —with which man has to share his shrinking planet. As he learns to observe their interdependence and their fragility, their variety and their complexity, he may remember that he, too, is a part of this single web and that if he breaks down too thoroughly the biological rhythms and needs of the natural universe, he may find he has destroyed the ultimate source of his own being. If somewhere in his community he leaves a place for silence, he may find the wilderness a great teacher of the kind of planetary modesty man most needs if his human order is to survive.

[BARBARA WARD AND RENÉ DUBOS, 1972]

Glacier Peak Wilderness, Washington

> choking for air. Police jabbed a young, blond-haired girl in the stomach. Despite her screams, police continued to hit her until she fell to the pavement. Gradually, the crowd dispersed, and the violence ended.

The next evening—the first day of the convention—police and demonstrators enacted an almost identical script. The demonstrators were more obscene and sullen than before, while the police were more violent. To millions watching both the convention and the disorders on television, it was becoming obvious that the important action was not only in the amphitheater but also in the streets and parks.

The next day battle lines were drawn even more severely. Early in the evening a leader of a radical black political group, Bobby Seale of the Black Panthers, told a crowd in Lincoln Park: "There are pigs—Lyndon Johnson, Hubert Humphrey, and Nixon—in this society." He was followed by Jerry Rubin, a young white radical, who attempted to tie black and white radicalism together: "We whites have been suppressed as blacks have for the past hundred years. We're going with the blacks. If they try to keep us out of the park, then we'll go to the streets. They bring out the pigs to protect the pigs they nominate."

Later, the police cleared Lincoln Park in what had by now become the customary manner. But much of the action had shifted to Grant Park, just across from the huge Conrad Hilton Hotel, the convention's official headquarters. The police declared the hotel off limits. The demonstrators rallied, heard speeches, and shouted insults. One or two even undressed and paraded naked to try to provoke the police. Finally the tired police were relieved by troops of the Illinois National Guard, who did not attempt to enforce the city's curfew. The crowd remained in Grant Park, undisturbed all through the night.

The next day, about 10,000 people gathered in Grant Park. The National Guard went off duty for a while, replaced by policemen. When the crowd declared its intention of marching to the amphitheater, police officials quickly forbade this.

By nightfall several thousand unorganized people were packed at one corner of the block-long Hilton. Nervous police lined up to protect the hotel. Other police tried to clear the streets. The crowd had no place to go—and no plan, either. The lights of television crews added to the unreality of the scene. On an upper floor in the hotel Hubert Humphrey waited for the vote that would nominate him. He could smell and taste faint tear-gas fumes floating up from below.

Just before 8 P.M. the "battle of Chicago" reached its climax. On millions of television sets around the country Americans watched in fascination as two events occurred together: The convention went on with the cumbersome and traditional speeches, demonstrations, and roll calls. Outside the police once more broke discipline and began to attack the demonstrators. A reporter for a Saint Louis newspaper described his experience this way:

> The crowd tried to reverse gears. People began falling over each other. I was in the first rank between police and the crowd and was caught in the first surge. You could hear shouting and screaming. I saw a youth running by me also trying to flee. A policeman clubbed him as he passed, but he kept running.

Another newspaper reporter experienced the battle this way:

> To my left, the police caught a man, beat him to the ground, and smashed their clubs on the back of his unprotected head. He was elderly, somewhere in his mid-fifties. As I stopped to help him, the police turned on me. It was the most slow and confused and the least experienced people who got caught and beaten.

Not all the violence was done by the police. Some demonstrators fought back with rocks, glass bottles, and kicks. Some policemen were hurt by bottles, ash trays, even pieces of furniture hurled from the hotel. About a hundred policemen claimed injuries (most of them delivered by thrown objects) at or near the Hilton. Nobody knows how many demonstrators were hurt. But,

With the Democrats about to nominate Hubert Humphrey inside, the passions of demonstrators outside intensified—but so did the reaction of the police. Here police are shown dispersing demonstrators outside convention headquarters.

on televison, what showed was the almost unbelievable picture of hundreds of nightsticks being raised and brutally lowered.

The main battle was over quickly. By 8:15 the police were in control. The crowd scattered to other parts of the city, where several small skirmishes occurred. Around midnight the police at the Hilton were again relieved by guardsmen. By 1 A.M. the remaining crowd in Grant Park was officially described as orderly. At the amphitheater the party had nominated Humphrey.

Oddly, there were almost no pieces to pick up. The federal government eventually indicted eight leaders on various charges. But a spectacular trial produced no convictions. Little or no disciplinary action was taken against the Chicago police.

What remained, for many people, besides confused memories of the battle, was one small but dramatic incident at the convention itself. Abraham Ribicoff, a liberal senator from Connecticut, was making a nominating speech for George McGovern of South Dakota, another liberal senator. In the middle of the speech Ribicoff stared down at Richard Daley, who had become a symbol of the kind of traditional party leadership that the protest centered on. If George McGovern were President, Ribicoff said coldly, there would be no "Gestapo tactics in the streets of Chicago." As the television camera zoomed in for a close-up of Daley's angry face, the mayor shouted back something unintelligible.

All too intelligible, however, was the open anger between Ribicoff and Daley. This was the real significance of the "battle of Chicago." It clearly demonstrated the bitter split in the Democratic coalition that had held power for so long. In that sense the battle almost assured Hubert Humphrey's defeat and Richard Nixon's election as President.

Politics at Home

During The Same summer of 1968 Russian tanks and troops stormed into Prague, Czechoslovakia, to stamp out a movement to liberalize that nation's communist government. The Americans demonstrating in Chicago drew parallels between themselves and the people of Prague. Both, they claimed, were victims of cruel and repressive regimes based only on military power. The parallel was false in several ways, however.

In 1968, the United States was ending almost four decades of national politics dominated by a Democratic party dedicated more or less to reform, not repression. In a dozen important areas of life—such as social welfare, education, or civil rights—defenders of the political system could point to many important successes. One of the strangest facts about the critical summer of 1968, then, was that hundreds of thousands—perhaps millions—of middle-class young people rebelled against a style of politics that had been, at least on the surface, devoted to improving the lot of the poor, the elderly, and several exploited minorities.

KENNEDY'S "THOUSAND DAYS"

The decade of the 1960s began on a note of hope and experimentation. John Fitzgerald Kennedy brought to the White House in 1961 a public personality full of energy, wit, and enthusiasm. But, basically, the political mind of the new President, like many members of his administration, was the product of Roosevelt's New Deal and Truman's Fair Deal. Most of the legislation Kennedy succeeded in getting from Congress during the thousand days he was President reflected this traditional reforming trend. Social Security was extended to cover more self-employed people. The minimum wage went up to $1.25 an hour. New money for public housing was appropriated. There was an increase in federal aid to education and in funding for urban renewal and redevelopment.

Still, compared to the promising rhetoric and style of the President and many of his key colleagues, the actual legislative achievement was embarrassingly small. Most of the Kennedy program was enacted in the first year of his presidency. After this his domestic record in Congress was even more skimpy.

Much of what President Kennedy wanted to accomplish was simply bottled up or defeated in Congress. He attempted to create a new Department of Urban Affairs, but Congress refused to approve the legislation. A bill providing federally assisted medical care for the elderly (Medicare) failed to pass the Senate. A new, strong civil rights act could not get off the ground in either house of Congress. Without much help from the President, Congress did approve the Twenty-fourth Amendment. It prohibits any state from requiring payment of a poll tax as a qualification for voting. The old opposition group of conservative Southern Democrats and Republicans that had formed in the 1930s remained very powerful.

TRAGEDY IN TEXAS

In the 1962 election a number of congressmen friendly to the administration lost their seats. It was clear, too, that the President had become increasingly unpopular among some Southerners because of his liberal position on civil rights. To smooth over some of these difficulties, Kennedy decided to visit Dallas, Texas, in November 1963 to make a speech. Before the scheduled speech there was a motorcade through downtown Dallas. The route was well publicized to attract a large crowd. As the car carrying the President passed the Texas School Book Depository, a rifle fired several times. The President jerked forward and fell to the floor of the car, bleeding. He was rushed to a hospital but died very quickly.

In the days that followed Americans watched in sorrow, confusion, and astonishment. Vice President Lyndon Johnson, also in Texas at the time, flew back at once to Washington in the presidential plane with Mrs. Kennedy. He took the oath of office on the aircraft, still uncertain whether the assassination was part of a larger plot. The mystery was soon cleared up. The disgruntled young assassin, Lee Harvey Oswald, was captured. But, as he was being moved from one jail to another, in full view of television cameras beaming their picture to another nationwide audience, Oswald was shot to death by a Dallas night-club owner named Jack Ruby.

Most of the young people who, six years later, were the radicals, hippies, and demonstrators in Chicago were high-school students at the time of the assassination. With their parents they watched the murder, the funeral, and then Oswald's murder.

Other generations of Americans had entered adult life against a background of depression or war. To this new generation—at least to its white, middle-class majority—the violence at Dallas was probably the single most memorable introduction to the realities of modern life. The lessons drawn from it were confirmed again and again as the decade passed.

JOHNSON'S GREAT SOCIETY

Lyndon Johnson set to work promptly to become, as he put it, "President of all the people." Taking full advantage of the wave of emotion following Kennedy's assassination, he made his motto, "Let us continue." He also used all the knowledge and skill he had accumulated during a long career in Congress. Within twelve months of Kennedy's death Johnson managed to move some of the most cherished and difficult liberal proposals through Congress. He called his program the Great Society.

First, and perhaps most significant, the new President made a passionate plea for a new civil rights law. The first Southerner in the White House since Woodrow Wilson, he demanded full equality for blacks and other racial minorities. He even quoted the most stirring song of the civil rights movement: "We shall overcome." The effect was electric. For the first time in its history the Senate voted to end a filibuster against civil rights legislation. It passed the Civil Rights Act of 1964.

The law required that every state apply exactly the same standards to blacks and whites for voting or face suits in special courts. More important, at least in the short run, the act forbade any kind of discrimination in such public accommodations as trains, hotels, swimming pools, and restaurants. (Amazingly, throughout the South, there was rapid and widespread acceptance of this revolutionary aspect of the new law.) But the Civil Rights Act went even further. It authorized the federal government to cut off aid to any school district that did not move toward racial integration. It also forbade discrimination on the basis of either race or sex in employment.

Aside from civil rights Johnson devoted major efforts to his "war on poverty." To create the Great Society, the President asked Congress to set up a new government agency, the Office of Economic Opportunity (OEO). Under the legislation that Johnson wrung from a suddenly cooperative Congress, the OEO would provide education and vocational training to unemployed young people, make grants to cities for their own antipoverty programs, and finance part-time jobs for students and others who needed support. The dollar amounts appropriated were not large at first. But the legislation moved the federal government into more direct assistance for the poor than at any time since the depression.

Obviously, Johnson would be the unanimous choice of the Democrats in 1964. The Republicans nominated Senator Barry Goldwater of Arizona. Goldwater was an outspoken conservative, more so than any Republican candidate since Herbert Hoover. His book, *Conscience of a Conservative,* set forth a political philosophy opposed to most of the reform legislation passed during the New Deal, the Fair Deal, Kennedy's New Frontier, and Johnson's Great Society. Goldwater even hinted that he might seek an end to the Social Security system. For the first time in at least a generation the voters had an apparently clear-cut choice between a frank conservative and a liberal who stood squarely in the Roosevelt-Truman-Kennedy tradition of reform.

Lyndon Johnson's legislative experience helped him get an impressive domestic program through Congress during his presidency. This same activism in foreign affairs, however, proved his downfall.

The outcome was spectacular. Johnson and his vice-presidential candidate, Hubert Humphrey, won 61 percent of the vote, the largest popular margin of victory in modern history. Goldwater carried only his own Arizona, plus five states in the Deep South. Johnson also swept large numbers of Democratic governors, congressmen, and senators into office. Jubilantly, he interpreted the election as a national referendum on public policy. He set to work with more energy than ever to perfect the Great Society.

IMPROVING THE GREAT SOCIETY

The next two years, 1965 and 1966, were unquestionably Johnson's most impressive. He won a doubled appropriation for OEO from Congress. A law providing $3 billion in federal aid to education at all levels was a victory long overdue. An old sore spot was at least partially cured when Congress agreed to eliminate the national-origins quota restrictions on immigration. The new system replaced the former quotas, so heavily weighted in favor of northern Europe. Two general limits, one for the Western Hemisphere, the other for the rest of the world were substituted.

Most significant of all for many Americans was the passage of the Medicare bill. Since the Truman administration Democrats had tried without success to provide some form of federal medical assistance for the elderly and the poor. The Medicare law, administered through the Social Security system, provided such medical insurance for the elderly.

As though the Civil Rights Act of 1964 had not been spectacular enough, Johnson asked for and won a new law, the Voting Rights Act of 1965. It aimed primarily at guaranteeing voting rights to blacks. For the first time since the Civil War and Reconstruction the national government stepped directly into the process of registering voters. The law provided that in any district where fewer than half the eligible voters had participated in the 1964 election, federal registrars could be sent to enroll new voters under carefully controlled conditions.

But landslide victories in American politics often turn sour. Lyndon Johnson's victory was to be no exception. Two years after his landslide the President was in deep political trouble. By the 1966 congressional elections a reaction was clearly building in the country against some elements of his Great Society program. Accordingly, the Republicans in 1966 took forty-seven seats from the Democrats in the House of Representatives, plus three in the Senate. From this point on Johnson found it difficult indeed to deal with Congress. His administration was nearly stagnant in the area of domestic legislation and reform. It also became badly divided and embattled over the issue of the war in Indochina.

Part of the obvious political reaction of 1966 was not due to Lyndon Johnson and his policies but to the Supreme Court. Under the vigorous leadership of Chief Justice Earl Warren, the Court continued to make determined rulings on minority rights and integration. It also threatened many established patterns in American politics by a revolutionary decision, neatly summed up as "one man, one vote." This ruling declared that electoral districts for Congress and the state legislatures had to be drawn so that they contained almost equal numbers of people. This seemingly innocent idea meant that longstanding imbalances between urban and rural areas would soon end. For generations cities had been underrepresented in both state and national legislatures. In contrast rural areas had enjoyed disproportionate political representation. The Court ruling threatened this practice and shifted the balance of political power toward the cities.

Also, in a dramatic series of decisions, the Court enlarged the rights of defendants in criminal cases. Critics said these rulings made it nearly impossible for state and local authorities to enforce criminal law properly. The Court also angered many conservatives when it forbade prayers of any kind in public schools. Billboards went up carrying the demand "Impeach Earl Warren." Because he publicly agreed with many of its rulings and because many Court members were clearly identified with the Democratic Presidents who had appointed them, President Johnson shared much of the criticism leveled at the Court.

THE FALL OF LYNDON JOHNSON

The Johnson administration could easily have survived criticism from those conservatives who opposed the war on poverty, the civil rights legislation, and the Supreme Court decisions. But the President was also coming under still wider and sharper attack because of the deepening American involvement in the Indochina War. As the presidential primaries of 1968 approached, the attack gained force. Senator Eugene McCarthy, a Democrat from Minnesota, announced that he would run in Democratic primaries against the President—a most unusual step for a politician. Waiting in the wings—hesitating about whether to become a candidate himself—was Robert F. Kennedy, now a senator from New York.

To the astonishment of a great many professional politicians, Senator McCarthy effectively utilized thousands of young volunteers in the New Hampshire primary in March. He did not actually defeat the President but came close enough to embarrass him. And it appeared likely that McCarthy might actually win the next important primary election in Wisconsin, just weeks away.

In this tense political atmosphere the President went on national television on the last day of March. He announced that he would cut American military activity in Indochina and would try to start negotiations to end the war there. Then, after a slight pause, he announced that he would not seek reelection. He spoke quietly, with the emotion that marked most of his public speeches. But he had done an astonishing thing.

Antiwar activists united around Senator Eugene McCarthy to give him a significant showing against President Johnson in New Hampshire's primary. Though McCarthy ultimately lost the nomination, the response he evoked probably led Johnson not to seek reelection.

Johnson's announcement meant that the Democratic nomination was open. Robert Kennedy quickly entered the race. Vice President Hubert Humphrey was on a few primary ballots as a kind of administration stand-in. But the primaries boiled themselves down to a contest between two liberals, McCarthy and Kennedy. Both shared much the same support and had very similar ideas. McCarthy won some primaries, Kennedy others. Gradually, attention focused on the last primary, in California. There, Kennedy won by a narrow margin. There, too, leaving a victory celebration in a Los Angeles hotel, he was murdered by a young Syrian immigrant, Sirhan Sirhan.

This assassination turned the Democratic convention into an unequal struggle between a liberal wing, led but not controlled by Eugene McCarthy, and the party regulars, who rallied behind Hubert Humphrey. The latter group had enough support to nominate Humphrey.

THE REPUBLICAN RETURN

Some of the young people who went to Chicago rejected normal politics and demanded "revolution." But many, probably a majority, had actually worked for the nomination of McCarthy or Robert Kennedy. For them Kennedy's assassination and McCarthy's impending defeat were just the events that made Chicago's violence seem the inevitable outcome of their political experience. They had come close to compelling a major party to take a fundamentally new political turn. But they had failed—or, as they saw it, the Democrats had failed them. It is this fact that explains why the Democratic party—not the Republican party—was the target of their opposition.

For their part the Republicans simply reached back into history to nominate Richard Nixon. They adopted a generally conservative

Governor George Wallace's third-party candidacy in 1968 siphoned off nearly 10 million votes, making that election one of the closest in recent history.

platform, including a virtual endorsement of the war in Indochina. To the Chicago "radicals"—and their supporters around the nation—the Democratic party was the more evil precisely because it had made the closer approach to virtue.

The election was complicated still further by the third-party candidacy of Governor George C. Wallace of Alabama. Wallace, a Democrat and conservative, was a blunt-spoken opponent of racial integration and federal power. He appealed to his supporters' distrust of big, impersonal government bureaucracy. He also tried to persuade working-class Americans that they had been taxed unfairly to support welfare programs and other federally financed social experiments. With these ideas Wallace attracted a large and mixed body of support.

Wallace's candidacy, the Republicans' continuing position as a minority party, and a late surge of loyalty by Democrats made the election fairly close. Richard Nixon won by a smaller percentage of the vote than he had received in losing in 1960. The percentage of people voting for President was also the lowest in years.

NIXON'S DOMESTIC POLICIES

The narrowness of the election and continued Democratic control of Congress weakened the Nixon administration. Clearly Nixon would not be able—even if willing—to reverse the long tendency toward increased federal power. The President did attempt to reduce the size of the Great Society's social welfare budget. Also, he appointed new members to the Supreme Court, including Chief Justice Warren Burger. They would, he believed, change the direction the Court had taken under Earl Warren.

In many ways, however, Nixon's hands were tied. The Senate rejected some of his appointees to the Supreme Court, questioning their qualifications and conservative political views. Congress also refused to act on one of Nixon's major domestic programs, a proposal to replace what he had called the welfare mess with a system of guaranteed incomes at $1,600 a year. The figure was below what was then the official definition of the poverty line. In addition, it was coupled with a demand that the unemployed either accept work or enroll in vocational-training programs. In short, the welfare reform proposal was simply too conservative for the Democratic Congress to accept.

Probably Nixon's most serious domestic concern during his first term of office was the economy. Despite continued growth it seemed unhealthy and unstable. The most important evidence of this—aside from serious and rising unemployment figures—was a decided rise in prices. Finally, under severe pressure the President acted in August 1971. He announced a "New Economic Policy," with several "phases" designed to impose federal controls on wages and prices. In the first phase all prices and wages were frozen. This assertion of government power was quite out of character with Nixon's long previous opposition to federal economic controls.

Aside from the New Economic Policy little that emerged on the home front during the President's first term was surprising. There was no major change in social welfare legislation and no new civil rights laws of any kind. There was a new amendment to the Constitution (the Twenty-sixth), allowing all citizens over eighteen years of age to vote. But this law was a result of congressional, not presidential, efforts.

CONFLICT IN 1972

Because of Nixon's domestic performance and the troubled state of the economy, the Democrats appeared to have a good chance to regain the presidency in 1972. Several candidates emerged as leaders in primaries and state conventions: George Wallace, Hubert Humphrey, Edmund Muskie of Maine (vice-presidential candidate with Humphrey in 1968), and George McGovern (the man who had tried to reorganize Robert Kennedy's support in the 1968 convention).

By careful organization and by taking skillful advantage of party reforms made in 1968 and afterward, McGovern won delegates faster than any other candidate. Finally, he defeated Humphrey and Wallace in a close California primary. McGovern was too liberal for most of the professionals in the party. Consequently, party regulars made determined efforts at the convention to block his nomination. But he had enough delegates (though barely enough) to win nomination and to name Senator Thomas Eagleton of Missouri as his running mate.

In many ways McGovern's success resulted from the Chicago convention of 1968. His support included many who had supported Robert Kennedy or Eugene McCarthy in 1968. He also had the help of thousands of people who had either been in the streets at Chicago or been appalled by the police violence there. But McGovern's nomination did not heal the party division that had caused Humphrey's defeat four years before.

On the contrary, McGovern's victory deepened the division. Many old-line Democratic politicians refused to rally behind him. He represented, at least to many of his followers, something new on the American political scene. The new politics, as it was called, centered on youth, the rights of ethnic minorities, and the liberation of women.

During the primary campaigns McGovern had proposed several controversial schemes. He suggested, for example, that every family whose income was below $10,000 should receive a yearly cash grant of $1,000. This was to be paid for, according to McGovern, by higher taxes in the high-income brackets. Many middle-class voters were unconvinced that it would not raise their taxes as well. After his nomination McGovern attempted to back away from such proposals, seeking the moderate support he would need to win. But the memory of some of his primary proposals lingered on. McGovern's program seriously alienated many customary sources of Democratic political power in labor unions, among farmers, and among middle- and lower-middle-class voters.

Still, McGovern's showings in various public-opinion polls were better than Humphrey's had been at convention time in 1968.

George McGovern, in attempting to open the Democratic party to groups shut out of the 1968 convention, alienated the traditional base of Democratic support—blue-collar workers. Richard Nixon capitalized on this to win in a landslide.

 But his candidacy was badly hurt when newspapers began to report that Eagleton had been treated for psychiatric disorders. McGovern at first announced his support for Eagleton. But soon he asked for the vice-presidential candidate's resignation, an act the voters interpreted as indecisiveness. Sargent Shriver, a brother-in-law of John and Robert Kennedy, became Eagleton's replacement. But the damage had been done. In November Nixon won almost 61 percent of the popular vote and all electoral votes except those of Massachusetts and the District of Columbia. The President entered his second term with a landslide reminiscent of Johnson's in 1964.

CONSTITUTIONAL CRISES

During the campaign the President had promised that if he won the victory he hoped for, then the first six months of his new term would be just as exciting as Franklin Roosevelt's "hundred days." In ways that he would not have predicted the President was correct. Not just the first six months of the new term but its first year was marked by more political surprises and turmoil than any period since the secession winter of 1860–61. By the first anniversary of his reelection the President's victory had turned to ashes. The Nixon administration entered a series of crises that finally rendered him almost powerless, brought his standing in public opinion polls to its lowest ever, and created a very real possibility of presidential impeachment.

The crisis began in an odd way. Early on the morning of June 17, 1972, policemen surprised five men in the headquarters of the Democratic party in a Washington building known as the Watergate. The men carried walkie-talkies, cameras, burglars' tools, and electronic "bugging" equipment. In the days that followed, embarrassing connections between the Watergate burglars and the Nixon administration began to emerge. One of the burglars was employed by the President's own reelection committee. Another carried the phone number of a White House consultant. Investigators soon discovered that the apparent leader of the burglary had received over $100,000 that could be traced to the Nixon campaign organization.

At first the White House dismissed the incident as a "third-rate burglary attempt." John Mitchell, who had resigned as attorney general to direct the Nixon campaign, brushed it aside as a "bizarre incident." When investigations led to the indictment of two middle-level employees of the White House and the Nixon campaign, McGovern tried to make "Watergate" an election issue. But the seven men accused in the crime pleaded guilty without involving the President or his administration, and the incident did not affect the outcome of the election. On inauguration day the President could still hope that the crime would not affect his second term either.

Then in the spring of 1973, from many different sources, new accusations and confessions began to spill. By the beginning of summer two former Cabinet members—Mitchell and Secretary of Commerce Maurice Stans—had been indicted in a related case. The current attorney general and two of the President's top assistants had been forced to resign because of their possible involvement in an attempt to "cover up" the Watergate crime. A number of powerful and less powerful men began publicly to confess to perjury and obstruction of justice.

The President was forced to appoint a Special Prosecutor with full power to investigate not only Watergate but other related accusations. In the meantime the Senate had created a special committee, headed by Democratic Senator Sam Ervin of North Carolina, to investigate the entire campaign of 1972. The committee held public hearings that attracted an even larger audience than the McCarthy hearings of 1954. Stunned and confused, Americans saw the President's own counsel, John Dean, accuse him of participating in an attempt to buy the silence of the Watergate burglars. They also saw the acting head of the FBI admit that he had burned evidence. For weeks a train of witnesses, including several Cabinet members and men with offices

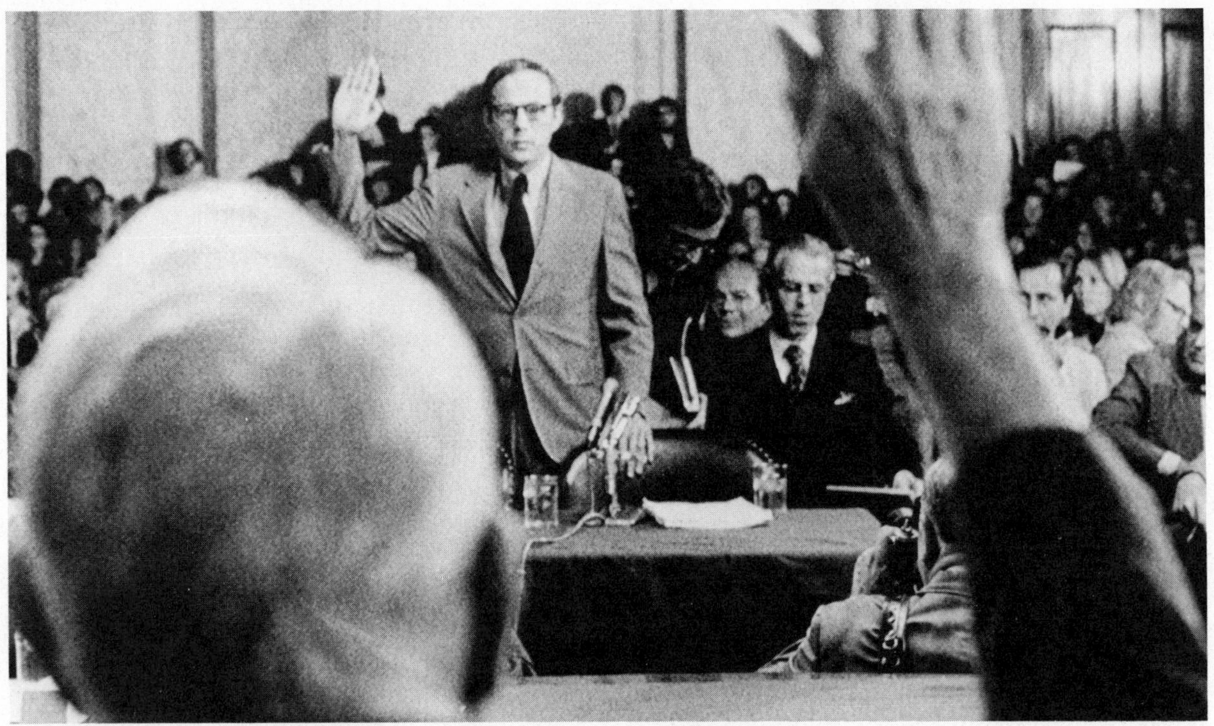

The Watergate hearings reached a dramatic climax with the testimony of John Dean, here being sworn in before the Senate investigating committee by its chairman, Sam Ervin. To test the truthfulness of Dean's testimony, Senate investigators subpoenaed presidential tapes, and a confrontation with the executive branch resulted.

only a few feet from the President's, painted a picture of intrigue and irregularity that threw serious doubt on the meaning of the 1972 election. Even more shockingly, the testimony sometimes appeared to implicate the President himself.

In the midst of these dramatic hearings a minor White House technician revealed that the President had systematically recorded his conversations. Immediately the Ervin committee and Special Prosecutor Archibald Cox subpoenaed the tapes. The President vigorously refused to surrender them, claiming that it was essential that any President be able to conduct conversations in private. The legal status of the tapes formed the basis for a constitutional encounter between the President on one side and the judiciary and Congress on the other—an encounter that everyone expected to be resolved only by a "definitive decision" of the Supreme Court.

While the President and the nation waited for such a decision, the administration suffered another serious blow. Vice President Spiro Agnew was under investigation for accepting bribes. According to the charges, both during his Maryland career and as Vice President, Agnew had taken large sums of money from construction executives who were anxious to secure government contracts. Agnew repeatedly and indignantly denied the charges until, early in October, he pleaded *nolo contendere* (no contest) to a charge of tax evasion—in an attempt to avoid further prosecution and a possible prison sentence. Simultaneously he resigned as Vice President. Making the first use of the Twenty-fifth Amendment, the President nominated Republican Congressman Gerald Ford of Michigan as his choice to replace Agnew. The nomination required congressional approval.

While the administration was digesting the

After pleading no contest to a tax evasion charge at a Baltimore federal court, Vice President Spiro Agnew resigned his office. He claimed that he acted to avoid a divisive struggle in the courts.

shock of the Vice President's resignation, a federal appeals court ruled that Nixon must turn over the presidential tapes and other documents to a federal judge. After a tense delay the President announced that he would neither obey the appeals court nor appeal the case to the Supreme Court. He was willing, however, to produce written versions of the tapes. At the same time he ordered Archibald Cox to take no further legal action to obtain the tapes. The Special Prosecutor refused, and the President ordered the attorney general to fire him. In his turn the attorney general refused and resigned. The assistant attorney general followed suit. Finally the solicitor general, third man in the Justice Department, agreed to carry out the President's order. Overnight the President had gotten rid of Cox but had also lost the first two men in the department that was investigating possible White House involvement in crimes.

The result was an outcry of public indignation that one of the President's own aids described as a "fire storm." Washington was suddenly flooded with letters and telegrams demanding the impeachment of the President. Then, just as suddenly, Nixon announced that he would obey the court's order and surrender the tapes. This gesture helped to cool the demands for impeachment. But several congressmen had already introduced impeachment resolutions, and a House committee announced that it was going to proceed at "full speed" with hearings on possible impeachment.

The President had steadily narrowed the circle of denials and refusals with which he had originally tried to surround himself. He was now laid open to the ultimate constitutional action that might be taken against him. He had seen his administration severely wounded by resignations and indictments. He had heard himself publicly accused of criminal behavior by other political leaders. After his promise to surrender the tapes—a promise he had refused to make until his impeachment seemed likely—the President appeared to have no remaining cards to play. The initiative had shifted almost completely to the courts and to Congress. Richard Nixon, a President who was extremely fond of making spectacular moves and decisions, could only wait while the other branches of government came to their decisions.

Neil Armstrong took this photograph of Edwin Aldrin preparing a scientific experiment on the surface of the moon. Their successful lunar landing fulfilled John Kennedy's promise of 1961 to put Americans on the moon before 1970.

THE MOONSHOT

It Was Not so much the height of the rocket as its weight that was remarkable. True, it was as tall as sixty of any of the men aboard it. But it weighed a fantastic 6 1/2 million pounds. It stood on a launch pad at Cape Kennedy, Florida, waiting to be shot into space toward the moon. Almost at its peak three astronauts waited. Two of them were destined to be the first human beings ever to step onto the moon. All over the United States people watched on television, just as they had watched the Democratic convention in Chicago a year before. This time, however, it was not violence they awaited but a spectacular triumph of human skill and technology.

The name of the rocket, "Saturn," was taken from antiquity. The moonshot was the eleventh in a series with another classical name, "Apollo." But the astronauts' capsule had a patriotic name, "Columbia." And the small "Lunar Excursion Module" in which two of them would drop onto the surface of the moon also bore a name Americans treasure as a national symbol, "Eagle."

When the Saturn roared to life on July 15, the three astronauts experienced only mild excitement. Their hearts speeded up a bit, but they were experienced, well-trained men for whom the moment of lift-off was almost routine. Slowly at first and then with almost unbelievable speed the rocket roared upward. Within minutes, the astronauts were orbiting the earth weightlessly. Then they were launched on a course aimed at the moon almost a quarter of a million miles away.

For the next two days the men moved farther and farther from the earth's field of gravity. Late on July 17 they passed that invisible point in space where the moon's gravity becomes stronger than the earth's. After this, they literally fell toward the moon, reaching a silent speed of over 5,000 miles per hour. Saturday night, July 18, they disappeared behind the moon, in the first of several orbits they would make while preparing to separate the Columbia from the Eagle. After separation the Eagle would aim for a target on the moon named the Sea of Tranquillity.

The separation was completed early Sunday. Several hours later the two astronauts in the Eagle fired the rockets that would slow their craft down. It began its final controlled fall toward the moon's surface. At the last moment two astronauts, Neil Armstrong and Edwin Aldrin, could see they were headed for a rough, rocky crater. Quickly, they took control of the awkward-looking little Eagle away from the computers. Firing rockets to slow their fall, they dropped farther. Armstrong's heartbeat increased to 156 per minute, more than twice the normal pulse.

Suddenly, the rockets stopped firing as the ship came to rest on the surface. Armstrong reported to the space headquarters in Houston, Texas: "Houston: Tranquillity Base here. The Eagle has landed." It was 4:17 P.M., Eastern Daylight Time, July 20, 1969.

Hours later, just before 11 o'clock that night, Armstrong opened the hatch of the Eagle and climbed carefully down a short ladder toward the surface. He moved uncertainly, clumsy in his pressurized white spacesuit. With him he carried a heavy back-pack to provide him with air and cool his suit against the 250-degree temperature of the moon's morning. Finally, he planted a heavy boot on the powdery moon and said, through the static of his radio, "That's one small step for man, one giant leap for mankind."

Aldrin followed Armstrong down the ladder. The astronauts planted an American flag, stiffened with wires to make it "fly" on the airless moon. Awkwardly, the astronauts stepped back and saluted the bit of red, white, and blue cloth that stood out oddly against the bleak, gray moonscape. Then they placed a plaque on the surface to mark their achievement. Unlike the flag, the plaque credited the event to the entire human race:

> Here men from the planet earth first set foot upon the moon, July, 1969, A.D. We came in peace for all mankind.

With these ceremonies completed, the two set out to explore the area around their spacecraft. They moved around in odd hops, six or eight feet long, in the moon's weak gravity. They took samples of lunar "soil" and collected forty-five pounds of moon rocks. These would be their only "payload" on the trip home. Finally, they crawled back up the ladder to the Eagle.

On Monday afternoon, after about one earth day on the moon, the Eagle's rockets were fired. Leaving its heavy base behind, the craft lifted precariously off the moon. There followed an orbital chase of the mother ship, Columbia, in which the third astronaut had been orbiting and waiting. The link-up was successful. Aldrin and Armstrong reentered the Columbia for the trip home. They pointed their craft across the darkness and cold of space to a spot in the Pacific where they would splash down. The trip home began. As though to remind himself and all people of the humility they ought to feel in the face of their own accomplishment, Aldrin read a verse from the Bible over the Columbia's radio: "When I consider the heavens, the work of Thy fingers, the moon and the stars which Thou has ordained, what is man that Thou art mindful of him?"

New Directions in the Economy

Aldrin's Scriptural passage, the use of patriotic names and the flag, the plaque declaring peace—all these aspects of the moon landing marked it as an achievement of the human spirit. But, at bottom, it was more significant as the most striking single symbol of America's rapid technological change and economic growth during the 1960s.

The rocket and the electronic and computer technology that made the moon flight possible exemplified a marked change in the nature of American economic life. The space program as a whole showed just how productive the economy had become. All during the post–World War II period productivity had steadily increased. Then in the 1960s the economy rose to a rate of production few economists could have predicted. The billions of dollars spent to send Armstrong and Aldrin after their forty-five pounds of rocks were billions that came out of what the government considered surpluses.

PATTERNS OF CHANGE

In several important ways the economy of the 1960s and 1970s differed noticeably from American economies of the past. First, it was oriented much more to consumer goods than to heavy industrial goods. The mainstay of the modern economy had clearly become, by 1960, the cars, clothing, household appliances, and other items that ordinary families bought from year to year.

Second, though continuing a long-term trend, the new economy was built more and more on credit. Home mortgages, bank loans, and installment purchases enabled Americans to buy more goods than most other people in the world could even dream of getting. From 1945 to 1970, in fact, the volume of consumer credit increased ten times. It was this, and not industrial technology, that some economists said was the most important American "invention."

Third, the new economy was characterized by an increasing reliance on computer technology. Computers ran banks, oil refineries, even some libraries. By the 1970s many ordinary supermarket cash registers were linked to large computers that regulated the flow of stock to the market shelves. Computers were changing the practice of medicine, too. Even professional football teams used computers to help determine strategies and player trades. Thus by 1969 the "on-board computer" that helped fly the astronauts to the moon and back was no longer a strange science-fiction fantasy. It was as common a feature of American society as the Ford automobile had been in the 1920s.

Fourth, and perhaps most important, the American economy was changing rapidly from a system that rested on a solid basis of production to one that centered on service. Economists divide economic activity into three principal types. The first (characteristic of the American economy in the colonial period) is called primary, or extractive. It involves taking goods directly from nature, as a tobacco planter, a fur trader, or a goldminer does. The second type (basic to the industrial revolution of the nineteenth and twentieth centuries) involves the production of artificial goods like automobiles, steam engines, and airplanes.

The third type of economic activity involves services. The money people spend on policemen's salaries or advertising or going to movies is spent not for a touchable, physical "good" (as economists call it). Rather, it goes for a service that cannot be resold or stored away for later use. In the simplest terms the United States had, by the beginning of the 1960s, developed a service economy. By 1960 more workers were employed to perform services than to produce goods, a trend that seems likely to continue into the future.

SIGNS OF GROWTH AND WEAKNESS

All these changes occurred in an atmosphere of growth and prosperity. Between 1961 and 1968 the United States experienced the longest and most spectacular period of peacetime economic expansion in its history. Inflation in the prices of goods and services was held down to a low of about 1 percent per year. Economic growth, on the other hand, occurred at a rate of about 5 percent. This meant that the total value of all goods and services Americans bought and sold and paid for in taxes doubled between 1956 and

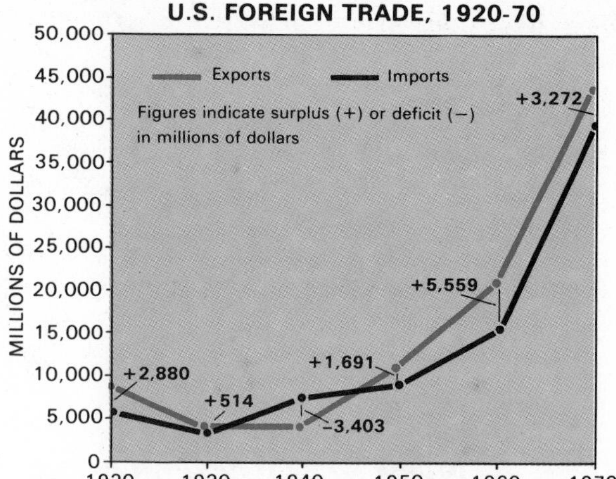

1971, from less than $500 billion to more than $1 trillion.

Americans took this kind of growth more or less for granted. About 1968, however, problems began to develop that cast doubt on both the stability and wisdom of these growth patterns. For one thing the rate of growth itself slowed down rather drastically. Also, between 1968 and 1973, inflation rose at a rate that frightened many economists, businessmen, and politicians. In fact, prices soared at a rate of about 6 percent a year, despite efforts by the Nixon administration to control them.

At the same time, the rate of increase in Gross National Product, the most convenient measurement of economic growth, slowed to less than half that of the period 1961–68. Unemployment then became a critical problem. Nationally, the unemployment figure hovered around 5 percent of the work force, or about one worker out of every twenty. But in some industrial states unemployment neared 10 percent in the early 1970s. All three factors—the slowing growth rate, inflation, and unemployment—became major political issues for the second Nixon administration and major daily worries for Americans.

The domestic economy's lack of strength also weakened the dollar abroad. Since World

War II the dollar had been the world's strongest currency. But America's leveling growth rate and rising inflation caused the dollar's value to decrease in relation to other currencies like the German mark and Japanese yen. President Nixon had to keep devaluing the dollar—that is, to accept official reductions in the amount of money it took to exchange an American dollar for another nation's currency.

PROBLEMS IN AN AFFLUENT SOCIETY

These weaknesses in the American economy were worrisome enough. But they were further complicated by other noneconomic problems. For one thing, it became more apparent than ever that affluence was not shared equally. In general, the history of the American economy has seen the spreading of wealth to middle- and lower-income groups. Thus in 1929 the richest 20 percent of Americans received almost 60 percent of the money every year. But by 1960 the same group received only about 45 percent. After 1960 this kind of democratic change slowed almost to a stop. Almost no shift occurred in the distribution of income over the next dozen years. Clearly, the problem of poverty was not being solved by economic growth and change.

A second nagging issue that became increasingly important after the mid-1960s was the mounting problem of urban decay. The failure of Americans to keep their great cities clean, safe,

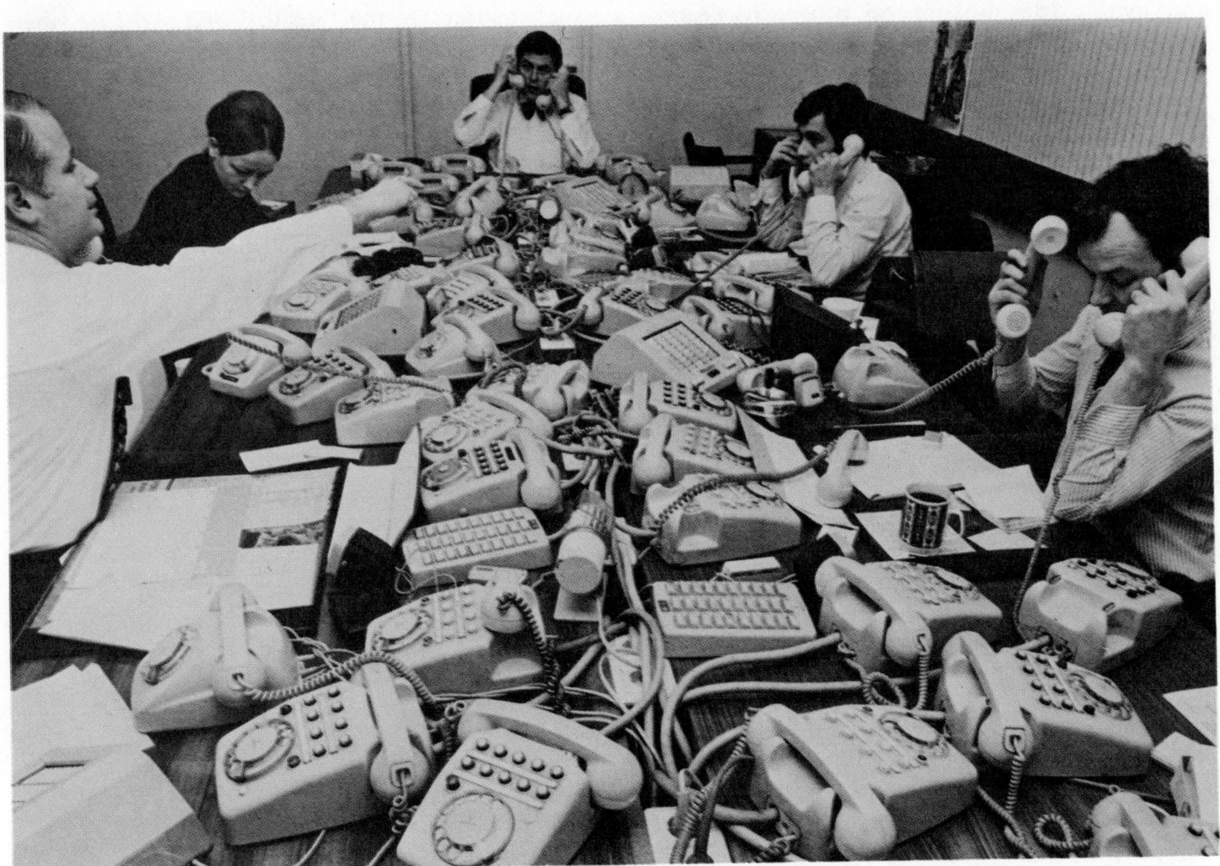

When the dollar was devalued in February 1973, brokers in international currency were deluged with calls. The dollar's weakness was a sign of the economy's illness.

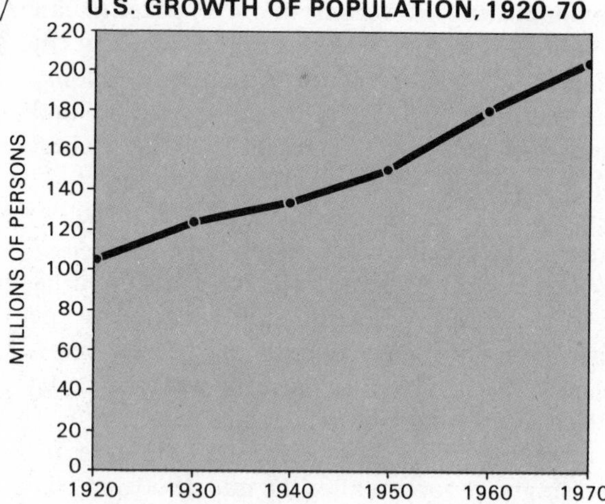

and livable (despite general prosperity) suggested to some observers that mere growth was not the solution. Partly because of the movement by blacks for civil rights and the rioting that often broke out in large cities, many Americans began to ask for a reexamination of national priorities. They challenged the use of valuable resources for superhighways or moon landings instead of for the more obvious and pressing problems of urban poverty and decay.

Finally, a new interest in the natural environment began to cast doubt on the wisdom of economic growth itself. This new concern for "ecology" (the delicate relationship between man and his natural surroundings) questioned the very concept of productivity. The criticism of growth by those interested in the environment took many forms. For one thing, ecologists insisted on the necessity of slowing down the rate of population increase, both in the United States and the whole world. Overpopulation threatened massive famines. For another, they warned that the world could support only so much economic activity before it began to collapse. In so doing they awakened a new consciousness of the fragility of the earth's resources and wildlife.

For the first time in their history large numbers of Americans began to worry about such matters as the "death" of Lake Erie, the disappearance of whole species of wildlife, and, by the 1970s, an "energy crisis" that actually threatened shortages of gasoline and electricity. Against such a background President Nixon announced the indefinite postponement of any more manned space explorations. Astronaut Aldrin's biblical question, "What is man?" seemed more urgent—and profound—than ever before.

Suds from phosphate detergents dumped into Lake Erie created a serious hazard to life along the lakefront. Pollution of the natural environment is one of the ongoing problems of industrial civilization.

Two hundred thousand people, black and white, filled the Washington Memorial mall in August 1968 to give a visible form to Martin Luther King's dream of racial harmony.

A Man and His Dream

MARTIN LUTHER KING, JR., stepped to the microphone and looked out on some 200,000 people still massed patiently on the mall before the Washington Monument. They had been coming to Washington for days. There a great march and demonstration for civil rights and racial equality was to be held. And now, on August 28, 1963, they had listened to speeches and sung hymns and freedom songs almost all day. Many of them were veterans of the 1955–56 bus boycott in Montgomery, Alabama, or of countless other sit-ins and demonstrations that had followed.

Huge as it was, the crowd was only a small part of what many participants called simply the movement. It represented hundreds of local groups that had organized and marched and sat-in and struggled for the integration of schools, lunch counters, hotels, and swimming pools. They worked for better jobs and equal pay for blacks, for the right to vote, for equal housing—for all those concrete goals summed up in the word "freedom." Now, in Martin Luther King, they were about to hear the man who, more than any other American, was the movement's voice.

His voice could captivate listeners. A well-trained voice of a professional minister, it was deep and strong—with a well-timed tremble on the important words that he wished to emphasize. He had all the skills of the country preacher, black or white: simplicity, repetition, and homely images.

It was the voice of an experienced political leader too. From the beginnings in Montgomery King had become not just a spokesman for the movement but also one of its strategists. He had already organized and led massive protests against segregation. He had learned how to provoke white leaders to serve his cause. Some of his younger followers already complained that he was too conservative, too committed to winning cooperation from white liberals. They would complain more and more as the years passed.

Some complained, too, that King's passionate devotion to nonviolence made the movement weak. In the end, they argued, the only thing white racists could understand was force and power. But King had so far managed to thread his way skillfully through such criticisms and the need to inspire passion in the blacks, who were the only real base of the movement.

King's voice was also that of a man whose courage few people doubted. He had lined up with his followers (many of them children) against policemen's clubs, firehoses, and dogs. Earlier in the year he had gathered thousands of blacks in Birmingham, Alabama, against what was probably the most vicious police repression of a protest demonstration in modern American history. And he had seen the insides of several jails and state prisons as a result of his work. Whenever blacks had become violent, he had gone into saloons and pool halls to plead with them to be gentle and forgive the violence they experienced.

In any other man such passion and such well-publicized courage might have looked a little foolish. It would have been easy for King to seem ridiculous or pretentious. But he always managed, somehow, to stop short of the point where he might become a holier-than-thou joke to less visionary people, white or black.

Today, before the immense crowd, with television cameras focused relentlessly on him, he would prove again that he could put meaning into words like "hope" and "freedom" and "faith." At first he read from the speech he had carefully prepared, hammering away at one point. It had been a hundred years since the Civil War, and still the promises of equality had not been redeemed. One hundred years and black Americans were still crippled, lonely, and poor.

Then King stopped reading and began to improvise, drawing on all his training and experience in the pulpit. He drew, too, on the encouraging shouts and cheers that began to roll up from the crowd. Soon something like an overpowering conversation began to take place. The crowd urged him on, and King repaid their cheering with one ringing phrase after another. "I have a dream today," he began. The noise of the crowd came back to him. It pushed him into a shouted, trembling meditation that soon brought the audience to its feet:

> I have a dream that my four little children will one day live in a nation where they will not be judged by the color of their skin but by the content of their character.

And then, again, the electrifying assertion:

> I have a dream today.

And again, the roar.

> I have a dream that one day the state of Alabama, whose governor's lips are presently dripping with the words of interposition and nullification,[1] will be transformed into a situation where little black boys and black girls will be able to join hands with little white boys and white girls and walk together as sisters and brothers.
>
> I have a dream today.

Then King passed swiftly into the comforting language of biblical faith:

> I have a dream that one day every valley shall be exalted, every hill and mountain shall be made low, the rough places will be made plain,

[1] Interposition is the idea that a state may oppose a federal policy, such as desegregation, with which it disagrees. Nullification means that a state fails to enforce a particular federal law within its territory.

> and the crooked places will be made straight, and the glory of the Lord shall be revealed, and all flesh shall see it together.

The speech already had tremendous emotional impact. But King had still more to say. He chose an American patriotic song for his final theme:

> This will be the day when all of God's children will be able to sing with new meaning, "My country, 'tis of thee, sweet land of liberty, of thee I sing. Land where my fathers died, land of the pilgrim's pride, from every mountainside, let freedom ring."

Probably no other man in America could have used such words so movingly. But King had an astonishing talent for giving new toughness to familiar language. So the massive crowd only cheered harder as he went on:

> And if America is to be a great nation, this must become true. So let freedom ring from the prodigious hilltops of New Hampshire. Let freedom ring from the mighty mountains of New York. Let freedom ring from the heightening Alleghenies of Pennsylvania!
>
> Let freedom ring from the snowcapped Rockies of Colorado!
>
> Let freedom ring from the curvaceous peaks of California!
>
> But not only that; let freedom ring from Stone Mountain of Georgia!
>
> Let freedom ring from Lookout Mountain of Tennessee!

Martin Luther King, Jr., was the most eloquent spokesman for racial justice in the 1960s. For many, his passionate plea for nonviolence was undercut by his own violent death at the hands of an assassin.

> Let freedom ring from every hill and mole-hill of Mississippi! From every mountainside, let freedom ring!
>
> When we let freedom ring, when we let it ring from every village and every hamlet, from every state and every city, we will be able to speed up that day when all of God's children, black men and white men, Jews and Gentiles, Protestants and Catholics, will be able to join hands and sing in the words of the old Negro spiritual, "Free at last! Free at last! Thank God almighty, we are free at last!"

Judged by his own professional standards, the speech was probably not Martin Luther King's best. But it was really not so much a speech as an event. What he and the crowd had managed to create together was one of those very rare moments when people give expression to their highest ideals and best hopes. Jefferson did it in the opening sentences of the Declaration of Independence. Lincoln did it at Gettysburg. In the last few minutes of his speech King somehow became the conscience of the America of the 1960s.

But against his dream some unhappy realities had to be placed. These realities called him and his movement quickly and regularly back to frustration and failure. Less than three weeks after King put his dream into words, he hurried back to Birmingham. There he had been leading a long protest against segregation. Someone had tossed a bomb into a black church, killing four young girls. In the same day, Birmingham police killed two blacks. At the funeral King spoke bitterly of the "stale bread of hatred and the spoiled meat of racism."

There were some victories for the dream, too. The Civil Rights Act of 1964 was at least as much the creation of King as of Lyndon Johnson. The Nobel Prize for peace he won the same year was one of the highest recognitions the world could give his talents and contributions. Yet there was always the hard and ever-present reality of poverty and racism. The movement stumbled on, often splintered by criticism within. King turned north, taking the movement to Chicago to demand attention for black poverty and deprivation in Northern cities. There he encountered resistance as stiff as any he had met in the South. He became increasingly concerned with the war in Indochina, which he considered an immediate evil almost as important as the old problem of race. The reality of Indochina, too, often seemed incurable.

Five years after his great speech, a frustrated King was trying to plan another march on Washington. This one, he said, would be a "last desperate demand" for an end to "the worst chaos, hatred, and violence any nation has ever encountered." In early April 1968, however, he interrupted the planning to go to Memphis, Tennessee, to help in a strike of black sanitation men against the city. On April 4 he walked onto a balcony outside his motel room and leaned over the rail to talk to a friend in the parking lot two stories below. In a nearby building a rifle fired. The bullet passed through King's jaw and neck; in a short time he was dead.

Social Dreams and Realities

OF ALL THE urges that move Americans probably none is more pronounced than the need to feel that their experience is somehow new and different from other peoples' in other times. Americans keep finding ways to assert they have been singled out for a unique destiny that will separate them from history and move them into a special future. This need is as old as the first English settlements of North America. John Winthrop was fond of reminding his fellow Puritans that they had embarked on an experiment that would set them apart from the rest of mankind.

The leaders of the American Revolution, too, had a deep sense of uniqueness and experimentation. In his turn, Lincoln asked for a "new birth of freedom." Similarly, in the twentieth century, one President after another has tried to identify himself with newness. So we have seen Theodore Roosevelt's New Nationalism, Woodrow Wilson's New Freedom, and Franklin Roosevelt's New Deal. Even conservatives have insisted on the newness of their ideas. Herbert Hoover bravely announced that the United States had entered a "New Era." And Dwight Eisenhower often spoke of a "new prosperity."

But perhaps no generation of Americans has been as touched by the rage for newness as that of the 1960s. John F. Kennedy enjoyed pointing out that the "torch" of leadership had at last been passed to men and women "born in this century." He even called his program the New Frontier.

But if there was any reason to think of the 1960s as truly new or different, the reason did not lie in politics at all. All the political campaigns and crises of the Kennedy, Johnson, and Nixon years were acted out against a background of deep social change and conflict that made presidential politics seem almost irrelevant. Part of the underlying meaning of the "battle of Chicago" was that national politics had continued in a more or less traditional pattern while society at large had undergone fundamental changes.

The enormous public pressure that finally forced Johnson and Nixon to try to end the war in Indochina was also a signal that traditional habits of foreign policy were being rejected by

Among those influenced by King's advocacy of nonviolent tactics was Cesar Chavez, leader of the Mexican American farm workers. Here he ends a twenty-three day fast in support of striking grape growers by breaking bread with Robert Kennedy.

growing numbers of Americans. The moon landing, too, suggested that if the 1960s and 1970s had any unique significance, it was not to be found primarily in politics but rather in deep changes in America's economics and technology.

MOVEMENTS FOR CHANGE

In such an atmosphere, it seemed possible to believe a new era had in fact arrived. In 1963 Martin Luther King's proclamation, "I have a dream," made as much sense as any dream in American history. Not just for the 200,000 or more whites and blacks who assembled to hear King but for millions of others it seemed reasonable to hope that a new era had at last arrived. Old promises of freedom and equality, long-denied and half-forgotten, surfaced again. They found expression in dozens of organized movements demanding peace, equality, or freedom.

The 1960s saw many such movements. As the symbolic leader of the most powerful movement of all, King stood nearer the center of his generation's struggles than any other American. Like the "radicals" at Chicago a few months after his murder, King demanded changes of a political nature–new civil rights laws, for example. But, again like the young demonstrators in Chicago, King expressed a dream that went well beyond politics. In his lifetime dozens of groups of Americans, many of them overlapping, joined militant movements that aimed at change. Women, blacks, Mexican Americans, Indians, homosexuals, college students–one group after another began to complain bitterly about their exploitation by the Establishment and to demand "liberation."

The civil rights movement, for which King spoke so effectively, was the largest and in some ways the most successful. But it was only one movement among many. Growing from it (and adopting many of its tactics) was the whole range of protests and organized demands that gave the period from 1960 onward so much of its unique flavor and tone.

College students on campuses from California to New York organized little "revolutions." They took over buildings, marched, sang, and issued manifestoes demanding an end to the Indochina war. Other Americans engaged in campaigns to legalize abortion, homosexuality, and the use of marijuana. Toward the end of the decade millions of women began crusading for women's liberation, an end to what they regarded as the injustices of a society dominated by men.

All these drives existed on the edges of politics, though they affected politics deeply. Certainly King's speech affected the passage of the Civil Rights Act of 1964, and the peace movement probably forced Lyndon Johnson's decision not to run for reelection in 1968. But they were far more than political phenomena. The movements of the 1960s went deeper into society than politics normally does. They also reflected, more accurately than surface political events, some of the profound changes in the nature of American society.

Moreover, the movements of the period seemed to thrive most on direct action outside the ordinary channels of politics. In the process they created a new vocabulary and a new style of behavior. The new vocabulary was full of words like "protest," "demand," "demonstration," and "confrontation." The new style was one of action, often illegal and sometimes violent and deadly.

The movement for black civil rights inspired other movements like Women's Liberation. These demonstrators use the foremost symbol of freedom as the backdrop for their demands for political and economic equality.

RESISTANCE AND POLARIZATION

To most Americans—especially to those who were not black or Puerto-Rican, young, or students in college—all these movements and their loud demands were frightening. Public opinion polls showed very clearly that a majority of Americans actually approved the way the Chicago police had handled the demonstrations. And, for all the vocal opposition to the Indochina war that students and others created, this war was supported most of the time by an equal number of citizens.

Such ordinary Americans—the people Richard Nixon called the silent majority, or middle America—were shocked by the "radicalism" of many of the groups of the 1960s. To them, and to most of their professional political leaders, it was painfully obvious that black "militants," "hippies," and student "revolutionaries" represented a critical danger to the country. It was among this decided majority of Americans that Republicans like Richard Nixon and conservative Democrats like George Wallace and Richard Daley found their base of support.

This conflict between a confused, sometimes frightened, and often angry middle America on one side and those demanding social change on the other gave the years after 1960 much of their air of crisis. The lines seemed clearly drawn. At one pole stood millions of people demanding changes in society, in laws, in politics, even in what many people regarded as simple good manners. At the other pole was the desire by this not-always-silent majority for "law and order." The slogan, a rather vague phrase, stood for the preservation of traditional patterns of family life, race relations, and attitudes toward drugs, pornography, abortion, plus many other social details.

Part of the genius of Martin Luther King's 1963 speech was the skill with which he attempted to cut through the atmosphere of polarization. His Washington audience was at least one-fourth white. The television audience was many times as large and doubtless had even more whites. For this audience King was able to link civil rights closely to the most cherished rhetoric of patriotic Americans—even to the music they had all learned in schools: "From every mountainside, let freedom ring."

BLACK MILITANCY

But King's experience after 1963 also mirrored the increasing tensions and frustrations of a divided society. In all the movements of protest and reform there were growing demands for more immediate change, more direct action, more violence. Long before King's assassination, a struggle had developed among young black leaders. It would eventually challenge the essentially nonviolent definition that King wanted his own group to have. The challenge focused on

Within a decade the tone of the civil rights movement changed dramatically. Quiet picketing gave way to strident mass protest. Rising expectations and growing frustrations offer some explanation.

what quickly became known as militancy. Some black leaders thought King's tactics were too slow, too peaceful, and too dependent on white cooperation. So they demanded a more aggressive strategy.

In 1966, two years before King's death, two of the most important black organizations underwent fierce struggles for control between militants and moderates. In the Student Nonviolent Coordinating Committee (the group that had begun the sit-ins of the early 1960s) a young man named Stokely Carmichael, whose slogan would soon become "Black Power," won control. The Congress of Racial Equality elected a young, aggressive leader named Floyd McKissick.

Even before this, another black, much more radical than King, Malcolm Little (or Malcolm X as he was known after he joined the religious and militant Black Muslims) had already presented a serious challenge to King's moderate leadership in New York and other Northern cities. Malcolm X himself was killed at a New York rally in 1965. His death—combined with King's and with the killing of several Black Panther party leaders in Chicago in 1970—opened the way for a more and more splintered contest for public leadership of black Americans.

UNANSWERED QUESTIONS

No one—not even King—really knew the answers to two critical questions: Who really spoke for black America? Even more fundamentally, did "the black community" really exist as a unified social and political whole? As far as voting statistics and other figures indicated, militant leaders had only a small following. Millions of blacks seemed to be going quietly about their daily lives. In the process they appeared to be changing an impressive range of statistics about the place of black people in American society.

In the 1960s, for example, the proportion of blacks whose jobs could be labeled skilled, clerical, or professional increased from about one out of every five to one out of every three. At the same time the proportion of blacks finishing high school jumped from a little over one-third to almost two-thirds. In the South the number of blacks attending integrated schools rose from only 6 percent in 1965 to 38 percent in 1969. In Northern cities family income among blacks rose from about 75 percent of the figure for whites in 1960 to practical equality in 1970.

But despite such encouraging statistics, a turn for the worse appeared about 1970. Over the next three years black family income actually declined in proportion to that of whites. And unemployment statistics (which had improved during the 1960s) once again became even worse for blacks than for whites. Educational statistics continued to improve. But in the tough reality of jobs and income the situation of blacks seemed to be starting a slide downward from some of the gains of the preceding decade.

At the same time it was also obvious that the poorest group of Americans by far was still the lower-income fifth of the black population. In Northern cities great black ghettos had been created in the years since World War II. Nothing could hide the fact that the millions who lived in them did not participate at all in whatever overall improvement took place in the general condition of blacks.

It was undeniably true that blacks who happened to be well off were making progress in political terms. Thurgood Marshall became the first black justice on the Supreme Court; Edward Brooke of Massachusetts was elected as the first black senator since Reconstruction; Robert Weaver was the first black man ever appointed to the Cabinet. The election of black mayors in Cleveland, Newark, and Los Angeles also appeared to be a sign of very real gains. Yet such facts as these could not hide the equally obvious truth that those blacks who were poor and obscure lived lives that were wracked with hunger, disease, drugs, crime, and early death.

Black poverty continued to provide the widespread potential constituency for such organizations as the Black Panther party and the Black Muslims. There was no lack of evidence of violent unrest among urban black populations in the cities outside the South. In 1964, just one

Slums such as this one in the Brownsville section of New York are a continuing reminder that King's dream of equality is still a task for the nation into its third century of existence.

year after King announced his hopeful dream, New York's Harlem exploded into rioting and burning that shocked and surprised the entire nation.

Similar outbreaks of violence followed during the next four years in the Watts area of Los Angeles, as well as in Chicago, Detroit, Newark, New Haven, Washington, Cleveland, and a dozen other important cities. The "disturbances" were not planned. They were not the result of any kind of "conspiracy" among black radicals. They even had some beneficial results. It was partially in response to urban violence that new antidiscrimination laws and programs for the relief of poverty were passed.

Still, the powerful fact that millions of poor black people packed into urban ghettos were deeply hostile to the system of law and stability was a source of anxiety to millions of Americans, both black and white. For reasons that were almost impossible to grasp, the intensity of urban violence, of confrontation of all kinds, in almost all the movements of the 1960s began to slacken off after 1970. Whatever the reason for the relative peace of these years, it was most certainly not that the problems of the 1960s had been solved. True, the war in Indochina appeared to be over. However, every other complaint of the troubled Kennedy and Johnson years still remained.

Above all, it remained an open question whether Americans could—or would—ever deal successfully with the problems of racism and black poverty that Martin Luther King had dreamed of solving. His dream was one kind of answer. His assassination was another. Both were answers rooted in the American past. But no one could tell which answer would be final—whether the riots and assassinations would continue a long history of blunders and failures or whether the dream of 1963 would ever be realized.

1. Was the agreement that led to the removal of Russian missiles from Cuba of greater advantage to the United States or to Russia?
2. How does the existence of "client" nations prevent the full relaxation of Soviet-American tensions? Which of these client relationships do you think is potentially the most dangerous?
3. In what way did the increasing cost of arms help bring on the detente? How did the increasing number of power centers in the world help?
4. Is the Alliance for Progress a continuation of dollar diplomacy? Is the military intervention in Indochina a justifiable extension of the containment policy?
5. Why did demonstrators gather in Chicago for the Democratic National Convention in 1968? Why were they so pessimistic about their chances of success?
6. Show how Kennedy's philosophy is basically New Deal–Fair Deal.
7. What programs made up Johnson's "Great Society"? Given his domestic record do you think he could have run successfully in 1968?
8. In what ways did Nixon try to change the political direction of the country?
9. Why is the American economy today referred to as a consumer economy? a service economy? What is the connection between this country's affluence and its ecological problems?
10. What was the significance of Martin Luther King's "I Have a Dream" speech? Why was King's leadership rejected by the militants?

Beyond the Text

1. American interventions in Laos, the Dominican Republic, and Vietnam seem to have been initiated on behalf of unpopular but anticommunist governments. Should the United States support such governments?
2. Debate the proposition: The Expenditure of Vast Sums of Money to Reach the Moon Is Money Unwisely Spent.
3. It is claimed that black liberation movements often set the style and tone of other movements in the 1960s. Compare the goals and tactics of women, Mexican Americans, Indians, and other minority groups to test this statement's validity.

Bibliography

Nonfiction

Ashby, Darell, ed., *The Discontented Society.**
Berman, Ronald, *America in the Sixties.**
Burner, David, Robert Marcus, and Thomas West, *A Giant's Strength: America in the 1960s.**
Cleaver, Eldridge, *Soul on Ice.**
Draper, Theodore, *Abuse of Power.**
Fall, Bernard B., *Viet-Nam Witness: 1953–1966.*
Friedan, Betty, *The Feminine Mystique.**
Goldman, Eric F., *Tragedy of Lyndon Johnson.**
King, Martin Luther, *Why We Can't Wait.**
Muse, Benjamin, *The American Negro Revolution.**
Phillips, Kevin, *The Emerging Republican Majority.**
Schlesinger, Arthur M., Jr., *Thousand Days.**
Shaplen, Robert, *Time Out of Hand: Revolution & Reaction in Southeast Asia.**
Sullivan, Walter, ed., *America's Race for the Moon.*
White, Theodore H., *The Making of the President, 1964,* 1968,* 1972.*

Fiction

Brown, Claude, *Manchild in the Promised Land.**
Kesey, Ken, *One Flew Over the Cuckoo's Nest.**
Wolfe, Tom, *Electric Kool-Aid Acid Test.**

*a paperback book

THE DECLARATION OF INDEPENDENCE

In Congress, July 4, 1776. *The unanimous Declaration of the thirteen united States of America,*

When in the Course of human events, it becomes necessary for one people to dissolve the political bands which have connected them with another, and to assume among the powers of the earth, the separate and equal station to which the Laws of Nature and of Nature's God entitle them, a decent respect to the opinions of mankind requires that they should declare the causes which impel them to the separation.—

We hold these truths to be self-evident, that all men are created equal, that they are endowed by their Creator with certain unalienable Rights, that among these are Life, Liberty and the pursuit of Happiness.—

That to secure these rights, Governments are instituted among Men, deriving their just powers from the consent of the governed,—

That whenever any Form of Government becomes destructive of these ends, it is the Right of the People to alter or to abolish it, and to institute new Government, laying its foundation on such principles and organizing its powers in such form, as to them shall seem most likely to effect their Safety and Happiness. Prudence, indeed, will dictate that Governments long established should not be changed for light and transient causes; and accordingly all experience hath shown, that mankind are more disposed to suffer, while evils are sufferable, than to right themselves by abolishing the forms to which they are accustomed. But when a long train of abuses and usurpations, pursuing invariably the same Object evinces a design to reduce them under absolute Despotism, it is their right, it is their duty, to throw off such Government, and to provide new Guards for their future security.—

Such has been the patient sufferance of these Colonies; and such is now the necessity which constrains them to alter their former Systems of Government. The history of the present King of Great Britain is a history of repeated injuries and usurpations, all having in direct object the establishment of an absolute Tyranny over these States. To prove this, let Facts be submitted to a candid world.—

He has refused his Assent to Laws, the most wholesome and necessary for the public good.—

He has forbidden his Governors to pass Laws of immediate and pressing importance, unless suspended in their operation till his Assent should be obtained; and when so suspended, he has utterly neglected to attend to them.—

He has refused to pass other Laws for the accommodation of large districts of people, unless those people would relinquish the right of Representation in the Legislature, a right inestimable to them and formidable to tyrants only.—

He has called together legislative bodies at places unusual, uncomfortable, and distant from the depository of their public Records, for the sole purpose of fatiguing them into compliance with his measures.—

He has dissolved Representative Houses repeatedly, for opposing with manly firmness his invasions on the rights of the people.—

He has refused for a long time, after such dissolutions, to cause others to be elected; whereby the Legislative powers, incapable of Annihilation, have returned to the People at large for their exercise; the State remaining in the mean time exposed to all the dangers of invasion from without, and convulsions within.—

He has endeavoured to prevent the population of these States; for that purpose obstructing the Laws for Naturalization of Foreigners; refusing to pass others to encourage their migrations hither, and raising the conditions of new Appropriations of Lands.—

He has obstructed the Administration of Justice, by refusing his Assent to Laws for establishing Judiciary powers.—

He has made Judges dependent on his Will alone, for the tenure of their offices, and the amount and payment of their salaries.—

He has erected a multitude of New Offices, and sent hither swarms of Officers to harrass our people, and eat out their substance.—

He has kept among us in times of peace, Standing Armies without the Consent of our legislatures.—

He has affected to render the Military independent of and superior to the Civil power.—

He has combined with others to subject us to a jurisdiction foreign to our constitution, and unacknowledged by our laws; giving his Assent to their Acts of pretended Legislation:—

For quartering large bodies of armed troops among us:—

For protecting them, by a mock Trial, from punishment for any Murders which they should commit on the Inhabitants of these States:—

For cutting off our Trade with all parts of the world:—

For imposing Taxes on us without our Consent:—

For depriving us in many cases, of the benefits of Trial by Jury:—

For transporting us beyond Seas to be tried for pretended offences:—

For abolishing the free System of English Laws in a neighbouring Province, establishing therein an Arbitrary government, and enlarging its Boundaries so as to render it at once an example and fit instrument for introducing the same absolute rule in these Colonies:—

For taking away our Charters, abolishing our most valuable Laws, and altering fundamentally the Forms of our Governments:—

For suspending our own Legislatures, and declaring themselves invested with power to legislate for us in all cases whatsoever.—

He has abdicated Government here, by declaring us out of his Protection and waging War against us.—

He has plundered our seas, ravaged our Coasts, burnt our towns, and destroyed the lives of our people.—

He is at this time transporting large Armies of foreign Mercenaries to compleat the works of death, desolation and tyranny, already begun with circumstances of Cruelty & perfidy scarcely paralleled in the most barbarous ages, and totally unworthy the Head of a civilized nation.—

He has constrained our fellow Citizens taken Captive on the high Seas to bear Arms against their Country, to become the executioners of their friends and Brethren, or to fall themselves by their Hands.—

He has excited domestic insurrections amongst us, and has endeavoured to bring on the inhabitants of our frontiers, the merciless Indian Savages, whose known rule of warfare, is an undistinguished destruction of all ages, sexes and conditions.

In every stage of these Oppressions We have Petitioned for Redress in the most humble terms: Our repeated Petitions have been answered only by repeated injury. A Prince, whose character is thus marked by every act which may define a Tyrant, is unfit to be the ruler of a free people.

Nor have We been wanting in attentions to our British brethren. We have warned them from time to time of attempts by their legislature to extend an unwarrantable jurisdiction over us. We have reminded them of the circumstances of our emigration and settlement here. We have appealed to their native justice and magnanimity, and we have conjured them by the ties of our common kindred to disavow these usurpations, which, would inevitably interrupt our connections and correspondence. They too have been deaf to the voice of justice and of consanguinity. We must, therefore, acquiesce in the necessity, which denounces our Separation, and hold them, as we hold the rest of mankind, Enemies in War, in Peace Friends.—

We, therefore, the Representatives of the united States of America, in General Congress, Assembled, appealing to the Supreme Judge of the world for the rectitude of our intentions, do, in the Name, and by Authority of the good People of these Colonies, solemnly publish and declare, That these United Colonies are, and of Right ought to be, Free and Independent States; that they are absolved from all Allegiance to the British Crown, and that all political connection between them and the State of Great Britain, is and ought to be totally dissolved; and that as Free and Independent States they have full Power to levy War, conclude Peace, contract Alliances, establish Commerce, and to do all other Acts and Things which Independent States may of right do.—

And for the support of this Declaration, with a firm reliance on the protection of divine Providence, we mutually pledge to each other our Lives, our Fortunes and our sacred Honor.

John Hancock

(MASSACHUSETTS)

NEW HAMPSHIRE
Josiah Bartlett
William Whipple
Matthew Thornton

MASSACHUSETTS
Samuel Adams
John Adams
Robert Treat Paine
Elbridge Gerry

DELAWARE
Caesar Rodney
George Read
Thomas McKean

NEW YORK
William Floyd
Philip Livingston
Francis Lewis
Lewis Morris

NEW JERSEY
Richard Stockton
John Witherspoon
Francis Hopkinson
John Hart
Abraham Clark

NORTH CAROLINA
William Hooper
Joseph Hewes
John Penn

MARYLAND
Samuel Chase
William Paca
Thomas Stone
Charles Carroll of Carrollton

SOUTH CAROLINA
Edward Rutledge
Thomas Heywood, Jr.
Thomas Lynch, Jr.
Arthur Middleton

RHODE ISLAND
Stephen Hopkins
William Ellery

CONNECTICUT
Roger Sherman
Samuel Huntington
William Williams
Oliver Wolcott

PENNSYLVANIA
Robert Morris
Benjamin Rush
Benjamin Franklin
John Morton
George Clymer
James Smith
George Taylor
James Wilson
George Ross

VIRGINIA
George Wythe
Richard Henry Lee
Thomas Jefferson
Benjamin Harrison
Thomas Nelson, Jr.
Francis Lightfoot Lee
Carter Braxton

GEORGIA
Button Gwinnett
Lyman Hall
George Walton

THE CONSTITUTION OF THE UNITED STATES OF AMERICA

We the People of the United States, in Order to form a more perfect Union, establish Justice, insure domestic Tranquility, provide for the common defence, promote the general Welfare, and secure the Blessings of Liberty to ourselves and our Posterity, do ordain and establish this Constitution for the United States of America.

The preamble establishes the principle of government by the people, and lists the six basic purposes of the Constitution.

ARTICLE I • LEGISLATIVE DEPARTMENT

Section 1. All legislative Powers herein granted shall be vested in a Congress of the United States, which shall consist of a Senate and House of Representatives.

Section 2. The House of Representatives shall be composed of Members chosen every second Year by the People of the several States, and the Electors in each State shall have the Qualifications requisite for Electors of the most numerous Branch of the State Legislature.

Representatives serve two-year terms. They are chosen in each state by those electors (that is, voters) who are qualified to vote for members of the lower house of their own state legislature.

No Person shall be a Representative who shall not have attained to the Age of twenty-five Years, and been seven Years a Citizen of the United States, and who shall not, when elected, be an Inhabitant of that State in which he shall be chosen.

Representatives and direct Taxes shall be apportioned among the several States which may be included within this Union, according to their respective Numbers, which shall be determined by adding to the whole Number of free Persons, including those bound to Service for a Term of Years, and excluding Indians not taxed, three-fifths of all other Persons. The actual Enumeration shall be made within three Years after the first Meeting of the Congress of the United States, and within every subsequent Term of ten

The number of representatives allotted to a state is determined by the size of its population. The 14th Amendment has made obsolete the reference to "all other persons"—that is, slaves.

A census must be taken every ten years to determine the number of representatives to which each state is entitled. There is now one representative for about every 470,000 persons.

Source: House Document #529. U.S. Government Printing Office, 1967.
[NOTE: *The Constitution and the amendments are reprinted here in their original form. Portions that have been amended or superseded are in brown type.*] *The words printed in the margins explain some of the more difficult passages.*

Years, in such Manner as they shall by Law direct. The Number of Representatives shall not exceed one for every thirty Thousand, but each State shall have at Least one Representative; and until such enumeration shall be made, the State of New Hampshire shall be entitled to chuse three, Massachusetts eight, Rhode Island and Providence Plantations one, Connecticut five, New York six, New Jersey four, Pennsylvania eight, Delaware one, Maryland six, Virginia ten, North Carolina five, South Carolina five, and Georgia three.

"Executive authority" refers to the governor of a state.

When vacancies happen in the Representation from any State, the Executive Authority thereof shall issue Writs of Election to fill such Vacancies.

The Speaker, chosen by and from the majority party, presides over the House. Impeachment is the act of bringing formal charges against an official. (See also Section 3.)

The House of Representatives shall chuse their Speaker and other Officers; and shall have the sole Power of Impeachment.

The 17th Amendment changed this method to direct election.

Section 3. The Senate of the United States shall be composed of two Senators from each State, chosen by the Legislature thereof, for six Years; and each Senator shall have one Vote.

The 17th Amendment also provides that a state governor shall appoint a successor to fill a vacant Senate seat until a direct election is held.

Immediately after they shall be assembled in Consequence of the first Election, they shall be divided as equally as may be into three Classes. The Seats of the Senators of the first Class shall be vacated at the Expiration of the second Year, of the second Class at the Expiration of the fourth Year, and of the third Class at the Expiration of the sixth Year, so that one third may be chosen every second Year; and if Vacancies happen by Resignation, or otherwise, during the Recess of the Legislature of any State, the Executive thereof may make temporary Appointments until the next Meeting of the Legislature, which shall then fill such Vacancies.

No Person shall be a Senator who shall not have attained to the Age of thirty Years, and been nine Years a Citizen of the United States, and who shall not, when elected, be an Inhabitant of that State for which he shall be chosen.

The Vice President may cast a vote in the Senate only in order to break a tie.

The Vice President of the United States shall be President of the Senate, but shall have no Vote, unless they be equally divided.

The president *pro tempore* of the Senate is a temporary officer; the Latin words mean "for the time being."

The Senate shall chuse their other Officers, and also a President pro tempore, in the absence of the Vice President, or when he shall exercise the Office of President of the United States.

No President has ever been successfully impeached. In 1868 the Senate fell one vote short of the two-thirds majority needed to convict Andrew Johnson. Twelve other officials —ten federal judges, one senator, and one Secretary of War—have been impeached; four of the judges were convicted.

The Senate shall have the sole Power to try all Impeachments. When sitting for that Purpose, they shall be on Oath or Affirmation. When the President of the United States is tried, the Chief Justice shall preside: And no Person shall be convicted without the Concurrence of two thirds of the Members present.

Judgment in Cases of Impeachment shall not extend further than to removal from Office, and disqualification to hold and enjoy any Office of Honor, Trust or Profit under the United States: but the Party convicted shall nevertheless be liable and subject to Indictment, Trial, Judgment and Punishment, according to Law.

Elections for Congress are held on the first Tuesday after the first Monday in November in even-numbered years.

Section 4. The Times, Places and Manner of holding Elections for Senators and Representatives, shall be prescribed in each State by the Legislature thereof; but the Congress may at any time by Law make or alter such Regulations, except as to the Place of chusing Senators.

The 20th Amendment designates January 3 as the opening of the congressional session.

The Congress shall assemble at least once in every Year, and such Meeting shall be on the first Monday in December, unless they shall by Law appoint a different Day.

Section 5. Each House shall be the Judge of the Elections, Returns and Qualifications of its own Members, and a Majority of each shall constitute a Quorum to do Business; but a smaller number may adjourn from day to day, and may be authorized to compel the Attendance of absent Members, in such Manner, and under such Penalties as each House may provide.

Each House may determine the Rules of its Proceedings, punish its Members for disorderly Behavior, and, with the Concurrence of two thirds, expel a Member.

Each House shall keep a Journal of its Proceedings, and from time to time publish the same, excepting such Parts as may in their Judgment require Secrecy; and the Yeas and Nays of the Members of either House on any question shall, at the Desire of one fifth of those Present, be entered on the Journal.

Neither House, during the Session of Congress, shall, without the Consent of the other, adjourn for more than three days, nor to any other Place than that in which the two Houses shall be sitting.

Each house of Congress decides whether a member has been elected properly and is qualified to be seated. (A quorum is the minimum number of persons required to be present in order to conduct business.) The House once refused admittance to an elected representative who had been guilty of a crime. The Senate did likewise in the case of a candidate whose election campaign lent itself to "fraud and corruption."

Section 6. The Senators and Representatives shall receive a Compensation for their Services, to be ascertained by Law, and paid out of the Treasury of the United States. They shall in all Cases, except Treason, Felony and Breach of the Peace, be privileged from Arrest during their Attendance at the Session of their respective Houses, and in going to and returning from the same; and for any Speech or Debate in either House, they shall not be questioned in any other Place.

No Senator or Representative shall, during the Time for which he was elected, be appointed to any civil Office under the Authority of the United States, which shall have been created, or the Emoluments whereof shall have been encreased during such time; and no Person holding any Office under the United States, shall be a Member of either House during his Continuance in Office.

Congressmen have the power to fix their own salaries. Under the principle of *congressional immunity,* they cannot be sued or arrested for anything they say in a congressional debate. This provision enables them to speak freely.

This clause reinforces the principle of separation of powers by stating that, during his term of office, a member of Congress may not be appointed to a position in another branch of government. Nor may he resign and accept a position created during his term.

Section 7. All Bills for raising Revenue shall originate in the House of Representatives; but the Senate may propose or concur with Amendments as on other Bills.

Every Bill which shall have passed the House of Representatives and the Senate, shall, before it become a Law, be presented to the President of the United States; If he approve he shall sign it, but if not he shall return it, with his Objections to that House in which it shall have originated, who shall enter the Objections at large on their Journal, and proceed to reconsider it. If after such Reconsideration two thirds of that House shall agree to pass the Bill, it shall be sent, together with the Objections, to the other House, by which it shall likewise be reconsidered, and if approved by two thirds of that House, it shall become a Law. But in all such Cases the Votes of both Houses shall be determined by Yeas and Nays, and the Names of the Persons voting for and against the Bill shall be entered on the Journal of each House respectively. If any Bill shall not be returned by the President within ten Days (Sundays excepted) after it shall have been presented to him, the Same shall be a Law, in like Manner as if he had signed it, unless the Congress by their Adjournment prevent its Return, in which Case it shall not be a Law.

Every Order, Resolution, or Vote to which the Concurrence of the Senate and House of Representatives may be necessary (except on a question of Adjournment) shall be presented to the President of the United States; and before the Same shall take Effect, shall be approved by him, or being disapproved by him, shall be repassed by two thirds of the Senate and House of Representatives, according to the Rules and Limitations prescribed in the Case of a Bill.

The House initiates tax bills but the Senate may propose changes in them.

By returning a bill unsigned to the house in which it originated, the President exercises a *veto.* A two-thirds majority in both houses can override the veto. If the President receives a bill within the last ten days of a session and does not sign it, the measure dies by *pocket veto.* Merely by keeping the bill in his pocket, so to speak, the president effects a veto.

The same process of approval or disapproval by the President is applied to resolutions and other matters passed by both houses (except adjournment).

These are the *delegated*, or *enumerated*, powers of Congress.

Duties are taxes on imported goods; *excises* are taxes on goods manufactured, sold, or consumed within the country. *Imposts* is a general term including both duties and excise taxes.

Section 8. The Congress shall have Power to lay and collect Taxes, Duties, Imposts and Excises, to pay the Debts and provide for the common Defence and general Welfare of the United States; but all Duties, Imposts and Excises shall be uniform throughout the United States;

To borrow money on the credit of the United States;

To regulate Commerce with foreign Nations, and among the several States, and with the Indian Tribes;

Naturalization is the process by which an alien becomes a citizen.

To establish an uniform Rule of Naturalization, and uniform Laws on the subject of Bankruptcies throughout the United States;

To coin Money, regulate the Value thereof, and of foreign Coin, and fix the Standard of Weights and Measures;

Government *securities* include savings bonds and other notes.

To provide for the Punishment of counterfeiting the Securities and current Coin of the United States;

To establish Post Offices and post Roads;

Authors' and inventors' rights are protected by copyright and patent laws.

To promote the Progress of Science and useful Arts, by securing for limited Times to Authors and Inventors the exclusive Right to their respective Writings and Discoveries;

Congress may establish lower federal courts.

To constitute Tribunals inferior to the supreme Court;

To define and punish Piracies and Felonies committed on the high Seas, and Offenses against the Law of Nations;

Only Congress may declare war. *Letters of marque and reprisal* grant merchant ships permission to attack enemy vessels.

To declare War, grant Letters of Marque and Reprisal, and make Rules concerning Captures on Land and Water;

To raise and support Armies, but no Appropriation of Money to that Use shall be for a longer Term than two Years;

To provide and maintain a Navy;

To make Rules for the Government and Regulation of the land and naval Forces;

Militia refers to national guard units, which may become part of the United States Army during an emergency. Congress aids the states in maintaining their national guard units.

To provide for calling forth the Militia to execute the Laws of the Union, suppress Insurrections and repel Invasions;

To provide for organizing, arming, and disciplining the Militia, and for governing such Part of them as may be employed in the Service of the United States, reserving to the States respectively, the Appointment of the Officers, and the Authority of training the Militia according to the discipline prescribed by Congress;

This clause gives Congress the power to govern what became the District of Columbia, as well as other federal sites.

To exercise exclusive Legislation in all Cases whatsoever, over such District (not exceeding ten Miles square) as may, by Cession of particular States, and the acceptance of Congress, become the Seat of the Government of the United States, and to exercise like Authority over all Places purchased by the Consent of the Legislature of the State in which the Same shall be, for the Erection of Forts, Magazines, Arsenals, dock-Yards, and other needful Buildings;—And

Known as the *elastic clause*, this provision enables Congress to exercise many powers not specifically granted to it by the Constitution.

To make all Laws which shall be necessary and proper for carrying into Execution the foregoing Powers, and all other Powers vested by this Constitution in the Government of the United States, or in any Department or Officer thereof.

This clause concerns the slave trade, which Congress did ban in 1808.

Section 9. The Migration or Importation of such Persons as any of the States now existing shall think proper to admit, shall not be prohibited by the Congress prior to the Year one thousand eight hundred and eight, but a tax or duty may be imposed on such Importation, not exceeding ten dollars for each Person.

The *writ of habeas corpus* permits a prisoner to appear before a judge to inquire into the legality of his or her detention.

The privilege of the Writ of Habeas Corpus shall not be suspended unless when in Cases of Rebellion or Invasion the public Safety may require it.

No Bill of Attainder or ex post facto Law shall be passed.

No capitation, or other direct, Tax shall be laid, unless in Proportion to the Census or Enumeration herein before directed to be taken.

No Tax or Duty shall be laid on Articles exported from any State.

No Preference shall be given by any Regulation of Commerce or Revenue to the Ports of one State over those of another; nor shall Vessels bound to, or from, one State, be obliged to enter, clear, or pay Duties in another.

No Money shall be drawn from the Treasury, but in Consequence of Appropriations made by Law; and a regular Statement and Account of the Receipts and Expenditures of all public Money shall be published from time to time.

No Title of Nobility shall be granted by the United States: And no Person holding any Office of Profit or Trust under them, shall, without the Consent of the Congress, accept of any present, Emolument, Office, or Title, of any kind whatever, from any King, Prince, or foreign State.

A *bill of attainder* is an act of legislation that declares a person guilty of a crime and punishes him or her without a trial. An *ex post facto* law punishes a person for an act that was legal when performed but later declared illegal.

The object of Clause 4 was to bar direct (per person) taxation of slaves for the purpose of abolishing slavery. The 16th Amendment modified this provision by giving Congress the power to tax personal income.

Section 10. No State shall enter into any Treaty, Alliance, or Confederation; grant Letters of Marque and Reprisal; coin Money; emit Bills of Credit; make any Thing but gold and silver Coin a Tender in Payment of Debts; pass any Bill of Attainder, ex post facto Law, or Law impairing the Obligation of Contracts, or grant any Title of Nobility.

No State shall, without the Consent of the Congress, lay any Imposts or Duties on Imports or Exports, except what may be absolutely necessary for executing its inspection Laws: and the net Produce of all Duties and Imposts, laid by any State on Imports or Exports, shall be for the Use of the Treasury of the United States; and all such Laws shall be subject to the Revision and Controul of the Congress.

No State shall, without the Consent of Congress, lay any duty of Tonnage, keep Troops, or Ships of War in time of Peace, enter into any Agreement or Compact with another State, or with a foreign Power, or engage in War, unless actually invaded, or in such imminent Danger as will not admit of delay.

States are hereby forbidden to exercise certain powers. Some of these powers belong to Congress alone; others are considered undemocratic.

States cannot, without congressional authority, tax goods that enter or leave, except for a small inspection fee.

ARTICLE II • EXECUTIVE DEPARTMENT

Section 1. The executive Power shall be vested in a President of the United States of America. He shall hold his Office during the Term of four Years, and, together with the Vice President, chosen for the same Term, be elected, as follows.

Each State shall appoint, in such Manner as the Legislature thereof may direct, a Number of Electors, equal to the whole Number of Senators and Representatives to which the State may be entitled in the Congress: but no Senator or Representative, or Person holding an Office of Trust or Profit under the United States, shall be appointed an Elector.

The Electors shall meet in their respective States, and vote by Ballot for two persons, of whom one at least shall not be an Inhabitant of the same State with themselves. And they shall make a List of all the Persons voted for, and of the Number of Votes for each; which List they shall sign and certify, and transmit sealed to the Seat of the Government of the United States, directed to the President of the Senate. The President of the Senate shall, in the Presence of the Senate and House of Representatives, open all the Certificates, and the Votes shall then be counted. The Person having the greatest Number of Votes shall be the President, if such Number be a Majority of the whole Number of Electors appointed; and if there be more than one who have such Majority, and have an equal

Federal officials are ineligible to serve as presidential electors.

The 12th Amendment superseded this clause. The weakness of the original constitutional provision became apparent in the election of 1800, when Thomas Jefferson and Aaron Burr received the same number of electoral votes. The 12th Amendment avoids this possibility by requiring electors to cast separate ballots for President and Vice President.

Number of Votes, then the House of Representatives shall immediately chuse by Ballot one of them for President; and if no Person have a Majority, then from the five highest on the List the said House shall in like Manner chuse the President. But in chusing the President, the Votes shall be taken by States, the Representation from each State having one Vote; a quorum for this Purpose shall consist of a Member or Members from two thirds of the States, and a Majority of all the States shall be necessary to a Choice. In every Case, after the Choice of the President, the Person having the greatest Number of Votes of the Electors shall be the Vice President. But if there should remain two or more who have equal Votes, the Senate shall chuse from them by Ballot the Vice President.

The Congress may determine the Time of chusing the Electors, and the Day on which they shall give their Votes; which Day shall be the same throughout the United States.

A naturalized citizen may not become President.

No person except a natural born Citizen, or a Citizen of the United States, at the time of the Adoption of this Constitution, shall be eligible to the Office of President; neither shall any Person be eligible to that Office who shall not have attained to the Age of Thirty-five Years, and been fourteen Years a Resident within the United States.

The Vice President is next in line for the presidency. A federal law passed in 1947 determined the order of presidential succession as follows: (1) Speaker of the House; (2) president *pro tempore* of the Senate; and (3) Cabinet officers in the order in which their departments were created. (So far, death has been the only circumstance under which a presidential term has been cut short.) This clause has been amplified by the 25th Amendment.

In Case of the Removal of the President from Office, or of his Death, Resignation, or Inability to discharge the Powers and Duties of the said Office, the same shall devolve on the Vice-President, and the Congress may by Law provide for the Case of Removal, Death, Resignation or Inabiltiy, both of the President and the Vice President, declaring what Officer shall then act as President, and such Officer shall act accordingly, until the Disability be removed, or a President shall be elected.

The President shall, at stated Times, receive for his Services, a Compensation, which shall neither be encreased nor diminished during the Period for which he shall have been elected, and he shall not receive within that Period any other Emolument from the United States, or any of them.

Before he enter on the Execution of his Office, he shall take the following Oath or Affirmation:—"I do solemnly swear (or affirm) that I will faithfully execute the Office of the President of the United States, and will to the best of my Ability, preserve, protect and defend the Constitution of the United States."

This clause suggests written communication between the President and "the principal officer in each of the executive departments." As it developed, these officials comprise the Cabinet—whose members are chosen, and may be replaced, by the President.

Section 2. The President shall be Commander in Chief of the Army and Navy of the United States, and of the Militia of the several States, when called into the actual Service of the United States; he may require the Opinion in writing, of the principal Officer in each of the executive Departments, upon any subject relating to the Duties of their respective Offices, and he shall have Power to Grant Reprieves and Pardons for Offenses against the United States, except in Cases of Impeachment.

Senate approval is required for treaties and presidential appointments.

He shall have Power, by and with the Advice and Consent of the Senate, to make by and with the Advice and Consent of the Senate, shall appoint Ambassadors, other Treaties, provided two thirds of the Senators present concur; and he shall nominate, and public Ministers and Consuls, Judges of the supreme Court, and all other Officers of the United States, whose Appointments are not herein otherwise provided for, and which shall be established by Law: but the Congress may by Law vest the Appointment of such inferior Officers, as they think proper, in the President alone, in the Courts of Law, or in the Heads of Departments.

Without the consent of the Senate, the President may appoint officials only on a temporary basis.

The President shall have Power to fill up all Vacancies that may happen during the Recess of the Senate, by granting Commissions which shall expire at the End of their next Session.

Section 3. He shall from time to time give to the Congress Information of the State of the Union, and recommend to their Consideration such Measures as he shall judge necessary and expedient; he may, on extraordinary Occasions, convene both Houses, or either of them, and in Case of Disagreement between them, with Respect to the Time of Adjournment, he may adjourn them to such Time as he shall think proper; he shall receive Ambassadors and other public Ministers; he shall take Care that the Laws be faithfully executed, and shall Commission all the Officers of the United States.

The President delivers a "State of the Union" message at the opening of each session of Congress. Woodrow Wilson was the first President since John Adams to read his messages in person. Franklin D. Roosevelt and his successors followed Wilson's example.

Section 4. The President, Vice President and all civil Officers of the United States, shall be removed from Office on Impeachment for, and Conviction of, Treason, Bribery, or other high Crimes and Misdemeanors.

ARTICLE III • JUDICIAL DEPARTMENT

Section 1. The judicial Power of the United States, shall be vested in one supreme Court, and in such inferior Courts as the Congress may from time to time ordain and establish. The Judges, both of the supreme and inferior Courts, shall hold their Offices during good Behaviour, and shall, at stated Times, receive for their Services, a Compensation, which shall not be diminished during their Continuance in Office.

Federal judges hold office for life and may not have their salaries lowered while in office. These provisions are intended to keep the federal bench independent of political pressure.

Section 2. The judicial Power shall extend to all Cases, in Law and Equity, arising under this Constitution, the Laws of the United States, and Treaties made, or which shall be made, under their Authority;—to all Cases affecting Ambassadors, other public Ministers and Consuls;—to all Cases of admiralty and maritime Jurisdiction;—to Controversies to which the United States shall be a Party;—to Controversies between two or more States;—between a State and Citizens of another State;—between Citizens of different States;—between Citizens of the same State claiming Lands under Grants of different States, and between a State, or the Citizens thereof, and foreign States, Citizens or Subjects.

This clause describes the types of cases that may be heard in federal courts.

The 11th Amendment prevents a citizen from suing a state in a federal court.

In all Cases affecting Ambassadors, other public Ministers and Consuls, and those in which a State shall be Party, the supreme Court shall have original Jurisdiction. In all the other Cases before mentioned, the supreme Court shall have appellate Jurisdiction, both as to Law and Fact, with such Exceptions, and under such Regulations as the Congress shall make.

The Supreme Court handles certain cases directly. It may also review cases handled by lower courts, but Congress in some cases may withhold the right to appeal to the highest court, or limit appeal by setting various conditions.

The trial of all Crimes, except in Cases of Impeachment, shall be by Jury; and such Trial shall be held in the State where the said Crimes shall have been committed; but when not committed within any State, the Trial shall be at such Place or Places as the Congress may by Law have directed.

The 6th Amendment strengthens this clause on trial procedure.

Section 3. Treason against the United States, shall consist only in levying War against them, or in adhering to their Enemies, giving them Aid and Comfort. No Person shall be convicted of Treason unless on the Testimony of two Witnesses to the same overt Act, or on Confession in open Court.

Treason is rigorously defined. A person can be convicted only if two witnesses testify to the same obvious act, or if he confesses in court.

The Congress shall have Power to declare the Punishment of Treason, but no Attainder of Treason shall work Corruption of Blood, or Forfeiture except during the Life of the Person attainted.

Punishment for treason extends only to the person convicted, not to his or her descendants. ("Corruption of blood" means that the heirs of a convicted person are deprived of certain rights.)

ARTICLE IV • RELATIONS AMONG THE STATES

States must honor each other's laws, court decisions, and records (for example, birth, marriage, and death certificates).

Section 1. Full Faith and Credit shall be given in each State to the public Acts, Records, and judicial Proceedings of every other State. And the Congress may by general Laws prescribe the Manner in which such Acts, Records and Proceedings shall be proved, and the Effect thereof.

Each state must respect the rights of citizens of other states.

Section 2. The Citizens of each State shall be entitled to all Privileges and Immunities of Citizens in the several States.

The process of returning a person accused of a crime to the governmental authority (in this case a state) from which he or she has fled is called *extradition*.

A Person charged in any State with Treason, Felony, or other Crime, who shall flee from Justice, and be found in another State, shall on demand of the executive Authority of the State from which he fled, be delivered up, to be removed to the State having Jurisdiction of the Crime.

The 13th Amendment, which abolished slavery, makes this clause obsolete.

No Person held in Service or Labour in one State, under the Laws thereof, escaping into another, shall, in Consequence of any Law or Regulation therein, be discharged from such Service or Labour, but shall be delivered up on Claim of the Party to whom such Service or Labour may be due.

A new state may not be created by dividing or joining existing states unless approved by the legislatures of the states affected and by Congress. An exception to the provision forbidding the division of a state occurred during the Civil War. In 1863 West Virginia was formed out of the western region of Virginia.

Section 3. New States may be admitted by the Congress into this Union; but no new State shall be formed or erected within the Jurisdiction of any other State; nor any State be formed by the Junction of two or more States, or parts of States, without the Consent of the Legislatures of the States concerned as well as of the Congress.

The Congress shall have Power to dispose of and make all needful Rules and Regulations respecting the Territory or other Property belonging to the United States; and nothing in this Constitution shall be so construed as to Prejudice any Claims of the United States, or of any particular State.

A *republican* form of government is one in which citizens choose representatives to govern them. The federal government must protect a state against invasion and, if state authorities request it, against violence within a state.

Section 4. The United States shall guarantee to every State in this Union a Republican Form of Government, and shall protect each of them against Invasion; and on Application of the Legislature, or of the Executive (when the Legislature cannot be convened) against domestic Violence.

ARTICLE V • AMENDING THE CONSTITUTION

An amendment to the Constitution can be proposed (a) by Congress, with a two-thirds vote of both houses, or (b) by a convention called by Congress when two-thirds of the state legislatures request it. An amendment is ratified (a) by three-fourths of the state legislatures, or (b) by conventions in three-fourths of the states. The twofold procedure of proposal and ratification reflects the seriousness with which the framers of the Constitution regarded amendments. Over 6,900 amendments have been proposed; only 26 have been ratified.

The Congress, whenever two thirds of both Houses shall deem it necessary, shall propose Amendments to this Constitution, or, on the Application of the Legislatures of two thirds of the several States, shall call a Convention for proposing Amendments, which, in either Case, shall be valid to all Intents and Purposes, as part of this Constitution, when ratified by the Legislatures of three fourths of the several States, or by Conventions in three fourths thereof, as the one or the other Mode of Ratification may be proposed by the Congress: Provided that no Amendment which may be made prior to the Year One thousand eight hundred and eight shall in any Manner affect the first and fourth Clauses in the Ninth Section of the first Article; and that no State, without its Consent, shall be deprived of its equal Suffrage in the Senate.

ARTICLE VI • GENERAL PROVISIONS

All Debts contracted and Engagements entered into, before the Adoption of this Constitution, shall be as valid against the United States under this Constitution, as under the Confederation.

This Constitution, and the Laws of the United States which shall be made in Pursuance thereof; and all Treaties made, or which shall be made, under the Authority of the United States, shall be the supreme Law of the Land; and the Judges in every State shall be bound thereby, any Thing in the Constitution or Laws of any State to the Contrary notwithstanding.

The *supremacy clause* means that if a federal and a state law conflict, the federal law prevails.

The Senators and Representatives before mentioned, and the Members of the several State Legislatures, and all executive and judicial Officers, both of the United States and of the several States, shall be bound by Oath or Affirmation, to support this Constitution; but no religious Test shall ever be required as a Qualification to any Office or public Trust under the United States.

Religion may not be a condition for holding public office.

ARTICLE VII • RATIFICATION

The Ratification of the Conventions of nine States shall be sufficient for the Establishment of this Constitution between the States so ratifying the Same.

The Constitution would become the law of the land upon the approval of nine states.

DONE in Convention by the Unanimous Consent of the States present the Seventeenth Day of September in the Year of our Lord one thousand seven hundred and eighty-seven and of the Independence of the United States of America the Twelfth. In Witness whereof We have hereunto subscribed our Names.

G° WASHINGTON
Presid^t and deputy from
VIRGINIA

Attest: *William Jackson,* Secretary

DELAWARE
Geo: Read
Gunning Bedford, jun
John Dickinson
Richard Bassett
Jaco: Broom

MARYLAND
James McHenry
Dan: of St Thos Jenifer
Danl Carroll

VIRGINIA
John Blair
James Madison Jr.

NORTH CAROLINA
Wm Blount
Richd Dobbs Spaight
Hu Williamson

SOUTH CAROLINA
J. Rutledge
Charles Cotesworth Pinckney
Charles Pinckney
Pierce Butler

GEORGIA
William Few
Abr Baldwin

NEW HAMPSHIRE
John Langdon
Nicholas Gilman

MASSACHUSETTS
Nathaniel Gorham
Rufus King

CONNECTICUT
Wm Saml Johnson
Roger Sherman

NEW YORK
Alexander Hamilton

NEW JERSEY
Wil: Livingston
David Brearley
Wm Paterson
Jona: Dayton

PENNSYLVANIA
B Franklin
Thomas Mifflin
Robt. Morris
Geo. Clymer
Thos. FitzSimons
Jared Ingersoll
James Wilson
Gouv Morris

AMENDMENTS

AMENDMENT I • (1791)

Establishes fredom of religion, speech, and the press; gives citizens the rights of assembly and petition.

Congress shall make no law respecting an establishment of religion, or prohibiting the free exercise thereof: or abridging the freedom of speech, or of the press; or the right of the people peaceably to assemble, and to petition the Government for a redress of grievances.

AMENDMENT II • (1791)

States have the right to maintain a militia.

A well regulated Militia, being necessary to the security of a free State, the right of the people to keep and bear Arms, shall not be infringed.

AMENDMENT III • (1791)

Limits the army's right to quarter soldiers in private homes.

No Soldier shall, in time of peace, be quartered in any house, without the consent of the Owner, nor in time of war, but in a manner to be prescribed by law.

AMENDMENT IV • (1791)

Search warrants are required as a guarantee of a citizen's right to privacy.

The right of the people to be secure in their persons, houses, papers, and effects, against unreasonable searches and seizures, shall not be violated, and no Warrants shall issue, but upon probable cause, supported by Oath or affirmation, and particularly describing the place to be searched, and the persons or things to be seized.

AMENDMENT V • (1791)

To be prosecuted for a serious crime, a person must first be accused *(indicted)* by a grand jury. No one can be tried twice for the same crime *(double jeopardy)*. Nor can a person be forced into self-incrimination by testifying against himself or herself.

No person shall be held to answer for a capital, or otherwise infamous crime, unless on a presentment or indictment of a Grand Jury, except in cases arising in the land or naval forces, or in the Militia, when in actual service in time of War or public danger; nor shall any person be subject for the same offence to be twice put in jeopardy of life or limb; nor shall be compelled in any criminal case to be a witness against himself, nor be deprived of life, liberty, or property, without due process of law; nor shall private property be taken for public use, without just compensation.

AMENDMENT VI • (1791)

Guarantees a defendant's right to be tried without delay and to face witnesses testifying for the other side.

In all criminal prosecutions, the accused shall enjoy the right to a speedy and public trial, by an impartial jury of the State and district wherein the crime shall have been committed, which district shall have been previously ascertained by law, and to be informed of the nature and cause of the accusation; to be confronted with the witnesses against him; to have compulsory process for obtaining witnesses in his favor, and to have the Assistance of Counsel for his defence.

[*The date following each amendment number is the year of ratification.*]

AMENDMENT VII • (1791)

In suits at common law, where the value in controversy shall exceed twenty dollars, the right of trial by jury shall be preserved, and no fact tried by a jury, shall be otherwise reexamined in any Court of the United States, than according to the rules of the common law.

A jury trial is guaranteed in federal civil suits involving more than twenty dollars.

AMENDMENT VIII • (1791)

Excessive bail shall not be required, nor excessive fines imposed, nor cruel and unusual punishments inflicted.

AMENDMENT IX • (1791)

The enumeration in the Constitution, of certain rights, shall not be construed to deny or disparage others retained by the people.

The listing of specific rights in the Constitution does not mean that others are not protected.

AMENDMENT X • (1791)

The powers not delegated to the United States by the Constitution, nor prohibited by it to the States, are reserved to the States respectively, or to the people.

Limits the federal government to its specific powers. Powers not prohibited the states by the Constitution may be exercised by them.

AMENDMENT XI • (1798)

The Judicial power of the United States shall not be construed to extend to any suit in law or equity, commenced or prosecuted against one of the United States by Citizens of another State, or by Citizens or Subjects of any Foreign State.

A state cannot be sued by a citizen of another state in a federal court. Such a case can be tried only in the courts of the state being sued.

AMENDMENT XII • (1804)

The Electors shall meet in their respective states and vote by ballot for President and Vice-President, one of whom, at least, shall not be an inhabitant of the same state with themselves; they shall name in their ballots the person voted for as President, and in distinct ballots the person voted for as Vice-President, and they shall make distinct lists of all persons voted for as President, and of all persons voted for as Vice-President, and of the number of votes for each, which lists they shall sign and certify, and transmit sealed to the seat of the government of the United States, directed to the President of the Senate;—The President of the Senate shall, in presence of the Senate and House of Representatives, open all the certificates and the votes shall then be counted;—The person having the greatest number of votes for President, shall be the President, if such number be a majority of the whole number of Electors appointed; and if no person have such majority, then from the persons having the highest numbers not exceeding three on the list of those voted for as President, the House of Representatives shall choose immediately, by ballot, the President. But in choosing the President, the votes shall be taken by states, the representation from each state having one vote; a quorum for this purpose shall consist of a member or members from two-thirds of the states, and a majority of all the states shall be necessary to a choice. And if the House of Representatives shall not choose a President whenever the right of choice shall devolve upon them, before the fourth day of March next following, then the Vice-President shall act as President, as in the case of

Revises the process by which the President and Vice President were elected (see Article II, Section 1, Clause 3). The major change requires electors to cast separate ballots for President and Vice President. If none of the presidential candidates obtains a majority vote, the House of Representatives—with each state having one vote—chooses a President from the three candidates having the highest number of votes. If no vice presidential candidate wins a majority, the Senate chooses from the two candidates having the highest number of votes. The portion printed in color was superseded by Section 3 of the 20th Amendment.

the death or other constitutional disability of the President.—The person having the greatest number of votes as Vice-President, shall be the Vice-President, if such number be a majority of the whole number of Electors appointed, and if no person have a majority, then from the two highest numbers on the list, the Senate shall choose the Vice-President; a quorum for the purpose shall consist of two-thirds of the whole number of Senators, and a majority of the whole number shall be necessary to a choice. But no person constitutionally ineligible to the office of President shall be eligible to that of Vice-President of the United States.

AMENDMENT XIII • (1865)

Abolishes slavery.

Section 1. Neither slavery nor involuntary servitude, except as a punishment for crime whereof the party shall have been duly convicted, shall exist within the United States, or any place subject to their jurisdiction.

Section 2. Congress shall have power to enforce this article by appropriate legislation.

AMENDMENT XIV • (1868)

This section confers full civil rights on former slaves. Supreme Court decisions have interpreted the language of Section 1 to mean that the states, as well as the federal government, are bound by the Bill of Rights.

Section 1. All persons born or naturalized in the United States, and subject to the jurisdiction thereof, are citizens of the United States and of the State wherein they reside. No State shall make or enforce any law which shall abridge the privileges or immunities of citizens of the United States; nor shall any State deprive any person of life, liberty, or property, without due process of law; nor deny any person within its jurisdiction the equal protection of the laws.

A penalty of a reduction in congressional representation shall be applied to any state that refuses to give all adult male citizens the right to vote in federal elections. This section has never been applied. The portion printed in color was superseded by Section 1 of the 26th Amendment. (This section has also been amplified by the 19th Amendment.)

Section 2. Representatives shall be apportioned among the several States according to their respective numbers, counting the whole number of persons in each State, excluding Indians not taxed. But when the right to vote at any election for the choice of electors for President and Vice-President of the United States, Representatives in Congress, the Executive and Judicial officers of a State, or the members of the Legislature thereof, is denied to any of the male inhabitants of such State, being twenty-one years of age, and citizens of the United States, or in any way abridged, except for participation in rebellion, or other crime, the basis of representation therein shall be reduced in the proportion which the number of such male citizens shall bear to the whole number of male citizens twenty-one years of age in such State.

Any former federal or state official who served the Confederacy during the Civil War could not become a federal official again unless Congress voted otherwise.

Section 3. No person shall be a Senator or Representative in Congress, or elector of President and Vice-President, or hold any office, civil or military, under the United States, or under any State, who, having previously taken an oath, as a member of Congress, or as an officer of the United States, or as a member of any State legislature, or as an executive or judicial officer of any State, to support the Constitution of the United States, shall have engaged in insurrection or rebellion against the same, or given aid or comfort to the enemies thereof. But Congress may by a vote of two-thirds of each House, remove such disability.

Section 4. The validity of the public debt of the United States, authorized by law, including debts incurred for payment of pensions and bounties for services in suppressing insurrection or rebellion, shall not be questioned. But neither the United States nor any State shall assume or pay any debt or obligation incurred in aid of insurrection or rebellion against the United States, or any claim for the loss or emancipation of any slave; but all such debts, obligations and claims shall be held illegal and void.

Makes legal the federal Civil War debt, but at the same time voids all Confederate debts incurred in the war.

Section 5. The Congress shall have power to enforce, by appropriate legislation, the provisions of this article.

AMENDMENT XV • (1870)

Section 1. The right of citizens of the United States to vote shall not be denied or abridged by the United States or by any State on account of race, color, or previous condition of servitude.

Gives blacks the right to vote.

Section 2. The Congress shall have power to enforce this article by appropriate legislation.

AMENDMENT XVI • (1913)

The Congress shall have power to lay and collect taxes on incomes, from whatever source derived, without apportionment among the several States, and without regard to any census or enumeration.

Allows Congress to levy taxes on incomes.

AMENDMENT XVII • (1913)

The Senate of the United States shall be composed of two Senators from each State, elected by the people thereof, for six years; and each Senator shall have one vote. The electors in each State shall have the qualifications requisite for electors of the most numerous branch of the State legislature.

Provides for election of senators by the people of a state, rather than the state legislature.

When vacancies happen in the representation of any State in the Senate, the executive authority of such State shall issue writs of election to fill such vacancies: *Provided,* That the legislature of any State may empower the executive thereof to make temporary appointments until the people fill the vacancies by election as the legislature may direct.

This amendment shall not be so construed as to affect the election or term of any Senator chosen before it becomes valid as part of the Constitution.

AMENDMENT XVIII • (1919)

Section 1. After one year from the ratification of this article, the manufacture, sale, or transportation of intoxicating liquors within, the importation thereof into, or the exportation thereof from the United States and all territory subject to the jurisdiction thereof for beverage purposes is hereby prohibited.

Legalizes *prohibition*—that is, forbidding the making, selling, or transporting of intoxicating beverages. Superseded by the 21st Amendment.

Section 2. The Congress and the several States shall have concurrent power to enforce this article by appropriate legislation.

Section 3. This article shall be inoperative unless it shall have been ratified as an amendment to the Constitution by the legislatures of the several States, as provided in the Constitution, within seven years from the date of the submission hereof to the States by the Congress.

AMENDMENT XIX • (1920)

Gives women the right to vote.

The right of citizens of the United States to vote shall not be denied or abridged by the United States or by any State on account of sex.

Congress shall have power to enforce this article by appropriate legislation.

AMENDMENT XX • (1933)

The "lame duck" amendment allows the President to take office on January 20, and members of Congress on January 3. The purpose of the amendment is to reduce the term in office of defeated incumbents—known as "lame ducks."

Section 1. The terms of the President and Vice-President shall end at noon on the 20th day of January, and the terms of Senators and Representatives at noon on the 3d day of January, of the years in which such terms would have ended if this article had not been ratified; and the terms of their successors shall then begin.

Section 2. The Congress shall assemble at least once in every year, and such meeting shall begin at noon on the 3d day of January, unless they shall by law appoint a different day.

Section 3. If, at the time fixed for the beginning of the term of the President, the President elect shall have died, the Vice-President elect shall become President. If a President shall not have been chosen before the time fixed for the beginning of his term, or if the President elect shall have failed to qualify, then the Vice-President elect shall act as President until a President shall have qualified; and the Congress may by law provide for the case wherein neither a President elect nor a Vice-President elect shall have qualified, declaring who shall then act as President, or the manner in which one who is to act shall be selected, and such person shall act accordingly until a President or Vice-President shall have qualified.

Section 4. The Congress may by law provide for the case of the death of any of the persons from whom the House of Representatives may choose a President whenever the right of choice shall have devolved upon them, and for the case of the death of any of the persons from whom the Senate may choose a Vice-President whenever the right of choice shall have devolved upon them.

Section 5. Sections 1 and 2 shall take effect on the 15th day of October following the ratification of this article.

Section 6. This article shall be inoperative unless it shall have been ratified as an amendment to the Constitution by the legislatures of three-fourths of the several States within seven years from the date of its submission.

AMENDMENT XXI • (1933)

Section 1. The eighteenth article of amendment to the Constitution of the United States is hereby repealed.

Repeals the 18th Amendment.

Section 2. The transportation or importation into any State, Territory, or possession of the United States for delivery or use therein of intoxicating liquors, in violation of the laws thereof, is hereby prohibited.

States may pass prohibition laws.

Section 3. This article shall be inoperative unless it shall have been ratified as an amendment to the Constitution by conventions in the several States, as provided in the Constitution, within seven years from the date of the submission hereof to the States by the Congress.

AMENDMENT XXII • (1951)

Section 1. No person shall be elected to the office of the President more than twice, and no person who has held the office of President, or acted as President, for more than two years of a term to which some other person was elected President shall be elected to the office of the President more than once. But this Article shall not apply to any person holding the office of President when this Article was proposed by the Congress, and shall not prevent any person who may be holding the office of President, or acting as President, during the term within which this Article becomes operative from holding the office of President or acting as President during the remainder of such term.

Limits a President to only two full terms plus two years of a previous President's term.

Section 2. This article shall be inoperative unless it shall have been ratified as an amendment to the Constitution by the legislatures of three-fourths of the several States within seven years from the date of its submission to the States by the Congress.

AMENDMENT XXIII • (1961)

Section 1. The District constituting the seat of Government of the United States shall appoint in such manner as the Congress may direct:

A number of electors of President and Vice-President equal to the whole number of Senators and Representatives in Congress to which the District would be entitled if it were a State, but in no event more than the least populous State; they shall be in addition to those appointed by the States, but they shall be considered, for the purposes of the election of President and Vice-President, to be electors appointed by a State; and they shall meet in the District and perform such duties as provided by the twelfth article of amendment.

By giving the District of Columbia three electoral votes, Congress enabled its residents to vote for President and Vice President.

Section 2. The Congress shall have power to enforce this article by appropriate legislation.

AMENDMENT XXIV • (1964)

Section 1. The right of citizens of the United States to vote in any primary or other election for President or Vice-President, for electors for President or Vice-President, or for Senator or Representative in Congress, shall not be denied or abridged by the United States or any State by reason of failure to pay any poll tax or other tax.

Forbids the use of a poll tax as a requirement for voting in federal elections.

Section 2. The Congress shall have power to enforce this article by appropriate legislation.

AMENDMENT XXV • (1967)

Outlines the procedure to be followed in case of presidential disability.

Section 1. In case of the removal of the President from office or of his death or resignation, the Vice-President shall become President.

Section 2. Whenever there is a vacancy in the office of the Vice-President, the President shall nominate a Vice-President who shall take office upon confirmation by a majority vote of both Houses of Congress.

Section 3. Whenever the President transmits to the President pro tempore of the Senate and the Speaker of the House of Representatives his written declaration that he is unable to discharge the powers and duties of his office, and until he transmits to them a written declaration to the contrary, such powers and duties shall be discharged by the Vice-President as Acting President.

Section 4. Whenever the Vice-President and a majority of either the principal officers of the executive departments or of such other body as Congress may by law provide, transmit to the President pro tempore of the Senate and the Speaker of the House of Representatives their written declaration that the President is unable to discharge the powers and duties of his office, the Vice-President shall immediately assume the powers and duties of the office as Acting President.

Thereafter, when the President transmits to the President pro tempore of the Senate and the Speaker of the House of Representatives his written declaration that no inability exists, he shall resume the powers and duties of his office unless the Vice-President and a majority of either the principal officers of the executive department or of such other body as Congress may by law provide, transmit within four days to the President pro tempore of the Senate and the Speaker of the House of Representatives their written declaration that the President is unable to discharge the powers and duties of his office. Thereupon Congress shall decide the issue, assembling within forty-eight hours for that purpose if not in session. If the Congress, within twenty-one days after receipt of the latter written declaration, or, if Congress is not in session, within twenty-one days after Congress is required to assemble, determines by two-thirds vote of both Houses that the President is unable to discharge the powers and duties of his office, the Vice-President shall continue to discharge the same as Acting President; otherwise, the President shall resume the powers and duties of his office.

AMENDMENT XXVI • (1971)

Lowers the voting age to eighteen.

Section 1. The right of citizens of the United States, who are eighteen years of age or older, to vote shall not be denied or abridged by the United States or any state on account of age.

Section 2. The Congress shall have the power to enforce this article by appropriate legislation.

ILLUSTRATION CREDITS

The initials **PE** *denote* Pictorial Essay.

CHAPS. 19 AND 20

Page 385, Library of Congress; **386,** Brady Collection–U.S. Signal Corps/National Archives; **388,** N.Y.P.L. Rare Book Division; **390,** Charles Colcock Jones Papers/Manuscript Dept. Special Collections Division–Tulane University Library; **391,** N.Y.P.L. Prints Division; **393,** Library of Congress; **394,** Library of Congress; **401,** Penn Community Services Cultural Program; **405(right),** Brady Collection–U.S. Signal Corps/National Archives; **408,** Valentine Museum–Richmond, Va.; **409,** Brady Collection–U.S. Signal Corps/National Archives; **412,** Library of Congress; **414,** National Archives; **416, 417, 419, 422, 423,** Library of Congress; **426,** Virginia State Library; **429,** Louisiana State Museum.

UNIT FIVE

Page 432, Culver Pictures, Inc.; **435,** Smithsonian Institution/National Anthropological Archives; **437,** U.S. Signal Corps/National Archives; **440, 441, 442,** Smithsonian Institution/National Anthropological Archives; **443 & 445,** U.S. Signal Corps/National Archives; **451,** Nebraska State Historical Society; **454,** Library of Congress; **455,** Minnesota Historical Society; **456,** N.Y.P.L.; **457,** Permission of Huntington Library–San Marino, Cal.; **458,** Southern Pacific Railroad; **461,** Library of Congress; **463,** Manitoba Archives; **465,** Smithsonian Institution/National Anthropological Archives; **466,** Naval Observatory/National Archives; **469,** Western History Department–Denver Public Library; **470,** Bureau of Reclamation/National Archives; **473,** Library of Congress; **474 & 477,** International Harvester Company Historical Archives; **491 & 492,** Library of Congress; **493,** A.T.&T.; **495,** Library of Congress; **PE 6-1,** Culver Pictures, Inc.; **PE 6-2(top),** N.Y. Historical Society; **(bottom),** Metropolitan Museum of Art; **PE 6-3(top & center),** Bettmann Archive; **(bottom),** N.Y.P.L. Picture Collection; **PE 6-4(top),** Los Angeles County Museum of Art; **(bottom),** Museum of the City of New York; **PE 6-5(top),** Bettmann Archive; **(bottom),** N.Y.P.L. Picture Collection; **PE 6-6(top left),** Wisconsin State Historical Society; **(top right),** Missouri Historical Society; **(bottom),** Chicago Historical Society; **PE 6-7(top),** Illinois Department of Conservation; **(bottom),** Chicago Historical Society; **PE 6-8(top),** Thomas Gilcrease Institute–Tulsa, Okla.; **(bottom),** Franklin D. Roosevelt Library–Hyde Park, N.Y.; **500,** Intern'l. Museum of Photography at George Eastman House; **501,** Photo by Jacob A. Riis–Jacob A. Riis Collection, Museum of the City of New York; **504,** Kansas State Historical Society–Topeka, Kan.; **505,** Museum of the City of New York; **509(newspaper),** Library of Congress; **(photo),** Culver Pictures, Inc.; **512,** Library of Congress; **514,** Photo by Elroy Sanford–Lake County Historical Society/President James A. Garfield Museum; **517 & 518,** Library of Congress; **519 & 522,** Culver Pictures, Inc.; **525,** Library of Congress; **528,** N.Y.P.L. Picture Collection; **529,** Culver Pictures, Inc.; **533,** N.Y.P.L. Picture Collection; **535 & 536,** Culver Pictures, Inc.; **538,** Bettmann Archive; **540,** Culver Pictures, Inc.

UNIT SIX

Page 542, Culver Pictures, Inc.; **545 & 547,** Brown Brothers; **549,** N.Y. Historical Society; **553, 554, 556, 559,** Brown Brothers; **560,** Library of Congress; **564,** Brown Brothers; **569(top & center),** Library of Congress; **(bottom),** Culver Pictures, Inc.; **570,** Cleveland Public Library Picture Collection; **571, 573, 574, 578,** Library of Congress; **581,** Bettmann Archive; **583,** Naval Photographic Center; **584,** U.S. Signal Corps/National Archives; **590 & 592,** Library of Congress; **594 & 595,** U.S. Signal Corps/National Archives; **596,** Library of Congress; **599,** N.Y. Historical Society; **603,** Library of Congress; **607,** U.S. Signal Corps/National Archives; **608,** Library of Congress; **610,** U.S. War Dept. General Staff/National Archives; **614,** Library of Congress; **615,** U.S. Signal Corps/National Archives; **619,** Culver Pictures, Inc.; **623,** National Air and Space Museum/Smithsonian Institution; **PE 7-1,** Painting of the Museum's Interior in 1881 by Frank Waller, Photo by Francis G. Mayer–Metropolitan Museum of Art; **PE 7-2(top),** Culver Pictures, Inc.; **(bottom),** Museum of Fine Arts of Boston; **PE 7-3(top),** Art Institute of Chicago; **(bottom left),** Metropolitan Museum of Art; **(bottom right),** Museum of Modern Art–Gift of Friends of the Sculptor in 1908; **PE 7-4(top),** N.Y.P.L. Picture Collection; **(bottom),** Phillips Gallery; **PE 7-5 (top),** Hedrich Blessing; **(bottom),** Amherst College Collection; **PE 7-6(top),** Culver Pictures, Inc.; **(bottom),** Museum of the City of New York; **PE 7-7(top),** Edward Steichen; **(bottom),** Courtesy Mr. Ira Gershwin and The Humanities Research Center–University of Texas at Austin; **PE 7-8(top),** Museum of Art of Ogunquit; **(bottom),** Brown Brothers; **625,** National Air and Space Museum/Smithsonian Institution; **627 & 630,** Brown Brothers; **634,** National Air and Space Museum/Smithsonian Institution; **638,** Westinghouse Broadcasting Company, Inc.; **640 & 641,** Ford Archives; **643,** Brown Brothers; **644,** Michigan History Division; **646 & 647,** Bettmann Archive; **648,** Culver Pictures, Inc.; **650,** United Press International; **652,** Wide World Photos.

UNIT SEVEN

Page 654, Art by Ed Malsberg; **657,** United Press International; **660,** Wide World Photos; **663,** United Press International; **665,** Wide World Photos; **666,** Acme News-Pictures, Inc.; **670,** Wide World Photos; **671,** United Press International; **672,** Underwood and Underwood; **673,** Wide World Photos; **675,** Wide World Photos; **677,** Cartoon by Alley–*Memphis Commercial Appeal;* **678, 681, 683, 686,** Wide World Photos; **687,** United Press International; **688(top),** Wide World Photos; **(bottom),** United Press International; **693,** Culver Pictures, Inc.; **697,** Navy Dept./National Archives; **698,** Naval Photographic Center; **701,** United Press International; **702,** U.S. Office of War Information/National Archives; **706, 707, 710,** Navy Dept./National Archives; **713,** United Press International; **715,** Acme Newspictures, Inc.; **717,** United Press International; **PE 8-1,** Detail of "The New Television Set" by Norman Rockwell–Permission Los Angeles County Museum of Art; **PE 8-2(top left),** Culver Pictures, Inc.; **(top right),** Eileen Darby/Graphic House; **(bottom),** Brown Brothers; **PE 8-3(top),** Globe Photos; **(bottom),** Time-Life Picture Agency; **PE 8-4(top left),** Acme Newspictures, Inc.; **(top right),** Hy Peskin/Time-Life Picture Agency; **(bottom),** Capricorn Art Gallery; **PE 8-5(top),** Francis Miller/Time-Life Picture Agency; **(bottom),** Ralph Crane/Time-Life Picture Agency; **PE 8-6(top),** Margaret Bourke-White/Time-Life Picture Agency; **(bottom),** Leonard McCombe/Time-Life Picture Agency; **PE 8-7(top),** Nina Leen/Time-Life Picture Agency; **(bottom),** University of Wisconsin Dept. of Photocinema; **PE 8-8(top),** Frank Scherschel/Time-Life Picture Agency; **(bottom),** Peter Stackpole/Life Magazine © Time Inc.; **721,** U.S. Information Agency/National Archives; **724,** Acme Newspictures, Inc.; **726,** U.S. Office of War Information/National Archives; **728,** U.S. Information Agency/National Archives; **730,** Estate of David Low; **731 & 732,** Wide World Photos; **735 & 738,** Wide World Photos; **740,** United Press International; **742, 745, 748, 751, 752,** Wide World Photos; **756 & 757,** Wide World Photos; **758,** Dorothea Lange Collection–Oakland Museum; **760,** United Press International; **763, 765, 767, 768, 770,** Wide World Photos.

EPILOGUE

Page 773, Art by Ed Malsberg; **774 & 775,** United Press International; **779,** Wide World Photos; **780 & 782,** United Press International; **783,** Wide World Photos; **PE 9-1,** Esther Henderson/Rapho Guillumette; **PE 9-2(top),** Charles Moore/Black Star; **(bottom),** V. Bucher/Photo Researchers; **PE 9-3(top),** Bruce Roberts/Rapho Guillumette; **(bottom left),** Fred J. Maroon/Photo Researchers; **(bottom right),** Porterfield Chickering/Photo Researchers; **PE 9-4 (top),** Ford Motor Company; **(center),** Charles E. Rotkin/Photography for Industry; **(bottom),** Hedrich-Blessing; **PE 9-5(top),** Lucio Woods/Photo Researchers; **(bottom),** F. Hulnegle/Monkmeyer; **PE 9-6(top),** Myron Wood/Photo Researchers; **(bottom left),** Georg Gerster/Rapho Guillumette; **(bottom right),** Ray Manley/Shostal Photos; **PE 9-7(top),** Russ Kinne/Photo Researchers; **(center),** Tom McHugh/Photo Researchers; **(bottom),** Joe Munroe/Photo Researchers; **PE 9-8(top),** Jack Fields/Photo Researchers; **(bottom),** Ray Ateson; **786, 789, 791,** Wide World Photos; **792,** United Press International; **793,** Wide World Photos; **795 & 796,** United Press International; **803 & 805,** Wide World Photos; **808 & 809,** United Press International; **810(left),** Wide World Photos; **(right),** United Press International; **812,** Wide World Photos.

Italicized page numbers preceded by *c, m,* or *p* refer to a chart *(c),* map *(m),* or picture *(p).* Italicized numbers preceded by PE indicate a pictorial essay; thus PE*6–1* refers to page 1 of Pictorial Essay 6. Subentries are arranged chronologically.